William Edmund Bunting Ball, Charles Greenstreet Addison

Principles of Torts and Contracts

A short digest of the common law, chiefly founded upon the works of Addison.

With illustrative cases.

William Edmund Bunting Ball, Charles Greenstreet Addison

Principles of Torts and Contracts
A short digest of the common law, chiefly founded upon the works of Addison. With illustrative cases.

ISBN/EAN: 9783337423964

Printed in Europe, USA, Canada, Australia, Japan

Cover: Foto ©Suzi / pixelio.de

More available books at **www.hansebooks.com**

PRINCIPLES

OF

TORTS AND CONTRACTS:

A SHORT

DIGEST OF THE COMMON LAW,

CHIEFLY FOUNDED UPON THE WORKS OF ADDISON.

WITH ILLUSTRATIVE CASES.

For the use of Students.

BY

W. EDMUND BALL, LL.B.

LATE "HOLT SCHOLAR" OF GRAY'S INN;
BARRISTER-AT-LAW OF GRAY'S INN AND OF THE MIDLAND CIRCUIT.

LONDON:
STEVENS AND SONS, 119, CHANCERY LANE,
Law Publishers and Booksellers.
1880.

TO

THOMAS E. WEBB, Esq., LL.D., Q.C.

OF THE IRISH BAR,

REGIUS PROFESSOR OF LAWS,

IN THE UNIVERSITY OF DUBLIN,

This Work

IS AFFECTIONATELY DEDICATED

BY

HIS NEPHEW.

PREFACE.

In theory, the Common Law of England consists of a system of immemorial rules, of which the cases decided in Her Majesty's Courts are only the exemplification. Practically, however, it is very well known that to a very large extent judicial decisions originate that which they profess only to apply. In books of practice, the conventional theory is rightly ignored: the form is immersed in the matter: instead of the case illustrating the rule, the rule is deduced from the case; and our text-books are, in fact, an index and guide to the Reports. To the beginner, however, the inversion of what might appear to be the natural order of legal study is not a little perplexing. The attention is constantly diverted, and the memory confused, by the necessity of separating the abstract from the concrete.

In the present work, which is designed to meet the requirements of the student, I have endeavoured to set forth the first principles of the Common Law in as brief and axiomatic a form as possible, and to each chapter I have appended a short summary of cases, which may serve to illustrate the principal positions laid down in the text.

I have adopted the general scope of the great works of Addison, as affording the best existing exposition of the law, in the hope that this merely elementary book may serve as a useful stepping-stone to the study of its more ponderous originals. Wherever practicable, I have followed the exact language employed by Addison, which in its turn is usually transcribed from the reported decisions of the judges.

The selected cases are referred to by the numerals beneath the marginal notes of the several paragraphs which they illustrate. I have preferred this arrangement to the plan of referring each case separately to the particular sentence of the text to which it applies, because I have wished to avoid unnecessarily encumbering the letter-press with that array of bracketed figures which renders the appearance of the ordinary law-book so repulsive to the reader; and, further, because I have thought it useful to group together, in some sort, cases of which the subject-matter is cognate.

Occasionally, where the case quoted is a mere re-echo of the text, without the addition of anything to explain the rule, or to impress it upon the memory, I have merely referred to its title, without stating its effect.

The task of selecting suitable cases for the purposes of illustration has been one of considerable difficulty. I cannot hope that I have always been fortunate enough to light upon those which are most appropriate, nor can I feel sure that I have illustrated all the most important points. I trust, however, that my scheme may prove in some degree convenient and useful for the purposes of elementary study. I cannot help thinking it better to lay before the average student a comparatively small number of cases, in an epitomized form, than to provide him with a multitude of mere references.

WILLIAM EDMUND BALL.

April, 1880.

CONTENTS.

BOOK I.

	PAGE
CHAPTER I. ACTIONABLE WRONGS	1
„ II. TITLE TO REALTY	11
„ III. TRESPASS ON REALTY	17
„ IV. NUISANCE	27
„ V. NATURAL AND CONVENTIONAL SERVITUDES	43
„ VI. WASTE	57
„ VII. DISTRESS FOR RENT	63
„ VIII. TRESPASS AND CONVERSION OF CHATTELS	70
„ IX. NEGLIGENCE	81
„ X. ASSAULT, BATTERY, MAYHEM, AND FALSE IMPRISONMENT	92
„ XI. MALICIOUS CONSPIRACY AND MALICIOUS ABUSE OF LEGAL PROCEEDINGS	100
„ XII. RESPONSIBILITY OF JUDGES, MAGISTRATES, AND MINISTERIAL OFFICERS	104
„ XIII. LIBEL AND SLANDER	115
„ XIV. FRAUD AND DECEIT	132
„ XV. MATRIMONIAL INJURIES AND SEDUCTION	142

BOOK II.

	PAGE
CHAPTER I. CONTRACTS GENERALLY	153
„ II. FORM OF CONTRACTS	161
„ III. INTERPRETATION OF CONTRACTS	175
„ IV. CAPACITY OF PARTIES	183
„ V. AGENCY	194
„ VI. PARTNERSHIP	204
„ VII. CORPORATIONS AND JOINT STOCK COMPANIES	212
„ VIII. MASTER AND SERVANT	218
„ IX. BAILMENTS AND LIEN	231
„ X. SALE	256
„ XI. BILLS OF SALE AND PLEDGES OF PERSONALTY	280
„ XII. PRINCIPAL AND SURETY	290
„ XIII. INSURANCE	299
„ XIV. NEGOTIABLE INSTRUMENTS	318
„ XV. VOID AND VOIDABLE CONTRACTS	337
„ XVI. TRANSFER OF CONTRACTS	356
„ XVII. DISCHARGE OF CONTRACTS	366

INDEX OF CASES.

A.

ABERDEEN Arctic Co. v. Sutter, 78
Abernethy v. Hutchinson, 8
Adams v. Broughton, 77
―― v. Lindsell, 157
Adamson v. Jarvis, 140
Alderson v. Pope, 209
Aldred's Case, 8
Alexander v. N. E. Rail. Co., 130
Allen v. Pink, 181
―― v. Wright, 98
Alston v. Scales, 24
Anderson v. Midland Rail. Co., 67
Andrews v. Askey, 152
―― v. Belfield, 229
Anon., 6 E. 4, p. 7, 23
Ansell v. Baker, 383
Applebee v. Percy, 38
Appleby v. Myers, 229
Armory v. Delamirie, 77, 272
Astley v. Johnson, 331
Atkinson v. Denby, 352
Attack v. Bramwell, 69
Att.-Gen. v. Gee, 42
―― v. Mathias, 54
Ayloff v. Scrimpshire, 381
Azema v. Casella, 354

B.

BAILEY v. Macaulay, 217
―― v. Sweeting, 173
Baily v. Crespigny, 376
―― v. Merrell, 139
Baines v. Ewing, 199
Baird v. Williamson, 52
Balch v. Symes, 254
Barber v. Richards, 330
Barnard v. Godscall, 362

Barnes v. Barnes, 151
Barnett v. Earl of Guilford, 25
Barraclough v. Johnson, 39
Barrett v. Deere, 377
―― v. Hartley, 230
Barton v Hanson, 209
Barwick v. English Joint-Stock Bank, 140, 199
Bascomb v. Beckwith, 354
Bateman v. Joseph, 333
Battersby v. Smyth, 349
Baxter v. Burfield, 228
Bayliss v. Att.-Gen., 180
―― v. Fisher, 79
Beard v. Webb, 192
Beatty v. Gibbons, 76
Beauchamp, Earl of, v. Winn, 354
Beckwith v. Philby, 98
Beely v. Parry, 363
Belding v. Read, 287
Bentley v. Craven, 202
Bermondsey, Vestry of, v. Brown, 39
Berry v. Head, 77
Bertie v. Beaumont, 15
Bickett v. Morris, 16
Biggs v. Lawrence, 348
Binks v. South Yorkshire, &c., Rail. Co., 39
Bird v. Boulter, 174
―― v. Holbrook, 36
―― v. Jones, 98
Birkenhead, &c., Rail. Co. v. Pilcher, 190
Blackhurst v. Cockell, 310
Blades v. Arundel, 113
―― v. Higgs, 79
Blake v. Peters, 62
Blithman v. Martin, 349
Bloxham v. Sanders, 277
Boardman v. Boardman, 150
Bodenham v. Purchas, 379

Bohtlingk v. Inglis, 278
Boll v. Dunsterville, 201
Bonomi v. Backhouse, 9
Borradaile v. Brunton, 140
Boss v. Litton, 88
Bourke v. Short, 348
—— v. Warren, 130
Bourne v. Gatliffe, 251
Bowdell v. Parsons, 375
Bowes v. Howe, 332
Bowker v. Burdekin, 170
Bracewell v. Williams, 158
Brandon v. Curling, 313
Brewer v. Sparrow, 9
Bridgland v. Shapter, 8
Bridges v. Hawksworth, 272
Brierly v. Kendall, 286
Briggs v. Oliver, 87
Brind v. Dale, 248
Broadbent v. Ramsbotham, 52
Broadwater v. Blot, 247
Broadwood v. Granara, 253
Bromage v. Prosser, 125
Brooker v. Scott, 189
Brown v. Dawson, 24
—— v. Edgington, 139
—— v. Glenn, 68
—— v. Wootton, 10
Browne v. Gosden, 129
—— v. Lee, 298
Brunswick, Duke of, v. Slowman, 114
Brydon v. Stewart, 90
Bryant v. Foot, 54
—— v. Wardell, 77
Burbridge v. Manners, 334
Burgess v. Clements, 253
Burling v. Read, 25
Burns v. Coulson, 89
Bushell v. Miller, 79
Busk v. Royal Exchange Assurance Co., 312, 315
Butcher v. Butcher, 24
Butler v. Hunter, 88
—— v. Wildman, 312
Byrne v. Boadle, 37

C.

CAILIFF v. Danvers, 248
Cairns v. Robins, 251
Calder v. Halkett, 111
—— and Hebble Navigation Co. v. Pilling, 10
Calye's Case, 253
Campanari v. Woodburn, 202
Campbell v. Allgood, 62

Capel v. Jones, 129
Carpenter v. Buller, 182
Carrol v. Blencow, 193
Carslake v. Mapledoram, 124
Carter v. Boehm, 311
—— v. Flower, 333
—— v. Ring, 375
—— v. Whalley, 211
Castle, Ex parte, 78
—— v. Sworder, 274
Caswell v. Worth, 90
Catherwood v. Caslon, 151
Caton v. Caton, 173
Catteris v. Cowper, 24
Caudle v. Seymour, 111
Cawkwell v. Russell, 41
Chandelor v. Lopus, 139
Chandler v. Doulton, 69
Chapman v. Speller, 114
Chapple v. Cooper, 189
Chase v. Westmore, 253, 254
Chasemore v. Richards, 52
Cheltenham Carriage Co., In re, 112
Cherry v. Heming, 170
Cheveley v. Fuller, 182
Child v. Affleck, 126
Chinery v. Viall, 279
Church v. Imperial Gas Light Co., 216
Churchward v. Studdy, 78
Churton v. Frewen, 16
Claringbould v. Curtis, 279
Clark v. Molyneux, 127
Clarke v. Earnshaw, 247
—— v. Spence, 277
Cleeve v. Mahany, 41
Clifford v. Watts, 375
Clift v. Schwabe, 317
Coates v. Railton, 278
Coats v. Chaplin, 255
Cochrane v. Willis, 159
Cockayne v. Hodgkisson, 126
Coggs v. Bernard, 247, 248
Colby v. Gadsden, 272
Coldham v. Showler, 173
Coles v. Hulme, 180
—— v. Trecothick, 272
Collins v. Martin, 329
Colmere, In re, 287
Cook v. Baker, 171
—— v. Beal, 97
Cooke v. Oxley, 157
—— v. Wildes, 127
Coombe v. Woolfe, 296
Coombes v. Dibble, 348
Coope v. Eyre, 209
Cooper v. Lloyd, 192
—— v. Hubbuck, 55

INDEX OF CASES.

Cooper v. Parker, 380
—— v. Willowmatt, 76
Corby v. Hill, 37
Couch v. Steel, 10
Cowing v. Cowing, 151
Cox v. Burbidge, 87
—— v. Glue, 51
Crane v. London Dock Co., 272
Crawford v. Cocks, 210
—— v. Middleton, 124
Cross v. Lewis, 55
Crossley v. Ham, 330
Crouch v. London & N. W. Rail. Co., 248
Crutchley v. Mann, 329
Cuckson v. Stones, 227
Cullen v. Butler, 313
—— v. Duke of Queensbury, 217
Cuming v. Hill, 228
Curtis v. Pugh, 273
—— v. Wheeler, 67

D.

Dalby v. Indian & London Life Insurance Co., 316
Dalton v. Midland Rail. Co., 191
—— v. Whittern, 68
Dansey v. Richardson, 253
Darby v. Darby, 211
Darling v. Clue, 55
Dartnall v. Howard, 246
Davies v. Davies, 225
Davis v. Bowsher, 254
—— v. Duncan, 128
—— v. Gardiner, 125
Davison v. Duncan, 128
—— v. Gill, 15
Dawes v. Hawkins, 40
Dawkins v. Lord Paulet, 126
—— v. Lord Rokeby, 102
Dawtrey v. Huggins, 23
Deane v. Keate, 246
De Grave v. Mayor of Monmouth, 216
De Hahn v. Hartley, 310
Delacroix v. Thevenot, 130
Denton v. G. N. Rail. Co., 250
—— v. Peters, 329
Dering v. Dering, 150
Devon v. Pawlett, 364
Dickenson v. Naul, 273
—— v. Watson, 8
Digby v. Thompson, 124
Dimes v. Grand Junction Canal Co., 111
Dixon v. Ball, 87
—— v. Hurrell, 192
Dobson v. Collis, 172

Dodd v. Morris, 152
Dodsley v. Varley, 275
Doe v. Pearsey, 15
Doswell v. Impey, 110
Dover v. Mills, 246
Drury v. Delafontaine, 348
Duncombe v. Reeve, 69
Dunlop v. Higgins, 157
Dunston v. Paterson, 99
Duppa v. Mayo, 68

E.

Eager v. Grimwood, 152
Earle v. Peale, 190
—— v. Rowcroft, 313
East India Co. v. Sandys, 351
Eastern Counties Rail. Co. v. Broom, 99
Eastwood v. Kenyon, 171
Eckhardt v. Wilson, 365
Edge v. Bumford, 329
Edmunds v. Brown, 216
Edwards v. Halinder, 37
Egerton v. Earl Brownlow, 350
Eicholz v. Bannister, 139
Elliott v. Kemp, 364
—— v. Turner, 179
Elsam v. Denny, 334
Elves v. Crofts, 350
—— v. Man, 61
Embery v. Owen, 52
Emblen v. Myers, 91
Emmerson's Case, 353
Emmerson v. Heelis, 174
England v. Bourke, 130
Essell v. Hayward, 211
Evans v. Powis, 381
Evelyn v. Ruddish, 62
Every v. Smith, 24
Exeter Carrier's Case, 255

F.

Fairlie v. Fenton, 200
Falcke v. Gray, 279
Farley v. Danks, 103
Farnham v. Atkins, 190
Farnsworth v. Garrard, 229
Farrant v. Barnes, 249
Farrow v. Wilson, 383
Fawcett v. York & North Midland Rail. Co., 39
Fawcus v. Sarsfield, 309
Feather v. Queen, 10
Featherstone v. Hutchinson, 352

Feise v. Parkinson, 315
Feltham v. England, 90
Fenn v. Bittlestone, 286
—— v. Harrison, 198
Field v. Adames, 26
Firth v. Purvis, 69
Fish v. Kempton, 200
Fitzgerald v. Midland Rail. Co., 250
Flindt v. Scott, 351
Flower v. Adam, 91
Foster v. Dawber, 381
Fowkes v. Joyce, 69
—— v. Manchester & London Life Assurance Co., 316
Fox v. Scard, 350
Foxhall v. Barnett, 103
Fragano v. Long, 277
Frame v. Dawson, 270
Francis v. Cockrell, 88
Franklin v. Neate, 288
Freeman v. Arkell, 103
—— v. Birch, 255
French v. Styring, 209
Frith v. Cartland, 79

G.

GAGE v. Smith, 61
Galliard v. Laxton, 98
Gallin v. London & N. W. Rail. Co., 250
Gardiner v. Gray, 140
Gardner v. Walsh, 296
Gawler v. Chaplin, 112
Gibbon v. Budd, 230
Giblin v. M'Mullen, 246
Gibson v. Carruthers, 365
Giles v. Jones, 348
—— v. Spencer, 67
Gilliat v. Roberts, 275
Gilpin v. Fowler, 127
Gipps v. Gipps, 150
Godin v. London Assurance Co., 315
Godsall v. Boldero, 316
Godwin v. Francis, 271
Godwyn v. Cheveley, 26
Goff v. G. N. Rail. Co., 99
Goodall v. Skelton, 277
Goodman v. Griffiths, 173
—— v. Pocock, 227
Gord v. Needs, 180
Gordon v. Rimmington, 312
Goss v. Lord Nugent, 151, 380
Gott v. Gandy, 37
Graham v. Furber, 78
—— v. Musson, 174

Grainger v. Hill, 98, 103
Grand Junction Canal Co. v. Shugar, 52
Grant v. Vaughan, 78
Grantham v. Hawley, 287
Gray v. Bond, 54
Great Northern Rail. Co. v. Shepherd, 251
Greaves v. Hepke, 276
Gregory v. Duke of Brunswick, 102
Green v. Bartlett, 203
—— v. Brown, 311
—— v. Goddard, 97
Greening v. Wilkinson, 79
Greville v. Atkins, 347
Griffin v. Dighton, 16
Griffiths v. Lewis, 124
Grose v. West, 16
Grote v. Chester & Holyhead Rail. Co., 38
Grove v. Dubois, 201
Grubb v. Earl of Burlington, 62
Grymes v. Boweren, 61
Guntor v. Astor, 152
Gurney v. Womersley, 332
Gutsole v. Mathers, 131

H.

HALFORD v. Hatch, 362
—— v. Rymer, 316
Hall v. Barrows, 211
—— v. Fuller, 335
—— v. North Eastern Rail. Co., 250
Hallen v. Runder, 172
Halstead v. Skelton, 329
Hanley v. Casson, 202
Harbidge v. Warwick, 55
Hargrave v. Le Breton, 131
Harley v. King, 362
Harmer v. Cornelius, 226
Harnett v. Maitland, 61
Harris v. Great Western Rail. Co., 252
—— v. James, 37
—— v. Morris, 192
Harrison v. Tennant, 211
Hartop v. Hoare, 288
Harvey v. Bridges, 25
Hasleham v. Young, 210
Hastings, Marquis of, v. Morley, 376
Hatton, In re, 383
Hawthorne v. Hammond, 252
Heane v. Rogers, 182
Hearn v. London & South Western Rail. Co., 249
Helyear v. Hawke, 199
Henly v. Mayor, &c., of Lyme, 9

INDEX OF CASES. xiii

Henfrey v. Bromley, 382
Hey v. Moorhouse, 24
Higgins v. Hopkins, 228
—— v. Senior, 201
Highmore v. Earl of Harrington, 130
Hill v. Balls, 8
—— v. Gray, 140
Hiscox v. Greenwood, 77
Hitchman v. Stewart, 298
Hoby v. Roebuck, 171
Hochster v. De la Tour, 376
Hodgson v. Anderson, 159
—— v. Loy, 277
—— v. Scarlett, 128
Holder v. Soulby, 253
Holliday v. Atkinson, 159
—— v. Morgan, 139
Holloway v. Holloway, 141
Holmes v. Bellingham, 15
—— v. Mather, 87
—— v. Mitchell, 295
—— v. Onion, 89
Holroyd v. Marshall, 287
Hooper v. Lane, 113
Hope v. Hope, 150
Hopkins v. Prescott, 351
Hopper v. Reeve, 97
Hopwood v. Thorn, 124
Hore v. Whitmore, 310
Horn v. Anglo-Australian Insurance Co., 316
—— v. Ivy, 216
Horton v. McMurtrey, 226
Hotson v. Browne, 180
Howes v. Ball, 68
Hughes v. Quentin, 91
Humble v. Hunter, 200
—— v. Langston, 362
—— v. Mitchell, 172
Hume v. Oldacre, 9
Humphries v. Brogden, 51
Hunt v. Hooper, 112
Hutchins v. Scott, 382
Huzzey v. Field, 89
Hyde v. Graham, 54

I.

IRELAND v. Thomson, 202
Irwin v. Dearman, 152

J.

JAMES v. Boston, 127
—— v. Hayward, 40

Jay v. Richardson, 362
Jayne v. Price, 15
Jeffereyes v. Legendra, 310
Jenkins v. Hutchinson, 140
Jenner v. Clegg, 67
Jennings v. Rundall, 190
Johnson v. Blenkensopp, 226
—— v. Hudson, 348
Jolly v. Rees, 191
Jones v. Ashburnham, 158
—— v. Bright, 139
—— v. Jones, 25
—— v. Owen, 111
Joyce v. Swann, 276

K.

KEEN v. Priest, 69
Keir v. Leeman, 349
Kelly v. Kelly 150
Kennedy v. Broun, 230
—— v. Panama, &c., Royal Mail Co., 352
Kerrison v. Cole, 351
Kershaw v. Ogden, 273
King v. Hoare, 10, 383
Kingston v. Phelps, 160
Kirby v. Duke of Marlborough, 296
Kirkman v. Shawcross, 254
Kirton v. Elliot, 189
Knapp v. Harden, 180
Koebel v. Saunders, 311

L.

LACY v. Kinaston, 382
Labouchere v. Dawson, 350
Laing v. Meader, 377
—— v. Whaley, 52
Laird v. Pim, 270
Lamert v. Heath, 355
Langridge v. Levy, 138
Latham v. Parry, 210
Laugher v. Brefitt, 80
Law v. London Indisputable Life Policy Co., 316
Leck v. Maestaer, 247
Lee v. Riley, 23, 87
—— v. Robinson, 272
—— v. Smith, 67
—— v. Stevenson, 53
Leicester, Earl of, v. Walter, 130
Levy v. Moylan, 112
Lewis v. Bingham, 383
—— v. Branthwaite, 25

Lewis v. Levy, 128
—— v. Rucker, 309
Lickbarrow v. Mason, 279
Lindley v. Lacey, 181
Liver Alkali Co. v. Johnson, 248
Liverpool Adelphi Loan Association v. Fairhurst, 190
Livie v. Janson, 314
Lloyd v. Howard, 330
—— v. Johnson, 347
London & N. W. Rail. Co. v. Glyn, 315
——, Birmingham, &c., Banking Co., In re, 377
——, Bishop of, v. Web, 62
——, City of, v. Wood, 110
Lougher v. Williams, 363
Loughton v. Bishop of Sodor and Man, 127
Lowe v. Govett, 16
—— v. London & N. W. Rail. Co., 216
Lucas v. Godwin, 229
Lyons v. De Pass, 272
Lysney v. Selby, 139

M.

M'CAWLEY v. Furness Rail. Co., 250
M'Dougal v. Claridge, 126
M'George v. Egan, 191
M'Gregor v. Thwaites, 128
M'Iver v. Richardson, 157
Maclean v. Dunn, 174, 199
M'Manus v. Lancashire & Yorkshire Rail. Co., 249
Mainwaring v. Brandon, 201
Malachy v. Soper, 131
Mallett v. Bateman, 295
Manchester & Altrincham Rail. Co. v. Fullarton, 38
Manley v. St. Helen's Canal & Rail. Co., 39
Manning v. Lunn, 376
March v. March, 151
Margetson v. Wright, 139
Marshall v. Broadhurst, 364
—————v. York & Newcastle Rail. Co., 255
Martin v. Gilham, 61
—— v. Great Northern Rail. Co., 38
—— v. Temperley, 89
Mary's Case, 99
Marzetti v. Williams, 9
Mason v. Pritchard, 296
Master v. Miller, 336
Mather v. Maidstone, 331

Matson v. Wharam, 171
Matthews v. Baxter, 193
—— v. L——e, 347
May v. Burdett, 38
Mayhew v. Herrick, 78
Mears v. London & S. W. Rail. Co., 88
Mentone v. Athawes, 229
Mercantile Bank of India v. Dixon, 334
Meredith v. Meigh, 274
Merest v. Harvey, 26
Merryweather v. Jones, 374
Metcalfe v. London & Brighton Rail. Co., 249
Meyer v. Haworth, 192
Micklethwaite v. Merrill, 288
Mills v. Mayor of Colchester, 54
Millard v. Harvey, 190
Miller v. David, 129
—— v. Race, 78, 335
Milligan v. Wedge, 88
Minshull v. Oakes, 363
Mitchell v. Edie, 314
—— v. Reynolds, 350
Moody v. Bell, 254
Morley v. Attenborough, 289
—— v. Boothby, 170
Morton v. Burn, 159
—— v. Tibbett, 273
Moss v. Hall, 332
Mounsey v. Ismay, 55
Mucklow v. Mangles, 276
Muller v. Moss, 78
Murgatroyd v. Robinson, 36
Murphy v. O'Shea, 202
Mussen v. Price, 278

N.

NASH v. Lucas, 68
Needler v. Guest, 228
Nesbit v. Lushington, 312
New Brunswick Rail. Co. v. Conybeare, 138
Newsome v. Coles, 211
Nicholson v. Revill, 298
Nixon v. Freeman, 68
Noble v. Kennoway, 311
Nokes v. Gibbon, 230
North East. Rail. Co. v. Crosland, 53
Northey v. Field, 278
Norris v. Baker, 41

O.

OAKES v. Turquand, 217

INDEX OF CASES.   xv

Oakes v. Wood, 97
Oakley v. Portsmouth & Ryde Steam Packet Co., 248
Ockenden v. Henley, 270
Oliver v. Oliver, 77
Olliet v. Bessey, 111
O'Mealey v. Wilson, 193
Ormrod v. Huth, 140
Osborn v. Gillet, 91, 99
Osborne v. Rogers, 158
Owens v. Dickenson, 192

P.

PADMORE v. Lawrence, 128
Parker v. Flint, 252
—— v. Patrick, 288
—— v. S. E. Rail. Co., 252
—— v. Winlow, 200
—— v. Wise, 295
Parmiter v. Coupland, 128
Partington v. Att.-Gen., 191
Partridge v. Bank of England, 336
Pasley v. Freeman, 9, 138
Passmore v. North, 329
Paterson v. Gandasequi, 201
—— v. Paterson, 150
Pattison v. Jones, 126
Paul v. Paul, 150
Payne v. Rogers, 38
Peacock v. Peacock, 211
—— v. Pursell, 377
—— v. Rhodes, 330
Pearce v. Brooks, 347
—— v. Ormsby, 129
Penruddock's Case, 41
Petty v. Anderson, 191
Pfleger v. Browne, 379
Phillips v. Foxhall, 297
—— v. Jones, 225
Phillipson v. Hayter, 191
Philp v. Squire, 151
Philpot v. Swann, 314
Philpott v. Jones, 379
Philpotts v. Evans, 279
Phipson v. Kneller, 333
Pickard v. Smith, 36
Pickering v. Busk, 199
Pigot v. Cubley, 288
Pinnell's Case, 380
Planché v. Colburn, 228
—— v. Fletcher, 313
Plimley v. Westley, 334
Pluckwell v. Wilson, 88
Pochin v. Pawley, 201
Polhill v. Walter, 138

Poole v. Adams, 315
Pooley v. Harradine, 295
Poplett v. Stockdale, 347
Potter v. Faulkner, 91
Powell v. Duff, 170
—— v. Hyde, 312
Price and Brown's Case, 217
—— v. Barker, 297
Pritchard v. Merchants' Life Assurance Co., 317
Proud v. Hollis, 26
Provost of Queen's College, Oxford, v. Hallett, 60
Pulsford v. Richards, 141
Pym v. Campbell, 181

Q.

QUARMAN v. Burnett, 89
Quebec Marine Insurance Co. v. Commercial Bank of Canada, 310

R.

RAITT v. Mitchell, 254
Ramsay v. Macdonald, 193
Rann v. Hughes, 170
Rawlings v. Till, 97
Raymond v. Fitch, 364
Read v. Coker, 96
Readhead v. Midland Rail. Co., 249
Reddie v. Scoolt, 152
Redman v. Wilson, 311
Regina v. Darlington Local Board, 38
—— v. Driscoll, 97
—— v. Evans, 141
—— v. Great Northern Rail. Co., 42
—— v. Musson, 16
—— v. Saintiff, 39
—— v. Stimpson, 111
—— v. Train, 40
Reynolds v. Wheeler, 298
Rex v. Birdbrooke, 225
—— v. Ecclesfield, 40
—— v. Great Bowden, 226
—— v. Great Wishford, 228
—— v. Hatfield, 15
—— v. Lyth, 225
—— v. Pagham Commissioners, 337
—— v. Pucklechurch, 225
—— v. Ragley, 40
—— v. Revel, 112
—— v. Russell, 41
—— v. Topham, 131
—— v. Weltje, 131

INDEX OF CASES.

Rex v. Williams, 131
Rich v. Basterfield, 37
Richards v. London & Brighton Rail. Co., 252
—— v. Rose, 53
Richardson v. Great Eastern Rail. Co., 88
Ricketts v. East & West India Dock and Rail. Co., 39
Ridgeway v. Wharton, 172
Riding v. Smith, 125
Ritchie v. Smith, 348
Robertson v. Kensington, 331
Robinson v. Cox, 346
—— v. Harman, 271
—— v. Hawksford, 335
Robson v. Drummond, 229
Roper v. Bumford, 378
Rose v. Groves, 40
Ross v. Estates Investment Co., 138
Rowe v. Tipper, 333
Rucker v. Cammeyer, 174
Rumball v. Ball, 375
Rushforth v. Hadfield, 254
Russel v. Langstaffe, 329
Russell v. Palmer, 88
Ryan v. Shilcock, 68

S.

St. Helen's Smelting Co. v. Tipping, 37
St. Paul v. St. Paul, 150
Sanderson v. Baker, 113
—— v. Piper, 179
Satterthwaite v. Dewhurst, 151
Saville v. Roberts, 102
Sayer v. Wagstaffe, 377
Schmaltz v. Avery, 201
Schneider v. Heath, 140
Scott v. Rayment, 209
—— v. Shepherd, 8
—— v. Stansfield, 127
Scottish N. E. Rail. Co. v. Stewart, 217
Scotson v. Pegg, 159
Seaman v. Fonerau, 310
Seare v. Prentice, 88
Selby v. Greaves, 67
Selway v. Fogg, 353
Semayne's Case, 113
Sergeson v. Sealey, 193
Seymour v. Greenwood, 89
—— v. Maddox, 90
Shadwell v. Hutchinson, 41
Sharp v. Grey, 88

Shaw v. Steward, 364
Shelley v. Westbrooke, 151
Shepheard v. Whitaker, 129
Shepherd v. Johnson, 279
Sherrington v. Yates, 191
Shore v. Wilson, 179
Shrewsbury v. Crompton, 61
Shuttleworth v. Le Fleming, 55
Sibree v. Tripp, 378
Sibthorpe v. Brunel, 160
Sillem v. Thornton, 315
Simpson v. Eggington, 378
—— v. Hartopp, 69
—— v. Penton, 294
—— v. Savage, 41
Simson v. Ingham, 379
Singleton v. Williamson, 26
Six Carpenters' Case, 26
Skaife v. Jackson, 379
Smith v. Braine, 330
—— v. Cook, 38
—— v. Dearlove, 253
—— v. Kenrick, 52
—— v. London Dock Co., 39
—— v. Neale, 172
—— v. Pritchard, 113
—— v. Surman, 172
—— v. Surridge, 314
—— v. Vertue, 332
—— v. Wilson, 180
—— v. Wood, 130
Smout v. Ilbery, 138
Smurthwaite v. Wilkins, 336
Smyth v. Carter, 60
Soames v. Spencer, 199
Solby v. Forbes, 179
Somerville v. Hawkins, 125
Southby v. Wiseman, 200
Southerne v. Howe, 140
Spencer's Case, 362
Spering v. Spering, 150
Spicer v. Cooper, 180
Spotswood v. Barrow, 226
Stafford, Mayor of, v. Till, 216
Standen v. Christmas, 363
Stanley v. Jones, 349
Staple v. Haydon, 53
Steiglitz v. Egginton, 201
Stevens v. Jeacocke, 10
Steward v. Gromett, 102
Stewart v. Cauty, 279
—— v. London & N. W. Rail. Co., 250
Stikeman v. Dawson, 190
Stone v. Compton, 297
Storr v. Crowley, 251
Summers v. Solomon, 200

Sutherland v. Pratt, 313
Sutton v. Moody, 78
Swan, *Ex parte*, 334
Swansborough v. Coventry, 53
Sweet v. Meredith, 348
——— v. Pym, 255
Swift v. Swift, 349

T.

TALLEY v. G. W. Rail. Co., 251
Tarleton v. M'Gawley, 8
Tarpley v. Blabey, 130
Tarrant v. Webb, 90
Tasker v. Shepherd, 227
Taylor v. Caldwell, 376
——— v. Chambers, 272
——— v. Jones, 158
——— v. Manners, 380
——— v. Stray, 203
——— v. Wakefield, 273
——— v. Whitehead, 53
Tempest v. Fitzgerald, 274
Tennant v. Golding, 36
Thompson's Case, 217
Thompson v. Davenport, 200
——— v. Hudson, 378
——— v. Ross, 151
Thornett v. Haines, 270
Thorogood v. Robinson, 79
Throgmorton v. Allen, 98
Tidman v. Ainslie, 129
Timothy v. Simpson, 98
Todd v. Flight, 38
——— v. Hawkins, 126
——— v. Ritchie, 313
Topham v. Braddick, 202
——— v. Duke of Portland, 349
Torrance v. Bolton, 353
Townend v. Toker, 158
Trustees of British Museum v. Finnis, 39
Tucker v. Newman, 24
——— v. Laing, 297
Tuff v. Warman, 91
Turley v. Bates, 276
Turner v. Ambler, 103
——— v. Stones, 332
Tupper v. Fowkes, 170
Tutton v. Darke, 68
Tutty v. Alewin, 124

U.

UNION Bank of Manchester v. Beech, 382
Usil v. Hales, 128

V.

VANE v. Lord Barnard, 62
Vaughan v. Menlove, 61
Venables v. Smith, 90
Vicars v. Wilcocks, 125
Viramy v. Warne, 230
Vivian v. Champion, 363
Vooght v. Winch, 383
Vowles v. Miller, 16

W.

WAKEMAN v. Robinson, 87
Waldo v. Martin, 350
Walker v. Brewster, 36
——— v. Chapman, 352
——— v. G. W. Rail. Co., 216
——— v. Macdonald, 331
——— v. Moore, 271
——— v. Neville, 381
——— v. Nussey, 275
Walter v. Holmes, 254
——— v. Selfe, 37
Ward v. Weekes, 125
Wason v. Walter, 127
Watbroke v. Griffith, 253
Watkins v. Vince, 199
Watson v. Threlkeld, 192
Watts v. Shuttleworth, 296
Waugh v. Morris, 347
Wayne v. Hanham, 289
Webb v. Fairman, 179
——— v. Fox, 365
——— v. Hewitt, 297
Wellock v. Constantine, 9
Wells v. Abraham, 9
——— v. Horton, 172
Western Counties Manure Co. v. Lawe's Chemical Manure Co., 124
Wheatcroft v. Hickman, 208
Wheelton v. Hardistry, 316
Whincup v. Hughes, 228
White v. Bass, 53
——— v. Crisp, 40
——— v. Cuyler, 201
——— v. Garden, 273
——— v. Spettigue, 77
Whitehead v. Anderson, 278
——— v. Tuckett, 199
——— v. Walker, 332
Whitfield v. S. E. Rail. Co., 129
Whistler v. Forster, 331
Wiffin v. Kincard, 97
Wigg v. Shuttleworth, 351
Wightman v. Townroe, 209

b

Wilby v. Elston, 8
Wild v. Harris, 375
Wiles v. Woodward, 182
Wilkes v. Hungerford Market Co., 9
Wilkinson v. Byers, 158
——— v. Haygarth, 25
——— v. Oliveira, 153
Wilks v. Back, 201
Williams v. Bailey, 353
——— v. Burgess, 275
——— v. James, 335
——— v. Lake, 172
——— v. Millington, 200
Williamson v. Allison, 138
——— v. Freer, 126
Willis v. De Castro, 382
Wiltshire v. Sidford, 16
Wilson v. Brett, 246
——— v. Kearne, 190
——— v. Lewis, 210
——— v. Ray, 352
——— v. Whitehead, 209
Winsmore v. Greenbank, 151
Wise v. Metcalfe, 61
Wiseman v. Easton, 210
Wood v. Clarke, 69
Woollam v. Hearne, 182
Wormer v. Biggs, 26

Worsley v. Wood, 315
Wotton v. Cooke, 363
Wright v. Clements, 129
——— v. London & N. W. Rail. Co., 91
——— v. Stavert, 171
Wyatt v. Harrison, 51
——— v. White, 102
Wythes v. Labouchere, 297

Y.

Yates v. Nash, 328
Yeatman v. Yeatman, 150
Yeomans v. Williams, 380
Yorke v. Greenhaugh, 255
——— v. Grindstone, 252
Young v. Glover, 329
——— v. Grote, 335
——— v. Macrae, 124
——— v. Matthews, 276

Z.

Zwinger v. Samuda, 336

INDEX OF STATUTES.

Statute	PAGE
5 Ric. II. c. 7	19, 93
32 Henry VIII. c. 34	358
5 & 6 Edward VI. c. 16	338
2 & 3 Ph. & Mary, c. 7	259
29 Eliz. c. 4	109
31 Eliz. c. 6	339
c. 12	259
21 Jac. I. c. 16	374
29 Car. II. c. 3, s. 4	163—169, 165, 167, 256, 257
s. 17	166, 167, 261—265, 290
c. 7	341
2 Will. & Mary, c. 5	23, 66
3 & 4 Anne, c. 9	325
7 Anne, c. 25, s. 3	ib.
8 Anne, c. 9, ss. 35—39	221
c. 14	109
ss. 6, 7	63
c. 19	6
12 Anne, st. 2, c. 12	339
7 Geo. II. c. 15	237
8 Geo. II. c. 13	6
11 Geo. II. c. 19	66
16 Geo. II. c. 18	104
19 Geo. II. c. 37, s. 1	300
24 Geo. II. c. 40	340
26 Geo. II. c. 33	237
7 Geo. III. c. 38	6
12 Geo. III. c. 73	29
14 Geo. III. c. 48, s. 1	307
c. 78	30, 307
26 Geo. III. c. 86	237
32 Geo. III. c. 60	122
47 Geo. III. c. 25	338
48 Geo. III. c. 88	325
49 Geo. III. c. 126	338
53 Geo. III. c. 159	86, 237
54 Geo. III. c. 56, s. 4	163
1 & 2 Geo. IV. c. 78, s. 1	319
5 Geo. IV. c. 74	340
c. 83	95
6 Geo. IV. c. 24	261
7 & 8 Geo. IV. c. 25	339
c. 31	22
9 Geo. IV. c. 14	132, 184
s. 7	167
ss. 1, 5	169
s. 15	183
c. 94	339
11 Geo. IV. & 1 Will IV. c. 68	234
s. 2	235
s. 4	236
1 & 2 Will. IV. c. 32	341
c. 37	340
c. 58	109, 245
c. 76	340
2 & 3 Will. IV. c. 71, s. 1	48
ss. 2, 3, 7	49
ss. 1, 2, 3	50
s. 4	51
3 & 4 Will. IV. c. 15	7
c. 27	373
s. 10	11
s. 3	12
s. 14	13
ss. 16, 17	374
c. 42	374
c. 98, s. 6	367
5 & 6 Will. IV. c. 37	341
c. 50	28
c. 63	340
c. 65	6
7 Will. IV. & 1 Vict. c. 55	110
1 & 2 Vict. c. 101	340
2 & 3 Vict. c. 12	342
c. 47	95
5 & 6 Vict. c. 39	283
c. 45, s. 17	6, 7
c. 100	7

INDEX OF STATUTES.

Statute	PAGE
6 & 7 Vict. c. 65	7
c. 73	243
c. 96, ss. 1, 2	122
s. 6	123
8 Vict. c. 20	95
8 & 9 Vict. c. 20, s. 47	31
c. 106, ss. 2, 3	162
c. 109, s. 18	339
9 & 10 Vict. c. 93	87, 96
c. 95	106
11 & 12 Vict. c. 44, s. 7	ib.
12 & 13 Vict. c. 92	23
14 & 15 Vict. c. 19	95
c. 25, s. 3	57
16 & 17 Vict. c. 119	339
17 & 18 Vict. c. 31	235, 238
s. 16	236
c. 60	30
c. 125	245, 368
s. 87	327
19 & 20 Vict. c. 97	374
s. 3	290
s. 5	294
s. 6	170, 319
c. 108	66
20 & 21 Vict. c. 85, ss. 28, 33, 35, 59	146
ss. 16, 21, 27	142
ss. 29, 30	143
s. 31	144
ss. 21, 26, 32, 45	145
21 & 22 Vict. c. 90	342
22 & 23 Vict. c. 56	340
c. 61, s. 5	146
23 & 24 Vict. c. 32	95
c. 111	325
c. 126	245
c. 144, s. 6	145
24 & 25 Vict. c. 96	71, 260
c. 97	95
c. 100, s. 31	27
ss. 53, 55	149
25 & 26 Vict. c. 38	340
c. 63	95
c. 68	7
c. 88	136
c. 89	213
s. 4	204
s. 38	215
26 & 27 Vict. c. 41	241
c. 88, s. 4	7
c. 92	235
27 & 28 Vict. c. 56, s. 1	300
28 & 29 Vict. c. 60	30
c. 86, ss. 1, 2	204
ss. 3, 4	205
29 & 30 Vict. c. 69, s. 6	234
30 Vict. c. 23	169, 300
30 & 31 Vict. c. 48, s. 5	257
c. 131	214
c. 134	95
c. 142	340
c. 144	309
31 & 32 Vict. c. 119	237
32 & 33 Vict. c. 24	342
c. 68	146
c. 70	2
c. 71, ss. 15, 23, 94, 95	73
ss. 6, 87	110
ss. 15, 17	360
ss. 23, 25, 54	361
s. 94	361
ss. 31—50, 125	373
c. 72, s. 33	221
c. 113	341
c. 117	ib.
33 Vict. c. 14	188
33 & 34 Vict. c. 23	189
c. 93	185, 187
34 Vict. c. 17	323
34 & 35 Vict. c. 79	65
c. 101, s. 7	341
35 & 36 Vict. c. 93, s. 18	285
ss. 27, 28	286
36 Vict. c. 12, s. 2	342
36 & 37 Vict. c. 66, s. 24	356
37 & 38 Vict. c. 50	187
c. 57	374
s. 1	11
ss. 3, 4, 5	11
s. 7	13
c. 62	155, 183
38 & 39 Vict. c. 77	206
c. 92	58
39 & 40 Vict. c. 81, ss. 4, 5, 7, 12	326
41 Vict. c. 19, s. 3	146
s. 4	142
41 & 42 Vict. c. 41	74, 170
s. 4	280
ss. 4, 10	281
ss. 4, 10, 11	282
s. 20	360

PRINCIPLES

OF

TORTS AND CONTRACTS.

BOOK I.—TORTS.

CHAPTER I.

ACTIONABLE WRONGS.

To constitute a tort there must be a conjunction of damage (*damnum*) done to the plaintiff, and a wrongful act (*injuria*) on the part of the defendant causing that damage. Tort.
(1)

By damage is meant loss, pecuniary or otherwise, of which the law takes cognizance. Damage.
(2)

All loss which ensues in the ordinary and natural course of events from the committal of a wrongful act constitutes legal damage; and this even though the damage was caused directly and immediately by the act of third parties who were set in motion by the primary wrong-doer, provided such acts were the necessary or legal and natural consequences of the original wrongful act.

Legal damage is not necessarily pecuniary. Every invasion of the plaintiff's right or unauthorized interference with his property imports legal damage; and even though the plaintiff be not a farthing the poorer through the wrongful act of the defendant the jury may nevertheless give more than nominal damages if they choose.

The least infringement of personal liberty or security is a cause of action in which substantial damages are recoverable.

Injury or wrongful act. (3) A person who puts a dangerous thing in motion, or who performs a possibly dangerous act in a place where an accident on his part would probably and naturally result in damage to others, is held responsible as for a wrongful act in case mischief ensues.

An individual who makes an improvement on his own land for his own benefit, and who thereby unintentionally causes damage to his neighbour, is responsible as for a wrongful act.

Where one maliciously persuades another to break a contract, or deprives a woman of her marriage by false representations, or, being a banker, refuses to pay a draft of a customer to whose credit there are sufficient funds lying in the bank, this is a wrongful act for which substantial damages are recoverable.

Loss not importing legal damage. (4) The obstruction of a view under any circumstances, or of light and air, the right to which has not been acquired by prescription, does not constitute legal damage.

Loss of reputation consequent on slander, by the use of words, not in themselves actionable, and where no *pecuniary* loss has been occasioned, does not constitute legal damage.

Where a loss has been occasioned, which would not under the ordinary course of events ensue from the wrongful act committed, or where it would not have ensued from the wrongful act, but for the intervention of circumstances for which the original wrong-doer is not responsible, there is no legal damage.

Injurious act without legal wrong. (5) There is no legal wrong where damage has been occasioned by inevitable accident, or in the performance of a legal act without negligence, or in necessary self-defence.

The sale of diseased horses, cattle, or sheep, in the absence of a warranty, is not a legal wrong, however injurious to the vendee (the vendor may, however, be held responsible for fraudulent concealment; also see 32 & 33 Vict. c. 70).

It is no legal wrong for a commanding officer to falsely and maliciously arrest and accuse a subordinate, nor for an infant to obtain money under false pretence that he is of full age, nor for a married woman to represent that she is a *feme sole*, whereby she obtains an invalid contract to be made with her, nor for a man to seduce a female infant who is neither actually nor constructively in her father's service. The maxim that there is no wrong without a remedy must be understood of course with reference to legal and not to moral wrong. But it must be admitted that there are many wrongs properly remediable by law which are not recognized in our judicial system.

Any injury to property, whether direct or brought about indirectly, by menaces, false representations, or fraud, constitutes a tort. *Injuries to property. (6)*

By property is meant not only landed estate and personal chattels, but also property of an incorporeal nature, as for example:—

(1). *A franchise.* Where one enjoys the monopoly of a ferry, it is actionable to erect a new ferry, except at such a distance from the old one as makes the new passage a real convenience to the public; or where anyone is owner of a fair or market, it is a disturbance of his rights, wilfully and intentionally to sell wares immediately beyond the limits of the market in order to avoid the payment of tolls.

(2). *Property in literary and artistic productions,* as unpublished manuscripts, lectures, paintings and photographs.

(3). *The right to the free exercise of one's trade.* It is actionable to prevent others by force or fraud from dealing at the plaintiff's shop, or from working on his premises, or from sending children to his school. But interference with a man's trade by fair competition is never actionable.

B 2

(4). *The right of the landowner or occupier to preserve game.* It is actionable to frighten your neighbour's grouse so that they are prevented from going on his land.

Breach of duty generally. (7)
Wherever a legal duty is imposed upon a person, whether by contract or otherwise, a breach of that duty constitutes a tort.

When a contract is broken, an action (*ex contractu*) may be brought for the breach of the contract, or an action *ex delicto* for the breach of the duty imposed by the contract.

Where the duty existed prior to the contract, an action of tort only can be brought.

In an action of tort founded upon contract, nominal damages are claimable, though no actual damage is proved.

Only parties to the contract can be sued *ex delicto* for the breach of it, and the cause of action is not transferable to one to whom the contract is not transferable.

Public officers are liable in tort if no special remedy is provided by statute for the refusal or neglect to perform ministerial (but not judicial) acts, and for the abuse of the powers confided to them.

Officers in public departments are responsible for their own negligence or misconduct, but not for that of their subordinates.

The law imposes upon consignors and bailors for hire or otherwise of dangerous goods the duty of giving notice of the nature of such articles, and an action of tort lies for the neglect to do so.

Fraud or falsehood. (8)
Where anyone by fraud or falsehood has caused damage to another, he is liable in tort. And when anyone knowingly makes a false statement intending that another shall act upon it, and the latter does act upon it, and suffers damage, the former is liable in tort.

Every malicious act which causes damage to another is actionable.

Once a tort not
An act innocent in its origin may be rendered tortious

by subsequent circumstances, and conversely a wrongful act may be deprived of its tortious character by ratification. *always a tort. (9)*

An act which is perfectly lawful in itself may operate so as to cause damage to another, and from the moment that it does so it becomes a tort; *e.g.*, a man may lawfully excavate his own land, but as soon as his neighbour's land begins to be caused thereby to sink, he becomes liable in tort.

Where a man has taken possession of property, and sold it without lawful authority, the owner may treat him as a wrong-doer, and sue him for damages, or he may affirm his act and treat him as his agent. And if the owner ratify such an act by receiving payment, or otherwise, he cannot subsequently treat it as a wrong.

Where a wrongful act amounts to a felony, the action of tort is suspended until a criminal tribunal shall have convicted or acquitted the wrong-doer. [Some doubt, however, has recently been thrown upon this rule.] *Torts which amount to crime. (10)*

But where stolen property is in the hands of an innocent third party, who did not purchase it in market overt, the owner may bring an action against him for its recovery before the thief is prosecuted.

Where the wrongful act amounts to a misdemeanour only, the civil remedy is not suspended until the offender is brought to trial for the criminal act. [Felonies are only distinguishable from misdemeanours by enumeration, and not by definition.]

For a public nuisance which affects all persons alike, the remedy is by indictment; but if special damage is suffered by an individual he may bring his action for damages.

When several persons have been jointly concerned in the commission of a wrongful act, they may in general all be charged jointly as principals, or the plaintiff may sue any one of the parties individually. *Joint tortfeasors. (11)*

Whenever two persons have so conducted themselves as to be liable to be jointly sued, each is responsible for the whole injury sustained by their common act.

If two commit a joint tort, the judgment against one is of itself, without execution, a sufficient bar to an action against the other for the same cause.

Wrongs under Statute Law.

Where a statute creates a right or duty, and no remedy is expressly provided, the remedy is by action of tort. But where a specific remedy is provided in the statute, that remedy and that only can be pursued, unless it fails to cover the whole right.

Penalties. (12) Where a statute creates no specific right, and imposes no specific duty, but merely prohibits a thing from being done under a penalty for doing it, the penalty only is recoverable, and an action for damages is not sustainable.

Penalty and damages. (13) Where a statute vests a right or imposes a duty, and at the same time imposes a penalty on those who infringe the right or neglect the duty, an injured party may bring his action for damages, and at the same time, if he be the first in the field, sue for the penalty.

Penalty *or* damages. Where a statute gives damages, and imposes a penalty in the alternative, the injured party may elect his remedy.

Damages only. Where a statute creating a new duty or obligation provides a special mode of obtaining compensation, and gives the amount recovered to the party aggrieved, no other remedy can be applied for the public or private wrong.

Statutes imposing penalties. The Copyright Act, 8 Anne, c. 19, imposed penalties for the infringement of copyright, which were cumulative on the common law remedy. This statute was, however, repealed by 5 & 6 Vict. c. 45 (see *infra*). Penalties are still imposed by the latter Act (sec. 17) upon the importation, sale or publication of books reprinted abroad. And these penalties are cumulative upon the remedy by action.

By 5 & 6 Will. IV. c. 65, anyone publishing, &c., a lecture of which statutory notice has been given, and without the consent of the lecturer, is liable to a penalty as well as damages.

By 8 Geo. II. c. 13, and 7 Geo. III. c. 38, anyone engraving, copying, &c., a print or engraving without the written consent of the proprietor is liable to a penalty as well as damages. The 25 & 26 Vict. c. 68 contains a similar provision with regard to paintings, drawings and photographs.

By 26 Vict. c. 88, s. 4, anyone using a counterfeit trade-mark or a false description of an article of manufacture is liable to a penalty as well as damages.

Penalties for the commission of nuisances under various statutes are also cumulative in the common law remedy by action.

3 & 4 Will. IV. c. 15, and 5 & 6 Vict. c. 45, impose penalties as an alternative remedy for the representation of dramatic and musical compositions without the written consent of the author or proprietor. The aggrieved party may either sue for the penalty *or* bring his action for damages.

The provisions of the Useful and Ornamental Designs Acts (5 & 6 Vict. c. 100, and 6 & 7 Vict. c. 65) are similar.

The Copyright Act, 5 & 6 Vict. c. 45, provides a special remedy by action on the case for damages against any person who publishes or causes a book to be printed for sale or exportation without the *written* consent of the proprietor of the copyright, or who imports for sale or hire such unlawfully printed book, or who, with guilty knowledge, sells or publishes, or exposes for sale or hire, such book without the consent of the proprietor. There is therefore now no *penalty* for the infringement of copyright in books, except under sec. 17 of the Act (see above).

Penalties imposed by bye-laws founded upon statute **Bye-laws.**
(14)

for the suppression of certain torts are cumulative upon the common law remedy by action.

Power to make bye-laws for certain specified purposes is given to municipal corporations, local boards, public companies, &c. Such powers are to be narrowly construed.

Patent law. (15) Patent law is derived from the prerogative of the Crown modified by statute, and the remedy for the infringement of a patent is by action for damages, with or without injunction.

ILLUSTRATIVE CASES.

(1) *Rex* v. *Pagham Commissioners*, 8 B. & C. 362.

Certain defences against the inroads of the sea having been erected for the benefit of the Pagham levels by commissioners appointed for the purpose, the sea was caused to flow with greater violence against and damaged the adjoining land not within the levels. It was held that the owner of the adjoining land could not obtain compensation; for although the act of the defendants caused him damage, that act was not a wrongful act, since landowners have the right to protect their land against the sea.

(2) *Scott* v. *Shepherd*, 3 *Wils.* 403.

An action of trespass was maintained against the person who originally threw a squib, which after having been thrown about in self-defence by other persons, at last put out the plaintiff's eye.

(3) *Dickenson* v. *Watson, Sir T. Jones*, 205.

A defendant having with him a pistol loaded with hail shot, discharged it in the open air, in a place where he thought no one was; the plaintiff, however, was passing, and the shot deprived him of the sight of his eye. The defendant was not held excused on the ground of accident.

(4) *Aldred's ca.*, 9 *Co.* 58 b.

"For prospect, which is a matter only of delight and not of necessity, no action lies for stopping thereof."

Wilby v. *Elston*, 8 C.B. 142.

The words "You are living by imposture. You used to walk St. Paul's Churchyard for a living," spoken of a woman with the intention of imputing that she was a swindler and a prostitute, were held not actionable without proof of special damage.

(5) *Hill* v. *Balls*, 2 H. & N. 299.

A declaration stated that the defendant had knowingly sold a glandered horse to the plaintiff, who believed it to be healthy. The horse was worthless and infected, and caused the death of another horse of the plaintiff's. Held, that the declaration disclosed no cause of action.

(6) *Bridgland* v. *Shapter*, 5 M. & W. 375.

A person brought sheep to a public house forty yards out of the limits of a market, left them there, went into the market in search of customers, whom he brought back to the public house, and there sold the sheep to them. Held, that this was a fraud upon the market for which the seller was actionable.

Abernethy v. *Hutchinson*, 1 *H. & Tw.* 28.

A person who attends oral lectures is not justified in publishing them for profit. An action will lie upon the implied contract by the lecturer against a pupil attending oral lectures who causes them to be published for profit, and an injunction will be granted against third persons so publishing them.

Tarleton v. *M'Gawley*, *Peake* 270.

An action was held to be maintainable against the master of a vessel for purposely firing off a cannon at negroes and thereby preventing them from trading with the plaintiff.

(7)   *Marzetti* v. *Williams*, 1 *B. & Ad.* 423.

A banker enters into an implied contract to pay a cheque drawn by a customer within a reasonable time after he, the banker, has received sufficient funds belonging to the customer. The banker is therefore guilty of a breach of duty in refusing to pay a cheque under such circumstances, and the customer may sue him in tort, although he has not sustained any actual damage.

Henly v. *Mayor, &c., of Lyme*, 5 *Bing.* 91.

The plaintiff, who had suffered loss in consequence of the decay of sea walls, which a corporation was directed to repair under the terms of a grant from the Crown, was held entitled to sue the corporation for damages. Best, C.J.: "I take it to be perfectly clear that if a public officer abuses his office either by an act of omission or commission, and the consequences of that is an injury to an individual, an action may be maintained against such public officer."

(8)   *Pasley* v. *Freeman*, 3 *T.R.* 51.

A false affirmation made by the defendant with intent to defraud the plaintiff, whereby the plaintiff received damage, was held to be ground for an action on the case; it was held not necessary to support the action, that the defendant should have been benefited by the deceit, or that he should have colluded with the person who was.

(9)   *Bonomi* v. *Backhouse*, *Ell. Bl. & Ell.* 622.

The plaintiff was owner of the reversion of a messuage entitled to the support of the underground mines and earth of the contiguous ground. The defendant, more than six years before action brought, worked the mines at 280 yards distance from the house in such a manner that the earth intervening between the place of working and the foundation of the house gradually gave way, and finally, within six years of action brought, the effect reached the foundation of the house, which was thereby injured. On these facts: held, that the plaintiff was entitled to verdict. [Here it will be seen that the act of the defendant was not originally tortious, but became such by subsequent circumstances.]

Brewer v. *Sparrow*, 7 *B. & C.* 310.

The assignees of a bankrupt having once affirmed the act of a person who wrongfully sold the property of the bankrupt, were held unable to treat him subsequently as a wrong-doer and sue him in tort.

(10)   *Wellock* v. *Constantine*, 7 *L.T.R., N.S.* 751.

In an action for assault, the evidence proved that the defendant had committed a rape on the plaintiff. The judge at the trial nonsuited the plaintiff on the ground that the complaint involved a charge of felony. A person is not allowed to make, in the first instance, a felony the foundation of a civil action. But see *Wells* v. *Abraham, L.R.,* 7 Q.B. 554.

Wilkes v. *Hungerford Market Co.,* 2 *Bing., N.C.* 281.

The plaintiff, a bookseller, having a shop by the side of a public thoroughfare, suffered loss in his business in consequence of passengers having been diverted from the thoroughfare by defendant's continuing an authorized obstruction across it for an unreasonable time. Held, that this was damage sufficiently of a private nature to form the subject of a civil action.

(11) *Hume* v. *Oldacre,* 1 *Stark.* 351.

In an action of trespass against a huntsman for hunting over the lands of another, damages may be recovered, not only for the mischief immediately occasioned by the defendant himself, but also for that done by the concourse of people who accompanied him.

Brown v. *Wootton, Cro. Jac.* 74.

Popham, C.J.: "If one hath cause of action [in trespass] against two, and obtain judgment against one, he shall not have remedy against the other."

The same is true with regard to joint contractors, but not with regard to joint and several contractors. (*King* v. *Hoare,* 13 *M. & W.* 494.)

(12) *Stevens* v. *Jeacocke,* 11 *Q.B.* 731.

By the 4 & 5 Vict. c. 57, it is enacted that certain fishing stations shall be bounded as therein defined, and that in cases of interference by one boat with another, under specified circumstances the fish taken by the party interfering shall be forfeited to the party interfered with, and the interfering party shall forfeit £50. The plaintiff declared in trespass on the case for general damages. Held, that the declaration showed no cause of action, the plaintiff stating no interference with any common law right, and the statute having only imposed a particular penalty for the act done, and having therefore given no general cause of action.

(13) *Couch* v. *Steel,* 3 *Ell. & Bl.* 410.

The statute 7 & 8 Vict. c. 112, s. 18, makes it the duty of the shipowner to have on board a proper supply of medicines: Held, that though the Act imposed a penalty, recoverable by a common informer, as the specific punishment for the breach of duty as to the public, sailors sustaining a private injury from the breach of that statutable duty are entitled to maintain an action to recover damages.

(14) *Calder and Hebble Navigation Co.* v. *Pilling,* 14 *M. & W.* 87.

A local Act empowered the company of proprietors of a public navigation to make bye-laws for the good and orderly using the navigation, and for the well governing of the bargemen, and to inflict reasonable fines, not exceeding £5, against persons offending against the same. The company made a bye-law that the navigation should be closed on every Sunday, and that no person should navigate any boat, &c., on Sundays under a penalty of £5. Held, that the making of such a bye-law was unauthorized and void.

(15) *Feather* v. *Queen,* 35 *L.J., Q.B.* 200.

See the judgment of Cockburn, C.J., in which the history and nature of patent right are discussed.

CHAPTER II.

TITLE TO REALTY.

IF a person is shown to be in receipt of rent he is presumed to be entitled to the reversion in fee of the land in respect of which the rent is received, unless this presumption can be rebutted by a contrary presumption arising from surrounding circumstances. Presumption in favour of fee-simple. (1)

Title to land has been protected by various Statutes of Limitations, by the last of which, 37 & 38 Vict. c. 57, s. 1, which came into operation January 1st, 1879, it is enacted that no person can bring an action for the recovery of lands, but within twelve years next after the time at which the right to bring such action shall have first accrued to him, or to some person through whom he claims. Statutes of Limitations.

Six years are allowed (37 & 38 Vict. c. 57, s. 3) for persons under disability from the time the disability ceases; but no action is to be brought after thirty years (sec. 5). The disabilities which have the effect of extending the period of limitation are infancy, coverture, idiotcy, lunacy, and unsoundness of mind. Absence beyond seas (sec. 4) is not now a disability. Disabilities, c. 57, s. 3.

The extension of the period of limitation is granted also from the death of the person under disability.

It is enacted by 3 & 4 Will. IV. c. 27, s. 10 (Statute of Limitations), that no person shall be deemed to have been in possession of land merely by reason of his having made an entry thereon, and that no continual or other claim upon or near any land shall preserve any right of making entry. But this section applies to a mere entry, without Possession by landowner.

any attempt or intention to take possession. And it is different when the entry was made *animo possidendi*, and possession was actually taken, to the exclusion of the adverse occupants. And such a re-entry and resumption of possession by a landowner before the period of limitation has elapsed is sufficient to preserve his rights; and it is immaterial how long such resumption of possession lasted, provided that the resumption was complete.

Occupation by servants. (2)

If a landowner allows a servant or workman to live in a cottage on his estate rent free, the possession of the servant or workman is the possession of the master.

And if a landowner, from motives of kindness or charity, allows a dependent, or relation, or friend, to occupy a cottage and land, and the landowner, during such occupation, continues to exercise acts of ownership over the property so occupied, as by repairing or otherwise, he has never parted with the possession.

But when a younger brother, or other relation of a person entitled as heir to the possession or receipt of the profits of land, or to the receipt of rent, enters into the possession or receipt thereof, such possession is not to be deemed the possession or receipt of the heir.

Possession by joint owners.

The possession of one or more co-parceners, joint tenants, or tenants in common, for his or their own benefit, is not to be deemed the possession of those entitled to the other shares.

Accrual of the right of action under Statute of Limitations.

When the person claiming, or the person through whom he claims, has been in possession or in receipt of rent, and has while entitled thereto been dispossessed, or has discontinued such possession, then the right is deemed (3 & 4 Will. IV. c. 27, s. 3) to have first accrued at the time of such dispossession or discontinuance.

By discontinuance is meant an abandonment of possession by one person, followed by actual possession by another person. Thus the title to minerals and right of entry to get them, being granted to a person other than the grantee of the surface, are not lost by non-user for however long a period, provided no other person has worked or been in possession of the mines.

By s. 14 of the 3 & 4 Will. IV. c. 27, when any acknowledgment of the title of the person claiming land or rent shall have been given to him in writing and signed by the person in possession or receipt of rent, the right of action of the former shall be deemed to have first accrued at, and not before, the time at which such acknowledgment or the last of such acknowledgments was given. *Acknowledgments.*

By the 37 & 38 Vict. c. 57, s. 7, a mortgagor is barred from bringing any action to redeem the mortgage at the end of twelve years from the time when the mortgagee took possession, or from the last written acknowledgment of the title of the mortgagor signed by the mortgagee. *Mortgagees.*

Title to Particular Species of Real Property.

The trustees of turnpike roads and highways have the control over them: but in presumption of law the landowners on either side are entitled to the soil of the road *ad medium filum viæ*. No legal presumption arises as to the ownership of soil in a road when the road is defined for the first time under a newly created authority, such as a board of commissioners for enclosing lands. *Title to soil of highways. (3)*

When a private way runs between the land of two adjoining owners it may be presumed that the soil of the way belongs half to one owner and half to another. But this presumption may be rebutted by proof of acts of ownership on the part of one only of the adjoining proprietors, or by proof of the reservation of the soil of the road by the grantor under whom both claim. *Title to soil of private road. (4)*

Waste land extending along the side of a public highway is presumed to belong to the owner of the adjoining land, and not to the lord of the manor. But proof to the *Waste lands adjoining highways. (5)*

contrary may be given; and if the narrow strip communicates with an open common this is evidence in favour of the supposition that the owner of the common is also owner of the narrow strip.

Title to sea-shore and bed of navigable river. (6) The sea-shore, or the bed of a tidal river, between high and low water-mark, is presumed to belong to the Crown. By ancient grant, however, it may be vested in a private individual, or in the lord of the adjoining manor.

Waste adjoining sea-shore. (7) Waste land adjoining the sea-shore, and situate above the high water-mark of ordinary, though not of extraordinary, spring tides, *primâ facie* belongs to the owner of the adjoining property.

Non-navigable rivers. (8) The soil of the bed of a non-navigable river belongs *primâ facie* to the owners of the land on either side *ad medium filum aquæ*. Neither, however, is entitled to use it so as to interfere with the natural flow of the stream; and an encroachment by one landowner on his side of the stream is actionable at the suit of the other, although no special damage can be proved.

Towing paths. Navigation companies, authorized to set out towing paths on the banks of navigable rivers and canals, first giving compensation to the owners of lands made use of for the purpose, do not acquire the soil of the towing paths, but only a right of way over them.

Boundary walls, ditches, and hedges. (9) Evidence of common user of a boundary wall by the adjoining proprietors, whose estates it separates, justifies the presumption either that the wall was originally built on land belonging in undivided moieties to the owners of the respective premises, and at their joint expense, or that it had been agreed between them that the wall and the land on which it stood should be considered the property of both as tenants in common.

A ditch is usually cut to the extremity of the land of the man making it, and the soil dug out is thrown on his own land, and forms a bank.

A boundary hedge generally belongs to the occupier who

has been in the habit of cutting and repairing it. Sometimes, however, the adjoining owners are tenants in common of the hedge. And where a tree stands in a hedge, the ownership of the tree follows the ownership of the hedge.

The freehold of the church and chancel, as well as of the churchyard, is in the rector, whether spiritual or lay. But where there is a lay rector, the right of possession is in the incumbent for the use of the parishioners. Title to church and churchyard. (10)

The immemorial occupation and repair of a private chapel or chancel attached to a parish church will entitle the lord of the manor by prescription to its exclusive use, although the freehold may be in another. And the immemorial repair of such a chapel is evidence of a right of freehold in it.

ILLUSTRATIVE CASES.

(1) *Jayne v. Price*, 5 Taunt. 326.

Proof of possession of land and pernancy of the rent was held to be *primâ facie* evidence of a seisin in fee.

But proof of forty years' subsequent possession by a daughter, while a son and heir lived near, and knew the fact, was held to be much stronger evidence that the first possessor had only a particular estate.

(2) *Bertie v. Beaumont*, 16 East, 33.

A servant was put into the occupation of a cottage, with less wages on that account. Held, that the master might properly declare on it as in his own occupation in an action on the case for a disturbance of a right of way over the defendant's close to such cottage.

(3) *Davison v. Gill*, 1 East, 69.

Lord Kenyon, C.J.: "As to the trustees of the turnpike road, the soil is not vested in them, but remains in the persons who were entitled to it before the Act passed by which they were appointed. The trustees have only the control of the highway."

King v. Inhabitants of Hatfield, 4 Ad. & E. 156.

When the herbage of a road became vested by the General Inclosure Act (41 Geo. III. c. 109) in the proprietors of allotments on each side: Held, that no presumption arose that the soil itself belonged to such proprietors.

(4) *Holmes v. Bellingham*, 7 C.B., N.S. 329.

The rule as to the soil being presumptively vested in the respective owners of the adjoining land *usque ad medium filum viæ*, Held to be the same in the case of a private as in that of a public road—independently of circumstances, such as the exercise of acts of ownership, by which the presumption might be rebutted.

(5) *Doe v. Pearsey*, 7 B. & C. 307.

A cottage having been erected on a strip of waste land by the side of a turnpike, adjoining to enclosed land, which was copyhold; on an action of ejectment :—Held, that the presumption is that waste land which adjoins a road belongs to the owner of the adjoining enclosed land, whether he be a freeholder, leaseholder, or copyholder, and not to the lord of the manor.

Grose v. *West*, 7 *Taunt.* 42.

A strip of land lying between a highway and the adjoining enclosure communicated with an open down or common. Held, that the evidence of ownership, which applied to the larger portions of land, applied also to the narrow strip communicating with it, and the presumption of the ownership of the strip by the owner of the adjoining enclosure was rebutted.

(6)   *Hale de Jure Maris, Hargrave's Law Tracts, pp.* 25—27.

The Queen v. *Musson*, 27 *Law J.*, *N.S.*, *M.C.* 100.

If the officers of a parish claim a right to rate a person for occupying that part of the sea-shore which lies between high and low water-mark, the onus lies upon them to show by evidence that such part is within the parish, and in the absence of evidence it must be presumed to be extra-parochial, and therefore not liable to be rated.

(7)   See *Lowe* v. *Govett*, 3 *B. & Ad.* 869.
(8)   *Bickett* v. *Morris*, *L.R.*, 1 *Scotch App. Ca.* 47.

The soil of the *alveus* of a running stream is not the common property of the respective owners on the opposite sides of the stream; the share of each belongs to them in severalty, and extends *usque ad medium filum aquæ*; but neither is entitled to use it in such a manner as to interfere with the natural flow of the stream. Any encroachment by one proprietor may be resisted by the other, and the onus of proving that the act is not an encroachment falls on the party doing it.

Per Lord Westbury: "An encroachment on the *alveus* of a running stream may be complained of without the necessity of proving that damage has been sustained, or is likely to be sustained."

(9)   *Wiltshire* v. *Sidford*, 8 *B. & C.* 259.

The reasonable presumption from the common use of a wall, Held *primâ facie* to be that the wall and the land upon which it was built were the undivided property of each. The case of *Matts* v. *Hawkins* (5 Taunt. 20), distinguished; in that case the quantity of land which each contributed was known.

Vowles v. *Miller*, 3 *Taunt.* 137.

Proof of the ancient width of a ditch, Held to be evidence that the owner's land did not extend beyond the outer edge thereof.

(10)   *Griffin* v. *Dighton*, 33 *Law J.*, *Q.B.* 29.

The lay rector of a church sued the vicar and churchwardens for taking off the lock of a door leading into the chancel. Held, that the freehold of a church, including chancel and churchyard, is in the rector, but the right to the corporal possession is in the spiritual incumbent after induction, and therefore, a lay rector has not, against the vicar, any right to the possession or control of the chancel.

Churton v. *Frewin*, *L.R.*, 2 *Eq. Ca.* 634.

Upon a bill filed to re-establish a right to a chancel as part of the parish church against the lord of the manor, who claimed it as appendant to the manor :—Held, that immemorial use and occupation, coupled with reparations, entitled the lord of the manor by prescription to the perpetual and exclusive use of the chancel.

CHAPTER III.

TRESPASS ON REALTY.

EVERY entry upon land in the occupation of another constitutes a trespass in respect of which an action for damages is maintainable, unless the act can be justified in the exercise of some legal right. *Definition. (1)*

Every trespass upon land is in law an injury to the land, although it consists merely in walking over it and no damage is done to the soil or grass. Every interference with the possession of the occupier is in law an injury to the property, and therefore, if a man is unlawfully turned out of his dwelling house, that amounts to an injury to his dwelling house.

It is an act of trespass for a man to throw stones, rubbish, or materials of any kind upon another man's land, or to allow his cattle, poultry, or domestic animals to stray upon another man's land, unless he can show that the proprietor of the land was bound to fence for his benefit and has failed to do so. *Trespass by cattle, &c. (2)*

Whether the cattle at the time of their straying were in the custody of the owner himself, or of the owner's servant, or of a stranger is immaterial, and if they are in the custody of a stranger, the latter may be sued as well as the owner. If, however, a servant, without the knowledge of his master, takes beasts and puts them in the fields of another, the servant is the trespasser, and not the master; for the servant by his wrongful act obtains a special property in them for the time.

If a landowner who has land abutting upon a highway neglects to fence the land from the highway, so that cattle stray from the highway and injure his crops, he cannot immediately distrain the beasts damage feasant, or treat the owner of the beasts as a trespasser, but must either drive them out himself, or allow a reasonable time for the drovers in charge of them to do so. But if the beasts are not lawfully using the highway, but are straying there away from their owner or his servants, and pass from thence to the adjoining unfenced land, this is a trespass for which the owner of the beasts is liable.

Rabbits and pigeons trespassing upon land may be killed, but the breeder of them is not responsible in trespass, for they are animals *feræ naturæ*. The owner of a dog which has strayed and done injury to crops will not generally be liable to an action of trespass, unless the dog is of a peculiarly mischievous disposition, so as to be unfit to be at large, and this is known to the master.

Who are entitled to bring an Action of Trespass.

Right of possession. (3) It is the right of possession of the land, and not the right of property in it, which entitles a person to bring an action for trespass. If the freehold of the *locus in quo* is proved to be in the plaintiff, the possession is also presumed to be in him, unless there is evidence to the contrary. But actual or constructive possession without proof of any title to the freehold is sufficient to support an action against a wrong-doer. And very slight evidence of possession is sufficient to establish a *primâ facie* title to sue for an injury to realty; mere occupancy of land, however recent, gives a good title to the occupier against all who cannot prove an older and better title in themselves.

Tenant and reversioner. (4) The owner of property, who has parted with possession of the property to a tenant or lessee, cannot maintain an action for trespass, but the tenant or lessee is the proper party to sue.

Where, however, the injury caused by the trespass is of a permanent nature and deteriorates the marketable value of the reversion, the landlord or reversioner may maintain an action on the case for damages. And the removal of the smallest portion of soil must in general be esteemed an injury to the reversion, because it tends to alter the evidence of title.

If a house or land is occupied, not by a tenant or lessee, but by a servant of the owner, the occupation of the servant is the occupation of the master, the latter therefore may sue for any act of trespass.

A person who has the freehold and a right to the possession of the land, may by a peaceable entry upon the land, acquire sufficient possession of it to enable him to maintain an action for a trespass against any person, who being in possession at the time of his entry, wrongfully continues upon the land. *Peaceable entry.* (5)

If a landlord, having a right to the possession of land on the expiration of a lease, sends his agent to the land to demand possession, and the agent enters and makes the demand, this is a sufficient entry to clothe the landlord with constructive possession, so as to enable him to sue in trespass all persons who subsequently come upon the land by the authority of the tenant.

Originally, if a man had a right to the possession of land, he might enter and obtain possession by force of arms. Forcible entry was forbidden, 5 Ric. II. c. 7. *Forcible entry.* (6)

A mere trespasser cannot, by the act of trespass, obtain any possession of the land upon which he has trespassed; he may consequently be expelled by main force. But if a trespasser is allowed to continue on the land; and the landowner sleeps on his rights and makes no effort to remove him, he will gain a possession, and although it is a wrongful possession, he cannot be forcibly ejected from it.

A mere intruder upon land, who has been allowed to run up a hut and occupy it, has no right to the possession of the hut, and the landlord may enter and pull down the hut about the ears of the occupants and remove the materials.

But a house cannot be pulled down, whilst persons are living in it, for the mere purpose of abating a nuisance or preventing interference with an incorporeal right, such as the right of common.

When the rightful owner has also the right of possession he is authorized in entering upon his own land peaceably; and if his entry is resisted by force, he may, it seems, repel force by force. If he assaults and expels persons who, having originally come into possession lawfully, continue to hold unlawfully after their title to occupy has been determined, he may be made responsible for the assault, and be indicted for a forcible entry; but he cannot in any case be made responsible for damages in trespass.

<small>Trespass to subsoil. (7)</small>
If land is demised generally to a lessee who enters under the lease, he is in possession of both the surface and the minerals; but he has no right to work the minerals without the license of the lessor, neither can the lessor work them without the permission of the lessee.

If, however, the adjoining occupier sinks a mine in his own land and makes lateral excavations trespassing upon the minerals of the lessee, without disturbing the surface of the land in his occupation, the lessee may maintain an action for the injury to his possessory interest, and the lessor may maintain an action for the injury to his reversionary estate.

<small>Heir at law. (8)</small>
The heir at law cannot maintain trespass for an injury done to lands descended to him without entry; but after entry his right of possession relates back so as to support an action against a wrong-doer for a trespass committed at an antecedent period.

<small>Tenant in common. (9)</small>
An action is maintainable by one tenant in common against his co-tenant, or the licensee of the latter, for digging up and carrying away the soil of the close of which they are tenants in common.

Justification of Trespass.

<small>Plea denying title or</small>
The defendant in an action of trespass, may show that the plaintiff is in fact the trespasser. He may plead that

the freehold of the land and the right of possession are in himself and not in the plaintiff, and thus the title of the plaintiff to the property and also his right of possession are in issue. *right to possession.* (10)

A defendant in an action of trespass may justify his trespass by showing that he has a right of way over the close of the plaintiff; and although the premises to which the right of way is appurtenant may be in the occupation of the tenant of the defendant, the right of way is nevertheless constructively in the occupation of the defendant, so that he may use it for any purpose connected with his rights as a landlord. *Plea of right of way.* (11)

If the defendant in an action of trespass relies on a plea of leave and license, he must prove either an express permission from the plaintiff to the defendant to come on the land, or circumstances from which such permission may fairly be implied. *Plea of license.* (12)

When a person has a special authority given him by law to enter upon lands for any purpose, and he exceeds his authority by doing on the land what he had no right to do, or by staying longer than he had a right to stay, he becomes a trespasser *ab initio*.

A trespass may be excused on the ground that it was committed in self-defence, in order to escape some pressing danger or apprehended peril, or in defence of the possession of a man's goods and chattels, or cattle, sheep, or domestic animals. *Self-defence.* (13)

An entry on the plaintiff's land may be justified on the ground that the plaintiff took the defendant's goods and carried them on his own land, wherefore the defendant entered upon the plaintiff's land and took them back again. But the entry is not justifiable from the mere fact of the defendant's goods being on the plaintiff's land. It must be shown that they came there by the plaintiff's act. *Recovery of goods.* (14)

Damages in Actions of Trespass on Realty.

If the trespass is not wilful and persevering, or insulting *Nominal damages.*

and no actual damage is done and no question of title arises, the damages recoverable will be merely nominal.

Exemplary damages. (15) If a trespass takes place after warning not to trespass, or if it is an impertinent intrusion upon a man's domestic privacy, or an insulting invasion of his proprietary rights exemplary damages will be recoverable.

Action against hundred. By 7 & 8 Geo. IV. c. 31, it is enacted that if any building or machinery shall be feloniously destroyed by persons riotously assembled together, the inhabitants of the hundred shall be liable, if the damage done exceeds £30, to yield full compensation to the persons damnified by the offence.

Injunction. Whenever trespasses have been repeated again and again so as to become a nuisance an injunction may be granted against the persevering wrong-doer.

Distress Damage Feasant.

When distress damage feasant may be made. (16) Every occupier of land has a right to seize animals and chattels trespassing upon and doing damage to his land and to detain them until he is tendered fair compensation. If many cattle are doing damage, a man cannot take one of them as distress for the whole damage, but he may distrain one of them for its own damage, and bring an action of trespass for the damage done by the rest.

Time and place of making distress damage feasant. (17) The distress must be taken at the time the damage is done, otherwise it is illegal. And cattle damage feasant may be distrained in the night. If cattle get out of a close before the party coming to distrain has got into it, they cannot be followed and distrained when off the land.

Things distrainable damage feasant. (18) The right to distrain animals and chattels damage feasant is limited to such animals and chattels as are not in the actual possession and use, and under the personal care of some human being, for otherwise a breach of the peace might be caused. But a dog is not under the care of a person unless it is under his immediate control. Shocks of corn and turves may be distrained damage feasant.

Tender before the distress makes the distress tortious. Tender after the distress and before the impounding makes the detainer unlawful. Tender of amends. (19)

The 2 W. & M. c. 5, which enables landlords to sell things distrained for rent, does not extend to distresses damage feasant. They remain, therefore, as they were at common law, mere pledges, and the sale of them will render the party distraining a trespasser *ab initio*. Distress a pledge.

But 12 & 13 Vict. c. 92, requires persons who impound animals to provide them with food.

And 17 & 18 Vict. c. 60, enacts that any person who has supplied such animal with food and water, may, after seven days, sell the animal openly in the public market, after having given three days' public printed notice. And the produce of the sale is to be applied in discharge of the value of the food supplied and the expenses of the sale, the overplus to be rendered to the owner of the animal.

For proceedings on writ of replevin, see under Distress for Rent, p. 66.

ILLUSTRATIVE CASES.

(1) *Mich. 6 E. 4, p. 7, pl. 18.*

An action was brought for trespass upon land and treading down the grass; the defendant pleaded that his land adjoined that of the plaintiff, and upon it there was a thorn hedge; he cut the thorns, and they *ipso invito* fell upon the plaintiff's land; the defendant removed them promptly from the plaintiff's land. Held, that the defendant was liable in damages; for though a man do a lawful thing, yet if any damage thereby befalls another, he must answer for it, if he could have avoided it.

(2) *Lee v. Riley, 34 Law J., C.P. 212.*

Through the defect of a gate which the defendant was bound to repair, the defendant's horse got out of his land into an occupation road, and strayed into the plaintiff's field, where it kicked the plaintiff's horse. Held, that the defendant was liable for the trespass by his horse, and that it was not necessary for the maintenance of the action to prove that the defendant's horse was vicious, and that the defendant was aware thereof. Held also, that the damage sustained by the plaintiff was not too remote.

Dawtry v. Huggins, Clayton, 32, pl. 56.

Hogs belonging to A. were in the custody of B., who kept them in his yard, they strayed thence into the land of C. adjoining, a servant of A. and a servant of B. both being in charge of them at the time. Held, that trespass might be brought against A.

2 Roll. Abr., 553.

"If my servant without my knowledge put my beasts in the close of another, my servant is the trespasser and not I."

(3)   *Every* v. *Smith*, 26 *Law J., Exch.* 344.

In an action for trespass the plaintiffs, who were owners of a street of houses, failed to show that the deed under which they claimed conveyed the soil of the street, and the trespass complained of was in pulling down the wall of a house they were building across one end of it, which had been commenced a short time before; the defendants, highway commissioners, pleaded "not possessed," and justified their act as the abatement of a nuisance on a highway, but did not justify under the owner of the soil. Held, that the plaintiffs had a possessory right sufficient to sustain the action.

Catteris v. *Cowper*, 4 *Taunt.* 547.

The plaintiff in an action for trespass could only prove as his title that two years since he had taken possession of the waste land in question, and twice mown the grass, and had since pastured a cow there. Held, that this was a good title, whereupon he might recover in trespass against all the world except such as could prove an older and better title in themselves.

(4)   *Tucker* v. *Newman*, 11 *Ad. & E.* 40.

The defendant built a roof with eaves, which discharged rain water by a spout into an adjoining yard, of which the plaintiff was the reversioner. Held, that if the jury considered that the dripping of water might be injurious to the reversion, they were justified in giving damages to the plaintiff.

Alston v. *Scales*, 9 *Bing.* 3.

The surveyor of a highway was held to be liable to the reversioner for the subtraction of a portion of his bank by the road side, although the property was actually better for what the surveyor had done.

(5)   *Butcher* v. *Butcher*, 7 *B. & C.* 339.

A party, having the legal title to land, acquires by entry the lawful possession of it, and may maintain trespass against any person, who, being in possession at the time of his entry, wrongfully continues upon the land.

Hey v. *Moorhouse*, 6 *B.N.C.* 52.

The term of a tenant having expired, and notice to quit having been given, the agent of the plaintiff went on the premises, and required the tenant to give up possession, which he refused; the tenant subsequently authorized the defendant to come upon the premises for the purpose of removing hay. Held, that the lessor, having entered by his agent, might sue in trespass the defendant, claiming under the late tenant, as well as the late tenant himself.

(6)   *Brown* v. *Dawson*, 12 *Ad. & E.* 629.

A master had possession of a schoolroom for the purposes of his office, but was summarily dismissed by the trustees, who took possession of the room and locked it up. The master returned next day, broke into the room, and held it for eleven days, at the end of which the trustees forcibly ejected him. He then brought an action of trespass, describing the premises as a "room of the plaintiff." Held, that the plaintiff had not, by his re-entry, a *primâ facie* right of possession against the trustees as wrong-doers.

Jones v. *Jones,* 31 *Law J., Exch.* 506.

To trespass for breaking and entering and pulling down the plaintiff's house whilst he and his family were therein and assaulting the plaintiff, and by so pulling down the house endangering the lives and injuring the persons of the plaintiff and his family, and ejecting them therefrom, and taking the materials of the house, the defendant, as to the breaking and entering and pulling down and destroying the house and taking away the materials, justified in the exercise of a right of common of pasture over the land on which the house was wrongfully built. Held, that the plea did not answer the action.

Harvey v. *Bridges,* 14 *M. & W.* 442.

The defendants, who were entitled to the freehold of a certain dwelling house, took possession of it without breach of the peace or forcible entry, and then expelled the plaintiff from the possession and occupation of the same. Held, that the defendants were justified.

(7) *Lewis* v. *Branthwaite,* 2 *B. & Ad.* 437.

In copyhold lands, although the property in mines be in the lord, the possession of them is in the tenant. The latter may therefore maintain trespass against the owner of an adjoining colliery for breaking and entering the subsoil and taking coal therein, although no trespass be committed on the surface.

(8) *Barnett* v. *Earl of Guildford,* 11 *Exch.* 19.

An infant copyholder, who had been admitted by the lord to his copyhold, and by his father and guardian had actually entered into possession in Nov. 1853, brought an action of trespass for the wrongful occupation by the lord of the land for a prior period of three months. Held, that although an heir at law cannot maintain at action without entry, after entry his possession relates back, so as to support an action against a wrong-doer for an antecedent trespass.

(9) *Wilkinson* v. *Haygarth,* 12 *Q.B.* 837.

One of several tenants in common sued the defendant in trespass for digging up and carrying away turf. The defendant pleaded license from another tenant in common. Held, that the plea was bad, since the tenant in common could not authorize any act which amounted to a destruction, and which therefore he could not have done himself. [But see *Job* v. *Potton, L.R.* 20 *Eq.* 84, where it was held that it was not trespass or destructive waste for a tenant in common of a coal mine to get, or to license another to get, the coals, he, the working tenant, not appropriating to himself more than his share of the proceeds.]

(10) *Burling* v. *Read,* 11 *Q.B.* 904.

To a declaration in trespass charging that the defendant broke and entered plaintiff's workshop, the defendant pleaded that the workshop was his and denied that it was the plaintiff's. Held, that the right of property and possession was in issue, and that the defendant was entitled to the verdict upon proof that he was entitled to the soil.

[The workshop in question was alleged to have been pulled down whilst the plaintiff was inhabiting it. This was held to be immaterial. *Perry* v. *Fitzhowe,* 8 *Q.B.* 757 (compare *Jones* v. *Jones* above), distinguished. Lord Campbell, C.J.: "I assume *Perry* v. *Fitzhowe* to be right; but that case is clearly distinguishable from this, where the house is not the dwelling house of the plaintiff, and where the act complained of is the act, not of a commoner who seeks to abate nuisance, but of the owner of the house."]

(11) *Proud* v. *Hollis*, 1 B. & C. 9.

"While the tenement is occupied by a tenant the landlord may use the way to view waste, or demand rent or to remove an obstruction."

(12) *The Six Carpenters' Ca.*, 8 Co. 146 ; *and see* 1 Sm. L.C.

The six carpenters entered into a tavern, and ordered wine, part of which they paid for, but refused to pay for the remainder. Thereupon the plaintiff brought an action for breaking his house and for assault and battery. Held (1) That if a man abuse an authority given to him by law he becomes a trespasser *ab initio* ; but otherwise when the authority is given by the party. (2) Mere nonfeasance, as in the case, does not amount to such abuse as to make a man a trespasser *ab initio*.

(13) 6 *Ed.* 4, 7, *pl.* 18.

"If I drive my beasts along the highway, and you have open uninclosed land adjoining the highway, and my beasts enter your land and eat the herbage thereof, and I come freshly and chase them out of your land, you shall not have an action against me, because the chasing them was lawful." Catersby arg., and see *Godwyn* v. *Cheveley*, 4 H. & N., 631.

(14) 2 *Roll. Abr.* 565, *pl.* 9.

(15) *Merest* v. *Harvey*, 5 *Taunt.* 443.

Upon declaration for breaking the plaintiff's close, treading his grass, and hunting for game accompanied by offensive demeanour. Held, that £500 was not excessive damages.

(16) *Gilbert on Distress*, pp. 21, 22.

(17) *Wormer* v. *Biggs*, 2 C. & K. 31.

The owner of a freehold seized and detained an animal which had done damage to the freehold, but which had ceased doing so, there being no necessity to detain the animal to prevent further damage. Held, that the freeholder was liable in damages to the owner of the animal.

(18) *Field* v. *Adames*, 12 Ad. & E. 649.

In an action of trespass, the defendants justified the taking of a horse, cart, and other chattels, damage feasant. It was replied that the horse, cart, &c., were at the time of the distress in the actual possession and under the personal care of the plaintiff. Held, that this reply sufficiently answered the plea, without allegation of actual danger of a breach of the peace.

And *see Six Carpenters' Ca.*, *ubi sup.*, Lord Coke's *Observations*, p. 147.

(19) Tender of amends after impounding is too late, see *Singleton* v. *Williamson*, 31 *Law J.*, *Exch.* 287.

CHAPTER IV.

NUISANCE.

CORRELATIVE with the rights of proprietors as against the world in general, are their duties towards the world in general. Derelictions of these duties constitute nuisances.

1. *Nuisances by Landowners.*

Every landowner is bound to prevent his sewers, drains, and cesspools from becoming an annoyance to others. <small>Sewers, drains, &c. (1)</small>

A riparian owner may not foul the stream running through his land to the prejudice of other riparian owners, or the public in general, unless he has obtained a prescriptive right to do so. <small>Fouling streams. (2)</small>

A proprietor may not collect together on his premises a crowd of persons to the annoyance of his neighbours. <small>Crowds. (3)</small>

A proprietor may not (24 & 25 Vict. c. 100, s. 31) place spring guns or man traps upon his estate, whereby a trespasser or other person might be injured; but guns or traps for the destruction of vermin are not illegal, and spring guns or man traps may be placed in a dwelling house for the protection thereof in the night time. <small>Spring guns, traps, &c. (4)</small>

Traps may be set for vermin; but if they are baited so as to attract dogs from adjoining premises, the owner of a dog so attracted and injured by the trap may recover damages.

Wells, mining shafts, quarries, &c., must be guarded or fenced, otherwise the owner is responsible for injuries sustained by persons, who fall into them, provided they were lawfully traversing the land in which the well, &c., is <small>Wells and shafts. (5)</small>

situated, and were not guilty of negligence. And even a trespasser may maintain an action if the well, &c., is situated within twenty-five yards of any carriage way.

Machinery. Steam engines, and other machines are required to be fenced round if within twenty-five yards of a carriage way; windmills, if within fifty yards; brick and lime kilns, if within fifteen yards (General Highway Act, 5 & 6 Will. IV. c. 50).

Private ways. (6) Landowners are responsible for injuries arising from the defective and dangerous condition of private ways and approaches to their dwelling houses, but not for injuries sustained by anyone whilst straying from the ordinary approach to the house and trespassing on the adjoining grounds.

Sea walls. (7) A proprietor whose land adjoins the sea may protect himself against its approaches by erecting sea-walls, &c., even although he may thereby injure his neighbour by causing a greater influx upon his land.

2. *Nuisances by Householders.*

Noisome trades. (8) A man may carry on a lawful trade in his house, although it render his neighbour's residence less pleasant and agreeable, so long as it does not interfere with the ordinary physical comfort of human existence. And a trade which creates a noisome and sickening smell may be a nuisance, although not actually injurious to health.

When the nuisance arising from the exercise of a trade is temporary or trifling the court will not interfere. And a right to exercise a noisome trade may be acquired by prescription.

Responsibility for nuisance. (9) The landlord as well as the occupier is generally answerable for the existence of a nuisance upon the demised premises. But if a landlord demises premises not in themselves a nuisance, but which may or may not become a nuisance, according to the way in which they are used by the tenant, the landlord is not responsible for a nuisance created upon them by the tenant.

And a landlord who creates a nuisance upon his premises, or purchases premises with an existing nuisance upon them, cannot get rid of his responsibility by conveying his property to others.

Every occupier of a house adjoining a highway is responsible for injuries to passers by, arising from things falling into the street, unless he can show that the fall was caused by some inevitable accident or from tempest. He is bound also to secure his shutters, swing doors, and things placed against his house, so that they cannot readily be thrown down on passengers by mischievous persons. *Injuries to passers by. (10)*

If one man overload the floor of a warehouse with merchandise, so that the floor breaks and crushes the goods of another on the floor beneath, the latter is entitled to damages against the former. If the floor is ruinous, the occupier must take care he does not put more on it than it will bear. *Fall of floors. (11)*

When damage is caused to the public by the fall of a building or part of it— *Fall of building. (12)*

(i). Where there is no agreement between the landlord and tenant as to repairs; if the house was ruinous and dangerous when demised, the landlord is responsible to the public, but not to the occupier.

(ii). If the landlord has agreed to keep the house in repair; even if it was in good repair at the time of the demise, and subsequently became ruinous, he is responsible to the public as well as to the occupier.

And the occupier is responsible to the public for the nuisance in any case. *Quoad* the public, however, he is not bound to repair, but only to shore up the building.

The master of a house is responsible to his neighbours for the safe keeping of the fires within his house. *Fire.*

He is not responsible, however (12 Geo. III. c. 73), for

the spreading of a fire which commenced by pure accident, *i.e.*, without negligence either of the master or his servants.

And the same principle applies (14 Geo. III. c. 78) to fires in outhouses and fields.

3. *Nuisances from Keeping Dangerous Animals.*

Ferocious animals. (13)
Whoever keeps on his premises an animal accustomed to attack mankind, with a knowledge of its dangerous propensities, is liable generally to an action for injuries inflicted by the animal, without proof of any negligence or a default in securing it. If the animal be *feræ naturæ*, as a lion or a tiger, the action lies without proof of knowledge of its mischievous disposition.

And now, by statute 28 & 29 Vict. c. 60, proof of a knowledge of previous mischievous propensity is not necessary to support an action against the owner of a dog which has worried sheep or cattle.

The maintenance of a mischievous animal is sufficient to render liable to an action for injuries without proof of ownership.

4. *Nuisances by Statutory Proprietors.*

Statutory powers. (14)
When power is given by statute to execute certain works, and the statute expressly contemplates the creation of a nuisance, no action will lie on account of it. But in general statutory powers are to be exercised with caution, and if they are exceeded, or are not strictly pursued, or if the things authorized to be done are done carelessly and negligently, an action for damages is maintainable.

Railway company's traffic. (15)
A railway company is not authorized to conduct its traffic so as to create a nuisance. The company, for example, although it is not responsible for unavoidable noises caused by its engines, is responsible in damages if the engine-driver unnecessarily puts on the whistle, or lets off

steam when crossing or running alongside of a public road, and by so doing frightens horses lawfully on the highway and causes them to upset a carriage.

Railway companies are required to manage their property so as not to make it a source of danger to their passengers, or others lawfully using their stations. Their stations must be lighted sufficiently for strangers as well as their own servants; and all mischiefs which could reasonably have been foreseen must be guarded against. Stations.
(16)

Every railway company is responsible for the maintenance of its bridges, viaducts, and embankments in good repair, and if these break down through original faulty construction by the contractor or engineer, the company is still responsible. Bridges, embankments, &c.
(17)

When a railway crosses a public road on a level, the company must maintain good and sufficient gates across such road, and employ persons to keep them shut, except when required to be open to permit the passage of cattle, horses, carts, &c., and such gates must be carefully closed for the protection of everything passing, *either lawfully or unlawfully*, along the highway (8 & 9 Vict. c. 20, s. 47). Level crossings.
(18)

The statutory obligation upon railway companies (8 & 9 Vict. c. 20) to maintain fences between their lines and adjoining lands amounts only to a servitude to make and repair fences for the benefit of adjoining occupiers, and does not impose a duty towards the world in general. Fences.
(19)

A railway company is not, therefore, responsible for the loss of animals which have strayed upon their line, through the defect of fences, if the animals were not lawfully upon the adjoining land, but were trespassing.

But when cattle are passing along a highway in charge of a servant, the latter is lawfully using the highway, and is deemed an adjoining occupier. If, therefore, cattle under his care stray upon the railway through a defect of fences and are killed or injured, the company is liable to damages.

**Canal companies.
(20)**
Canal companies are bound to take reasonable care for the safety of the lives and property of those who navigate their canal and for the protection of the public. Sufficient bridges must, therefore, be provided, also lights, railings, &c. A canal company is not bound, however, to fence off its canal from an adjoining thoroughfare, unless it be so near the thoroughfare as to be dangerous to persons using it.

**Docks and wharfs.
(21)**
Similar duties towards the public are imposed upon the trustees and commissioners of wharfs and docks.

5. *Nuisances in respect of Public Property.*

Public property.
There are certain species of real property over which the public have rights of user with correlative duties, a breach of which constitutes a nuisance.

**Highways.
(22)**
All ways open to all the Queen's subjects, whether cart, horse, or footways, are highways.

The soil of highways belongs to the owners of the lands which adjoin; but the control over them is vested in trustees for the public use, *e.g.*, trustees appointed by the parish vestry, and commissions appointed by district boards.

**Origin of highways.
(23)**
Public ways become such (i) by dedication, (ii) by necessity.

(i). A mere tenant cannot dedicate without the consent of his landlord or reversioner. Such consent may, however, be presumed after long user by the public.

No particular time is necessary to constitute evidence of dedication. If the act of dedication be unequivocal it may take place at once. User by the public is only evidence of dedication and no more. If the owner throws a bar or chain across the road, or prohibits its use by notice, or altogether closes it, even if for only one day in the year, there is no *animus dedicandi*.

If a man build a double row of houses opening at each end into an ancient street and sells or lets the houses, that is instantly a highway; but if the footpaths or the paving are not completed, the evidence of dedication is not sufficient. And the same applies to the case of a new street forming a *cul de sac.*

(ii). Where there is only one road to a place and no other way of getting to it, this is a highway of necessity, whether it was laid out with the intention of dedicating it to the public or not.

The dedication of a highway cannot be limited in duration—once dedicated it is a highway for ever; nor can it be limited to a particular part of the public, but its dedication may be limited in extent of user, *e.g.*, it may be dedicated subject to the right of adjoining owners to throw rubbish on the soil of the way, or subject to other risks and inconveniences. Limited dedication. (24)

It is a nuisance to erect a gate across a highway where none previously existed, or to obstruct a thoroughfare by building a projecting house or bridge, or wilfully to interfere with the free right of passage of another along a highway. Neither vestry trustees nor commissioners of highways can authorize the obstruction of a highway, nor can they, for the convenience of one part of the community, permit acts to be done on a highway which are a nuisance to another part of the community. Obstructions to highways. (25)

The parish is generally bound to repair its own highways, and it may levy rates for the purpose. A parish may, however, be relieved from its liability by an order of magistrates. Repair of highways. (26)

A particular township may by immemorial usage be liable to repair its own roads independently of the parish of which it forms part.

District boards may be formed for the repair of highways within their district.

The right of soil in navigable rivers is vested in the Crown, subject to the rights of public passage. Every grantee from the Crown must take subject to this right. Such grantee or any other person is therefore Navigable rivers. (27)

liable to an action or indictment, if he place any obstruction in the river.

Sunken vessels. (28) The owner of a vessel sunk by accident, without default or misconduct, in a navigable river, if he retain possession of the vessel, is bound to take reasonable care to prevent the occurrence of accidents to other vessels from the obstruction, and to remove it with reasonable speed; and these duties will be transferred to a purchaser of the sunken vessel. If, however, the owner abandons the vessel his responsibility entirely ceases.

Erection in river or port. (29) An erection in a navigable river or port is not a nuisance merely because it infringes on the water way. Whether it is a nuisance is a question for the jury.

[The liability for nuisance is modified by the doctrine of contributory negligence (see p. 85) and by the relation of master and servant (see p. 83).]

Remedies.

Abatement. (30) A man may justify a peaceable entry to abate an existing nuisance, but not to prevent the commission of a nuisance.

If the continuance of the nuisance endangers life, the injured party may enter and abate it without notice. In other cases, notice should be given, and a request made for the abatement of the nuisance before entry.

After notice, commoners may pull down a house on their common, even though the wrong-doer and his family are in it.

Nuisances arising from the exercise in excess of limited rights may be abated by stopping the exercise of the right altogether, until it is reduced to its proper limits.

A private person cannot abate an obstruction on a highway or in a navigable river, unless it does him special injury, and he is prevented from passing up or down the road or river with reasonable convenience and safety whilst the obstruction remains.

Unless the injury is of a permanent nature, the occupant or tenant should bring the action, and not the landlord or reversioner. ^{Action.} (31)

If the action is brought against the originator of the nuisance, no notice is necessary. If brought against a continuer of a pre-existing nuisance, notice must be given, with a request to abate the nuisance, before action commenced.

Whenever a public nuisance inflicts special damage upon a private individual, he may bring his action for damages.

For every nuisance, the continuance of which would inflict permanent injury upon premises demised to a tenant, and diminish their value in the market, damages are recoverable by the reversioner in respect of the injury to the inheritance, as well as by the tenant in respect of the immediate residential injury. ^{Damages.} (32)

The continuance of a nuisance is a fresh injury, for which a fresh action can be brought for every day of its continuance. Damages cannot therefore be recovered in respect of any injury subsequent to the day of the commencement of the action, for this is the subject of a fresh action.

In actions for injuries from keeping ferocious animals, the plaintiff is entitled to recover substantial damages in respect of the bodily anguish he has endured, together with all surgical and other expenses which have been reasonably and necessarily incurred in consequence of the injury.

The High Court of Justice will prevent the continuance of a nuisance by injunction. ^{Injunction.} (33)

But the court will not interfere where the injury is trifling or of a temporary nature, or when the applicant has virtually encouraged the erection of the nuisance by passing it by without protest.

In the case of public nuisances the Attorney-General usually sues on behalf of the public; but persons who have individually sustained damage may apply for injunctions for the protection of their own property.

D 2

An interlocutory injunction before the hearing of the case will not be granted, except where necessary for the protection of property, or the prevention of some threatened injury thereto.

Indictment. (34) In the case of public nuisances, such as the obstruction of highways or navigable rivers, an indictment lies for the public injury, as well as an action for special damage sustained by individuals. A corporation or a railway company is as much amenable to indictment for obstruction of a thoroughfare as a private person. A parish is indictable for non-repair of its highways.

ILLUSTRATIVE CASES.

(1) *Tenant* v. *Golding*, 1 *Salk.* 21.

The plaintiff was possessed of a cellar contiguous to the defendant's privy; for want of repair the filth ran through into the plaintiff's cellar. Held, that the plaintiff was entitled to damages, and that of common right, without any proof of prescription.

(2) *Murgatroyd* v. *Robinson*, 7 *Ell. & Bl.* 391.

The owner of a mill brought an action against the owner of a mill higher up the stream for throwing cinders into the stream at his works, whence they were carried down to the plaintiff's mill-pool and filled it up, to the obstruction of the plaintiff's right of water. The defendants pleaded that they had for more than twenty years of right thrown cinders, &c., into the stream. The issue on this plea having been found for the defendant: Held, that the plea was bad, *non obstante veredicto*, as not showing that defendants had during twenty years of right caused the cinders, &c., to go into the plaintiff's pond; as till the occupiers of the mill sustained some damage from the defendants' user, no right as against them began to be acquired.

(3) *Walker* v. *Brewster*, L.R., 5 *Eq. Ca.* 25.

The collection of a crowd of noisy and disorderly people, to the annoyance of the neighbourhood, outside grounds in which entertainments with music and fireworks are being given for profit, Held, to be a nuisance for which the giver of the entertainments is liable to an injunction; even though he has excluded all improper characters from the grounds, and the amusements within the grounds have been conducted in an orderly way.

(4) *Bird* v. *Holbrook*, 4 *Bing.* 628.

The defendant, for the protection of his property, set a spring gun in a walled garden, at a distance from his house: the plaintiff, who climbed over the wall in pursuit of a stray fowl, having been shot, Held, that the defendant was liable in damages.

(5) *Pickard* v. *Smith*, 10 *C.B.*, *N.S.* 470.

Refreshment rooms and a coal cellar at a railway station were let by the company to the defendant, the opening for putting coals into the cellar being on the arrival platform. A train coming in whilst the servants of a coal merchant were shooting coals into the cellar for the defendant, the plaintiff, a passenger, whilst passing in the usual way out of the station, without any fault of his own, fell into the cellar opening, which the coal merchant's servants had negligently left insufficiently guarded. Held, that the defendant, being the occupier of the refreshment rooms and cellar, was responsible for this negligence. And *semble* that the railway company also would be liable, but not the coal merchant.

(6)   *Corby* v. *Hill,* 4 *C.B., N.S.* 556.

Byles, J.: "The rule of law is precisely the same in respect of a private way, whether by prescription or by license (as it is in respect of a public way). . . . If the obstruction was placed upon the road with the unqualified leave of the owners of the soil, all persons contributory to the injury sustained by the plaintiff therefrom would be jointly and severally responsible to him for it."

(7)   *Rex* v. *Pagham Commissioners,* 8 *B. & C.* 362.   *Vide supra,* p. 8.

(8)   *St. Helen's Smelting Co.* v. *Tipping,* 35 *Law J., Q.B.* 66.

In actions brought for a nuisance a difference is to be marked between an action brought for a nuisance on the ground that the alleged nuisance produces material injury to property, and an action brought for a nuisance on the ground that the alleged nuisance is productive of sensible personal discomfort. In certain cases a submission is required from persons living in society to that amount of discomfort which may be necessary for the legitimate and free exercise of the trade of their neighbours which would not be required to circumstances the immediate result of which is sensible injury to the value of property. In the case, noxious vapours from smelting works had injured the trees and shrubs on the adjoining property, and it was held that the judge had rightly directed the jury, who were satisfied of this, to find for the plaintiff.

Walter v. *Selfe,* 4 *De G. & Sm.* 315.

Burning bricks on a man's own ground so as to be offensive to his neighbour, Held, to be a nuisance, irrespective of the consideration as to whether it was or was not noxious to health.

(9)   *Rich* v. *Basterfield,* 4 *C.B.* 783.

An action was brought against A., the owner of premises, for a nuisance arising from smoke issuing out of the chimney to the prejudice of the plaintiff in his occupation of an adjoining messuage, on the ground that A., having erected the chimney and let the premises with the chimney so erected, had impliedly authorised the lighting of a fire therein. Held, that the action would not lie. The premises demised were capable of being used without making fires and creating the nuisance. [Compare *Harris* v. *James,* 25 *L.T.* 240, where a landlord who let his field to another for the purpose of making and using a lime-kiln on it was held liable for the nuisance which was thereby caused.]

(10)   *Byrne* v. *Boadle,* 33 *Law. J., Exch.* 13.

The plaintiff, while walking in a street in front of the house of a flour dealer, was injured by a barrel of flour falling upon him from an upper window. Held, that the mere fact of the accident, without any proof of the circumstances under which it occurred, was evidence of negligence to go to the jury in an action against the flour dealer.

(11)   See *Edwards* v. *Halinder, Popham,* 46.

(12)   *Gott* v. *Gandy,* 2 *Ell. & Bl.* 845.

The plaintiff, who was tenant from year to year, brought an action against his landlord for neglecting to do substantial repairs after notice that the premises were in a dangerous state through want of them; *per quod* the premises, during the tenancy, fell and injured the plaintiff's goods. Held, that the declaration was bad in substance. "Though in the absence of an express contract a tenant from year to year is not bound to do substantial repairs, yet in the absence of an express contract he has no right to compel his landlord to do them."

Todd v. *Flight*, 30 *Law J.*, *N.S.*, *C.P.* 21.

The defendant, who was owner of a building and a stack of chimneys near to a building of the plaintiff, demised them when the chimneys were known by him to be ruinous and in danger of falling upon the building of the plaintiff, and the chimneys afterwards, during the occupation of the tenant of the defendant, fell upon the plaintiff's building. Held, that an action for the injury of the plaintiff would lie against the defendant, although he was not the occupier at the time of the fall.

Payne v. *Rogers*, 2 *H. Bl.* 350.

Buller, J.: "The tenant as occupier is *primâ facie* liable to the public, whatever private agreement there may be between him and the landlord. But if he can show that the landlord is to repair, the landlord is liable for neglect to repair."

(13)   *May & Wife* v. *Burdett*, 9 *Q.B.* 101.

The female plaintiff was bitten and injured by a monkey; the defendant, who was the owner of the monkey, knew its mischievous and ferocious nature. Held, that an action on the case was maintainable without averment of negligence or default on the part of the defendant in securing or taking care of the monkey. [As to what amounts to evidence of the *scienter*, see *Applebee* v. *Percy*, *L.R.*, 9 *C.P.* 647. See *Smith* v. *Cook*, *L.R.*, 1 *Q.B.D.*, where it was held that the doctrine of *scienter* is not to be extended to the case of a defendant who has contracted to take reasonable care : *e.g.*, an agister of cattle.]

(14)   *Regina* v. *Darlington Local Board*, 5 *B. & S.* 515.

The defendants made certain sewers in pursuance of the powers of two Acts of Parliament, and in doing so injuriously affected the water of a stream on which the prosecutor had a mill. Blackburn, J.: "The rule is well established that for any act which is injurious to property, but which an Act of Parliament has authorised to be done, though the consequence of the act is *damnum* to the owner, it ceases to be *injuria*, and no damages can be recovered in an action."

(15)   See *Manchester & Altrincham, &c., Railway Co.* v. *Fullarton*, 13 *C.B.*, *N.S.* 54.

(16)   *Martin* v. *Great Northern Railway Co.*, 16 *C.B.* 180.

The plaintiff arrived at the station of the defendants about two minutes before the time of departure of the train, and in running along the line at a place where he ought not to have gone, in order to reach the train, which was on the opposite side of the railway, through an insufficiency of light, he fell over a switch handle, and was considerably hurt. The judge left it to the jury to say whether the injury was occasioned by the negligence of the defendants, and the jury found for the plaintiff.

(17)   *Grote* v. *Chester and Holyhead Railway Co.*, 2 *Exch.* 255.

In an action against a railway company for compensation for injury received by the plaintiff by the breaking down of a bridge over which he was passing in a passenger train, Held, that it was a proper question for the jury whether the defendants had engaged the services of competent engineers, who had adopted the best method and had used the best materials, and that if the defendants had done so, they would not be liable; but that the mere fact of their having engaged the services of a competent person would not relieve them from the consequences of an accident arising from a deficiency in the work.

(18) *Fawcett* v. *York & North Midland Railway Co.,* 16 Q.B. 618.

The plaintiff's horses strayed from his field into the highway and thence through gates at a level crossing, which were open on to the defendants' railway, and were in consequence killed by a train. Held, that by 5 & 6 Vict. c. 55, s. 9, an obligation was imposed on the company to keep the gates closed against stray cattle as well as against cattle lawfully on the road.

(19) *Ricketts* v. *East & West India Docks & Railway Co.,* 12 C.B. 174.

The plaintiff's sheep escaped from his close, through his own defect of fences, and getting into the intervening close of a third party, escaped thence on to the defendants' railway and were killed. Held, that the company were not liable.

(20) *Manley* v. *St. Helen's Canal & Railway Co.,* 2 H. & N. 840.

A boatman on a canal having opened a swivel bridge to allow his boat to pass through, a person who was coming along the road walked into the water just as the boat was coming up to the bridge, and was drowned. When the bridge was open, the end of the highway abutting on the canal was wholly unfenced. Two lamps had formerly been kept burning, one of which had been removed and the other was out of repair. In an action brought under Lord Campbell's Act, the jury found that the deceased was drowned by reason of the neglect of reasonable precautions on the part of the company. Held, that the jury were justified in finding the bridge in question insufficient, whether it had been sufficient or not at the time when it was built.

And see *Binks* v. *South Yorks, &c., Co.,* 3 B. & S. 244.

(21) *Smith* v. *London Dock Co.,* L.R., 3 C.P. 326.

The defendants, a dock company, provided gangways from the shore to the ships lying in their dock. The plaintiff went on board a ship in the dock at the invitation of one of the ship's officers, and while he was on board the defendants' servants, for the purposes of the business of the dock, moved the gangway so that it was, and was to their knowledge, insecure. The plaintiff, in ignorance of this insecurity, returned along it to the shore, and was injured. Held, that the defendants were liable in damages.

(22) *Holt, C.J., in Reg.* v. *Saintiff,* 6 Mod. 256.

(23) *Barraclough* v. *Johnson,* 8 Ad. & E. 105.

In determining whether or not a way has been dedicated to the public, the proprietor's intention must be considered. If it appear only that he has suffered a continual user, that may prove a dedication; but such proof may be rebutted by evidence of acts showing that he contemplated only a license resumable in a particular event.

The common course to rebut the presumption of dedication by user of a way is to shut it up one day in the year. See *Trustees of British Museum* v. *Finnis,* 5 C. & P. 460.

(24) *Vestry of Bermondsey* v. *Brown,* L.R., 1 Eq. Ca. 204.

The dedication by the owner of the soil of a right of way from continuous user can only be presumed in favour of the public, not of the inhabitants of a particular parish.

Dawes v. *Hawkins*, 8 *C.B.*, *N.S.* 848.

An ancient highway over a common was, without the authority of the owner of the soil, diverted by an adjoining proprietor, who substituted for it a new road, which was used by the public for more than twenty years. After the lapse of that period the original road was re-opened to the public, and the then owner of the soil over which the substituted road was, built a wall across the substituted road.

In an action against the defendants for pulling down the wall: Held, that there was no evidence of a dedication of the substituted road to the public. Byles, J.: "It is clear there can be no dedication of a way to the public for a limited time certain or uncertain. If dedicated at all, it must be dedicated in perpetuity. It is an established maxim—'Once a highway always a highway,'—for the public cannot release their rights."

(25)   *James* v. *Hayward*, *Cro. Car.* 184.

If a new gate be erected across a public highway, it is a common nuisance, although it be not fastened, and any of the King's subjects passing that way may cut it down and destroy it.

Queen v. *Train*, 31 *Law J.*, *M.C.* 169.

Upon the trial of an indictment for making a tramway upon a public highway in the parish of Lambeth, the jury found that the tramway was a nuisance, and that it rendered the highway unsafe. The defendants offered evidence that a great number of persons were carried along the tramway, and that a great saving of money was effected thereby. Held, that the finding of the jury amounted to a verdict of guilty, and that the evidence tendered by the defendants was inadmissible. Blackburn, J.: "If the defendants are right in their contention that this introduction of a tramway upon the public highway is an advantage to the public, they ought to go before a Committee of the Houses of Parliament in order to obtain an Act for the purpose."

(26)   *Rex* v. *Ragley*, 12 *Mod.* 409.

Holt, C.J.: "The parish of common right ought to repair their highway; but by prescription one parish may be bound to repair the way in another parish."

Rex v. *Ecclesfield*, *B. & Ald.* 348.

Indictment against the inhabitants of a parish for not repairing a road. Plea, that the inhabitants of a particular district within the parish have immemorially repaired all the roads within that district of which the road indicted for was one. Held, that this plea was good, although it did not state any consideration for the liability of the inhabitants of the district.

(27)   *Rose* v. *Groves*, 6 *Scott's N.R.* 645.

The plaintiff carried on the business of a licensed victualler in a house abutting on the river Thames, the defendants wrongfully and maliciously placed beams and spars, so that at certain states of the tides they floated opposite the plaintiff's house, thereby obstructing access thereto from the river and preventing customers from coming to the plaintiff's house for refreshments. Held, that this was such a private and particular damage to the plaintiff as to entitle him to maintain an action for obstruction.

(28)   See *White* v. *Crisp*, 10 *Exch.* 312.

(29) *Rex* v. *Russell*, 6 B. & C. 566.

Upon the trial of an indictment for a nuisance in a navigable river by erecting staiths there for loading ships with coals, the jury were directed by the judge to acquit the defendants, if they thought that the abridgment of the right of passage occasioned by these erections was for a public purpose, and produced a public benefit, and if the erections were in a reasonable situation, and a reasonable space was left for the passage of vessels on the river. Held, that this direction was proper.

(30) *Norris* v. *Baker*, 1 Roll. Rep. 393.

The plaintiff had set up poles on his own land in order to build a house, which, when erected, would be a nuisance to the adjoining dwelling-house of the defendant, and the latter entered upon the plaintiff's land and knocked down the poles to prevent the nuisance. Held, that the entry was wholly unjustifiable.

Cawkwell v. *Russell*, 26 Law J., Exch. 34.

When a party who is entitled to a limited right exercises it in excess, so as to cause a nuisance (as where a window or a drain is enlarged or applied to other purposes than originally authorized), as the entire nuisance may be abated, an action for an obstruction of the original right of easement cannot be maintained until its exercise has been reduced within its original limits.

(31) *Simpson* v. *Savage*, 1 C.B., N.S. 347.

In an action by a reversioner for an injury to his reversion by the erection of workshops and a forge and chimney on land adjoining his houses in the occupation of his tenants, and causing smoke to issue from the chimney and making loud noises—Held, that there was no evidence to go to the jury to prove injury to the reversion, and in order to entitle the plaintiff to maintain the action, the injury complained of must be of a permanent character.

Penruddock's Ca., 5 Co. 100.

There is this distinction between the beginning and continuance of a nuisance by building a house that hangs over or damages the house of a neighbour. Against the beginner an action may be brought without laying a request to remove the nuisance; but against a continuer a request is necessary.

(32) *Shadwell* v. *Hutchinson*, 4 C. & P. 333.

A reversioner recovered in an action for obstructing an ancient light, to the injury of his reversionary interest; the obstruction was not removed. Held, that he might maintain a second action for the continuance of the injury, and that on issue taken whether this was the "same identical grievance" for which he has previously recovered, the reversioner was entitled to verdict.

(33) *Cleeve* v. *Mahany*, 9 W.R. 882.

When the owner of houses, who lives at a distance from them, applies for an injunction on the ground of nuisance to the inhabitants of such houses, the court will not interfere by interim injunction where there is no evidence of such inhabitants in support of the application.

When the court has good ground for concluding that a present nuisance is temporary, it will not grant an interim injunction.

Att. Gen. v. *Gee, L.R.,* 10 *Eq. Ca.* 131.

Bill and information filed to restrain the local board of health of a town from discharging sewage into a river. Dismissed with costs on the ground that the injury was trifling.

(34) *Reg.* v. *G. N. Railway Co.,* 9 *Q.B.* 325.

A railway company held properly indicted for cutting through and obstructing a highway by works performed in a manner not conformable to the powers conferred on the company by Act of Parliament.

CHAPTER V.

NATURAL AND CONVENTIONAL SERVITUDES.

I. *Natural Servitudes.*

CERTAIN rights and duties attach to adjoining proprietors from the mere fact of their vicinity. Others are derived from contract, or from prescription founded on a supposed contract.

Rights and duties naturally incident to adjoining ownership are called natural servitudes.

Every proprietor has a right to such support from the adjoining land of his neighbour as will suffice to support his land in its natural condition, *i.e.*, unburdened by buildings. Lateral support. (1)

Where one possesses the surface and another the subsoil, the former has a right to such support from the lower strata as will suffice to maintain the surface in its natural state, *i.e.*, unburdened by buildings. And the owner of the surface may not dig into the subsoil beyond what is necessary for the cultivation of the land or its proper enjoyment. Support of surface. (2)

Every proprietor has a right to the continued flow of a natural stream running through his land and to the use of its water to a reasonable extent. He may not seriously lessen the quantity of the water which would naturally descend, or defile it so as to render it unfit for use. Natural streams, &c. (3)

A landowner may deal with casual and intermittent surface waters on his estate as he may choose; but he may not cut off the natural and apparent supply of surface water from natural streams.

A landowner must receive and discharge rain water and

spring water which naturally flows into his land from a higher level.

Although a proprietor may have no right to the flow of water upon his premises, yet if by the permission of the adjoining proprietor he has such flow of water, and a third party wrongfully interferes with it and fouls it, the latter is liable in damages.

Well water. (4) The law with regard to underground water is different. A proprietor may sink a well, although by doing so he drains the well of his neighbour, or diminishes the volume of water in an adjoining river. But a landowner will be restrained from drawing off the subterranean water in the adjoining land if in so doing he draws off water which has once flowed in a defined surface channel through such land.

And a mine owner may not flood his neighbour's mine by pumping up water from a lower to a higher level for the purpose of his own mining operations.

Rights more extensive than those of ordinary riparian proprietors are given by statute to companies incorporated for the purpose of rendering rivers navigable.

Natural servitudes are appurtenant to the land; they cannot be alienated from the land and held in gross.

The right to natural servitudes may be destroyed or lost by the creation of a conventional servitude contradictory to that right.

II. *Conventional Servitudes.*

Origin of conventional servitudes. Conventional servitudes arise (i) by implication of the law from grants to which they are deemed accessory; (ii) by express grant; (iii) by custom; (iv) by prescription founded on the presumption of a lost grant.

Easements and profits à prendre. An easement strictly so called consists in the right of entering upon the land of another or using that land for the purpose of some convenience, unaccompanied by any interest in the soil itself.

Where the right exists of entering upon the land of another and taking therefrom a profit from the soil, this is called a *profit à prendre*.

Thus the right to dry nets or clothes upon one's neighbour's land, or to discharge water thereon from the eaves of one's house, or a right of way across his field, is an easement. Whilst the right to depasture cattle upon another's land, or to cut and carry away turf or wood for domestic use, or to shoot and sport over his land and carry away the game killed, is a *profit à prendre*.

1. *Accessorial Servitudes.*

Accessorial servitudes, or servitudes of necessity, are founded generally upon the principle that a man shall not derogate from his own grant.

Where one man grants land to another to which there is no access but over the land of the grantor or the land of a stranger, the grantee has a right of way over the grantor's land. Ways of necessity. (5)

When a landowner grants a part of his land expressly for building, the grantee has an easement of lateral support for his building from the grantor's adjoining land. Lateral support. (6)

Where houses are built together so as to receive mutual support, and the owner sells one of them, or sells two or more of them to different owners, each house has a right to the easement of mutual support. And the same principle holds good where different stories of the same house are granted to different individuals. Mutual support of houses. (7)

If the owner of a house and the surrounding land sells the house and retains the land, an easement of necessary light and air is accessorial to the grant of the house; so that the owner of the unsold land may not build upon it so as to obstruct the access of light and air to the windows of the house. Light and air. (8)

But the converse does not hold good. If the owner sells the surrounding land and retains the house, the purchaser may build as close to the house as he pleases.

On the grant by an owner of an entire heritage of part of that heritage, as it is then used and enjoyed, there will pass to the grantee all continuous and apparent easements, used by the owner of the entirety, for the benefit of the parcel granted.

But, in such case, there is no implied reservation to the grantor of easements over the parcel of ground granted away.

Easements accessorial to other easements. (9) The grantee of a right of way or water-course is bound to keep it in repair. He has, therefore, as a necessary accessorial easement, the right of going upon the land over which the easement is enjoyed to execute necessary repairs.

2. *Servitudes arising by Express Grant.*

Deed required. (10) Easements are incorporeal hereditaments, and can therefore only be granted under seal.

When a conveyance of land (which must be under seal) contains words reserving certain easements or privileges to the grantor, his heirs, and assigns, these words will operate as a grant from the grantee to the grantor of the easements and privileges in question.

Licenses. (11) Mere permission by parol to go upon another's land justifies an entry upon that land, but it may be revoked at pleasure, and so of parol licenses generally for other purposes.

3. *Easements founded upon Custom.*

Antiquity of custom. (12) In order to justify an easement the custom upon which it is founded is presumed to have existed from time immemorial; but proof is only required of its continuance as of right and without interruption during the period required by the Prescription Act. Such custom must be *certain* and *reasonable*, and its reasonableness is a question of law and not of fact.

Whilst easements strictly so called (see p. 44) may be founded upon custom, *profits à prendre* cannot generally arise in this way. There are certain cases, however, in which *profits à prendre* may be claimed by custom:—

(i). *Common appendant*, or the right claimed by copyholders to common of pasture in their lord's wastes, may be claimed by custom, because the tenants cannot prescribe in their own names, for want of permanence, nor in their lord's name, since he cannot prescribe against himself.

(ii). The right of tin-bounders in Cornwall to search for tin on the wastes of a manor may be claimed by custom.

Title by Prescription.

Title by prescription is a title acquired by use and time and allowed by law. From immemorial enjoyment, the law will presume a grant which has been lost, and immemorial enjoyment is presumed from proof going back to the extent of living memory.

Prescription. (13)

Nothing but incorporeal hereditaments can be claimed by prescription. No prescription can give a title to lands or other corporeal substances; though the same effect of confirming ancient possession is arrived at with regard to them by the Statute of Limitations, which forbid actions to be brought after the lapse of certain periods.

All prescriptions must be either in a man and his ancestors or in a man and those whose estate he has, which last is called prescribing in a *que* estate. If a man prescribes in a *que* estate, nothing is claimable by this prescription except such things as are incident, appendant, or appurtenant to lands. But if a man prescribes in himself and his ancestors, he may prescribe for things in gross.

A prescription must always be laid in him that is tenant of the fee. A copyholder must, therefore, prescribe under cover of his lord's estate, and the tenant for life under cover of the tenant in fee simple.

Requisites for the presumption of a lost grant. (14)

To raise a presumption of a grant of an easement or profit from long continued, uninterrupted enjoyment of the privilege, the enjoyment must have been open and notorious, and exercised as a matter of right, and not of grace and favour.

As a general rule, a grant will not be presumed against an ignorant man, and therefore, if an easement or profit has been enjoyed on land let on lease, the landlord is not to be prejudiced in his rights and the inheritance burdened through the *laches* or acquiescence of tenants in matters affecting the inheritance without the knowledge and sanction of the landlord. But when the user and enjoyment are had and exercised under circumstances of notoriety, a jury may infer the landlord's knowledge and acquiescence.

Proof of immemorial enjoyment before the Prescription Act.

Proof of immemorial enjoyment was in ancient times essential to the legal presumption of a lost grant; but for a long time before the passing of the Prescription Act, judges were in the habit of directing juries to presume a lost grant of an easement or profit, from an uninterrupted enjoyment of the privilege as of right for twenty years—adopting that period by analogy to the Statute of Limitations. But this presumption was liable to be rebutted by showing the commencement of the enjoyment within the period of "legal memory."

The Prescription Act, sec. 1.

By the Prescription Act, 2 & 3 Will. IV. c. 71, it is enacted (sec. 1) that no claim by custom, prescription, or grant to any right of *common*, or other *profit*, or *benefit*, to be taken or enjoyed from or upon any land (except tithes, rent, and services) shall, where such right, &c., has been actually taken and enjoyed by any person claiming right thereto, without interruption for the full period of *thirty* years, be defeated by showing merely that such right, &c., first commenced within the time of legal memory, but that such claim may be defeated in any other way in which it was previously liable to be defeated; and that, when such right has been so enjoyed for the full period of *sixty* years, the right thereto shall be deemed absolute and indefeasible, unless it shall appear that the same was taken and enjoyed by some agreement in writing expressly made for that purpose.

The second section of the Prescription Act makes similar provision with regard to *ways, or other easements, watercourses, or the use of any water*, with this difference that the periods of prescription are *twenty years* and *forty years*, instead of *thirty* years and *sixty* years respectively. Prescription Act, sec. 2.

By the third section of the Prescription Act it is provided that when *the access and use of light* to and for any dwelling-house, workshop, or other building shall have been actually enjoyed therewith for the full period of *twenty years* without interruption, the right thereto shall be deemed absolute and indefeasible, unless it shall appear that the same was enjoyed by some covenant or agreement in writing expressly made for that purpose. Prescription Act, sec. 3.

The period during which a party capable of resisting the claim is an infant, idiot, *non compos mentis, feme covert*, or tenant for life, or during which any action shall have been pending, is to be excluded (sec. 7) from the computation of the periods mentioned, except only in cases where the claim is thereby declared to be absolute and indefeasible. Periods excluded from computation.

Under the Prescription Act, easements and *profits à prendre* cannot be claimed by user and enjoyment, unless the benefit or profit has been used, exercised, and taken for the more beneficial use and enjoyment of some neighbouring tenement. Easements in gross and profits in gross cannot, therefore, be claimed under the Act. And a right which can be of no benefit to any tenement, such as a right to cut down and carry away and sell trees growing on a neighbour's land, or a right to go upon land for recreation or amusement, cannot be prescribed for under the statute. Easements in gross. (15)

To bring a right within the term easement in the second

section of the statute, it must be a right analogous to a right of way or a right of water-course, and must be a right of utility and benefit, and not of mere amusement; but a right of mere amusement may be claimed by custom.

Peculiarities of sec. 3. (16)

The right to access of light dealt with in the third section is a *negative* easement, whereas the various rights dealt with in sections 1 and 2 are *positive* easements. The third section differs from the first and second (i) in that a far less time gives an indefeasible right, and no intermediate period is appointed for the accrual of a conditional title; (ii) the proviso of the seventh section with regard to the infancy, idiotcy, &c., of persons capable of objecting does not apply to the third section; (iii) the third section does not in express terms require that the enjoyment should be by a person "claiming right."

In spite, however, of the absence of the words "claiming right," it has been held that section 3 converts into a right such an enjoyment only of the access of light over contiguous land as had been had for twenty years, in the character of an easement distinct from the enjoyment of the land itself.

When, therefore, the owner in fee of an ancient house and the land surrounding it, having enjoyed the access of light to his windows across such adjoining land, his own property, for more than twenty years, sells such adjoining land, and the purchaser builds thereon, so as to shut out the light from the ancient house, the owner has no remedy, as his enjoyment of light having been over his own land, was not such an enjoyment as the statute contemplates.

When the windows and the land across which the light comes are in the occupation of different parties, and there is no unity of possession of the dominant and servient tenements, a prescriptive right is gained by twenty years' uninterrupted enjoyment, although the servient land across which the light comes is held on lease, and the landlord or reversioner has no means of redress.

If an ancient window is supplanted by a new window varying in size, elevation, or position from the ancient window, the new window may be obstructed by the adjoining landowner, but not the space occupied by the ancient aperture.

By section 4 of the Prescription Act it is enacted that no act or other matter shall be deemed to be an interruption, unless the same shall have been submitted to or acquiesced in for one year, after the party interrupted shall have had notice thereof. *Interruption of enjoyment preventing prescription.* (17)

The enjoyment of the privilege must be continuous, but the exercise of the right need not be continuous. "Without interruption" does not mean "without intermission." By interruption is meant an obstruction by the act of some person other than the claimant; and a mere cesser of enjoyment on the part of the claimant does not necessarily raise the inference of interruption.

When a prescriptive right has once been gained by twenty or thirty years' uninterrupted enjoyment as of right, it is not lost again by mere non-user. The evidence, therefore, to sustain a prescriptive claim need not come down to the commencement of the action, nor to any definite period.

ILLUSTRATIVE CASES.

(1) *Wyatt* v. *Harrison*, 3 B. & Ad. 871.

The possessor of a house which is not ancient cannot maintain an action against the owner of adjoining land for digging away that land so that the house falls in. But otherwise if it had appeared that the plaintiff's house was ancient, or if the complaint had been that the digging occasioned a falling in the soil of the plaintiff to which no artificial weight had been added. See also Lord Campbell's judgment (p. 744) in *Humphries* v. *Brogden*, next cited.

(2) *Humphries* v. *Brogden*, 12 Q.B. 739.

Action on the case by the occupier of the surface of land for negligently and contrary to the custom of the country working the subjacent minerals *per quod* the surface gave way. The surface was not built on. The jury found that the defendant had worked the mines carefully and according to the custom of the country, but without leaving sufficient support for the surface. Held, that on this finding the plaintiff was entitled to verdict.

Cox v. *Glue*, 5 C.B. 551.

The plaintiff was seised in fee of a close upon which the burgesses of an adjoining town had a right, during a certain portion of the year, to depasture their cattle, having during that period exclusive possession of the close. Held, that the plaintiff could maintain an action of trespass against a person who during that period committed a trespass in the subsoil by digging holes.

(3) *Embrey* v. *Owen*, 6 *Exch.* 353.

To an action by the plaintiffs, the occupiers of a water-grist mill, the defendant, a riparian proprietor, pleaded that at certain periods of the year when the water was more than sufficient for the use of the mill, the defendant diverted small and reasonable quantities for the purpose of irrigating certain closes, which quantities of water, except that which was absorbed in the irrigation, were returned into the stream above the mill, and that the quantity which was absorbed was inappreciable. Held, that this was not such an unreasonable use of the water as was prohibited by law.

Broadbent v. *Ramsbotham*, 11 *Exch.* 602.

The plaintiff's mill for more than fifty years had been worked by the stream of a brook, which was supplied by the water of a pond filled by rain, a shallow well supplied by subterraneous water, a swamp, and a well, formed by a stream springing out of the side of a hill, the waters of all which occasionally overflowed and ran down the defendant's land in no definite channel into a brook. Held, that the plaintiff had no right as against the defendant to the natural flow of any of the waters.

Laing v. *Whaley*, 3 *H. & N.* 685.

The plaintiff, by permission of a canal company, made a cut from the canal to his own premises, and by the water, got thus from the canal, fed the boilers of his engines. The defendant, without any right or permission from the company, fouled the water in the canal, whereby the water as it came into the plaintiff's premises was fouled, and by the use of it the plaintiff's boilers were injured. Judgment was given for the plaintiff.

(4) *Chasemore* v. *Richards*, 7 *H.L.C.* 349.

The plaintiff, a landowner and mill-owner, who had for above sixty years enjoyed the use of a stream which was chiefly supplied by percolating underground water, lost the use of the stream after an adjoining owner had dug on his own ground an extensive well for the purpose of supplying water to the inhabitants of the district, many of whom had no title as landowners to the use of the water. Held, that the plaintiff had no right of action. [Compare *Grand Junction Canal Co.* v. *Shugar*, *L.R.*, 6 *Ch. App.* 483.]

Smith v. *Kenrick*, 7 *C.B.* 515.

The proprietor of a mine, for the purpose of obtaining coal and so working his mine in the manner most advantageous to himself, removed a block of mineral, and by so doing caused water to flow through certain openings and flood an adjoining mine. Held, that in the absence of any servitude, and in the absence of negligent or malicious conduct on the part of the defendant, he was not responsible for the injury.

Baird v. *Williamson*, 33 *Law J.*, *C.P.* 101.

The owner of the upper of two adjoining mines is not liable for injury by water flowing by gravitation into the lower mine from works conducted by him in the usual and proper manner for the purpose of getting minerals from any part of his mine ; but he must not interfere with such gravitation so as to make it more injurious to the lower mine or advantageous to himself.

(5) *Staple* v. *Haydon*, 6 *Mod.* 4.

"If A. has an acre of ground surrounded by ground of B., A. for necessity has a way over a convenient part of B.'s ground to his own soil as a necessary incident to his ground."

(6) *N. E. Railway Co.* v. *Crosland*, 32 *Law J.* 353.

A railway company, under the powers of their Act, bought land for the purposes of their line, and purchased also from various landowners the right of making a tunnel through their lands. Minerals were excepted under the Act from purchases made in pursuance of it. The defendant Crosland, who derived title as landowner from the vendors to the company, gave notice to the company of his intention to work for minerals within a certain distance of the tunnel. An injunction was granted to restrain him on the ground that his workings would injure the tunnel.

(7) See *Richards* v. *Rose*, 9 *Exch.* 221.

(8) *Swansborough* v. *Coventry*, 9 *Bing.* 305.

The plaintiff purchased a house of A., and the defendant at the same time purchased of A. the adjoining land upon which an erection of one storey high had formerly stood. In the conveyance to plaintiff his house was described as bounded by *building ground* belonging to defendant. Held, that defendant was not entitled to build to a greater height than one storey, if by so doing he obstructed plaintiff's light.

White v. *Bass*, 7 *H. & N.* 722.

The owners in fee of a house and adjoining land granted to trustees a lease, and subsequently the reversion, of the land, and then conveyed the house in fee simple to a person under whom the plaintiff obtained possession. The defendant, by the authority of the trustees, built on the land so as to obstruct the light and air which for upwards of twenty years had come to the windows of the plaintiff's house. Until the lease was granted there had never been any severance of title or occupancy of the land and house, and the same had been occupied, and used together, by the proprietors thereof for upwards of fifty years. Held, that the plaintiff could maintain no action against the defendant for building on the land so as to obstruct the light and air of the plaintiff's house.

(9) *Taylor* v. *Whitehead*, 2 *Doug.* 745.

The defendant, who had a right of way over part of the plaintiff's land, went over the adjoining land, and, on action brought, justified his trespass on the plea that the way was out of repair. Lord Mansfield: "I entirely agree that by common law he who has the use of a thing ought to repair it. The grantor *may* bind himself [to do so], but here he has not bound himself. Highways are governed by a different principle. They are for the public service, and if the usual tract is impassable, it is for the public good that people should be entitled to pass in another line."

(10) *Lee* v. *Stevenson*, *E.B. & E.* 512.

Lease of land by plaintiff to defendant, reserving to plaintiff power to enter upon the land, and to dig and make a covered sewer and watercourse through it in order to convey away the drainage from plaintiff's premises. Plaintiff made a sewer accordingly; defendant made a drain from his own premises and carried it into the sewer. Held, that the plaintiff was entitled to the exclusive use of the sewer, and that he could recover in an action against defendant for so interfering with such exclusive use.

(11)   *Hyde v. Graham,* 32 *Law J. Exch.* 27.

To trespass for entering the plaintiff's land and breaking open his gate the defendant pleaded that there was a dispute between himself and others and the plaintiff as to whether there was a highway over the land, and that a memorandum had been drawn up and signed by the plaintiff, the defendant, and others, by which it was agreed that the way should remain open and unobstructed, without prejudice to the question of right, until the parties had come to a definite arrangement as to the manner in which the disputed question should be tried. The plea then alleged that the trespasses were committed before any such arrangement had been come to. Held, that the plea was no answer to the action either at law or in equity.

(12)   *Bryant v. Foot,* L.R. 2 Q.B. 161.

From the year 1808 to the date of trial (1867) the fee paid on the celebration of a marriage in a parish church was proved to have been almost uniformly 13s. There was no evidence extending beyond 1808. Held, that the amount of the fee being so great as to lead to the irresistible inference that it could not have existed in point of fact in the time of Richard I. was sufficient in itself to rebut the presumption arising from modern enjoyment, that the fee had an immemorial legal existence.

Mills v. Mayor, &c., of Colchester, L.R. 2 C.P. 476.

The owners of an oyster fishery had, since the reign of Elizabeth, held courts, and granted for a reasonable fee licences to fish to all persons inhabiting certain parishes who had been apprenticed for seven years to a duly licenced fishermen. In an action against the owners of the fishery by a person so qualified for not granting him a licence to fish on payment of the usual fee—Held, that as every act of fishing had been by licence, there had been no enjoyment as of right so as to give rise to a custom.

(13)   *Att.-Gen. v. Mathias,* 4 *K. & J.* 592.

The defendants claimed as foresters of the Crown a right to grant to certain free miners licences for working stone quarries in uninclosed lands, and to exact certain fees or rents in respect thereof. Held, that no such right could exist in point of law, for with regard to the free miners it was a claim to carry away the substratum without stint, which could not be established (1) by custom, for it was a *profit à prendre* which cannot be claimed *in alieno solo ;* nor (2) by prescription, for prescription to be good must be both reasonable and certain, and this was neither ; nor (3) by presuming a *lost grant,* for prescription presupposes such a grant, and if such grant cannot be presumed before, *à fortiori* it cannot after, the period of legal memory ; and, further, with regard to the defendants, besides the foregoing objections, they could not show a valid prescription exempting them as officers of the Crown from accounting for the proceeds of the Crown's soil which they had sold.

(14)   *Gray v. Bond,* 5 *Moore,* 534.

The lessees of a fishery had for sixty-four years been in the constant habit of landing their nets openly on a river-bank in the occupation of a tenant, and had from time to time sloped and pared the bank, and exercised other acts of ownership on the land. Held, that a jury was justified in inferring that the landlord knew of and acquiesced in the enjoyment of the easement.

(15) *Shuttleworth* v. *Le Fleming,* 34 *Law J., C.P.* 309.

To an action of trespass, defendants pleaded a right of free fishery in gross by a prescription of sixty years. Held, that rights in gross are not within the Prescription Act (2 & 3 Will. IV. c. 71).

Mounsey v. *Ismay,* 1 *H. & C.* 729.

A custom from time whereof the memory of man runneth not to the contrary for the freemen and citizens of a town on a particular day of the year to enter upon a close for the purpose of holding a horse racing, held to be a good custom.

(16) *Harbidge* v. *Warwick,* 3 *Exch.* 552.

The plaintiff and his father, whom he had succeeded, had occupied a house, of which they were seised in fee for more than sixty years, and during all that time had enjoyed access of light to their window over contiguous land. The house was an ancient house, and the window was also ancient and necessary for the convenient occupation of the house. The contiguous land in question was a garden, which, from the time of their occupation of the house by the plaintiff and his father, had been also occupied by them as tenants from year to year, until two years before action brought. It was then occupied by defendant, who built a wall obstructing the access of light to the window. Held, on the construction of 2 & 3 Will. IV. c. 71, s. 3, that the unity of possession prevented the acquirement of any right to the light in question. See *White* v. *Bass, supra,* p. 53.

Cross v. *Lewis,* 2 *B. & C.* 686.

Plaintiff's windows overlooked defendant's premises, which were for more than twenty years in the occupation of a tenant, the defendant never visiting them. Held, that the plaintiff had gained a prescriptive right to the access of light, and was entitled to recover against the defendant, who had obstructed it.

(17) *Darling* v. *Clue,* 4 *F. & F.* 334.

Willes, J.: "If there is proof to your satisfaction of a long enjoyment of the alleged way, you must not negative it merely because there was a time during which there was no enjoyment." And see *Cooper* v. *Hubbuck,* 12 *C.B., N.S.* 470.

CHAPTER VI.

WASTE.

BESIDES the payment of rent reserved, if any, and the observance of the covenants of the demise, there are other duties imposed upon the tenant towards the landlord or reversioner. A dereliction of these duties constitutes waste. Similar duties are imposed on tenants for life, or years, with regard to their remaindermen.

<small>Commissive and permissive waste.</small> Waste is either commissive or permissive. Commissive waste consists in the doing of some wilful injury by the tenant to the premises demised. Permissive waste consists in the tenant's remaining passive whilst decay or ruin is progressing.

1. *Waste by Tenants for Life or for Terms of Years.*

<small>Permissive waste. (1)</small> A tenant for life, or for a term of years, is responsible for both commissive and permissive waste. He must use all reasonable endeavours to keep the demised buildings wind and water-tight, and must generally execute such repairs as are necessary to secure this. He is not bound, however, to repair the principal timbers of the roof.

If the building should perish from time and natural decay, he is not bound to rebuild it, unless he has contracted to do repairs.

If the building be destroyed by fire arising from his negligence or that of his servants, this is permissive waste, for which he is responsible.

It is waste to remove virgin soil, to open new mines or quarries, to convert arable land into pasture, or *vice versâ*; to dig for lime, gravel, clay, &c., except to execute repairs to which he is bound; to divert the course of a stream, to destroy fences, to dry up ancient fish-ponds or to make new ones, or to destroy game. *Commissive waste on the land. (2)*

It is waste to pull down houses, out-buildings, or walls, to remove wainscots or floors, to build up old windows or doors or to open new ones, to change one species of building into another, as a water-mill into a wind-mill, or a corn-mill into a malt-mill. *Commissive waste to buildings. (3)*

It is waste to fell timber trees except for the repair of the house, when the tenant has covenanted to repair; (and what are timber trees depends upon the custom of the country); to destroy saplings, to cut down trees which are not timber, but which afford shelter to a dwelling-house or to cattle, or which support a bank. But a tenant may cut underwood, if in accordance with the custom of the country; and he may generally take sufficient wood for necessary repairs of buildings and fences. *Commissive waste to trees. (4)*

As between landlord and tenant, the tendency of the law is to allow considerable latitude in the removal of fixtures. There are certain classes of fixtures, however, which may not be disannexed from the soil, and the removal of them by the tenant constitutes waste. *Commissive waste by removal of fixtures. (5)*

(i). Tenant's fixtures which may not be disannexed:—
Buildings let into the ground, and not merely placed upon the surface, locks, keys, bars, and shutters put up for the security of the premises.

(ii). Tenant's fixtures which may be disannexed:—
Vessels and machinery used for purposes of trade, ornamental furniture, such as pier-glasses and carved chimney-pieces, grates and gas-fittings, Dutch barns, fowl-houses, conservatories, or other wooden buildings merely attached by screws or bolts to their foundations, buildings, &c., erected under 14 & 15 Vict. c. 25, s. 3, with the consent of

the landlord, and giving him the option of purchase instead of removal.

Other fixtures may be removable by local custom

The tenant may abandon his right to remove fixtures, which he may erect during his term, by express covenant.

The right to remove fixtures must be exercised by the tenant before his term has expired. He cannot re-enter for the purpose of removing them.

But if a tenant has mortgaged his fixtures to a third person, and allows his term to expire without removing them, the mortgagee may, nevertheless, enter to remove them. [As to compensation to tenant for the erection and enlargement of buildings during the term, and for other improvements, see the Agricultural Holdings Act, 38 & 39 Vict. c. 92.]

Commissive waste by fire. (6) Whilst the destruction of the demised premises by fire through the negligence of the tenant is permissive waste, yet, if the negligence be so gross as to give the appearance of a wilful act, this is regarded as commissive waste.

2. *Waste by Tenants from Year to Year.*

Tenants from year to year. (7) Tenants from year to year are liable for commissive waste, like tenants for life, or for a term of years. They are not, however, generally liable for permissive waste, but they are bound to repair windows, so as to prevent the rain from entering and damaging the building.

3. *Waste by Tenants at Will.*

Tenants at will. (8) Tenants at will are not liable for permissive waste. If they are guilty of commissive waste, this is itself a determination of the tenancy, and they may at once be treated as mere trespassers.

4. *Waste by Incumbents.*

Incumbents. (9) An incumbent is bound to restore and rebuild as well as to repair. He may alter the condition of the land for the good of the benefice. He may cut down timber for repairs.

The liabilities of incumbents are regulated by 34 & 35 Vict. c. 43.

5. *Waste by Copyholders.*

In strictness a copyholder guilty of waste thereby forfeits his estate. Clear proof is, however, required of an act which is injurious to the inheritance. Copyholders. (10)

Equitable Waste.

When a life estate is given "without impeachment of waste" the tenant for life will still be restrained from committing what is known as "equitable waste," *i.e.*, wanton or malicious waste—such as damaging or destroying buildings or boundary walls, cutting down wood unfit for timber, or trees grown for shelter or ornament to the mansion, or destroying a field by carrying away brick earth. By tenant for life. (11)

Similarly a lessee for a term of years without impeachment of waste will be restrained from causing lasting injury to the inheritance. Lessee for years.

When direct licence to commit waste is given by the lease to the lessee, such permission vests the property in that which is the subject of waste in the lessee, provided he avail himself of it during the term.

A tenant in fee simple, subject to an executory devise over, will be restrained from committing equitable waste. Tenant in fee simple subject to executory devise over. (12)

Trustees of a term for special purposes without impeachment of waste are not even permitted to cut down timber. Trustees. (13)

Waste by Strangers.

The lessee, whether for life or years, is liable for commissive waste, even when it is committed by third persons, for the lessee is presumed to be capable of preventing it. The lessor has his action against the lessee for waste; and the lessee has his action of trespass against the wrong-doer.

Inspection of Waste.

Lessors or reversioners have the right of entry upon the lands of their lessees to see whether there is any waste, and the lessee resisting this right is liable in substantial damages, although no waste has been committed.

Remedies for Waste.

Action and injunction. (14)
In an action for waste the actual damage sustained may be recovered and an injunction obtained against the recurrence of the mischief.

The action for waste must generally be brought by the person next entitled in remainder; and, if the latter has only a life estate, he is only entitled to such damages as are commensurate with the injury done to his life estate.

An injunction may be obtained to restrain a lessee for lives renewable for ever from committing waste on the demised property.

When waste is committed by a stranger in collusion with a tenant an injunction will be granted against such stranger as well as such tenant.

The right to an injunction against waste may be lost by long delay and practical acquiescence.

It is no answer to an action of waste to say that the value of the property is enhanced by the changes made. The lessor is entitled to have the premises kept in the state in which he demised them.

ILLUSTRATIVE CASES.

(1)   2 *Roll Abr. Waste* (*C*).

(2)   *Provost, &c., of Queen's College, Oxford* v. *Hallett*, 14 *East* 489.

An action on the case for an injury to the inheritance held to lie by the reversioners, pending the term, against a tenant, for inclosing and cultivating waste land included in the demise.

(3)   *Smyth* v. *Carter*, 18 *Bear.* 78.

Sir John Romilly, M.R.: "This court will restrain a tenant from pulling down a house and building any other which the landlord dislikes. It is not sufficient to show that the house proposed to be built is a better one. The landlord has a right to exercise his own judgment and caprice."

(4) *Gage* v. *Smith, Godb.* 209.

An action of waste was brought by the reversioner against the lessee for committing waste in uncovering a barn and in destroying the stocks of elms, ashes, whitethorn, and blackthorn. Held (*inter alia*) that the eradicating of whitethorn is waste, but not of blackthorn, but if blackthorn grow in a hedge, and the whole hedge be destroyed, the same is waste. It was also held that it is not waste to cut quick-set hedges, but rather good husbandry, and that a tenant may cut underwoods of hazel, willows, and thorns according to usage, but not dig them up.

(5) *Elwes* v. *Maw,* 3 *East* 53.

A tenant in agriculture who erected, at his own expense, and for the necessary and convenient occupation of his farm, a beast-house, carpenter's shop, fuel-house, pump-house, and fold-yard wall, which buildings were of brick and mortar, and tiled, and let into the ground, cannot remove the same though during the term, and though he thereby leave the premises in the same state as when he entered. Had the buildings been erected for the purposes of trade or manufacture, the decision would have been otherwise.

Grymes v. *Boweren,* 6 *Bing.* 437.

A pump was erected by a tenant, during his term, very slightly affixed to the freehold. Held, that it was removable as a tenant's fixture. Tindal, C.J. : " The rule as to fixtures has always been relaxed more as between landlord and tenant than as between persons standing in other relations. It has been holden that stoves are removable during the term ; grates, ornamental chimney pieces, wainscots fastened with screws, coppers and various other articles."

(6) *Shrewsbury* v. *Crompton,* 5 *Co.* 136.

On an action against a tenant at-will for negligently permitting the premises to be burnt down, held that the action was not maintainable, for a tenant at-will is not liable for permissive waste.

For an example of such gross negligence as would render either a stranger or a tenant liable for damage caused by fire see *Vaughan* v. *Menlove,* 3 *B.N.C.* 468.

(7) *Martin* v. *Gilham,* 7 *Ad. & E.* 540.

An action was brought against the defendant, a lessee from year to year, for certain acts of commissive waste, and for "otherwise using the said premises in so untenant-like and improper manner " that they became dilapidated and in bad condition. The only waste proved was permissive. Held, that the tenant was not liable.

(8) *Harnett* v. *Maitland,* 16 *M. & W.* 262.

A declaration in case set forth that the defendant was tenant to the plaintiff of a certain messuage, and that the defendant had wrongfully permitted the premises to be waste and ruinous. Held, on general demurrer, that the declaration was bad for not showing that the defendant was more than a tenant-at-will, who is not liable for permissive waste.

(9) *Wise* v. *Metcalfe,* 10 *B. & C.* 313.

An incumbent of a living is bound to keep the parsonage house and chancel in good and substantial repair, restoring and rebuilding when necessary, according to the original form, without addition or modern improvement ; but he is not bound to supply or maintain anything in the nature of ornament, such as painting (unless that be necessary to preserve exposed timber from decay) and whitewashing and papering.

(10) *Grubb* v. *Earl of Burlington*, 5 B. & Ad. 507.

A copyholder pulled down a barn without any intention of rebuilding it. Held that the lord could not recover the place from him on the ground of a forfeiture, if the jury found that the pulling down of the barn was no injury to the property.

(11) *Vane* v. *Lord Barnard*, 2 Vern. 738.

The defendant, in consideration of marriage, settled Raby Castle to the use of himself for life without impeachment of waste, remainder to his son, &c. The defendant, upon some displeasure with his son, employed several persons to pull down the castle, whereupon the court granted a perpetual injunction to stop him, and ordered him to repair what he had already pulled down.

Bishop of London v. *Web*, 1 P. Wms. 528.

The defendant, a tenant under a long lease, without impeachment of waste, was restrained at the instance of the plaintiff, who was remainderman in fee, from digging the ground for brick.

(12) See *Blake* v. *Peters*, 31 Law J., Ch. 889.

(13) *Campbell* v. *Allgood*, 17 Beav. 623.

Trustees in whom an estate is vested ought not to cut down ornamental trees, alleged to be prejudicial, without first applying to the parties beneficially interested for their assent, or to the court for its authority.

(14) *Evelyn* v. *Ruddish*, Holt N.P.C. 543.

Freehold premises were out to lease, and there were several interests in the property, viz., tenant for life, remainder in tail, and reversion in fee. A breach of covenant occurred, giving the tenant for life a right of action. Held, that he could only recover damages for the injury done to his life estate, and not such as might be sustained by the reversioner.

CHAPTER VII.

DISTRESS FOR RENT.

By the Common Law landlords to whom rent is due, and who are immediate reversioners, may enter in person upon the demised premises and seize certain moveables and hold them as a pledge for the payment of rent. And by statute they may sell the thing distrained. *Definition. (1)*

A tenant from year to year underletting from year to year has a reversion which enables him to distrain for rent reserved upon such underlease. *Tenant from year to year. (2)*

Where the tenant holds over at the determination of a demise, whether adversely or with permission, the landlord has no right to distrain in respect of such occupation. But a renewal of the tenancy will be presumed on slight evidence. And as to rent accrued due before the determination of the tenancy, see 8 Anne, c. 14, ss. 6 & 7. *Tenant holding over. (3)*

If the tenant become bankrupt, the landlord may still distrain, but if he does so after the commencement of the bankruptcy, the distress is not available for more than one year's rent accrued due. *Tenant bankrupt.*

Where a tenant enters under an executory contract for a future lease, if the agreement was for a tenancy at a fixed rent, or if by payment of rent, or otherwise, an agreement for a tenancy at a fixed rent can be implied, the landlord may distrain for all rent subsequently accruing due. *Tenant in possession under executory contract. (4)*

A mere receiver of rents has no authority to distrain, unless he be a receiver appointed by the Court of Chancery.

Rent payable in advance. (5) Rent may be payable in advance so as to entitle the landlord to distrain for it at the commencement instead of the end of each quarter.

Agreement not to distrain. (6) The right to distrain may be made conditional, or may be postponed, or abandoned by the contract of the parties.

Licence to distrain. (7) A debtor may give his creditor a licence to enter upon the debtor's land and distrain all the goods and chattels on his premises, and sell them in discharge of his debt. But a licence of this sort cannot be made to extend to and bind those who are not parties to it.

Time, place, and mode of distraining. (8) Distress cannot be made until the day after the day appointed for payment of rent. It cannot be made before sunrise or after sunset. It cannot be made upon land which is not parcel of the demise, unless the tenant has fraudulently removed his goods.

A landlord or his bailiff cannot lawfully break open gates, or break down inclosures, or force open the outer door of a building, or enter by a window which is shut though not fastened.

A distress is made if the lessor in person or by deputy enters on the premises and announces to the tenant or his servants that he detains certain chattels for rent.

Things not distrainable. (9) Amongst things not distrainable, some are absolutely privileged from distress, and others only conditionally. Belonging to the first class are:—

(i). Things annexed to the freehold.

(ii). Things delivered to a person exercising a public trade to be carried, worked up, or managed by him in the way of his trade or employ. (See *infra*, "The goods of third persons.")

(iii). Cocks and sheaves of corn and other things which cannot be restored in the same plight.

(iv). Things in actual use.

(v). Animals *feræ naturæ*.

(vi). Things in the custody of the law.

DISTRESS FOR RENT.

Belonging to the second class are :—

(i). Beasts of the plough, instruments of husbandry, and beasts which profit the land, as sheep.

(ii). The instruments of a man's trade or profession.

Things belonging to the last two classes are only privileged, provided there be other sufficient distress on the premises.

The property of third persons found upon the demised premises is not distrainable, if it remain in their own use and possession, or if it be placed there with the leave of the landlord, or if it be the subject of a bailment. By 34 & 35 Vict. c. 79 the goods of a lodger are exempt from distress by the superior landlord, on his serving the landlord with notice and an inventory of the said goods and tendering to the landlord any balance of rent which may be due from him to the tenant. <small>The goods of third persons. (10)</small>

A distress is wrongful, if it be made before the rent has become due. And the tenant may resist such seizure by force, and after seizure he may rescue the goods before they are impounded Tender of rent before distress renders the distress wrongful *ab initio*. The abuse of the right of distress renders the landlord a trespasser *ab initio*. Thus, if an outer door be broken and goods in the house seized, this is not a distress but a trespass. <small>Wrongful distress. (11)</small>

If the landlord distrains goods and chattels beyond what is reasonably necessary to realise the rent and expenses, he renders himself liable to an action for damages, even though the tenant has in fact sustained none.

A landlord cannot lawfully distrain twice for the same rent, unless the distress has been withdrawn at the instance of the tenant, or unless there has been some mistake as to the value of the things taken, or unless the distress has been rendered abortive by the threats or misconduct of the tenant. If distress has been relinquished on receiving a bill or note, and the bill or note

F

is dishonoured at maturity, the landlord may distrain again

Impounding distress. (12) No formal impounding is now required; the goods are impounded as soon as the distrainor has made out and delivered to the tenant, or has left upon the premises, an inventory of the goods he has taken. And any one who takes or drives away things impounded, is guilty of pound-breach and liable to treble damages, and subject to an indictment. If the distrainor uses or consumes things distrained and impounded, he is subject to an action for damages, and the owner may interfere to prevent the abuse without being guilty of pound-breach.

Sale of things distrained. 2 W. & M. c. 5 enacts that if within five days the distress be not replevied (see *infra*) with sufficient security, the distrainor may cause the goods to be appraised and sold in satisfaction of the rent and charges. The tender of rent and costs within the five days allowed by the statute will also render the sale unlawful.

The 11 Geo. II. c. 19 enacts that when a distress has been made for rent justly due, and the distrainor shall afterwards have committed some irregularity or unlawful act, he shall not be deemed a trespasser *ab initio*, but the party aggrieved may recover full satisfaction for the special damage received.

Replevin.

By the writ of replevin, the thing distrained is ordered to be restored to the tenant, who at the same time gives security to prosecute an action with success and make out the unlawfulness of the taking.

And the 19 & 20 Vict. c. 108 empowers the registrar of the county court of the district in which the distress is taken, to approve of replevin bonds, and to grant replevins on security being given. This was formerly the duty of the sheriff of the county.

ILLUSTRATIVE CASES.

(1) *Selby v. Greaves, L.R. 3 C.P. 594.*

A. let to B. a defined portion of a room in a factory, with steam power for working lace-machines belonging to B., at a certain sum per annum, payable quarterly, a deduction to be allowed in the event of hindrances in the supply of power beyond seven days in each quarter. Held a sufficient devise to enable A. to distrain.

(2) See *Curtis v. Wheeler, M. & M. 493.*

(3) *Jenner v. Clegg, 1 M. & Rob. 213.*

A house was let to certain tenants from the 1st of April, 1830, for one year, and, from and after the expiration of that term, as long as the parties might please at the rent agreed upon payable half-yearly (the half-year's rent to be payable in advance), and for such rent in advance the landlord was to have the right to distrain. On the 29th of September, 1831, the tenants gave notice to quit on the 1st of April then next. They did not, however, quit in pursuance of their notice but held over, and whilst they did so the landlord distrained for half a year's rent due on the 1st of April, 1832, as he contended, in advance, in respect of the half-year commencing on that day. Parke, J.: "I am clearly of opinion that the defendant had no right to distrain. The tenants have not waived the notice to quit by holding over. The landlord may recover double value during the period of the holding over, or he may bring an action for use and occupation; but he cannot distrain unless he can show an agreement between the parties to hold on at the same rent."

(4) *Anderson v. Midland Railway Co., 30 Law J., Q.B. 96.*

The plaintiff entered into an agreement with M. that a valid lease in law should be forthwith duly executed by the plaintiff and M., of a house and premises to M. to hold for a term of three years. The agreement specified how the rent should be paid and what covenants should be contained in the lease, and then proceeded, "And it is hereby mutually agreed that these presents shall operate as an agreement only; and that, until a lease shall be executed, the rents, covenants, and agreements, agreed to be therein reserved and contained, shall be paid and observed, and the several rights and remedies shall be enforced, in the same manner as if the same had been actually executed." Held, that a tenancy was created which gave M. a right to distrain.

(5) *Lee v. Smith, 9 Exch. 665.*

A. became tenant to the defendant of certain premises under the terms of a written agreement (not under seal) for a term exceeding three years, the rent payable quarterly in advance. A. occupied the premises for some time, and paid several quarters' rent, and the receipts given to him by the defendant's agent stated that such payment was in advance although, in fact, A. never paid the rent in advance. Held, that although the agreement was void under the 8 & 9 Vict. c. 106 as not being under seal, still the receipt taken was ample evidence of the tenancy being upon the terms of the rent being payable quarterly in advance.

(6) *Giles v. Spencer, 3 C.B., N.S. 244.*

A., the tenant of a house, let certain rooms on the ground floor to B. under a written agreement from year to year, subject to a quarter's notice, with a stipulation, that no action or distress should be prosecuted by A. in respect of such rent, unless he should have previously paid the rent due from himself to the superior landlord, and should have produced his receipt for the same to B. Held, that under this agreement trespass might be maintained against a broker employed by A. to distrain without having previously complied with the condition.

(7) *Howes* v. *Ball*, 7 B. & C. 481.

A. agreed to give B., a coachmaker, £100 for a coach, and to pay for the same by four bills of £25 each, and that B. should have a claim upon the coach until the debt was duly paid. The bills were given but not paid. A. died, and B. obtained possession of the coach. Held, that the agreement amounted to a sale, subject to a personal licence to resume possession of the coach, if the bills were not paid. Tenterden, C.J. : " Construing it as a licence, it is a personal licence, not available against any person to whom Howes might transfer the property. It could not therefore be available against his administrator, to whom the property came by operation of the law."

(8) *Duppa* v. *Mayo*, 1 Saund. 287.

Though rent must be demanded or tendered before sunset to take advantage of or save a forfeiture, yet it is *not due* until midnight of the day upon which it is made payable.

Brown v. *Glenn*, 16 Q.B. 254.

A landlord cannot break open an outer door of a stable, though not within the curtilage, to levy an ordinary distress for rent.

Nash v. *Lucas*, L.R., 2 Q.B. 590.

A broker went with a warrant of distress to certain demised premises and found the door of the house fastened. A workman was employed by the tenant to do some repairs in the area in front of the house ; the tenant subsequently left the house, fastening the front door of the house and the door communicating between the area and the house. The workman, after finishing his work, found himself unable to get out, and was advised by the broker to get into the house by means of a window which looked into the area, and which was shut and not fastened. The workman did this, and then unfastened the house door from the inside to let himself out. On the front door being thus opened, the broker entered and distrained. Held, that the transaction must be taken as one, and that as the entry was by the opening of a window, the distress was unlawful.

Ryan v. *Shilcock*, 7 Exch. 72.

A landlord, in order to distrain, may open the outer door by the usual means adopted by persons having access to the building ; and therefore he may open it by turning the key, by lifting the latch, or by drawing back the bolt.

Tutton v. *Darke*, 5 H. & N. 647 ; *Nixon* v. *Freeman*, ibid.

An entry to make a distress through an open window is lawful. A distress for rent before sunrise, or after sunset, is illegal, although there may be daylight. *Sed quære* whether the time of sunrise is to be reckoned from the first appearance of the beams of the sun above the horizon, or from the time when the whole sun has emerged.

(9) *Dalton* v. *Whittern*, 3 Q.B. 961.

If a landlord, under a distress for rent, sever fixtures from the freehold and dispose of them he is liable in trover.

Keen v. *Priest,* 4 *H. & N.* 236.

Cart, colts, and young steers, not broken in, or used for harness, or the plough, are not privileged from distress as beasts which profit the land under 51 Hen. III. stat. 4. And sheep are privileged, not only under that statute, but at common law, if there are other goods on the premises sufficient to satisfy the rent.

Simpson v. *Hartopp, Willes* 512.

Implements of trade are privileged from distress for rent, if they are in actual use at the time, or if there be any other sufficient distress on the premises. And see the notes on this case in 1 *Sm. L. C.,* where the whole subject is treated of.

(10)   *Fowkes* v. *Joyce,* 2 *Vern.* 129.

A grazier, driving a flock of sheep to London, is encouraged by an innkeeper to put his sheep into pasture grounds adjoining the inn. The landlord, seeing the sheep, consents that they shall stay there one night, and then distrains them for rent. Grazier relieved against this distress.

Wood v. *Clarke,* 1 *Cr. & J.* 484.

Materials delivered by a manufacturer to a weaver to be by him manufactured at his own home are privileged from distress for rent due from the weaver to his landlord; but a frame or other machinery delivered by the manufacturer to the weaver together with the materials for the purpose of being used in the weaver's house in the manufacture of such materials is not privileged, unless there be other goods upon the premises sufficient to satisfy the rent due.

(11)   *Attack* v. *Bramwell,* 32 *Law J.,* Q.B. 146.

When a landlord to whom rent is due for a house enters the house in a way which is unlawful, and seizes and takes possession of the goods in the house as a distress for the rent, he is liable in trespass; and the value of the goods is the measure of damages which the tenant is entitled to recover.

Chandler v. *Doulton,* 34 *Law J., Exch.* 89.

In an action for an excessive distress the plaintiff is entitled to nominal damages, though he proves no actual damage.

(12)   *Firth* v. *Purvis,* 5 *T.R.* 432.

A landlord distrained four casks of beer in a cellar, giving due notice of distress to the tenant, and left the casks in the cellar, without placing them under lock, or leaving anyone in charge of them. Held, that this was a sufficient impounding, and that a subsequent tender of rent was no answer to the distress.

Duncomle v. *Reeve, Cro. Eliz.* 783.

Certain hides were taken in distress, and after the distress the distrainor tanned the hides in order to prevent them rotting. Held that the tanning was unlawful, because the property was "*quasi* altered." "Although one may in some cases meddle with and use a distress where it is for the owner's benefit, as where one distrains armour he may cause it to be scoured to avoid rust, so, if one distrains raw cloth, he may cause it to be fulled, for it is for the owner's benefit. But here the tanning is not for his benefit; for it takes from him the notice of the thing, and so is a means of taking away the thing itself; for he cannot have any knowledge thereof to have it again."

CHAPTER VIII.

TRESPASS AND CONVERSION OF CHATTELS.

OF the right to possession of chattels and injury to that right, viz., trespass and conversion.

Ownership. (1) Ownership or the right of general property in chattels draws to it the right of possession, and one in whom the general property in a chattel is vested may maintain an action against anyone who takes or injures it, although he himself has never had possession of it in fact.

Bailment. (2) When the owner has parted with the possession of chattels for a certain time, he cannot sue a wrongdoer for trespassing upon or converting the property. But if the bailee alters or changes the nature of the chattels, or does anything to destroy their identity, or if the chattels are taken out of the possession of the bailee by a wrongdoer, the right of possession reverts to the bailor.

A bailee having the temporary right to possession may sue any third person who wrongfully seizes them for conversion.

And a person who has a right as against an owner to the temporary possession of a chattel may sue the owner, if the latter refuse to deliver up the chattel on demand.

If the bailor has no title to personal chattels at the time of the bailment, the bailee can have none, and a claimant may bring his action against the latter. The bailee may, however, interplead, and leave the respective rights of the claimant and the bailor to be judicially decided as between themselves.

When a person has merely a lien upon goods he has no right to sell them, and if he does sell them this is an act of conversion which determines his lien, and the right of possession of the goods accrues to their owner. *Lien.* (3)

[As to the transfer of the right of property in chattels, and the right to possession generally by sale or otherwise, see Part II., Contracts.]

In an action of conversion the plaintiff, in recovering damages for the wrong done, loses his right of property in the thing converted, which, if the judgment has been satisfied, is transferred to the defendant. And this transfer dates back by relation to the time of the conversion. *Converted property.* (4)

The innocent finder of a lost article is entitled to the possession of it against all the world except its owner. And an "innocent finder" is one who has not taken possession of the lost article feloniously or fraudulently, knowing, or having the means of knowing, the owner of it. *Lost property.* (5)

When by design or accident one man alters or improves the chattel of another without authority, he has no right to detain it from the owner until the alterations or improvements have been paid for. *Things altered or confused by a wrongdoer.* (6)

If anyone mixes his own money in one heap, or his corn in one sack with the money or corn of another, so that the money or corn of the former cannot be distinguished or separated from the money or corn of the latter, then the whole heap of money, or the whole sack of corn, shall belong to the latter.

The right of property in the thing sold is at Common Law changed permanently by sale in market overt to a *bond fide* purchaser. But (24 & 25 Vict. c. 96) when the person from whom goods have been stolen prosecutes and obtains a conviction against the thief, the right of ownership is revested in the person robbed, and he may follow the goods, even though they have been sold in market overt. *Stolen property.*

And when stolen property is sold out of market overt no right of property is conveyed to the purchaser, and the person robbed may follow his property, even though the thief has not been prosecuted. [See *supra*, Chapter I., and *infra*, Part II., Chapter X.]

Timber. (7)
Although the property in timber trees which are cut down on an estate is in the lessor, and he may maintain an action against anyone who carries them away, yet the lessee has sufficient possession to bring an action for the conversion of the timber also.

Letters. (8)
The right of property in letters is in the person to whom they are addressed and delivered, but he has no right to publish them without the permission of the writer.

Negotiable and non-negotiable instruments. (9)
When lost or stolen bills of exchange and promissory notes assignable by delivery, or bank notes, come into the possession of *bonâ fide* holders for value without notice, they become lawful owners of them, and may retain or pay them away. And mere negligence in taking a negotiable security and giving full value for it does not fix such *bonâ fide* holder with the defective title of the person from whom he received it.

If a bill or note is assignable only by endorsement, neither thief nor finder can make a valid endorsement so as to confer the right of possession on a *bonâ fide* holder for value.

Dock warrants, delivery orders, and wharfingers' receipts are not negotiable instruments, and their possession is no stronger evidence of title than the naked possession of the goods.

Untamed animals. (10)
There is no ownership or absolute proprietary right in animals *feræ naturæ*. So long as they remain on a man's land he has the right of possession in them; but the moment they leave his land his right is lost. If a man hunt and kill a wild animal in another man's grounds, the property in the dead animal is in the latter. But if one start a wild animal in another's grounds, and chase it from thence into the grounds of a third person, and then kill it, the property in the dead animal will be in the

TRESPASS AND CONVERSION OF CHATTELS. 73

hunter, who is nevertheless liable to actions for trespass on the part of both of the proprietors upon whose grounds he ventured.

Until a fisherman has got a fish into his power, or under his dominion or control, he can have no right of possession in it. Fish.
(11)

When a chattel is held in partnership, in joint tenancy, or in tenancy in common, and one partner, &c., sells the chattel not in market overt, the sale operates only as to his own share, and he cannot, therefore, be sued by his co-partner, &c., for conversion. But if he sell the chattel in market overt or destroy it this would amount to a conversion. Joint property.
(12)

All the property of a bankrupt, except property held by him in trust, his tools, wearing apparel, and bedding, to the value of £20, vests (32 & 33 Vict. c. 71) in the registrar of the court until the appointment of a trustee, and then passes to the latter, and the title of the trustee relates back to the act of bankruptcy. The trustee may, however, s. 23, disclaim onerous or unmarketable property, even after he has taken possession of it and endeavoured to sell it; but such property is in no case restored to the bankrupt. And by ss. 94 and 95 dealings with a bankrupt before the date of the order of adjudication made in good faith for valuable consideration and without notice of any act of bankruptcy are not to be deemed invalid. Bankrupt's property.

By s. 15 of the Act the property of the bankrupt divisible amongst his creditors shall comprise all goods and chattels being at the commencement of the bankruptcy in the possession, order, or disposition of the bankrupt with the consent of the true owner, of which goods and chattels the bankrupt is the reputed owner, or of which he has taken upon himself the sale or disposition as owner. Reputed ownership.
(13)

But if, before the adjudication, and without notice of the act of bankruptcy, the true owner has actually re-taken possession of the goods, his title will prevail.

Reputation of ownership arises where the bankrupt has once been the actual and visible owner of the goods and chattels, and has made over all his right or interest in them to a third person, either absolutely, or by way of mortgage, and nevertheless remains in possession of them.

But if the change of ownership has been made notorious to the world in which the bankrupt moves, the presumption of ownership is rebutted.

And now by the Bills of Sales Act, 1878, there is no reputation of ownership in a bankrupt over goods and chattels comprised in a duly registered bill of sale. Nor does the presumption exist with regard to goods which are left with the vendor, in accordance with a known custom of trade, until the purchaser shall choose to remove them, nor with regard to raw material furnished to the bankrupt to be manufactured or repaired.

Trust property. (14)
If a trustee destroy trust property, he makes himself responsible for it to the *cestui que trust*. But if he invest the proceeds in other property, and the latter can be traced, he is still in possession of the trust property, and he can assert no other right in it.

Trespass upon Personalty.

Trespass may be committed upon goods and chattels in the possession of another by laying hold of, or removing them, or in the case of cattle, sheep, and domestic animals by striking, chasing, or driving them away.

Conversion of Chattels.

Conversion of chattels. (15)
The removal of goods in the possession of another constitutes trespass; but if the goods so removed are removed by the wrongdoer for the purpose of taking them away from the person who is in possession of them, or for the purpose of exercising some dominion or control over them,

for the benefit of himself or of some third person, this constitutes conversion.

If a man has a chattel which he knows, or has the means of knowing, to belong to another, and nevertheless refuses to deliver it up, this is a conversion of the chattel.

If a vendor who sells goods on credit resells the goods before the day of payment has arrived, this is a conversion of them.

If a man take the property of another by abuse of the powers of law, this is an act of conversion.

When the goods of one man have not been wrongfully taken possession of by the person who holds them, but if they came into the hands of the latter in a lawful manner, he cannot be made responsible for a conversion of them, until they have been demanded from him by the person entitled to possession, and he has refused to deliver them up. And a refusal, coupled with a condition which the holder has no right to impose, is tantamount to an absolute refusal. But, if the demand is too large, a refusal to comply with it is no evidence of a conversion of such part of the goods as could properly be demanded. Demand when necessary. (16)

Remedies.

A man is justified in committing an assault or breach of the peace in order to recapture from a thief or felonious receiver a chattel of which he was in actual possession when it was taken away from him. Recaption. (17)

When the goods and chattels of one man have been wrongfully taken away by another, the wrongdoer may be sued either for a trespass or for a conversion of them. But if the chattels have come lawfully into the possession of the defendant in the first instance, and his wrongful act consists in unlawfully withholding them after demand by the plaintiff, entitled to the possession of them, the action should be for conversion and not for trespass. Action. (18)

In actions of trespass substantial damages are recoverable, although no pecuniary damage can be proved to have been sustained.

In actions for the conversion of chattels the full value of the chattels at the time of the conversion is the measure of damages when no special damage has been received and the goods have not been tendered and received back after action. But the jury may give the value of the goods at any subsequent time at their discretion.

When no special damage has been incurred the defendant may obtain an order for a stay of proceedings, on a delivery of the goods to the plaintiff, and the payment of nominal damages and costs.

But when special damage has been received the plaintiff may recover all that at the commencement of the suit he has lost through the wrongful seizure of his goods, and the defendant cannot show in mitigation of damages that after action brought he paid to the plaintiff the value of the goods.

When the bailee or hirer brings an action against one who has wrongfully taken goods out of his possession he is entitled to recover as against a stranger the entire value of the goods. But if the action is brought by the bailee or hirer against the owner of the goods, he is only entitled to damages in respect of his limited interest.

ILLUSTRATIVE CASES.

(1) *Beatty* v. *Gibbons*, 16 *East* 116.

Where the outgone tenant had covenanted with his landlord to leave the manure made by him on the farm and sell it to the incoming tenant at a valuation made by certain persons, the effect of such covenant is that the possession of, and the property in, the manure remain in the outgone tenant ; and, therefore, if the incoming tenant remove and use it before such valuation he is liable to the outgone tenant in trespass.

(2) *Cooper* v. *Willowmatt*, 1 *C.B.* 672.

A. conveyed goods by bill of sale to B. B. allowed A. to use the goods at a weekly rent, A. undertaking to deliver them up upon demand. A. afterwards sold and delivered the goods to C., a *bond fide* purchaser. Held, that B. might maintain trover against C.

Bryant v. *Wardell*, 2 *Exch.* 479.

Certain goods having been lent by the plaintiff to the defendants for a term, were used by the defendants in contravention of the agreement, and were not re-delivered at the end of the term. Held, that the bailment had been determined, and that the plaintiff might maintain trover. Pollock, C.B.: "When there has been a misuser of the thing lent, as by its destruction or otherwise, there is an end of the bailment, and the action of trover is maintainable for the conversion."

(3) *White* v. *Spettigue*, 13 *M. & W.* 608.

An action of trover was brought to recover the value of certain books which had been stolen from the plaintiff, and which the defendant had innocently purchased and resold. In defence it was represented that the defendant had a lien upon the books. Alderson, B.: "The utmost extent of the defence set up in this case is that the defendant was entitled to the *possession* of the books until the plaintiff had prosecuted the felon. He clearly had no right to sell the goods, as he had no property in them; he does sell the goods and thereby puts an end to the lien if any existed."

(4) *Adams* v. *Broughton*, *Andr.* 19.

"The property in the goods is entirely altered by the judgment, and the damages recovered are the price thereof, so that he (the defendant in trover) hath the same property therein as the original plaintiff had, and that against all the world."

(5) *Armory* v. *Delamirie*, 1 *Str.* 505; 1 *Sm. L.C.*

The plaintiff, a chimney sweeper's boy, found a jewel and carried it to the defendant's shop (who was a goldsmith) to know what it was, and delivered it to the defendant, who, under pretence of weighing it, took out the stones, and offered the boy three halfpence for them, the boy refused to take the money, and insisted on having the stones restored to him; the defendant gave him back the socket without the stones. Held, that the plaintiff, by finding the jewel, acquired such property in it as to enable him to maintain trover against a wrongdoer.

(6) *Hiscox* v. *Greenwood*, 4 *Esp.* 174.

The plaintiff's chaise was broken by the negligence of his servant, and the latter, unknown to his master, employed the defendant to repair it, the defendant never having previously been employed by the plaintiff in any way. When the repairs were completed the defendant refused to deliver the coach to the plaintiff until paid the amount which he demanded for the work done. Held, that the defendant had no lien on the coach, since he was not employed by the authority of the plaintiff.

(7) See *Berry* v. *Head*, *Cro. Car.* 242.

(8) *Oliver* v. *Oliver*, 11 *C.B., N.S.* 139.

An action of detinue for letters. The plaintiff and defendant were brothers. The letters for the recovery of which the action was brought, which related to family matters, were written and sent by the defendant to the plaintiff, and had been given back by the plaintiff to the defendant. There was contradictory evidence as to whether the letters had been given by the plaintiff to the defendant to be kept as his own property, or whether they had merely been handed to him to be re-delivered on request. Held, that taking the latter view, the jury were right in finding a verdict for the plaintiff, the property in letters, or, at least, of the paper upon which they are written, being in the receiver.

(9) *Miller* v. *Race*, 1 Burr. 452 ; 1 *Sm. L.C.*

Property in a bank-note passes like that in cash, and a party taking it *bonâ fide* and for value is entitled to retain it against a former owner from whom it has been stolen. This rule was held in *Grant* v. *Vaughan*, 3 *Burr.* 1516, to extend to the case of a draft by a merchant on his banker, and to bills and notes, payable to bearer, or payable to order, and endorsed in blank, generally.

(10) *Churchward* v. *Studdy*, 14 *East* 249.

The plaintiff's dogs, having hunted and caught on the defendant's land a hare, started on the land of another, the property is thereby vested in the plaintiff, who may maintain trespass against the defendant for afterwards taking away the hare; and so it would be though the hare being quite spent had been caught by a labourer of the defendant for the benefit of the hunter. [The plaintiff would be, however, liable to an action for trespassing on the grounds of the defendant. See *Sutton* v. *Moody*, 1 Ld. Raym. 250.]

(11) *Aberdeen Arctic Co.* v. *Sutter*, 6 *Law T.R., N.S.* 229, *H.L.*

The A. whaling brig, on a whaling excursion, engaged B., a native Esquimaux, to assist, and sent him out to catch a whale. B. first harpooned the whale, and after his lines were run out, fixed an inflated seal-skin to the end of them, and threw it overboard. B. then looked out for the whale ; but when it re-appeared a boat belonging to the C. ship was nearest to it, and first captured it, and claimed property. Held, that the whale was a " loose fish " until it was captured by the A. vessel.

(12) *Mayhew* v. *Herrick*, 7 *C.B.* 249.

The defendant, an officer of the Palace Court, seized under a *fi. fa.* against A. partnership effects of A. and B., and sold them to various purchasers who carried them away. In trover, at the suit of the assignees of B. (who had become bankrupt)—Held, that the seizure and sale did not, under the circumstances, amount to a conversion ; but that in the absence of any evidence to show in what proportions the partners were interested in the partnership property, the assignees were entitled to a moiety of the proceeds of the sale.

(13) *Graham* v. *Furber*, 14 *C.B.* 134.

The taking of goods by the true owner out of the possession, order, or disposition of a bankrupt, after a secret act of bankruptcy, but before the date of the fiat or filing of the petition, held to be a " dealing or transaction " with the bankrupt within the protection of 12 & 13 Vict. c. 106.

Ex parte Castle, 3 *M.D. & De G.* 124.

A father by deed assigned to his son, in consideration of natural love and affection, certain pictures and effects, upon trust to permit the father to have the present use and enjoyment of them during his life, and subject thereto, to the proper use and benefit of his son. Formal possession was delivered to the son, upon the execution of the deed, by the delivery of one picture in the name of the whole; but the father remained in possession till his bankruptcy. Held, that the assignees were entitled to the goods.

Muller v. *Moss*, 1 *M. & S.* 335.

An agreement was entered into between A. and B. that B., in consideration of a certain sum of money, should convey to A. a dwelling-house and deliver possession to him of all the household furniture and stock, and that after formal possession delivered to A., B. should be allowed to remain in possession for three months without paying rent, which agreement was notorious in the neighbourhood and was carried out. Before the expiration of the three months B. became bankrupt. Held, that B. was not "reputed owner" of the furniture and stock.

(14) *Frith* v. *Cartland*, 34 *Law J.*, *Ch.* 301.

Property was entrusted to E. upon certain terms. E. mixed this with property of his own, and absconded. He was immediately afterwards made a bankrupt. Subsequently E. was taken with money in his hands, which was clearly shown to be the produce of portions of the mixed property. On a bill filed by the *cestui que trust*, against the assignees in bankruptcy— Held, that the whole trust fund must be made good out of the money remaining in E.'s hands before the assignees could establish any claim on behalf of the general creditors.

(15) *Bushel* v. *Miller*, 1 *Str.* 129.

The plaintiff and defendant, who were porters on the Custom House Quay, had each small boxes in a hut on the quay for storing small parcels until they could be put on board ship; and the plaintiff placed some goods in the hut in such a manner that the defendant could not get to his box without removing them, which he accordingly did, but forgot to put them back again, and the goods were lost. Held, that the defendant had a right to remove the goods, and so far was not in fault; but as he had not returned them to the place where he found them, there might be ground for an action of trespass in meddling with them, but that there was no conversion of them, as the defendant had not in any wise disturbed the plaintiff's dominion or ownership over the property.

(16) *Thorogood* v. *Robinson*, 6 *Q.B.* 772.

When plaintiff's goods and servants were on land which defendant had recovered in ejectment, and defendant on entering under the writ of possession turned plaintiff's servants off the land, and would not let them remain for the purpose of removing the goods; there having been no subsequent demand or refusal,—Held, that the jury might find that there was no conversion.

(17) *Blades* v. *Higgs*, 10 *C.B.*, *N.S.* 713.

To a count for assaulting the plaintiff, the defendants pleaded that the plaintiff had wrongfully in his possession dead rabbits belonging to the Marquis of Exeter, and was about wrongfully and unlawfully to carry away and convert them to his own use, whereupon the defendants, as the servants of the Marquis, and by his command, requested the plaintiff to refrain from carrying away and converting the rabbits, which he refused to do. Whereupon they, by the order of the Marquis, took the rabbits away from the plaintiff, using no more force than was necessary. Held a good plea.

(18) *Bayliss* v. *Fisher*, 7 *Bing.* 153.

The defendant wrongfully seized goods, and placed a man in possession of them for some days. Held, that the owner might recover damages, although he had the use of the goods all the time.

Greening v. *Wilkinson*, 1 *C. & P.* 626.

In an action in trover, evidence was given that the cotton, which was the subject-matter of the action, was worth 6d. per lb. at the time of the refusal to deliver it up ; but that at the time of action it was worth, through a rise in the market, as much as 10½d. The jury gave damages according to the higher value. Held, that they were justified in so doing.

Laugher v. Brefitt, 5 B. & Ald. 765.

In trespass against custom-house officers for taking plaintiff's goods, which had been returned before action brought in a deteriorated state, a verdict was found for the plaintiff, for the difference in price between the value of the goods at the time of the seizure, and the time when they were returned. The judge certified that there was probable cause for seizure under the 28 Geo. III. c. 37, s. 24.

By that statute it is enacted that in case any action shall be brought against any person for seizing goods under the Revenue Acts, and a verdict shall be given against the defendants, if the judge shall certify that there was probable cause for the seizure, then the plaintiff, besides the thing so seized or the value thereof, shall not be entitled to above 2d. damages nor to any costs of suit.

Held, that the damages given by the jury might be recovered.

CHAPTER IX.

NEGLIGENCE.

OF negligence, or neglect of duties towards the world in general, incumbent upon those who own or who are entrusted with the care of goods and chattels.

The owner or person in charge of goods and chattels is bound to exercise care to prevent such goods and chattels causing injury to others, and if by his negligence injury should accrue to others, he is liable in damages.

<small>Responsibility of those in charge of goods and chattels. (1)</small>

And this is the case although the injury complained of arose accidentally or by misfortune, but not if it resulted from circumstances over which the defendant had no control.

In general, affirmative evidence of negligence must be given in order to sustain an action.

<small>Evidence of negligence. (2)</small>

But where the accident is one which could not in all probability have happened with the use of ordinary care, and when the machine causing the accident was in the sole management of the defendant, there is a presumption of negligence which it rests with the defendant to rebut.

A person guilty of negligence is not responsible for all consequences which may arise under any circumstances, but only for such as might reasonably be anticipated.

<small>Remote consequences of negligence. (3)</small>

Coach proprietors are responsible for injuries which arise from the defective construction of the vehicles which they let out to hire, if such defect could have been discovered by due inspection, and for accidents which arise from overloading.

<small>Negligence of coach proprietors, &c. (4)</small>

A person causing a temporary building to be erected, as a stand at a racecourse, is liable for injuries caused to those who use it, and who pay money for admission, although the injuries have arisen from a defect in the construction of the building which was not capable of being discovered by inspection.

Negligence of persons driving. (5) Persons driving are responsible for injuries caused by their want of care or caution; and if injury is caused by them to a foot passenger, it is no answer to say that the foot passenger was on the carriage way, for a foot passenger has a right to walk on the carriage way as well as on the pavement.

Negligence of skilled workmen, &c. (6) All kinds of skilled workmen and all persons belonging to the learned professions (except barristers) are responsible, if they undertake works of skill without being possessed of sufficient skill, or if they apply less than the occasion requires.

A solicitor is liable for the consequences of ignorance or non-observance of the rules of practice of his court, and for mismanagement, or want of care, in so much of the conduct of a cause as is usually allotted to his department of the profession. And, although a barrister is not liable for negligence, he is of course liable for malice, fraud, or treachery.

Who may sue for negligence. (7) A person who has let chattels out to hire may nevertheless sue for damages in respect of a permanent injury to his reversionary interest. When there are several joint owners of a chattel which has been injured by negligence, all should be joined as plaintiffs; otherwise the defendant may object to the non-joinder in order that he may not be harassed by several actions for the same cause.

Who may be sued for negligence. (8) The person who actually inflicts the injury through his own negligence is always responsible for it.

If one person orders another to do a certain act the result of which is inevitable injury to a third person, the person giving the order is responsible for the injury as well as the person executing it, although the relationship of master and servant does not exist between the two.

But if the act ordered to be done *can* be lawfully done without injury to others, and injury arises from the negligence of the person who executes the order, the person who ordered the act is not responsible unless he stands in the relation of master to the other.

Thus, when anyone entrusts the execution of work to a person who exercises an independent employment and who has the immediate control over the workmen engaged in the work, the latter and not the former is responsible for injuries done to third persons from the negligent execution of the work; unless the execution of the work creates a nuisance on the premises of the person ordering the work, or is otherwise in itself unlawful, and in this case the person ordering the work and not the sub-contractor is liable. Contractor and sub-contractor. (9)

A master is responsible for the negligence of a servant appointed and paid directly or indirectly by himself. Liability of master for negligence of servant. (10)

The test for determining whether a master is responsible for the wrongful act of his servant is the enquiry whether the act done by the servant was or was not within the scope of his employment, in furtherance of his master's business, and for his master's benefit. If this is the case the master is responsible, although the act done be reckless, wilful, or malicious, and contrary to the duty of a servant towards his master.

A master against whom damages have been recovered by reason of the negligence of his servant may recover the amount of these damages from the latter.

If the person for whom the work is done selects the particular servant who is to do it, that will not relieve the master of such servant from the responsibility for his negligence.

A master is not relieved from his responsibility for the wrongful act of his servant because an Act of Parliament limits his choice to a particular class of skilled or educated persons.

An officer in Her Majesty's service is not responsible in damages for injuries occasioned by the negligence of inferior officers in carrying out orders given by him in the discharge of his duty.

When carriages and horses are let out to hire, the driver being appointed by the owner of the carriage, the latter is responsible for all injuries arising from the negligent driving of the vehicle, although the hirer may be in possession and in control of it. But if the hirer drives himself or provides a coachman, the hirer and not the owner is responsible for injuries arising from negligent driving.

Liability of a master for negligence causing injury to his servant. (11)

A master is bound to take all reasonable precautions for the safety of servants and workmen whom he employs. If dangers exist known to him but not to his servants or workmen it is his duty to disclose them, so that they may take precautions against them.

But the master is not responsible when the dangers are known to his *employés* and the latter have accepted the employment, knowing of the attendant risks and having the opportunity of guarding against them.

A servant is not bound to risk his life in the service of his master, and he may decline any service in which he reasonably apprehends injury to himself.

It has been held that the owner of a mine is bound to exercise ordinary care to keep the shaft and hoisting tackle of the mine in a secure condition. And in all cases, if the master himself interfere in the conduct or management of work, it is his duty to select safe and sound materials for the scaffolding, tackle, &c., of his workmen; and if he knowingly neglect to do so, he is responsible for damage which may ensue. But if he does not himself interfere in the work, but appoints a competent foreman to superintend the work and select materials, and the latter selects unsound materials, and injury is sustained therefrom by a workman, the default is not in the master but in the foreman.

When rules for regulating a dangerous employment are carelessly and improperly framed by the employer, so that risks are caused which might have been guarded against by proper rules, the employer will be responsible for injuries arising to his workmen through his negligence; and so also when statutory rules for the management of a colliery are culpably neglected with the knowledge of the owner of the mine.

When several servants are employed by the same master in a common employment, the master is not responsible for injury resulting to one of them from the negligence of another, provided he has taken due care not to expose his servant to unreasonable risk, and has been guilty of no want of care in the selection of proper servants. *Injuries by fellow-servants.* (12)

It is not enough that the servant injured and the servant causing the injury should be employed by the same master: they must be employed in the same work. Thus, if a gentleman's coachman should negligently drive over his game-keeper, the master would be responsible for the coachman's negligence.

If a person, who voluntarily comes forward to assist servants engaged in a dangerous work, should receive injury from the negligence of one of the servants, the employer is not responsible for the injury.

When the plaintiff has himself helped to bring about the accident of which he complains he cannot recover damages. *Contributory negligence.* (13)

The negligent act of a third party will not, however, exonerate the defendant, if the negligence of the defendant was the proximate cause of the damage to the plaintiff.

The negligent act of the plaintiff which contributed to the accident must, in order to disentitle him to an action for compensation, be such as he is legally responsible for.

Contributory negligence on the part of the plaintiff will not disentitle him to recover damages, (i) unless it were such that, but for that negligence, the accident could not have happened; (ii) nor if the damage be not the necessary, or ordinary, or likely result of such contributory negligence; (iii) nor if the plaintiff might, by the exercise of ordinary care on his part, have avoided the consequences of the plaintiff's neglect.

Damages. (14) The damages recoverable in actions for injuries caused by negligence will mainly depend upon the nature and character of the injury, *i.e.*, whether it is the mere result of such negligence as amounts to little more than accident, or whether it is of a wilful and insolent character. In cases of injuries to chattels from negligence, the measure of damages is the actual deterioration in the value of the chattel, and if the owner has been deprived of the use of the chattel, and has been put to expense, and has sustained special damage which is the natural and necessary result of the wrongful act, such damages are recoverable.

The liability of a ship-owner for damage done by the negligent management of his vessel, causing a collision with another vessel, is limited (53 Geo. III. c. 159) to the value of the vessel and its freight at the time of the collision, and if his own vessel founder immediately afterwards, the owner is not thereby exempted from liability.

By Lord Campbell's Act (9 & 10 Vict. c. 93) it is enacted that when the death of a person has been caused by any wrongful act, neglect, or default, which, if death had not ensued, would have entitled the injured party to maintain an action for damages, the person who would have been liable, if death had not ensued, shall be liable to an action for damages although the death shall have been caused by circumstances amounting to felony. Such action is to be for the benefit of the wife, husband, parent, or child of the deceased, and to be brought in the name of his executor or administrator, and the damages apportioned amongst the above-mentioned relatives in such shares as directed by the jury.

The loss of the benefit of education, and the enjoyment

of the comforts and conveniences of life, through the death of a father whose income ceases with his life, are an injury in respect of which damages may be given.

ILLUSTRATIVE CASES.

(1) *Dixon* v. *Ball*, 5 *M. & S.* 198.

The plaintiff and defendant both lodged at the house of A., where the defendant kept a loaded gun. The defendant, being out of the house, sent B., his servant, a mulatto girl fourteen years of age, for the gun, desiring A. to give it her and to take the priming out. A. accordingly took out the priming, told the girl so, and delivered the gun to her. She took it up and presented it in play at the plaintiff's son, a child of eight years of age, saying she would shoot him, and drew the trigger. The gun went off and severely injured the child. Held, that the defendant was liable in damages.

Wakeman v. *Robinson*, 1 *Bing.* 213.

The defendant, driving a high-spirited horse, did not use a curb-chain, and whilst endeavouring to check the horse pulled the wrong rein; the horse taking fright ran the shaft of the vehicle against the plaintiff's waggon-horse and caused its death. Held, that although the defendant was innocent of any intention to injure, yet, as some degree of blame attached to him, the accident could not be regarded as inevitable, and therefore he was liable in damages. And see *Holmes* v. *Mather*, *L.R.* 10 *Ex.* 261.

(2) *Briggs* v. *Oliver*, 35 *Law J., Exch.* 163.

The plaintiff, going to the doorway of a house in which the defendant had offices, was pushed out of the way by a servant of the defendant, who was watching a packing case which belonged to the defendant, and was leaning against the wall of the house. The plaintiff fell, and the packing case fell on his foot and injured him. There was no evidence as to who placed the packing case against the wall, or what caused its fall. Held, that there was a *primâ facie* case against the defendant to go to the jury, the fall of the packing case being some evidence that it had been improperly placed against the wall.

(3) *Cox* v. *Burbidge*, 13 *C.B., N.S.* 430.

The owner of a horse negligently allowed his horse to stray on the high road, and whilst there it kicked and injured a child who was passing. Held, that although the owner would have been responsible for such damage as in the ordinary sequence of events might have been expected to occur from the straying of the horse, such as its walking into a neighbouring corn-field and trampling down the corn, yet he could not be held liable for the injury done to the child, unless it could be shown that the horse was naturally of a vicious disposition and wont to kick, and that the owner was aware of its propensity.

Lee v. *Riley*, 34 *Law J., C.P.* 212.

Through the defect of a gate which the defendant was bound to repair, the defendant's horse strayed into the plaintiff's field, where it kicked the plaintiff's horse. Held (distinguishing *Cox* v. *Burbidge*), that the defendant was liable in trespass, and that it was not necessary for the maintenance of the action to prove that the defendant's horse was vicious, and that the defendant was aware thereof. Held, also, that the damage which the plaintiff had sustained by the injury to his horse was not too remote, but was sufficiently the consequence of the defendant's neglect to be recoverable in such action.

(4) *Sharp* v. *Grey*, 9 *Bing.* 459.

Assumpsit against a coach proprietor for failing in his undertaking to convey the plaintiff safely from C. to L. The axletree of the defendant's coach broke on the journey, whereby the plaintiff was thrown off and injured. Before the journey the defendant's servants examined this part of the vehicle in the usual way, when no defect was obvious, and it was subsequently found that the defect to which the accident was due could not have been discovered without taking the coach to pieces. Held, that the coach proprietor was liable. And see *Francis* v. *Cockrell, L.R.*, 5 *Q.B.* 184, and *Richardson* v. *G. E. Ry. Co.*, 1 *C.P.D.* 342.

(5) *Pluckwell* v. *Wilson*, 5 *C. & P.* 375.

A person driving a carriage is not bound to keep on the regular side of the road; but if he does not, he must use more care and keep a better look out to avoid a collision than would be necessary, if he were on the proper part of the road.

Boss v. *Litton*, 5 *C. & P.* 407.

A foot passenger, though he may be infirm from disease, has a right to walk in the carriage way, and is entitled to the exercise of reasonable care on the part of persons driving carriages along it.

(6) *Seare* v. *Prentice*, 8 *East* 352.

An action on the case lies against a surgeon for gross ignorance and want of skill in his profession, as well as for negligence and carelessness to the detriment of a patient.

Russell v. *Palmer*, 2 *Wils.* 325.

Action upon the case held to be sustainable by the plaintiff against his attorney, who, after judgment against a third party at the suit of the plaintiff, neglected to take proper steps to obtain execution, whereby the plaintiff suffered loss.

(7) *Mears* v. *Lond. & S. W. Railway Co.*, 11 *C.B., N.S.* 850.

The owner of a barge, which is out on hire for an unexpired term, may maintain an action against a third person for a permanent injury thereto.

(8) *Butler* v. *Hunter*, 7 *H. & N.* 826.

The plaintiff and defendant were owners of adjacent ancient houses, and an architect employed by the defendant to superintend the repairs of his house, having considered it necessary to pull down and rebuild the front wall, agreed with a contractor to do the work for an estimated price, and the workmen of the contractor, in pulling down the wall, removed a breastsummer which was inserted in the party-wall between the defendant's and the plaintiff's house without taking any precautions by shoring or otherwise, in consequence of which the front wall of the plaintiff's house fell. Held, that there was no evidence for the jury of any liability on the part of the defendant.

(9) *Milligan* v. *Wedge*, 12 *Ad. & E.* 737.

The buyer of a bullock employed a licensed drover to drive it from Smithfield Market. By the bye-laws of London no one but a licensed drover could be so employed. The drover employed a boy to drive the bullock to the owner's slaughter-house. Mischief was occasioned by the bullock, owing to the careless driving of the boy. Held, that the owner was not liable for the injury, the boy not being in point of law his servant.

(10) *Huzzey v. Field,* 2 Cr. M. & R. 432.

Where the owner of a boat, which was accustomed to ply for hire and to carry passengers across a haven, employed a servant for that purpose, and the servant on one occasion received a passenger on board, and carried him across the haven near the line of an ancient ferry, and paid the fare over to his master—Held, that the servant was acting at that time in the course of his master's service and for his master's benefit, and that the master was answerable for his act, and would have been liable in an action of case for such act, if it had been distinctly proved to have amounted to an invasion of the ferry.

Seymour v. Greenwood, 6 H. & N. 359.

The plaintiff, a passenger by an omnibus, while being forcibly removed from it by the guard in charge was thrown on the ground and seriously injured. The proprietor of the omnibus, on being applied to for compensation, stated that the plaintiff was drunk and had refused to pay his fare. On cross-examination the plaintiff did not deny that he had been drinking. Held, that there was evidence for the jury of a wrongful act having been done by the servant in the course of his employment about his master's business. And see *Burns v. Coulson,* L.R. 8 C.P. 563.

Holmes v. Onion, 2 C.B., N.S. 790.

The defendant, who was a harness maker, hired one S., a skilful thatcher, to do for him such thatching as he could procure during a period of six weeks, paying him for his services 6s. per week and his board. Within the six weeks S. engaged himself to thatch some stacks for the plaintiff, the latter not knowing of his engagement with the defendant until after the work was commenced. The thatching having been carelessly done—Held, that the defendant was responsible to the plaintiff in damages.

Martin v. Temperley, 4 Q.B. 298.

By 7 & 8 Geo. IV. c. 75, and by the bye-laws in pursuance thereof, no one besides freemen, or apprentices to freemen, of the Watermen and Lightermen's Company might navigate craft on the river for hire within certain limits. The owner of a barge hired two properly qualified persons to navigate it within the limits, and by their negligent management of the barge another vessel was injured. Held, that the owner of the barge was liable in damages.

Quarman v. Burnett, 6 M. & W. 499.

Two old ladies, being possessed of a carriage of their own, were furnished by a job-master with a pair of horses and a driver by the day or drive. They gave the driver a gratuity for each day's drive, provided him with a livery-hat and coat, which were kept in their house, and after he had driven them constantly for three years, and was taking off his livery in their hall, the horses started off with their carriage and inflicted an injury upon the plaintiff. Held, that the defendants were not responsible, as the coachman was not their servant, but the servant of the job-master. "It is undoubtedly true, however," observes Parke, B., "that there may be special circumstances which may render the hirer of job-horses and servants responsible for the neglect of a servant, though not liable by virtue of the general relation of master and servant. He may become so by his own conduct, as by taking the actual management of the horses, or ordering the servant to drive in a particular manner which occasions the damage complained of." [Where a cab proprietor lets out a cab to a driver at so much a day, the driver is the servant of the proprietor, and not a bailee : see *Venables* v. *Smith*, 2 Q.B.D. 279.]

(11) *Seymour* v. *Maddox*, 16 Q.B. 332.

The defendant was possessed of a theatre and of a stage therein, on which dramatic entertainments were given, and of a dressing-room for chorus singers, and of a floor underneath the stage in which floor was a hole cut, and along which floor the performers at the theatre were accustomed to pass from the said dressing-room to the back of the stage. The plaintiff, who was hired by the defendant as a chorus singer, brought an action against the defendant for neglecting to cause the floor to be sufficiently lighted, and for leaving the hole open without any sufficient fence, so that the plaintiff was injured by falling into the hole. Held, that the plaintiff could not recover.

Brydon v. *Stewart*, 2 *Macq.* 34.

It is no answer to a claim of damages by the surviving relations of a workman accidentally killed in a mine, "which was not in a safe and sufficient state," to say that he was at that moment of time in the act of leaving the work for a purpose of his own. The master who lets a servant down a mine is bound to bring him up safely, even though he come up on his own business and not for that of his master.

Feltham v. *England*, L.R. 2 Q.B. 33.

The defendant was a maker of locomotive engines, and the plaintiff was in his employ. An engine was being hoisted for the purpose of being carried away by a travelling crane moving on a tramway resting on beams of wood, supported by beams of brickwork. The piers had been recently repaired and the brickwork was fresh. The plaintiff, in obedience to orders, got on the engine to clean it ; the crane was then moved, the piers gave way, the engine fell, and the plaintiff was injured. This was the first time the crane had been used. Held, that, in the absence of evidence to show that there was any personal negligence on the part of the defendant, as that he had employed unskilful or incompetent persons to build the piers, or that he knew or ought to have known that they were insufficient, the plaintiff could not recover.

Caswell v. *Worth*, 5 *Ell. & Bl.* 855.

Action by plaintiff, employed in a factory, against defendants, the occupiers, for not sufficiently fencing a shaft while in motion, as required by 7 & 8 Vict. c. 15, s. 21, whereby plaintiff got entangled with it and injured. Plea, admitting that the shaft was not sufficiently fenced, but alleging that plaintiff, contrary to the express command of defendants, and knowing that it was dangerous to meddle with the shaft, took hold of it and set it in motion, whereupon the injury occurred. Held, on demurrer, a good plea.

(12) *Tarrant* v. *Webb*, 18 *C.B.* 805.

The plaintiff, a painter in the employ of the defendant, sustained an injury from the failure of a scaffolding upon which he was working, and which had been erected by another servant of the defendant. In leaving the case to the jury the judge told them that if they were of opinion that the scaffolding was erected under the personal direction and interference of the defendant and was insufficient, *or* that the person employed by the defendant for the purpose of erecting it was an incompetent person, the plaintiff was entitled to recover. Held, a misdirection. Jervis, C.J. : "The rule is, that no action lies against the master for the consequences to a servant of the mere negligence of his fellow. That, however, does not negative responsibility in every case. The master *may* be responsible where he is personally guilty of negligence; but certainly not where he does his best to get competent persons. He is not bound to warrant their competency. The summing up, I apprehend, fails in this, that the jury might have been of opinion that the defendant used every possible care to employ a competent person to erect the scaffolding, and yet that he was liable, because it turned out that the person employed was incompetent."

Potter v. *Faulkner*, 1 B. & S. 800.

While the defendant's porters were lowering bales of cotton from the defendant's warehouse, and his carter was receiving them into his lorry, the plaintiff, at the request of the defendant's carter, assisted him, and in consequence of the negligence of the defendant's porters, a bale of cotton fell upon, and injured him. Held, that the defendant was not liable. [Compare *Wright* v. *L. & N. W. Ry. Co.*, L.R. 10 Q.B., where the injured person was not a mere volunteer, but a licensee of the defendants, and the latter were held responsible.]

(13) *Flower* v. *Adam*, 2 Taunt. 314.

A. placed lime rubbish in a highway; the dust blown from it frightened the horse of B., and nearly carried him into contact with a passing waggon, in avoiding which he unskilfully drove over other rubbish placed in the road by C., and was overthrown and hurt. Held, that upon these facts B. could not recover against A.

Tuff v. *Warman*, 5 C.B., N.S. 573.

In an action to recover damages for an injury occasioned by a collision between two vessels—Held, by the Exchequer Chamber, that the proper question for the jury was, whether the damage was occasioned entirely by the negligence or improper conduct of the defendant, or whether the plaintiff himself so far contributed to the misfortune by his own negligence or want of ordinary and common care and caution that, but for such negligence or want of ordinary care and caution on his part, the misfortune would not have happened; in the first place, the plaintiff would be entitled to recover; in the latter not, as, but for his own fault, the misfortune could not have happened. The plaintiff would not, however, be disentitled to recover if the defendant might, by the exercise of care on his part, have avoided the consequences of the neglect or carelessness of the plaintiff.

(14) *Emblen* v. *Myers*, 6 H. & N. 54.

In an action for wilful negligence, the jury may take into consideration the motives of the defendant, and if the negligence is accompanied with a contempt of the plaintiff's rights and convenience, the jury may give exemplary damages.

Hughes v. *Quentin*, 8 C. & P. 703.

In an action for negligent driving, whereby the plaintiff's horse was injured, it appeared that the horse was sent to a farrier's for six weeks for the purpose of being cured, and that at the end of that time it was found that the horse was permanently damaged to the extent of £20. Held, that the proper measure of damages was the keep of the horse at the farrier's, the amount of the farrier's bill, and the difference between the value of the horse at the time of the accident and at the end of the six weeks.

Osborn v. *Gillet*, L.R. 8 Ex. 88.

Declaration against defendant for injuries caused to E., plaintiff's daughter and servant, by reason whereof she afterwards died; claiming as special damage the loss of E.'s services, and her burial expenses. Held, that the plaintiff could not recover. See judgment of Bramwell, B., as to the meaning and construction of Lord Campbell's Act.

CHAPTER X.

ASSAULT, BATTERY, MAYHEM, AND FALSE IMPRISONMENT.

Assault, Battery, and Mayhem.

Assault.
(1)

EVERY blow or push constitutes an assault, in respect of which an action for damages is maintainable, unless the act can be justified or excused on the ground that it was done in self defence, or in defence of one's property, or in pursuance of some legal warrant or authority, or was the result of inevitable accident. Striking at a person with or without a weapon, holding up the fist in a threatening way sufficiently near to be able to strike, presenting a gun or pistol, whether loaded or unloaded, in a hostile manner within range, and any gesture or threat of violence exhibiting an intention to assault with the means of carrying that threat into effect, constitute an assault.

If the person of one man is violently struck through the carelessness and negligence of another this is an assault, and it is no answer that it was unintentional.

If a constable orders an unconvicted prisoner to be handcuffed when there is no attempt to escape, nor any reasonable ground to fear a rescue, the constable is responsible in damages for assault.

Assault and battery.
(2)

A battery, as distinguished from an assault, is where the person of a man is actually struck or touched in a violent, angry, rude or insolent manner. But every laying on of hands is not a battery. The intention of the party must be considered.

When an assault has been carried to the extent of maiming, crippling, or wounding, the person injured will recover heavy damages, unless the act amounts to a felony, in which case criminal proceedings must be taken; or, unless it can be justified. *(Mayhem and wounding. (3)*

If the assault was in self-defence, and the party complaining was the aggressor, his action is met by the plea of "*son assault demesne.*" *(Justifiable assault and battery. (4))*

If one person strikes another, and in the heat of anger the person struck returns the blow with a stick or bludgeon, the battery is excusable; but he has no right to revenge himself; and if when danger is past he strikes a blow not necessary for self-defence, this is an assault and battery.

If a man enters the house or grounds of another with force and violence, the latter is justified in turning him out without a previous request; but if he enters quietly he must be requested to retire before hands can be lawfully laid on him. At the request of the master of a house a policeman may turn out an intruder, but he is not bound to do so.

When goods and chattels are seized by force, although the person using it has a right to the possession he seeks to acquire, nevertheless force may be opposed by force.

Forcible entries by landlords are forbidden by law (5 Ric. II. c. 7). And if a man enters peaceably into a house, but turns the occupant out of possession either by force or threats, this is a forcible entry. But if the tenant voluntarily leave the premises vacant, the landlord may at once enter.

Any person who witnesses an affray may, during the continuance of the affray, for the purpose of putting a stop to it, lay hands on the affrayers.

When a person has been assaulted in such a way as to endanger life he is justified in maiming and wounding the attacking party. *(Justifiable maiming and wounding. (5))*

False Imprisonment.

Definition. (6) False imprisonment consists in unlawfully arresting a man and detaining him without any legal authority. The arrest or detention of the person by an officer without a warrant, or by an illegal warrant, or by a legal warrant executed at an unlawful time, may constitute a false imprisonment.

Actual contact is not necessary to constitute an imprisonment. Any restraint put upon the freedom of another by show of authority or force constitutes an imprisonment.

Authority of judges. (7) Judges of a court of record have power during the sitting of the court to commit to the custody of their officer by oral command without any warrant made at the time.

Authority of constables. (8) A constable not having obtained a warrant of justices, or not having such warrant with him at the time, is not justified in making an arrest except for felony or for suspicion of felony, if he has reasonable ground for such suspicion.

If an assault be committed within view of a constable, he has authority to arrest the offender at the time or immediately after.

Arrest by private persons. (9) Private persons may arrest for felony without warrant. To justify a private person in arresting on suspicion of felony, he must not only, like a constable, make out a reasonable ground of suspicion, but he must also prove that a felony has actually been committed.

Any bystander may and ought to arrest an affrayer at the moment of the affray and detain him until his passion be cooled, and then deliver him to a peace officer to be carried before a justice of the peace to be compelled to find sureties for the peace. But a private person cannot give affrayers into custody after the affray has ceased, unless there is reasonable apprehension of a renewal of the affray.

By the Larceny Amendment Act, 24 & 25 Vict. c. 96, persons "found committing" offences against the Act may be apprehended by any person without a warrant. And persons to whom property is offered to be sold, pawned, or delivered may apprehend upon reasonable cause of suspicion that an offence against the Act has been committed with respect to such property. *Arrest by constables or private persons under certain statutes.*

By 14 & 15 Vict. c. 19, a private person may apprehend anyone "found committing" any indictable offence during the night time (*i.e.*, between 9 p.m. and 6 a.m.).

The Vagrant Act, 5 Geo. IV. c. 83, authorizes any person to apprehend anyone committing certain acts of vagrancy.

By 24 & 25 Vict. c. 97, a landlord or occupier may apprehend any person found committing malicious injury to property.

By 23 & 24 Vict. c. 32, a churchwarden may arrest anyone guilty of riotous, violent, or indecent conduct in a place of worship.

Arrest by private persons may be justified also in certain cases under the Merchant Shipping Act, 25 & 26 Vict. c. 63; under 8 Vict. c. 20, relating to railway companies; under the Annual Mutiny Act, and under 2 & 3 Vict. c. 47 and 30 & 31 Vict. c. 134, relating to the Metropolitan police district.

If the wrong person is arrested by mistake, all persons causing the arrest are liable in trespass for the injury, unless the party complaining has brought it upon himself by his own misstatements and misrepresentations. *Arrest of wrong party. (10)*

Actions for Assault and Battery and False Imprisonment.

Most Acts of Parliament conferring special powers and authorities upon constables and others for the accomplishment of particular purposes contain protective clauses for *Protective clauses in statutes.*

the benefit of persons acting in the execution of the Act: making the cause of action local, requiring the action to be commenced within a certain limited period (usually six calendar months), requiring also one month's notice of action to be given, enabling the defendant to plead the general issue, and prohibiting the plaintiff from recovering, if tender of sufficient amends shall have been made before action brought, or if a sufficient sum of money shall have been paid into court after action.

These clauses are appended to the various statutes enabling constables or private persons to arrest persons found in the commission of a felonious or prohibited act.

Who may bring action for assault. (11) The person assaulted is generally the proper plaintiff; but if the assault has caused his death, the action may be brought (Lord Campbell's Act) by his personal representative. If the person assaulted is a servant, and if the master has lost the benefit of his service by reason of the assault, then both master and servant have their action for damages; but if the master has not lost the benefit of his servant's services, he has not an action, but only the servant.

Responsibility for assault by agent or servant. (12) An action for assault and battery will lie against a corporation whenever the corporation can authorize the act to be done, and it has been done by their orders or authority. But it is otherwise if the corporation cannot legally authorize the act to be done. Thus, railway companies are responsible for assaults committed by their servants, if the latter have express or implied authority for their acts. And an action will lie against every person who has ratified and adopted an act of imprisonment effected or ordered by his servant or agent for his use and benefit.

ILLUSTRATIVE CASES.

(1) *Read v. Coker*, 13 *C.B.* 860.

The plaintiff being in the defendant's workshop, and refusing to quit when desired, the defendant and his servants surrounded him, and, tucking up their sleeves and aprons, threatened to "break his neck" if he did not go out; whereupon the plaintiff, apprehending violence, departed. Held, an assault.

Hopper v. Reeve, 7 Taunt. 698.

It is a direct trespass to injure the person of another by driving a carriage against the carriage wherein such person is sitting, although the last-mentioned carriage be not the property nor in the possession of the person injured.

(2)   *Rawlings* v. *Till*, 3 *M. & W.* 28.

Trespass for assaulting the plaintiff, *seizing and laying hold of him* and imprisoning him. The defendant having pleaded not guilty and a justification under a writ of *capias*, the plaintiff, at the trial, recovered a farthing damages. Held, that the judge could not certify under the statute 43 Eliz. c. 6 to deprive the plaintiff of costs, for that the seizing and laying hold of the plaintiff amounted to a *battery*.

Wiffin v. Kincard, 2 B. & P., N.R. 472.

A constable touched the plaintiff with his staff in order to engage his attention, and subsequently took him by the collar and carried him to the watch-house.

The court were of opinion that the touch given by the constable's staff did not amount to a battery. With regard to the seizing by the collar, the court were agreed that it was an imprisonment, but differed as to whether it amounted to a battery.

(3)   See *Bac. Abr. Maihem.*

(4)   *Oakes* v. *Wood*, 3 *M. & W.* 150.

Trespass for assaulting plaintiff and striking him with a bludgeon. The defendant pleaded that he was possessed of a public-house, and that the plaintiff made a great noise and disturbance therein, and obstructed the business; whereupon the defendant requested him to cease doing so, and to leave the house, which he refused, whereupon the defendant, in defence of his possession, *molliter manus imposuit* to remove the plaintiff. The defendant also pleaded *son assault demesne*. At the trial the judge directed the jury that even though the plaintiff assaulted the defendant first, if the defendant struck the plaintiff with a bludgeon he was not justified. Held, that this was a misdirection.

Reg. v. Driscoll, 1 Car. & M. 214.

If one man strikes another a blow, that other has a right to defend himself and to strike a blow *in his defence*, but he has no right to *revenge himself*; and if when all the danger is past he strikes a blow not necessary for his defence, he commits an assault and battery.

Green v. Goddard, 2 Salk. 640.

Per curiam, "There is a force *in law* in every trespass *quare clausum fregit*; as if one enters into my ground, in that case the owner must request him to depart before he can lay hands on him to turn him out. The other is an *actual force*; and in that case it is lawful to oppose force to force; and if one breaks down the gate, or comes into my close *vi et armis*, I need not request him to be gone, but may lay hands on him immediately."

(5)   *Cook* v. *Beal*, 1 *Ld. Raym.* 177.

Per curiam, "A man cannot justify a maim for every assault, as if A.

strike B., B. cannot justify the drawing his sword and cutting off his hand; but it must be such an assault whereby in probability the life may be in danger."

(6) *Grainger* v. *Hill*, 4 B.N.C. 212.

Placing a party under restraint of a sheriff's officer who holds a writ of *capias* is an arrest without proceeding to actual contact.

Bird v. *Jones*, 7 Q.B. 742.

A part of a public highway was enclosed and appropriated for spectators of a boat-race. The plaintiff, desiring to reach a certain spot, climbed over the enclosure, but was prevented from proceeding further in the direction he wished by the defendant, a policeman, but he was allowed to remain where he was, and was told that he was at liberty to go in the only other direction by which he could pass to the spot he wished. Held, that this did not amount to an imprisonment, and this, whether the plaintiff had or had not a right to pass in the first-mentioned direction; since there was only a partial and not a complete restraint of the will of the plaintiff.

(7) See *Throgmorton* v. *Allen*, 2 *Roll. Abr.* 558.

(8) *Galliard* v. *Laxton*, 31 *Law J.*, *M.C.* 123.

A justice issued a warrant directed to the constable of the township of N. and all the officers of the peace in and for the county of C., commanding him or them to apprehend W. G., who had been adjudged the putative father of a bastard child, and to convey him before two justices to answer for not obeying an order for the payment of money to the mother of the child. A police-officer arrested W. G., but at the time of doing so the warrant was actually at the police-station, and not in the possession of the officer, although it had been previously. Held, that the arrest was illegal. And see *Codd* v. *Cabe*, 1 *Ex. D.* 352.

Beckwith v. *Philby*, 6 B. & C. 635.

A constable, having reasonable cause to suspect that a felony has been committed, is justified in arresting the party suspected, although it afterwards appears that no felony has been committed.

(9) *Allen* v. *Wright*, 8 C. & P. 522.

In an action of false imprisonment, the defendant justified on the ground that the plaintiff had been his lodger, and after she had left her apartments he discovered that some feathers were missing from the bed she had occupied, and suspecting her to be the person who had stolen them he caused her to be apprehended. It appeared that the defendant took a policeman at night to the new lodgings of the plaintiff, and had her apprehended and taken to the police station, and the next day she was examined before the magistrate and discharged. Held, that as the defendant had taken the law into his own hands, instead of adopting the prudent course of having a previous investigation by a magistrate and obtaining a warrant from him, it was incumbent upon him to prove to the jury not only that a felony had been committed, but also that the circumstances were such that any reasonable person would fairly have suspected the plaintiff of being the person who had committed it.

Timothy v. *Simpson*, 1 C.M. & R. 757.

The plaintiff entered the defendant's shop to purchase an article in the shop, when a dispute arose between the plaintiff and the defendant's shopman; the plaintiff being requested to leave the shop refused to do so, and the shopman endeavoured to turn him out: an affray ensued between them, during which the defendant came into the shop. The affray continued a short time after his entrance, and he then requested the plaintiff to leave quietly ; the plaintiff refused to do so, and the defendant then gave him in charge of a policeman who took him to the police-station. Held, that the defendant was justified in giving the plaintiff in charge for the purpose of preventing a renewal of the affray.

(10) *Dunston* v. *Paterson*, 2 *C.B.*, *N.S.* 495.

The sheriff having a writ commanding him to arrest A., took B., who represented herself to be the person named in the writ. Held, that though B. might be estopped by her misrepresentation from suing the sheriff for the original taking, he could not justify detaining her after he had notice that she was not the real party.

(11) *Robert Marys's Case*, 9 *Co.* 113.

"If my servant is beat the master shall not have an action for this battery, unless the battery is so great that by reason thereof he loses the services of his servant, but the servant himself for every small battery shall have an action." [See *Osborn* v. *Gillet*, *supra*, p. 91.]

(12) *Goff* v. *G. N. Railway Co.*, 30 *Law J.*, *Q.B.* 148.

A railway company, though a corporation, is liable in an action for false imprisonment, if the act be committed by the authority of the company ; the authority need not be under seal ; but it lies on the plaintiff to give evidence justifying the jury in finding that the company's servants who imprisoned him, or some of them, had authority from the company to do so. The fact that subordinate servants of the company referred to the superintendent of the line as the authority to determine whether a passenger should be apprehended (under 8 Vict. c. 20, ss. 103, 104) for travelling without a ticket, Held to be sufficient evidence that he was an officer having authority to act in the matter.

Eastern Counties Railway Co. v. *Broom*, 6 *Exch.* 327.

An assault committed on behalf of and for the benefit of a corporation is capable of being ratified by them, and if ratified renders them liable in trespass for the act. The servant of a railway company took the plaintiff, a passenger upon the company's line, into custody for an alleged breach of one of the company's bye-laws, and carried him before a magistrate. The attorney of the company attended before the magistrate to conduct the charge. Held, that this was no evidence that the company ratified the act of their servant.

CHAPTER XI.

MALICIOUS CONSPIRACY AND MALICIOUS ABUSE OF LEGAL PROCEEDINGS.

Malicious conspiracy. (1)
A CONSPIRACY to do an unlawful act is in itself ground for criminal proceedings, but not for a civil action, unless some act done in pursuance of the conspiracy has caused actual legal damage to the plaintiff.

Malicious prosecution. (2)
To put the criminal law in force maliciously and without reasonable or probable cause is wrongful, and if injury is thereby caused to the property or person of another, he has his action for damages. It is a malicious prosecution if anyone attend before a magistrate and maliciously and without reasonable and probable cause make a complaint by which the magistrate is induced to issue a warrant against the plaintiff. But if, acting upon a *bonâ fide* statement or deposition, the magistrate erroneously treats that as a felony which is only the matter of a civil action, and issues his warrant, the complainant is not responsible for the erroneous judgment of the magistrate.

If an indictment preferred by the defendant contains several charges against the plaintiff, and he is convicted on some and acquitted on others, the plaintiff may maintain an action for malicious prosecution in respect of the charges of which he was acquitted.

Exhibition of articles
To maintain an action for malicious prosecution it is necessary to prove that the proceedings terminated in

favour of the plaintiff, if from their nature they be capable of such a termination. But an action for malicious exhibition of articles of the peace is maintainable, although the accused person has been obliged to find sureties and been imprisoned in default; for the truth of the articles cannot be controverted before the magistrates, who have no discretion in the matter, but are bound to act on the statement sworn to before them. *of the peace. (3)*

An action will not lie at the suit of a subordinate officer against his commanding officer for maliciously and without reasonable and probable cause bringing him to a court-martial. *Prosecution by court-martial. (4)*

No action lies for prosecuting a civil action against another maliciously and without reasonable and probable cause. If a man fancies he has a cause of action, he may sue and put forward his claim, however false and unfounded it may be. In some cases, however, an action may be maintainable for litigation which is manifestly vexatious. *Malicious civil actions. (5)*

An action for malicious prosecution will lie against persons who petition for an adjudication in bankruptcy without reasonable or probable cause, and knowingly or wilfully and recklessly swear to depositions false in fact; provided the proceedings have been superseded or set aside before the commencement of the action. *Malicious proceedings in bankruptcy. (6)*

Whoever makes use of the process of the court for some private purpose of his own, not warranted by the exigency of the writ or the order of the court, is liable to an action for damages. *Malicious abuse of legal process. (7)*

By malice is meant any indirect motive of wrong. And want of reasonable and probable ground for setting the criminal law in motion is of itself evidence of malice. On the other hand, the want of probable cause cannot be implied from the most express malice. *Malice and reasonable and probable cause. (8)*

In order to recover damages in an action for malicious prosecution the plaintiff must show that he has suffered either in person, or reputation, or pocket, and every expense *Damages. (9)*

the plaintiff has necessarily incurred in order to defend himself from the false and malicious charge brought against him is recoverable as part of the damages.

ILLUSTRATIVE CASES.

(1) *Gregory* v. *Duke of Brunswick*, 6 *M. & Gr.* 205.

Action maintainable for conspiring to prevent the plaintiff, who was about to perform as an actor at a theatre, from acquiring fame and profit in that performance, and for hiring persons to hoot, hiss, groan and yell at the plaintiff during the performance, and for hooting, hissing, &c., together with such persons.

(2) *Wyatt* v. *White*, 5 *H. & N.* 371.

The defendant, a miller, saw a number of sacks partly covered with a tarpaulin lying on a quay alongside a vessel. Seeing his mark on one of the sacks, he cut it open and found it contained pieces of sacks, new and old. He removed the tarpaulin and saw some sacks on which was his mark, and on others it was cut away. Being informed that the sacks were about to be shipped by the plaintiff for the manufacture of paper, he laid an information before a magistrate that he had reason to suspect that some sacks, his property, had been stolen and were then in the possession of the plaintiff. The magistrate thereupon issued a warrant to search for the goods, and if they should be found, to bring them and the plaintiff before him to be dealt with according to law. The plaintiff was accordingly apprehended and taken before the magistrate, who dismissed the charge. In an action for maliciously causing the search warrant to be issued and the plaintiff apprehended—Held, that there was no absence of reasonable and probable cause, and consequently the defendant was not liable either in respect of the search warrant or arrest.

(3) See *Steward* v. *Gromett*, 7 *C.B.*, *N.S.* 191.

(4) *Dawkins* v. *Lord Rokeby*, 4 *F. & F.* 806.

Four years before action brought the defendant, who was the plaintiff's superior officer, had decided against him on some dispute with his brother officers; the plaintiff had after this been put under arrest by the defendant for some supposed slight, for which he was kept in custody more than eight days, and not brought to a court-martial, and ultimately, in consequence of the plaintiff's complaints against his commanding officers, including the defendant, a court of enquiry sat, before which the defendant, with others, gave evidence against him of want of temper and proper respect, &c., for which the court reported him unfit for command, and upon this he was compelled by the commander-in-chief to retire. Held, that there was no cause of action, as the matters were purely military. Willes, J.: "I will lay it down that even if it had been made out that Lord Rokeby had maliciously and without reasonable and probable cause given the evidence he did before the courts of enquiry . . . the plaintiff could not have obtained redress in these courts."

(5) *Saville* v. *Roberts*, 1 *Ld. Raym.* 380.

"If A. sues an action against B. for mere vexation, in some cases, upon particular damage, B. may have an action; but it is not enough to say that A. sued him *falso et malitiose*, but he must show the nature of the grievance

specially, so that it may appear to the court to be manifestly vexatious."
See *Daw* v. *Swain*, 1 *Sid.* 424, where the special cause was the holding to excessive bail.

(6) *Farley* v. *Danks*, 4 *Ell. & Bl.* 499.

Declaration charged that defendant falsely and maliciously, and without any reasonable or probable cause, filed a petition for adjudication of bankruptcy against plaintiff and procured him to be declared a bankrupt. Held, that this charge was established by proof that defendant petitioned for the adjudication, and by depositions, false in fact and maliciously made, induced the commissioner to adjudicate the bankruptcy, although it appeared that, even if the depositions had been true, the adjudication could not have been supported in law.

(7) *Grainger* v. *Hill*, 5 *Sc.* 561.

In an action on the case for maliciously issuing a writ against the plaintiff (no debt being due, and the defendant knowing the plaintiff to be unable to procure bail) for the purpose of compelling the plaintiff to part with property, and under pressure of arrest extorting it from him, it is not necessary either to aver or to prove that the action in which such process issued has been legally determined, or that the process was sued out without reasonable or probable cause.

(8) *Turner* v. *Ambler*, 10 *Q.B.* 257.

In an action for malicious prosecution, the facts material to the question of probable cause must be found by the jury; and the judge is then to decide, as a point of law, whether the facts so found establish probable cause or the want of it. Among these facts are the defendant's knowledge of the alleged ground of accusation at the time when he prosecuted, and his belief at that time that the conduct forming such ground of accusation amounted to the offence charged. If the defendant did not so believe, the want of reasonable and probable cause is established, though the imputed offence appear *primâ facie* to have been committed by the plaintiff and the fact to have been known to the defendant before the charge was made. The absence of belief must be proved by the plaintiff. And if it is not proved, the defect is not supplied (for the purpose of showing want of probable cause) by evidence that the defendant made use of the charge as a means of obtaining an unfair advantage over the plaintiff.

(9) *Freeman* v. *Arkell*, 3 *D. & R.* 671.

A count for maliciously indicting for an assault held not supportable without some proof of consequential injury sustained by the plaintiff.

Foxhall v. *Barnett*, 23 *Law J.*, *Q.B.* 7.

The plaintiff, who had been committed to gaol for manslaughter by a coroner's warrant, was afterwards admitted to bail, and subsequently got the inquisition under which he had been committed quashed. In an action against the coroner for false imprisonment, alleging as special damage that he had been obliged to pay money in procuring his discharge from custody—Held, that he was entitled to recover the costs of quashing the inquisition.

CHAPTER XII.

RESPONSIBILITY OF JUDGES, MAGISTRATES, AND MINISTERIAL OFFICERS.

Responsibility of Judges and Magistrates.

<small>Acts beyond the scope of authority. (1)</small>   IF judges or other judicial officers do any act beyond the limit of their authority causing injury to another, they become liable to an action for damages; but if the act done be within the limit of their authority, but through an erroneous or mistaken judgment, they are not liable to an action; and the same holds good of arbitrators chosen by consent.

<small>Interest in suit. (2)</small>   If the judge has any private or pecuniary interest in the subject-matter of a suit, he cannot adjudicate upon it. Such interest, however, must be direct and certain, and not merely remote or contingent. And although any direct pecuniary interest, however small, in the subject of enquiry disqualifies a person from acting as judge, the mere possibility of bias in favour of one of the parties will not have that effect.

And 16 Geo. II. c. 18 enables justices of the peace within their jurisdiction to do all acts appertaining to their office as justices relating to the laws for the relief of the poor, notwithstanding that they are chargeable with poor rates. But no such justice is to act in the determination of any appeal to the Quarter Sessions from any order relating to the place where he is taxed or chargeable.

RESPONSIBILITY OF JUDGES AND MAGISTRATES. 105

Every judge of a court of inferior jurisdiction must have before him some cause of action into which he has by law authority to enquire; otherwise his proceedings are extra-judicial, and he will be responsible for the injurious consequences that result from them to others. But if he has *primâ facie* jurisdiction in the matter, and has not the knowledge or the means of knowledge of his want of jurisdiction, he is not responsible in damages. Jurisdiction. (3)

A justice of the peace has no power to do any judicial act out of his county, but he may do a ministerial act, such as taking an information. Limitation of jurisdiction of justices of the peace. (4)

Various Acts of Parliament give to justices of the peace a particular jurisdiction over particular offences; and this jurisdiction is in some cases to be exercised by one justice, and in some cases by two. Whenever these statutory powers are exercised by justices care must be taken that the special authority is strictly pursued, otherwise they will act without jurisdiction.

In some cases the magistrate is authorized by statute to act upon his own view; but where this is not the case he must have before him some information or complaint in order to give him jurisdiction over the matter.

When there is no evidence at all before justices of the facts necessary to give them jurisdiction they cannot lawfully adjudicate or convict.

When a criminal statute authorizes justices to punish trespassers on land, and a question of title is raised, and there is fair and reasonable evidence in support of it, they ought not to proceed, for they have no jurisdiction to decide whether the claim is well or ill founded in fact.

If a corporation or a local board exceed their powers in making a bye-law, a justice exceeds his jurisdiction in convicting on it.

All judgments, orders, and proceedings of courts of inferior jurisdiction may be removed into the Queen's Bench Division of the High Court of Justice for the Certiorari.

purpose of being examined on the ground of want of jurisdiction or excess of jurisdiction.

Contempt. (5) A court of record has power to punish by commitment for contempt a libel on the court when the court is not sitting as well as when it is sitting; and the question whether the particular publication be libellous or contemptuous or not is a question for the court which commits.

A county court judge (9 & 10 Vict. c. 95) may commit for any insults wilfully offered to him or his officers, or for any wilful interruption of the proceedings of the court, or for any other misbehaviour in court.

When words are spoken in the presence and hearing of a justice of the peace, reflecting upon him in the execution of his duty, he may punish the offender immediately.

Actions against judges of courts of inferior jurisdiction. All judges of courts of inferior jurisdiction acting under the authority of an Act of Parliament are in general entitled to notice of action and to an opportunity of tendering amends and paying money into court; and an action against them must in general be brought within a certain limited period [see 11 & 12 Vict. c. 44, s. 7].

Responsibility of Ministerial Officers.

Every ministerial officer of a court of justice is liable to an action for neglecting the duties of his office.

Duty of sheriff. (6) It is the duty of the sheriff as soon as a writ of execution is lodged in his hands to ascertain what goods the execution debtor possesses within his bailiwick, to seize them without any unnecessary delay and sell them to the best advantage. He is responsible in damages, if he sells them for much less than they ought to have realized, or if he seizes and sells goods of much greater value than would suffice to satisfy the execution, poundage, and expenses.

As between himself and different execution creditors, the sheriff is bound to execute that writ which is first delivered to him to be executed. *Priority of writs.* (7)

If, after the sheriff has been desired to suspend the execution of a writ, he receives orders to execute it, this order will not relate back so as to give the execution of the writ any priority over writs which have been placed in the hands of the sheriff in the interim.

If a sheriff act under a writ which turns out to be forged, he is not protected, but is liable for all damages occasioned by its execution. But if the writ be genuine, although irregular on the face of it, the sheriff is protected by it, but not the persons who issued it. *Void and irregular writs.* (8)

When a house is recovered in ejectment the sheriff is justified in breaking the house to execute the writ of possession. *Trespasses in execution of writs.* (9)

In all cases where the king is a party the sheriff may break the party's house, if admittance is denied him after request.

In all cases whatever, if the door of the house be open, the sheriff may enter to do execution; but except in the cases above mentioned, if entry be denied, it is not lawful for the sheriff to break the house.

It is not "breaking" to open the outer door of a house by lifting the latch or drawing back a sliding bar in the ordinary way in which persons going into the house open the door.

If the officer has obtained peaceable entrance, and is expelled by force, he may then lawfully break the outer door in order to re-enter. And after peaceable entry at an outer door an inner door may be broken, and that without demand.

The principle that a man's house is his castle extends only to himself and his own family and goods. It extends only to his dwelling-house, not to a barn or out-house. (But a barn or an outhouse may not be broken open in order to make a distress for rent.)

If a sheriff enters the house of a stranger, believing that the goods of the execution debtor are there, he is justified only in the event of his finding them. He enters at his own peril.

When the original act of entry was unlawful, the subsequent execution of the writ is also unlawful, and if after lawful entry he remains an unreasonable time, he becomes a trespasser *ab initio*.

Goods of a third party. (10)
The sheriff may not take in execution the goods of a stranger, although they are in the possession of the execution debtor as ostensible owner, and although he is assured by the execution creditor that the goods in question belong to the debtor.

The sheriff is bound at his peril to take notice whose the goods are, and for that purpose may impanel a jury.

Responsibility of sheriff for acts of his officers. (11)
The high sheriff is responsible for the acts of the under-sheriff in the execution of his office; for the latter is the general agent of the former.

The bailiff is the special agent of the sheriff for the execution of each particular writ. The sheriff is responsible for what he does in its execution, but he is not responsible when the act done is not done in execution of the warrant.

The liability of the sheriff in case of mistake or misconduct on the part of his officer is confined to cases where there is a misdoing of something which the sheriff commands him to do.

Mode of execution of writ. (12)
It is not sufficient for a sheriff to enter a house with a writ of *fieri facias* in his hands and to demand the debt and costs, together with the expenses of levying. He must do some overt act. If he does not actually seize anything he must leave someone in possession. By the Mercantile Law Amendment Act (19 & 20 Vict. c. 97) the delivery of a writ of *fieri facias* is not to affect any title to the goods seized which has been acquired *bonâ fide* without notice before the actual levy.

By 8 Anne, c. 14, if the rent of the premises on which the levy is to be made is in arrear, there are no goods out of which the sheriff is bound to levy until the arrear, not exceeding one year's rent, has been paid to the landlord. The sheriff is not called upon by law to advance the money to pay the rent, but such advance must be made by the execution creditor. *Landlord's claim for rent.*

By 19 & 20 Vict. c. 108, it is enacted that the 8 Anne, c. 14, shall not apply to goods taken in execution under the warrant of a county court; but the landlord may, within five days of the taking, or before the removal of the goods, make a claim in writing for rent, signed by himself or his agent; and if such claim be made, the officer making the levy is to distrain for the rent so claimed and the costs of distress. But when the tenement is let by the week, no more than four weeks' rent can be distrained for; the rent for two terms of payment when the tenement is let for any other term less than a year, and the rent for one year in any other case.

By 1 & 2 Will. IV. c. 58, when claim is made by a third party to goods taken, or intended to be taken, in execution by the sheriff, the sheriff may apply to the court from which process has issued to call before it by rule of court the party issuing process and the third party making claim, for the adjustment of their respective rights, and the protection of the sheriff. *Interpleader.*

In selling goods under a writ of execution the sheriff can convey no better title to the goods than the execution debtor himself possessed at the time of the sale, and he does not warrant the title of the purchaser. *Title to goods sold by sheriff. (13)*

If the sheriff makes a false return to a writ of execution, he is responsible in damages to the execution creditor, if any actual damage has resulted to him from the false return, but not otherwise. *False return.*

If a sheriff or his officer receive any fee or gratuity other than those allowed by 29 Eliz. c. 4 and 7 Will. IV. & *Extortion.*

1 Vict. c. 55, he is guilty of extortion, and liable to an action for treble damages, or punishable for contempt of court.

Action against sheriff for money had and received.
After a return to a *fieri facias* that the money is levied, the sheriff is liable to an action for money had and received, without any demand of payment.

But the Bankruptcy Act, 1869 (32 & 33 Vict. c. 71), provides (sec. 6) that any execution for £50 and upwards levied by seizure and sale on the property of a trader shall be an act of bankruptcy; and it is further provided (sec. 87) that the sheriff or bailiff of the county court shall in such cases retain the proceeds of the sale in their hands for a period of fourteen days, in trust to pay them over to the trustee in bankruptcy, if a petition for adjudication or liquidation by arrangement be presented within that time; but if no petition be presented, then to the execution creditor.

Nominal damages.
For any negligence or breach of duty on the part of the sheriff, nominal damages are recoverable, although there is no proof of actual pecuniary damage.

Special damages.
All special and extraordinary damage which is the natural and direct result of the sheriff's wrongful act is recoverable by the party aggrieved.

Exemplary damages. (14.
When trespasses of a serious nature have been committed by officers of the law under cover of legal process, exemplary damages are recoverable.

ILLUSTRATIVE CASES.

(1) *Doswell* v. *Impey*, 1 B. & C. 169.

Commitment by commissioners of bankrupts of a bankrupt for not fully answering to their satisfaction lawful questions proposed by them to the bankrupt, whom they have authority to examine, and upon a subject on which they have authority to inquire. Held, to be within the limits of their authority; and they are consequently not liable in damages for any such commitment.

(2) *City of London* v. *Wood*, 12 Mod. 688.

An action brought in the Lord Mayor's Court in the names of the Lord Mayor and Commonalty of the City of London against Wood for four hundred pounds as a forfeiture for that he, being duly chosen sheriff, did not serve or otherwise discharge himself. Held, that the action could not be sustained in that court, for although the Recorder presides in the Lord Mayor's Court, yet he only sits as deputy for the Lord Mayor and aldermen.

Dimes v. *Grand Junction Canal Co.*, 3 *H.L.C.* 759.

A public company which was incorporated filed a bill in equity against a landowner in a matter largely involving the interests of the company. The Lord Chancellor (Cottenham) had an interest as shareholder in the company to the amount of several thousand pounds, a fact which was unknown to the defendant. The cause was heard before the Vice-Chancellor, who granted the relief sought by the company. The Lord Chancellor on appeal affirmed the order of the Vice-Chancellor. Held, that the Lord Chancellor was disqualified on the ground of interest from sitting as judge in the cause, and that his decree was therefore voidable, and must be reversed. (Held, also, that the Vice-Chancellor was, under the 53 Geo. III. c. 24, a judge subordinate to, but not dependent on, the Lord Chancellor, and that consequently the disqualification of the Lord Chancellor did not affect him; but that his decree might be made the subject of an appeal to the House of Lords.)

(3) *Olliet* v. *Bessey*, 2 *W. Jones* 214.

One arrested by a process out of an inferior court, for a cause of action which did not arise within its jurisdiction, may maintain an action against the plaintiff who levied the plaint, and who must be taken to know where the cause of action arose, but not against the judge or officer who entered the plaint, or the officer who executed it, for they have no means of knowing that the cause of action did not arise within their jurisdiction. And see *Calder* v. *Halkett*, 3 *Moore P.C.C.* 77.

(4) 2 *Hale P.C.* 50.

Jones v. *Owen*, 2 *D. & R.* 602.

The statute 13 Geo. III. c. 78, s. 60, imposing a penalty on the driver of a cart, &c., for riding thereon under certain specified circumstances, authorizes a justice on his own view, or upon the oath of one witness, to convict the offender, and in case the offender refuses to discover his name or the name of the owner of the cart, &c., he is subjected to a penalty, and may without warrant be apprehended forthwith by the person seeing the offence committed. Where the driver of a waggon committed an offence within this Act in the view of a justice, and having placed himself before the board on which his master's name was painted so as to prevent the discovery of the owner, and the justice, in order to ascertain the name, stopped the horses, and laid hands on the driver, and removed him from his position before the board, and thereby informed himself of the ownership—Held, on demurrer, that this was a trespass, and gave the driver a right of action.

Caudle v. *Seymour*, 1 *Q.B.* 892.

A justice's warrant, commanding a constable to apprehend and bring before him the body of A. B. to answer all such matters and things as on Her Majesty's behalf shall be objected against him on oath by C. D., for an assault committed upon C. D., is bad, as not showing any information upon oath upon which the warrant issues. An information was in fact taken, but not by the justice, but by his clerk in his absence. In an action against the justice for false imprisonment—Held, that the warrant having been framed, and 'the information taken, as above stated, the defendant had no jurisdiction, and the action lay.

Reg. v. *Stimpson*, 4 *B. & S.* 307.

Upon an information under 24 & 25 Vict. c. 96, s. 24, against the defendant for attempting to take, otherwise than by angling, fish in a river in which the prosecutor had a private right of fishery, the prosecutor gave evidence in support of his right, and the defendant gave evidence that the river was a tidal navigable river, and called two witnesses who said that they had fished in it for forty years without interruption. The justices convicted the defendant. Held, that a *bond fide* claim of title to fish in that place was made by the defendant before the justices, and that there was no reasonable evidence on which they could find that it was not made *bond fide*, and the conviction was quashed.

(5) *Re Cheltenham Carriage Co., L.R. 8 Eq. ca. 580.*

A petition for winding-up a company, containing charges of fraud against the directors, was published *in extenso* in a newspaper before the hearing of the petition. Held, that the publishers of the newspaper had committed a contempt of court; and they were ordered to pay the costs of a motion to commit.

Levy v. Moylan, 10 C.B. 211.

A warrant of commitment under 9 & 10 Vict. c. 95, s. 113, recited that A. "did wilfully insult the judge of the county court during his sitting, and therefore the said judge did order that A. should be taken into custody and detained until the rising of the court;" it then proceeded, "these are, therefore, to require you, the high bailiff, &c., to take the said A., and to deliver him to the governor of the house of correction, &c., to be there detained for seven days, &c." Held, that the warrant was good upon the face of it, and justified the officer and the gaoler in taking and detaining A.

Rex v. Revel, 1 Str. 421.

The words "you are a rogue and a liar" were spoken of a justice of the peace in his presence and in the execution of his duty. Held, that in such a case the justice might either commit the offender immediately for contempt or proceed by way of indictment.

(6) *Gawler v. Chaplin, 2 Exch. 506.*

Action against sheriff for seizing under a *fi. fa.* goods of much greater value than sufficient to satisfy the writ, and for selling such goods for a much less sum than he ought to have done. Held, a good cause of action. It was contended in argument that the sheriff was bound to provide for any rent that might be due to the landlord, as well as for the sum endorsed on the writ. Parke, B.: "We think the duty to seize in respect of a year's rent does not arise in the first instance, until the landlord has made his claim: then if the plaintiff refuses to pay the amount of the rent, the sheriff may levy the amount under the original writ."

(7) *Hunt v. Hooper, 10 Q.B. 561.*

In an action against a sheriff for not levying and for a false return of *nulla bona* it appeared that a writ of *fi. fa.* was issued by the plaintiff against the goods of W., and was delivered to the sheriff on the 7th of June with a direction to issue the warrant immediately, and the seizure took place the day after. Previously (on the 1st of June), B. had delivered a writ of *fi. fa.* against W. to the sheriff, with directions to execute it, at the same time suggesting that the next morning would be the best time for the purpose, but he did not order the sheriff to restrain the execution until that time. Subsequently (W. having offered him £50 to stay the execution) B. verbally desired the sheriff, and on the 2nd of June gave him written notice, not to execute the writ until further orders. The £50 not being paid on the 9th of June, B. requested the sheriff to proceed, and the sheriff accordingly entered, but found plaintiff's bailiff in possession. The sheriff then sold the goods, paid the money to B., and returned *nulla bona* to the plaintiff's writ. The jury found that B.'s writ was in the first instance intended to be executed. Held, that the notice by B. not to execute the writ until further order was equivalent to a withdrawal of his writ, which could not be considered as in the hands of the sheriff *to be executed*, within the meaning of 29 Car. II. c. 3, s. 16, until the order to proceed; and, therefore, that the plaintiff was entitled to a verdict for the amount levied.

(8) *Hooper* v. *Lane*, 10 Q.B. 561.

Case against a sheriff for negligence in not arresting B. on a *ca. sa.* issued by the plaintiff; alleging further, as a breach, that defendant wrongfully arrested B. under another writ which was void, and falsely imprisoned B., by reason of which B. was ordered by a judge to be discharged, and immediately departed out of defendant's bailiwick; whereby defendant deprived himself of the means of lawfully taking B., under plaintiff's writ. Judgment in the Court of Queen's Bench for the plaintiff. Held, in error, in the Exchequer Chamber, that at the trial the judge ought to have left it to the jury whether the defendant knew, or ought to have known, that the writ upon which B. was arrested was a void one.

(9) See rules laid down in *Semayne's Case*, 5 Co. 91 & 1 Sm. L.C.

(10) *Sanderson* v. *Baker*, 3 Wils. 309.

Trespass *vi et armis* held to lie against sheriffs for taking the goods of A. by mistake, instead of the goods of B., by his bailiff upon the sheriff's warrant upon a *fi. fa.*, the bailiff having received notice from B. after the seizure that the goods were his. Gould, J.: "If the bailiff had made any doubt whether the goods seized were the property of the plaintiff or not, it was the duty of him and the sheriff to have made an enquiry by a jury under a writ of *proprietate probandâ.*"

(11) *Smith* v. *Pritchard*, 8 C.B. 588.

Where a warrant issues upon a judgment of a county court against a party resident within another jurisdiction, and is sealed there by the clerk of the court, under the 104th section of the 9 & 10 Vict. c. 95, the high bailiff of the court out of which the warrant originally issued is not responsible for any irregularities in its execution by the under-bailiff of the foreign jurisdiction, even though his own under-bailiff assists therein. Under a warrant so issued by one court and sealed by the clerk of another court the officers broke and entered the premises of a third person, under a mistaken impression that the party against whom the warrant was directed was there; and upon the owner of the premises resisting their entry, the bailiffs, under colour of the 114th section of the statute, took him into custody and carried him before a magistrate. Held, that the high bailiff of the court from which the warrant was re-issued was liable with the under-bailiffs for the breaking and entering, which was an act done by the latter under the supposed authority of the writ; but not for the assault, which was committed in the assertion of a power given by the statute to the individual officer obstructed.

(12) *Blades* v. *Arundel*, 1 M. & S. 711.

Where a sheriff's officer executed a writ of *fi. fa.* by going to the house and informing the debtor he came to levy on his goods, and laying his hand on a table, and saying, "I take this table," and then locked up his warrant in the table drawer, took the key, and went away without leaving anyone in possession, and after the *fi. fa.* was returnable, but not continued, the landlord distrained the goods for rent—Held, that the sheriff could not maintain trespass against him.

(13)   *Chapman* v. *Speller*, 14 Q.B. 621.

The defendant, at a sheriff's sale, bought goods from the sheriff for £18 ; the plaintiff, who was also at the sale, bought defendant's bargain of him for £5 and paid him the £23. The sheriff began to deliver the goods to the plaintiff, but they were then claimed as not being the property of the execution creditor, and were recovered by the true owner. Held, that there was no implied warranty by the plaintiff that he had title, nor any failure of consideration, the plaintiff having paid the £23 to the defendant not for the goods, but for the right which defendant had acquired by his purchase ; and that this consideration had not failed.

(14)   *Duke of Brunswick* v. *Slowman*, 8 C.B. 381.

A., a sheriff's officer, to whom a writ of *fi. fa.* was directed, offered for a pecuniary consideration to delay its execution for a few days. B., who exercised the office of bailiff to the sheriff, in partnership with A., afterwards illegally executed the writ by breaking open an outer door, and A. subsequently withdrew his men from possession on payment of the amount indorsed on the writ, and of a bonus to himself. The jury gave £720 damages, observing that that sum was meant to include the £220 paid by the plaintiff to induce the defendants to withdraw. Held, that in such a case, the damages were peculiarly within the discretion of the jury, and might include the sum of £220 as specified.

CHAPTER XIII.

LIBEL AND SLANDER.

ALL publications in writing or print imputing to another disgraceful or dishonest conduct, or which are injurious to the private character or credit of another, or hold a man up to ridicule or contempt, are libellous, and an action for damages is maintainable against the writer and publisher, unless the publication is privileged, or unless the libeller can prove the truth of the libel. *Definition of libel. (1)*

Verbal slander is not generally actionable without proof of special damage. But— *Verbal slander. (2)*

(i) Words imputing an indictable offence are actionable *per se*, without proof of any special damage. But such words are not actionable if they are applied merely as terms of abuse; if they convey a mere vague suspicion; if they are spoken by way of warning, or in grief and sorrow.

(ii) Words imputing that a man is afflicted with a contagious disorder are actionable *per se;* but not if the imputation refers merely to the past.

(iii) Defamatory words concerning tradesmen and professional men, spoken of them in the way of their trade or profession, are actionable *per se*. Thus it is actionable to say of a tradesman that he is in the habit of cheating his customers, or that he is in the habit of selling goods which he knows to be bad. But it is not actionable for one tradesman to depreciate the wares of a rival tradesman in comparison with his own, unless he does so fraudulently and maliciously, and special damage has ensued.

(iv) Words imputing misconduct, or gross ignorance, or

incapacity to professional men in the discharge of their professional duties, are actionable *per se*. Thus, to say of a practising physician that he is a quack, or of a practising attorney that he betrays the secrets of his profession, or of a beneficed clergyman that he preaches sedition, is actionable. But mere general abuse of a professional man, without reference to his conduct in his profession, is not actionable without proof of special damage.

(v) Words imputing official misconduct to a person in an office of profit or trust are actionable *per se*.

Special damage. (3)
Slanderous words not actionable *per se* may be rendered actionable if they cause special damage to the plaintiff. Thus, it is no cause of action to say of a spinster that she has had a child. But if she is about to be married, and the utterance of the slander causes her to lose her marriage, a cause of action arises. Whenever proof of special damage is necessary to maintain an action of slander, it must appear that the special damage is the immediate and natural consequence of the words spoken. The wrongful dismissal of a slandered servant by his master is not the natural consequence of the utterance of the slander, and such dismissal is not special damage sufficient to support an action for words not actionable *per se*.

The unauthorized repetition of slanderous words is not the necessary consequence of the original uttering of the words; and the original utterer, therefore, is not responsible in damages for the subsequent repetition of the slander by persons who had no authority from him to repeat what he said. The person who repeats the slander, and not the original utterer, is responsible, unless he can show that he repeated it on a justifiable occasion.

Malice. (4)
Malice is the gist of an action of libel or slander. But by malice is meant, in its legal sense, a wrongful act done intentionally and without just cause. In every libel or slander which is not a privileged communication the law implies malice from the fact of publication.

A communication is privileged when it is made by one *Privileged writings and communications.* (5)
person to another in the discharge of some public or private
duty, whether legal, moral, or social, or in the conduct of
his own affairs in matters where his interest is concerned.
In these cases the presumption of malice is repelled; but
the privilege is taken away if evidence be given of actual
malice. Whether the circumstances under which a communication was made constitute it a privileged communication or not is a question for the judge. But if
there is any dispute about those circumstances, that must
be submitted to a jury.

Communications between relations respecting the *Confidential disclosures.* (6)
character of a person proposing marriage with one of the
parties; communications between friends to prevent an
injury to one of them; communications made by a person
who has a pecuniary interest in the subject matter to
which it relates, for the purpose of protecting his own
interests; or answers to enquiries where the person
answering is bound morally or socially to protect the
interests of the enquirer, are privileged, if the person
making the communication does so without malicious
motive, and in the honest belief that it is true. But his
belief is not an honest belief if it is formed in a reckless
and inconsiderate manner, and without enquiry into the
facts where the means of enquiry exist.

Disclosures made *bonâ fide* in answer to enquiries made
by the plaintiff himself, or by another person acting at his
request, are also privileged and protected.

A communication with regard to the character of a *Communications respecting the character of servants.* (7)
servant, made by a former master, with honesty of purpose,
to a person interested in the enquiry, is privileged, although
made in the presence and hearing of a stranger. Even
though the statement be untrue in fact, the master will
be protected unless it can be shown to have proceeded
from a malicious mind. If the master volunteers to give
the character, stronger evidence will be required that he

acted *bonâ fide* than in the case where he has given the character after being requested to do so.

If a former employer has received credible information of the misconduct of a servant after the latter has left his situation, it is his duty to disclose the fact in answer to enquiries to character.

Communications made by public officers. (8)
No action will lie for statements made in the course of his duty by a superior military or naval officer respecting his inferior officer, even though made maliciously and without reasonable and probable cause.

A criminatory communication made by a clerk of the peace at Quarter Sessions is privileged if it is confined to a statement of facts which it is his duty to investigate, and contains nothing but what he believes to be true.

Clergymen. (9)
If a minister of religion publishes or circulates amongst his charge letters casting serious imputations on the character and conduct of private persons, such letters are actionable, although written and published under the gravest sense of duty, or the sincerest desire to improve the morals of the community.

Defamatory letters respecting clergymen, addressed to the bishop of the diocese, are privileged if there was fair and reasonable ground for resort to the bishop; but not if they were written on light and frivolous grounds.

Parliamentary privilege. (10)
A member of Parliament may make what reflections he pleases upon the character of others from his place in Parliament, and a faithful report by a public newspaper of an entire debate in either House of Parliament, containing matter disparaging to the character of an individual as having been spoken in the course of the debate, is not actionable.

Defamatory petitions to Parliament, or to the Queen, or to ministers or officers of State, respecting the conduct of magistrates and officers, and containing statements honestly believed to be true, are privileged communications.

Privilege
Judges are not responsible for slanderous words spoken

by them in their judicial capacity concerning private individuals. *Of judges and advocates.* (11)

Statements and comments made by advocates in the conduct of a cause are privileged. So, also, are defamatory statements made by a party in open court conducting his own cause if they are relevant to the enquiry, or are spoken during the heat and excitement of a trial.

An action will not lie for anything sworn or stated in the course of a judicial proceeding before a court of competent jurisdiction. But the libeller may of course be prosecuted for perjury. *Witnesses.* (12)

Charges and communications which would otherwise be slanderous are protected if made *bonâ fide* in the prosecution of an enquiry into a suspected crime.

Reports of legal proceedings, whether *ex parte* or not, are not actionable unless the account published is false or highly coloured, or the reporter has added comments, allegations, and opinions of his own, reflecting upon the character or conduct of others, or unless the matters given in evidence and published are of a grossly scandalous, blasphemous, or immoral character. *Reports of legal proceedings.* (13)

When a magistrate thinks fit to conduct a preliminary enquiry, relating to an indictable offence, in private, the publication of the proceedings before him is unlawful.

The publication of reports, speeches, and proceedings at vestries, meetings of commissioners appointed to be held by statute for public purposes, or public meetings generally, are not privileged. *Reports of public meetings.* (14)

The writings of authors and journalists, the works of artists, and the public character of public men, such as ministers of state, judges, generals, and actors, are the fair subject of criticism, exposure, or ridicule; but the critic is not justified in making calumnious remarks upon the private character of the individual, or in imputing to him sordid and dishonest motives, or base and dishonourable conduct. *Criticism in public papers.* (15)

Parties to be made defendants. (16)

In case of verbal slander, when the action is maintainable only in respect of special damage, the person whose wrongful act is the direct and immediate cause of the special damage can alone be made defendant. But in case of written slander, every publisher and disseminator of the libel is liable to an action for damages as well as its original author or inventor.

A corporation aggregate may be made answerable for a libel published by its directions, although the body corporate had no ill-will to the plaintiff, and did not mean to injure him.

Interpretation of the words used. (17)

The statement of claim in an action for libel or slander should set forth the very words used, specifying the defamatory sense in which they were used, but if the words used are libellous in themselves, no innuendo to explain their meaning is required. It is for the judge to decide whether the words used are capable of receiving the innuendo or interpretation put upon them.

When the words used are susceptible of a harmless meaning, the burden of proof rests with the plaintiff to show that they were used in a libellous sense.

When the words used have an equivocal meaning, but are well understood and known in a libellous sense, it is for the jury to say whether they were used in that sense or not.

If the meaning of the words is so obscure and doubtful as to render the document incomprehensible, they are not actionable, although the publication may have been evidently intended to vex and annoy the plaintiff.

If the words themselves are not of a defamatory character, they are not actionable, although special damage may have resulted to the plaintiff from the utterance of them.

In an action for libel, the defendant has a right to have the whole of the publication read, or, in an action for verbal slander, to have the whole of the conversation of which the slanderous words formed part given in evidence, in order to explain the meaning of particular expressions.

When the words of the slander charged are equivocal, evidence may be given of subsequent slanders in order to explain the import of the former, and such evidence may be given to show the malicious intention of the defendant, but not for the purpose of increasing the damages.

If the libellous words do not avowedly point to any particular person, it is for the jury to say whether they do or do not apply to the plaintiff. But it is not necessary that all the world should understand who is pointed at in the libel, it is sufficient if those who know the plaintiff can make out who is meant. *Application of the libel to the plaintiff.* (18)

Every sale of a newspaper is a fresh publication of a libel contained in it. *Publication.* (19)

If a man writes a libel and puts it into his desk, this is no publication of it.

It is no publication of a libellous caricature to show a copy of it to a person who requests to see it.

Libellous matter, contained in a private letter addressed to the person libelled himself and delivered into his hands only, is not "published" within the meaning of the law. But if the writer of the letter knows that a clerk of the plaintiff's is in the habit of opening his letters in his absence, there is evidence for the jury to consider whether the defendant intended to put the clerk in possession of the letter, and in this case there would be a publication of its libellous contents.

When the defendant pleads justification of the libel, and shows that his defamatory charge against the plaintiff is true in substance, he sufficiently answers the claim for damages. *Justification.* (20)

And when the defendant justifies words which impute a felony to the plaintiff, he may go into proof of his justification, although the plaintiff has been tried and acquitted on the charge; but if the plaintiff has been convicted the conviction may be given in evidence.

Damages.
(21)

In actions of libel and slander the damages are almost altogether within the discretion of the jury, and the court will not interfere with them, unless they are manifestly extravagant.

Mitigation of damages.
(22)

When the plaintiff claims damages on the ground of the disparagement of his character, evidence, in mitigation of damages, may be given that his character was blemished before the publication of the libel or slander.

In mitigation of damages, the defendant may show that he was provoked to publish the libels concerning the plaintiff by libels against him published by the plaintiff.

By 6 & 7 Vict. c. 96, s. 1, the defendant in an action for defamation may give in evidence, in mitigation of damages, that he made or offered an apology to the plaintiff before the commencement of the action, or as soon afterwards as he had opportunity. And with regard to public newspapers, see s. 2 of the Act.

Verdict.

32 Geo. III. c. 60, enacts that in trials for libel the jury may give a general verdict of guilty or not guilty, and shall not be required or directed to find the defendant guilty, merely on proof of publication of the paper charged to be a libel, and of the sense ascribed to the same.

Indictment.
(23)

An indictment for misdemeanour lies for defamation as well as a civil action. With regard to slanderous *writings*, wherever an action will lie for composing or publishing them, without proof of special damage, an indictment may also be maintained. But an indictment cannot be maintained for mere verbal slander unless it is seditious or blasphemous, or directly tending to a breach of the peace, or is uttered respecting a magistrate in the execution of his office.

Although the person libelled be dead at the time of the publication of the libel, it is nevertheless indictable if its tendency is to stir up others to break the peace, or if it be a libel upon a magistrate or public officer.

A person may be indicted for a libel upon a class

of persons, as the residents in a particular locality, if the tendency of the publication is to stir up riot and disorder.

Libel against a private individual is only a misdemeanour, and does not therefore suspend or interfere with the right of action for damages.

Formerly, in all cases of indictment or information for the criminal offences of libel, it was immaterial whether the libel was true or false. But now by 6 & 7 Vict. c. 96, s. 6, it is enacted that on the trial of any indictment or information for a defamatory libel, the defendant, having pleaded such plea as in the statute mentioned, may have the truth of the libel inquired into, but that the truth of it shall not amount to a defence, unless it was for the public benefit that the matters charged as libellous should be published.

Slander of Title.

If lands or chattels are about to be sold, and a man declares that the vendor's title is defective, that the lands are mortgaged, or that the chattels are stolen property, and so deters people from buying, or causes the property to be sold for a less price than it would otherwise have realized, this is a slander of the title of the owner, and gives him a claim to compensation in damages, unless the slanderer can prove the truth of his statement. Slander of title. (24)

The action for slander of title is in fact an action on the case for special damage. Special damage must in all cases be proved, whether the slander be spoken or written. Action for slander of title. (25)

To maintain the action there must be malice, either express or implied, on the part of the slanderer, and the words spoken must go to defeat the plaintiff's title. If the words are spoken by a stranger who has no right or business to interfere, the law presumes malice; but if he is himself interested in the matter, and announces the defect of title *bonâ fide*, either for the purpose of protecting his Proof of malice. (26)

own interest or preventing the commission of a fraud, the legal presumption of malice is rebutted, and the plaintiff must then show that there was no reasonable or probable cause for the statement.

ILLUSTRATIVE CASES.

(1) *Digby* v. *Thompson*, 4 *B. & Ad.* 821.

The following words published in a newspaper:—"D. has had a tolerable run of luck. He keeps a well spread sideboard; but I always consider myself in an hotel when my legs are under his table, for the bill is sure to come in sooner or later, though I rarely dabble in the mysteries of *écarté* or any other game. The fellow is as deep as *Crockford*, and as knowing as the marquis:"—Held, sufficient to support a declaration for libel without explanatory averments, for they tend generally to disgrace the plaintiff.

(2) *Crawford* v. *Middleton*, 1 *Lev.* 82.

The defendant falsely and maliciously said that he had met one upon the road who said to him, "What, are you carrying W. to gaol? I shall follow you shortly and bring with me H. C. (the plaintiff) for stealing a mare." In fact no one had said this to him. Held, that the defendant was liable for slander. [*Per curiam*, if the words had been spoken in grief and sorrow at the news, then, as there would have been no malice, the defendant would not have been liable.]

Carslake v. *Mapledoram*, 2 *T.R.* 475.

Charging a person with *having had* a contagious disorder not actionable, because it is no reason why the company of a person so charged should be avoided.

Griffiths v. *Lewis*, 7 *Q.B.* 65.

Plaintiff enquired of defendant whether he had accused her of using false weights in her trade. Defendant, in presence of a third person, answered, "To be sure I did. You have done it for years." Held, that the latter words were actionable, and not privileged by reason of the plaintiff's enquiry, the evidence showing that such enquiry was caused by a former statement of the defendant himself. [An untrue statement disparaging a man's goods, published without lawful occasion and causing him special damage, Held actionable. *Western Counties Manure Manufacturing Co.* v. *Lawe's Chemical Manure Co.*, L.R. 9 *Ex.* 218—distinguishing *Young* v. *Macrae*, 32 *Law J.*, Q.B. 6. Such an action is not strictly an action for defamation of character, but resembles an action for slander of title.]

Tutty v. *Alewin*, 11 *Mod.* 221.

The defendant said of an apothecary, "It is a world of blood he has to answer for in this town through his ignorance; he did kill a woman and two children at Southampton, &c." Held, that the words were actionable *per se*.

Hopwood v. *Thorn*, 8 *C.B.* 313.

The defendant spoke words concerning the plaintiff, who was a Dissenting minister, but who had previously been a draper in partnership with his brother-in-law, conveying the imputation that whilst so in partnership he had taken advantage of his brother-in-law. Held, that in the absence of proof of special damage the words charged, not being spoken of the plaintiff in reference to his office of minister, were not the subject of an action.

(3) *Davis* v. *Gardiner*, 4 Co. 16.

The plaintiff, being about to be married to a substantial citizen, the defendant said of her that she had had a bastard child, upon hearing which her intended husband refused to marry her. Held, that this was a good ground of action. "If the defendant had charged the plaintiff with bare incontinency, yet the action should be maintainable." [See also *Riding* v. *Smith*, L.R. 1 *Ex. D.*, where an action for slander and libel, attributing to plaintiff's wife, who assisted him in the business, an act of adultery on the business premises, was held maintainable, as injury to the business was the natural result of such slander: Held, also, that special damage might be proved by general evidence that the business fell off.]

Vicars v. *Wilcocks*, 8 *East* 3.

The defendant said of the plaintiff, who was a journeyman in the employment of A., that he had been guilty of unlawfully cutting his (the defendant's) cordage, upon hearing which A. dismissed the plaintiff before the end of the term for which he had been hired. Held, that such wrongful dismissal could not be laid as special damage in order to support an action of slander.

Ward v. *Weeks*, 4 *M. & P.* 796.

Action for slander; special damage alleged that by reason thereof one B. refused to give the plaintiff credit. It appeared that the defendant had spoken the words to one E., and that E. had communicated the statement as the statement of the defendant to B. Held, that the defendant was not responsible for the repetition of the slander by E. to B.

(4) *Bromage* v. *Prosser*, 4 *B. & C.* 255.

A. B. met the defendant and said, "I hear that you say that the (plaintiffs') bank at M. has stopped. Is it true?" Defendant answered, "Yes, it is. I was told so. It was so reported at C., and nobody would take their bills, and I came to town in consequence of it myself." It was proved that C. D. had told the defendant that there was a run upon the plaintiffs' bank at M. At the trial for the slander the judge, after observing that the defendant did not appear to have been actuated by any ill will against the plaintiffs, directed the jury to find their verdict for the defendant if they thought the words were not maliciously spoken. Held, upon motion for a new trial, that in ordinary actions for slander malice in law must be inferred from the publishing the slanderous matter; but in actions for slander, *primâ facie* privileged, malice in fact must be proved. Held, therefore, in this case that the judge ought first to have left it as a question for the jury, whether the defendant understood A. B. as asking for information, and whether he had uttered the words merely by way of honest advice to A. B. to regulate his conduct, and if they were of that opinion; then, secondly, whether in so doing he was guilty of any malice in fact.

(5) *Somerville* v. *Hawkins*, 10 *C.B.* 583.

The defendant dismissed the plaintiff from his service on suspicion of theft, and upon the latter coming into his counting-house for his wages, the defendant called in two other of his servants, and addressing them in the presence of the plaintiff, said :—" I have dismissed that man for robbing me; do not speak to him any more, or I shall think you as bad as he is."

Held, a privileged communication, for that it was the *duty* of the defendant and also his *interest* to prevent his servants from associating with a person of such a character as the words imputed to the plaintiff. To entitle the plaintiff in such a case to have the question of malice left to the jury, it is not enough that the facts proved are *consistent* with the presence of malice, as well as with its absence, for in cases of privileged communication malice must be expressly proved.

Williamson v. *Freer*, L.R. 9 C.P. 393.

A communication which would have been privileged if sent by post, Held to have lost that privilege by having been unnecessarily sent by telegraph.

(6) *Todd* v. *Hawkins*, 2 M. & Rob. 21.

A letter from a son-in-law to his mother-in-law, volunteering advice respecting her proposed marriage, and containing imputations upon the person whom she was about to marry, is a privileged communication, and not actionable unless actual malice be shown.

M'Dougall v. *Claridge*, 1 Campb. 266.

A letter written confidentially to persons who employed A. as their solicitor, conveying charges injurious to his professional character in the management of certain concerns which they had entrusted to him, and in which B., the writer of the letter, was likewise interested, cannot be considered a libel.

Cockayne v. *Hodgkisson*, 5 C. & P. 543.

A., being a tenant of B., was desired by B. to inform him if he saw or heard anything respecting the game on the estate. A. wrote a letter to B. informing him that his gamekeeper sold game. Held, that if A. had been so informed, and believed it to be a fact, this was a privileged communication.

(7) *Pattison* v. *Jones*, 8 B. & C. 578.

A., having discharged his servant, and hearing that he was about to be engaged by B., wrote a letter to B. and informed him that he had discharged him for misconduct. B., in answer, desired further information, which A. gave in a second letter. Held, that assuming the letter to be a privileged communication, it was properly left to the jury to consider whether the second letter was written by A. *bonâ fide* or with an intention to injure the servant.

Child v. *Affleck*, 9 B. & C. 403.

The defendant, with whom the plaintiff had lived as servant, in answer to enquiries respecting her character, wrote a letter imputing misconduct to her whilst in that service and after she left it. Held, that as no malice was proved the letter was a privileged communication.

(8) *Dawkins* v. *Lord Paulet*, L.R. 5 Q.B. 94.

To a declaration for libel it was pleaded that the defendant was the superior military officer of the plaintiff, and made the reports, complained of as a libel on the plaintiff, to the Commander-in-Chief in the course of military duty. Replication, that the libel was written by the defendant of actual malice, and without any reasonable, probable, or justifiable cause, and not *bonâ fide*, or in the *bonâ fide* discharge of the defendant's duty. On demurrer—Held, that the replication was bad : for that no action would lie against a military officer for an act done in the ordinary course of his duty as such officer, even if done maliciously and without reasonable and probable cause.

Cooke v. *Wildes,* 5 *Ell. & Bl.* 340.

Defendant was deputy clerk of the peace, and in the course of his duty submitted to the Quarter Sessions his account of the expenses of printing the register of county voters. Previously to this he addressed a letter to the finance committee of magistrates, explaining that he had taken away the contract for printing from the plaintiffs (whom he had formerly employed) on the ground of misrepresentation and fraud on their part. Held, that the occasion was privileged ; but that from the terms of the letter there was evidence of express malice, and that it was a question for the jury whether there was such malice.

(9) *Gilpin* v. *Fowler,* 9 *Exch.* 615.

The plaintiff was master of a "national school" in the parish of C., of which the defendant was rector and also one of the managers of the school. Defendant requested plaintiff to teach also in the Sunday school. Plaintiff declined, and was in consequence dismissed from his post. Plaintiff then set up a school on his own account in the parish. On this the defendant wrote and distributed a pastoral letter, in which he denounced the plaintiff's conduct, and warned his parishioners against affording any countenance to the school. At the trial the judge ruled that this letter was privileged. Held, in the Exchequer Chamber, on a bill of exceptions, that the communication was not privileged. [But see *Loughton* v. *Bp. of Sodor and Man,* L.R. 4 *P.C.* 495, where a bishop's charge, containing strictures on the conduct of a layman who had attacked his character, was held privileged.]

James v. *Boston,* 2 *C. & K.* 8.

A letter written to a bishop, informing him of a report current in a parish in his diocese that the incumbent of a district in that parish had fought with the schoolmaster, is a privileged communication, if written honestly to call the bishop's attention to a rumour which was bringing scandal to the church, and not from any malicious motive ; and it is not material that the writer of the letter did not live in the district to the incumbent of which the letter refers. [And see *Clark* v. *Molyneux,* 3 *Q.B.D.* 237.]

(10) *Wason* v. *Walter, L.R.* 4 *Q.B.* 73.

The plaintiff presented a petition to the House of Lords, charging a high judicial officer (Sir F. Kelly, C.B.) with having thirty years before made a statement, false to his own knowledge, in order to deceive a Committee of the House of Commons, and praying enquiry and removal of the officer, if the charge were found true. A debate ensued in which the charge was utterly refuted, and the plaintiff's conduct in making it severely animadverted upon. The debate was reported in the "Times," and a leading article appeared in the same paper, commenting strongly upon the plaintiff's conduct. Held, that a faithful report in a public newspaper of a debate in either House of Parliament, containing matter disparaging to the character of an individual, is privileged, and that the subject was one upon which a writer in a public newspaper had a full right to comment, and the occasion was, therefore, so far privileged that the comments would not be actionable, so long as a jury should think them honest, and made in a fair spirit, and such as were justified by the circumstances disclosed in an accurate report of the debate.

(11) *Scott* v. *Stansfield, L.R.* 5 *Exch.* 220.

Plea, to a declaration for slander, that the defendant was a county court judge, and the words complained of were spoken by him in his capacity as such judge, while sitting in his court and trying a cause in which the present plaintiff was defendant. Replication, that the said words were spoken falsely and maliciously, and without any reasonable, probable, or justifiable cause, and without any foundation whatever, and not *bonâ fide* in the discharge of the defendant's duty as judge, and were wholly irrelevant in reference to the matter before him. Held, that the replication was bad and the action not maintainable.

Hodgson v. *Scarlett*, 1 B. & Ald. 244.

Action against a barrister for the following words, spoken by him as counsel, in a cause concerning the plaintiff, one Hodgson, an attorney in the cause:—"This was one of the most profligate things I ever knew done by a professional man. Mr. Hodgson is a fraudulent and wicked attorney." Held, that as the words spoken were relevant and pertinent to the cause, no action was maintainable.

(12) <center>*Padmore* v. *Lawrence*, 11 Ad. & E. 380.</center>

Defendant, in presence of a third person, not an officer of justice, charged plaintiff with having stolen his property, and afterwards repeated the charge to another person, who was called in to search the plaintiff with the consent of the latter. Held, that the charge was privileged, if the defendant believed in its truth, acted *bonâ fide*, and did not make the charge before more persons, or in stronger language than necessary, and whether this was or was not the case, was a question for the jury.

(13) <center>*Lewis* v. *Levy*, 27 Law J. 282.</center>

It is a good defence to an action for a libel that it consists of a fair and impartial report of a trial in a court of justice; but if it contains other libellous matter, such as comments reflecting upon any of the parties whose names appear in it, it entirely loses the privilege which it might otherwise claim.

M'Gregor v. *Thwaites*, 3 B. & C. 24.

Declaration for a libel purporting to contain an account of a proceeding which had taken place before a magistrate respecting a matter in which he was merely asked for advice, and not called upon to act in his magisterial capacity. Held, that the defendant could not justify the publication, on the ground of its being a correct account of the proceedings. And see *Usil* v. *Hales*, 47 L.J. 324.

(14) <center>*Davison* v. *Duncan*, 7 Ell. & Bl. 229.</center>

The publication of matter defamatory of an individual is not privileged because the libel is contained in a fair report in a newspaper of what passed at a public meeting. [But see *Davis* v. *Duncan*, L.R. 9 C.P. 396, in which *Davison* v. *Duncan* was discussed, and it was held that the conduct of persons at a public meeting, held for the purpose of promoting the election of a candidate for a seat in Parliament, might be made the subject of a fair and *bonâ fide* discussion by a writer in a public newspaper, and that unfavourable comments made upon such conduct in the course of such discussion were privileged.]

(15) <center>*Parmiter* v. *Coupland*, 6 M. & W. 108.</center>

Action for libels published of the plaintiff, the late mayor of Winchester, in a local newspaper, imputing to him partial and corrupt conduct and ignorance of his duties. Held, that although a publication may be a libel on a private person which would not be any libel on a person in a public capacity, yet any imputation of unjust or corrupt motives is equally libellous in either case.

(16)   *Tidman* v. *Ainslie*, 10 *Exch.* 63.

In an action for libel it is no justification that the libellous matter was previously published by a third person, and that the defendant, at the time of his publication, disclosed the name of that person, and believed all the statements contained in the libel to be true. As to the repetition of slander, see *Ward* v. *Weeks*, *supra*.

Whitfield v. *South Eastern Railway Co.*, 27 *Law J.*, *Q.B.* 229.

Action brought against a railway company for falsely publishing through their electric telegraph that the plaintiffs' bank had stopped payment. Held, that the company was responsible in damages, and that in such an action it was not necessary to show that the defendants had any ill-will to, or that they meant to injure the plaintiffs.

(17)   *Wright* v. *Clements*, 3 *B. & Ald.* 509.

Declaration stated that the defendant published a libel containing false and scandalous matters concerning the plaintiff *in substance* as follows ; and then set out the libel with innuendoes. Held, a bad declaration.

Shepheard v. *Whitaker*, *L.R.* 10 *C.P.* 502.

A local paper by mistake inserted a dissolution of partnership under the head of "first meetings under the Bankruptcy Act." In an action for libel, the innuendo laid was "that the plaintiff was bankrupt." Held, that the innuendo was good.

Broome v. *Gosden*, 1 *C.B.* 732.

A declaration for a libel to the effect that on a certain night a gentleman was hocussed and robbed in a public house kept by the plaintiff—*innuendo* that the defendant intended to cause it to be believed that the public house was the resort of thieves and bad characters. Witnesses were called for the plaintiff, that they understood the libel as an imputation upon the character of the plaintiff and his house, and had in consequence ceased to frequent the plaintiff's house. The jury returned a verdict for the defendant, and the court above refused to grant a rule for a new trial.

Capel v. *Jones*, 4 *C.B.* 263.

In this case the alleged libel was of an exceedingly ambiguous and equivocal character. There was no innuendo or averment of special damage. Judgment for the defendant. V. Williams, J. : "It is not enough to show that the alleged libel has a malicious or caluminous tendency; it must be distinctly shown what the particular imputation is."

Miller v. *David*, *L.R.* 9 *C.P.* 118.

A statement false and malicious, but only possibly injurious, Held, not sufficient to support an action, though damage has actually resulted.

Pearce v. *Ornsby*, 1 *M. & Rob.* 456.

Abinger, C. B. : "You may give evidence of subsequent words to explain the words in the declaration ; but when there is nothing equivocal in the words charged, you cannot give evidence of subsequent words of the same import, for which subsequent words another action may be brought and damages recovered. The evidence now offered would tend to aggravate the damages in this."

K

(18) *Bourke* v. *Warren*, 2 C. & P. 307.

In a libel, asterisks were used instead of the name of the party libelled. Held, that to make this actionable it was sufficient that the party should be so designated that those who knew the plaintiff could understand that he was the person meant.

(19) *Smith* v. *Wood*, 3 Campb. 323.

The defendant had a caricature print, entitled "The inside of a parish workhouse, with all abuses reformed." A witness stated that, having heard the defendant had a copy of this print, he went to his house and requested liberty to see it. The defendant thereupon produced it, and pointed out the figure of the plaintiff and the other persons it indicated. Held, that this was not sufficient evidence of publication to support an action.

Delacroix v. *Thevenot*, 2 Stark. 63.

Action for a libel contained in a letter written by the defendant to the plaintiff; proof that the defendant knew that letters sent to the plaintiff were usually opened by his clerk. Held to be evidence to go to the jury of the defendant's intention that the letter should be read by a third person.

(20) *Alexander* v. *North Eastern Railway Co.*, 34 Law J., Q.B. 152.

The plaintiff charged as a libel upon him a notice published by the defendants, a railway company, which stated that the plaintiff had been convicted by justices of an offence against the defendants' bye-laws and fined, with an alternative of three weeks' imprisonment; the alternative in the conviction was really fourteen days. Held, that it was a question for the jury whether the statement charged as libellous was or was not substantially true, and the inaccuracy of the statement did not necessarily make it libellous.

England v. *Bourke*, 3 Esp. 80.

Action for libel; the words laid in the declaration were, "You are a thief and a murderer."

The plaintiff had been tried for murder and acquitted. *Per* Lord Kenyon: "There is no plea of justification of the truth of the words; had there been, notwithstanding the acquittal, I would have tried the truth of the plea."

(21) *Highmore* v. *Earl and Countess of Harrington*, 3 C.B., N.S. 142.

The court refused to grant a new trial on the ground that the damages were excessive where the jury had given £750 in an action for defamatory words spoken of a beneficed clergyman to his curate, imputing to the former gross immorality and dishonesty.

(22) *Earl of Leicester* v. *Walter*, 2 Campb. 251.

In an action for a libel the defendant may prove, in mitigation of damages, that before and at the time of the publication of the libel the plaintiff was generally suspected to be guilty of the crime thereby imputed to him, and that, on account of this suspicion, his relations and friends had ceased to associate with him.

Tarpley v. *Blabey*, 2 B.N.S. 437.

In order to the admission in evidence of libels by the plaintiff in mitigation of damages, it must be shown with precision that such libels were connected with, and related to the same subjects as, the libels by the defendant.

(23) See *Hawkins' Pleas of the Crown*, ch. 73.

Rex v. *Weltje*, 2 *Campb.* 142.

Held, that an indictment would not lie for the words, "he is a scoundrel and a liar," spoken of the prosecutor as a justice of the peace in his absence.

Rex v. *Topham*, 4 *T.R.* 126.

An indictment for publishing libellous matter reflecting on the memory of a dead person—Held not supportable, as it did not allege that the libel was published with a design to bring contempt on the family of the deceased, and to stir up the hatred of the king's subjects against them, and to excite the relations of the deceased to a breach of the peace.

Rex v. *Williams*, 5 *B. & Ald.* 595.

The court granted a criminal information for a libel upon the clergy of the diocese of Durham stating that none of the bells in the several churches in Durham had been tolled upon the decease of Queen Caroline, ascribing this omission to the clergy, and severely animadverting upon their conduct.

(24) *Gutsole* v. *Mathers*, 1 *M. & W.* 501.

In an action for slander of title, as in an action for defamation of character, the plaintiff must set out the exact words used by the defendant. A declaration for words imputing that tulips of the plaintiff, about to be sold by auction, were stolen property, whereby purchasers were deterred from bidding, and the sale was defeated, was held bad in arrest of judgment for not setting out the words *verbatim*.

(25) *Malachy* v. *Soper*, 3 *Sc.* 723.

In an action for slander of title, it appeared that the defendant had published a paragraph in a newspaper, stating that "the petition in a bill filed in the Court of Chancery against the plaintiff and certain other persons as shareholders in a certain mine, for an account and an injunction, had been granted by the Vice-Chancellor, and that persons duly authorized had arrived on the workings." Held, that the action could not be maintained without proof of special damage, and that an allegation that "the shares possessed by the plaintiff in the mine had become depreciated in value, and that the plaintiff had been hindered and prevented from selling or disposing of his shares in the said mine, and from working and using the same in so ample and beneficial a manner as he might have done but for the slander," was not a sufficient allegation of special damage.

(26) *Hargrave* v. *Le Breton*, 4 *Burr.* 2423.

Action for slander of title. Judgment of Lord Mansfield: "To maintain such an action as this, there must be malice, either express or implied, and the words spoken must go to defeat the plaintiff's title. Whereas, here is no malice, either express or implied. The words of the message sent are true; and they proceed from a person called upon to give notice, either to protect his own property, or to save another from being cheated.

CHAPTER XIV.

FRAUD AND DECEIT.

False representation. (1)

IF a falsehood be knowingly told with an intention that another should believe it to be true and act upon it, and that person does act upon it, and thereby suffers damage, the party telling the falsehood is responsible in damages in an action of deceit.

In order to maintain an action for deceit it is not necessary to prove that the false representation was made from a corrupt motive of gain to the defendant, or a wicked motive of injury to the plaintiff, nor is it material whether the defendant has any interest in the matter respecting which the representation is made, nor whether the representation be made to the plaintiff, or to a third party with the intention that it should be communicated to the plaintiff. A false representation is actionable though made under the pretence of a claim of right. And it is equally actionable for a man to undertake to assert that to be true which he does not know to be true, and which he has no ground for believing to be true, as to affirm that to be true which he knows to be false.

Representations concerning credit, &c.

By 9 Geo. IV. c. 14, representations concerning the conduct, credit, ability, trade or dealings of third persons must be authenticated by a writing, signed by the defendant, in order to support an action. Under this statute, representations by one member of a company as to the circumstances, credit and condition of the company must be in writing and signed in order to be made the foundation of an action.

Thus, directors of public companies are liable for prospectuses, &c., to which their signatures are annexed, containing false statements. Directors so acting may also be punished for misdemeanour under various statutes; but this does not suspend or interfere with the civil remedy. *Directors of public companies. (2)*

It is no answer to an action for deceit, brought against the directors of a public company, to say that the plaintiff might have ascertained the truth by proper inquiry. But the plaintiff is bound to make himself acquainted with the provisions of the articles of association, if they are in existence at the time of the contract, or within a reasonable time after they are in existence.

Although a shareholder may thus sue the directors for fraudulent misrepresentation, or plead fraud to an action for calls brought by the company, or within a reasonable time rescind, and be relieved from, the contract on the ground of fraud, he will still be liable as a contributory in case the company winds up, so far as his original contract extends, unless it was annulled on the ground of misrepresentation, or otherwise, before the commencement of the winding up.

The representations of a director, or manager, or a clerk are not the representations of the company, so as to make it responsible, unless they are adopted and ratified at a general meeting of the company. But the representations of a promoter may be in certain cases.

Whenever a representation amounts to a warranty of the fact stated, and is untrue, it is fraudulent in law whether there was knowledge, or want of knowledge, of its untruth on the part of the person making it. *Breach of warranty. (3)*

Warranty does not cover defects which are patent. Thus, if a horse be warranted sound, this is construed to mean, saving those manifest defects which are visible to all mankind and known to the purchaser at the time of the sale. But a purchaser, who relies upon a warranty, is not bound to make any particular examination of a horse before he buys it to ascertain whether a defect exists.

A representation may amount to a warranty, although made before the sale, if it was made pending the negotiation for the sale. But private representations made prior to a sale by auction form no part of the negotiation ending in the purchase. And representations made after a sale do not amount to a warranty.

If the means of information lie peculiarly or exclusively within the reach of the person making the representation, and he pretends to know the truth of the matter, he must be taken to warrant his knowledge of the fact. Thus the statement by a jeweller to a purchaser that a glittering stone is a diamond amounts to a warranty of the fact.

Representations not amounting to warranty. (4)

Representations concerning matters which are obvious to ordinary intelligence, and which lie as much within the knowledge of one party as the other, and where they are not made for the purpose of preventing inquiry or examination, do not amount to a warranty of the knowledge of their truth on the part of the person making them.

When the representation is made concerning something which is mere matter of opinion, and the person giving his opinion does not possess any exclusive means of knowledge, there is no fraud, however erroneous may be the statements made.

Warranty of title on sale of chattels. (5)

The bare affirmation on the part of a person who sells a personal chattel, that it is his, amounts to a warranty. And in the ordinary sale of goods in a shop, the seller does in effect warrant that the goods are his own. But if a man does not sell as owner, but in some other capacity, as sheriff or pawnbroker, and does not make any representation as to title, he is presumed to sell only such a title as he actually possesses.

If a manufacturer represents the article he makes to be of some superior or peculiar quality, or to be fit for some particular purpose, in order to recommend it to a purchaser, his representation amounts to a warranty of the fact. Warranty of goods by manufacturers. (6)

When the vendor is not himself the manufacturer of the goods he sells, and the purchaser is afforded the means of inspection and examination, the representations made by the vendor of the quality of the goods amount merely to assertions of his own opinion and belief, and not to a warranty. Representations by vendors who are not manufacturers. (7)

But if a man goes to a shop and asks the shopkeeper for an article fit for a particular purpose, and it is the clear understanding of the parties that the purchaser relies upon the skill and judgment of the shopkeeper for the supply of an article fit for the purpose specified, there is an implied warranty on the part of the shopkeeper that the article he furnishes is reasonably fit for that purpose.

A person, who exhibits a sample of goods for sale, warrants that the sample has been fairly taken from the bulk, and he does no more than this. The purchaser takes the risk of all latent defects and infirmities inherent in the article and unknown to the seller, whether they arise from natural causes or from fraudulent dealings with the goods by third parties through whose hands they have passed. Sale by sample. (8)

Wherever the purchaser has no opportunity of inspecting the goods he buys, the rule *caveat emptor* does not apply. Therefore a representation, made by a vendor to an absent purchaser, as to the quality of goods he offers for sale, amounts to a warranty. Representations to absent purchasers. (9)

If a vendor is aware of any serious secret defect, materially deteriorating the value of the goods in the market, and, nevertheless, offers them for sale at the ordinary market price, and knows that the purchaser is deceived by the appearance of the goods, and is labouring under a mistake respecting them, and the vendor takes no trouble to Concealment of defects. (10)

disclose the real facts to the purchaser, he is responsible in damages for wilful deceit; and so if the vendor resorts to any contrivance to conceal the defect. But if the defect is patent, and the purchaser has the means of examination at hand, the maxim *caveat emptor* will apply.

Warranty of trade marks, &c. By 25 & 26 Vict. c. 88, it is enacted that when any person shall sell goods bearing, or accompanied with, a trade mark, the sale shall be deemed to be made with a warranty that the trade mark is genuine, unless the contrary be expressed in writing, signed by the vendor, and accepted by the vendee. And when goods are sold upon which, or accompanying which, there is any statement respecting the number, quantity, or weight of such goods, or of the place or country at which they were manufactured or produced, such sale shall be deemed to be made with a warranty of the truth of such statement, unless the contrary be expressed in some writing signed by the vendor and accepted by the vendee.

Sale "with all faults." (11) A sale of a chattel " with all faults " does not mean that the purchaser is to take it with all frauds. Such a stipulation will not protect the vendor from an action for deceit, if he has resorted to any artifice to conceal a defect, or has made any false representation for the purpose of preventing examination or inquiry by the purchaser.

False representation of authority. (12) If an agent, who has no authority to make a contract in the name of his principal, nevertheless makes a contract as having such authority, he is responsible to the party with whom the contract is made in an action of deceit. And this is the case, whether he knows that he is acting without authority, or whether he *bonâ fide* believes that he has it, unless, in the latter case, he discloses the grounds upon which he believes that he has authority.

A man, who employs another to do an act which the employer assumes to have, and appears to have a right to authorize him to do, impliedly warrants that he has the authority which he assumes to have, and if he has no such authority, he is liable to an action for deceit, and is bound to indemnify his servants or agents.

A principal is not responsible for the fraud or deceit of his agent, unless it is committed by the agent in the transaction of the ordinary business of the principal, or unless the principal adopts and takes the benefit of it. *Responsibility of principal for fraud of agent.* (13)

Remedies.

In an action for misrepresentation, deceit, or breach of warranty, special damages are recoverable, provided they are such as might fairly and reasonably be considered, in the ordinary course of things, to be the probable result of the plaintiff's acting on the faith of the representation or warranty. But if there are circumstances which render the misrepresentation or deceit peculiarly injurious to the plaintiff, the defendant will not in general be responsible for the increased damages resulting therefrom, unless the special circumstances were known to him at the time of making the representation. *Damages recoverable.* (14)

Where a false representation is made by one man to induce another to enter into a contract, and the person making the representation is no party to the contract, equity will compel the latter to make good his assertion as far as possible. And this is so even when the statement made was believed by the person who made it to be true, if in the due discharge of his duty he ought to have known the fact which negatives the representation. *Remedy in equity.* (15)

All deceitful practices for defrauding others are indictable at common law; and various statutes have been passed for the repression of particular kinds of fraud, which, however, "were never meant to apply to a mere fraud committed in the course of a commercial transaction, and to make it the subject of an indictment, unless the matter was really and wholly a designed piece of swindling." *Indictment.* (16)

Injunction.
(17) Wherever a person has been injured in his trade or business, or has sustained some special injury from a fraud committed by another, he is entitled to an injunction to prevent the continuance of the injury as well as to compensation in damages. Thus an injunction will be granted to prevent the fraudulent use of the trade marks and business designations of others.

ILLUSTRATIVE CASES.

(1) *Polhill* v. *Walter*, 3 B. & Ad. 114.

A bill was presented for acceptance at the office of the drawee when he was absent. A., who lived in the same house, being assured by one of the payees that the bill was perfectly regular, was induced to write on the bill an acceptance as by the procuration of the drawee, believing that the acceptance would be sanctioned and the bill paid. When due, the bill was dishonoured, and the indorsee sued A. for falsely, fraudulently, and deceitfully representing that he was authorized to accept by procuration. On the trial the jury negatived all fraud in fact. Held, notwithstanding, that A. was liable.

Langridge v. *Levy*, 2 M. & W. 519.

Declaration that L., the father of the plaintiff, bought a gun of the defendant for the use of himself and his sons, the defendant falsely and fraudulently warranting the gun to have been made by N. and to be a good and safe gun. The gun was not made by N. and was a bad and dangerous gun. In consequence of its ill-construction, the gun exploded in the hands of the plaintiff, and severely injured him. Held, that the action was maintainable.

Pasley v. *Freeman*, 3 T.R. 51.

The plaintiff received damage by a false affirmation made by the defendant with intent to defraud. Held, that in such an action, it is not necessary that the defendant should be benefited by the deceit, or that he should collude with the person who is.

Smout v. *Ilbery*, 10 M. & W. 1.

Where a man, who had been in the habit of dealing with the plaintiff, went abroad, leaving his wife and family resident in this country, and died abroad—Held, that the wife was not liable for goods supplied to her after his death, but before the information of his death had been received, the revocation of her original authority to contract for her husband, being by the act of God, and the continuance of the life of the principal being equally within the knowledge of both parties.

(2) See *New Brunswick Railway Co.* v. *Conybeare*, 31 Law J., Ch. 297, and *Ross* v. *Estates Investment Co.*, L.R. 3 Eq. Ca. 122.

(3) *Williamson* v. *Allison*, 2 East 450.

In an action on the case in tort for breach of a warranty of goods—Held, that the *scienter* need not be proved.

Margetson v. *Wright, 5 M. & P.* 606.

On the sale of a race-horse, the seller told the purchaser that the horse was a crib-biter; the horse also had a splint, which was apparent. Held, that a warranty that the horse was sound, wind and limb, at the time of the sale, did not extend to those defects.

Holliday v. *Morgan,* 1 *Ell. & Ell.* 1.

A warranty of soundness, on the sale of a horse, is broken by a malformation existing from the birth of the horse which at the time of the sale renders the horse less fit for reasonable use. An extraordinary convexity of the cornea of the eye, producing short sightedness, in consequence of which the horse is liable to shy, is not so patent a defect that a purchaser with express warranty is bound to notice it.

Lysney v. *Selby,* 2 *Ld. Raym.* 1118.

An action will lie against the seller of an estate for affirming the rents to be more than they are, while he is in treaty about the sale, if the party to whom the affirmation is made relies upon it, and thereupon buys the estate.

Chandelor v. *Lopus,* 2 *Cro.* 2, 1 *Sm. L.C.*

The defendant sold the plaintiff a stone, which he affirmed to be a Bezoar stone. Held, that no action lay against him, unless he either knew that it was not a Bezoar stone, or warranted it to be a Bezoar stone.

(4) *Baily* v. *Merrell,* 3 *Bulstr.* 94.

In an action for deceit it appeared that the defendant, having a load of wood to be carried, came to the plaintiff, a carrier, and bargained with him for the carriage of it at 2s. a hundredweight, representing that there were eight hundredweight. The plaintiff, relying upon the representation, caused the wood to be put into his cart and carried; but finding that he had got an overpowering load, and having killed two of his horses in dragging it along, he caused the wood to be weighed, when he found the weight to be twenty hundredweight; and thereupon brought his action for damages. Held, that the action was not maintainable, as it was his own fault that he did not have the wood weighed before putting it in his cart.

(5) See *Eicholz* v. *Bannister,* 34 *Law J., C.P.* 105.

(6) *Jones* v. *Bright,* 3 *M. & P.* 174.

The defendant supplied copper sheathing for the plaintiff's vessel; the sheathing turned out to be defective in a short time after it was used, and the jury found that the decay was occasioned by some intrinsic defect in the quality. Held, that the plaintiff was entitled to recover in an action in the nature of deceit, although no fraud was imputed to the defendant; for that, as he manufactured the copper, and knew the purpose to which it was to be applied, and said "he would supply the plaintiff well," it amounted to a warranty that it should be fit for that purpose.

(7) *Brown* v. *Edgington,* 2 *M. & Gr.* 289.

A., a wine merchant, ordered a crane rope of B., a dealer in ropes. B.'s foreman, on being told the nature and dimensions of the rope and the purpose for which it was required, said that one would have to be manufactured specially. B. sent an order to his manufacturer, who employed a third person to make the rope. Held, that A. might recover against B. damages resulting from the insufficiency of the rope.

(8) *Ormrod* v. *Huth*, 14 *M. & W.* 664.

Where cotton was sold by sample, upon a representation that the bulk corresponded with the sample, but no warranty was taken by the purchaser, and the bulk of the cotton turned out to be of inferior quality, and to have been falsely packed, though not by the seller—Held, that an action on the case for a false and fraudulent representation was not maintainable without showing that such representation was false to the knowledge of the seller, or that he acted fraudulently in making it.

(9) *Gardiner* v. *Gray*, 4 *Campb.* 145.

Where, at the time of sale, a specimen of goods was exhibited to the buyer, and there was a written contract which merely described the goods as of a particular denomination, and the buyer had no opportunity of inspecting the goods—Held, that this was not a sale by sample; but as there was no opportunity of inspecting the goods, the maxim *caveat emptor* did not apply, and there was an implied warranty that the goods should be of a merchantable quality of the denomination mentioned in the contract.

(10) *Hill* v. *Gray*, 1 *Stark.* 434.

The agent of the vendor of a picture, knowing that the vendee laboured under a delusion, with respect to the picture, which materially influenced his judgment, permitted him to make the purchase without removing that delusion. Held, that the sale was void.

Southerne v. *Howe*, 2 *Roll.* 5.

"If I sell a horse which has lost an eye, no action lies, but otherwise if I sell him with a counterfeit eye."

(11) *Schneider* v. *Heath*, 3 *Campb.* 506.

The vendor of a ship, which was worm-eaten, and had its keel broken and was entirely unseaworthy, represented her to be "nearly as good as when launched." The ship was sold "to be taken with all faults." Held, that the vendor could not avail himself of that stipulation.

(12) See *Jenkins* v. *Hutchinson*, 13 *Q.B.*; Judgment of Erle, C.J., *p.* 748.

Adamson v. *Jarvis*, 4 *Bing.* 72.

The plaintiff, an auctioneer, sold goods under order of the defendant, who had no right to dispose of them; and the true owner afterwards recovered against the plaintiff. In an action by the plaintiff against the defendant for the representation of the latter that the goods were his. Held, that the plaintiff might recover.

(13) *Barwick* v. *English Joint Stock Bank*, *L.R.* 2 *Exch.* 259.

The defendants being asked to guarantee one J. D., whom the plaintiff was supplying with goods on credit, the manager of the defendants gave the plaintiff a written guarantee, which the manager knew to be unavailing, and fraudulently concealed from the plaintiff the fact which would render it unavailing. Held, that the defendants were liable for the fraud of their agent.

(14) *Borradaile* v. *Brunton*, 2 *Moore* 582.

In an action for the warranty of a chain cable, it appeared that one of the links was partly broken, and the master of the vessel ordered the cable to be slipped to avoid danger. Held, that the defendants were liable upon such warranty, and that the plaintiff might recover the value of the cable and the anchor to which it was attached.

(15)   See *Pulsford* v. *Richards*, 17 *Beav.* 94.

(16)   *Reg.* v. *Evans*, 32 *Law J.*, *M.C.* 38.

The prisoner and two other persons entered into articles of partnership, by the terms of which the profits were to be divided equally among them. By a subsequent verbal arrangement the prisoner was to act as agent for the sale of partnership goods, and was to receive a commission on all orders obtained by him, which commission was to be paid out of the partnership funds before any division of profits was made. The prisoner, by falsely pretending that he had obtained some orders, induced his fellow-partners to pay him a sum for commission. Held, that he was not indictable for obtaining money by false pretences, as his charges were payable out of the partnership funds, and his false statement was a misrepresentation respecting a partnership matter, and would have had to be investigated, and the sum paid duly considered, in taking the partnership accounts in order to ascertain the profits.

(17)   *Holloway* v. *Holloway*, 13 *Beav.* 209.

The plaintiff, Thomas Holloway, sold a medicine as "*Holloway's* pills." The defendant, Henry Holloway, commenced to sell " *H. Holloway's* pills " in boxes similar to the plaintiff's, and with a view of passing off his pills as the plaintiff's. The defendant was restrained by injunction.

CHAPTER XV.

MATRIMONIAL INJURIES AND SEDUCTION.

Matrimonial Injuries.

Divorce.
By the Divorce Act, 20 & 21 Vict. c. 85, s. 27, a husband may petition the court for the dissolution of marriage on the ground of adultery on the part of his wife. And a wife may petition for the dissolution of the marriage on the ground that her husband has been guilty of incestuous adultery, or of bigamy with adultery, or of rape, sodomy, or bestiality, or of adultery coupled with cruelty, or of adultery coupled with desertion for two years or upwards without reasonable excuse.

Judicial separation.
By 20 & 21 Vict. c. 85, s. 16, a sentence of judicial separation may be obtained by either husband or wife on the ground of adultery or cruelty, or desertion without cause, for two years and upwards. A judicial separation corresponds to the old divorce *a mensâ et thoro*. And by 41 Vict. c. 19, s. 4, if a husband be convicted of an aggravated assault upon his wife, the court or magistrate before whom he is convicted may, if satisfied that the future safety of the wife is in peril, order that the wife shall be no longer bound to cohabit with her husband; and such order shall have the force and effect in all respects of a decree of judicial separation on the ground of cruelty.

Protection order.
By 20 & 21 Vict. c. 85, s. 21, a wife, deserted by her husband without reasonable cause, may at any time after such desertion apply, if resident within the metropolitan district,

to a police magistrate, or, if resident in the country, to justices in petty sessions, or in either case to the Divorce Court, or the judge ordinary thereof, for an order to protect any money or property she may acquire by her own lawful industry, and property which she may become possessed of after such desertion, against her husband or his creditors, or any person claiming under him. Such order, however, if made by a police magistrate or justices at petty sessions, must within ten days be entered with the registrar of the county court within the jurisdiction of which the wife is resident, and the husband or creditor, or other person claiming under him, may apply to the court, or to the magistrate or justices by whom such order was made, for the discharge thereof.

If, after notice of such order, the husband, or any person claiming under him, shall seize or continue to hold any property of the wife, he may be compelled, at the suit of the wife, to restore the specific property and a sum equal to double the value of the property so seized or held.

Where the husband has deserted the wife, or the wife the husband, an application may be made to the Divorce Court for the restitution of conjugal rights; but the power of the court only extends to compelling the parties to live under the same roof. A deed of separation is no bar to a suit for the restitution of conjugal rights. But a suit for the restitution of conjugal rights cannot be maintained by a wife who has committed adultery. *Restitution of conjugal rights.* (1)

Adultery will form no ground for divorce or judicial separation, if the petitioner has been in any way accessory to, or conniving at, the adultery, or has condoned it (Divorce Act, sect. 29), or if the petition is prosecuted in collusion with the respondent or co-respondent (sect. 30). And the court may refuse to act, if the petitioner has been guilty of unreasonable delay in presenting the petition, or of cruelty towards the other party to the marriage, or of having deserted, or wilfully separated from, the other party to the *Adultery, connivance, condonation.* (2)

marriage, before the adultery complained of, and without reasonable excuse, or of such wilful neglect or misconduct as has conduced to the adultery (sect. 31). And misconduct conducing to adultery is not mere carelessness, but a knowledge by the husband of an intimacy distinctly dangerous, and a purposed or reckless disregard of it. The neglect of the husband, in order to bar a divorce, must be neglect which conduced to the wife's original fall, not neglect conducing to any particular act of adultery committed subsequently to her fall.

Connivance by the husband to any one act of criminal intercourse on the part of the wife may deprive him of redress for a subsequent act of adultery not tolerated or connived at.

An agreement on the part of the wife to live separate would amount to connivance, if it were made with a knowledge of the adultery committed by the husband, and the probability of its continuance.

Condonation of adultery is forgiveness of the offence, with full knowledge of all the circumstances, accompanied or followed by reconciliation and conjugal cohabitation.

Cruelty. (3)
It is cruelty on the part of a husband to strike his wife, or threaten her with personal violence without adequate provocation, and so conduct himself as to give her a reasonable apprehension of bodily harm if she continues to reside with him; if he puts her unnecessarily under personal restraint; if he spits in her face; if he treats her with gross insult, attempts to debauch her maid-servants, or charges her with gross offences in the presence of third parties. Everything is in legal construction cruelty which tends to bodily harm. And moral force alone, if systematically exerted in order to compel the submission of the wife, in such a manner, and in such a degree, as to injure her health, amounts to legal cruelty.

Habitual drunkenness on the part of either husband or wife, although accompanied by much annoyance and extraordinary conduct, does not amount to cruelty. But the wilful communication to the wife of venereal disease is cruelty, and the wilfulness is presumed in the absence of evidence to the contrary.

Mere turbulence of temper does not amount to cruelty; and the court will not interfere in cases in which the party complaining has pursued a course of retaliation.

Desertion, in order to entitle the wife to a protection order under s. 21 of the Divorce Act (20 & 21 Vict. c. 85), means not only that the husband has absented himself from his wife, but also that he has left her unprovided for, and such desertion must continue at the time of making the order. *Desertion. (4)*

Desertion, in order to form the ground of a judicial separation, or, accompanied by adultery, to form a ground for divorce, must be without cause, without the consent of the petitioner, and it must have continued two years at the time of making the petition, and it is not necessary to show that the husband has left his wife unprovided for.

After a decree for dissolution of marriage, or judicial separation, the wife acquires the legal status of a *feme sole*, and the same is true in respect of a married woman who has obtained a protection order during the continuance of the order (Divorce Act, s. 21, s. 26). *Status of divorced or separated wife.*

After a decree of divorce or judicial separation, the court may order the husband to secure such a sum of money for the support of the wife as it may deem reasonable (Divorce Act, s. 32). *Alimony. (5)*

And where a decree of divorce or judicial separation has been founded on the adultery of the wife, the court may order a settlement of her property for the benefit of the innocent party and the children of the marriage (Divorce Act, s. 45; 23 & 24 Vict. c. 144, s. 6).

And where there are either ante-nuptial or post-nuptial settlements, and there are children of the marriage, the court may make such orders as it thinks fit as to the application of the whole, or a part, of the property settled, either

L

for the benefit of the children of the marriage, or of their respective parents, or of both (22 & 23 Vict. c. 61, s. 5). And where there are no children of the marriage, the court may now vary or alter the marriage settlements (41 Vict. c. 19, s. 3).

Custody of children. (6) In any suit for obtaining a decree of nullity of marriage, or for dissolving marriage, or for obtaining judicial separation, the court may make provision for the custody, maintenance, and education of the children of the marriage, or it may place such children under the protection of the Court of Chancery (Divorce Act, s. 35).

At common law, the father has a right to the exclusive custody of his legitimate infant children, and with this right the Court of Divorce will not generally interfere, unless the father has by immorality and misconduct disqualified himself from being the legal guardian of his children.

Without any proceedings in the Divorce Court, the Court of Chancery will restrain the father from acquiring the custody of his infant children where he has deserted their mother and his conduct is such as to render the interference of the court necessary to protect the children from temporal ruin or spiritual peril.

Hearing of petition. Either party to a petition for a dissolution of marriage may insist on having the contested matters of fact tried by a jury. This is not the case in a suit for judicial separation. But in any case the court may in its discretion direct questions of fact to be tried by jury (Divorce Act, s. 28).

By the 32 & 33 Vict. c. 68, the parties to any proceeding instituted in consequence of adultery, and the husbands and wives of such parties, are competent to give evidence, provided that no witness, whether a party to the suit or not, shall be bound to answer any question tending to show that he or she has been guilty of adultery, unless such witness has already given evidence in disproof of his or her alleged adultery.

Petitions for By s. 59 of the Divorce Act (20 & 21 Vict. c. 85) the action of criminal conversation is abolished, but by s. 33 it is enacted that any husband may, either in a petition for dissolution of marriage, or for judicial separation, or by petition for that purpose only, claim damages from any person on the ground of his having committed adultery with the wife of such petitioner.

damages from adulterers. (7)

In a claim for damages of this character it is necessary to prove a legal marriage between the petitioner and the person alleged to be his wife.

The injury suffered by the husband from the seduction of his wife depends upon the circumstances and situation in life of the husband at the time of the seduction, upon the mode in which he fulfilled his marital duties, and the terms upon which the husband and wife were living together, and upon the general character of the wife at the time she was led astray. But the jury ought to give compensation without regard to the wealth of the defendant, unless the latter has employed his wealth to corrupt the wife.

After verdict or decree, the court is to direct the application of the damages; and the whole or any part thereof may be settled for the benefit of the children of the marriage, or as a provision for the maintenance of the wife.

It is a tort at common law, for which damages may be recovered, to persuade and procure a wife to live separate from her husband. And every person who receives a married woman into his house, and suffers her to continue there after he has received notice from her husband not to harbour her, is liable to an action for damages, unless the husband has, by his cruelty and misconduct, forfeited his marital rights, or has turned his wife out of doors, or has by some insult or ill-treatment compelled her to leave him.

Harbouring wife. (8)

And in actions for persuading wives to leave their husbands, as in actions for enticing away servants (see *infra*), the jury are justified in giving ample compensation for all the damage resulting from the wrongful act, as for example the loss of the advantage of a fortune left to her separate use.

L 2

Seduction.

Loss of service of servants.
It is actionable to procure a servant to leave his master's service, or to harbour him and keep him as servant after he has quitted his place, and before the expiry of his term of service, against the will of his master and with notice of the desertion of service.

Loss of service of children.
A parent has no remedy for an injury done to his child by the tortious act of another, unless the child was old enough to be capable of rendering, and did render, some service, however trifling.

Loss of service through seduction. (9)
The law gives no remedy to the parent for the mere seduction of a daughter unless she was living with her parent at the time of the seduction, and the seduction is followed by pregnancy and illness, whereby the parent is deprived of the services which she previously rendered.

If it is proved that, although the defendant seduced the girl, he was not the father of the child of which she was subsequently delivered, there is no cause of action against him.

If the father has so neglected his parental duties, and encouraged his daughter in improper intimacies as to invite the injury of which he complains, he has no ground of action for redress.

Who may sue. (10)
Any person with whom the girl was residing at the time of the seduction, either in the character of daughter and servant, or as ward and servant, or as a servant only, may sue for damages. And in the case of an orphan living with a relation or friend, who stands towards her *in loco parentis*, and is thus entitled to sue, such relation or friend may recover damages beyond the mere loss of service, as when (*vide infra*) the action is brought by the actual parent.

Damages in actions
If a servant or contractor is induced through the malicious persuasion of the defendant to abandon the work or

contract he has undertaken to perform, the measure of the damages is not to be confined to the loss of the services of those who were thus enticed away; but the jury may give ample compensation for all the damage resulting from the wrongful act. *for loss of service. (11)*

In estimating the damages to be given to a father, or one standing *in loco parentis* for the loss of service of his daughter from seduction, the jury are not confined to a consideration of the mere loss of service, but may also give damages for the distress of mind which he has sustained in being deprived of the society and comfort of his child, and by the dishonour which he receives. The jury may also take into consideration the situation in life and circumstances of the parties. *Damages in actions for seduction. (12)*

It is inadmissible to show, in aggravation of damages, that the defendant accomplished his purpose through the medium of a promise of marriage; for a breach of promise of marriage is a distinct ground of action; but the question may be asked "whether the defendant paid his addresses in an honourable way," and if this is shown, liberal damages may be given.

In mitigation of damages, it may be shown that the girl seduced was not of moral and virtuous character at the time of the seduction; but where evidence of this kind is given, it may be met by evidence of her previous good character.

24 & 25 Vict. c. 100, s. 55, makes it an indictable misdemeanour to take an unmarried girl under the age of sixteen out of the possession, and against the will, of her father, or mother, or any other person having the lawful care of her. *Indictment for abduction.*

And by the same statute, s. 53, it is a felony to fraudulently allure, take away, or detain any woman under the age of twenty-one, who has any interest in any real or personal estate, or who is presumptive heiress, &c., to any-one having such interest, out of the possession and against the will of anyone who has the lawful care of her, with intent to marry or carnally know her. It is also a felony to take and detain from motives of lucre any woman over twenty-one, entitled to any real and personal estate, &c., against her will, with intent to marry or carnally know her. And in either case, on conviction, the person convicted becomes incapable of taking any estate or interest in any property of the woman.

ILLUSTRATIVE CASES.

(1) *Spering* v. *Spering*, 3 *Sw. & Tr.* 211.

An agreement between husband and wife to live separate, Held, no bar to a suit for restitution of conjugal rights.

Hope v. *Hope*, 27 *Law J., Prob. & Matt.* 43.

A suit for restitution of conjugal rights, Held, not maintainable by a wife who has committed adultery, although the husband also has committed adultery.

(2) See *Dering* v. *Dering*, *L.R.*, 1 *P. & D.* 531.

St. Paul v. *St. Paul*, *L.R.*, 1 *P. & D.* 739.

Gipps v. *Gipps*, 32 *Law J., P. & M.* 78.

(3) *Paterson* v. *Paterson*, 3 *H.L.C.* 328.

Neglect, silence, and shunning the wife's company do not constitute that cruelty and maltreatment in respect of which a judicial separation will be granted.

Kelly v. *Kelly*, 2 *P. & D.* 31.

If force, whether physical or moral, is systematically exerted to compel the submission of a wife, in such a manner, to such a degree, and during such length of time, as to injure her health, and render a serious malady imminent, this is such cruelty as will entitle her to a judicial separation.

And see *Boardman* v. *Boardman*, 1 *P. & D.* 233.

(4) *Yeatman* v. *Yeatman*, 1 *P. & D.* 489.

A husband who withdraws from cohabitation with his wife may be guilty of the offence of "desertion" within the meaning of s. 16 of the Divorce Act, although he continues to support her. Desertion "without cause" means "without reasonable cause." Such reasonable cause is not necessarily a distinct matrimonial offence on which a decree of judicial separation or dissolution could be founded; but it must be grave and weighty. Mere frailty of temper and habits which are distasteful to a husband are not reasonable ground for desertion.

(5) *Paul* v. *Paul*, *L.R.*, 2 *P. & D.* 93.

On the marriage of the parties (which marriage was subsequently dissolved by reason of the adultery of the wife) the father of the respondent settled property, in the first place, for the benefit of his daughter for life, then for the benefit of her husband, and on the death of the survivor of them, for the benefit of their children. No property was settled on behalf of the petitioner. The court varied the settlement by ordering the whole income of the settled property to be applied during the joint lives of the petitioner and respondent for the benefit of their children.

(6)   See *March* v. *March*, L.R., 1 P. & D. 437.

Barnes v. *Barnes*, L.R., 1 P. & D. 463.

Pending a suit in which the mother was the respondent, the court made an order granting the custody of two infant children, aged respectively three years and eighteen months, to the mother, on the ground that her health was suffering from being deprived of their society, and that they were living with a stranger and not with their father.

Shelley v. *Westbrooke*, Jac. 266.

On a petition presented to the Lord Chancellor, his lordship restrained a father's authority over his children on the ground of his professing and acting on irreligious and immoral principles.

(7)   See *Catherwood* v. *Caslon*, 13 M. & W. 265, *and*

Cowing v. *Cowing*, 33 Law J., P. & M. 149.

(8)   *Philp* v. *Squire*, 1 Peake, 115.

The plaintiff's wife came to the house of the defendant (to whose wife she was related) and *represented herself* to have been very ill-used by her husband, who, she said, had turned her out of doors. Upon this representation the defendant received her into his house, and at her request permitted her to continue there after he had received notice from her husband not to harbour her. It was not proved that the husband had in fact ill-treated his wife. Held, that the defendant was not liable to an action for harbouring the wife, as he had acted from motives of humanity.

Winsmore v. *Greenbank*, Willes, 577.

The plaintiff alleged that his wife left him and lived apart from him, during which time a fortune of £30,000 was left to her separate use, and that she being willing to return to the plaintiff, the defendant unlawfully persuaded her to continue to live away from the plaintiff, whereby he lost the assistance of his wife in his domestic affairs and the advantage of her fortune. The jury found for the plaintiff, giving him £3000 damages. On a motion for a new trial: Held, that this sum was not excessive.

(9)   *Satterthwaite* v. *Dewhurst*, 4 Doug. 315.

Action brought by the plaintiff, a widow, for the seduction of her daughter. The daughter, previously to her seduction and consequent confinement, had maintained herself. During her illness and subsequently she and her infant were maintained by the mother, who claimed damages on this account. Held, that the action could not be maintained, since the mother could not allege the loss of her daughter's services.

Thompson v. *Ross*, 5 H. & N. 16.

A parent cannot maintain an action for the seduction of a daughter not residing in the house with such parent, but being a domestic servant living in the house of her master, though, with the permission of her master, she had been in the habit, during any leisure time, of assisting in the work by which her parent earned a livelihood.

Eager v. *Grimwood*, 1 *Exch.* 61.

It appeared that the defendant had debauched the plaintiff's daughter, and she was delivered of a child, but the jury found that the child was not the defendant's. Held, that the jury were rightly directed to find a verdict for the defendant.

Reddie v. *Scoolt*, 1 *Peake*, 316.

A father who has permitted a married man, knowing him to be such, to visit his daughter as a suitor cannot maintain an action against him for seducing her.

(10) *Irwin* v. *Dearman*, 11 *East*, 23.

The plaintiff, an officer in the army, adopted and bred up in his own house the daughter of a deceased soldier in his regiment. In an action against the defendant for her seduction he obtained £100 damages, although the only actual damage proved was the loss of the young woman's service for five weeks. The court refused to set aside the verdict.

(11) *Gunter* v. *Astor*, 4 *Moore*, 15.

The defendants clandestinely sent for the plaintiff's workmen, and, having caused them to be intoxicated, induced them to sign an agreement to leave him and come to them, by which the plaintiff was nearly ruined. The plaintiff's yearly income was about £800. The jury gave him £1600 damages. Held, that this was not an excessive sum. Richardson, J.: "The measure of damages the plaintiff is entitled to receive from the defendants is not necessarily to be confined to those servants he might have in his employ at the time they were so enticed, or for that part of the day on which they absented themselves from his service, but he is entitled to recover damages for the loss he sustained by their leaving him at that critical period."

(12) *Andrews* v. *Askey*, 8 *C. & P.* 9.

In an action for the seduction of a daughter, the jury are not confined to the mere loss of service, but may give damages for the distress and anxiety of mind which the parent has felt. And it is for the jury to take into consideration the situation in life of the parties, and say what they think to be a reasonable compensation.

Dodd v. *Morris*, 3 *Campb.* 520.

In an action for seducing the plaintiff's daughter, the daughter is not bound to answer in cross-examination whether she had not previously been criminal with other men. In such action evidence cannot be admitted that the defendant accomplished by means of a promise of marriage, but the question may be put to the daughter whether the defendant paid his addresses in an honourable way. The mere cross-examination of the daughter, to show that she had been guilty of improper conduct, does not entitle the plaintiff to call other witnesses to her character.

BOOK II.—CONTRACTS.

CHAPTER I.

CONTRACTS GENERALLY.

A CONTRACT is an agreement by which two parties mutu- Definition. ally promise and engage, or one of them promises and engages to the other, to give some particular thing, or to do or abstain from doing some particular act.

When there is a mutual contract binding each party to the other, the contract is bilateral.

When the contract binds one person to another, without any engagement being made by the latter, it is unilateral.

Every contract is founded on a concurrence of intention between two parties, and the communication of that intention. Such communication consists of a proposal or offer and an acceptance of that offer.

A mere proposal is not in itself binding; it may be Proposal revoked at any time before acceptance, but not afterwards; (1) and, even if a definite time for acceptance be fixed, the proposer is free to withdraw his proposal before that time has elapsed. And a proposal is held to be revoked from the time that the intention to revoke it is communicated.

If a time for acceptance be prescribed in the proposal, Acceptto form a valid contract the acceptance must be within ance. that time. If no time be prescribed, the acceptance must (2) be within a reasonable time. Acceptance dates from the communication of the intention to accept. And where an acceptance is by post, there is a binding contract from the time that the letter accepting the offer is posted.

To conclude a binding contract, the acceptance must be absolute and unconditional.

Implied contract. The communication of the proposal or the acceptance, or both, may be by conduct as well as by word.

Implied contracts may be divided into Inferred Contracts and Constructive Contracts, or obligations *quasi ex contractu.*

An inferred contract is where the intention of the parties may be gathered from their acts and from surrounding circumstances.

A constructive contract is where the parties have not, in fact, entered into any contract at all, but where circumstances have arisen between them which make it just that one should have a right and the other be subject to a liability.

Consideration. (3) In order that a contract not under seal should be binding, it is necessary that it should be made on valid consideration. A mere verbal, gratuitous promise to give any particular thing, unaccompanied by a transfer of possession, is not enforceable by law.

There is a sufficient consideration to render a promise binding in law if anything be performed which the party is under no legal obligation to perform, or if anything is given or done, at the request of the promisor, as the inducement for the promise, whereby the promisor derives benefit or advantage, or whereby the promisee sustains trouble or loss, or suffers injury or inconvenience.

It is a sufficient consideration that loss or inconvenience has been sustained by one party at the request of the other, although no actual benefit has thereby accrued to the latter.

Any service, benefit, or advantage rendered to a third person at the request of the promisor is a sufficient consideration for the promise.

Bygone acts or services are a sufficient consideration to support a promise if they were performed or rendered pursuant to the previous request of the promisor, and not otherwise. And if the defendant has accepted and retains the benefit or advantage of the consideration, the law will imply a request where there really was none.

The only duties of the nature of mere moral obligations, the performance of which will amount to a consideration which will support an express promise, are such as could be enforced at common law but for the intervention of some statutory enactment or positive rule of law which exempts a class to which the particular party belongs. Thus, previously to the Infants' Relief Act (37 & 38 Vict. c. 62), the express promise of a person arrived at full age operated to revive his liability for debts contracted whilst he was an infant, and which he was therefore not legally, but only morally, bound to pay.

The forbearance of legal or equitable rights forms a good consideration; and in case of all unliquidated claims and demands, where the precise amount due has not been fixed by the agreement of the parties, satisfaction for a part of the demand is good consideration for the discharge of the residue (see *infra*, p. 370).

When money or goods are entrusted to a man on the faith of his promise to deal with them in a certain way, the confidence reposed in him is deemed sufficient consideration for his promise, although he undertook the duty or trust gratuitously.

It is not requisite that the consideration for a contract should be adequate in point of value. If there be *any* consideration, the extent of it will not be weighed. Inadequacy of consideration may, however, be evidence of fraud. **Adequacy of consideration. (4)**

Natural affection, blood relationship, friendship, or voluntary courtesy are not sufficient consideration to render a promise or undertaking, not under seal, binding in law, nor is the performance of any mere moral obligation, except as above stated. The payment of part of an ascertained and liquidated debt is no consideration for a discharge of the residue (see *infra*, p. 370). And the performance of any **Invalid considerations. (5)**

act which the party is under a legal obligation to perform is no consideration for a promise. (The performance of an act which a person is bound towards another to perform may, however, form a good consideration to support a promise by a third person if the latter derives a benefit from the performance.) Bygone transactions cannot be made a good consideration for a promise unless, as above stated, they have been performed pursuant to the request of the party making the promise.

Failure of consideration. (6) If a consideration, apparently good, should turn out to be false or a nullity, the promise founded upon it becomes void. Thus, when the consideration was the forbearance of a suit, and there turns out to have been no cause of action, the promise founded upon such consideration is not legally binding.

Unilateral promise. (7) In the case of unilateral promises, there is no binding engagement to perform the executory consideration; but the performance of the consideration is a condition precedent to the performance of the promise. Thus, where the promisor agrees that, if the promisee will furnish goods to a third person, he, the promisor, will guarantee the payment, the promisee does not become bound to furnish the goods, but if he does so, the promisor becomes bound to pay for them.

Mutual promises. (8) Mutual promises are those in which the promise of the one party to do one thing is the consideration for the promise of the other party to do another. Thus, in contracts of sale, the promise of the one party to sell forms the consideration of the promise of the other party to buy.

All contracts founded upon mutual promises between persons of full age must be binding on both parties, so that each may have an action upon it, or neither will be bound.

But when one of the parties to a contract, founded upon mutual promises, is an infant, and the other a person of full age, the former may take advantage of his or her minority, and resist the completion of the contract; but the other party cannot refuse to complete the contract on the ground that there was no mutuality of obligation.

If there be a day set for the payment of the money, or the doing of the thing which one promises to do for another thing, and that day is to happen, or may happen, before the other thing can be performed, an action may be brought for the money, &c., before the other thing is done.

<small>Independent promises.
(9)</small>

ILLUSTRATIVE CASES.

(1) *Cooke* v. *Oxley*, 3 *T.R.* 653.

A. having proposed to sell goods to B. gave him a certain time, at his request, to determine whether he would buy them or not; B. within the time determined to buy them, and gave notice thereof to A.; yet A. was not liable in an action for not delivering them, for B., not being bound by the original contract, there was no consideration to bind A. [If B. had given A. some consideration for keeping the offer open; the case would have been otherwise. Compare *Great Northern Railway Co.* v. *Whitham*, L.R. 9 C.P. 16.]

(2) *M'Iver* v. *Richardson*, 1 *M. & S.* 557.

The plaintiffs having refused to furnish goods to A. on his credit alone, the defendant wrote to the plaintiffs in the following terms:—" You will be perfectly safe in crediting A.; indeed, I have no objection to guaranty you against any loss from giving them this credit." The goods were thereupon furnished. Held, that the paper did not amount to a guaranty, there being no notice given by the plaintiffs to the defendant that they accepted it as such, or any consent of the defendant that it should be a conclusive guaranty.

Adams v. *Lindsell*, 1 *B. & Ald.* 681.

A. by letter offered to sell to B. certain specified goods, "*receiving an answer by return of post:*" the letter being misdirected, the answer notifying the acceptance of the offer arrived two days later than it ought to have done. On the day following that on which it would have arrived if the letter containing the offer had been properly directed, A. sold the goods to a third person. Held, that there was a contract binding the parties, from the moment the offer was accepted, and that B. was entitled to recover against A. in an action for not completing his contract.

Dunlop v. *Higgins*, 1 *H.L.C.* 381.

A letter offering a contract does not bind the party to whom it is addressed to return an answer by the very next post after its delivery, or to lose the benefit of the contract; an answer posted on the day of receiving the offer is sufficient.

A contract is accepted by the posting of a letter declaring its acceptance.
A person who has put into the post a letter declaring his acceptance of a contract offered has done all that it is necessary for him to do, and is not answerable for casualties occurring at the post-office and causing delay.

(3) *Wilkinson* v. *Oliveira*, 1 *B.N.C.* 490.

The declaration stated that, in consideration that the plaintiff at the request of the defendant had given defendant a letter written by O., since deceased, by means of which letter defendant was enabled to and did determine certain disputes in his own favour, and obtain a large portion of O.'s effects, defendant promised to give plaintiff £1000. Held, that a sufficient consideration was disclosed to sustain an action on the promise.

Jones v. *Ashburnham*, 4 *East*, 194.

The plaintiff declared that A., since deceased, was indebted to him so much, and that, after his death, in consideration of the premises, and that he, at the instance of the defendant, "would forbear and give day of payment" of the debt (not stating to whom he was to forbear), the defendant promised, &c. Held, on demurrer, that there was no consideration for the promise; for a promise can only be sustained on a consideration of benefit to the defendant or detriment to the plaintiff; and unless there were some person whom the plaintiff could have sued for the debt, his forbearance was no detriment to him.

Taylor v. *Jones*, 1 *Raym.* 312.

The plaintiff, a captain in the army, at the instance of the defendant, gave leave of absence to A., a private soldier. Held, that this was a good consideration for a promise by the defendant to pay a sum of money to the plaintiff if A. continued absent for more than ten days.

Osborne v. *Rogers*, 1 *Saund.* 264, *n.* 1.

"Where a man pays a sum of money, or buys goods for me without my knowledge or request, and afterwards I agree to the payment, or receive the goods, this is equivalent to a previous request to do so."

Bracewell v. *Williams*, *L.R.* 2 *C.P.* 196.

A promise not to apply for costs under 12 & 13 Vict. c. 106, s. 85, is a sufficient consideration to support a contract to pay the amount of such costs.

A promise to conduct proceedings in bankruptcy, so as to injure as little as possible the debtor's credit, is not a good consideration to support a contract.

Wilkinson v. *Byers*, 1 *Ad. & E.* 106.

Payment by the defendant of an agreed sum in discharge of an unliquidated demand, Held, a good consideration for a promise by the plaintiff to stay proceedings, where an action had been actually commenced, and to pay his own costs.

(4) *Townend* v. *Toker*, *L.R.* 1 *Ch.* 446.

A lady, who was entitled in fee to an estate subject to mortgages, proposed to her nephew that she should come and live with him, and that he

should remove into a larger house for the purpose, she contributing a yearly
sum towards the housekeeping. The nephew agreed to this, provided she
would settle the estate, limiting it to him after her death. She agreed to
this, and a settlement was accordingly executed by which the nephew
covenanted to indemnify her from all liability in respect of the mortgages,
except the payment of the interest during her life. He removed to a
larger house at considerable expense, and they lived together for some
time; his aunt afterwards ceased to live with her nephew, and agreed to
sell the estate to a purchaser, who filed a bill against the aunt and nephew
for specific performance. Held, that the settlement could not be set aside
as voluntary, as against the purchaser; the covenant of indemnity and the
expenses incurred by the nephew on the faith of the settlement being
severally sufficient to support it as made for value.

(5)   *Holliday* v. *Atkinson*, 5 B. & C. 501.

A promissory note, expressed to be for value received, was made in favour
of an infant aged nine years; in an action upon the note by the payee
against the executors of the maker, no evidence of consideration being
given, the judge told the jury that the note being expressed for value
received, imported that a good consideration existed, and that gratitude to
the infant's father, or affection to the child, would suffice. Held, that
although the jury might have presumed that a good consideration was
given, yet that those pointed out were insufficient; and a new trial was
granted.

Scotson v. *Pegg*, 6 H. & N. 295.

A declaration stated that, in consideration that the plaintiff would deliver
to the defendant a cargo of coals on board the plaintiff's ship, the defendant
promised to discharge the same at the rate of forty-nine tons a day. Plea,
that the plaintiff had made a previous contract with third parties for the
delivery of the said coals in the manner mentioned, that such third parties
had ordered the delivery to the defendant, and that there was no consideration for the defendant's promise to the plaintiff other than the doing of
that which the defendant was already bound to do by his contract with
such third parties. Held, that the plea was bad, for, as the plaintiff
derived a benefit under the former contract, the performance of such contract was a sufficient consideration for the defendant's promise to the
plaintiff.

(6)   *Cochrane* v. *Willis*, L.R. 1 Ch. 58.

A tenant in tail expectant on the death of a tenant for life, who was
insolvent, being desirous of preserving the timber on the estate from being
cut, signed an agreement with the assignee of the tenant for life, agreeing
that the assignee should have the same right to the timber as if he had
actually cut it on a past day named; and the assignee agreed to refrain
from cutting it for a month. It turned out that the tenant for life was
dead at the date of the agreement, though not at the date mentioned in the
agreement; both the tenant in tail and the assignee were ignorant of his
decease. Held, that the agreement was founded on a mistake, and was
without consideration, and the Court refused to enforce it.

(7)   See *Morton* v. *Burn*, 7 Ad. & E. 23.

(8) *Kingston* v. *Phelps, Peake R.* 229.

A written agreement to submit disputes to arbitration is not binding upon any of the parties unless all have signed it, as the obligation by all to obey the award of the arbitrator is the consideration to each for his entering into the contract.

(9) *Sibthorpe* v. *Brunel, 3 Exch.* 826.

If there are mutual covenants for the sale and purchase of an estate, and a fixed day is appointed for the payment of the purchase money, and another and later day for the conveyance of the property, the money must be paid on the day appointed, although the purchaser has not got the estate.

CHAPTER II.

FORM OF CONTRACTS.

CONTRACTS are, (i.) by Matter of Record, (ii.) by Deed, (iii.) by Parol.

(i.) *Contracts by Matter of Record.*

Contracts by matter of record are contracts acknowledged in open court before an officer of the court, and recorded in the presence of the party making the acknowledgment, and the contract is proved by the mere production of the record. Recognizances are contracts by record, and so are the disused statutes merchant and statutes staple. Contracts by matter of record.

(ii.) *Contracts by Deed.*

Contracts by deed are contracts sealed and delivered by the parties to them. The essential requisites of a deed are, writing, sealing, and delivery. A deed is good whether printed or written. It is good although it mentions no time or place of making. Signing is not essential to it at common law, and the Statute of Frauds, which requires certain writings to be signed, does not extend to deeds. The sealing, or the acknowledgment of the seal, must be made after the deed is written and before its delivery. Until the sealed writing is delivered it is not a deed, and the delivery may be made by the party making the deed, Contracts by deed. (1)

or by any one else with his authority, previous or subsequent.

Escrow. (2) A sealed writing may be delivered not to take effect at once, but only subject to the performance of a condition precedent; in this case it is called an escrow.

Deeds poll and indentures. When a deed is made by one person alone, it is called a deed poll; when between two or more parties, it is called an indenture.

Effect of deed. (3) When a contract is made by deed, the necessity of a consideration is dispensed with [except in the case of certain deeds under the Statute of Uses, and in the case of deeds disposing of the goodwill of a business]. And a party to a deed is estopped in general from averring anything in contradiction to what is stated therein.

When deed is required. (i.) All unilateral engagements, where there is no consideration on the one side for the promise on the other, must be made by deed in order to be effectual.

(ii.) Incorporeal hereditaments (such as a reversion or contingent remainder, or right of common, or an advowson) have always required a deed to effect their transfer.

(iii.) By the 8 & 9 Vict. c. 106, s. 2, it is enacted that all corporeal hereditaments shall, as regards the conveyance of the immediate freehold, be deemed to lie in grant as well as in livery. Freehold estates must therefore be transferred by deed, as the alternative to the ancient livery of seisin.

(iv.) By s. 3 of the same statute, leases required by the Statute of Frauds (*q. v. infra*) to be in writing, must be made by deed. [But a lease by simple contract, though void as a lease, will operate as an agreement to grant a lease for the term specified.]

The statute 8 & 9 Vict. c. 106, s. 2, does not apply to equitable estates, which may be assigned by writing without seal.

(v.) The authority of an agent to make or execute a deed for his principal must be under seal, except in the case of joint contractors, one of whom may execute a deed for himself and the others, without an authority under seal for the purpose, provided he does so in the presence of the others.

(vi.) At common law the contracts of corporations are required to be by deed; but to this rule there are many exceptions (see *infra*, p. 212).

(vii.) Assignments of copyright in sculpture are required by 54 Geo. III. c. 56, s. 4, to be by deed attested by two witnesses.

(viii.) By the Merchant Shipping Act (17 & 18 Vict. c. 104, s. 55) the transfer of British ships, or shares therein, is required to be made by deed or bill of sale, in the form given in the schedule to the Act. And the mortgage of a British ship, or the transfer of such mortgage, is required to be by deed.

(iii.) *Parol Contracts,—Statute of Frauds.*

A contract not by matter of record and not under seal, is said to be parol, whether it be written or merely oral. But by statute certain contracts are required to be in writing. Parol contracts.

The 4th section of the Statute of Frauds enacts that *no action shall be brought*, Statute of Frauds, 4th section.

(*a*)—whereby to charge any executor or administrator upon any special promise to answer damages out of his own estate;

(*b*)—or, whereby to charge the defendant with any special promise to answer for the debt, default, or miscarriage of another person;

(*c*)—or, to charge any person upon any agreement made upon consideration of marriage;

(*d*)—or, upon any contract, or sale of lands, tenements, or hereditaments, or any interest in or concerning them;

(*c*)—or, upon any agreement which is not to be performed within the space of one year from the making thereof;

unless the agreement upon which such action shall be brought, or some note or memorandum thereof, shall be in writing and signed by the party to be charged therewith, or some other person thereunto by him lawfully authorized.

Promise of executor to be personally answerable. (4)

The promise of an executor or administrator to answer damages out of his own estate would be invalid without some consideration for the promise; and putting the promise into writing pursuant to the statute does not do away with the necessity of a consideration.

Guaranty. (5)

A promise is not within the statute unless there is, or is to arise, a debt or duty of some other person, for which that other is to remain primarily liable.

A promise to be primarily liable, or to be liable at all events for goods supplied to or work done for a third party, is not within the statute.

Where one, in order to obtain some direct personal advantage, promises to pay the debt of another, this is not within the statute.

If the original contract is discharged and extinguished by the substitution of a new contract by a third person to pay the amount of the debt, the new contract is not within the statute.

A mere promise of indemnity is not within the statute.

A contract to give a guaranty at a future time is as much within the statute as the guaranty itself.

By the 19 & 20 Vict. c. 97, s. 3, it is rendered unnecessary that the consideration for a promise to answer for the debt, default, or miscarriage of another should appear on the note or memorandum required by the Statute of Frauds. The consideration may therefore be supplied by oral evidence, but not the nature and extent of the promise itself, or the name of the party to whom it is given. (And see further as to guaranties, *infra*, Chap. XII.)

A promise to marry is not within the statute, for the consideration of a promise to marry is not marriage, but the other party's reciprocal promise to marry.   *Promise in consideration of marriage.* (6)

When anything is done which substantially amounts to a sale or parting with an interest in land, the contract is within the statute. Thus agreements for leases, and for the sale, assignment, or surrender of leasehold estates, must be in writing in order to support an action. (And see *supra*, p. 162, as to requirement of deed.)   *Contracts for the sale of interests in land.* (7)

Leases not exceeding three years from the making, and on which a rent of two-thirds at least of the full improved value of the land is reserved, are expressly excepted from the operation of the statute.

Contracts for the letting and hiring of furnished houses and lodgings are contracts for an interest in land. But a contract to board and lodge a man generally, without giving him a right to any specific rooms, is not a contract for an interest in land.

Agreements to make alterations and repairs, entered into between a landlord and an intended lessee in connection with the agreement for the lease, are contracts for an interest in land. But when the tenant is in actual occupation, an agreement to make alterations or repairs is not a contract for an interest in land, but for work and services.

Agreements between adjoining proprietors concerning the building of boundary walls and fences are not contracts for an interest in land.

An agreement for the sale and purchase of growing grass, growing timber and underwood, or growing fruit or hops, is a contract for the sale of an interest in land; unless the agreement is made with a view to their immediate severance from the soil and delivery as chattels to the purchaser.

But growing crops of turnips, potatoes, and corn, and other annual productions of the soil, raised by the labour of man, are considered as goods and chattels, and contracts for their sale need never be in writing, under the 4th section of the Statute of Frauds. But where a contract of sale is not required to be in writing under the 4th section, it may still be required to be in writing under the 17th section (*q. v. infra*).

Contracts for the sale of fixtures and railway shares, or shares in the profits of a mine, do not come within either the 4th or the 17th section of the Statute of Frauds. They are deemed to be neither interests in land nor goods and chattels within the meaning of the Act. But the actual transfer of shares in fulfilment of a contract of sale is in general required by statute to be made in writing, and in some cases by deed.

Agreements not to be performed within a year. (8)

This clause relates to agreements which on the face of them cannot be performed within a year.

A contract which is contingent upon the happening of some uncertain event, and which therefore may or may not be performed within the year, is not within the statute. Nor does the statute apply when the contract is wholly executed, or intended to be so, within the year, although there are some acts to be done by the other party beyond the prescribed limit.

But if a contract be for more than a year, the fact that it is defensible within the year will not take it out of the operation of the statute.

Statute of Frauds, 17th section.

By the 17th section of the Statute of Frauds, no contract for the sale of any goods, wares, and merchandise for the price of £10 or upwards shall be allowed to be good except

- the buyer shall accept part of the goods so sold and actually receive the same ;
- or give something in earnest to bind the bargain or in part payment ;
- or except some note or memorandum in writing of the bargain be made and signed by the parties to be charged by such contract or their agents thereunto lawfully authorized.

By the 9 Geo. IV. c. 14, s. 7, the provisions of the 17th section of the Statute of Frauds are declared to extend to all contracts for the sale of goods for the price of £10 or upwards, notwithstanding the goods may be intended to be delivered at some future time, or may not be actually made, procured, or provided, or fit or ready for delivery.

[See further as to the contract of sale, Chap. X., *infra.*]

Construction of the Statute of Frauds.

The 4th section of the Statute of Frauds does not avoid contracts not authenticated in the manner therein prescribed, but only precludes any right of action upon them. The 17th section is stronger and avoids contracts not made as it directs. Effects of non-compliance.

The "agreement" of the 4th section includes the consideration of the contract. With regard to guaranties, however, the necessity for the consideration to appear in writing or by necessary inference from the written document has been taken away (19 & 20 Vict. c. 97, s. 3). The "bargain," of which a memorandum or note is required by the 17th section, does not include the consideration. Requisites of memorandum. (ʙ)

The memorandum under both sections must show the names of the parties and the terms of the contract, and where a price is agreed upon at the time of the sale, it must be set forth on the face of the memorandum.

It is not necessary to show that the agreement has been signed by both parties in order to make the one who has signed it liable upon the contract. And if a written and signed proposal is verbally accepted, the contract becomes complete, and the written proposal is a sufficient memorandum of it.

Any printed papers or written communications which may have passed between the parties, forming on the face of them part of one connected transaction, may be incorporated, and construed together, in order to establish the requisite written evidence of an agreement.

A letter admitting the essential particulars of the contract, but containing a repudiation of the bargain upon bad or insufficient grounds, will constitute a good memorandum of the contract within the statute.

Signature. (10) The signature required by the statute need not be placed in any particular part of the instrument, but it must be introduced so as to authenticate every material part of it. A man may sign by his initials or by his mark, or by a stamp.

The signature must be made with the intention of authenticating the document as a concluded contract, and not with the mere intention of altering or settling a draft. But the acknowledgment of a signature previously made to a document constituting a proposal, the document having been altered in the meantime with the assent of the party making the proposal, is equivalent to an actual signature of the document as finally settled.

Signature by agents. (11) Where a note or memorandum is signed by an agent, it is not necessary that the authority given to the agent should be in writing. And where the signature is in print, the printer may be deemed a person "lawfully authorized" within the statute.

A partner may bind his co-partner by signing the customary trading name of the firm to contracts in the usual course of the partnership business.

A clerk or traveller of one party cannot be treated as an agent to bind the other party, unless he has received express authority to do so.

An auctioneer effecting a sale by auction, or an auctioneer's clerk taking down the biddings in the presence of the purchaser, is during the continuance of the sale the authorized agent of the purchaser as well as of the vendor, and may sign for both or either of the parties to satisfy the Statute of Frauds. An auctioneer who signs the defendant's name by his authority, cannot afterwards sue the latter upon the contract authenticated by such signature. But if the signature was made by the auctioneer's clerk, the auctioneer may then sue upon the contract.

A broker is also agent for both parties, and his signature to "bought and sold notes" is sufficient to satisfy the statute.

Other Contracts requiring Authentication in Writing.

By 9 Geo. IV. c. 14, s. 5, every ratification after full age of any promise or simple contract made during infancy must be in writing and signed by the party to be charged. But now, by the "Infants Relief Act," 37 & 38 Vict. c. 62, no action can be brought upon any ratification made after full age of any promise or contract made during infancy. Confirmation of promises by infants.

By the 9 Geo. IV. c. 14, s. 1, no action can be brought upon a promise to pay a debt which has become barred by the Statute of Limitations, unless such promise be in writing and signed by the debtor. Acknowledgment of barred debts.

By the Merchant Shipping Act, 1854, the transfer of British ships, or of any share in them, is required to be either by bill of sale or deed, in the form therein prescribed. But informal executory agreements for the sale or mortgage of ships are now valid as between the parties to them. Transfer of ships.

By the 30 Vict. c. 23, s. 7, marine insurances must, with certain exceptions, be expressed in a written policy. Marine insurance.

By various statutes, assignments of copyright are required to be in writing, and in the case of sculpture, by deed. Assignments of copyright.

Acts of Parliament relating to particular companies, or particular classes of companies, usually prescribe certain forms in writing for the transfer of shares. Transfer of shares.

Negotiable instruments must from the nature of the case be in writing. Bills of exchange and promissory notes.

Bills of sale.

And by the 19 & 20 Vict. c. 97, s. 6, the acceptance of a bill of exchange must be in writing.

The formalities to be observed with regard to bills of sale are regulated by the 41 & 42 Vict. c. 31 (*see infra*, Chap. XI.).

ILLUSTRATIVE CASES.

(1)   *Cherry* v. *Heming*, 4 *Exch.* 637.

Rolfe, B.: "I am strongly inclined to think that the Statute of Frauds does not extend to deeds, because its requirements would be satisfied by the parties putting their mark to the writing. The object of the statute was to prevent matters of importance from resting on the frail testimony of memory alone. Before the Norman time, signature rendered the instrument authentic. Sealing was introduced because the people in general could not write. Then there arose a distinction between what was sealed and what was not sealed, and that went on until society became more advanced, when the Statute of Frauds ultimately said that certain instruments must be authenticated by signature. That means, that such instruments are not to rest on parol testimony only, and it was not intended to touch those which were already authenticated by a ceremony of a higher nature than a signature or mark."

Powell v. *Duff*, 3 *Campb.* 181.

If a party executes a bail bond before the condition is filled up, it is void.

Tupper v. *Foulkes*, 9 *C.B.*, *N.S.* 797.

A deed was executed by a son of the defendant, thus,—" John William Foulkes for Thomas Foulkes" (the defendant). In an action upon a covenant contained in the deed, the defendant pleaded *non est factum*. It was proved that, the deed being shown to the defendant executed as above, he was asked whether his son had authority to execute it for him, and whether he adopted his son's act, to which the defendant answered in the affirmative. Held, that this amounted to a re-delivery of the deed and sustained the issue.

(2)   *Bowker* v. *Burdekin*, 11 *M. & W.* 147.

It is not necessary that the delivery of a deed as an escrow should be by express words. If, from the circumstances attending the execution, it can be inferred that it was delivered not to take effect as a deed until a certain condition were performed, it will operate as a delivery as an escrow only.

(3)   *Morley* v. *Boothby*, 3 *Bing.* 111.

Best, C.J.: "The common law protected men against improvident contracts. If they bound themselves by deed, it was considered that they must have determined upon what they were about to do before they made so solemn an engagement; and therefore it was not necessary to the validity of the instrument that any consideration should appear on it."

(4)   *Rann* v. *Hughes*, 7 *T.R.* 350 n.

Skynner, C.B.: "The declaration states that the defendant being indebted as administratrix, promised to pay when requested. The being indebted is of itself a sufficient consideration to ground a promise, but the promise must be co-extensive with the consideration, unless some particular consideration of fact can be found here to warrant the extension of it against the defendant in her own capacity. If a person indebted in one right, in consideration of forbearance for a particular time, promise to pay in another right, this convenience will be a sufficient consideration to warrant an action against him or her in the latter right ; but here there is no such sufficient consideration."

(5)   *Eastwood* v. *Kenyon*, 11 *Ad. & E.* 438.

The defendant promised the plaintiff to pay A. B. a debt due from the plaintiff to A. B. Held, not within section 4 of the Statute of Frauds, for that contemplates only promises made to the person to whom another is liable.

Matson v. *Wharam*, 2 *T.R.* 80.

A tradesman was induced to send goods upon credit to another by a promise made in these words, "If you do not know him you know me, and I will see you paid." Held, void by the Statute of Frauds, not being in writing. There is no distinction between a promise to pay for goods furnished for the use of another, made before they are delivered and after.

Hodgson v. *Anderson*, 5 *D. & R.* 746.

A. was indebted to B., and C. was indebted in a large sum to A. An arrangement for the mutual convenience of the parties having been entered into, C.'s agents verbally promised B. to pay him the sum owed to him by A. Held, that C.'s promise was not to pay the debt of a third person, and, therefore, was not within the Statute of Frauds. Bayley, J.: "I think the case is not within the Statute of Frauds, because it was a promise by C. to pay his own debt with his own money, only paying it to B. instead of to A.; it was not a promise to pay with his own money the debt of a third person."

(6)   *Cook* v. *Baker*, 1 *Str.* 34.

The Statute of Frauds extends only to contracts in consideration of marriage, and not to contracts to marry.

(7)   *Wright* v. *Stavert*, 2 *Ell. & Ell.* 721.

By a parol agreement between plaintiff, a boarding-house keeper, and defendant, defendant agreed to pay plaintiff for the board and lodging of himself and man, at the boarding-house, with accommodation for his horse, £200 a-year, from a fixed day ; the agreement to be terminable by a quarter's notice on either side. Held, that though the agreement was unwritten, the action was maintainable ; for the contract was not one for any interest in or concerning land within the Statute of Frauds. Compton, J.: "The contract was merely that the defendant should become an inmate of the plaintiff's establishment; it was not intended to create the relation of landlord and tenant, or to give the defendant the exclusive occupation of any part of the house."

Hoby v. *Roebuck*, 7 *Taunt.* 157.

Where the lessee of a house agreed to pay the lessor annually during the residue of the lessee's term 10 *per cent.* on the cost of new buildings, if the lessor would erect them—Held, that this agreement was not required by the Statute of Frauds to be in writing.

Smith v. *Surman*, 9 *B. & C.* 568.

A. being the owner of trees growing on his land, verbally agreed with B., while they were standing, to sell him the timber *at so much per foot.* Held, that the contract was not a contract for the sale of an interest in or concerning land within the 4th section of the Statute of Frauds, but that it was a contract for the sale of goods within the 17th section. Littledale, J.: " Here the vendor was to cut the trees himself. His intention clearly was not to give the vendee any property in the trees, until they were cut and ceased to be part of the freehold."

Hallen v. *Runder*, 1 *C.M. & R.* 266.

Action brought for £40, the price of fixtures sold under a verbal agreement. Held, that the action was maintainable, and that this was not a sale of an interest in land under the 4th section of the Statute of Frauds, nor a sale of goods under the 17th section. [*Lee* v. *Risdon*, 7 *Taunt.* 188, previously decided that fixtures could not be treated as goods in an action for the price.]

Humble v. *Mitchell*, 11 *Ad. & E.* 205.

Shares in a joint-stock banking company are not goods, wares, or merchandise within the 17th section of the Statute of Frauds, nor an interest in land within the 4th section.

(8) *Wells* v. *Horton*, 12 *Moore*, 182.

A. being largely indebted to B., in consideration that B. would forbear to sue him during his lifetime, verbally promised B. that his (A.'s) executor should pay the amount of the debt to B. after his (A.'s) decease. Held, that the promise was binding on the executor, although it was not in writing; for the death of A. was a contingency which might occur within a year from the making of the contract.

Dobson v. *Collis*, 1 *H. & N.* 81.

A contract for service for more than a year, but subject to determination within the year on a given event—Held, to be within the 4th section of the Statute of Frauds.

(9) *Smith* v. *Neale*, 2 *C.B., N.S.* 67.

A written proposal, containing the terms of a proposed contract, signed by the defendant, and assented to by the plaintiff by word of mouth—Held, a sufficient agreement within the 4th section of the Statute of Frauds.

Ridgway v. *Wharton*, 6 *H.L.C.* 238.

If there is a signed paper in which there is an agreement to do something, leaving the subject-matter unexplained, but referring to another paper which contains the full particulars of the explanation, the two may be connected together so as to constitute a contract valid under the Statute of Frauds.

Williams v. *Lake*, 2 *Ell. & Ell.* 349.

Defendant wrote, signed, and handed to T. and O. the following document: "Sir, I beg to inform you that I shall see you paid the sum of £800 for the ensuing building, which you undertake to build for Messrs. T. and O. I am—Thomas Lake." He intended it to be handed over by T. and O. as a guaranty to J., who was then negotiating with T. and O. to erect for them the building referred to. T. and O., however, having agreed with the plaintiff instead of J. that plaintiff should erect the building, delivered the document to plaintiff. Defendant afterwards heard of and ratified this delivery. Plaintiff having erected the building sued defendant on the document as a guaranty. Held, that the document was not sufficient to satisfy the Statute of Frauds, inasmuch as the name of the person for whom the document was intended did not in any way appear upon the face of it, so that it did not contain the names of both the parties to the contract.

Goodman v. *Griffiths*, 1 *H. & N.* 574.

The defendant agreed to purchase of the plaintiff certain goods at a discount of 25 per cent. from a list of goods with prices annexed, and he signed an order for the goods referring to the list. The terms as to discount were not mentioned in the order. The defendant afterwards wrote to the plaintiff requesting him to send the invoice, which he did. The defendant wrote in reply a letter, signed by him, returning the invoice, and declining to take the goods. Held, first, that the order was not a sufficient memorandum of the bargain within the 17th section of the Statute of Frauds, as it did not contain the price; secondly, that the letter returning the invoice was not a sufficient admission of the contract as stated in the invoice so as to satisfy the statute.

Bailey v. *Sweeting*, 9 *C.B.*, *N.S.* 843.

A. upon one and the same occasion bought several parcels of goods of B., one parcel (consisting of chimney-glasses, amounting to £38 10s. 6d.) for ready money, the rest on credit. The goods were sent to A. at different times. The chimney-glasses being damaged in the carriage, A. declined to receive them. A. afterwards, in answer to an application by B. for payment of the whole of the goods, wrote to him as follows: "The only parcel of goods selected for ready-money was the chimney-glasses, amounting to £38 10s. 6d., which goods I have never received, and have long since declined to have, for reasons made known to you at the time." On action brought to recover the price of the whole of the goods, A. paid into court sufficient to cover all but the price of the chimney-glasses, and the jury found that the chimney-glasses were sold under a separate contract from the rest of the goods. Held, that the letter—inasmuch as it contained an admission of the bargain, and of all the substantial terms of it—was a sufficient note or memorandum of the contract to satisfy the 17th section of the Statute of Frauds, notwithstanding the subsequent attempted repudiation of liability.

(10)   *Caton* v. *Caton*, 36 *Law J.*, *Ch.* 886.

The mere circumstance of the name of a party being written by himself in the body of a memorandum of agreement will not of itself constitute a signature under the Statute of Frauds. It must be inserted in such a manner as to govern, or to have the effect of authenticating, the whole instrument.

Coldham v. *Showler*, 3 *C.B.* 312.

A. contracted to purchase of B. the goodwill, &c., of a public-house. On the back of the agreement was the following memorandum, written and signed by C., after the execution of the agreement by A. and B.: "I hereby undertake that my daughter, B., shall perform all the covenants and conditions named in the annexed agreement, and hold and consider myself responsible for her." In an action against C. to recover back the deposit, on the purchase going off by the default of the vendor: Held, that the agreement and indorsement might be looked at together for the purpose of making out a consideration for the defendant's promise. Tindal, C.J.: "It is perfectly indifferent whether the signature was on one side of the paper or the other; the whole being one transaction, the signature of the defendant applies to all that precedes it."

(11) *Maclean* v. *Dunn*, 1 *Moo. & P.* 761.

A broker made a contract in writing for the sale of goods, not being authorized by one of his principals at the time, which the latter afterwards assented to. Held, that the broker was an agent duly authorized to bind his principal under the Statute of Frauds at the time the contract was entered into.

Graham v. *Musson*, 5 *B.N.C.* 603.

A buyer of goods requested D., the agent of the seller, to write a note of the contract in the buyer's book ; D. did so, and signed the note with his own name. Held, that such note was not sufficient under the Statute of Frauds to bind the buyer.

Emmerson v. *Heelis*, 2 *Taunt.* 38.

An auctioneer is an agent lawfully authorized by the buyer to sign a contract for him, whether it be for a purchase of an interest in land, or of goods. His authority is given by the auctioneer bidding aloud.

Bird v. *Boulter*, 4 *B. & Ad.* 443.

In *assumpsit* by an auctioneer against a purchaser for goods sold, an entry in the sale-book by the auctioneer's clerk, who attended the sale, and as each lot was knocked down named the purchaser aloud, and on a sign of assent from him, made a note accordingly in the book, is a memorandum in writing by an agent lawfully authorized within section 17 of the Statute of Frauds. The clerk is not identified with the auctioneer (who sues). In the business which he performs, of entering the names, &c., he is impliedly authorized by the persons attending the sale to be their agent.

Rucker v. *Cammeyer*, 1 *Esp.* 105.

A broker who is employed to sell goods for any person, and who agrees for the sale of them, and gives to the purchaser and to his employer a sale note, is to be considered as agent for both parties, and such note is a sufficient note in writing within the Statute of Frauds.

CHAPTER III.

INTERPRETATION OF CONTRACTS.

THE terms of a contract are to be understood in their plain, ordinary, and popular sense, unless, by the usage of trade or otherwise, they have, in respect of the subject-matter, acquired a peculiar sense. Technical words of law, however, are to have their legal effect, unless it is clear that the parties used them in a sense different from their legal meaning. Ordinary grammatical construction is to be followed, unless repugnant from the general context. _{General construction. (1)}

One part must be so construed with another that the whole may, if possible, stand; but a particular clause or sentence, totally repugnant to the general intent of the contract, is void and must be rejected.

When the figures and the words in a written contract disagree, the courts will give force to the words at length in preference to the figures.

The word "month" is construed to mean a calendar month, unless it appears from the general context that a lunar month was intended. And, when time is to be computed from a particular day, such day is to be excluded from the computation.

Admissibility of Oral Evidence in Written Contracts.

The general rule is, that oral evidence shall not be given to add to, to subtract from, or alter, or vary any description of written contract. _{General rule.}

Evidence of surrounding circumstances.
(2)

Evidence may be given, however, for the purpose of identifying the subject-matter of the contract; and evidence may be given with regard to the persons, facts, and circumstances which are the subjects of the allusions and statements in the writing, so that the meaning of the words used, and their application to the things described, may be arrived at.

Ambiguity.
(3)

From the admission of evidence as to surrounding circumstances, an ambiguity, not apparent upon the face of the contract (therefore called a latent ambiguity), may arise as to the application of the words used to the object to which they refer. And since a latent ambiguity is introduced solely by the admission of extrinsic evidence, it may be rebutted and removed by the production of further evidence of the identity of the objects described. But when there is a patent ambiguity, *i.e.*, an ambiguity evident on the face of the document, as, for example, where a blank is left in a deed, or an important clause or word has been omitted by mistake, the defect cannot be cured by extrinsic evidence.

If, however, an important word has been omitted by mistake, and it clearly appears from the context and the nature of the transaction, and the surrounding circumstances, what the parties intended, the courts will construe the instrument as though the word had been inserted.

Evidence of custom and usage.
(4)

Oral evidence of custom and usage is always admissible to elucidate the real meaning of the parties, but not to contradict the express provisions of the contract.

Where, by the usage of trade or by custom, a word has acquired, in respect of the subject-matter of the contract, a peculiar meaning different from the ordinary popular meaning, evidence is admissible to show that the parties used the word in its peculiar or trade acceptation, and not in its ordinary popular sense.

Terms of art and specifications of weight, measure, &c., are controlled by local custom, unless a definite meaning has been expressly attached to the terms in question by statute.

And to vary the meaning of plain words, clear, cogent, and irresistible evidence of the custom must be given.

When a contract is not required by law to be in writing, oral evidence is admissible in aid of incomplete written evidence. *Evidence where writing does not form a complete contract.* (5)

Such evidence does not alter, or add to, a written contract, for no contract exists independently of it. And oral evidence is admissible to show that a writing, although apparently forming a complete contract, does not contain, and was not intended to contain, the whole agreement between the parties.

And where a contract is required by law to be in writing, and there is only a proposal in writing, evidence may be given that the proposal was verbally accepted; but evidence may not be given of what passed at the time of the proposal to vary the contract.

A loose and incomplete memorandum of sale will not exclude oral evidence of a warranty, although the memorandum is silent as to the fact of such warranty.

An agreement upon a distinct matter may be shown to have been made by word of mouth, either previously to, or concurrently with, the written contract. *Concurrent verbal contract.* (6)

If two parties sign a memorandum of contract, upon the strength of a clear oral agreement that the writing is not to be binding, until the happening of a certain event, and the event has not happened, evidence may be given of the verbal agreement, and the written contract cannot be enforced. *Evidence of conditional assent.* (7)

A written contract may, before breach of it, be added to, subtracted from, or qualified by, a subsequent verbal contract, which may be proved, partly by the written agreement, and partly by the subsequent verbal terms engrafted upon it. *Subsequent verbal contract varying written contract.* (8)

But this is not the case where the new contract, thus

sought to be established in the place of the original written contract, is a contract of such a nature that it is required by law to be in writing; for it cannot be proved partly by written and partly by oral evidence; and the original written contract will therefore remain in force. In other words, a contract required by the Statute of Frauds to be in writing, cannot be varied by a subsequent parol agreement.

Subsequent verbal contract annulling written contract. (9)
Where a contract has been reduced to writing, whether required by law to be in writing or not, it may be waived or annulled, before breach of it, by a subsequent verbal agreement between the parties.

Specific performance with variation. (10)
In equity a defendant may prove a parol variation to a written contract where he is resisting specific performance of the contract; and a plaintiff may also make use of a parol variation where there has been such a part performance as would enable the court to decree specific performance in the case of an original independent agreement, or where the omission has occurred by fraud, or, in cases not within the Statute of Frauds, by clear mistake.

Court to decide whether writings amount to contract. (11)
Where a contract is evidenced by letters or writings, it is for the court to interpret them, and determine whether they do or do not amount to a concluded contract.

Estoppel by deed. (12)
The rule that a party is estopped from contradicting what he has affirmed by deed does not extend to strangers to the deed. A party to a deed is not estopped in an action by another party to it, not founded on the deed, from disputing the truth of certain facts recited and set forth in the deed. Where a recital in a deed is intended to be a statement which all the parties have agreed to be true, it is an estoppel upon all. But where it is intended to be the statement of one party only, that party only is estopped. And the intention must be gathered from the construction of the whole instrument.

Estoppel by parol. (13)
Although a party to a written contract, not under seal, may have made express admissions in the contract, he may

yet show that such admissions were mistaken or untrue; and he is not estopped from contradicting them, unless another person has been induced by them to alter his position; and the same is the case with regard to representations by words or conduct.

ILLUSTRATIVE CASES.

(1) *Elliott* v. *Turner,* 2 *C.B.* 446.

In covenant on an indenture by which B. was licensed to make and sell buttons according to A.'s patent, the issue was whether certain buttons made by B. were made under the licence. The specification described the invention to consist in the application to the covering of buttons of figured woven fabrics, "wherein the ground, or the face thereof, is produced by a warp of *soft or organzine silk,* such as is used in weaving satin." The jury asked how they were to understand the word "or" in the specification; whether it was used disjunctively, or, whether "organzine" was the construction of the word "soft." The judge told them that, in his opinion, unless the silk were *organzine* it was not within the patent. Held, upon a bill of exceptions, that this direction was erroneous; for the judge should not have told the jury that, in his opinion, soft and organzine silk were absolutely the same, but that the words were *capable* of being so construed, if the jury were satisfied that at the date of the patent there was only one description of soft silk—and that organzine, used in satin weavings; but otherwise, that the proper and ordinary sense of the word "or" was to be adopted, and the patent held to apply to every species of soft silk, as well as to organzine silk.

Solly v. *Forbes,* 4 *Moore,* 448.

In the construction of a deed, regard must be had to all its parts, and general words are to be restrained by a particular recital contained therein; and if a deed operate two ways, the one consistent with the intent of the parties, and the other repugnant to it, the court will put such a construction on it as to give effect to such intent, which is to be derived from the whole of the instrument.

Sanderson v. *Piper,* 7 *Sc.* 408.

A bill of exchange, by which the drawer required the drawee to pay "two hundred pounds, value received," purported by the figures at the top to be a bill of £245, to which latter sum the stamp was applicable. Held, that parol evidence was not admissible to show that the bill was intended to be drawn for the larger amount.

Webb v. *Fairmaner,* 3 *M. & W.* 473.

Goods were sold on the 5th of October, to be paid for in two months. Held, that an action for the price could not be commenced until after the expiration of the 5th of December.

(2) *Shore* v. *Wilson,* 9 *Cl. & Fin.* 355.

Lady Hewley left certain charities in trust for "such poor and Godly preachers of Christ's holy gospel" as the trustees for the time being should think fit. Held, that for the purpose of determining the objects of Lady Hewley's charity under the terms used, extrinsic evidence was admissible to show the existence of a religious party by whom such phraseology was used, and that she was a member of that party.

(3) *Gord* v. *Needs*, 3 M. & W. 129.

A testator devised a house to George Gord, the son of John Gord; another to George Gord, the son of George Gord; and a third to "*George Gord, the son of Gord.*" Held, that evidence of the testator's declarations was admissible to show that he intended that the house devised to "George Gord, the son of Gord," should go to George Gord, the son of George Gord.

Bayliss v. *Att.-Gen.*, 2 Atk. 239.

A testator left £200 to the Ward of Bread Street, London, to be applied "according to Mr. ———'s will." Parol evidence to explain whom the testator intended by the blank, not allowed.

Coles v. *Hulme*, 8 B. & C. 568.

The condition of a bond recited that A. was indebted to B. in various sums of money, which were all stated in pounds sterling, and money of a smaller denomination, and that the bond was given to secure payment of those sums. In the obligatory part of the bond, the word *pounds* was omitted; it merely stated that the obligor became bound in 7700, without stating the description of money. Held, that the word *pounds* might be supplied.

(4) *Smith* v. *Wilson*, 3 B. & C. 728.

In a lease of a rabbit warren, the lessee covenanted that at the expiration of the term he would leave on the warren ten thousand rabbits, the lessor paying for them £60 per thousand. Held, in an action by the lessee against the lessor for refusing to pay for the rabbits left at the end of the term, that parol evidence was admissible to show that, by the custom of the country where the lease was made, the word *thousand* applied to *rabbits* denoted *twelve hundred*.

Spicer v. *Cooper*, 1 Q.B. 424.

Declaration stated that defendant had sold plaintiff eighteen pockets of Kent hops at the price of £5 per cwt., but failed to deliver according to promise. It appeared in evidence that the contract was in writing, as follows: "Sold, 18 pockets Kent hops, at 100s.," and that a pocket contained more than a cwt. Held, that evidence might be given to show that by usage of the hop trade a contract so worded was understood to mean £5 per cwt.

(5) *Knapp* v. *Harden*, 1 Gale, 47.

A letter signed by both parties, specifying the prices to be charged for some work to be done, Held, not in itself a complete contract, and parol evidence, therefore, admissible of a contemporaneous agreement as to the period of payment.

Hotson v. *Browne*, 9 C.B., N.S. 442.

The plaintiff, the publisher and proprietor of "Hotson's Local Time Tables," received from one M. (who was a canvasser for orders on commission) the following memorandum: "Insert my advertisements for one year in Hotson's Local Time Tables, the Great Northern, and [six other railways —naming them], space to be two squares in back page; and charge for insertion to be 10s. per month each book. (Signed) B. Browne & Co."

The signature and the words "10s. per month each book" were in the handwriting of the defendant. The defence being that the defendant was induced to sign the contract by the representation of M. at the time that the charge was to be 10s. per month for the seven books, it was proposed at the trial to ask the defendant, who was called as a witness, what representation M. had made to him when he obtained the order from him, but the judge declined to allow the evidence to be put, inasmuch as it was an attempt to vary by parol a written contract. Held, that the evidence was properly rejected.

Allen v. *Pink*, 4 M. & W. 140.

The defendant gave a verbal warranty of a horse, which the plaintiff thereupon bought and paid for, and the defendant then gave him the following memorandum: "Bought of G. P., a horse for the sum of £7 2s. 6d. G. P." Held, that parol evidence might, notwithstanding, be given of the warranty.

(6) *Lindley* v. *Lacey*, 17 C.B., N.S. 578.

Upon a negotiation between the plaintiff and the defendant for the sale of the fixtures, furniture, and goodwill of a business (the agreement for which was afterwards reduced into writing), a distinct and separate promise was made by the defendant, in consideration of the plaintiff's signing the agreement, that he, the defendant, would settle an action then pending against the plaintiff at the suit of one C. Held, that evidence of this oral agreement was admissible, notwithstanding that the written agreement contained an authorization to the defendant to settle C.'s action out of the purchase-money.

(7) *Pym* v. *Campbell*, 6 Ell. & Bl. 370.

Action on an agreement for sale. On the trial, plaintiff produced an agreement signed by defendant. Defendant gave evidence that plaintiff and defendant having negotiated as to the purchase, it was arranged that they should draw up and sign a memorandum of an agreement of sale, but that it should not be a bargain until A., a third person, on being consulted, approved. A. did not approve. The judge directed the jury to find for defendant, if satisfied that it was arranged that the writing should be no agreement until A. approved.

(8) *Goss* v. *Lord Nugent*, 2 N. & M. 28.

A purchaser in his written contract stipulated for a good title; he subsequently, by verbal agreement, waived the stipulation for a good title. Held, that he could not be compelled to complete the purchase upon a defective title. Denman, C.J.: "If the present contract had not been subject to the control of any Act of Parliament, it would have been competent for the parties, by word of mouth, to dispense with requiring a good title to be made to the lot in question, and that the action might be maintained. But the object of the Statute of Frauds was to exclude all oral evidence as to contracts for the sale of land, and that any contract which is sought to be enforced must be proved by writing only. But in the present case the written contract is not that which is sought to be enforced; it is a new contract which the parties have entered into, and that new contract is to be proved, partly by the former written agreement, and partly by the new verbal agreement."

(9) *Ibid*, p. 34.

Denman, C.J.: "As there is no clause in the Statute of Frauds which requires the dissolution of such contracts to be in writing, it seems that a written contract concerning the sale of lands may still be waived and abandoned by a new agreement not in writing, so as to prevent either party from recovering on the contract which was in writing."

(10)   See *Woollam* v. *Hearne*, 2 W. & T.L.C. in Equity.

(11)   *Cheveley* v. *Fuller*, 13 C.B. 122.

A. wrote to B. on the 15th of July, proposing a partnership, saying : "As to the time, I certainly should wish it by the end of August." To this B. answered on the 16th : "I am ready to accede to your proposal. With regard to time, if you could possibly defer my coming until the second week in September, it would suit much best." On the 19th A. again wrote: "The time is very important, and ought not to be later than August." Held, that these letters did not constitute an absolute agreement ; and the judge of the county court, having *left it to the jury to determine* whether B.'s letter of the 16th of July was a positive acceptance of A.'s proposal of the 15th, held, a misdirection.

(12)   *Carpenter* v. *Buller*, 8 M. & W. 209.

Where a distinct statement of a particular fact is made in the recital of a bond or other instrument under seal, and a contract is made with reference to that recital, it is not, as between the parties to the instrument, and in an action upon it, competent to the party bound to deny the recital. But a party to an instrument is not estopped, in an action by another party not founded on the deed, and wholly collateral to it, from disputing the facts so admitted ; but evidence of the circumstances under which such admission was made is receivable to show that the admission was inconsiderately made, and is not entitled to weight as proof of the fact which it is used to establish.

Wiles v. *Woodward*, 5 Exch. 557.

The plaintiff and the defendant had been in partnership together as paper manufacturers and iron merchants. The partnership was dissolved by a deed, which recited that it had been agreed that the business of a paper manufacturer should belong exclusively to the defendant, and the business of an iron merchant to the plaintiff, but that the plaintiff should receive out of the stock, paper to the value of £898, which should remain in the paper mill for a year at his option. The deed also recited that in performance of that arrangement *paper to the value of £898 had been delivered to the plaintiff*, and the same was then in the mill, as the plaintiff acknowledged. In fact, no paper whatever was set apart or delivered to the plaintiff. Held, that the parties were estopped by the deed from saying that no such delivery had taken place.

(13)   *Heane* v. *Rogers*, 9 B. & C. 586.

In an action of trover, brought by a person against whom a commission of bankruptcy had issued, against his assignees to recover goods which they had, as such assignees, sold, it appeared that the bankrupt had assisted the assignees by giving directions as to the sale of the goods. Held, that the interference of the plaintiff in the sale of his goods was referable to an intention on his part to take care of the property, and see that the most was made of it, and that it did not amount to an assent to the sale, and that he was not thereby estopped from bringing an action against his assignees.

CHAPTER IV.

CAPACITY OF PARTIES.

(i) *Incapacity from Infancy.*

AT common law the contracts of persons below the age of twenty-one are not binding upon them, but are, with certain exceptions, voidable at their option, either during infancy or after attaining their majority. *Contracts by infants.*

Before the Infants Relief Act, 1874, an action might be brought upon a ratification or acknowledgment (required by 9 Geo. IV. c. 14, s. 15, to be in writing and signed) made after full age of any debt or simple contract made during infancy. *Ratification.*

By the Infants Relief Act (37 & 38 Vict. c. 62) loans of money to infants, contracts for the sale to them of goods, other than necessaries, and accounts stated with them, are absolutely void; and no action can be brought on a ratification of any contract made during infancy. *Infants Relief Act, 1874.*

Infants not residing under the parental roof, and not provided by their parents with the necessaries of life, may bind themselves by contract to pay for their necessary food, clothing, physic, and education. An infant may be made liable for the rent of a fit and proper lodging, and for necessaries furnished to his wife and children residing with him. The infant cannot bind himself to the payment of any particular sum for necessaries. This must be left to the decision of the jury. The question as to what things *Valid contracts by infants.* (1)

are and what things are not necessaries is a mixed question of law and fact, to be determined by the circumstances of each case.

If money is laid out by a third person in the purchase of necessaries for an infant, such money may be recovered from the latter. But money lent to an infant for the purchase of necessaries cannot be recovered. Nor can an action be brought upon a bill of exchange accepted by an infant, although it was accepted on account of necessaries furnished to him.

Certain contracts by infants which are now voidable only. (2)
There are certain cases in which contracts made by infants might be adopted or confirmed without writing under Lord Tenterden's Act (9 Geo. IV. c. 14), and to these cases the Infants Relief Act does not apply. Thus, a marriage settlement made by an infant is sufficiently confirmed by tacit acquiescence after full age. An infant partner is bound by the terms of the partnership, unless he repudiates on arriving at majority; and an infant shareholder, not repudiating at full age, is liable for calls.

An infant purchaser of real estate, who has taken possession, becomes liable to all the obligations attached to the estate, unless during infancy, or on arriving at full age, he elects to avoid the purchase. And an infant lessee, continuing to occupy after full age, is liable for arrears of rent contracted during infancy.

Torts connected with contract. (3)
An infant is liable for his torts; but he cannot be sued for a wrong when the cause of action is in substance *ex contractu*. An action of deceit will not lie upon an assertion by a minor that he is of full age. But a minor, representing himself to be of full age, is liable in equity to the extent of any advantage he has gained thereby.

Infants' rights ex contractu. (4)
An adult party, who has contracted with an infant, is liable to be sued by the infant, although the latter has incurred no corresponding legal obligation, for infancy is a personal privilege of which no one can take advantage but the infant himself.

An infant cannot, however, obtain specific performance against an adult contracting party. And although an infant cannot be compelled to complete a contract for the purchase of an estate, yet, if he has paid a deposit under such a contract, he cannot recover it back merely because he declines to complete the purchase.

(ii) *Incapacity from Coverture.*

At common law a married woman is incapable of binding herself by contract. A married woman is answerable for torts committed by her during coverture, and may be sued for them jointly with her husband, or separately, if she survives him; but she cannot be sued for a fraud when it is directly connected with a contract with her, as, for example, when she has induced a contract by the false representation that she is a *feme sole*. Contracts by married women. (5)

Although a contract made by a married woman is void as far as she is concerned, her husband may enforce it if he thinks fit, even though it was made without his knowledge. And if the wife die before the husband has reduced any *chose in action* into possession, his right remains, and he may enforce it on taking out letters of administration to his wife's estate. Rights of husband on wife's contracts. (6)

A wife may recover in an action on a contract brought in her own name, unless her coverture is specially pleaded. Rights of wife on her own contract. (7)

If a contract has been made either by a wife alone, or by her jointly with her husband, and if the husband has not sued upon the contract in his lifetime, the wife, surviving, may sue upon it, and take the benefit of it.

By the 33 & 34 Vict. c. 93, a married woman may now maintain an action in her own name for the recovery of any wages or earnings acquired by her in any employment or trade in which she is engaged, or which she carries on separately from her husband, or for any money acquired Married Woman's Property Act.

through the exercise of any literary, artistic, or scientific skill; and such money, earnings, &c., are to be deemed to be property settled to her separate use, independent of any husband to whom she may be married.

Liability of husband upon wife's contracts. (8)
Where a wife has entered into a contract with the express or implied sanction of her husband, he becomes bound just as by the act of any other authorized agent.

The wife is not her husband's agent in respect of the management of his estate and business, unless he has entrusted her with the general management of it. But she is presumed to be his general agent in all matters connected with the domestic economy of the house and family.

Implied agency. (9)
A wife has therefore an implied authority to pledge her husband's credit for such things as fall within the domestic department ordinarily entrusted to the wife's management, and are necessary and suitable to the style in which her husband chooses to live; or if she carries on a separate trade with the concurrence of her husband, for goods suitable for such trade.

This presumption may, however, be rebutted by proof that the husband had furnished her with ready money to pay for what was necessary, and had forbidden her to pledge his credit.

If a husband, living under the same roof as his wife, sees her wearing costly dresses or ornaments, and fails to manifest his disapprobation, and gives no intimation to the tradesmen who supply them of his intention not to pay for them, he will be assumed to assent to his wife's proceedings.

Those who furnish a wife with necessaries, after a separation by reason of the wife's adultery, have no claim against the husband in respect thereof, whether they had notice of the adultery or not.

If the husband has deserted the wife and left her destitute, without being able to prove that she has forfeited her marriage rights by adultery, or if the wife has been compelled to leave her husband by reason of his cruelty, or from any other justifiable cause, the husband's liability for necessaries furnished to her still continues.

Where husband and wife separate by mutual consent, the husband remains responsible for necessaries furnished to her, unless she has competent provision from him, or from funds at her own disposal.

The death of the husband does not render the wife responsible for contracts made by her during coverture; nor is she responsible on any promise made after the death of her husband to pay for things furnished to her during his lifetime, as such a promise is without consideration.

Where a wife has a separate income over which her husband has no control, and contracts are entered into by her with reference to, and upon the credit of, that property, effect will be given to such contracts, not as personal liabilities, but by laying hold of the separate property in the hands of the trustees. *Liability of wife's separate estate.* **(10)**

If a man has permitted a woman to whom he was not married to use his name and pass for his wife, and in that character to contract debts, he is liable for those debts, whether the tradesman who furnished the goods knew or did not know that she was not his wife. *Reputed marriage.* **(11)**

By the Married Woman's Property Act (33 & 34 Vict. c. 93) a wife may be sued alone for debts contracted by her before marriage, and any property belonging to her for her separate use is liable to satisfy such debts. But by the Amending Act (37 & 38 Vict. c. 50) a husband and wife, married after July 30th, 1874, may be jointly sued for the wife's ante-nuptial debts, and the husband is liable to the extent of the assets acquired by him in right of his wife. *Husband's liability on wife's ante-nuptial contracts.*

A *feme covert* trader may, by the custom of London, be sued in the courts of the City of London upon contracts made by her in the course of trade. *Custom of City of London.* **(12)**

By the common law the wife of the King of England may sue and be sued as a *feme sole*. *Queen Consort.* **(13)**

Wife of person civilly dead. (14) The wife of a person who is outlawed or convicted of felony, and not lawfully at large under any licence, may sue and be sued as a *feme sole*.

(iii) *Incapacity from Lunacy.*

Simple contract. (15) If a party to a contract was, at the time he entered into the engagement, a lunatic, or of unsound mind, and any imposition appears to have been practised upon him, the contract will be void; but not if the contract is fair and honest, and bears no sign of the infirmity of mind of the party sought to be charged.

Contract by deed. (16) A lunatic will not be bound by any deed entered into by him, unless it be shown to have been entered into during a lucid interval; and the nature of the contract may be *primâ facie* evidence of its having been entered into during a lucid interval.

(iv) *Incapacity from Drunkenness.*

Contract by drunken man. (17) A party who makes a contract in such a state of drunkenness as not to know what he is doing, cannot be compelled to perform the contract by the other party who knew him to be in that state. But a contract made by a man in a state of drunkenness is voidable only, and not void. And if the drunken man chooses to ratify it after he becomes sober, it will be binding upon him.

(v) *Incapacity of Aliens.*

Alien friends. By the 33 Vict. c. 14, real and personal property of every description may be held and disposed of by an alien friend in the same manner, in all respects, as by a natural born

British subject. But nothing in the act is to qualify an alien to be the owner of a British ship.

All alien enemies, and all British subjects, and subjects of neutral nations, domiciled in an enemy's country, or engaged in the service of a hostile power, are incapacitated from contracting with British subjects, unless they have obtained a licence to trade. Alien enemies. (18)

(vi) *Incapacity from Outlawry, &c.*

Where a person has been outlawed he is civilly dead, and is incapable of enforcing any contract he may have entered into; but he is liable to be sued thereon. Outlaws. (19)

When a person has been convicted of treason or felony, and has been sentenced to death or penal servitude, he is precluded by the 33 & 34 Vict. c. 23 from alienating any property, or making any contract. This disability ceases when the term of penal servitude is accomplished, or when the convict has obtained a pardon. And the convict may lawfully enter into contracts when he is lawfully at large under a licence. Convicts.

ILLUSTRATIVE CASES.

(1) *Kirton* v. *Elliot*, 2 *Bulstr.* 69.

In an action of debt against an infant for rent in arrear, Held that the infant was liable. Dodderidge, J.: "If a greater rent be reserved than the land is worth, then, peradventure, the infant shall not be charged with it."

Chapple v. *Cooper*, 13 *M. & W.* 252.

An infant widow is bound by her contract for the furnishing of the funeral of her husband, who has left no property to be administered.

Brooker v. *Scott*, 11 *M. & W.* 67.

Dinners, confectionery, or fruit supplied to an infant, an undergraduate in the University, having lodgings in the town, are not *primâ facie* necessaries; and in an action brought against him for such articles, no special circumstances being shown, the court directed a non-suit.

Earle v. *Peale*, 1 *Salk.* 387.

Parker, C.J. : "An infant may buy necessaries, but he cannot borrow money to buy them, for he may misapply the money, and therefore the law will not trust him, but at the peril of the lender, who must lay it out for him, or see it laid out, and then 'tis his providing, and his laying out so much money for the infant."

(2)   *Birkenhead, &c., Railway Co.* v. *Pilcher*, 5 *Exch.* 121.

Where nothing but the simple fact of infancy was pleaded to an action for railway calls against a purchaser who had been registered, and had thereby become a shareholder in a permanent character : Held, that such plea was insufficient.

(3)   *Jennings* v. *Rundall*, 8 *T.R.* 335.

The plaintiff declared that, at the defendant's request, he had delivered a mare to the defendant, to be moderately ridden, and that the defendant wrongfully and injuriously rode the mare, so that she was damaged. Held, that the defendant might plead his infancy in bar, the action being founded on contract.

And see *Stikeman* v. *Dawson*, 1 *De G. & Sm.* 90.

(4)   *Farnham* v. *Atkins*, 1 *Sid.* 446.

Action by a female infant against another woman. The latter covenanted to teach the infant to sing and to dance, and to find her in food and lodging, and the infant covenanted to perform domestic services in return. The infant assigned as a breach, that her mistress did not find her in food. Judgment was given for the plaintiff; and the court held, that although the infant was not bound by her agreement, yet the other was bound towards the infant by hers.

Wilson v. *Kearse*, *Peake's Ad. Cas.* 196.

The plaintiff, an infant, contracted with the defendant to purchase of him the goodwill and stock of a public-house, and made a deposit of £20. Being afterwards called on to complete the contract, he refused. Held, that the plaintiff could not recover the £20.

(5)   *Liverpool Adelphi Loan Association* v. *Fairhurst and Wife*, 9 *Exch.* 422.

An action will not lie against a husband and wife for a false and fraudulent representation by the wife to the plaintiff that she was *sole* and unmarried at the time of her signing a promissory note as surety to him for a third person, whereby the plaintiff was induced to advance a sum of money to that third person ; for this is a tort directly connected with the contract of the wife.

(6)   *Millard* v. *Harvey*, 34 *Beav.* 237.

A wife, unknown to her husband, requested her father to sell a field, to be paid for out of her savings. The father at first refused, but he received the money, and shortly afterwards put the husband into possession. For ten years the money was retained by the father without payment of interest, and the field by the husband without payment of rent. The father then attempted to eject the husband, who, being made acquainted with the circumstances, insisted on retaining the field. Held, that the father was bound to convey it to the husband.

Partington v. *Att.-Gen.*, *L.R.* 4 *H.L.* 100.

If a married woman becomes entitled to the property of a deceased relation situated in England, and her husband takes no steps to reduce her rights into possession, and she dies, and her husband does not take out administration to her, and he dies, the child of these married persons must take out two administrations—one to his father, the other to his mother.

(7) *Dalton* v. *Midland Counties Railway Co.*, 13 *C.B.* 474.

The plaintiff, a married woman, bought, with moneys earned by her partly before and partly during coverture, railway stock in her own name, and was registered as the proprietor thereof. Held, that she might (subject to being met by a plea in abatement) maintain an action for the same in her own name.

Sherrington v. *Yates*, 12 *M. & W.* 885.

The assignees of a bankrupt cannot maintain an action in their own names alone on a promissory note made to the wife of the bankrupt before her marriage.

(8) *McGeorge* v. *Egan*, 7 *Sc.* 112.

In an action for a school bill, it appeared that the defendant's wife took the child (her niece) to the plaintiff's school, and that the defendant had visited her while there; but there was no evidence of any communication between the plaintiff and the parent of the child: Held, that the fact of the defendant having paid for articles of domestic use ordered by his wife was evidence for the jury of her authority to charge him with the education of the child.

Petty v. *Anderson*, 10 *Moore*, 577.

The defendant, a baker and confectioner, was discharged under the Insolvent Debtors Act; and the business, during his absence, and after his return from imprisonment, was carried on by his wife, who purchased goods in her own name. The wife was acknowledged by the landlord as tenant of the house in which they lived, and was rated in the books of the parish as the occupier. The defendant was aware of, and assented to, the dealings of his wife, and, being with her, partook of the profits of the trade. Held, that he was liable in an action for the price of the goods, notwithstanding that the invoices were made out in the name of the wife alone, she being his agent.

(9) *Phillipson* v. *Hayter*, *L.R.* 6 *C.P.* 38.

The plaintiff sued the defendant, a clerk with an income of £400 a-year, for £20, the price of goods sold to the wife. The goods consisted of costly trinkets, none of which were seen by the husband until after his wife's elopement with another man. Held, that the plaintiff could not recover.

Jolly v. *Rees*, 15 *C.B.*, *N.S.* 643.

In 1851 the defendant forbade his wife to incur debts for clothing for herself and two daughters, telling her that he would allow her £50 a-year for that purpose, in addition to £65 per annum which was settled upon her to her separate use. In 1860 and 1861 the wife contracted a debt with the plaintiff for clothing. The plaintiff had no notice of the revocation of the wife's authority. In an action against the husband to recover the price of these goods, the jury found that the articles supplied were necessaries suitable to the estate and degree of the parties ; that the wife's authority to pledge her husband's credit was revoked in 1851 ; that if the £115 per annum had been regularly paid to the wife, and applied by her to the clothing of herself and daughters, it would have been sufficient ; that (beyond the £65) it was not regularly paid ; and that so much of it as was paid was insufficient. Held, that the plaintiff was not entitled to recover.

Cooper v. *Lloyd*, 6 *C.B.*, *N.S.* 643.

The adultery of a wife, living apart from her husband, destroys her implied agency to bind him by her contracts for necessaries. And in such a case the wife herself is an admissible witness to prove the adultery.

Harris v. *Morris*, 4 *Esp.* 41.

A husband, who suspected his wife of adultery, but could produce no proof of it, turned her out of doors. He then advertised in the newspapers and gave particular notice to individuals that his wife had no authority to pledge his credit. Held, that this did not exempt him from a demand for necessaries furnished to her while subsequently living apart from him.

Dixon v. *Hurrell*, 8 *C. & P.* 717.

If a husband and wife separate by mutual consent, the husband is liable for reasonable maintenance for his wife, unless she has a competent provision either from the husband or from some fund of her own ; and if she has such provision, it lies on the husband to show it. A mere notice by the husband that he will not pay for goods supplied to his wife, will not avail him if, under the circumstances of the separation, he is liable; but if the husband and wife both deal with the same tradesman, and the latter agrees with the husband not to charge him for goods to be supplied to the wife, the tradesman cannot, after that, charge the husband for such goods.

Meyer v. *Haworth*, 8 *Ad. & E.* 467.

Coverture being pleaded to a declaration in assumpsit for goods sold and delivered, plaintiff replied that defendant was, at the time of the contract, separated from her husband, and living in open adultery; that plaintiff did not know of the marriage or adultery, and that defendant, after her husband's death, and before action brought, in consideration of the premises, promised to pay. Held, that no consideration appeared for the promise in the replication ; and that the plaintiff could not recover.

(10) See *Owens* v. *Dickenson*, 1 *Cr. & Ph.* 48.

(11) *Watson* v. *Threlkeld*, 2 *Esp.* 637.

Assumpsit for goods sold and delivered. The plaintiff proved the delivery of the goods to a woman who passed for the defendant's wife, at the defendant's lodgings. The defendant proved that in fact this woman was not his wife, though she lived with him as such, and that that circumstance was known to the plaintiff when the goods were furnished. Held, that the defendant was liable. Lord Kenyon : "What I have said must not be taken to apply to the case of a common strumpet, who may assume the name of a person without his authority ; it must be where the man permits the woman to assume his name, where she lives in his house, and is part of his family."

(12) *Beard* v. *Webb*, 2 *Bos. & P.* 93.

A *feme covert* sole trader in the City of London held not liable to be sued as such in the courts at Westminster, though she might in the City courts.

(13) See *Co. Litt.* 133 a.

(14) *Carrol* v. *Blencow*, 4 *Esp.* 27.

A married woman, whose husband has been transported for seven years, may maintain an action as a *feme sole*, on the ground of the husband having abjured the realm, even though the term of his transportation has expired.

(15) *Manby* v. *Bewicke*, 3 *K. & J.* 342.

Held, that a suit could not be maintained under the 26th section of the Statute of Limitations (3 & 4 Will. IV. c. 27) to set aside a compromise of an action to recover large estates, made eighty years before, upon the ground that the compromise was a fraud upon the plaintiff in the action, and that he was a man of such dull intellect, that, though cognisant of all the facts, it was necessarily a concealed fraud as to him. Any man, who is not a lunatic, must be considered competent to agree to a compromise of litigation in which he is engaged, the circumstances, under which the compromise was made, not being such as to afford evidence of fraud.

(16) *Sergeson* v. *Sealey*, 2 *Atk.* 411.

In 1724 A. made a purchase of real estate, with the approbation of his eldest son, and the other members of his family. In 1726, on inquisition, he was found a lunatic with a retrospect of eight years. The purchase appearing to have been a reasonable act, the court refused to set it aside, and change the disposition of the sum of money so expended.

(17) *Matthews* v. *Baxter*, *L.R.* 8 *Exch.* 132.

The defendant entered into a contract when he was too drunk to know what he was about; afterwards, when he became sober, and capable of transacting business, he confirmed the contract. Held, that he was liable upon it.

(18) *O'Mealey* v. *Wilson*, 1 *Campb.* 481.

If a British subject voluntarily resides in an enemy's country, and carries on commerce there, he is disqualified as an alien enemy to sue in our courts of justice, although naturalized by a neutral state, and recognised as a citizen of that state both by its diplomatic agents and by the enemy's government. And *semble*, that if a neutral voluntarily resides and carries on commerce in an enemy's country, he is an alien enemy to all civil purposes.

(19) *Ramsay* v. *Macdonald, Foster* 61.

While M. lay under sentence of death, R., a creditor of his, obtained leave of the Lord Chief Justice at his chambers to charge M., in custody of the sheriff, in an action for a considerable sum of money. "The person of a man under an attainder is not absolutely at the disposal of the Crown. It is so for the ends of public justice, and for no other purpose. The King may order execution to be done upon him according to law, notwithstanding he may be charged in custody at the suit of creditors. But till execution is done, his creditors have an interest in his person for securing their debts."

CHAPTER V.

AGENCY.

Particular agency. (1)
AN agent, expressly employed to do some particular act, cannot bind the principal who employs him, if he exceeds the authority with which he is clothed. But he has an implied authority to do all such incidental acts as are usual and necessary.

General agency. (2)
General agents may be such by express authority, or by implication of the law. Any person who accredits another by employing him in a particular course of dealing, is bound by what has been done by such agent in the course of his usual employment. The liability of the principal is measured by the nature and extent of the previous employment of the agent.

Revocation.
The authority of an agent may be revoked at any time, but in order to determine the responsibility of the principal to third parties who have dealt with the agent, the revocation should be made as notorious as the previous authority.

Agent exceeding his authority. (3)
If an agent exceeds his authority, in cases where it is notorious that an agent's authority is usually limited, the principal will not be liable beyond the extent of the authority given.

Ratification by principal. (4)
Where an agent has exceeded his authority, or has acted without authority, and the principal subsequently acquiesces either expressly or impliedly, the principal will be liable just as if he had given his authority previously.

A principal is liable to an action for the fraudulent Misrepresentation by agents. (5)
misrepresentation of his agent, acting in the course of his business and for the master's benefit, though no express command or privity of the master be proved, except in cases where the principal has not in anywise sanctioned, or adopted, or elected to take the benefit of the fraud.

The agent is not clothed by law with any authority to Warranties by agents. (6)
warrant, unless he be the general agent of a tradesman employed in the business of buying and selling, as, for example, the servant of a horse-dealer. And an agent having a general authority to sell may give a warranty so as to bind his principal, although he has received express directions not to give a warranty, except where the principal has notified to the world that the authority of the agent is circumscribed.

If a man send his servant with ready-money to buy Purchases by a servant. (7)
goods, and the servant buys them upon credit, the master is not chargeable. But if a servant has been in the habit of purchasing goods for his master upon credit, and he purchases some things without the master's order, the master is nevertheless bound, if the tradesman gave credit to him and not to the servant.

A foreman, intrusted with the general management of a Foremen and managers. (8)
trade or business, has an implied general authority from his employer to enter into all such contracts as are usually and necessarily entered into in the ordinary conduct of the business.

Liability on Contracts by Agents.

If an agent, who makes a contract, contracts only in the (i.) When the agent contracts for a disclosed principal. (9)
name of the principal, intending to bind the latter and not himself by the contract, the principal and not the agent will have the right of action upon it.

But if the agent has an interest or special property in the subject-matter of a contract, he may maintain an action upon it. Thus, an auctioneer has a special property in goods which he is employed to sell, and he may, therefore, maintain an action against the buyer for the price of goods sold by him.

But where an agent professes to contract for, and on behalf of a named principal, but contracts in his own name and signs his name to the contract, he may be made personally liable, if it appears from the general context of the written instrument that he was to be responsible for the fulfilment of the contract.

<small>(ii.) Where the agent contracts for an undisclosed principal—rights and liabilities of principal. (10)</small>

Where an agent contracts for an undisclosed principal, and (a) *where the agent is apparently himself the principal*, the principal may, so long as the contract remains executory, come forward and claim the benefit of it: but in doing so he is bound by all the equities raised by his agent whilst dealing apparently as principal.

But there are cases in which those who have contracted with an apparent principal may refuse to fulfil the contract with any other person who comes forward as the real principal, as, for example, when the character and credit of the person describing himself as principal have been the inducement of the contract.

(b) *Where an agent acts for an undisclosed principal, and the other contracting party knows him to be an agent, but does not know who is his principal*, and, consequently, debits the agent, in the first instance, he may, nevertheless, on ascertaining who is the real principal, proceed against him.

(c) *When an agent acts for an undisclosed principal, and the other contracting party knows him to be acting as the agent of a particular known principal*, and the agent pledges his own credit, and the other contracting party gives credit to the agent, and makes him his debtor, he cannot afterwards resort against the principal.

<small>Rights and liabilities of agent</small>

Wherever an agent contracts as an apparent principal, and the real principal does not come forward and claim the benefit of the contract, the agent may do so. And in every case, even where the undisclosed principal is known to the other contracting party, the agent who has contracted as principal is himself liable in the contract. Evidence may be admitted to prove who is the real principal, in order to charge him, but not in order to discharge the agent who has contracted as apparent principal. contracting for undisclosed principal. (11)

But if a person is placed in a situation which renders his character of agent notorious, he cannot be made personally liable in respect of his transactions in the usual course of his employment.

An officer acting in a public capacity in discharge of his duty to the Crown or the country, cannot be made personally liable on contracts made in discharge of such duty, unless he expressly makes himself liable upon them.

The liability in the case of deeds is confined to the person who has contracted therein in his own name, and does not extend to the person on whose behalf, or for whose benefit, the contract is expressed to be made. If an agent contracts under seal in his own name, although his representative character is disclosed on the face of the contract, he is personally bound. But if an agent is authorized by power of attorney under seal to enter into, and execute, a deed for his principal, and the principal is made to contract in his own name, and the agent merely executes the deed for him, the principal and not the agent is bound. Contracts under seal by agents. (12)

Liability of Agent to Principal.

It is the duty of an agent to keep regular accounts, and if after demand he refuses to account, he is responsible in damages. Accounts. (13)

Del credere commission is a species of agency in which the agent, in consideration of an additional commission, guarantees to his principal the payment of all debts which become due through his agency to the principal. Del credere commission. (14)

Responsibility of brokers, &c. (15) Brokers, factors, and commission agents impliedly contract to execute commissions intrusted to them in a careful, skilful, and diligent manner, and to obey the orders and directions they receive. They cannot become purchasers of the property intrusted to them to sell, unless they do so openly, and with full disclosure of all they know about it; nor can they purchase their own goods for their principals.

Sub-agent. (16) Every agent is responsible for money received by a sub-agent employed by him for the purpose of receiving money, whether the principal had or had not reason to suppose that there was any necessity for the employment of a sub-agent; and the sub-agent so employed to receive money is accountable only to the agent, his employer, and cannot be sued by the principal. But if the sub-agent has received direct instructions from the principal, or is in any respect his agent, he will be accountable to the principal.

Commission. (17) The amount of commission due to those who undertake the duties of agent is generally governed by the usage of trade, in the absence of express agreement.

An authority to sell upon certain terms and for a certain commission is revoked by the death of the principal before the authority has been acted upon.

An agent to sell is entitled to his commission, if the relation of buyer and seller has been brought about by his act, although the actual sale was not effected by him.

Indemnification. (18) The principal is bound to indemnify his agent in respect of all payments which may be made by the latter in the due course of his employment.

ILLUSTRATIVE CASES.

(1) *Fenn v. Harrison*, 3 *T.R.* 757.

The holder of a bill of exchange desired A. to get it discounted, but positively refused to indorse it, and A. delivered it to B. for the same purpose, informing him to whom it belonged, and B. finding that he could not dispose of it without indorsing it, was prevailed upon to do so by A.'s telling him that he would indemnify him; but the indorsee took it upon the credit of the names on the bill without any knowledge of the real owner: Held, that as A. was a special agent under a limited authority, his principal was not bound by any act beyond scope of such limited authority. [On a third trial of this case, the defendant was, however, held liable on the ground of a subsequent ratification. See *Fenn* v. *Harrison*, 4 *T.R.* 177.]

(2) *Watkins* v. *Vince*, 2 *Stark.* 388.

Evidence that the defendant's son, a minor, had in three or four instances signed bills of exchange for his father, is sufficient, in the absence of rebutting evidence, to charge the father on a guarantee purporting to be a guarantee of the father, but in the handwriting of the son.

Whitehead v. *Tuckett*, 15 *East.* 400.

A firm of brokers were in the habit of buying and selling and receiving the value for sugars in their own names for their principal. Sometimes, when the market was low, under an unlimited authority as to quantity and price, at other times under special instructions; but keeping only a general account, without accounting separately for each particular lot sold or purchased. The brokers sold a particular parcel of sugars under the price directed by their principal, and received the money for him, but afterwards failed. Held, that the principal was bound by the sale. The general authority of the brokers to sell, so as to bind their principal in respect of the purchaser, must be collected from their general dealing, and not merely from their private instructions as to the particular parcel of goods.

(3) *Baines* v. *Ewing*, L. R. 1 *Exch.* 320.

The defendant authorized an insurance broker at Liverpool to underwrite policies of marine insurance in his name and on his behalf, the risk not to exceed £100 by any one vessel. The broker, acting in excess of his authority, and without the knowledge of the defendant, underwrote a policy for the plaintiff for £150. The plaintiff was not aware that the broker's authority was limited by any particular sum; but it is notorious in Liverpool that in nearly all cases there is a limit of some sort, which remains undisclosed to third persons, imposed on brokers by their principals. In an action on the policy: Held, 1st, that the defendant was not liable for the whole amount underwritten, the broker having exceeded his authority; and, 2nd, that the contract whereon the action was founded was not capable of division, and therefore, the defendant was not liable to the extent of the £100.

(4) *Maclean* v. *Dunn, vide supra*, *p.* 174.

Soames v. *Spencer*, 1 *D. & R.* 32.

A. and B. being jointly interested in a quantity of oil, A. entered into a contract for the sale of it, without the authority or knowledge of B., who, upon receiving information of the circumstance, refused to be bound by it, but afterwards assented by parol. Held, in an action against the vendors, that B.'s subsequent ratification of the contract rendered it binding.

(5) *Barwick* v. *English Joint Stock Bank, vide supra*, *p.* 140.

(6) *Helyear* v. *Hawke*, 5 *Esp.* 72.

Action of assumpsit on the warranty of a horse. The defendant having employed an agent to sell the horse for him, Held that what such agent said as a warranty or representation, at the time of the sale, respecting the horse, was evidence against his principal.

Pickering v. *Busk*, 15 *East.* 45.

Bayley, J.: "If the servant of a horse dealer, with express directions not to warrant, do warrant, the master is bound ; because the servant having a general authority to sell, is in a condition to warrant, and the master has not notified to the world that the general authority is circumscribed."

(7) *Southby* v. *Wiseman*, 3 *Keb.* 625.

Wild, J.: "If I give my servant money, I shall not answer for what he buyeth in trust ; but if I send sometimes on trust, or pay scores, I shall answer."

(8) *Summers* v. *Solomon*, 26 *Law J.*, *Q.B.* 301.

The defendant owned a jeweller's shop at Lewes, living himself in London, and visiting the shop monthly. The shop was managed by a shopman, H., from whom the plaintiff had for some years received orders at Lewes, in the defendant's name, for goods, which were sent to the shop, and afterwards paid for by the defendant. He absconded and came to London and ordered jewellery there of the plaintiff in the defendant's name : Held, that the plaintiff was justified in assuming that H. had general authority to order goods for the shop on the defendant's credit, and that the defendant was therefore liable for the goods obtained by H. in London.

(9) *Fairlie* v. *Fenton*, *L.R.*, 5 *Exch.* 169.

A broker cannot sue in his own name upon contracts made by him as broker. The plaintiff, a broker, signed and delivered to the defendants a bought note for cotton in the following form : " I have this day sold you on account of T.," &c. (Signed E. F., broker) : Held, that he was not a contracting party, and could not sue the defendants for breach of the contract in refusing to accept the cotton.

Williams v. *Millington*, 1 *H. Bl.* 81.

An auctioneer, employed to sell the goods of a third person by auction, may maintain an action for goods sold and delivered against a buyer, though the sale was at the house of such third person, and the goods were known to be the property of the latter ; for an auctioneer has a possession coupled with an interest in goods which he is employed to sell.

Parker v. *Winlow*, 7 *Ell. & Bl.* 670.

A memorandum of charter-party was expressed to be made " between P., of the good ship C., and W., agent for E. W. & Son," to whom the ship was to be addressed. It was signed by W., without any restriction. Held, that W. was personally liable as charterer.

(10) *Fish* v. *Kempton*, 7 *C.B.* 692.

A. buys goods of B., knowing that B. is selling them as factor. A. cannot, in an action by the principal for the price, set off a debt due to him from B., although it is found that A. made the purchase *bond fide.*

Humble v. *Hunter*, 12 *Q.B.* 310.

In assumpsit on a charter-party, executed not by plaintiff, but by a third person, who in the contract expressly described himself as "owner" of the ship : Held, that evidence was not admissible to show that such person contracted merely as the plaintiff's agent. Lord Denman, C.J.: " You have a right to the benefit you contemplate from the character, credit, and substance of the party with whom you contract."

Thomson v. *Davenport*, 9 *B. & C.* 78.

At the time of making a contract of sale, the party buying the goods represented that he was buying them on account of persons resident in

Scotland, but did not mention their names, and the seller did not inquire who they were, but debited the party who purchased the goods: Held, that the seller might afterwards sue the principals for the price.

Paterson v. *Gandasequi*, 15 *East.* 62.

If the seller of goods, knowing at the time that the buyer, though dealing with him in his own name, is in truth the agent of another person, and knows also who that other person is, but nevertheless elects to give credit to such agent, he cannot afterwards recover against the known principal.

(11) *Schmaltz* v. *Avery*, 16 *Q.B.* 659.

Assumpsit on a charter-party by freighter against ship-owner for not receiving cargo. Proof was given of a charter-party expressed to be by defendant of one part, "and G. S. & Co. (agents of the freighter), of the other part," and containing a memorandum as follows: "This charter being concluded on behalf of another party, it is agreed that all responsibility on the part of G. S. & Co. shall cease as soon as the cargo is shipped." G. S. & Co. now brought the action. Held, that notwithstanding the terms of the charty-party, plaintiffs might prove that they were the freighters, and their own principals, and on proof of this being the case, were entitled to recover in their own name.

Higgins v. *Senior*, 8 *M. & W.* 834.

In an action on a written agreement, purporting on the face of it to be made by the defendant, and subscribed by him for the sale and delivery by him of goods above the value of £10, it is not competent for the defendant to discharge himself, by proving that the agreement was really made by him by the authority of, and as agent for a third person, and that the plaintiff knew those facts at the time the agreement was made and signed.

Pochin v. *Pawley*, 1 *W. Bl.* 670.

The surveyor of a turnpike road, in the employment of the commissioners for highways, Held, not personally liable to the labourers employed in the repair of the road for their wages; for the contract is by implication of law, made with the commissioners.

(12) *White* v. *Cuyler*, 6 *T.R.* 176.

One who executes a deed for another under a power of attorney, must execute it in the name of his principal.

Wilks v. *Back*, 2 *East.* 142.

Though the act done must be the act of the principal, and not of the attorney who is authorized to do it; yet, if the deed be executed in the principal's name, it matters not in what form of words, such execution is denoted by the signature of the name; as if opposite the seal be written "for J. B. (the principal), M. W. (the attorney), L.S."

Steiglitz v. *Egginton*, 1 *Holt.* 141.

If one partner give another partner authority to execute a deed, that authority must be by deed, and a mere acknowledgment that such authority was given is not sufficient.

Boll v. *Dunsterville*, 4 *T.R.* 313.

If A. execute a deed for himself and partner by the authority of his partner, *and in his presence*, it is a good execution, though only sealed once.

(13) *Topham* v. *Braddick*, 1 *Taunt.* 572.

If goods are consigned to a factor on commission, the law will raise a contract to account for such as are sold, to pay over the proceeds, and to re-deliver the residue unsold, on demand.

(14) See *Grove* v. *Dubois*, 1 *T.R.* 112.

(15) *Mainwaring* v. *Brandon*, 2 *Moore*, 125.

A., in Holland, commissioned B., in London, to purchase and ship tobacco of the best quality. B. employed C. as his broker for that purpose, who accordingly made a purchase from D. On the arrival of the tobacco in Holland, it turned out to be of a very bad quality; and A. brought an action and recovered against B. Held, that B. was entitled to recover from C. the whole of the damages he had sustained in the action brought against him by A., although he had received a bought note from C., in which the tobacco was not described as of the best quality.

Murphy v. *O'Shea*, 2 *Jones & Lat.* 422.

If, in a transaction between a principal and agent, it appears that there has been any underhand dealing by the agent, *ex gr.*, that he has purchased the estate of the principal in the name of another person, instead of his own, however fair the transaction may be in other respects, it has no validity in a court of equity. An agent may, however, purchase from his principal, provided he deals with him at arm's length, and after a full disclosure of all he knows with respect to the property.

Bentley v. *Craven*, 17 *Beav.* 75.

One of several partners was employed to purchase goods for the firm. He, unknown to his co-partners, purchased goods of his own, at the market price, but he made a considerable profit thereby. Held, that the transaction could not be sustained, and that he was accountable to the firm for the profit thus made.

(16) *Ireland* v. *Thomson*, 4 *C.B.* 149.

Where, in consequence of damage to a ship during the voyage, it becomes impossible to prosecute the adventure, the master has the authority to sell her for the benefit of all parties interested; and a person employed by the master to superintend the sale is accountable to him for the proceeds, and not to the ship-owner.

Hanley v. *Cassan*, 11 *Jur.* 1088.

When a creditor employs a country solicitor to recover a debt, and the country solicitor employs a London solicitor to set the legal machinery in motion, and the debt is paid to the London solicitor, the latter is accountable to his client for the money, and cannot retain it in satisfaction and discharge of a debt due to him from his immediate employer, the country solicitor; for the London solicitor is to be regarded as the agent of the client.

(17) *Campanari* v. *Woodburn*, 15 *C.B.* 400.

A. agreed with B. that he would endeavour to sell a picture belonging to B., and that if he succeeded in selling the same, B. should pay him £100. B. died before the picture was sold. Having sold the picture, A. brought an action against the administratrix of B., alleging in his declaration that she had "confirmed the sale" of the picture. Held, that such declaration disclosed no cause of action, inasmuch as the authority from B. to A. to sell the picture was revoked by A.'s death, and the defendant's confirmation of the *sale*, in the absence of an allegation that she was aware of the contract between A. and B., was no adoption of the *contract* by her, so as to make her liable to pay the £100.

Green v. *Bartlett,* 14 *C.B.,* N.S. 681.

An auctioneer and estate agent was employed to sell an estate under an agreement, by which he was to receive a commission of 2½ per cent. "if the estate should be sold," and "in case the estate should not be sold," he was to be paid £25 as a compensation for his trouble and expense. Having put up the estate to auction, and failed to sell it, the agent being asked by a person who had attended the sale, who was the owner of the property, referred him to his principal; and, ultimately, that person, without any further intervention of the agent, became the purchaser : Held, that the sale having been effected through the means of the agent, he was entitled to the stipulated commission.

(18) *Taylor* v. *Stray,* 2 *C.B.,* N.S. 175.

The plaintiffs, stockbrokers and members of the London Stock Exchange, on the 28th of August, at the request of the defendant, bought for him twenty shares in a joint-stock bank, to be paid for on the "settlement day," which was the 15th of September, and duly forwarded to him the usual broker's contract-note. The bank stopped payment on the 3rd of September, and ultimately became bankrupt. On the 11th the defendant repudiated the transaction, and gave the plaintiffs notice not to pay the price on his account. The plaintiffs having been compelled, according to the rules of the Stock Exchange, to pay for the shares on the settlement-day, sent the defendant the certificates and transfers, and upon his declining to accept them, sued him for money paid : Held, that they were entitled to recover.

CHAPTER VI.

PARTNERSHIP.

<small>What constitutes partnership.</small>
Any number of persons, not exceeding twenty, may constitute themselves partners by associating together and contributing in equal or unequal proportions, money, labour, skill, or care for the furtherance of a joint undertaking, upon the express or implied understanding that they are to share in certain proportions the profit and loss of the transaction. (25 & 26 Vict. c. 89, s. 4.)

<small>Participation in profits.</small>
Mere participation in profits does not of itself constitute a partnership. And by the 28 & 29 Vict. c. 86 it is enacted:—

That the advance of money by way of loan to a person engaged, or about to engage, in any trade, upon a contract in writing with such person that the lender shall receive a rate of interest varying with the profits arising from such trade, shall not of itself constitute the lender a partner, or render him responsible as such. (Sec. 1.)

That no contract for the payment of a servant or agent of any person engaged in any trade, by a share of the profits of such trade, shall of itself constitute such servant or agent a partner, or render him responsible as such. (Sec. 2.)

That no person being the widow or child of the deceased partner of a trader, and receiving by way of annuity a portion of the profits made by such trader, shall, by reason only of such receipt, be constituted a partner, or be rendered responsible as such. (Sec. 3.)

That no person receiving by way of annuity, or otherwise, a portion of the profits of any business, in consideration of the sale by him of the good-will of the business, shall, by reason only of such receipt, be deemed a partner, or rendered responsible as such. (Sec. 4.)

A participation in the profits, it is therefore seen, is not of itself a conclusive proof of partnership. Where it is sought to render a person liable as a partner, the true test would appear to be whether he has constituted the other alleged partner his agent in respect of the partnership business. *Test of partnership.* (1)

A secret or dormant partner stands to those who contract with the firm in the position of an undisclosed principal. He is equally responsible with acting and ostensible partners. And private agreements between partners exempting dormant partners from liability do not affect the liability of such partners as regards third persons. *Dormant and secret partners.* (2)

Persons suffering themselves to be held out to the world as partners by permitting their names to be used in the business, or otherwise, are responsible to third persons as partners, although in fact they have no share or interest in the business. But if anyone contracts with a firm in partnership, knowing that a person whose name appears in the firm as an ostensible partner is not in fact a partner, and has no share or interest in the partnership, he cannot afterwards make that person responsible upon the contract which he entered into with notice of the fact. *Nominal partners.* (3)

If several persons join together in making a purchase of goods, and are *also* jointly concerned in the subsequent disposal of the goods, they become partners *inter se* in the transaction. *Joint purchasers of goods.* (4)

Tenancy in common of a chattel, as, for example, of a horse, does not constitute a partnership.

Partnership in profits.
(5)

There may be a partnership as regards the accruing profits of a business or joint speculation when there is no partnership or even community of interest in the capital stock of the business.

Specific performance.
(6)

The courts will not generally decree specific performance of a contract for a partnership; but when a partnership has commenced they will carry into effect the articles of partnership.

Contracts of partners inter se.

Formerly, at common law, a partner could not maintain an action against his co-partner, or against the firm of which he was a member, for goods sold, work done, or money had and received on account of the partnership. Nor could one mercantile firm maintain an action against another firm when the same person was a partner in both houses. In some cases, however, an action might be brought by a partner against the firm to which he belonged, as, for example, where the subject matter was nowise connected with the partnership, or where the partnership was at an end, and a partner sued for a balance found to be due on the settlement of accounts.

Under the Judicature Act the rules of equity have now superseded those of the common law.

Liabilities of partners upon partnership contracts.
(7)

Each member of a complete partnership is liable for himself, and as agent for the rest binds them upon all contracts made in the ordinary course of the business of the co-partnership. The implied general authority to enter into contracts on behalf of the firm does not extend to partnerships in particular transactions, nor to limited partnerships in profits where the partner has no interest in the capital stock.

As to the liability of partners upon deeds, see *supra*, p. 201.

Transactions out of ordinary course of business.
(8)

If the trading name of the firm be used by one partner in transactions outside the ordinary scope of the partnership business, the other partners will not be bound, unless they have expressly consented to such use of the name of the firm.

Where a partner gives a bill or note in the name of the firm to secure his own private debt, the party taking it cannot enforce it against the firm unless he can show that it was given with the authority or consent of the firm. But if the bill has passed into the hands of a *bona fide* holder, the latter may enforce the bill against the firm, whether it was given with their authority or not. Bills and notes in name of firm. (9)

Representations by partners touching partnership business and dealings, made in the ordinary course of business, will bind all the members of the firm as between themselves and third parties who have acted on the faith of such representations. Representations by partners. (10)

An incoming partner cannot be made responsible for the non-performance of contracts entered into before he became an actual or a nominal member of it. Liability of incoming partners. (11)

An incoming partner cannot be charged with the payment of the price of goods sold to the co-partnership before he became a member of it, although they may have been delivered subsequently thereto.

The transfer of the accounts of an old firm to a new firm taking its place, and the acceptance by the creditor of a new simple contract security from the new firm for the debt due to him, is not of itself sufficient to discharge a retiring partner. There must be an agreement, either express or fairly to be inferred, to discharge the old firm.

If no time has been limited for the dissolution of a general trading partnership, it is a partnership at will, and may be dissolved at the pleasure of any one or more of the partners. Dissolution of partnership. (12)

If the partners have agreed that the partnership shall continue for a definite period, it can only be dissolved before the expiration of the term limited by the mutual consent of all the parties, or by the bankruptcy, outlawry, embezzlement, felony, or death of any one or more of the partners, or by the assignment of any partner of his share in the partnership.

If the co-partnership has been contracted by parol, it may be renounced by parol, but if it has been established by deed, the renunciation and disclaimer of it by the party withdrawing should also be by deed.

Distribution of effects on dissolution. (13) — The share of a deceased partner in the partnership business is distributable between his representatives; and where a part of the partnership property consists of land which was purchased for the purpose of carrying on the business, it will be dealt with as personalty. The partnership stock to be distributed includes the good-will of the business and the right to use the trade mark.

Effect of dissolution quoad third parties. (14) — If once a person holds himself out as being a partner, until he gives out that he has ceased to be so, those who deal with the firm upon the faith of the supposed partnership may consider him as a partner, and he is bound by that representation.

The retirement of an ostensible partner ought to be made as notorious as his connexion with the firm. Besides notice in the *Gazette*, the fact should be repeatedly advertised in the newspapers circulated in the neighbourhood where the partnership was carried on, and express notice should be sent to customers residing at a distance.

Dormant and secret partners may release themselves from further responsibility by simply relinquishing their share in the business. And where a partnership or trading association is carried on by trustees or directors, the other partners or shareholders are in the position of dormant partners.

ILLUSTRATIVE CASES.

(1) *Wheatcroft* v. *Hickman*, 9 *C.B.*, *N.S.* 47.

A. and B., who carried on the business of iron-masters in co-partnership, by a deed, purporting to be made between A. and B. of the first part, five persons named, as trustees of the second part, and the several persons whose names were contained in a schedule as creditors for the sums therein mentioned, and who should execute the deed, of the third part,—reciting that the said A. and B. were indebted to the several parties thereto of the third part, and that they had agreed to assign all their estate and effects for the benefit of such creditors,—assigned the works and all their property and effects to the trustees, upon trust, amongst other things, *to carry on the business* under the name of the Stanton Iron Company, and *out of the profits* to pay interest on mortgages, &c., and *to pay and divide the nett income of the business remaining after answering the purposes aforesaid, unto and among all and singular the creditors of A. and B., in rateable proportions, according to the amount of their respective debts.* Held, by the House of Lords, that under this deed, the *creditors* executing it, did not become liable *as partners* for debts contracted by the trustees in carrying on the trade. Lord Wensleydale : "It cannot be collected from the trust deed that each of the subscribing creditors is a partner with the trustees, and by the mere signature of the deed constitutes them his agents for carrying on the business for his account and the rest of the creditors."

(2) *Wightman* v. *Townroe*, 1 *M. & S.* 412.

Where the executors of a deceased partner continued his share of the partnership property in trade for the benefit of his infant daughter : Held, that they were liable upon a bill drawn for the accommodation of the partnership, and paid in discharge of a partnership debt ; although their names were not added to the firm, but the trade was carried on by the other partners under the same style as before, and the executors, when they divided the profits and loss of the trade, carried the same to the account of the infant, and took no part of the profits themselves.

(3) See *Alderson* v. *Pope*, 1 *Campb.* 403, *n.*

(4) *Coope* v. *Eyre*, 1 *H. Bl.* 37.

A., B., C. and D. entered into an agreement to purchase goods in the name of A. only, and to take aliquot shares of the purchase ; but it did not appear that they agreed *jointly to re-sell* the goods. On failure of A. Held, that B., C. and D. were not answerable to the vendor as partners with A.

French v. *Styring*, 2 *C.B., N.S.* 357.

A. and B., being joint owners of a racehorse, it was agreed between them that A. should keep and train and have the management of the horse, conveying him to, and entering him for, the different races ; that 35*s.* per week should be allowed for his keep ; and that the expenses of his keep, &c., should be borne jointly by A. and B., and the horse's winnings equally divided between them. Held, that this did not constitute them partners in the horse, but that A. might recover from B. a moiety of the expense he had incurred, there having been no winnings, for this was in the nature of an advance of capital by A. to B.

(5) *Barton* v. *Hanson*, 2 *Taunt.* 51.

Where several persons unite together for the purpose of carrying on the business of common carriers of passengers and goods, and one finds the coach, and the others divide the road into districts, and each horses and conveys the coach through his own district, finding his own horses, harness, stables and equipments, servants, and coachmen, and all things necessary for the purpose ; there is no partnership in the stock in trade, although there is a partnership in the accruing profits.

(6) See *Scott* v. *Rayment*, *L.R.* 7 *Eq.* 112.

(7) *Wilson* v. *Whitehead*, 10 *M. & W.* 503.

A., B. and C. verbally agreed that they would bring out and be jointly interested in a periodical publication. A. was to be the publisher, and to

P

make and receive general payments, B. was to be the editor, and C. the printer; and after payment of all expenses, they were to share the profits of the work equally. C. was to furnish the paper, and charge it to the account at cost price. No profits were ever made, nor any accounts settled. The plaintiff furnished paper to C. for the purpose of being used by him in printing the periodical. Held, that A. and B. were not jointly liable with C. for the price of it.

(8) *Hasleham* v. *Young*, 5 Q.B. 833.

One of two solicitors who were in partnership together, in order to obtain the discharge of a client from custody, signed the partnership name to an undertaking to pay the debt and costs. Held, that the other partner who had given no express authority to his colleague to give such an undertaking, could not be sued thereon, as the giving of guarantees and undertakings of such a description is not within the usual course of the business of solicitors.

(9) *Wiseman* v. *Easton*, 8 L.T.R., N.S. 637.

A bill of exchange accepted in the name of a firm, in the hands of a *bonâ fide* holder, Held, to be valid against the firm, although the partner who accepted had no authority to do so, and his doing so was fraudulent.

(10) *Latham* v. *Parry*, 2 B. & Ald. 801.

A. employed B. and C., who were partners as wine and spirit merchants, to purchase wine, and sell the same upon commission. C., the managing partner, represented that he had made the purchases, and that he had sold a part of the wines so purchased at a profit; the proceeds of such supposed sale he paid to A., and rendered accounts, in which he stated the purchases to have been made at a certain rate per pipe. In fact, C. neither bought nor sold any wine. The transactions were wholly fictitious, but B. was entirely ignorant that this was the case. Upon the whole account a larger sum had been repaid to A., as the proceeds of that part of the wine alleged to have been re-sold, than he had advanced; but the other part of the wine, which C. represented as having been purchased, was unaccounted for. Held, that B. was liable for the false representations of his partner; and that A. was entitled to retain the money that had been paid to him upon these fictitious transactions as though they were real. Held, also, the supposed purchases having been represented to have been made at a certain specified rate per pipe, that A. might maintain an action for money had and received, to recover the specific sums advanced for the number of pipes unaccounted for.

(11) *Wilson* v. *Lewis*, 2 Sc., N.R. 115.

Action on a bill of exchange for £49 14s. 6d. against three partners. Two of the partners having become bankrupt, suffered judgment by default. The third pleaded that the bill was accepted by the other two in the name of the firm, without his knowledge, privity, or consent, for a debt due from them before he became a member of the firm. It appeared that the consideration for the acceptance was a debt due to the plaintiff for the hire of horses, gigs, and harness, upon a contract entered into and partly executed before the defendant became a partner with the other two; but that a part of the consideration, viz., £1 15s., accrued since the day on which the partnership commenced. Held, that the plaintiff was entitled to have a verdict entered for him for the £1 15s.

Crawford v. *Cocks*, 6 Exch. 291.

Where a banking firm makes payments, professedly on behalf of a customer (who has a banking account with the firm), but without his authority, and the sum so paid is entered to his debit in the books of the firm, and the firm afterwards admits new partners, the new firm is not liable to the customer for such payments, unless there be an agreement between the two firms and the customer that the new firm shall take upon themselves the *actual* liabilities of the old firm.

(12) *Peacock* v. *Peacock*, 16 *Ves.* 49.

Partnership without any provision as to its duration may be determined without previous notice, subject to the accounts, to wind up the concern.

Essell v. *Hayward*, 30 *Beav.* 158.

A partnership between two solicitors for their joint lives may be dissolved *instanter*, if one of the parties fraudulently sells out trust funds and applies the produce to his own use.

Harrison v. *Tennant*, 21 *Beav.* 482.

The court dissolved a partnership entered into for a term of years, when without any breach of the partnership articles, circumstances had so altered that it could not be carried on upon the footing originally contemplated, and the confidence mutually reposed had ceased, and given place to mistrust, so that it was apparent that the partnership could not go on without mutual injury.

(13) *Darby* v. *Darby*, 3 *Drew.* 495.

A. and B. purchased land on a joint speculation with their joint moneys for the purpose of laying it out in building plots, and re-selling it at the joint profit or loss of A. and B. Held, that it was converted out and out; and the share of one of the partners in the unsold real estate passed on his death to his personal representatives.

Hall v. *Barrows*, 33 *Law J.*, *Ch.* 204.

Partnership stock includes the goodwill of the business and the right to use the trade mark; and on the purchase, by a surviving partner from the executors of a deceased partner, of the partnership stock at a valuation, the value of the goodwill and the trade mark must be taken into account.

(14) *Newsome* v. *Coles*, 2 *Campb.* 617.

If, after a dissolution of partnership, and notice of this published in the "London Gazette," and sent round to the customers of the house, one of the partners carries on the business under the old firm, and draws and accepts bills in the name of that firm, the other partners are not bound to apply for an injunction against his doing so, and are not liable upon such bills, to a person ignorant of the dissolution of partnership.

Carter v. *Whalley*, 1 *B. & Ad.* 11.

S. and others carried on business under the name of the "Plas Madoc Colliery Company." S. withdrew from the firm, which afterwards became indebted to C., no notice having been given to C. or to the public of S.'s withdrawal. Held, that S. was not liable for the debt, there being no sufficient evidence that he had ever, while a partner, represented himself as such to C., or appeared so publicly in that character that C. must have been presumed to know of it.

CHAPTER VII.

CORPORATIONS AND JOINT STOCK COMPANIES.

Definition. (1)
A CORPORATION is an aggregate body with an existence, rights, and liabilities separate and distinct from the individual existence, rights, and liabilities of its members.

A body corporate, from the mere fact of its incorporation, has the power of making bye-laws for its government, subject and subordinate to the laws of the realm (see *supra*, p. 9), of electing its own officers, of suing and being sued in the corporate name, of holding and enjoying property in that name, and of acting and speaking through its common seal. Corporations cannot lawfully purchase or hold lands, however, without the license of the Crown or the authority of Parliament.

Contracts by corporations to be by seal. (2)
The common law rule is that contracts entered into by corporations must be made in the name and under the seal of the body corporate; and that, if the common seal has not been affixed to the contract, it is not the contract of the corporation, but of the individual members concerned in making it. This rule, however, has been subjected to important exceptions.

Exception in favour of executed contracts. (3)
If a corporation has contracted with another party without seal, and has had the benefit of the fulfilment of the contract, although the contract could not have been enforced against the corporation whilst it remained executory, the law will raise an implied promise in its favour upon which it may sue in its corporate capacity. And, on the other hand, where a corporation has had the

benefit of an informal contract, it cannot retain that benefit and refuse to pay on the ground that the contract was not under seal.

A corporation with a head, such as a municipal corporation, may transact trifling matters of business, and enter into such ordinary contracts as are of constant recurrence, and the making of which forms part of its usual functions, without the employment of its common seal. Thus, ordinary servants may be hired, and articles for the use of the corporation may be purchased without a deed.

Exception in favour of trifling transactions. (4)

A corporation established for trading purposes may contract without the use of its common seal in the ordinary course of the trade for the purpose of which it was incorporated, and may maintain actions upon such contracts *whether executed or executory.* It may also draw and accept bills and promissory notes.

Exception in favour of trading corporations. (5)

Contracts by the officers of trading corporations are binding upon the corporation, if they are within the scope of their regular employment.

Where a corporation is created by Act of Parliament for particular purposes, and with special powers, its deed, though under the corporate seal regularly affixed, does not bind it, if it plainly appears by the express provisions of the statute creating the corporation, or by necessary or reasonable inference from its provisions, that the deed was *ultra vires.* But a corporation is fully capable of binding itself by any contract, except where it is plain that the Legislature meant that such a contract should not be made.

Contracts ultra vires. (6)

Joint Stock Companies.

The Companies' Act (25 & 26 Vict. c. 89) enables seven or more persons by subscribing their names to a memorandum of association, and obtaining registration, to form themselves into an incorporated company, with unlimited

Formation of joint stock companies.

liability, or with liability limited by shares, or by guarantee. The Act prohibits more than ten persons from carrying on in partnership the business of banking, or more than twenty persons from carrying on any business having gain for its object, unless they are registered as a company under that Act, or under some previous Act. After registration, a certificate of incorporation is granted to the company, and it becomes a corporation, having perpetual succession and a common seal, with power to hold lands.

<small>Contracts of registered joint stock companies.</small> By the 30 & 31 Vict. c. 131, contracts on behalf of a joint stock company registered under the Companies' Act, 1862, are regulated as follows : A contract which, if made between private persons, would be required to be under seal, may be made on behalf of the company under the company's common seal. A contract required by law to be in writing and signed by the party to be charged, may be made on behalf of the company and signed by any person acting under the express or implied authority of the company. And a contract, not required by law to be in writing, may be made by word of mouth on behalf of the company by any person acting under its authority, express or implied.

<small>Rights inter se of members of a joint stock company.</small> The rights *inter se* of members of a joint stock company are regulated by the Joint Stock Companies' Acts, and the memorandum and articles of association. When these are silent the ordinary law of partnership applies.

<small>Winding up of joint stock companies.</small> In the event of a company formed under the Companies' Act, 1862, being wound up, every member, present and past, is to be liable to contribute to the assets of the company to an amount sufficient to pay the debts and liabilities of the company, the costs of the winding up, and for the adjustment of the rights of the contributories amongst themselves. No past member is to be liable to contribute, if he has ceased to be a member for one year prior to the winding up. And no past member is to be

liable to contribute in respect of any debt or liability of the company contracted after he ceased to be a member. No past member is to be liable to contribute, unless the existing members are unable to satisfy the liabilities of the company.

In the case of a company limited by shares, no contribution is to be required from any member exceeding the amount unpaid on the shares in respect of which he is liable as past or present member.

In the case of a company limited by guarantee, no contribution is to be required of any member exceeding the amount of the undertaking entered into in his behalf by the memorandum of association (25 & 26 Vict. c. 89, s. 38).

All persons who have purchased shares and received dividends, or who have applied for and accepted and received an allotment of shares, or who have agreed to take shares and subscribe capital, are liable to be made contributories, whether they have executed the deed, or signed the contract, or hold their shares as trustees, or in their own right, or as mortgagees or creditors. Contributories. (7)

Where parties have been induced by the fraudulent representations of directors to become shareholders, they may be able to resist a claim to enforce the contract for the purchase of the shares; but as against creditors they are nevertheless liable as contributories. Fraudulent representations by directors. (8)

Every person who holds himself out or permits himself to be published to the world as a provisional director or acting committeeman or manager of a projected company, may become chargeable to parties who subsequently to such announcement have dealt with the managing committee. Provisional directors and committeemen. (9)

The members of the managing committee of a club or charity are personally responsible for the payment of tradesmen who have supplied goods, or to servants who have performed work for the benefit of the club or charitable Committees of clubs and charities. (10)

institution, by order of the committee. The credit is deemed to have been given to the committee rather than to the fluctuating body of subscribers.

ILLUSTRATIVE CASES.

(1) *Edmunds* v. *Brown*, 1 *Lev.* 237.

A corporation sealed a bond, and particular members of the corporation signed it. The corporation was dissolved: Held, that the particular persons who signed were not chargeable.

(2) See *Bro. Abr. Corporations, pl.* 47—63.

(3) *Mayor, &c., of Stafford* v. *Till*, 4 *Bing.* 75.

A corporation aggregate brought an action for use and occupation against a tenant who had occupied lands of the corporation without a deed. Best, C.J.: "Where a party has occupied land, the contract between him and his landlord must be considered as executed. If the contract were executory, there would be no mutuality of benefit, and consequently no consideration. But in the present case, the land having been enjoyed by the defendant, the promise to pay for it is implied, and there is a good consideration for the promise."

Lowe v. *London and N. W. Railway Co.*, 21 *Law J.*, Q.B. 361.

Where a corporation have actually used and occupied land for the purpose of their incorporation by the permission of the owner, *semble*, that they are liable to be sued in assumpsit for use and occupation, notwithstanding that they have not entered into a contract under their common seal. And in the case of a railway company sued under the above circumstances, where the 8 Vict. c. 16, s. 97, provides that any contract which, if made between private persons, would be valid, although made by parol only, may be made by parol, on behalf of the company by the directors, and shall be binding on the company: Held, that such a contract might be presumed to have been entered into, and that the company was therefore liable to the action.

De Grave v. *Mayor of Monmouth*, 4 *C. & P.* 111.

The mayor of a town ordered certain weights and measures from the plaintiff; and when supplied they were examined at a full meeting of the corporation. Held, that this was such a recognition of the contract as would make the corporation liable to pay for them, although the order for them was not under the common seal of the corporation.

(4) See *Bro. Abr. Corporations*, 56, and *Horn* v. *Ivy*, 1 *Ventr.* 47.

(5) *Church* v. *Imperial Gaslight Co.*, 6 *Ad. & E.* 846.

A corporation created for the purpose of supplying gas may maintain assumpsit for breach of a contract by the defendant to accept gas from year to year at £12 16s. per annum, the consideration being alleged to be the promise of the plaintiffs to supply it on those terms. Such promise by the company, though not under seal, is valid, and a good consideration.

Walker v. *Great Western Railway Co.*, L.R. 2 *Ex.* 228.

Held, that the general manager of a railway company has, as incidental to his employment, authority to bind the company to pay for surgical attendance, bestowed at his request on a servant of the company injured by an accident on their railway. [In *Cox* v. *Midland Railway Co.*, 3 *Exch.* 268, it was held that a station-master had no authority to bind the company for surgical attendance on injured passengers.]

(6) *Scottish North Eastern Railway Co.* v. *Stewart*, 3 *Macq. H.L.C.* 382.

Acts of Parliament authorizing companies to make railways are now regarded as *enabling* statutes which give powers, but do not render compulsory or obligatory the exercise of these powers. *Per* Lord Wensleydale : " A corporation is capable of binding itself by any contract, except when the statutes by which it is created or regulated expressly or by necessary implication prohibit such contract between the parties."

(7) *Thomson's ca.*, 34 *Law J., Ch.* 525.

A., upon his appointment as agent to a limited assurance company, agreed to take shares upon the terms that the payment for them should be deducted from his commission as agent, and no deposit was ever paid by him upon them, but he was registered as the holder of the shares. The company, very soon after his appointment, dismissed him ; but, as he contended, wrongfully. On the winding-up of the company, Held, that the company's cancellation of A.'s appointment as agent, whether justifiable or not, could not operate as a cancellation of A.'s agreement to become a shareholder, and that A. was liable as a contributory.

Price & Brown's case, 4 *De G. & S.* 146.

Shares were deposited by the allottees with creditors as security, and having been called in were exchanged by the creditors for others in their own names. The fact that they held the shares as security only was known to the directors of the company. Upon the company being wound up :— Held, that the creditors had been properly placed upon the list of contributories in respect of the shares.

(8) *Oakes* v. *Turquand*, 26 *Law J., Ch.* 949.

A contributory, under the Companies Act, 1862, is a person who has agreed to become a member of the company, and whose name is on the register. It matters not that his consent was obtained by fraud. The contract between a shareholder, who has been deceived by a fraudulent prospectus, and the company is voidable, not void, and can only be avoided subject to the rights of the creditors.

(9) *Bailey* v. *Macaulay*, 13 *Q.B.* 815.

In an action against a member of the committee of a projected railway company, for work and labour, goods supplied, and money paid, Held, that the jury were to consider whether the defendant, by taking upon him the character of a committee man, and afterwards acting in the affairs of the company, has authorized the company's solicitor, or secretary, or any member of the committee, to hold him out to the world as personally responsible for the reasonable and necessary expenses incurred in forming such a company, and on its behalf; and then, whether the credit was given on the faith of his being so personally responsible.

(10) *Cullen* v. *D. of Queensbury*, 1 *Br. P.C.* 404.

A., B. and C., on behalf of themselves and other members of a club, entered into articles with D. to provide necessaries for the use and accommodation of the club : Held, that they were personally bound by such articles ; and that D. was not bound to resort to any of the other members for satisfaction of his demands.

CHAPTER VIII.

MASTER AND SERVANT.

Contract of service.
IN order to constitute a contract of hiring and service there must be a mutual engagement, either express or implied, binding one party to employ and remunerate, and the other to serve for some determinate period. The contract of hiring and service may be complete and valid, although the servant is never actually called upon to do any work. The readiness and willingness on the part of the servant are construed as equivalent to actual service, and entitle him to an action for his wages.

A contract for hiring and service need not be authenticated by writing, unless the hiring exceeds a year in duration.

Implied contract. (1)
In the absence of an express contract a hiring may be presumed from the fact of service. But when the service has been with the parent or other near relation of the party serving, an express hiring must be proved in order to support a claim for wages.

Yearly hirings. (2)
When the employment of a servant is of a permanent nature, and annual wages are reserved, the hiring cannot, except by custom or usage of trade, be terminated by either party without the consent of the other before the termination of the current year, in the absence of misconduct.

Reservations of quarterly, monthly, or weekly wages are not inconsistent with a yearly hiring. But where there has been no long-continued service, and in the absence of custom or usage, from which a yearly hiring must be inferred, the payment of weekly or monthly wages raises a presumption in favour of a weekly or monthly hiring.

A general hiring of domestic or menial servants, when no time is mentioned for the duration of the service, is a hiring for a year, and so on from year to year, defeasible by custom and usage at the option of either of the parties on giving a month's warning, or paying, or tendering a month's wages. *Defeasible yearly hiring.* (3)

So, by the custom of particular trades, a general hiring of a commercial traveller is a hiring for a year, subject to an implied understanding that either party may terminate the engagement by giving three months' notice.

By special agreement the power of defeasance may be on one side only. The servant may agree to serve during a certain fixed period, subject to the right of the master to dismiss him at any time during that period.

Where the transaction between the employer and employed amounts to a mere authority to serve upon certain terms, there is only a service at will. If the work is actually performed and accepted, the law raises an implied promise to pay for it. But the employer is not bound to provide work, nor is the workman bound to execute it. *Service at will.* (4)

If a servant professes to be skilled in some particular art, and has been hired as a skilled servant, and has been found utterly incompetent to do what he has undertaken, the employer may at once dismiss him without notice. *Dismissal for incompetency.* (5)

If a servant habitually neglects the just and reasonable orders of the master; if he absents himself repeatedly, or refuses to perform his work, or to submit to the domestic regulations of the house, or is guilty of gross immorality, or of fraudulent misrepresentation and deceit in the discharge of his duties, to the injury of his employer, the latter may at once dismiss him without notice. *Dismissal for misconduct.* (6)

If a justifying cause of dismissal exists, the master may

avail himself of it as a defence to an action, although it may not have formed the ground of dismissal, and although the master may not have known of its existence at the time of the dismissal.

Notice to leave.   In the case of a yearly hiring, not made defeasible by custom or agreement, reasonable notice must be given on either side of the intention to terminate the contract. A quarter's notice, given a quarter of a year before the expiration of the current year of hiring, would in all cases be amply sufficient; and a month's notice is often all that is required by custom and usage.

Disability from sickness. (7)   If a household servant falls sick, or is hurt whilst doing his master's business, the master is not entitled to make any deduction from the agreed wages for the period during which the servant is unable to work. But if the servant has been struck down by disease and permanently disabled, so that he cannot be expected to return to his work, the master may dismiss him.

Death of master. (8)   A contract of hiring and service is dissolved by the death of either party. If the contract is made with a firm in partnership, it is dissolved by the death of one of the partners.

Damages for wrongful dismissal. (9)   If an employer renounces the contract he has made with a workman, and refuses to employ him, or, having employed, wrongfully dismisses him, the measure of damages is an indemnity for all the loss sustained by the plaintiff. The damages should be assessed so as to include the wages of the servant up to the time of dismissal, as well as the loss he has sustained by being prevented from continuing his services. The action may be brought as soon as the dismissal takes place; and if the servant has not succeeded in finding other equally eligible employment, he may recover damages far exceeding the salary agreed upon. But it seems to be considered that a servant, who is wrongfully dismissed, ought not to keep himself in a state of readiness to serve during the remainder of the term of hiring, but should at once endeavour to procure another situation.

Apprenticeship.

Every contract to serve, on the one hand, and to employ and instruct on the other, amounts to a contract of apprenticeship. As the contract is always to last for more than one year, it must be authenticated by writing to satisfy the Statute of Frauds. And by the immemorial custom of some towns and the bye-laws of some corporations, contracts of apprenticeship must be made by deed. Contracts of apprenticeship. (10)

It is necessary that the consideration or premium should be set forth in the instrument of apprenticeship, in order that the proper amount of stamp duty may be secured thereon (8 Anne c. 9, ss. 35—39).

By the custom of the city of London, an infant above the age of fourteen is responsible upon covenants contained in an indenture of apprenticeship executed by him. But at common law the infant is exempt from liability *ex contractu,* and therefore his friends usually become bound for his faithful service and good conduct during the term of the apprenticeship; and if, upon his coming of age, the infant should repudiate the contract of apprenticeship, they are bound to make good any damage which may be caused thereby to the master.

The contract of apprenticeship may be discharged by cancelling the indentures, or by the death or (32 & 33 Vict. c. 72, s. 33) bankruptcy of the master, or by the death of the apprentice. And if the master die within the term, his representatives are not bound to return any part of the premium, because there is only a partial failure of consideration. Dissolution or discharge. (11)

The contract may also be discharged by an award of justices at Quarter Sessions, or, if the master resides in a borough, by the mayor, with the assent of three other of his brethren or men of best reputation in the borough, who may also, in certain cases, order a part of the premium to be repaid.

Task-work.

Contract for letting out work. A contract for the letting out of task-work is a contract for the doing of work in the lump or job for an express or implied remuneration.

If the materials for the work, as well as the work itself, are furnished by the workman, the contract will generally be that of sale; but if the employer furnishes the materials and the workman contributes his labour merely, the contract is for the letting and hiring of work.

Contracts for work executed and executory. (12) As soon as mutual promises are exchanged, the right to the labour of the workman passes to the employer, and the right to the benefit or reward passes to the workman. If there is no engagement between the parties, both for the one to do the work and for the other to pay for its execution, there is no mutuality of obligation, and therefore no binding contract, unless the engagement is under seal.

But when the work has actually been done, the person at whose request, and by whose orders, it was executed must pay for it, although the workman was originally under no legal obligation to do the work, nor the employer to employ him. The law generally implies a promise to pay a reasonable compensation for services rendered, unless it appears that the services were to be gratuitous, or that the workman relied upon a particular fund, and not on the personal responsibility of the employer.

Rights of workman. (13) Where, after a contract for work by the job, the employer refuses to permit the workman to perform his task, the workman may sue for compensation for being prevented from earning the stipulated hire. And if the contract was defeasible at the will of the employer, and the workman has done anything under the contract, he may sue for remuneration on a *quantum meruit*.

If the contract is in its nature entire and indivisible, as for the building of a house for a certain price, or for conveyance between stipulated places for a certain price, the workman or coachman, who undertakes the performance of the contract, will not be able to recover the price agreed upon until the whole contract is performed. But where the contract is divisible, as where a builder agrees to build a house, to be paid for his work and labour and the materials supplied by measure and value, the undertaker of the work is entitled to demand payment from time to time as the work proceeds. <small>Conditions precedent to payment. (14)</small>

The approval of the employer of the work done may be a condition precedent to payment of the price. But where the produce of the workman's labour cannot be returned, as, for example, where an artist has been engaged to paint the ceiling of a room, although the employer should disapprove of the work, he must pay a reasonable remuneration for the labour which has been bestowed.

And when a contract has been substantially performed, the exact performance of every minute particular of the contract cannot be made a condition precedent to payment, but the employer may be entitled to such deductions from the contract price as would be necessary to enable him to have the work completed in exact accordance with the contract.

If, however, work has been so negligently and unskilfully done as to make it utterly useless to the employer, the latter cannot be called upon to pay for it, for there has been no beneficial service.

Time is frequently of the essence of a contract with regard to its commencement. But when the work has been commenced, its completion by a certain day will not in general be a condition precedent to the workman's right to the stipulated hire. But the employer may recover compensation from the undertaker of the work for damage which he has sustained by reason of the non-completion of the work at the appointed time.

Destruction of work before payment. (15) — If the contract is entire for the performance of a specific work for a specified sum, so that the performance of the whole work is a condition precedent to payment for any part of it, the workman will be deprived of all legal right to remuneration if the work is destroyed before completion. But if the workman is entitled to payment from time to time as the work proceeds, the destruction of the work before its completion will not deprive the workman of his hire.

Delegation of work. (16) — In most cases the workman may accomplish the work intrusted to him through the medium of inferior agents and workmen; but if the work is a work of art and genius, and the contract is founded upon the personal genius and capacity of the artist, he impliedly undertakes to perform the work himself.

Honorary and gratuitous services. (17) — The law raises no implied promise of remuneration for the services of trustees. The office of an arbitrator is generally honorary, and unless there is an express promise of payment, or such a promise can be inferred from the circumstances of the submission, he cannot maintain an action for remuneration.

The profession of the bar is honorary, and a barrister cannot maintain an action to recover his fees or for remuneration stipulated for by an express contract.

A physician may sue for his services, if he is registered as a physician under the Medical Act, and if he is not prohibited by the college to which he belongs from bringing an action for his charges.

If a service appears to have been rendered as a gratuitous act of kindness, or in discharge of a public duty, the presumption of a contract for payment is repelled. Thus, if a man undertakes a journey to become bail for his friend, or attends as a witness in a court of justice, he is not entitled to be paid for his trouble. In the last case, as the attendance to give evidence is a duty of a public nature, an express promise to remunerate the witness for so doing is invalid; but the witness is entitled to compensation according to a fixed scale framed by the judges.

ILLUSTRATIVE CASES.

(1) *Phillips* v. *Jones*, 1 *Ad. & E.* 333.

Defendant agreed with plaintiff's father to receive plaintiff (a minor) into his service on trial, and to take him as apprentice if approved of. Plaintiff went into the service, and worked for defendant nearly two years. After several applications made during that time by the father, defendant told the father that plaintiff should serve out the two years, and then be bound, the father paying defendant £10. This was agreed to, but defendant shortly after quarrelled with plaintiff, and sent him home. Plaintiff's father applied to defendant for an explanation, which defendant declined to give; and he refused either to take the plaintiff as his apprentice or to recompense him for his work. The judge put it to the jury on these facts, whether or not the defendant's conduct was such as warranted the father in considering the contract for an apprenticeship rescinded; and he stated that, if they thought it was, they were to give plaintiff such compensation for his work as they thought proper. The jury found a verdict for the plaintiff, with damages by way of compensation for his services. Held, that the judge's direction was right, and the verdict not to be disturbed.

Davies v. *Davies*, 9 *C. & P.* 87.

A. and his wife boarded and lodged in the house of B., the brother of A., and both A. and his wife assisted B. in carrying on his business. A. brought an action for the services, to which B. pleaded a set off for board and lodging :—Held, that neither the services on the one hand, nor the board and lodging on the other, could be charged for, unless the jury were satisfied that the parties came together on the terms that they were to pay and to be paid.

(2) *Rex* v. *Lyth*, 5 *T.R.* 327.

If a husbandman serve for a year, it is strong presumptive evidence that he served under a yearly hiring.

Rex v. *Birdbrooke*, 4 *T.R.* 245.

Lord Kenyon, C.J. : " It is said, this cannot be considered to be a hiring for a year, because there was a reservation of weekly wages, and because each party was to be at liberty to put an end to the agreement by giving a fortnight's notice; but whether the wages be to be paid by the week, or by the year, cannot make any alteration in the duration of the service, if the contract were for a year. This was a contract for a year, at so much a week."

Rex v. *Pucklechurch*, 5 *East* 382.

Where nothing is said in a contract of hiring about time, but there is a reservation of weekly wages, it is a weekly hiring only. Therefore, where the contract was for the servant to live with his master, the latter finding him board and lodging, and paying him 2s. 6d. per week—Held, that no settlement in the parish could be gained by service for more than a year under such contract.

(3) *Johnson v. Blenkensopp, 5 Jur. 870.*

By a written memorandum of agreement between the defendant and the plaintiff, the plaintiff was "to have 6s. a week, three bolls of wheat, to set potatoes for his family's use, to have a cow kept, house and firing, to keep the gardens and pleasure grounds in clean and good order, to assist in the stables, and, when required, at hay and corn harvest, and to make himself generally useful. To enter May 12th, 1838." The defendant had dismissed the plaintiff upon a month's warning. In an action brought by the plaintiff to recover a quarter's wages, as being a yearly servant: Held, that he was a menial servant, and was therefore by the general rule of law entitled to a month's notice only; and that the memorandum of agreement contained nothing which showed an intention in the parties to exclude that rule.

(4) *Rex v. Gt. Bowden, 7 B. & C. 249.*

Upon a special case, the Court of Quarter Sessions found that a pauper had hired himself as ostler to an innkeeper, that no earnest or wages were given, but he was to have what he could get as ostler, and be lodged and boarded in his master's house, and that either the master or servant might have determined the service when he pleased. It was held, that upon this finding, there could not be taken to have been any general or yearly hiring, and that no settlement in the parish was gained by serving under it.

(5) *Harmer v. Cornelius, 5 C.B., N.S. 236.*

Where a skilled labourer, artizan, or artist is employed, there is on his part an implied warranty that he is of skill reasonably competent to the task he undertakes. The plaintiff, who represented himself as an experienced scene painter, was hired by the defendant for a month. He was, however, found to be so incompetent that the defendant discharged him at the end of the second day. In an action for wrongful dismissal, Held, that the defendant was justified in dismissing the plaintiff.

(6) *Horton v. McMurtrey, 29 Law J., Exch. 260.*

The plaintiff was employed by the defendant to serve him faithfully in the business of a certain manufacture. Without the knowledge of his master, the plaintiff entered into a contract with a merchant (not dealt with by the defendant) for the supply of certain articles used in the manufacture, the result of which was a claim to a considerable amount by the merchant against the plaintiff's master, who thereupon dismissed him. Held, that the dismissal of the plaintiff was justifiable, and that a verdict for the defendant must be supported.

Spotswood v. Barrow, 5 Exch. 110.

To an action for wrongfully discharging the plaintiff from the defendants' service as traveller and salesman, the defendants pleaded that the plaintiff refused to obey the lawful and reasonable commands of the defendants in the said employ, and that the plaintiff received from divers customers of the defendants divers moneys, which he wrongfully appropriated to his own use; wherefore the defendants did, by reason of the premises, refuse to continue the plaintiff in their employ. At the trial it was proved that the plaintiff had misappropriated the defendants' moneys, but the fact of such misappropriation was not known to the defendants until after they had discharged the plaintiff. Held, that the defendants, having justifiable cause for discharging the plaintiff, the learned judge was wrong in leaving it to the jury to say whether they discharged him for that cause.

(7) *Cuckson* v. *Stones*, 1 *Ell. & Ell.* 248.

Plaintiff, by agreement in writing, agreed to serve defendant for the term of ten years in the capacity of a brewer. In consideration of the premises, and "of the due, full, and complete service" of plaintiff, "as aforesaid," defendant agreed to pay plaintiff £20 on execution of the agreement, to furnish him with a house and coals "during the whole of the said term of ten years," and to pay him "the weekly sum of £2 10s. during the said term of ten years." Plaintiff entered into defendant's service under the agreement. Some years afterwards plaintiff fell ill, and was unable to attend personally to business. Defendant refused to pay plaintiff his wages for the period during which he had been ill, but retained him in his service; and after he was able to attend again personally to business, paid him as before under the agreement. To an action by plaintiff to recover wages for the period during which he had been ill, defendant pleaded, that plaintiff was not, during any part of the time for which such wages were claimed, ready and willing or able to render, and did not in fact during any part of such time render, the agreed, or any service. Held, that the averment that plaintiff was not ready and willing, &c., was not supported by his physical inability, for a time only, and not through his own default, to attend personally to business; and that the contract not having been rescinded, the defendant was not entitled to suspend the weekly payments during that time.

(8) *Tasker* v. *Shepherd*, 6 *H. & N.* 575.

A declaration stated that by agreement in writing between B., since deceased, and the defendant, of the one part, and the plaintiff of the other part, B. and the defendant, who at the date of the agreement were carrying on business as stone merchants in co-partnership, appointed the plaintiff their sole London agent for a period of four years and a-half, and the plaintiff, in consideration of the premises, agreed to accept the appointment upon the terms (amongst others) that B. and the defendant should pay the plaintiff 2½ per cent. on all accounts received by them for stone sold by the plaintiff, or supplied by B. and the defendant to any person originally introduced to them by the plaintiff. Breach: that the defendant did not nor would employ the plaintiff as his sole agent for the whole period of four years and a-half, and did not nor would execute certain orders for stone procured by the plaintiff in his said capacity as agent. On demurrer: Held, that the parties contracted with reference to the then existing partnership business, and that the contract was to employ the plaintiff for a period of four years and a-half, subject to the condition that all the parties so long lived.

(9) *Goodman* v. *Pocock*, 15 *Q.B.* 576.

A clerk dismissed in the middle of a quarter brought an action for wrongful dismissal. The jury were directed not to take into account the services actually rendered during the broken quarter, as no special claim was made in respect of them; and damages were given accordingly. The plaintiff then brought a second action to recover under an indebitatus count for his services during the broken quarter. Held, that the action was not maintainable; because the plaintiff, by his former action on the special contract, had treated it as an open contract, and he could not afterwards recover under the indebitatus count, as for services under a rescinded contract.

Held also, that in the former action the jury ought to have been directed to take the services rendered during the broken quarter into account in awarding damages under the special count for the wrongful dismissal.

(10) *Rex* v. *Gt. Wishford*, 5 *N. & M.* 540.

The true test whether an agreement was a contract of hiring, or of apprenticeship, is the apparent object of the parties, and if that object is for one party to teach and the other to learn, the agreement is a contract of apprenticeship. And it is not necessary that the precise words "to teach" or "to learn" should occur in the agreement.

Cuming v. *Hill*, 3 *B. & Ald.* 59.

Action of covenant upon an indenture of apprenticeship, by the master against the father; breach, that the apprentice absented himself from the service; plea, that the son faithfully served till he came of age, and that he then avoided the indenture. Held, that this was no answer to the action.

(11) *Baxter* v. *Burfield*, 2 *Str.* 1266.

An apprentice is not bound to serve the executor of the master. Lee, C.J.: "The binding was to the *man*, to learn *his* art, and to serve *him*, without any mention of executors. And, as the words are confined, so is the nature of the contract, for it is fiduciary, and the lad is bound from a personal knowledge of the integrity and ability of the master."

Whincup v. *Hughes*, *L.R.* 6 *C.P.* 78.

The plaintiff apprenticed his son to a watchmaker and jeweller for the term of six years, paying to the master a premium of £25. The master duly instructed the apprentice for a year, and then died. The plaintiff sought in an action against the master's executrix for money had and received, to recover the whole or some part of the premium, on the ground of failure of consideration. Held, that such failure being only partial, the action was not maintainable.

(12) *Higgins* v. *Hopkins*, 3 *Exch.* 166.

Parke, B.: "If a party merely speculates on the chance of being paid, taking the risk whether funds will be collected and appropriated to his demand, there is no contract. If he does work on the order of another, under such circumstances as that it must be presumed that he looks to be paid as *a matter of right* by him, then a contract would be implied with that person.".

(13) *Planché* v. *Colburn*, 1 *M. & Sc.* 51.

The plaintiff contracted for a certain sum to write for the defendant a treatise, to be published in a periodical work called "The Juvenile Library." Before the completion of the treatise the defendant ceased to publish "The Juvenile Library." Held, that the plaintiff might recover on a *quantum meruit* for the part of the work he had done, notwithstanding that he had neither delivered nor tendered the treatise or any part of it.

(14) *Needler* v. *Guest*, *Aleyn* 9.

An attorney covenanted to pay his clerk 2*s.* for every quire of paper he copied out. Held, that this was an entire covenant of which no apportionment could be made *pro ratâ*, and that the clerk consequently could not maintain an action to recover remuneration for copying out any less number of sheets than a quire.

Andrews v. *Belfield*, 2 *C.B.*, *N.S.* 779.

A. gave an order to B., a coach-builder, in the following terms: " I now give you the order in general terms only, and on the assumption that you undertake to execute it in a manner which shall meet my approval, not only on the score of workmanship, but also that of convenience and taste." The carriage was thereupon built and forwarded to A., who found many faults with it, and rejected it. Held, that the order having been given and accepted on the express condition that the carriage should meet the approval of A. on the score of "convenience and taste," the latter was entitled, acting *bonâ fide* and not from mere caprice, to reject it.

Lucas v. *Godwin*, 3 *B.N.C.* 744.

Plaintiff contracted to build cottages by the 10th of October; they were not finished till the 15th. Defendant having accepted the cottages—Held, that plaintiff might recover the value of his work, on a declaration for work and labour and materials.

Farnsworth v. *Garrard*, 1 *Campb.* 38.

Where the plaintiff declares on a *quantum meruit* for work and labour done, and materials found, the defendant may reduce the damages by showing that the work was improperly done; and may entitle himself to a verdict by showing that it was wholly inadequate to answer the purpose for which it was undertaken to be performed.

(15) ### *Appleby* v. *Myers*, *L.R.* 2 *C.P.* 651.

Where A. contracts to do work and supply materials upon the premises of B. for a specific sum, to be paid on the completion of the whole, A. is not entitled to recover anything until the whole work is completed, unless it be shown that the performance of his contract was prevented by the default of B.

The plaintiffs contracted to erect certain machinery on the defendant's premises, the price to be paid on the completion of the whole. After some portions of the work had been finished, and others were in course of completion, the premises, with all the machinery thereon, were destroyed by an accidental fire. Held, that both parties were excused from the further performance of the contract, but that the plaintiffs were not entitled to sue in respect of those portions of the work which had been completed, whether the materials used had become the property of the defendant or not.

Mentone v. *Athawes*, 3 *Burr.* 1592.

If a shipwright is employed to repair a ship; and if the completion of the work is not made by custom or agreement a condition precedent to the payment, and the ship is accidentally burnt, the loss of the materials supplied by him, as well as of the value of the work and labour employed upon them, is the loss of the employer and not of the workman, and the employer, consequently, must pay the fair value of the labour and materials, although he can reap no benefit from what has been done.

(16) ### *Robson* v. *Drummond*, 2 *B. & Ad.* 308.

A., a coachmaker, entered into an agreement to furnish B. with a carriage for the term of five years, at seventy-five guineas a year. At the time of making the agreement, C. was a partner with A., but this was unknown to B., the business being carried on in the name of A. only. Before the expiration of the first three years the partnership between A. and C. was dissolved, A. having assigned all his interest in the business, and in the contract in question, to C., and the business was afterwards carried on by C. alone. B. was informed by C. that the partnership was dissolved, and that he (C.) had become the proprietor of the carriage, then in B.'s service. B. answered that he would not continue the contract with C., and that he would return the carriage to him at the end of the then current year, and he did so return it. An action having been brought in the names of A. and C. against B. for the two payments, which, according to the terms of the contract, would become due during the last two years of its continuance: Held, that the action was not maintainable, the contract being personal, and A. having transferred his interest to C., and having become incapable of performing his part of the agreement.

(17) *Barrett* v. *Hartley, L.R. 2 Eq.* 789.

A trustee has no right to exact or charge any remuneration or bonus in respect of great advantages accrued to the *cestui que trust* from services incident to the performance of the duties imposed by the deed of trust. A settled account by a *cestui que trust*, allowing a bonus to the trustee, set aside.

Viramy v. *Warne, 4 Esp.* 47.

Action brought by an executor to recover a sum of money alleged to be due to the testator for acting as an arbitrator on the part of the defendant, in a dispute which he had with his partner. Held, that the appointment of an arbitrator was not of such a nature as to raise a demand for payment, and that in the absence of an express promise the action was not maintainable.

As to barristers, see—*Kennedy* v. *Broun*, 13 *C.B., N.S.* 677.
As to physicians, see—*Gibbon* v. *Budd*, 2 *H. & C.* 92.
As to witnesses, see—*Nokes* v. *Gibbon*, 26 *Law J., Ch.* 208.

CHAPTER IX.

BAILMENTS AND LIEN.

Bailments Generally.

It is usual to divide bailments into six classes—(i) *Depositum;* (ii) *Mandatum;* (iii) *Commodatum;* (iv) *Vadium;* (v) *Locatio rei;* (vi) *Locatio operis faciendi.*

Depositum is a gratuitous bailment, in which goods are delivered to the bailee to keep for the use of the bailor. The bailee is only responsible for gross negligence; and if he keeps the goods deposited as he keeps his own, although he keeps his own but negligently, he is not responsible for damage which may happen to them; or rather, this is "a good argument in favour of his honesty." *Depositum.* (1)

Mandatum is where one acts by commission for another gratuitously. In this case, as in *Depositum*, the bailor alone benefits, and the bailee is responsible only for gross negligence. *Mandatum.* (2)

Commodatum is a gratuitous loan. The bailee alone benefits, and he is therefore answerable for the least neglect; but he is not chargeable when the goods are taken from him by superior force. *Commodatum.* (3)

Vadium, or pawn, gives a special property to the pawnee. Both the pawnor and the pawnee benefit; and the care required of the pawnee in keeping the goods is that "of a most careful householder"—a phrase which is construed to imply "ordinary diligence." *Vadium.* (4)

A creditor taking a pawn is obliged to restore it on payment of the debt; but if the pawnee use true diligence in keeping it, and it is lost, he may nevertheless resort to the pawnor for his debt.

The pawnee may not use the pawn if it be such as will be the worse for use, as clothes, &c.; but if it be such as will not be the worse, as a jewel, he may use it, but if he does so it is at his own peril, and even if he be robbed of it he will be answerable. [See further as to Pledge, Chapter XI.]

Locatio rei. (5) In *locatio rei*, or lending for hire, the bailee pays the bailor for the temporary use of the goods lent. The bailment is for the benefit of both parties, and the hirer is required to exercise the care of the most diligent householder, *i.e.*, ordinary diligence.

Locatio operis faciendi. In *locatio operis faciendi*, the bailor pays the bailee for keeping, carrying, managing or doing something to the thing bailed. Of this kind of bailment there are two classes—(i) Where the bailee does not exercise a public employment; and in this case the bailee is only bound to exercise ordinary diligence. (ii) Where the bailee exercises a public employment, as a common carrier, innkeeper, &c., he becomes, as will be seen, in fact an insurer, and is answerable for the goods committed to him, at all events.

It will be convenient to consider here the former of these two classes, and to reserve the consideration of the law relating to common carriers and innkeepers for the following sections.

Warehousemen, wharfingers, and depositaries for hire. (6) All persons to whom goods and chattels are delivered to be kept for hire, and who are paid expressly for the exercise of their labour and care in keeping them, and not merely for finding a place of deposit, are bound to exercise the same amount of care in their preservation as the most prudent and careful of men exercise in keeping their own property (*i.e.*, ordinary diligence).

Workmen, agisters. (7) And the same is the case with regard to a workman who has in his possession the chattels of another for the purpose of altering, mending, manufacturing, or making them up. So also an agister of cattle or other living animals is bound to take the utmost care of them.

Every man who undertakes to keep or carry goods is liable to an action if, through his neglect, they are lost, or come to any damage, although he is not a common carrier, and even although he receive no reward for his labour. "The confidence reposed in him is sufficient consideration to create a duty." *Bailees to carry who are not common carriers.* (8)

The bailee may make any fair and reasonable terms with the bailor, and may make his responsibility for the goods bailed dependent upon the observance of the conditions which he imposes. But such terms must not be devised for the purpose of fraud, or extortion, or for the purpose of exonerating the bailee from responsibility for his own negligence and misconduct. *Bailment of goods under special contract.*

If the subject-matter of the bailment be secretly stolen by the servant of the bailee, the latter is responsible, unless he can show that by the greatest vigilance he could not have guarded against or prevented the theft. But the bailee is not responsible for a robbery by irresistible violence. The mere fact of the loss of the thing bailed is *primâ facie* proof of negligence, and this presumption can only be rebutted by showing that the greatest care has been taken. *Theft or loss of thing bailed.* (9)

If the owner of the chattel bailed has conduced in any way to its loss, as by bringing persons to inspect it at the place where it is deposited, or otherwise, the bailee is absolved from responsibility. *Contributory negligence of bailor.* (10)

Common Carriers.

Every person is a common carrier who plies with a carriage by land or with a vessel by water between different places, and professes openly to carry goods for hire. The *Definition of common carrier.* (11)

owner of a conveyance, who merely lets it out by the hour, day, or job, is not a common carrier.

Whether carriers of passengers are, or are not, to be regarded as "common carriers," their responsibility, as will be seen, varies from that of common carriers of goods.

Normal responsibility of common carriers. (12) A common carrier is bound to the strictest diligence, and not only this, but he is made in fact an insurer, and compelled to answer for all loss and injury whatever, except such as is occasioned by the act of God, or the king's enemies, or such as arises from natural deterioration or inherent vice.

By the "act of God" is meant something in opposition to the act of man, such as storms, lightning, and inevitable accidents, not resulting from human agency. By the king's enemies are meant hostile armaments, and not mere predatory bands.

The common carrier is obliged to carry the goods of any person who proffers payment, unless the conveyance is full, or the goods are such that, from the construction of the conveyance, he cannot carry them, or such as he does not profess to carry, or, unless the risk is extraordinary, or the goods are "specially dangerous" under 29 & 30 Vict. c. 69, s. 6.

Limitation of normal responsibility of common carriers (i) with regard to certain valuable articles. (13) At common law, a carrier receiving goods has a right to ask necessary questions with regard to them; and if he ask no questions he is responsible, in the absence of fraud, for the parcel, of whatever value it may prove to be.

Under the Carriers' Act (11 Geo. IV. & 1 Will. IV. c. 68) a carrier is not liable for the loss of gold, silver, jewels, watches, and other costly articles therein enumerated, of value exceeding £10, unless the nature of the article has been declared; and for carrying such goods the carrier may demand an increased tariff. In cases within the Act, that is, where loss or damage has occurred to any of the articles mentioned in the Act, their value not having been declared, the carrier is not liable even for gross negligence. He is, however, still liable for delay or omission, and for damage arising from his own misfeasance, or the felonious acts of his servants.

The carrier must announce, by notice, the increased tariff which he requires for undertaking the carriage of the valuable articles mentioned in the Act. If he omit this notice he cannot claim any extra charge, nor is he entitled to any benefit under the Act. (Carriers' Act, sec. 2.)

Where an increased rate has been charged, as provided by the Act, and the goods are lost, such increased charge may be recovered as well as the value of the goods. The carrier is not concluded as to the value of the goods by the declaration which has been made, but he may demand further evidence from the plaintiff claiming damages.

The Carriers' Act applies solely to carriers by land. But where the contract is for carriage, partly by land, and partly by water, and the loss occurs during the carriage by land, the carrier is entitled to the benefit of the statute.

By the Railway and Canal Traffic Act (17 & 18 Vict. c. 31, extended to railway companies' steamboats by the 26 & 27 Vict. c. 92) a railway or canal company is exempted from liability for loss or damage to horses, cattle, and other animals mentioned, to a greater extent than certain sums named in the Act, unless the sender has declared them to be of greater value at the time of delivery, and paid an increased charge accordingly. For animals not mentioned in the Act, full compensation may be claimed, although no declaration of value has been made.

The same rules with regard to the notification of the increased tariff apply under the Railway and Canal Traffic Act as under the Carriers' Act.

At common law, a common carrier might by notice exonerate himself from liability, except for gross negligence, by public notice, provided such notice could be brought home to the knowledge of the consignor.

<small>Limitation of normal responsibility of common carriers (ii) by notice.</small>

But by the Carriers' Act (see above) the carrier is concluded from limiting his responsibility by notice with respect to articles not mentioned in the Act. (Carriers' Act, sec. 4.)

And, by the Railway and Canal Traffic Act, all notices which affect to limit the responsibility of railway and canal companies, beyond its own provisions, and those of the Carriers' Act, are declared null and void (sec. 16).

Railway companies may, however, by notice declare themselves not responsible for the luggage of passengers by certain trains—as excursion trains.

And a ticket upon which notice is printed (as a railway passenger's ticket) may in some cases avail as in fact forming a special contract. See *infra*.

Limitation of normal responsibility of common carriers by special contract. (14) The Carriers' Act took away the right of the carrier to limit his responsibility with regard to articles not mentioned in the Act *by notice*, but it left untouched the right to do so by special contract. And carriers were able to contract themselves out of liability for gross negligence, misconduct, and even fraud. And this is still the law with regard to special contracts, where the Railway and Canal Traffic Acts do not apply, and in the case of passengers.

Under the Railway and Canal Traffic Act (sec. 7), railway and canal companies can only limit their responsibility by special contract when that contract is signed by the consignor or his agent, and when its provisions are such as a court of law deems reasonable. And a condition in a special contract, which seeks to exempt a company from liability for gross negligence or misconduct, has been held to be unreasonable.

Limitation of responsibility in case of carriers by water. Carriers by water enjoy special limitations of responsibility beyond the common law exemptions, where loss has arisen by the act of God, or of the king's enemies.

Ship-owners, whether common carriers or not, are by 26 Geo. III. c. 86 exempted from liability in respect of loss or damage to ships by fire, and in respect of the loss of gold, silver, watches, or jewels by robbery or embezzlement, unless their value has been declared.

Ship-owners are exempted also from responsibility for loss occasioned by the incompetency of a licensed pilot. By the 7 Geo. II. c. 15, ship-owners are not liable beyond the value of their vessel and freight, where loss has occurred by the misconduct of the mariners or ship-master. This provision was extended by 26 Geo. II. to all cases of loss by robbery, and by 53 Geo. III. to all cases of loss. But the ship-master is never relieved from responsibility in these cases, though he be part owner of the vessel.

Ship-owners are permitted to contract themselves out of responsibility, even for the negligence or default of the master, or mariners, or others. But a condition that a ship-owner should not be liable for breakage and leakage does not discharge him for gross negligence.

By the 31 & 32 Vict. c. 119, a company which books goods partly by land and partly by sea may have the benefit of the conditions usually inserted in a charter-party, if such conditions be publicly notified at the office of booking, and printed on the receipt or freight note. [By invariable usage charter-parties contain express stipulations against liability for loss occasioned by any accident of navigation.] *Carriers partly by land and partly by water.*

Where a consignor fraudulently conceals the value of goods the carrier is relieved from responsibility if they are lost or stolen. Where goods are specially dangerous, and the consignor neglects to give notice to that effect to the carrier, the former will be responsible for any damage which the said goods may occasion, either to the carrier or to another consignor. *Concealment by consignor. (15)*

The responsibility of a carrier of passengers is greater than that of a mere bailee to carry (who, as we have seen, is responsible only for ordinary diligence), but it is less than that of a common carrier of goods. He does not, like the latter, become an insurer of safe conveyance, but he undertakes that, "so far as human care and foresight can go," he *Carriers of passengers. (16)*

will provide the same. He is liable for unskilfulness as well as for negligence. He impliedly warrants that his carriages are carefully constructed; but he is not responsible where a defect in their construction could not be discovered by an ordinary examination. The breaking down of a coach is *primâ facie* proof of negligence, and where an overloaded coach breaks down, the accident is attributed to the overloading. A coachman is bound to warn passengers of special dangers. A passenger may, as we have seen, agree by special contract to travel at his own risk. And the carrier is released from responsibility where the negligence of the passenger himself has contributed towards the accident, but not where it caused a part only of the accident. Railway companies may be sued by passengers for loss or damage caused by their not running trains in accordance with their printed time bills.

If a railway should become blocked by snow, or otherwise, the company is bound to use all reasonable exertions, and if necessary to incur extra expense to forward the passengers. [In the case of animals and goods this is not so.]

Passengers' luggage. (17) Railway companies are common carriers of passengers' luggage. Under this term are included all such things as a traveller usually carries for his own personal use or convenience. But merchandise is not luggage, and the railway company is not bound to carry it, unless the passenger is ready to pay the customary hire for merchandise.

In the case of excursion trains, where the railway company does not profess to receive luggage for conveyance, but allows the passenger to carry a small quantity under his own care, he does so at his own risk.

Delivery by carrier. (18) By the Railway and Canal Traffic Acts the carrier is bound to forward goods delivered to him without partiality and without delay. If the destination of the goods is marked out, the carrier must forward them to the house or place of business of the consignee at the earliest opportunity;

and if he suffers them to remain in his warehouse before forwarding them he is responsible as a common carrier for loss or damage which may happen to them whilst there, for they are still *in transitu*. But if the goods, after having been carried, are received into the warehouse of the carrier to await the orders of the consignee or owner as to their destination, the carrier is clothed only with the responsibilities of a warehouseman or bailee for hire. The carrier is justified in varying the place of destination by notice from the consignee, or by notice received *during transit* from the consignor.

If the carrier tender the goods at the house or place of business of the consignee, and is ready to deliver them on payment of the hire, he has fulfilled his contract as a carrier; and if the hire is not paid, he is not bound to part with the possession of the goods; but he may take them back to his own warehouse; and he holds them henceforward as a bailee for hire, or as a gratuitous bailee, according as he does or does not charge warehouse rent. The master of a foreign vessel is discharged from liability when he has delivered his cargo, after proper notice to the consignee, at the wharf of the port of destination. A railway passenger's luggage is delivered when it is placed on the platform of the station at the place of destination. But the responsibility of the company continues so long as the luggage remains in the custody of the servants of the company who are employed to convey it from the platform to a vehicle.

Innkeepers.

Every person who makes it his business to entertain travellers and passengers, and provide lodging and necessaries for them and their attendants and horses, is a common innkeeper. Definition. (19)

Duty of innkeepers. (20)

An innkeeper is bound to afford such shelter and accommodation as he possesses to all travellers who apply for it, and are ready to pay the customary hire, and who are not drunk, or disorderly, or labouring under contagious or infectious disease. He is also bound to provide for the horses of travellers, if he has room in his stables; even (*semble*) if the travellers themselves resort elsewhere for lodging and entertainment. He is not bound to receive the goods of a person who professes merely to make use of the inn as a place of deposit, and not to lodge there as a guest.

The extent of the duty of an innkeeper depends mainly upon the nature of his public profession. Thus, if he professes only to receive the ordinary luggage accompanying a traveller, he is not bound to take in articles of extraordinary bulk, nor goods which do not accompany the person of the traveller.

Liability of innkeeper at common law. (21)

The innkeeper is not answerable for those things which are not within the inn and the adjacent offices and stables. Thus, if an innkeeper lodges a man and his horse, and the owner requires that the horse be put out to pasture, and there he is stolen, the innkeeper is not answerable; but if the innkeeper, of his own accord, and without the request of the owner, puts the horse out to grass, and it is stolen, the innkeeper is answerable.

The innkeeper is bound by law to keep safely all the goods and chattels of his guest within his inn; and although the guest does not deliver his goods to the innkeeper to hold, nor acquaints him with them, yet if they be carried away or stolen the innkeeper is answerable, although it is not known who carried them away or stole them. But the innkeeper is not chargeable for the loss of his guest's goods, unless there be a default in him or his servants in the well and safe keeping and custody of them. If the guest's servant, or he who comes with him, or he whom he desires to be lodged with him, steals or carries away his goods, the innkeeper shall not be charged; but if the innkeeper appoints one to lodge with him he shall answer for him.

If the innkeeper declines to be answerable for the goods of his guest, unless the latter will keep them in a particular chamber, under lock and key, and the guest does not do so, the innkeeper is not responsible for their loss.

If a guest take upon himself the exclusive charge of the goods which he brings into the house of an innkeeper, he cannot afterwards charge the innkeeper with their loss.

By 26 & 27 Vict. c. 41 it is enacted that no innkeeper shall be liable to make good to any guest any loss of, or injury to, goods or property brought to his inn, not being a horse or any other live animal, or any gear appertaining thereto, or any carriage, to a greater amount than £30; except where such goods or property shall have been stolen, lost, or injured through the wilful act, default, or neglect of such innkeeper, or any servant in his employ; or where such goods shall have been deposited expressly for safe custody with such innkeeper. *Statutory limitation of the common law liability of innkeepers.*

The innkeeper may require, in the case of such deposit for safe custody, that the goods be placed in a box, or other receptacle, fastened and sealed by the guest.

A copy of the first section of the Act is required to be exhibited in a conspicuous part of the hall or entrance of the inn. And if such copy be not exhibited, or if the innkeeper refuse to receive for safe custody such goods, the innkeeper is not entitled to the benefit of the Act.

The innkeeper is relieved from liability, if the negligence of the guest so far occasions the loss that, if the latter had used the ordinary care of a prudent man, the loss would not have happened. *Contributory negligence of the guest.*

The length of time which a man remains in an inn does not alter his character as a traveller; but if a man takes apartments at an inn for a term, as by the week, month, or year, or if he resides at the inn under a special contract *Who are guests and travellers.* (22)

R

as to board and lodging, he is not staying at the inn as a traveller. He is to be regarded as a lodger at a private boarding-house.

If a man who has been a guest gives up his room, and asks permission to leave his goods at the inn, and the innkeeper takes charge of them, the latter is clothed only with the ordinary responsibilities of a bailee.

Liability of lodging-house keeper. (23) A lodging-house keeper, not being an innkeeper, is not responsible for the robbery of the goods of his guest, whether by his own servants or by others; but it is his duty to take such care of his house as every prudent householder might be expected to take, and to be careful in his choice of servants. If articles belonging to the lodger are actually placed in his hands, he is responsible for them like any other bailee; but he is not a bailee of them merely by reason of their having accompanied the person of the lodger. The lodger must take care of his own goods.

Lien of Bailees.

Lien. Lien is the right to retain the property of another until some pecuniary demand upon, or in respect of, it has been satisfied by the owner. Liens are of two kinds, particular and general.

Particular lien. (24) A particular lien consists in the right to retain goods in respect of labour or money expended upon them, and liens of this kind are favoured by law.

Thus, workmen and artificers have a lien upon chattels upon which, at the request of the owner, they have exercised their skill for a fair and reasonable remuneration, or if a price has been fixed by agreement, for that price.

General lien. (25) General lien is the right of a manufacturer, or workman, factor, broker, commission agent for the sale of goods, warehouseman, or wharfinger, into whose hands goods have been placed in the ordinary course of their employment, to retain possession of them, not only until they have received payment of the hire due to them for their services in the particular employment, but also for the general balance due to them from their employer in the ordinary course of dealing for work and services of the like nature, bestowed at other times upon goods of the employer. This right depends either upon the custom and usage of the particular trade, or upon the express agreement of the parties, and general liens are not like particular liens, favoured by law.

The usage, when it exists, must be shown to be long established and notorious, fair and reasonable, and not contrary to any established principle of law.

Bankers have a lien upon all the securities for money (notes, bills, negotiable instruments, &c.) of their customers, in their hands, for their advances to such customers in the ordinary course of business. Bankers. (26)

Solicitors have a lien upon all money recovered by them in actions in which they are employed, and upon deeds and papers of their clients, for the costs due to them generally by their clients. But where deeds are delivered for a specific purpose, the right of lien is extinguished as soon as the particular purpose has been accomplished, and it may be superseded altogether by the solicitor's taking from the client security for his costs. The town agent of a country solicitor has a lien only upon the money recovered, and upon the papers in his hands in the particular cause in which he is engaged, for the amount due to him in that particular cause. He cannot set up a claim of lien for the general balance due to him from the country solicitor who employs him, and his lien is limited to the debt actually due from the client to the country solicitor, so that, if the country client pays the country solicitor, the lien is discharged, for the country solicitor cannot give the town agent a lien which he does not himself possess. Solicitors. (27)

Every workman or artificer, not being a public innkeeper, General

lien by notice. (28) common carrier, or common ferryman, and not, therefore, being bound to exercise his calling in favour of all persons who may require his services, has a right to prescribe the terms upon which he will receive goods into his possession, to be dealt with in the ordinary course of his trade; and he may by express notice reserve to himself a general lien.

Agreements inconsistent with lien. (29) A person cannot set up a right of lien, either particular or general, which is at variance with the terms, or conditions, or implied understanding, upon which he received the property. Thus a lien is wholly inconsistent with a dealing on credit, and can only exist where payment is to be made in ready money, or where security is to be given the moment the work is completed.

Lien originating in tort. (30) A mere wrong-doer, who gets possession of property without the consent of the owner, cannot in general so deal with it as to create a lien as against the true owner, unless the person in whose possession the property is placed by the wrong-doer is a common carrier or public innkeeper; for persons exercising public employment of this nature are compelled to exercise their calling in favour of all who require their services.

Extinguishment of lien. (31) If a bailee, who has a right of lien upon property in his possession, *voluntarily* parts with the possession of such property, the lien is gone, and if he afterwards recover possession of the property, his right of lien does not revive.

Actions against Bailees.

Detinue. If the bailee retains the goods bailed to him, and refuses to return them to the bailor when the latter is entitled to their possession, and has requested that they should be delivered to him, this is an adverse or wrongful detention on the part of the bailee sufficient to support an action of detinue.

By the Common Law Procedure Act, 1854, in an action of detinue, the judge has power, on the application of the plaintiff, to order the return of the chattel detained, and if the chattel cannot be found, the judge may order the defendant to be distrained by all his lands and chattels in the bailiwick, until he render such chattel, or, at the option of the plaintiff, the assessed value of the chattel may be made of the defendant's goods.

When an action is brought against the bailee by a third party claiming the thing bailed, the bailee may interplead, and the bailor may be made defendant in the action instead of the bailee (1 & 2 Will. IV. c. 58, and 23 & 24 Vict. c. 126).

An action against a bailee for loss of goods should be brought by the owner of the goods. Where goods are delivered to a carrier to be conveyed to a purchaser in fulfilment of a contract of sale, the consignee is the owner of the goods; so that if they are lost he must sue for the loss of them. But if goods are not delivered to the carrier in pursuance of a contract of sale; or if from fraud, or non-compliance with the Statute of Frauds, no actual sale has taken place, and no interest has vested in the consignee, then the consignor is the proper person to sue for the loss of the goods. Where the bailee of goods, who has a special property in them, employs a carrier to convey the goods to the bailor, and the bailee pays the carrier, either the consignor or the consignee may sue the carrier for the loss of the goods, and whichever first obtains damages, it is a full satisfaction. *Loss of goods by carrier. (32)*

Every person who has been injured by the negligent performance of the work of carrying, may maintain an action against the carrier, although the work was done under a special contract to which he was not a party. Thus, a servant may maintain an action against a railway company for injuries arising from their negligence, although his master contracted and paid for his conveyance. *Injury to passenger. (33)*

ILLUSTRATIVE CASES.

(1) *Giblin* v. *M'Mullen, L.R.* 2 *P.C.* 317.

The plaintiff, a customer, deposited with the defendant's bank a strong box containing securities, himself retaining the key. The box was placed in the strong room where the securities of the bank were kept, and to which the cashier of the bank had access. The bank received nothing for keeping the box. Some of the securities in question were abstracted from the box by the cashier, who absconded, and the plaintiff having obtained a verdict in an action against the bank—Held, on appeal, that there was no evidence of gross negligence for which alone the defendant as gratuitous bailee could be held liable.

(2) *Dartnall* v. *Howard,* 4 *B. & C.* 345.

The declaration stated, that in consideration that the plaintiff, at the request of the defendants, would employ them to lay out £1400 in purchasing an annuity, the defendants promised to perform and fulfil their duty in the premises, and that they did not perform or fulfil their duty, but on the contrary, laid out the money in the purchase of an annuity on the personal security of G. and A., who were both in insolvent circumstances. The court, after verdict, arrested judgment on the ground that the defendants appeared to be *gratuitous* agents, and it was not averred that they had acted either with negligence or dishonesty.

(3) *Wilson* v. *Brett,* 11 *M. & W.* 113.

A. rode the horse of B. gratuitously, at the request of B., for the purpose of showing it for sale. A. was shown to be a person conversant with and skilled in the management of horses. Held, that he was liable to B. for injuries received by the horse through his riding it in a careless and improper manner.

(4) *Anon,* 2 *Salk.* 522.

"If the pawn be somewhat that will be the worse for wearing, as clothes, &c., the pawnee cannot use it. But if it be somewhat that will not be the worse for wearing, as jewels, the pawnee may use them, but then it must be at peril; for if the pawnee be robbed in wearing them, he is answerable; also, if the pawn be of such a nature that the keeping is of charge to the pawnee, as if it be a cow or a horse, the pawnee may milk the cow or ride the horse; and this is in recompense of the keeping.

"In case the pawn is lost, the pawnee hath still his remedy for the money against the pawnor; for the law requires nothing extraordinary of the pawnee; but only that he shall use an ordinary care for the restoring of the goods."

(5) *Dean* v. *Keate,* 3 *Camp.* 4.

A hired horse being taken ill, the hirer, instead of calling in a farrier, prescribed for the horse himself, and from unskilfulness gave it a medicine which caused its death. Held, that the hirer was liable to the owner of the horse as for gross negligence.

(6) *Dover* v. *Mills,* 5 *C. & P.* 175.

A booking-office keeper, who also kept a wine vault, held to be liable for his negligence in allowing goods which had been booked with him to remain in front of the bar, exposed to persons coming in for liquor, and this although the goods were too large to be conveniently taken inside the bar, behind the counter.

(7) *Leck v. Maestaer*, 1 *Camp.* 137.

A workman for hire is not only bound to guard the thing bailed to him against ordinary hazards, but likewise to exert himself to preserve it from any unexpected danger to which it may be exposed.

The defendant was the proprietor of a dry-dock, into which a ship of the plaintiffs had been put to be repaired. Whilst she lay there, during a remarkably high tide, the dock gates were burst open by the water, and she was thereby forced against another vessel and greatly injured. When the accident happened, although it was in the day time, the workmen were all absent, and there was only a watchman left to take charge of the shipping in the dock. It was proved that the dock gates were rotten, but that with a proper number of hands they might have been shored up so as to resist the extraordinary pressure of the water. Held, that the defendant was answerable for the damage done to the plaintiffs' ship.

Broadwater v. Blot, *Holt*, 547.

If cattle be agisted, and the agister leave the gate of his field open, he uses less than ordinary diligence ; and if the cattle stray out and are stolen he is answerable.

(8) *Coggs v. Bernard*, 2 *Ld. Raym.* 909, *and* 1 *Sm. L.C.*

The plaintiff declared that the defendant undertook safely and securely to take up several hogsheads of brandy then in a certain cellar at D., and safely and securely to lay them down again in a certain other cellar in W., and that the said defendant, his servants and agents, so negligently and carelessly put them down again into the said cellar at W. that one of the casks was staved and a great quantity of brandy was spilt. After verdict for the plaintiff, it was moved in arrest of judgment that it was not alleged in the declaration that the defendant was a common porter, nor averred that he had anything for his pains. Held, nevertheless, that the defendant was liable.

[In this case, it will be observed that the defendant undertook to lay the goods down *safely*. But it would seem that whether a man undertakes gratuitously " to keep or carry safely," or merely to " keep or carry," he is equally responsible for gross negligence. See notes to *Coggs* v. *Bernard* in 1 *Sm. L.C.*]

(9) *Clarke v. Earnshaw*, *Gow*, 30.

A chronometer, bailed to a watchmaker to be repaired for hire, was placed by the bailee in a drawer in his shop amongst a variety of common watches, some of which belonged to the bailee and the rest to his customers, which drawer was locked at night, and in a recess in the same room stood a strong iron chest, in which watches belonging to the bailee of the value of several thousand pounds were deposited and locked up, and in the night the drawer was broken open by the bailee's servant who slept in the shop, and the chronometer was stolen by him, together with the other watches there deposited, but the watches in the iron chest remained untouched. It was held that as the bailee had taken more care of his own watches by locking them up in an iron safe than he had taken of the bailor's chronometer, he was responsible for the loss.

(10) *Cailiff* v. *Danvers*, 1 *P.N.P.C.* 155.

Assumpsit against the defendant, a warehouse-keeper, for negligently keeping a quantity of ginseng, whereby it had been destroyed and spoiled. It appeared that the box containing the ginseng had been opened by the plaintiff's directions for the purpose of showing it to intending purchasers. Every night the lid of the box was shut down but not nailed. Many cats were kept in the warehouse, and all possible care taken to destroy vermin, notwithstanding which the rats had got at the ginseng and destroyed it. Held, that the responsibility of a warehouseman is not like that of a carrier. He is only bound to exert reasonable diligence, and is not liable at all events; and that the defendant having exerted all due and common diligence for the preservation of the ginseng was not liable for this damage, which he could not prevent.

(11) *Brind* v. *Dale*, 8 *C. & P.* 207.

A town carman whose carts ply for hire near the wharfs, and who lets them by the hour, day, or job is not a common carrier.

Liver Alkali Co. v. *Johnson*, *L.R.* 9 *Ex.* 338.

A barge-owner, who lets out his barges to separate persons, under separate agreements for each voyage, the hirer fixing the termini, between which the vessel is to ply, incurs the liability of a common carrier. But *per* Brett, J.: "He is not a common carrier, but liable as such under custom."

(12) See *Coggs* v. *Bernard*, *ubi supra*, judgment of Holt, C.J.

"If the delivery be to one that exercises a public employment, and he is to have a reward, he is bound to answer for the goods at all events. And this is the case of the common carrier, common hoyman, &c. The law charges this person, thus intrusted, to carry goods against all events but acts of God and of the enemies of the king. For though the force be never so great, as if an irresistible multitude of people should rob him, nevertheless he is chargeable."

Oakley v. *Portsmouth & Ryde Steam Packet Co.*, 11 *Exch.* 618.

The defendants, who were common carriers, contracted with the plaintiff to carry his goods between Gosport and Ryde. The goods were put in a boat, and towed by a steam vessel of the defendants, which proceeded to Portsmouth pier to take in passengers. There was another vessel of the defendants' alongside the pier; and it was the usual and most safe course for the steam-boat so approaching to stop, until the other vessel had left. On this occasion, the steam-boat with the boat in tow was twice stopped, in consequence of the stopping of the other vessel, and on the second time of stopping, the tide lifted up the tow-boat, and pitched it on the rudder of the steam-boat, whereby the tow-boat sprung a leak, and the plaintiff's goods were damaged. There was no negligence on the part of the captain of either vessel. Held, that the damage was not caused by the act of God; and therefore the defendants were liable.

Crouch v. *London & North Western Railway Co.*, 14 *C.B.* 255.

One who holds himself out as a carrier of goods between two places, one of which is beyond the confines of England, is still subject to the common law liability of a carrier for hire, and is bound to accept all goods which are reasonably tendered to him for conveyance between those limits. A common carrier has no general right to refuse to receive a parcel tendered to him for conveyance, unless informed of the nature of its contents. A railway company acting as common carriers, and bound by statute to deal equally with all persons, cannot make a regulation for the conveyance of goods which in practice affects one person only.

(13) *Hearn* v. *London & South Western Railway Co.*, 10 *Exch.* 793.

The loss or injury to goods against which a carrier is protected by the 11 Geo. IV. & 1 Will. IV. c. 68, is a loss *by the carrier* of the articles committed to him, or injury to them whilst in his care, and not a loss sustained *by the owner* in consequence of the non-delivery of the article in due time or altogether, or the loss of the use of the article by him. Therefore, where the plaintiff sued for damage which accrued to him from the temporary loss of luggage, comprising certain valuable title deeds, owing to the negligence of the defendants to whom it had been delivered to be carried ; and the defendants pleaded that the package in question contained goods exceeding in value the sum of £10 ; but that the value had not been declared nor the increased charge paid—Held, that the plaintiff was nevertheless entitled to recover.

Metcalfe v. *London & Brighton Railway Co.*, 4 *C.B., N.S.* 307.

Action against a common carrier for the loss of a parcel ; plea, founded upon the Carriers' Act, that the value exceeded £10 and was not declared at the time of delivery to the carrier ; reply, that the loss arose from the felonious acts of the defendant's servants. Held, a good answer to the plea, and the plaintiff entitled to recover.

(14) *M'Manus* v. *Lancashire & Yorkshire Railway Co.*, 4 *H. & N.* 327.

The 17 & 18 Vict. c. 31, s. 7, which makes void all notices, conditions, and declarations made and given by a railway company, limiting their liability, unless such as the court or judge trying the cause may adjudge to be just and reasonable, extends to cases where a special contract has been signed in conformity with the subsequent provision in the statute. The plaintiff, on sending a horse by the defendants' line, signed a ticket containing a memorandum to the effect that the company would not be "responsible for any damage or injury howsoever caused to live stock" travelling on their railway. During the journey the horse was injured by a defect in the truck in which it was carried. Held, that the above condition was not just and reasonable, and was therefore void, and that the defendants were not protected from liability in respect of the defect in the truck.

(15) *Farrant* v. *Barnes*, 11 *C.B., N.S.* 553.

The defendant being desirous of sending a carboy of nitric acid to Croydon, his foreman gave it to one R., the servant of a railway carrier, who (as the railway company would only carry articles of that dangerous character on one day in each week) handed it to the plaintiff, the servant of a Croydon carrier, without communicating to him (and there being nothing in its appearance to indicate) its dangerous nature. Whilst being carried by the plaintiff to the cart, the carboy from some unexplained cause burst, and its contents flowed over and severely injured the plaintiff. Held, that the defendant was liable to the plaintiff for the injury.

(16) *Readhead* v. *Midland Railway Co.*, *L.R.* 4 *Q.B.* 379.

The contract made by a general carrier of passengers for hire with a passenger is to take due care (including in that term the use of skill and foresight) to carry the passenger safely ; and it is not a warranty that the carriage in which he travels shall be in all respects perfect for its purpose ;

that is to say, free from all defects likely to cause peril, although those defects were such that no skill, care, or foresight could have detected their existence.

McCawley v. *Furness Railway Co.*, *L.R.* 8 *Q.B.* 57.

Declaration, that plaintiff was a passenger by defendants' railway, and they so negligently conducted the management of their railway that an engine and tender came into collision with the train in which defendant was travelling, and he was injured thereby. Plea, that defendants received plaintiff to be carried under a free pass, as the drover accompanying cattle, one of the terms of which free pass was that plaintiff should travel at his own risk. Replication, that it was by reason of the gross and wilful negligence of defendants that the accident happened. On demurrer: Held, that the replication was bad; for that, whatever gross or wilful negligence might mean, plaintiff, by the terms on the pass, had agreed that defendants should not be liable for the consequences of any accident happening in the course of the journey for which they would otherwise have been liable. [And see *Gallin* v. *London and N. W. Railway Co.*, *L.R.* 10 *Q.B.* 212, and *Hall* v. *N. E. Railway Co.*, ibid. 437.]

Denton v. *Great Northern Railway Co.*, 5 *Ell. & Bl.* 860.

The Great Northern Railway Company, whose line communicated with the line of the North Eastern Railway Company at M., had arrangements by which their trains starting from P. at 7 p.m. and going to M., there met a train of the North Eastern Company running from M. to H., by which passengers from P. to H. were forwarded. The Great Northern Company published monthly time tables, in which they stated, in the usual way, that the 7 p.m. train from P. carried to H. At the end of a month, after the Great Northern time tables were prepared in this form and printed, but before they were published, the North Eastern Company discontinued the train from M. to H. The Great Northern made no alteration in their time tables already printed, but published and circulated them after they knew that there was no such train. Plaintiff, having seen one of these time tables, made his arrangements on the faith of it to go from P. to H. by the 7 p.m. train; he came to P. in time, went to the station, and then for the first time learned that he could go no further than M. by that train. He was delayed in his journey and sustained damage, for which he sued the Great Northern Company. On a case stated, Held, that he was entitled to recover, on the ground that the circulation of the time tables amounted to a representation on the part of the defendants that there was a train, which was false to the knowledge of those making it, and calculated to induce the plaintiff to act as he did. Held, also, that the time table amounted to a contract on behalf of the company with those who should come to the station to forward them as stated in the table. [As to delay occasioned by *vis major*, see *Fitzgerald* v. *Midland Railway Co.*, 34 *Law J.* 771.]

(17) *Stewart* v. *London & North Western Railway Co.*, 33 *Law J., Exch.* 199.

The holder of a railway excursion ticket—expressed to be "issued subject to the conditions contained in the company's excursion bills," one of which conditions was that "luggage under 60 lbs. should be carried free, at passenger's own risk"—is bound by the terms of this special contract, which is not void under the Railway and Canal Traffic Act; and he has consequently no claim against the company for the loss of his luggage, although it be proved that he did not know the condition on which it was being carried.

Great Northern Railway Co. v. *Shepherd,* 8 *Exch.* 30.

A carrier of passengers for hire is at common law only bound to carry their *personal* luggage; therefore, if a passenger has merchandise among his personal luggage, or so packed that the carrier has no notice that it is merchandise, he is not responsible for its loss. But if the merchandise is carried openly, or so packed that its nature is obvious, and the carrier does not object to it, he will be liable. The luggage of a passenger by railway, though never delivered to any servant of the company, but kept by the passenger during the journey, may nevertheless be, in point of law, in the custody of the company, so as to render them responsible for its loss. [But if the passenger carries his luggage in the carriage with him he must take ordinary care of it, otherwise, if it is lost, the company will not be responsible: see *Talley* v. *G. W. Railway Co.,* L.R. 6 *C.P.* 44.]

(18) *Cairns* v. *Robins,* 8 *M. & W.* 263

Goods were forwarded by a carrier's waggon to A. in London, and delivered by the carrier to him. A. sent them back to the carrier's warehouse, with directions that they were to await his orders. They remained there for upwards of a year, when they were lost out of the warehouse. A printed bill issued by the carrier, and sent to A. with the goods, stated that "any goods that should have remained three months in the warehouse without being claimed, or on account of the non-payment of the charges thereon, would be sold to defray the carriage or other charges thereon, or the general lien, as the case might be, together with warehouse rent and expenses." The carrier had often before carried goods for A., but no goods of his had before lain in the carrier's warehouse. Held, that the carrier was not, under these circumstances, a mere gratuitous bailee of the goods at the time of their loss; and therefore, that A. might recover against him the value of the goods, on a declaration in assumpsit alleging that they were delivered to the defendant to be safely kept for the plaintiff for a reasonable compensation and reward to be therefore paid him.

Storr v. *Crowley,* *M'Cl. & Y.* 129.

Common carriers received goods of S. at L. on an undertaking to carry them to W. and deliver them to S., for his use, on payment of the hire. The goods were carried to W., and sent from the warehouse, nearly half a mile, to the house of S.; but, the hire not being ready to be paid, were taken back to the warehouse. Applications to send the goods again to the house were refused, not on the ground that the contract had been performed by the proffer, but until satisfaction of a lien set up on one side and resisted by the other, and which proved to have been unfounded in fact. Held, under these circumstances, that the carriers had waived the benefit which would probably have resulted to them from insisting on the proffer as an execution of their undertaking; that both parties had treated the contract as one continuing contract from the commencement of the transaction till an actual delivery should have taken place; and that, the carriers not having performed their part of the agreement, the consignee was entitled to recover the value of the goods in an action of assumpsit.

Bourne v. *Gatliffe,* 3 *Sc. N.R.* 1.

Goods of the plaintiff were consigned to the defendant, a ship-owner, to be delivered at the port of London to the plaintiff or his assigns. The defendant landed the goods at the F. wharf at the port of London, but before a reasonable time for the plaintiff or his assigns to come and receive the goods had elapsed, they were destroyed by an accidental fire. Held, that the mere landing of the goods at the F. wharf without due notice to the consignee was not a sufficient delivery under the bill of lading, unless the usage and practice of the port of London made it so (which it did not), and that the defendants were liable for the loss, although they were not common carriers.

Richards v. *London, Brighton, &c., Railway Co.*, 7 C.B. 839.

The wife of the plaintiff became a passenger by a first-class carriage on the defendants' railway to be conveyed from A. to B.; her luggage, including a dressing case, was placed in the carriage, under the seat; on the arrival of the train at B., the porters of the company took upon themselves the duty of carrying the lady's luggage from the railway carriage to the hackney carriage which was to convey her to her residence; and on her arrival there the dressing case was missing. Held, that the duty of the defendants, as common carriers, continued until the luggage was placed in the hackney carriage; and that the plaintiff, on proof of the above facts, was entitled to a verdict. [As to the responsibility of railway companies for luggage deposited in cloak-rooms, see *Parker* v. *S. E. Railway Co.*, 1 C.P.D. 618, and *Harris* v. *G. W. Railway Co.*, 1 Q.B.D. 515.]

(19) *Parker* v. *Flint*, 12 Mod. 254.

By the statute of 4 & 5 W. & M. c. 13, s. 18, it was enacted "that constables should quarter soldiers upon innkeepers and such as keep ale-houses and victualling-houses, livery stables, or sell brandy, metheglin, or cider by retail." In an action brought by the plaintiff against a constable for quartering a dragoon and horse upon him, the jury found "that there were wholesome wells at Epsom, and that the plaintiff, during the season for drinking the waters, indefinitely let lodgings to such as went thither to drink the waters, for the air, or for their pleasure, and did dress victuals for them and sell them ale and beer, and entertained their horses at eightpence *per diem*, but sold no victuals, drink, &c., to any but the lodgers." Resolved, *per curiam*, that the plaintiff's house was not a house within the description of the statute. First, it was no inn; for the verdict found he let lodgings only, which shows him not compellable to entertain anybody, and that none could come there without a previous contract; that he was not bound to sell at reasonable rates, nor to protect his guests. Secondly, it was not an alehouse, or victualling house, for those words extend only to such alehouses and victualling houses as are known and described by certain Acts of Parliament, and which it is a crime to keep without licence. Judgment therefore for plaintiff.

(20) *Hawthorn* v. *Hammond*, 1 C. & K. 404.

A person who keeps a public-house is bound to admit all persons who apply peaceably to be admitted as guests. A declaration against an innkeeper stated that the defendant kept an inn, and that the plaintiff was travelling at night, and the inn being shut up, the plaintiff knocked at the door of the inn, in order that he should be admitted as a guest; and that, although the defendant heard the knocking, and had notice of the premises, she would not admit the plaintiff to the inn. The defendant pleaded that she did not hear the knocking, and had not notice of the premises. Held, that on this issue, it was for the jury to say whether the defendant heard the knocking, and if so, whether she ought to have concluded from it that the person, so knocking at the door, was a person requiring to be admitted as a guest.

York v. *Grindstone*, 2 Ld. Raym. 860.

If a traveller leave his horse at an inn, and lodge elsewhere, he is to be deemed a guest, "because it must be fed, by which the innkeeper hath gain; otherwise if he had left a dead thing." *Per* three judges against the opinion of Holt, C.J.

Broadwood v. Granara, 10 *Exch.* 423.

Parke, B. : " The principle upon which an innkeeper's lien depends is that he is bound to receive travellers and the goods which they bring with them to the inn. The lien cannot be claimed, except in respect of goods which, in performance of his duty to the public, he is bound to receive. The obligation to receive depends on his public profession. If he has only a stable for a horse, he is not bound to receive a carriage."

(21) See *Calye's case,* 8 *Co.* 32 ; 1 *Sm. L. C.,* and the five rules therein laid down by the judges of the Court of King's Bench with regard to the liability of innkeepers.

Burgess v. Clements, 4 *M. & S.* 306.

Goods belonging to a factor were lost out of a private room in the inn, chosen by the factor for the purpose of exhibiting them to his customers for sale, the use of which was granted to him by the innkeeper, who, at the same time, told him that there was a key, and that he might lock the door, which the guest, however, neglected to do, although on two occasions, while he was occupied in showing the goods to a customer, a stranger had put his head into the room. The judge told the jury, that *primâ facie,* the innkeeper was answerable for the goods of his guest in his inn, but that the guest might by his own conduct discharge him from responsibility, and left it for them to say whether he had done so here. Held, that this direction was correct.

(22) *Watbroke v. Griffith,* Moore 877.

Per Warburton, J. : " If a person hire a chamber in an inn for a term, the innkeeper is not chargeable for any robbery in it, because the guest is '*quasi* a lessee.' "

Smith v. Dearlove, 6 *C.B.* 132.

An innkeeper received a carriage and horses to stand at livery ; whilst they were there the owner took occasional refreshment at the inn, and also for a short time had a friend supplied with lodging and refreshment there on his credit. Held, that these circumstances were insufficient to give the innkeeper a lien on the carriage and horses for his charges, since that right depends upon the fact that the goods came into " the innkeeper's possession in his character of innkeeper, as belonging to a guest."

(23) *Holder v. Soulby,* 8 *C.B., N.S.* 254.

Certain property of a lodger, who was about to quit, was stolen by a stranger, who in the absence of the lodger had been permitted by the occupier of the house to enter the rooms for the purpose of viewing them. Held, that the lodging-house keeper was not responsible for the loss.

Dansey v. Richardson, 3 *Ell. & Bl.* 145.

A boarding-house keeper is not bound to keep a guest's baggage safely to the same extent as an innkeeper ; but he undertakes by implication of the law, although nothing is expressed, to take due and proper care of a guest's baggage, and if he neglects to take due care of an outer door, so that a theft of the goods is facilitated, he may be held responsible for their loss.

(24) *Chase v. Westmore,* 5 *M. & S.* 183.

A workman, having bestowed his labour upon a chattel, in consideration of a price fixed in amount by his agreement with the owner, may detain the chattel until the price be paid; and this though the chattel be delivered to the workman at different times, if the work to be done under the agreement be entire. But where the parties contract for a particular time or mode of payment, the workman has no right to set up a claim to the possession inconsistent with the terms of the contract.

(25) *Rushforth* v. *Hadfield*, 6 *East* 528.

The lien for a general balance may arise in point of law from an implied agreement to be inferred from a general usage of trade, proved by clear and satisfactory instances sufficiently numerous and general to warrant so extensive a conclusion affecting the custom of the realm. Such a right of lien is not, however, to be favoured, nor can it be supported by a few recent instances of detention of goods by four or five members of the same trade for their general balance; but such lien may be inferred from evidence of the particular mode of dealing between the respective parties.

(26) *Davis* v. *Bowsher*, 5 *T.R.* 488.

A customer lodged bills of exchange in the hands of his banker generally, and when the banker advanced money to him he applied it to the discount of such of the bills as happened to be nearest in value to the sum advanced, but without any special agreement to that effect. Held, that this did not invalidate the banker's general lien upon all the other bills in his hands, but that he might retain them in order to secure the payment of his general balance.

(27) *Balch* v. *Symes*, *Turn. & R.* 87.

A solicitor has no lien upon the will of his client, and his lien upon other documents is superseded by his taking security. In a suit instituted against a solicitor, who had also acted in the capacity of steward, for an account and for delivery of title deeds, the court upon motion ordered the deeds to be delivered up to the plaintiff, upon payment into court of so much of the balance claimed by the answer as was not covered by any security.

Moody v. *Bell*, 2 *D. & R.* 6.

A town agent held to have no lien for the general balance due to him from a country attorney, upon the money of a client of the latter, coming to his hands in a cause in which he acts as the town agent; and see *Waller* v. *Holmes*, 30 *Law J., Ch.* 24.

(28) *Kirkman* v. *Shawcross*, 6 *T.R.* 14.

The dyers, dressers, bleachers, printers, and calenderers of Manchester and the neighbourhood held a public meeting in Manchester, and came to a resolution that they would receive goods to be dyed, dressed, &c., on the condition that such goods should not only be subject to the debts for the work and labour performed on them, but also for the general balance due from the persons employing them for work and labour of the same kind, performed upon goods which they had already delivered out of their possession. Held, that persons who had sent goods to a dyer, with notice of this resolution, had conceded a lien for their general balance.

(29) *Raitt* v. *Mitchell*, 4 *Campb.* 146.

A shipwright in the River Thames has no lien on a ship taken into his dock to be repaired without an express agreement for that purpose, credit being given by the usage of trade to the owner of the ship for the repairs; and see *Chase* v. *Westmore*, *supra*, p. 253.

(30) *Yorke v. Greenaugh,* 2 *Ld. Raym.* 866.

An innkeeper held to be justified in retaining for its keep, against its right owner, a horse left with him to be kept, although the persons who left it had no right with it.

Exeter Carrier's case, cited by Holt, C.J., in the last case.

A. stole goods, and delivered them to the Exeter carrier to be carried to Exeter. The right owner finding the goods in possession of the carrier, demanded them of him, upon which the carrier refused to deliver without being paid for the carriage. The owner brought trover, and it was held, that the carrier was justified in detaining the goods against the right owner, for the carriage; for when A. brought them to him, he was obliged to receive them and carry them, and since the law compelled him to carry them, it will give him remedy for the premium due for the carriage.

(31) *Sweet v. Pym,* 1 *East* 4.

One who has a lien on goods in his possession, if he deliver them to a carrier by water to be conveyed on account of, and at the risk of, his principal, cannot recover his lien by stopping the goods *in transitu,* and procuring them to be re-delivered to him by virtue of a bill of lading signed by the carrier in the course of his voyage.

(32) *Coats v. Chaplin,* 3 *Q.B.* 483.

The traveller of M., a tradesman residing in London, verbally ordered goods for M. of the plaintiff, a manufacturer at Paisley. No order was given as to sending the goods. Plaintiff gave them to defendant, a carrier, directed to M., to be taken to him, and also sent an invoice by post to M., who received it. The goods having been lost by defendant's negligence, and not delivered to M.: Held, that the property in the goods had not passed to the consignee, there having been no acceptance, so as to satisfy the Statute of Frauds, and, therefore, that the carrier was liable to the consignor.

Freeman v. Birch, 1 *N. & M.* 420.

A laundress sent linen which she had washed to the owner by the carrier, whom she paid. The carrier having lost it—Held, that the laundress was entitled to sue the carrier for the loss, she having, as bailee of the goods, a special property in them, which did not pass from her by their delivery to the carrier.

(33) *Marshall v. York, Newcastle, &c., Railway Co.,* 11 *C.B.* 655.

In an action against a railway company by a passenger for the loss of his personal luggage, it appeared that the fare of the plaintiff had been paid by his master, with whom he was travelling. Held, that although the plaintiff was not a party to the contract with the company, it was nevertheless the duty of the defendants towards him to carry him and his luggage safely and securely, and that for a breach of that duty they were liable to him.

CHAPTER X.

SALE.

Contracts for the Sale of Land.

<small>Sale of lands and corporeal hereditaments.</small>

It has already been noticed [*ante*, p. 163] that, under the 4th section of the Statute of Frauds, no action can be brought whereby to charge any person upon any contract for the purchase of lands, tenements, or hereditaments, or any interest in or concerning them, unless the contract, or some memorandum or note thereof, is in writing and signed by the party to be charged, or by some other person by him lawfully authorized to sign it.

The note or memorandum need not be drawn up in any particular form; but it is requisite that the subject matter of the sale, the price to be paid, and the name of the purchaser should be specified. And if there has not been a clear offer and acceptance of one and the same set of terms, if the property has not been clearly described and defined, or if any material particulars are left unsettled between the parties, there is no concluded contract capable of supporting an action for damages or specific performance.

<small>Sales by auction. (1)</small>

In the case of sales by auction, the assent of the parties is manifested by the knocking down of the auctioneer's hammer. The bidding is a mere offer, which may be retracted at any time before the hammer is down and the offer accepted.

A sale by auction is void, if the vendor, unknown to the bidders, employ a puffer, or anyone to bid on behalf of the vendor.

The 30 & 31 Vict. c. 48, s. 5, requires that the particulars or conditions of sale shall state whether the land is to be sold without reserve, or subject to a reserve price, or whether a right to bid is reserved.

As soon as the hammer of the auctioneer is down, and the bidding has been accepted, an agreement for the sale and purchase of the land should be signed by the parties themselves, or by the auctioneer as their agent, in order that the Statute of Frauds may be satisfied.

If an oral contract is made for the purchase of a freehold estate, or of a leasehold estate of more than three years duration, and the purchaser is actually put into possession of the property agreed to be sold to him, he will only obtain (Statute of Frauds, sec. 4) an estate or lease at will. But the purchaser so let into possession may be entitled to a conveyance of the estate, and equity will compel the vendor to execute such conveyance, notwithstanding the provisions of the Statute of Frauds, on the ground that there has been a part performance of the contract. *Oral contracts for the purchase of land. (2)*

But the mere naked transfer of possession is not generally a sufficient part performance of the contract, unless it is accompanied by acts on the part of the purchaser inconsistent with the notion of a contract for a yearly tenancy, or unless the vendor admits the existence of the contract.

(i.) If the estate agreed to be sold has been actually conveyed by the vendor to the purchaser, and the vendor sues for the non-payment of the purchase-money, the measure of damages is the price agreed to be paid, with interest. *Non-performance by purchaser. Damages. (3)*

(ii.) If no conveyance has been executed, the vendor is entitled, in case of the non-completion of the contract by the purchaser, to re-sell the estate, and if the re-sale takes place within a reasonable time, the measure of damages will be the difference between the price agreed to be paid by the purchaser and the price realised on the re-sale, together with the costs, charges, and expenses of the re-sale.

(iii.) If the vendor does not re-sell the estate, but elects to keep it in his own hands, he will be entitled to recover the difference, if any, between the agreed price and the presumed marketable value of the property, together with his costs, charges, and expenses.

Non-performance by the vendor. Damages. (4)

(i.) If the vendor has acted in good faith, and is only prevented from completing his agreement by the discovery of an unexpected defect in title, the purchaser will only be entitled to recover nominal damages, together with his deposit, if he has paid any; and, if before investigating the title of his vendor he re-sells the property, he does so at his own peril.

(ii.) If the breach of the contract arises not from any inability on the part of the vendor to make a good title, but from his refusal to take the necessary steps to give the purchaser possession, the purchaser may recover not only his deposit, if any, but also damages for the loss of his bargain, which will be measured by the difference between the contract price and the value at the time of the breach of contract; and the profit which the purchaser might have made by a re-sale will be evidence of this enhanced value.

Specific performance. (5)

An estate agreed to be sold vests in equity in the purchaser from the moment of signing the agreement; the court will, therefore, in all ordinary cases, decree a specific performance by the vendor of all such acts as are necessary to be done by him to transfer the legal estate to the purchaser, and thus carry the contract into complete effect.

But specific performance will not be decreed in favour of a purchaser who has been guilty of unreasonable delay in performing his part of the agreement, or who has slept on his rights.

Extravagance, unreasonableness, or inadequacy in price form no ground in general for refusing specific performance, unless it is such as amounts to conclusive evidence of fraud. But sales by heirs of their expectancies or reversions are closely scrutinised and generally discountenanced.

Contracts for Sale of Goods and Chattels.

1. *Title to Goods and Chattels.*

Title to goods and chattels is founded *primâ facie* upon visible possession and apparent ownership. And the mere possessor of goods by finding is entitled to hold them against everybody but the true owner. Title. (6)

Possession is not, however, conclusive evidence of ownership; and a purchaser cannot be secure of a safe title to goods which he buys, unless the purchase has taken place in *market overt*, and not then if the goods should turn out to have been stolen.

By market overt is meant a public market or fair, or a shop in the City of London. But a wharf in the City of London is not a market overt, nor is a shop in the City of London a market overt for the sale of other goods than those which are customarily sold there. A sale by sample is not a sale in market overt; and it is doubtful whether a sale *to* the shopkeeper himself, although of goods to be added to his stock in trade, is a sale in market overt. Market overt. (7)

Originally a sale of goods in market overt gave to the purchaser an indefeasible title to the goods against all the world. Sale of stolen goods in market overt.

But the 2 & 3 Ph. & M. c. 7, and 31 Eliz. c. 12, render the sale of horses in market overt void, unless accompanied by specified formalities, and prevent the property in a stolen horse being altered by sale in market overt, until six months have elapsed since the time of sale, and enable the owner at any time after to recover the horse, on payment of the price to the purchaser.

And by the 24 & 25 Vict. c. 96, amending earlier statutes, the property in all chattels which have been stolen reverts, on conviction of the thief, to the original owner from whom they were stolen, so as to enable him to maintain an action against the purchaser for the goods, or the value of them, without obtaining an order of restitution.

Sale out of market overt. (8) It is a rule, with some important exceptions, that a vendee out of market overt cannot obtain a better title than his vendor. Thus, although a person from whom goods have been stolen cannot bring an action for damages against the thief until he has prosecuted him for felony, this does not prevent him from recovering from an innocent third person stolen property which has been sold to the latter.

But if a man obtains possession of goods by a pretended contract of sale, paying for them by a cheque on a bank where he has no funds, or by a fictitious bill of exchange, he has himself no title to the goods when they are demanded back by the vendor, but if he has re-sold and delivered them to a *bonâ fide* purchaser, the title of the latter cannot be defeated.

If the owner of goods has intrusted another with the possession of them, or with documentary evidence of title to them, for purposes of sale, and the party so intrusted has sold contrary to the express directions of the owner, the purchaser will nevertheless acquire a perfect and complete title by the sale. If the owner of goods stands by, and voluntarily allows another to deal with goods as if he were the owner, and thereby induces a third party to purchase them, he cannot afterwards, although he acted under a mistake, claim them from such third party;

but he may claim the price of them, unless it has been paid over.

By the 6 Geo. IV. c. 94, contracts for sale and purchase of goods intrusted to agents and factors are made binding against their principals, if the contract was made in the ordinary course of business, and if the party dealing with the agent was not aware of want of authority on the part of the agent to sell the goods or receive the purchase-money.

2. *Legal Authentication of Executory Contracts for the Sale of Goods and Chattels.*

It has already been mentioned [page 166] that it is enacted by the 17th section of the Statute of Frauds that no contract for the sale of any goods, wares, or merchandise, for the price of ten pounds sterling or upwards, shall be allowed to be good:— Statute of Frauds, sec. 17.

    unless the buyer shall *accept* part of the goods so sold, and actually *receive* the same;

    or give something in earnest to bind the bargain, or in part payment;

    or unless some note or memorandum in writing of the bargain be made and signed by the party to be charged, or his agent thereunto lawfully authorized.

The requisites of the memorandum and the mode of signature have already been referred to. It remains to consider what is to be understood by the words "accept," "receive," and "earnest money."

The acceptance of goods may be either previous to, or contemporaneous with, their receipt. Thus, if a purchaser selects goods himself, and orders them to be sent to his house, and the goods so selected are delivered at his house, there is evidence of an acceptance and an actual receipt of the goods within the meaning of the statute. Acceptance and receipt under Statute of Frauds, sec. 17. (9)

Where there has been an acceptance and actual receipt of the thing only for an instant, the purchaser is bound and cannot withdraw from the bargain except on the ground of fraud.

If an intending purchaser has not selected specific articles, but articles are received by him for examination or trial, and returned within a reasonable time, there is no acceptance and receipt; and if a purchaser sends a servant for goods, and after they have been brought to him, sends them back, there is no acceptance and receipt

Acceptance and receipt by bailee purchasing. (10) When goods are in the hands of a bailee, and an oral bargain is made between him and the owner for the purchase of the goods, and the purchaser then changes the character in which he holds them, it is an acceptance as against him, and there will be a binding contract for the purchase of the goods.

Constructive acceptance. (11) There may be a constructive acceptance, sufficient to satisfy the statute, of things which are incapable of manual occupation or transfer. The acceptance may be manifested by acts of ownership, or acts inconsistent with the right of property or possession being in anyone else but himself.

But, so long as the vendor retains his right of lien over the whole commodity sold, there can be no such acceptance as the statute requires.

Possession of goods may, however, be given up and the right of lien extinguished, although the goods are never actually removed from the premises of the vendor. Thus, if an oral bargain is made for the purchase of goods, and the purchaser desires the vendor to keep them in his possession for a special purpose, and the vendor assents, this may be a constructive acceptance and receipt sufficient to satisfy the statute. In cases of this sort, the question will be whether the vendor had the subject matter of the sale in his own possession, retaining his right of lien for the price, or whether he had the bare custody of the chattel as the servant of the purchaser, having no possession or right of lien.

The acceptance of a bill of lading of goods on board ship, *in transitu* to the purchaser, is not an acceptance of the goods, unless the purchaser exercises dominion and ownership over the bill of lading, and deals with it so as to transfer the right of property in the goods to some third party. The acceptance and receipt by a purchaser of a delivery order or dock-warrant is not an acceptance and actual receipt of the goods comprised therein, until it has been presented to the warehouse-keeper or dock-keeper, and the latter has consented to hold the goods to the account of the purchaser. <small>Acceptance of bills of lading, &c. (12)</small>

Although the carrier, wharfinger, or forwarding agent has been appointed by the purchaser, his acceptance and receipt of the goods to be forwarded is not the acceptance and receipt of the purchaser. But if a purchaser directs goods to be taken to a place of deposit indicated by him, and they are sent there, it is the same as though they were sent to his own house. <small>Acceptance by carriers. (13)</small>

If the purchaser receives and keeps a portion of the bulk, he is responsible in damages for the non-acceptance of the whole of the commodity which he agreed to buy under the same contract. <small>Part acceptance and actual receipt. (14)</small>

The acceptance and actual receipt of goods takes the whole contract out of the operation of the Statute of Frauds, and leaves it open to the parties to supply the terms of the bargain by oral evidence. <small>Effect of acceptance and receipt. (15)</small>

The giving of any quantity of money, however small, by way of earnest or part payment has the effect of taking the whole contract out of the operation of the statute. It binds the bargain between the parties, and operates as a transfer of the right of property to the purchaser. The vendor cannot sell to another until he has requested the vendee to remove the goods and pay the price, and the latter has neglected to comply with the requisition within <small>Earnest and part payment. (16)</small>

a reasonable period. If there is a bargain for the sale of goods at a certain price, and it is subsequently agreed that a debt due to the purchaser shall be wiped off from the amount of the price, and the debt is accordingly discharged, this may be equivalent to earnest and part payment.

3. *Transfer of the Right of Property in the Thing sold.*

Contracts of sale transferring or not transferring the right of property. (17)

A contract for the sale of goods, wares, or merchandise, duly authenticated by writing, if within the Statute of Frauds, or merely oral, if not within the Statute of Frauds, may operate as a direct transfer of the right of property in the thing sold to the purchaser, or may merely amount to an agreement for a future transfer, without effecting any alteration of ownership.

A transfer of the right of property is accompanied by a transfer of the risk of loss, so that, if between the time of the bargain and the delivery the thing sold is destroyed without the neglect of the vendor, the loss is the loss of the purchaser.

Generally, in order to constitute a complete sale, sufficient to transfer the right of property, the price must be ascertained and fixed; and the precise thing sold must be ascertained and identified, except where the sale is of shares and undivided quantities expressly sold as such. Thus, if the bulk of the commodity has been identified, and the sale is a sale of an undivided quantity thereof, expressly sold as such, at an ascertained price, the ownership of the share and the risk of loss pass to the purchaser, just as though the shares had been separated and divided.

If it appears by the terms of the contract that it was the intention of the parties that the property should pass to the buyer, it will pass, although the goods have still to be weighed, measured, or tested, provided the subject matter of the sale is ascertained and identified. And there may be a complete contract so as to pass the property in the goods, although the price has not been definitely agreed on, or although the goods are still unfinished.

Where a specific chattel is ordered to be made, the right of property is not vested in the person giving the order, nor the right to the price in the manufacturer, until the thing ordered is completed and approved of by the purchaser. Contracts for sale and manufacture of goods. (18)

But when the contract provides that the article shall be manufactured under the supervision of a person appointed by the purchaser, and also fixes the payment by instalments at certain stages of the work, the materials employed vest in the purchaser at the time when they are put together, or at any rate from the time that the first instalment is paid, subject to the right of the builder to retain the fabric, in order to complete it, and earn the rest of the price.

If the vendor is authorized to select the goods, and forward them to the purchaser, the delivery of the goods by the vendor into the hands of the carrier transfers the ownership and risk to the purchaser, provided the contract of sale is binding under the Statute of Frauds. Delivery to carrier. (19)

And when goods are consigned to a merchant abroad under a bill of lading, expressing that the goods are shipped by order and on account of the consignee, the property vests in the consignee from the time they are put on board.

4. *Transfer of the Right to Possession of the Thing sold.*

Although the contract of sale is perfect and complete, and the right of property and the risk of loss are transferred to the purchaser, the *right of possession* may continue in the vendor, until the purchase-money has been paid or tendered. When different times are not expressly appointed for payment and delivery, the acts of payment and delivery are concurrent, and constitute mutual conditions to be Right to possession. (20)

performed at the same time. The purchaser cannot demand the thing sold without paying or offering to pay the price, nor can the vendor demand the price without delivering, or offering to deliver, the subject matter of the sale.

Sale on credit. (21) If goods are sold on credit, the vendor cannot sue for the price until the period of credit has expired, unless the giving of credit has been made conditional upon the performance of some precedent act by the purchaser.

Actual and constructive delivery of possession. (22) Goods sold may be delivered by manual transfer, or by removal to the premises of the purchaser. But there is a constructive delivery, if the vendor gives the purchaser a delivery order for the removal of the goods, or the key of the warehouse in which they are contained, provided that the particular goods to be removed have been separated from the bulk and identified.

When goods and chattels are incapable of manual occupation and delivery, such as a hay-stack standing in a meadow, it may be enough to show that the purchaser was to have fetched away the article, and that the vendor has given him the power and opportunity of removing it. But the mere placing of goods at the disposal of the purchaser, or putting it in his power to remove them, will not in any case constitute a delivery if the vendor retains his lien for the price, or possesses any dominion or control over them.

To constitute delivery there must be proved a virtual change of possession as well as of ownership.

Stoppage in transitu. (23) If the purchaser of goods becomes bankrupt before payment of the price, the vendor is entitled, so long as the goods remain *in transitu*, to re-take the goods, and put himself in the same position as though he had never parted with the actual possession of them.

This right is not defeated by part payment of the purchase-money, or by the acceptance of a bill or note for a part of the price. It is, however, strictly confined to those who stand in the position of unpaid vendors, and does not extend to those who have forwarded goods to a creditor by way of payment.

Goods delivered to a carrier to be conveyed to a purchaser are *in transitu*, although they may have been consigned to a carrier specially appointed by the purchaser to receive them. But goods are not *in transitu* when they are being conveyed in the purchaser's own cart or carriage, under the care of his own servant or agent.

If a charter-party amounts, as it usually does, merely to a contract for the conveyance of merchandise, the goods will be received by the ship-master in the character of a carrier, and will be *in transitu*. But if the charter-party amounts to a bailment of the ship to the purchaser of the goods, the purchaser becoming temporary owner of the vessel, the possession of the goods by the master of the ship will be the possession of the purchaser, and the vendor will have no right to stop them *in transitu*, unless the bill of lading expressly reserves to him the dominion and control over them.

The *transitus* is not determined by the arrival of the goods at their place of destination, but continues until they have come into the actual possession of the purchaser.

Goods in the hands of the purchaser's *agents for custody* are not *in transitu*, but are in the actual possession of the purchaser, and cannot be re-taken by the vendor.

So long as a carrier retains the goods in his character of carrier they remain *in transitu*, but if the carrier expressly, or impliedly, enters into a new agreement with the purchaser to hold the goods for the purchaser, as his agent, and on his account, the *transitus* is at an end, and the goods are constructively in the possession of the purchaser.

Notice to a carrier from the vendor to stop goods *in transitu* is sufficient; but, if given to an employer whose servant has the custody of the goods, it must be given in such time, and under such circumstances, as will enable the employer to communicate it to his servant in time to prevent a delivery to the consignee.

Rights of sub-purchasers. (24)
If the purchaser re-sells the goods whilst they are *in transitu*, and then becomes insolvent, the first vendor may stop the goods at any time before they have come into the possession of such second purchaser, and hold them as security for the due payment of the original purchase-money, *unless the second purchaser claims as the* bonâ fide *indorsee and holder for value of a bill of lading.* But the vendor may annex terms to the bill of lading preserving his control over the cargo and the *jus disponendi* of the goods on their arrival, although they may be shipped on board the purchaser's ship.

5. *Damages for Non-Performance of Contract of Sale of Goods.*

Non-performance by purchaser. (25)
If a vendor brings an action against a purchaser for the non-payment of the price of goods, sold at a fixed price, and delivered to the purchaser, the measure of damages is the price agreed to be paid.

If no price was determined upon, the measure of damages will be the usual and customary price for goods of a similar quality and description.

If the goods have not been delivered to the purchaser, but the ownership and right of property therein have been transferred by the bargain to the purchaser, the measure of damages is, in like manner, the price agreed upon, without deduction for losses which have occurred without the negligence of the vendor.

If the right of property has not been transferred to the purchaser, the measure of damages will be the difference between the agreed price and the marketable value of the goods at the time they were tendered to, and refused acceptance by, the purchaser, in addition to the expenses necessarily incurred by the vendor in fulfilling his part of the bargain. And if the purchaser has given notice that he will not accept the goods, the measure of damages will not be the difference between the contract price and the market price on the day when the notice was given, but at the time when the contract ought to have been fulfilled by the acceptance of the goods.

If the goods have been re-sold by the vendor within a reasonable time after the breach of contract by the purchaser, the measure of damages will be the difference between the contract price and the price realised by the re-sale, with the costs and expenses of the re-sale.

If a purchaser brings his action against the vendor for a breach of contract in not delivering goods sold, or not tendering them for acceptance, or for re-selling them and converting them to his own use, the measure of damages will be the difference between the price agreed to be paid and the marketable value of the goods at the time and place when and where they ought to have been delivered to the purchaser. *Non-performance by the vendor. (26)*

In case of a contract for the sale and purchase of shares, when the vendor holds in his hands the money of the purchaser, and thereby prevents him from using it, and from buying other shares therewith, the proper measure of damages would seem to be the highest price for which the same number of shares might be purchased in the market, either on the day the contract was broken, or at any time between that day and the day of trial, if the action has been brought without unreasonable delay.

Specific performance of a contract for the sale of goods and chattels will not generally be decreed. But a contract for the sale of a specific chattel, such as a particular vessel, or a chattel having a peculiar value resting on its individuality, such as old family pictures and heir-looms, will be enforced in specie. And whenever the object of the *Specific performance. (27)*

sale is such that there is an uncertainty whether the purchaser can procure another chattel of the same kind and value, or the possession of it is desirable for certain purposes which no other chattel of the same kind will answer, specific performance may be decreed.

[*As to Warranty on Sale*, see Pt. I., Chap. XIV., on Fraud and Deceit.]

ILLUSTRATIVE CASES.

(1) *Thornett* v. *Haines*, 15 *M. & W.* 272.

A sale by auction was stated by the auctioneer to be "without reserve;" but the vendor, without notice to the purchasers, employed a puffer to bid for him. Held, that the sale was rendered void, and that the purchaser was entitled to recover back his deposit from the auctioneer.

(2) *Frame* v. *Dawson*, 14 *Ves.* 386.

Verbal agreement for the renewal of a lease for a further term of ten years not enforced upon the ground of part performance, where the tenant rebuilt a party wall, such act being equivocal and easily admitting of compensation. So a tenant's possession and cultivation would not sustain a parol agreement to purchase. The act must be unequivocal and such as of itself to raise the inference of an agreement, the terms of which may then be proved by parol.

(3) *Laird* v. *Pim*, 7 *M. & W.* 474.

When a party has been let into possession of lands under a contract of purchase, but does not complete the purchase, and refuses to pay the purchase-money, and no conveyance is executed, the vendor cannot recover from him the whole amount of the purchase-money, but only the damages actually sustained by his breach of contract. Parke, B.: "The question is, how much worse is the plaintiff by the diminution in the value of the land, or the loss of the purchase-money, in consequence of the non-performance of the contract. It is clear he cannot have the land and its value too. The measure of damages in an action of this nature is the injury sustained by the plaintiff by reason of the defendant not having performed his contract."

Ockenden v. *Henly*, *Ell. Bl. & Ell.* 485.

Plaintiff put up for sale by auction real property, upon conditions of sale which stipulated that the purchaser of each lot should "forthwith pay into the hands of the auctioneer a deposit of 20 per cent. on the purchase-money, and sign the agreement to pay the remainder;" and "that if the purchaser of either lot shall fail to comply with these conditions, the deposit money shall be actually forfeited to the vendor, who shall be at full liberty to re-sell such lot, either by public auction or private contract; and any deficiency that may arise on such re-sale, together with all expenses attending the same, shall immediately after such second sale be made good by such defaulter; and on non-payment thereof, such amount shall be recoverable by the vendor as and for liquidated damages." Defendant became a purchaser at the auction, but did not pay the deposit, or complete the purchase. Plaintiff re-sold at a price below that for which defendant had purchased; and the deficiency, with the expenses of sale, exceeded the amount of the deposit. Held, that plaintiff was entitled to recover from defendant the amount of the deficiency and expenses only, and not, in addition to this, the amount of the deposit. *Per curiam:* Had the deposit been paid and the bargain completed, the deposit would have gone in part payment of the purchase-money; and in case of the non-completion of the bargain, if the deficiency and expenses had together been less than the deposit, the purchaser would have been entitled to the whole deposit, but nothing more.

(4) *Robinson* v. *Harman,* 1 *Exch.* 850.

Where a party agreed to grant a good and valid lease, having full knowledge that he had no title—Held, that the plaintiff, in an action for the breach of such agreement, might recover, beyond his expenses, damages resulting from the loss of his bargain.

Walker v. *Moore,* 10 *B. & C.* 416.

A. having contracted with B. for the purchase of a real estate, the vendor, acting *bonâ fide,* delivered an abstract showing a good title, and A., before he examined it with the original deeds, contracted to re-sell several portions of the property at a considerable profit. Upon a subsequent examination of the abstract with the deeds A. discovered that the title was defective, and thereupon the sub-purchasers refused to complete their purchases, and he refused to complete his purchase from B., and brought an action wherein he claimed as damages the expense which he had incurred in the investigation of the title, the profit which would have accrued from the re-sale of the property, the expense attending the re-sale, and the sums which he was liable to pay to the sub-contractors for the expenses incurred by them in investigating the title. Held, that he was entitled to recover only the expenses that he had incurred in the investigation of the title and nominal damages for the breach of the contract, as no fraud could be imputed to the vendor.

Godwin v. *Francis, L.R.* 5 *C.P.* 295.

F. and four others were joint owners of an estate which they were desirous of selling, and had advertised for sale. F., representing that he had authority from his co-owners to do so, contracted to sell the estate to the plaintiff, and sent him an abstract of title. The co-owners repudiated the contract, and concluded a sale at a higher price to another person. The plaintiff sued the four owners for breach of contract, and continued his action against them after they had all sworn, in answer to interrogatories, that F. had no authority to make the contract, and was non-suited. In an action against F. for this misrepresentation—Held, that the proper measure of damages was: 1, the costs of investigating the title; 2, the costs incurred and paid by the plaintiff in the action against the four, down to the time when the answers to the interrogatories had been received and considered by the plaintiff's legal advisers; 3, the difference between the contract price and the market price of the estate, and that the sum for which the estate was afterwards sold was *primâ facie* evidence of the latter; but that the plaintiff could not recover for the loss on the re-sale of horses, &c., bought for the purpose of stocking the land without notice to F., and before the title had been investigated or possession of the land given.

(5) *Colby v. Gadsden,* 34 Beav. 416.

A purchaser was let into the receipt of the rents before completion, and without payment of his purchase-money. Great delay having occurred and no payment having been made to the vendor, he gave notice to the tenants, and prevented any further receipt of the rents by the purchaser. Held, that this did not deprive the vendor of his right to have the contract specifically performed.

Coles v. Trecothick, 9 Ves. 246.

Eldon, L.C. : "Unless the inadequacy of price is such as shocks the conscience, and amounts in itself to conclusive and decisive evidence of fraud in the transaction, it is not itself a sufficient ground for refusing a specific performance. Accidental subsequent advantage made of a bargain is nothing."

(6) *Bridges v. Hawkesworth,* 21 Law J., Q.B. 75.

A person entering a shop found on the floor a bundle of bank notes, which had been accidentally dropped there by a stranger. The party who lost them could not be found. Held, that as against everyone but the true owner, the property in the notes belonged to the finder, and not to the owner of the shop, notwithstanding that the finder had immediately on picking up the bundle handed it over to the latter, with a view of its being restored to the true owner if he should return, and the owner of the shop had advertised the finding in the newspapers, the finder not having intended to waive his title, and having, before he demanded the notes back, offered to repay the expense of the advertisements and to indemnify the shopkeeper against any claim. [See also *Armory v. Delamirie, supra*, p. 77.]

(7) *Lyons v. De Pass,* 11 Ad. & E. 326.

A sale within the City of London, in an open shop, of goods usually dealt in there, is a sale in market overt, though the premises are described in evidence as a warehouse, and are not sufficiently open to the street for a person on the outside to see what passes within.

Taylor v. Chambers, Cro. Jac. 68.

A shop in London held not to be a market overt, except for goods proper to its trade.

Crane v. London Dock Co., 5 B. & S. 313.

Opium belonging to the defendants was stolen from them, and bought by sample by the plaintiff, a shopkeeper in the City of London, without knowledge of its having been stolen. Held, that a sale by sample was not within the privilege of market overt. [Whether a sale to a shopkeeper can be a sale in market overt doubted by the court.]

(8) *Lee v. Robinson,* 25 Law J., C.P. 249.

A. lost a horse and found it at R.'s stable, and R. refused to deliver it up, and said it belonged to B., and then both B. and R. refused. Afterwards B. said he bought it at X.'s (not being market overt), which turned out to be true. A. then offered R. and B., separately, an indemnity if they would deliver the horse up ; but R. refused to let it go, and B. said he left the matter entirely to R. Held, in an action of trover against B. and R., that there was sufficient evidence of conversion by R. If R. had been the mere servant or agent of B. it might have been otherwise ; for a servant or agent, who has received goods from his master or principal, may, on a demand made by the true owner of the goods, give a qualified refusal to deliver them up without being liable to an action of trover ; but where a bailee sets up, or relies upon, the title of his bailor, in answer to such demand, his refusal is evidence of a conversion by him.

White v. Garden, 10 C.B. 919.

A contract for the sale of goods obtained by fraud on the part of the purchaser is void only at the election of the vendor ; and it is too late to declare such election after the goods have passed into the hands of a third person who is a *bond fide* purchaser.

Dickenson v. Naul, 4 B. & Ad. 638.

An auctioneer, employed by a supposed executrix, sold goods of the testator, but, before payment, the real executrix claimed the money from the buyer. Held, that the auctioneer could not afterwards maintain an action against the buyer, though the latter had expressly promised to pay on being allowed to take away the goods.

(9)   *Kershaw* v. *Ogden*, 3 *H. & C.* 717.

The defendant verbally agreed to purchase of the plaintiff four stacks of cotton waste, then in his warehouse, at 1*s*. 9*d*. per lb. The defendant sent his packer and sacks and his cart to remove it. The packer packed the waste into eighty-one sacks, twenty-one of which were weighed, and taken in the defendant's cart to his premises, with a delivery order stating the weight. The remainder were not weighed. On the same day the defendant returned the twenty-one sacks to the plaintiff, alleging that the waste was of inferior quality, and the plaintiff replaced them in his warehouse. Held, that there was evidence for the jury of an acceptance and actual receipt of part of the goods, within the 17th section of the Statute of Frauds.

Curtis v. Pugh, 10 Q.B. 111.

If a purchaser receives goods into his warehouse and, intending to examine into their quality, treats them in a manner which materially alters their condition (as by removing glue from hogsheads into bags), it is not necessarily to be inferred from that fact alone that he finally accepts the goods.

(10)   *Taylor* v. *Wakefield*, 6 *Ell. & Bl.* 769.

It was verbally agreed, between the owner of goods and a person who was in possession of those goods as his tenant, that the tenant might, if he pleased, at the termination of the tenancy, purchase the goods for a sum which exceeded £10, but was not to take them until the money was paid. At the expiration of the tenancy the buyer tendered the price ; but it was refused by the vendor, who denied the validity of the bargain. After this the buyer proceeded to take away the goods ; the vendor prevented him, and took possession of them. In an action of trover by the buyer against the vendor—Held, that on these facts there was no evidence to go to the jury of an acceptance and actual receipt to bind the bargain, as, at the time when the buyer took the goods as owner, the parol contract had been already disaffirmed by the vendor. *Semble*, that if the buyer had been authorized to take the goods as owner, and had, without any fresh authority from the vendor, taken to them as owner, before the contract was disaffirmed, it would have bound the contract, not only in favour of the vendor, but also in favour of the buyer.

(11)   *Morton* v. *Tibbett*, 15 *Q.B.* 428.

Defendant purchased wheat of plaintiff by sample, and directed that the bulk should be delivered on the next morning to a carrier named by himself, who was to convey it to the market town of W., and defendant himself took the sample away with him. On the following morning the bulk was delivered to the carrier, and the defendant sold it at W. on that day by the same sample. The carrier conveyed the wheat, by order of the defendant, who had never seen it, to the sub-vendee, who rejected it as not corresponding with the sample; and defendant, on notice of this, repudiated his contract with plaintiff on the same ground. Held, that there was evidence to warrant a jury in finding acceptance and actual receipt by defendant, within the meaning of 29 Car. II. c. 3, s. 17.

Tempest v. Fitzgerald, 3 B. & Ald. 684.

The defendant, being on a visit at the plaintiff's house, orally agreed to purchase a horse of him for 45 guineas, and the horse was taken out of the stable by his orders, and was mounted, galloped, and leaped, both by himself and servant, and was afterwards cleaned by the latter, and various things were done to the animal by the defendant's directions, and the defendant then asked the plaintiff to keep the horse for him until he could send for it, and the horse died before it was fetched away, whereupon the defendant refused to pay the price. Held, that there had been no acceptance and receipt of the horse wit .in the meaning of the statute, the plaintiff never having parted with the possession or control of the horse, or lost his lien for the price.

Castle v. Sworder, 6 H. & N. 828.

The plaintiffs, wine and spirit merchants, kept a bonded warehouse, where they took in other persons' goods as well as their own, charging warehouse rent. Of this warehouse the plaintiffs had one key and the Custom-house officer another. The defendant agreed to buy of the plaintiffs two puncheons of rum, which were to remain in bond till wanted, the defendant to have six months' further credit. The plaintiffs sent to the defendant an invoice, describing the puncheons by marks and numbers, with the words "free six months," which was explained to mean that they might remain in the plaintiffs' warehouse without charge for six months. The plaintiffs entered in the rum book of their warehouse the puncheons of rum as sold to the defendant, and proved that after this entry they had no power to get the goods out. The rum remained in the warehouse two years, during which time the defendant on several occasions asked the plaintiffs to take back the goods, or buy them of him. Held, that there was evidence to go to the jury that the character in which the plaintiffs held the goods was changed, and that, if they held as warehousemen for the defendant, there was evidence of an acceptance and receipt of the goods by the defendant, so as to satisfy the 17th section of the Statute of Frauds.

(12)   *Meredith v. Meigh*, 22 Law J., Q.B. 401.

Upon a verbal order for the supply of china-stone from Cornwall, to be sent to the Anderton Carrying Company at Liverpool, to be by them forwarded to Hanley in Staffordshire, the vendors, on April 21st, shipped the stone on board a vessel not named by the vendees, and the captain signed a bill of lading for delivery of the stone to the Anderton Company at Liverpool, a copy of which was sent by post, on April 23rd, to the Anderton Company. On April 24th the vendees were informed by letter that the stone had been shipped and consigned to the Anderton Company. On May 4th the vendees were informed by letter of the loss of the vessel and cargo on April 25th, and thereupon they repudiated the contract, and refused payment of the price. Held, in an action for the price, that there was no evidence of an acceptance and receipt, within the 17th section of the Statute of Frauds, so as to bind the defendants.

(13) *Dodsley* v. *Varley*, 12 *Ad. & E.* 632.

Defendant, having bargained with plaintiff for the purchase of wool from plaintiff at a certain price, removed it to a warehouse used by defendant for that purpose, but belonging to a third party; there the wool was weighed and packed in sheeting of the defendant's. The course of dealing was that the wool remained on these premises till paid for. The wool in question was not removed or paid for. Held, that there was a sufficient delivery and acceptance of the goods, within section 17 of the Statute of Frauds, to ground an action for goods sold and delivered, though the plaintiff retained a special interest in them (not properly a lien) in respect of the understood engagement not to remove them till paid for.

(14) *Gilliat* v. *Roberts*, 19 *Law J., Exch.* 410.

A. bought a certain quantity of wheat, in value above £10, which wheat was to be reduced to a certain standard by dressing. After the making of the contract, A. sent for a small portion of the wheat, which was then sent him, but not dressed, whereby it fell short of the standard agreed on, but he retained it without objecting to it. Held, that this was a part acceptance within the Statute of Frauds; and that retaining the portion so sent amounted to a waiver of the full performance of the contract by the plaintiff as to that portion.

(15) *Williams* v. *Burgess*, 10 *Ad. & E.* 499.

Plaintiff entered into a parol agreement to sell to defendant a mare for £20, subject to the condition that if it should prove to be in foal defendant should, on receiving £12 from plaintiff, return it on request. Plaintiff delivered the mare and received £20. On its proving to be in foal he tendered to defendant £12, and requested him to return the mare, which defendant refused to do. Held, that the contract to return it on payment of £12 was not a distinct contract of sale, but one of the conditions of the original sale to the defendant; and that the delivery of the mare to defendant took the whole agreement out of the 17th section of the Statute of Frauds, so as to enable plaintiff to sue defendant for the refusal to return it.

(16) *Walker* v. *Nussey*, 16 *M. & W.* 302.

Plaintiff owed defendant £4 14s., and while it remained due sold him goods by sample to an amount exceeding £10, without note or memorandum in writing of the bargain for sale. Part of that bargain was that the debt due from plaintiff was to go in part payment by defendant to him; but no actual payment of money was made by either, nor was any receipt given by defendant for plaintiff's debt to him. The goods were supplied to defendant, who returned them as inferior to sample, and the jury found that he had never accepted them. Verdict for defendant. Held, on motion for a new trial, that nothing had been given in earnest to bind the bargain, or in part payment within the 17th section of the Statute of Frauds, so as to make the contract binding on the buyer. Parke, B.: "The 'part payment' mentioned in the statute must take place either at or subsequently to the time when the bargain was made. Had there been a bargain to sell the goods at a certain price, and *subsequently* an agreement that the sum due from the plaintiff was to be wiped off from the amount of that price, or that the goods delivered should be taken in satisfaction of the debt due from the plaintiff, either might have been an equivalent to part payment. But as the stipulation respecting the plaintiff's debt was merely a portion of the contemporaneous contract, it was not a giving something to the plaintiff by way of earnest or in part payment then or subsequently."

(17) *Greaves* v. *Hepke*, 2 B. & Ald. 131.

By the usage of Liverpool the vendor of goods was to pay warehouse rent for two months after the sale, if the goods remained there so long. Held, however, that where the vendor of such goods had, within the two months, given the usual order for delivery to the purchaser, the property in the goods from that time vested in the latter, and that he became responsible for all accidents which might happen to them ; and that the circumstance of the goods having within that time been distrained for warehouse rent was an accident which must fall on the purchaser.

Turley v. *Bates*, 2 H. & C. 200.

If, upon a contract for sale of goods, anything remains to be done by the buyer, such as weighing, measuring, or testing the goods, if it appears by the terms of the contract that it was the intention of the parties that the property should pass to the buyer, it will pass, though he has not done the act. Therefore, when the plaintiff sold the defendant a quantity of fire-clay at a certain price per ton, the clay to be carted away by the defendant at his own expense, and weighed by him at the weighing-machine of a third person :—Held, that the property in the clay passed to the defendant on the completion of the bargain, and that the plaintiff might recover the price under a count for goods bargained and sold, although the clay had never been weighed.

Joyce v. *Swann*, 17 C.B., N.S. 84.

There may be a complete contract so as to pass the property in goods from the seller to the buyer, although the *price* has not been definitively agreed on between them. Where from all the facts it may fairly be inferred that it was the intention of the seller to pass the property in goods shipped to order, the mere circumstance of the bill of lading being taken in the name of the seller, and remaining unendorsed, will not prevent its passing.

Young v. *Matthews*, L.R. 2 C.P. 127.

It depends upon the intention of the parties whether the property in goods, to which something remains to be done before they are ready to be delivered, passes to a buyer at the time of the sale or on the completion of the goods. A., a brickmaker who was in embarrassed circumstances, sold to B., to whom he was largely indebted, a large quantity of bricks. B sent an agent to the brickfield with an order for the delivery of the bricks, and A.'s foreman told him he was ready to commence delivering them, if a man who was in possession, under a distress put in by the landlord, was paid out ; and he pointed out three clamps, one consisting of finished bricks, a second of bricks still burning, and a third of bricks moulded but not burnt, as those from which he should make the delivery. A. having become bankrupt, the landlord sold some of the bricks, and B. sold the remainder to C., who removed them. In an action of trover by the assignees against C. for the bricks—Held, that the conduct of A.'s foreman was a sufficient appropriation of the bricks, and that the property in the whole of them, though some were unfinished, passed to B. at the time, such having been apparently the intention of the parties.

(18) *Mucklow* v. *Mangles*, 1 Taunt. 318.

A., a barge-builder, contracted to build a barge for B. Before the work was begun B. advanced money on account, and afterwards, and before the work was finished, he paid him further sums, making up the whole amount of the price. When the barge was nearly finished B.'s name was painted on the stern. Two days after the completion of the work, and before a commission of bankruptcy had issued, C., an officer of the sheriff of Middlesex, under an execution against A., took this barge, which had not then been delivered to B. Held, that C. was justified in so doing, the property not having passed to B.

Clarke v. *Spence,* 4 *Ad. & E.* 470.

P. contracted with a ship-builder to build him a ship for a certain sum, to be paid by instalments as the work proceeded; the first instalment when the vessel was rammed, the second when she was timbered, &c. An agent to P. was superintending the building. The vessel was built under such superintendence, all the materials being approved by the agent before they were used. The builder became bankrupt before the ship was completed. Afterwards the assignees completed the ship. All the instalments were paid or tendered. In an action of trover by P. against the assignees for the ship: Held, that on the first instalment being paid the property in the portion then finished became, by virtue of the above contract, vested in P., subject to the right of the builder to retain such portion for the purpose of completing the work and earning the rest of the price; and that such material subsequently added became, as it was added, the property of P. as the general owner. Held, further, that under the above circumstances the ship did not pass to the assignees, as having been in the "order or disposition of the bankrupt, by consent of the true owner."

(19) *Fragano* v. *Long,* 4 *B. & C.* 219.

A., resident at Naples, sent an order to M. & Co., handware-men at Birmingham, to despatch to him certain goods, insurance being effected, "terms, three months' credit from the time of arrival." M. & Co. having marked the package with A.'s initials, dispatched the goods by the canal to Liverpool, and effected an insurance, declaring the interest to be in A. At Liverpool the goods were delivered by the agent of M. & Co. to the owner of a vessel bound to Naples, through whose negligence they were damaged. Held, that the property in the goods vested in A. as soon as they were dispatched from Birmingham, and that the terms of the order did not make the arrival of the goods at Naples a condition precedent to A.'s liability to pay for them; and that he might, therefore, maintain an action for the injury done to the goods through the negligence of the shipowner.

(20) *Bloxham* v. *Sanders,* 4 *B. & C.* 941.

A., a hop merchant, on several days in August, sold to B., by contract, various parcels of hops. Part of them were weighed, and an account of the weights, together with samples, delivered to the vendee. The usual time of payment in the trade was the second Saturday subsequent to the purchase. B. did not pay for the hops at the usual time, whereupon A. gave notice that unless they were paid for by a certain day they would be resold. The hops were not paid for, and A. re-sold a part, with the consent of B., who afterwards became bankrupt, and then A. sold the residue of the hops without the assent of B., or his assignees. Account sales of the hops so sold were delivered to B., in which he was charged warehouse rent from August 30. The assignees of B. demanded the hops of A., and tendered the warehouse rent, charges, &c.; and A., having refused to deliver them, brought trover. The jury found that defendant had not rescinded the contract of sale. Held, that the assignees were not entitled to maintain trover to recover the value of the hops, inasmuch as, in order to maintain that action, the party must have not only a right of property, but also a right of possession; and that although a vendee of goods acquires a right of property by the contract of sale, yet he does not acquire a right of possession to the goods, until he pays, or tenders the price.

(21)   *Mussen* v. *Price,* 4 *East* 147.

Where goods were sold upon a contract that the vendee was to pay for them *in three months by a bill of two months:* Held, that the contract was for five months, and therefore that assumpsit for goods sold and delivered could not be brought at the end of three months, upon the neglect of the vendee to give his bill at two months, the remedy being by a special action on the case for damages for the breach of contract in not giving such bill.

(22)   *Goodall* v. *Skelton,* 2 *H. Bl.* 316.

A. agreed to sell goods to B., who paid a certain sum of money as earnest. The goods were packed in cloths furnished by B., and deposited in a building belonging to A. till B. should send for them, but A. declared at the same time that they should not be carried away till he was paid. Held, that A.'s declaration prevented this from operating as a delivery to B.

(23)   *Hodgson* v. *Loy,* 7 *T.R.* 440.

Consignor's right of stopping goods *in transitu* held not taken away by the consignee's having partly paid for the goods.

Coates v. *Railton,* 9 *D.R.* 593.

Goods, purchased by an agent at Manchester for the avowed purpose of being sent to his principal at Lisbon, are *in transitu* until they arrive at Lisbon, and, on the insolvency of the principal, may be stopped by the seller in the warehouse of the agent at Manchester.

Bohtlingk v. *Inglis,* 3 *East* 20.

A trader in England chartered a ship, on certain conditions, for a voyage to Russia, and to bring goods home from his correspondent there, who accordingly ships the goods on account, and at the risk of the freighter, and sends him the invoices and bills of lading of the cargo. Held, that the delivery of the goods on board such chartered ship does not preclude the right of the consignor to stop the goods while *in transitu* on board the same in case of the vendee's insolvency before actual delivery, any more than if they had been delivered on board a general ship for the same purpose. [Otherwise in the case of *Fowler* v. *McTaggart,* 1 *East* 522, where the ship had been chartered by the consignees for a term of three years, and they had absolute control of her during that period, finding stock and provisions, and paying the master. There, delivery on board the vessel was held to complete the *transitus,* and to amount to delivery to the consignees.]

Northey v. *Field,* 2 *Esp.* 614.

Where goods were consigned, but the duties not being paid, were lodged in the Government Stores: Held, that the consignor might stop them *in transitu,* if he claimed them before they were actually sold for the payment of the duties; or that, if they were sold, he was entitled to the proceeds.

Whitehead v. *Anderson,* 9 *M. & W.* 518.

Timber was sent from Quebec to be delivered at Fleetwood, in Lancashire; a notice of stoppage was given to the ship-owner at Montrose, while the goods were on their voyage, whereupon he sent a letter to await the arrival of the captain at Fleetwood, directing him to deliver the cargo to the agents of the vendor. Held, not a sufficient notice of stoppage *in transitu,* for such notice ought to be given either directly to the ship-master in custody of the goods, or else to the ship-owner, in such time as that by reasonable diligence he may communicate with the master in time to prevent the delivery to the consignee. Here delivery might have been made to the consignees before the master went ashore to receive his letter.

(24) *Lickbarrow* v. *Mason*, 6 *East* 20, *and* 1 *Sm. L.C.*

Although the consignor, in case of the insolvency of the consignee, may stop goods *in transitu* before they get into the hands of the consignee ; yet if the consignee assign the bills of lading to a third person for a valuable consideration, the right of the consignor, as against such assignee, is divested ; and there is no distinction in this respect between a bill of lading indorsed in blank and one indorsed to a particular person.

(25) *Phillpotts* v. *Evans*, 5 *M. & W.* 475.

Where A. contracted for the purchase of wheat, "to be delivered at Birmingham as soon as vessels could be obtained for the carriage thereof," and subsequently (the market having fallen) gave the seller notice that he would not accept it if it were delivered, the wheat being then on its way to Birmingham—Held, in an action against A. for not accepting the wheat, that the proper measure of damages was the difference between the contract price and the market price on the day when the wheat was tendered to him for acceptance at Birmingham and refused, and not on the day when notice was received by the seller.

Stewart v. *Cauty*, 8 *M. & W.* 160.

In an action for the non-acceptance of railway shares : Held, that the proper measure of damages is the difference of the prices of the shares on the day when they ought to have been accepted, and on the day when they were re-sold by the vendor, such sale being within a reasonable time.

(26) *Chinery* v. *Viall*, 5 *H. & N.* 288.

A. having bought some sheep on credit, left them in the custody of the vendor. Without any default on the part of A., the vendor re-sold the sheep. Held, first, that though the price had not been paid or tendered by A., the re-sale was a conversion of the sheep by the vendor, in respect of which A. was entitled to maintain trover ; secondly, that the measure of damages was not the value of the sheep, but the loss sustained by A. by not having the sheep delivered to him at the price agreed on.

Shepherd v. *Johnson*, 2 *East* 211.

In estimating the measure of damages in an action for breach of an engagement to replace stock on a given day : Held, that it was not enough to take the value of the stock on that day, if it had risen in the meantime ; but the highest value as it stood at the time of trial must be taken, there having been no offer on the part of the defendant to replace it in the intermediate time, while the market was rising.

(27) *Claringbould* v. *Curtis*, 21 *Law J., Ch.* 541.

Specific performance decreed of the purchase of a certain barge and the stores contained in her.

Falcke v. *Gray*, 29 *Law J., Ch.* 28.

Suit for specific performance of a contract giving the plaintiff the option of purchasing two valuable china jars. Held, that as the articles were of "unusual distinction and curiosity, if not unique," the contract was one which a court of equity could specifically enforce ; but as it appeared that the price was greatly inadequate, and that the purchaser knew it to be so, the court declined to grant the decree.

CHAPTER XI.

BILLS OF SALE AND PLEDGES OF PERSONALTY.

<small>Mortgage of goods and chattels. (1)</small>
A MORTGAGE of goods and chattels may be made by simple contract as well as by deed. If by the terms of a bill of sale, or assignment of chattels by way of mortgage, the mortgagor is to hold and enjoy the chattels as the mere servant or agent of the mortgagee, the latter is entitled to the possession of them whenever he thinks fit to call for it, and may seize, and carry away, and sell the property. If the mortgage debt is to be paid by a day named, and the mortgagor is to hold possession until default has been made, there is a re-grant and bailment of the goods to the mortgagor for the intervening period, and the mortgagee has no right to the possession of them until the mortgagor's time of holding has expired. But if the mortgagor deals fraudulently with the mortgaged goods thus left in his possession, as if he attempts to sell them, the bailment is determined, and the mortgagee may immediately commence an action for the recovery of the goods or their value.

<small>Bills of sale.</small>
The law relating to bills of sale of personal chattels is now regulated by the Bills of Sale Act, 1878 (41 & 42 Vict. c. 31).

By sec. 4, the term "bills of sale" is expressed to include bills of sale, assignments, transfers, declarations of trust without transfer, inventories of goods with receipt attached thereto, or receipts for purchase-money of goods and other assurances of personal chattels, and also powers of attorney, authorities, or licences to take possession of personal chattels as security for any debt, and also any agreement, whether intended or not to be followed by the execution of any other instrument, by which a right in equity to any personal chattels, or to any charge or security thereon, shall be conferred. But it shall not include assignments for the benefit of creditors, marriage settlements, transfers of ships or shares therein, transfers of goods in the ordinary course of business, bills of sale of goods in foreign parts or at sea, bills of lading, India warrants, or other documents used in the ordinary course of business as proof of the possession and control of goods.

Sec. 4 of the Act defines the expression "personal chattels" to mean goods, furniture, and other articles capable of complete transfer by delivery, and (when separately assigned) fixtures and growing crops, but it is not to include chattel interests in real estate, nor fixtures (except trade machinery), when assigned together with a freehold or leasehold interest, nor growing crops, when assigned together with any interest in the land on which they grow, nor shares, nor stocks, nor choses in action. *What are personal chattels.*

Sec. 10 of the Act requires that the execution of every bill of sale shall be attested by a solicitor, and that the attestation shall state that before the execution of the bill of sale, its effect has been explained to the grantor by the attesting solicitor. *Attestation of bills of sale.*

Sec. 10 also requires every bill of sale, together with an affidavit of the time when it was made, and of its due execution and attestation, to be registered within seven clear days after its making. *Registration.*

If a bill of sale is not attested and registered, as provided in the Act, within seven days after its making, it will be deemed fraudulent and void as against the trustee in bankruptcy or execution creditor of the person whose goods are comprised in it, so far as regards any chattels *Effect of non-registration.*

comprised in the bill of sale which, after the expiration of the seven days, are in the possession, or apparent possession, of the person making the bill of sale (sec. 10). And the registration of a bill of sale must be renewed once at least every five years (sec. 11).

Apparent possession. Personal chattels are to be deemed to be in the apparent possession of the person making a bill of sale, so long as they are in or upon any premises occupied by him, or are used and enjoyed by him in any place whatever, notwithstanding that formal possession (sec. 4) may have been given to any other person.

Bills of sale of after-acquired property. (2) A contract, which purports to transfer property not in existence, cannot operate as an immediate alienation. But if a person agrees to sell property of which he was not possessed at the time of the making of the contract, and he receives consideration for the contract, and afterwards becomes possessed of the property, and the property is of such a nature that specific performance would be decreed, the beneficial interest in the property is transferred to the purchaser as soon as the property is acquired.

A bill of sale of after-acquired property generally gives the grantee a power of seizing such property when it comes into existence; and when the power or authority has been executed to the extent of taking possession of the after-acquired property by the grantee, it is the same as if the grantor had himself put the grantee in actual possession of it.

Mortgages void as against creditors. If a mortgagor of goods and chattels is largely indebted at the time of the execution of the mortgage, and the security is contrived for the purpose of protecting the mortgaged property from the grasp of the creditors of the mortgagor, and not as a *bonâ fide* security for a debt, the mortgage will be invalid.

Mortgage constituting an act of bankruptcy. (3) A mortgage by a trader of all his goods and chattels, stock-in-trade and visible property, made for a pre-existing debt, has generally been considered an act of bankruptcy;

for it enables a trader to continue his trade under a false appearance, and to gain a delusive credit. It has been held, however, that a bill of sale, by way of mortgage, of the whole of the mortgagor's personal property, to enable him to obtain pecuniary advances for the purpose of carrying on his trade, a fair equivalent being received which can be made available for the payment of debts, is not an act of bankruptcy.

If an assignment is an act of bankruptcy as being fraudulent against creditors, it is also void as against the parties to it.

Pledge.

In the contract of pledge, the possession only of goods and chattels is transferred, the right of property remaining in the transferror. Pledge.

All kinds of goods and chattels, title deeds, and securities for money, and even money itself, if marked or enclosed in a bag or parcel, may be pledged.

As a general rule only the owner of goods can make a valid pledge of them. If a servant takes his master's jewels and pledges them, the pledgee acquires no right to detain them as against the owner. But if a man obtains goods under colour of a contract intended to transfer the property in the goods to him, and then pledges them, the pledgee will have a lien upon the goods to the amount of his advances. But if the property has not passed—if, for instance, the article has been stolen, or possession thereof has been obtained by false pretences—and it has then been pledged, the pledgee will have no lien upon it against the owner. Parties entitled to pledge. (4)

By the 5 & 6 Vict. c. 39, it is enacted that any agent who shall be intrusted with the possession of goods, or of the documents of title to goods, shall be deemed and taken to be the owner of such goods and documents, so far as to give validity to any contract, or agreement by way of pledge, lien, or security, *bonâ fide* made by any person with such agent, notwithstanding that the person claiming lien or pledge may have had notice that the person with whom such contract or agreement is made is only an agent.

Implied warranty by pledgor. (5) Every person who pledges goods and chattels impliedly warrants that the property pledged is his own; and if it turns out not to be so, the pledgee may restore it to the lawful owner coming forward and claiming it, and may set up the *jus tertii* in answer to an action by the pledgor for the recovery of the pledge.

Right of redemption. A thing may be pledged for a certain period, or it may be pledged indefinitely, no time being fixed for its redemption. In the first case, the pledgee cannot demand payment of the debt, nor the pledgor the restoration of the pledge, until the time appointed has expired. In the second case, the pledgor is entitled to redeem at any time by tendering the amount due, and the pledgee may compel the pledgor to redeem, or be foreclosed and lose his right of redemption altogether.

Sale of pledge by pledgor. (6) As the right of property in the pledge remains in the pledgor, he may sell the pledge, subject to the lien of the pledgee, and substitute the purchaser in his place, so as to entitle the latter to redeem.

Forfeiture. A debtor and creditor may agree that, if the debtor does not pay his debt within a specified period, the pledge shall be forfeited and become the absolute property of the pledgee, and in the case of pledges of movables the courts will not relieve against the forfeiture, unless the value of the pledge greatly exceeds the amount of the debt which it was intended to secure.

Sale by pledgee. (7) So long as the right of property in the pledge has not been vested in the pledgee by foreclosure, the pledgee cannot sell more than his own lien or claim upon the pledge, and can only transfer the pledge burdened with the pledgor's right of redemption, unless a power of sale has been expressly or impliedly reserved to him by contract. And if the deposit has been made to secure the payment of a sum of money by a day certain, there is, it has been held, an implied authority to sell, in case of non-payment by the day named.

When there is no express or implied reservation to the pledgee of the right of sale, in case of default in payment of the debt secured, in order to bar the right of the pledgor to redeem, the pledgee must obtain a decree of foreclosure. After foreclosure the pledge may be sold, and the proceeds applied in liquidation of the debt, the surplus, if any, being paid over to the debtor; or if the value of the pledge does not exceed the amount of the debt and the expenses of a sale, the creditor will be allowed to appropriate the pledge to his own use, and hold it as his own property. *Foreclosure. (8)*

The pledgee must take the same care of goods and chattels pledged to him as a prudent man ordinarily takes of his own property. If the pawn be something that will be worse for wear, the pawnee cannot use it. If the pawn will not be the worse for wear the pawnee may use it, but if he does so it will be at his own peril, and if he is robbed whilst doing so he will be answerable (see Bailments, Chapter IX.). *Duty of pledgee.*

The rights and liabilities of pawnbrokers are regulated by the Pawnbrokers' Act, 1872 (35 & 36 Vict. c. 93), which, however, only applies to loans of £10 and under. *Statutory rights and liabilities of pawnbrokers.*

Under this Act pledges may be redeemed within twelve months from the day of pawning, exclusive of that day, and seven days of grace are allowed in addition. Pledges for amounts of 10s., or under, become the absolute property of the pawnbroker, if not redeemed within that time; but by sec. 18, pledges for larger amounts remain, as at common law, redeemable until sale.

In cases where the loan is above 40s., the pledge may be made upon the terms of a special contract.

By sec. 27, an absolute liability is imposed upon the pawnbroker to make good, subject to certain deductions, the value of pledges damaged or destroyed by fire; and he is empowered to insure to the extent of such value.

By sec. 28, courts of summary jurisdiction may award a reasonable satisfaction to owners of pledges, in respect of depreciation arising by the default, neglect, or wilful misbehaviour of the pawnbroker.

Warranty on sale of unredeemed pledges. (9)
In sales by pawnbrokers of unredeemed pledges, expressly sold as such, the pawnbroker only warrants the subject-matter of the sale to be a pledge, the time for the redemption of which has expired. He sells merely his own title, and it is the duty of the purchaser to investigate that title; and if he is evicted by reason of the want of title in the pledgor to make the pledge, he has no remedy against the pawnbroker, unless the latter expressly warranted the title.

ILLUSTRATIVE CASES.

(1) *Brierly v. Kendall*, 17 Q.B. 937.

By indenture of sale, A. assigned all his household goods, &c., to secure a debt due from him to the assignees, subject to a proviso that the deed should become void upon payment of the said sum on a certain day, or on some earlier day to be appointed by the assignees by a notice in writing to be served on A. twenty-four hours before the day of payment so appointed: interest to be paid in the meantime. It was also agreed by the deed, that after default made in payment, contrary to the said proviso, it should be lawful for the assignees to enter and take possession of the goods, and to sell them and reimburse themselves out of the proceeds, and that until such default it should be lawful for A. to hold, use, and possess the said goods without any hindrance from the assignees. Held, that A. had, under the deed, the right of possession of the goods, defeasible only by default in payment after due notice; and that he might, therefore, sue the assignees in trespass for having entered and sold without due notice.

Fenn v. Bittlestone, 7 Exch. 152.

A., by deed dated Sept. 28th, 1845, conveyed certain goods to B., subject to a proviso that if he should pay B. the sum thereby secured on March 22nd, 1850, or at such earlier day as B. should appoint by giving A. fourteen days' notice, and should pay interest in the meantime half-yearly, the conveyance should be void; and it was thereby agreed between the parties that, until default should be made in the payment of the principal sum secured, at the time therein specified, or the interest, after fourteen days' notice, it should be lawful for A., his executors or administrators, to hold and enjoy the chattels. A. continued in possession of the chattels according to the agreement until Dec. 13th, 1849, when he became bankrupt, and his assignees (the defendants) on Feb. 19th, 1850, sold the whole of the chattels absolutely, and not merely the bankrupt's interest in them. No demand had been made on A. by B. or by the plaintiffs (the assignees of B.) for the principal or interest in the meantime. Held, first, that the deed did not give a mere possession and use of the goods to A. as bailee or tenant at will, but the right of possession and use for the term ending March 22nd, 1850, defeasible by non-payment of principal or interest according to the terms of the deed; but, secondly, that the sale by the assignees of A. destroyed the bailment; and, thirdly, that the sale by the assignees was equivalent to a sale by A., the bailee himself; and, consequently, that trover would lie by the assignees of the mortgagee, against the assignees in bankruptcy of the mortgagor, for the conversion by the sale of the goods during the term.

(2) *Grantham* v. *Hawley*, Hob. 132.

"The land is the mother of all fruits. Therefore he that hath it may grant all fruits that may arise upon it after; and the property shall pass as soon as the fruits are extant. A person may grant all the tithe wool that he shall have in such a year, yet perhaps he shall have none; but a man cannot grant all the wool that shall grow upon his sheep that he shall buy hereafter; for then he hath it neither actually nor potentially."

Belding v. *Read*, 3 H. & C. 955.

A. being indebted to the defendant, assigned to him by bill of sale all his household furniture, and all other effects whatsoever, being, or thereafter to be, upon or about his dwelling-house, farm, or premises at R. or elsewhere in Great Britain, upon trust to sell and satisfy his debt. Power was given to the defendant to enter premises where the goods *assigned* might be, and take possession of such goods; and a further power, in case the sum due should not be paid *upon demand*, to enter upon any premises which might from time to time be in A.'s occupation and "distrain the goods there found for the sum due; and if it should not be paid within one day to sell;" and it was declared that, until the defendant should think fit to take possession of the assigned premises, A. might retain possession. The defendant, five years after, entered A.'s premises, and having demanded payment of A.'s wife, forthwith seized (along with other goods of A.) goods which A. had acquired since the execution of the bill of sale, and after remaining in possession six days sold them. The day after the sale A. became a bankrupt. Held, that the first power did not extend to the after-acquired goods, for they could not be said to have been *assigned;* that the second power did extend to the after-acquired goods, but that the defendant had not exercised it according to its terms; and therefore that the assignees of A. were entitled to recover the value of the after-acquired goods from the defendant. Channell, B. : "As regards the after-acquired property, the contract was operative to this extent, that it conferred on the defendant certain rights to be executed in accordance with the power which the deed gave, and had the defendant so exercised them, although the after-acquired property could not pass by the deed itself, it might have passed by the defendant's subsequent act of intervention." [*Holroyd* v. *Marshall*, 10 H.L.C. 191, distinguished.]

(3) *In re Colemere*, L.R. 1 Ch. 128.

An assignment by a trader of all his property, as security for an advance of money, which he afterwards applies in payment of existing debts, is not necessarily fraudulent within the meaning of the Bankruptcy Acts. In order to make such an assignment fraudulent, the lender must be aware that the borrower's object was to defeat or delay his creditors. Such an assignment cannot be an act of bankruptcy unless it is also void as being fraudulent.

(4) *Hartop* v. *Hoare*, 3 *Atk.* 43.

Sir J. H., in 1729, lodged jewels for safe custody in the hands of S., a jeweller, enclosed in a paper that was sealed and put in a bag, which was also sealed with Sir J. H.'s seal. The same day S.'s clerk gave a receipt for them in these words, "Which bag, so sealed, I promise to take care of for my master S.—Signed M. ;" and in the receipt all the jewels were specified. In February, 1735, S. broke both seals, took out the jewels, and carried them to the shop of the defendant, a banker, borrowed £300 of the defendant, and deposited the jewels as his own proper goods, and as a security for the £300, and gave the defendant a promissory-note for the same sum. On the defendant's refusing to deliver the jewels to Sir J. H., the latter brought his action for trover and conversion of the jewels. On special verdict, judgment was given for the plaintiff.

Parker v. *Patrick*, 5 *T.R.* 175.

Goods were obtained from A. by fraud, and pawned to B. without notice. A. prosecuted the offender to conviction, and re-obtained possession of his goods. Held, that B. might maintain trover for them, for as pledgee he had a lien for his advances.

(5) *Cheesman* v. *Exall*, 6 *Exch.* 344.

The plaintiff, in order to defeat a judgment creditor, deposited certain plate with the defendant. In trover by plaintiff for the plate—Held, that the defendant was entitled to set up the right of the judgment creditor. Where a person pledges property to which he has no title, the pledgee may deliver it to the real owner ; there being in the ordinary case of a pledge an implied undertaking on the part of the pledgor that the property pledged is his own, and, on the part of the pledgee, that he will return it to the pledgor, provided it be not the property of another.

(6) *Franklin* v. *Neate*, 13 *M. & W.* 486.

Action of trover for a chronometer. The chronometer had been pledged by G. to the defendant, a pawnbroker. Whilst it was in the defendant's hands plaintiff bought the chronometer from G., tendered defendant the amount due upon it, and demanded possession. Held, that he was entitled to recover.

(7) *Micklethwaite* v. *Merrill*, 19 *L.T.R.* 61.

Action of trover for paintings. The plaintiff had deposited the pictures with the defendant upon a memorandum to the following effect :—" I have this day given into the care of J. M. (the defendant) twenty-six paintings, for him to hold and keep for me, and as a security for any sums which I may owe to his firm for goods supplied by them." Goods were supplied by the firm upon credit ; but not being paid for, the defendant, when the period of credit had expired, sold the pictures. Held, that the plaintiff was entitled to recover. Erle, J. : " A power of sale is by no means necessarily incident to every deposit of goods by way of security. A deposit with power to hold, and a deposit with power to sell, are quite different things."

Pigot v. *Cubley*, 15 *C.B., N.S.* 701.

Goods were deposited as security for the repayment of a loan of money on a day certain, but without any express stipulation that the pawnee should have power to sell in default of payment on that day. By a subsequent agreement the stipulated time was rendered indefinite. Held, that it was not competent to the pawnee to sell without a proper demand and notice. But, by the court, if it had not been for the subsequent agreement, and if the day of payment had remained certain, a power of sale would have been implied by law from the nature of the transaction.

(8) *Wayne* v. *Hanham*, 9 *Hare*, 62.

A mortgagee of a reversionary interest in stock, filing a bill to realise his security, is entitled to a decree for foreclosure in default of payment, that being the ordinary method by which the court excludes the right of redemption ; and although he may in some cases be entitled to a decree for sale, there is no rule or practice of the court which compels him to submit to such a decree.

(9) *Morley* v. *Attenborough*, 3 *Exch.* 500.

A pawnbroker, who sold a harp for £15 15s. as a forfeited pledge, Held, merely to have undertaken with regard to it that it was a pledge, and irredeemable, and that he was not cognisant of any defect of title to it.

CHAPTER XII.

PRINCIPAL AND SURETY.

Suretyship. (1) THE contract of suretyship is an agreement by one person to be answerable for the payment of some debt, or the performance of some act or duty, in case of the failure of some other person who is himself primarily liable.

From the terms of a contract it is frequently doubtful whether the contract is one of suretyship, or whether it is the contract of a person stipulating for some benefit or advantage for a third party, who is not bound by the contract, and on whom no liability attaches. In such cases the surrounding circumstances must be looked to in order to ascertain what the contract really was.

Authentication. It has been seen (*ante*, pp. 163, 164) that, by the 4th section of the Statute of Frauds, no action shall be brought upon any special promise to answer for the debt, default, or miscarriage of another person, unless the agreement, or some memorandum or note thereof, shall be in writing and signed by the party to be charged therewith, or some other person by him lawfully authorized.

Consideration. (2) Formerly, if the guarantee or undertaking was made by contract not under seal, the consideration for the promise, as well as the promise itself, was required to be disclosed upon the face of the writing. But by 19 & 20 Vict. c. 97, s. 3, it is enacted that a guarantee shall not be invalidated because the consideration of the promise does not appear in writing. But parol evidence is not admissible to prove the promise; and therefore the whole promise must be in writing, or the memorandum will be insufficient.

Where two or more persons sign a joint and several promissory note as principals, the effect of the contract cannot be modified by showing that one of them signed only as surety for the other without notice to the promisee; but this fact may be pleaded and given in evidence, for the purpose of giving the party so signing the equitable rights of a surety. *Joint and several promissory notes. (3)*

If a bond or guarantee is given by a surety to secure the re-payment of advances of money to the principal, provided such advances do not exceed in the whole, at any one time, a certain limited amount, the proviso protects the surety from being answerable beyond the amount named, but does not render the obligation void, if the advances go beyond it, unless that clearly appears to have been the intention of the parties. *Limitation of surety's liability. (4)*

In the case of contracts of suretyship under seal, the courts lean in favour of a construction limiting the liability of the surety to some particular supply or advance, rather than extending it to a general and continuous supply, creating an indefinite liability. Where, however, the continuing liability of the surety under a sealed instrument is established, he has no means of escape at common law; he cannot recall the bond, covenant, or obligation that he has entered into, and say that he will be no longer responsible for advances or supplies to the principal, unless in the contract of suretyship he has expressly reserved to himself such a power. *Continuing liability in contracts under seal. (5)*

In the case of simple contracts there is no leaning against the continuing liability of the surety. For the surety (though liable for all advances and supplies that have been made on the faith of his promise) may at any time revoke such promise, and discharge himself from the future and continuing liability by giving notice to that effect. *Continuing liability in contracts by parol. (6)*

If the person to whom a guarantee is given does any act injurious to the surety, or omits any act which his duty *Duty of person to whom a*

U 2

guarantee is given. (7) enjoins him to do, and the omission proves injurious to the surety, the latter will be discharged. Thus, in the case of bonds and guarantees given to an employer to secure the faithful services of a clerk or servant in his employment, the surety has a right to expect from the employer that he will call upon such clerk or servant to account in the ordinary course of business, and that he will not trust him beyond the bounds of ordinary prudence.

Alteration of principal obligation. (8) If a new contract is substituted in the place of the original contract, or if the original contract is altered in any material particular without the surety's knowledge and consent, so as to constitute a new agreement varying substantially from the former, the surety is no longer bound.

Extension of time of payment. (9) Any enlargement of the time of payment by a binding contract with the principal debtor which ties up the hands of the creditor, and prevents him from suing the principal debtor upon the original obligation, discharges the surety, if it has been made without his consent.

A mere promise, without consideration, not to sue the principal debtor for a certain time is not a binding contract, and will not discharge the surety. Neither will a parol agreement to enlarge the time of payment discharge the surety when the principal obligation is under seal, inasmuch as the legal operation of a deed cannot be affected by a parol agreement. Mere laches, or forbearance, or an omission on the part of the creditor to press the debtor and sue him for the money, will not discharge the surety.

If, after the principal debtor has made default, and the surety has become liable for the payment of the debt, the creditor, by a binding contract, agrees to give his principal debtor time for payment, and in the same contract expressly stipulates for the reservation of all his remedies against the surety, the latter will still remain liable, notwithstanding the arrangement between the principal and the creditor.

If the principal debt be unconditionally released or satisfied the engagement of the surety is also at an end. But if the principal debtor has made default, so that the liability of the surety has accrued and the creditor has an immediate right of action against him, the creditor may compound with the principal debtor, receiving a portion only of the debt, and may release him from the payment of the residue, and at the same time reserve all his rights and remedies against the surety. A deed of release of this sort, with reserve of remedies against the surety, is construed as a covenant not to sue, in order that effect may be given to the intention of the parties and the right of recourse to the principal reserved. *Release of principal debt.* (10)

A creditor is not bound to inquire under what circumstances his debtor has obtained the concurrence of a surety, unless the dealings are such as fairly to lead a reasonable man to believe that fraud must have been used in order to obtain such concurrence. *Fraud on surety.* (11)

If, when a person agrees to become surety, any material part of the contract between the debtor and creditor is misrepresented or concealed from the surety, with the knowledge of the creditor, this amounts to a fraud upon the surety, which will discharge him from his engagement.

If a person, whose honesty is guaranteed, makes defalcations which the employer condones without notice to the guarantor, the latter is not liable for subsequent defalcations.

A release by the creditor of one of two or more co-sureties releases all. *Co-sureties.* (12)

If several persons together become surety for one principal in respect of the same debt and transaction, either jointly or severally, or by the same or different contracts, and one of such co-sureties, after the liability of the principal has arisen, satisfies the whole debt or claim, or more than his own proportion of it, he may have recourse to his co-sureties for contribution. And, by the rule of equity, where one of three sureties has paid the debt, he is entitled to recover one moiety from another of the co-sureties, the third having become insolvent.

All persons who, by common consent, put their names to an accommodation bill, whether as drawers, acceptors, or indorsers, in order that one of them may get the bill discounted for his own benefit, are co-sureties for the due payment of the bill.

Indemnification of surety. (13) Money paid by the surety for the purpose of discharging the claim against the principal is money paid for the use of the principal at his request, which may be recovered from the latter. The surety need not wait for the commencement of an action against the principal, but he cannot accelerate the liability of the latter.

Every person who, being surety for the debt or duty of another, or being liable with another for any debt or duty, shall pay such debt or perform such duty, is entitled (19 & 20 Vict. c. 97, s. 5) to have assigned to him, or to a trustee for him, every judgment, specialty, or other security held by the creditor in respect of the debt or duty, whether such judgment, specialty, or other security shall or shall not be deemed at law to have been satisfied by the payment of the debt or the performance of the duty; and such person is entitled to stand in the place of the creditor, and use all the remedies, and, if need be, and upon proper indemnity, to use the name of the creditor in any action or other proceeding, in order to obtain from the principal debtor, or any co-surety, co-contractor, or co-debtor, indemnification for the advances made and loss sustained by the person who has paid the debt or performed the duty.

ILLUSTRATIVE CASES.

(1) *Simpson* v. *Penton,* 2 Cr. & M. 430.

A. introduced B. to C., an upholsterer, and A., in B.'s presence, asked C. whether he had any objection to supply B. with some furniture, and said that if he would "he would be answerable." C. asked A. how long credit he wanted, and A. replied "he would see it paid at the end of six months."

C. agreed to this, and A. gave him the order, and the goods were supplied accordingly. At the end of six months, B. not having paid the amount, C. applied to A. for payment, and he paid the money. The entry in C.'s book was "Mr. B., *per* Mr. A." Held, that the jury were warranted in finding that the undertaking on the part of A. was not a collateral but an original undertaking. Bayley, B.: "The expressions 'I'll be answerable,' and 'I'll see you paid,' are equivocal; and then the circumstances ought to be looked to to see what the contract between the parties was. It is quite clear that the goods were furnished for B.'s benefit, but it does not appear that he said one word by which he pledged himself, so as to give C. a right to call upon him for payment. It was left to the jury to say whether A. was the original debtor, and they found that he was. I think the jury were warranted in that finding."

Mallett v. *Bateman*, L.R. 1 C.P. 163.

B. verbally promised that if M. would supply C. with iron, and take C.'s acceptances, he would discount them. Held, that this was a promise to answer for the default of another, and that as it was not in writing, M. could not recover against B. on his refusing to discount the acceptances.

(2) <center>*Holmes* v. *Mitchell*, 7 C.B., N.S. 361.</center>

In a letter written to the plaintiff, relating to a proposed mortgage, the defendant used the following words, "I will take any responsibility myself respecting it, should there be any." Held, not a sufficient guarantee within the Statute of Frauds. Williams, J.: "The letter, if read by itself, would be a promise to be responsible for any sum of money, however large, at any rate of interest, secured by any kind of mortgage, on any land with any title. That, however, would be an unreasonable construction, and is not its true meaning; it evidently refers to previous conversations in which these particulars were supplied. The whole promise, therefore, is not in writing as the statute requires that it should be. It cannot be made out without reference to previous conversations. A consideration expressed in writing formerly discharged two offices, it sustained the promise and might also explain it. Now, however, parol evidence, though it may supply the consideration, cannot go further and explain the promise."

(3) <center>*Pooley* v. *Harradine*, 7 Ell. & Bl. 431.</center>

Action on a promissory note; plea, on equitable grounds, that defendant made the note jointly with J. for J.'s accommodation and as surety for J.; and that the note was delivered to plaintiff and taken by him on an agreement between them that defendant should be liable as surety only, and with notice that he was surety only; and that afterwards plaintiff, without defendant's consent, gave time to J., but for which he might have obtained payment. On demurrer, Held, that the plea was good, for though the absolute written contract between plaintiff and defendant, contained in the note, could not be varied by parol in equity any more than at law, yet an equity arose from the relation of surety and principal between the defendant and J., and the notice thereof to plaintiff at the time he took the note.

(4) <center>*Parker* v. *Wise*, 6 M. & S. 246.</center>

Bond by defendant as surety for Messrs. W., with a condition, reciting that obligees were bankers, and Messrs. W. paper manufacturers, and had overdrawn their account with obligees to the amount of £4822, and in order to enable them to carry on their business had applied to obligees to allow them for a time to overdraw such further sums as they should require, *so as that the same, together with the £4822, should not exceed in the whole, at any one time*, £5000, which obligees had agreed to do, and the condition was for the payment by Messrs. W. or defendant of the sum of £4822, and also such further sums as obligees should or might thereafter advance to Messrs. W. in the course of their business, not exceeding in the whole £5000: Held, not to be avoided by the obligees having allowed Messrs. W. to overdraw to an amount which, together with the £4822, exceeded £5000. If it had been intended that the bond should be void in case the amount named were exceeded, express words should have been used to that effect. The defendant must stand liable to the extent of £5000, but no more.

(5) *Kirby* v. *D. of Marlborough*, 2 *M. & S.* 22.

A bond entered into by A. and B. to the plaintiffs to enable A. to carry on his trade, conditioned for the payment of all such sums not exceeding £3000 which should at any time thereafter be advanced by plaintiffs to A., Held, not to be a continuing guarantee to the extent of £3000 for advances made at any time, but only a guarantee for advances once made to the extent of £3000.

(6) *Mason* v. *Pritchard*, 12 *East* 227.

A guarantee, not under seal, by the defendant to the plaintiff "for any goods he hath supplied, or may supply W. P. with, to the amount of £100," is a continuing guarantee to that extent for goods which may at any time have been supplied to W. P. until the credit was recalled, although goods to more than £100 had been before supplied and paid for.

(7) *Watts* v. *Shuttleworth*, 29 *Law J., Ex.* 229.

The defendant became surety for the performance by H. of a contract with the plaintiff W. for the fittings of warehouses at a fixed price. The contract between W. and H. contained a stipulation that W. should insure the fittings from fire, at such time and to such amount as the architect might consider necessary, and deduct the insurance from the amount of the contract. W. did not insure the fittings, and they were accidentally burnt in the workshop, and H. was unable to complete his contract. Held, that as W. did not insure in pursuance of his agreement, the defendant was released in equity from the guarantee.

(8) *Gardner* v. *Walsh*, 24 *Law J., Q.B.* 284.

A. being indebted to the plaintiffs, it was arranged between them that B. and the defendant should join as sureties for A. in a promissory note for the amount payable to the plaintiffs. The defendant, in ignorance of the arrangement that B. should sign the note, signed a joint and several note for the amount, together with A., and as A.'s surety. The note so signed was then handed to the plaintiffs, who procured it to be signed by B., without the defendant's consent or knowledge. Held, that assuming the note to have been completely issued when it was signed by B., this was an alteration of the note, and of the defendant's liability, in a material point, and that the defendant was consequently discharged. Lord Campbell, C.J.: "Under certain circumstances which might have supervened, this alteration might have been prejudicial to the defendant. But we conceive that he is discharged from his liability, if the altered instrument would operate differently from the original instrument, whether the alteration be or be not to his prejudice."

(9) *Coombe* v. *Woolf*, 8 *Bing.* 156.

Defendant guaranteed the payment of porter to be delivered by the plaintiff to J. The guaranty contained no stipulation as to the credit to be given to

J. The custom of the plaintiff was to give six months' credit, and then sometimes to take a bill at two months. The plaintiff having, without the knowledge of the defendant, given J. eleven months' credit, Held, that the defendant was discharged from his guaranty.

Tucker v. *Laing*, 2 *K. & J.* 745.

A letter written by the agent of a bond creditor to the principal obligor, giving him eighteen months further time to pay the bond debt, upon condition of his paying off at once the arrear of interest, and keeping down the interest to accrue in future : Held, to be a mere promise without consideration, and not binding ; and therefore, held, that the co-obligor, who had joined in the bond as surety only, was not thereby discharged.

(10)   *Webb* v. *Hewitt*, 3 *K. & J.* 438.

An agreement between a bond debtor and his creditor, that the latter shall take all the debtor's property, and shall pay his other creditors five shillings in the pound, operates in equity as a satisfaction of the debt, and it is not possible, upon such a transaction, to reserve any rights against the surety; and any attempt to do so would be void, as being inconsistent with the agreement.

Price v. *Barker*, 4 *Ell. & Bl.* 760.

B. and defendant, the latter as surety, gave plaintiff a joint and several bond for £600. Plaintiff afterwards by deed poll, without the knowledge or authority of defendant, released and for ever discharged B. from all claims and demands whatsoever, expressly, however, reserving his right to proceed against the sureties of B. Held, that the deed poll was not a release, but a covenant not to sue B. ; and that plaintiff was not precluded from suing defendant in respect of breaches accruing before the execution of the deed poll.

(11)   *Wythes* v. *Labouchere*, 5 *Jur.*, *N.S.* 499.

Concealment, on the part of a creditor, must, in order to avoid a guarantee, be of some material part of the transaction itself between the creditor and the debtor to which the suretyship relates, and there is no legal obligation on the part of the creditor to disclose to the intended surety matters affecting the credit of the debtor, or any other circumstances unconnected with the particular transaction.

Stone v. *Compton*, 5 *B.N.C.* 142.

Plaintiffs advanced £2600 to C., upon the security of an indenture of mortgage executed by C., and a promissory note for £2600, in which defendant joined as a surety. At the time of the advance, C. owed plaintiffs £800, which was deducted from the £2600, but the recital of the mortgage deed, which was read by plaintiffs' agent in the presence of defendant, stated untruly that the £800 had been paid. Held, that this was a fraud in law which released defendant from his liability on the promissory note.

Phillips v. *Foxhall*, 41 *Law J.*, *Q.B.* 293.

The defendant guaranteed that he would be answerable for any loss, not exceeding £50, which the plaintiff might sustain through any breach of duty by S., her servant, in receiving, collecting, and paying over to her moneys due from customers. To an action brought upon such guarantee, the defendant, in respect of moneys received by S. on account of the plaintiff, after the giving by the defendant of the guarantee, and before Nov. 12th,

1869, paid money into court. With respect to the residue of the plaintiff's claim, the defendant pleaded that after the giving of the guarantee of the defendant, and before Nov. 12th, 1869, S. embezzled moneys received by him to the amount of £57, that the plaintiff became aware of this on or about Nov. 20th, 1869, and that, without informing the defendant thereof, she agreed with S. that he should continue in her service, and should pay her £3 a month in liquidation of the said sum of £57; and thereupon S. continued in the service of the plaintiff until April 4th, 1871; that during that time he repaid to the plaintiff sums of money amounting to £48; that, during the continuance of S. in such service, he collected the moneys for, and on behalf of, the plaintiff, comprised in the residue therein pleaded to; that, during the whole of the time S. collected the said sums of money, the defendant was ignorant of the embezzlements prior to Nov. 20th 1869; and that the defendant was so prevented from revoking the guarantee and compelling S. to pay to him, the defendant, the moneys he was liable under the guarantee to pay to the plaintiff: Held, on demurrer, to be a good plea to the action.

(12) *Nicholson* v. *Revill*, 4 *Ad. & E.* 675.

A., B., and C., the two latter as sureties, gave the plaintiff three joint and several promissory notes, the first for £52 18s. 8d. at thirteen months, the second and third respectively for £110 13s. 4d. and £56 13s. 8d. at longer periods, as a satisfaction and security for a debt of £200 due from A. to the plaintiff. The first note being due and unpaid, and the second (now sued upon) not yet due, B. agreed with the plaintiff to pay, and did pay him, £100 in discharge of his (B.'s) liability on the three notes, and plaintiff accepted the same in such discharge, and gave up to B. the first of the three notes, indorsed upon the note now sued upon a receipt for £47 1s. 4d. on account, erased B.'s name from this note, and discharged him from further liability thereon. In an action against C. on the second note these facts were admitted by the plaintiff, and it was not denied that the transaction between B. and the plaintiff took place without C.'s knowledge or consent. Held, that the discharge of B. by the plaintiff also discharged C.

Hitchman v. *Stewart*, 3 *Drew.* 271.

Five sureties, one of whom was the plaintiff, guaranteed a debt of £800. The principal debtor and one of the sureties having become insolvent, the plaintiff paid the debt. Held, that the plaintiff in equity was entitled to recover from each of the three solvent sureties one-fourth of the sum paid by him, with interest from the time of his payment. [Formerly, *at law*, in such a case the plaintiff would only have been able to recover one-fifth of the sum paid by him from each of the three solvent sureties. See *Browne* v. *Lee*, 6 *B. & C.* 697.]

(13) *Reynolds* v. *Wheeler*, 10 *C.B., N.S.* 561.

A., for the purpose of raising money, drew a bill upon B., which B. accepted. Being unable to get the bill discounted without a third name, A. procured C. to indorse it. The bill being unpaid at maturity, the holder agreed to renew it; and accordingly a fresh bill was *drawn by B. upon A.*, and indorsed by C. B. having been compelled to pay the whole amount, Held, that he was entitled to sue C. for contribution.

CHAPTER XIII.

INSURANCE.

THE contract of insurance is one by which one of the contracting parties agrees to take upon himself the risks and accidents to which any particular property, or any particular individual, may be exposed, and promises, in consideration of a sum of money which the other contracting party agrees to pay, to indemnify the latter against these risks and accidents. The party undertaking to indemnify is called the insurer or underwriter, the party protected by the contract the insured, the money paid by the latter as the price of the indemnity, the premium, and the written instrument which evidences the contract, the policy.   Contracts of insurance.

(i.) *Marine Insurance.*

When the insurance is on a voyage from one port to another, without reference to time, the policy is called a voyage policy; but when it is from one fixed period to another, the policy is a time policy.   Voyage and time policies.

When the value of the property insured, as between the insured and the underwriter, is expressed on the face of the policy, the policy is called a valued policy. When it is not so expressed, but is left to be estimated in case of   Valued and open policies. (1)

loss, the policy is called an open policy. In the absence of fraud or wagering, a valued policy is valid, however largely in excess of the true value; but, if a policy be enormously over valued, this may be evidence of fraud.

Wagering and gaming policies.

By the 19 Geo. II. c. 37, s. 1, it is enacted that no insurance shall be made by any person on any ship, or on any goods or merchandise laden on board thereof, interest or no interest, or without further proof of interest than the policy, by way of gaming and wagering, or without benefit of salvage to the insurer; and that every such insurance shall be void.

By the 30 Vict. c. 23, ss. 7 and 8, contracts of insurance are required to be expressed in a policy, which must specify the particular risk or adventure, the names of the subscribers and the sums insured. If any of these particulars are omitted, or if the policy is for any time exceeding twelve months, it is void.

Formerly the interest which the underwriter himself acquires in the safety of the property he has insured could not have been re-insured. But by the 27 & 28 Vict. c. 56, s. 1, re-insurance may now be effected upon any ship or vessel, or upon any goods.

Implied warranties.
(2)

There is an implied warranty in voyage policies on the part of the insured that the ship insured is seaworthy, tight, staunch, and strong, properly equipped, and sufficiently manned at the time of the commencement of the voyage; but in the case of time policies there is no such warranty.

The insurer is entitled to expect that the ship-owner will do all that can be reasonably expected to be done to limit the risk, covered by the insurance, to those perils incidental to navigation which the care and skill of man cannot provide against.

If by accident or mistake a vessel sails out of port in an unseaworthy state, and the defect is remedied before any loss occurs, and she then sails again in a seaworthy state, the insurer will not be liable on the policy for a subsequent loss.

Every positive averment or allegation on the face of a policy of insurance of facts material to the risk, forming the basis of the contract, amounts to a warranty; and if such allegation be not strictly true, the insured cannot recover on the policy, to whatever cause the loss be owing. *Express warranties. (3)*

When there is a warranty that the vessel is "well" on the day the insurance is effected, the warranty is complied with, if the vessel was safe at any time on the day named, so that, if the vessel should have been lost in the morning of that day, and the insurance be effected in the afternoon, the underwriters will be liable. *Warranty that the ship is "well." (4)*

When the vessel is warranted to sail by a particular day, the underwriter will be discharged, if she does not sail at the time appointed; and the circumstance of her being prevented by inevitable accident, or restraint, or detention of princes in nowise exonerates the insured from the consequences of his breach of contract. *Warranty as to time of sailing. (5)*

If a vessel warranted "to depart with convoy" is proceeding from her loading port to the nearest place of rendezvous for convoy, and is captured, the underwriters are nevertheless responsible, as the vessel was fulfilling the warranty at the time of the capture in the only mode in which it could be fulfilled, and was proceeding to secure convoy and departing with convoy, in the mercantile sense of the term, and according to the usage of trade. A warranty that the vessel shall "depart with convoy" generally means that she is to have convoy for the whole voyage insured, unless prevented by stress of weather. *Warranty as to sailing with convoy. (6)*

Oral evidence of representations and statements, made at the time the policy was effected, are inadmissible in evidence to control, alter, or affect the liability upon the policy, unless they are fraudulent representations. *Fraudulent misrepresentation and concealment. (7)*

Fraudulent concealment of circumstances materially affecting or enhancing the risk to be incurred by the insurer or underwriter avoids all policies of insurance, and prevents the insured from recovering in respect of a loss wholly unconnected with the circumstances concealed. The keeping back of any such circumstance avoids the policy, although the suppression may have occurred through mistake.

Custom and usage. (8) Everything done in the usual course of navigation and trade is presumed to have been foreseen and in contemplation by the parties to every contract of insurance at the time they entered into the engagement. Every underwriter is presumed to be acquainted with the practice of the trade he insures.

Risks covered. The risks that underwriters generally take upon themselves by the common form of policy are perils of the sea, fire, pirates, letters of mart and countermart, takings at sea, restraint of princes and people, and barratry of the masters and mariners.

Perils of the sea. (9) As between the carrier of goods by sea and the owner of such goods, losses which, though caused immediately by the violence of the winds and waves, are imputable to the ignorance or negligence of the master or mariners, are not losses by perils of the sea. But, as between the insurer and insured, the immediate and not the remote cause of the loss is regarded, so that, if a vessel is wrecked through the incompetence or misconduct of the captain and crew, the loss is nevertheless a loss by perils of the sea, and is covered by the policy, provided the insured—if the insurance is on the vessel itself—had appointed a sufficient crew and a captain who appeared to have competent skill at the commencement of the voyage. Loss or damage resulting from ordinary wear and tear, or from some inherent vice or defect, is not covered by the policy.

If a vessel has sailed out of port on her intended voyage,

and does not arrive at her port of destination within a reasonable period, and no intelligence can be gained respecting her, this is evidence of the loss of the vessel from perils of the sea.

When fire is one of the perils insured against, and the ship is lost by fire, it is of no consequence whether this was occasioned by a common accident, or by lightning, or by an act done in duty to the state to prevent the vessel from falling into the hands of the enemy, or by the gross negligence of the captain or crew. Perils of fire. (10)

When jettison is one of the risks insured against, the policy will cover a loss occasioned by the throwing of the goods overboard to prevent their falling into the hands of the enemy. Jettison. (11)

When capture is insured against, the circumstance that the capture was illegal, or that it was occasioned by the fraud of the master, does not affect the liability of the insurer. Loss by capture. (12)

In the clause relating to restraints, &c., of kings, princes, and people, which is usually inserted in insurance policies, the word "people" is understood to refer to nations in their collective capacity, and not to bodies of insurgents acting in opposition to their rulers. The insurance against the risk of detention by princes will not extend to cover any loss happening in the course of any contraband adventure in which the goods become liable to seizure by the laws of this country. But as our laws do not take notice of the revenue laws of foreign governments, if the underwriter has notice of the intention of the insured to engage in a foreign smuggling transaction, and accepts the increased risk, he will be liable upon the policy. Restraints, &c., of kings, princes, and people. (13)

By barratry of the master and crew is meant any species of fraud by which the owners or insurers are injured. But barratry does not include simple negligence, nor any act done in obedience to the commands of the Peril of barratry. (14)

ship-owner, or from ignorance or error of judgment. Barratry is an act of fraud, not directed against the owner of goods which are lost, but against the owner of the ship. And if the owner of the ship (he being sole owner) concurs in the act which causes the loss, that takes from it the character of barratry.

Perils, &c., generally. (15) A clause is usually inserted in policies, extending the insurance to "all other perils, losses, and misfortunes that have or shall come to the hurt, detriment, or damage of the said goods, merchandise, and ship." These general words are, however, restrained in construction to perils of the same kind as those particularly enumerated in the policy.

Commencement of risk. (16) If the policy is on a ship or goods "lost or not lost," the indemnity extends to all past as well as all future damage. In policies of insurance on ships, the risk is generally expressly appointed to commence "from the time of the vessel's being ready to sail," or, "from the time of clearing," or, "at and from" her arrival at a particular place. If there is any voluntary or unreasonable delay, the underwriter will be discharged. In policies of insurance on goods there is usually an express stipulation that the risk upon the policy shall commence from the loading of the goods on board the ship.

Termination of the risk. It is generally provided in the policy that the risk shall continue as regards the ship, until she has arrived at her port of destination or port of discharge, and has been moored at anchor in safety for twenty-four hours, and, as regards the goods, until they have been safely discharged and landed.

Freight policies. (17) The freight to be earned by the vessel in the performance of the voyage may be insured, as well as the vessel itself, and the cargo laden on board. But to recover for loss of freight, a total loss by perils of the sea must be proved.

Deviation. (18) Every policy of insurance is effected upon the implied understanding that the vessel will proceed straightway, and without unnecessary delay, to the place of destination. If, therefore, she voluntarily deviates from her course to put into port, and is afterwards lost, the underwriters will be discharged; and unreasonable delay at any place at which the vessel is authorized to touch is equivalent to a deviation.

If a ship insured for a particular voyage grounds on a sandbank, and cannot be got off, the loss is a total loss, although the ship still exists *in specie*. If she is so disabled by stress of weather as not to be worth repairing the loss is a total loss, although she still exists as a ship in the dockyard. And when a vessel is wrecked, the cargo is totally lost, if no part of it can be recovered for the benefit of the insured. But in all cases where the subject-matter of the insurance is not totally destroyed, the insured, in order to recover the full amount of the insurance as for a total loss, must abandon what remains, and, by giving notice of abandonment to the underwriters, make cession to them of all his proprietary rights. When the subject-matter of the insurance totally perishes, no notice of abandonment is necessary. *Total loss and abandonment. (19)*

When there is a constructive total loss and abandonment, the risk of saving what remains to be saved is thrown upon the underwriter; but where there is a constructive total loss, and the insured neglects to give due notice of abandonment, the insured must make the best of what he can save, and resort to the underwriter for the actual loss, after deducting the value of what is recovered.

If a vessel loses part of its gear, as a mast, by a peril insured against, and is refitted, the loss is a partial loss; and if the vessel then puts to sea, and is totally lost, the insured is entitled to be indemnified in respect of the partial loss as well as the total loss; but if before the vessel is refitted she is totally lost, the insured cannot then recover in respect of the partial loss. *Partial loss. (20)*

x

A memorandum is frequently introduced at the foot of the policy exempting the underwriters from all partial losses upon certain articles and descriptions of merchandise, and from all partial losses not amounting to £5 per cent. upon other classes of goods, and upon all partial losses upon ship and freight not amounting to £3 per cent., unless the loss be a general average and contribution loss.

General average. By general average is meant loss arising from the general contribution, made by all parties interested in a ship and cargo, toward a loss sustained by some for the benefit of all; as, for example, when goods are thrown overboard, or masts and cables cut away for the purpose of preventing shipwreck.

Particular average. By particular average is meant a partial loss sustained by the insured, not connected with the loss of any other party, and not occasioned by a general average contribution.

An insurance on goods "warranted free of average, unless general," is equivalent, therefore, to an insurance against their total loss only.

Void policy. (21) If a policy is rendered void by reason of a written misrepresentation, or misstatement, made by the insured by mistake, and without fraud, the insured will be entitled to a return of his premium.

(ii.) *Fire Insurance.*

Insurable interest. (22) The insurer must have a pecuniary interest in the property exposed to risk, or he must be accountable, or responsible, to some person for the safety or security of the property. A bailee, or one who has a lien upon goods, may insure them.

Alteration of premises. (23) In every policy of insurance of property against fire there is an implied promise on the part of the insured that he will not, after the making of the policy, alter the premises so as to add to the risk; and if he does so the underwriter is discharged.

Negligence, whether of the servants or agents of the insured, or of the insured himself, is no defence against the claim of the insured. But the underwriters do not take upon themselves extraordinary risks, unless these risks are expressly brought to their notice, and are accepted and insured against by them. *Negligence. (24)*

By the terms of most contracts of fire insurance, the insured is required to give notice of the loss within a certain time to the insurer, together with a certificate of good character. When a reasonable suspicion exists that buildings have been insured for more than their value, and purposely fired, but proof is wanting, the insurers may rebuild or repair at their own expense, and resist the claim of the insured for the money secured by the policy (14 Geo. III. c. 78, s. 83). *Notice of loss. (25) Insurance money laid out in re-building.*

If the insured has effected two or more insurances upon the same property, he can recover no more than his actual loss. He may resort to which insurer he pleases, and the latter may resort to the others for contribution. *Double insurance. (26)*

A purchaser of property which is insured does not, by the mere fact of the purchase, and in the absence of any agreement to that effect, acquire any right to the insurance money. *Assignment of fire policies. (27)*

(iii.) *Life Insurance.*

A contract of life insurance is a contract to pay a certain sum of money on the death of a person, in consideration of the due payment of a certain annuity for his life. *Contracts of life insurance.*

By the 14 Geo. III. c. 48, it is enacted (sec. 1) that no insurance shall be made on the life of any person, wherein the person for whose use or benefit, or on whose account, the policy shall be made, shall have no interest. The *Interest of the insured. (28)*

interest of the person insured must be a pecuniary interest in the duration of the life insured.

The liability upon a life policy is not, however, affected by the question whether the party claiming the benefit of the policy has or has not been damnified by the happening of the contingency upon which the money becomes payable. The contract of life insurance is a mere contract to pay a certain sum of money upon the death of a person, in consideration of the due payment of certain annual premiums during his life. It is not, like a policy of marine insurance or fire insurance, a contract of indemnity.

Conditions. (29) A statement respecting the life insured does not amount to a warranty unless it is made the basis of the contract, and was intended by the parties to have that effect. But policies are generally granted subject to the condition that, if any untrue statement is contained in any of the documents addressed to the insurers in relation to the life insured, the policy shall be void. By untrue statement is sometimes meant a statement that is wilfully and designedly untrue. In other cases the policy will be void if the statement is unintentionally untrue.

Risks covered by the policy. (30) When insurance is made upon a life generally, without any representation of the state of the life insured, the insurer takes all the risks, unless there was some fraud on the part of the person insuring, either by his suppressing circumstances which he knew, or alleging what was false. Where, therefore, there is no express provision in the policy that, in the event of the insured dying by his own hand, the policy shall become void, the policy is not avoided by the circumstance of his having died by his own hand while in a state of temporary insanity, but the policy will be avoided if he is killed in a duel, or feloniously destroy himself, or is executed.

In most policies, where parties insure their own lives, a condition is inserted making the policy void if the party shall die by his own hands; and where there is such a condition in a policy, the insurers will be discharged from liability if the insured destroy himself, even though he does so in a fit of madness.

The assignment of life policies is regulated by the 30 & 31 Vict. c. 144. Such assignment may be made either by indorsement on the policy, or by a separate instrument in the form given by the Act. *Assignment of life policies.*

Policies of fire insurance and of life insurance, like policies of marine insurance, are avoided by fraudulent misrepresentation, or fraudulent concealment, of circumstances material to be known to the underwriter. And some policies go so far as to make the insurance company itself the sole judge of the materiality or immateriality of the misstatement. *Fraudulent misrepresentation and concealment.*

In policies of fire insurance and of life insurance, when the policy is to become forfeited, if the premium is not paid by a given day, but the policy may nevertheless be revived by the payment of the premium within a certain number of "days of grace," it is essential to the revival of the policy that the premises insured are safe, or that the life insured is in being at the time of the payment and acceptance of the premium. Many policies, however, expressly provide that the insurance shall be continued and the property or life covered until the expiration of the days of grace. *Forfeiture of policies. (31)*

ILLUSTRATIVE CASES.

(1)   *Lewis* v. *Rucker,* 2 Burr. 1171.

Lord Mansfield : " A valued policy is not to be considered as a wager policy. The only effect of the valuation is fixing the amount of the prime cost ; just as if the parties admitted it at the trial ; but in every argument, and for every other purpose, it must be taken that the value was fixed in such a manner as that the insured meant only to have an indemnity. If it be under valued, the merchant himself stands insurer of the surplus. If it be *much* over valued it must be done with a bad view, either to gain, contrary to the 19 Geo. II. c. 37, or with some view to a fraudulent loss. Where valued policies are used merely as a cover to a wager, they would be considered an evasion of the law."

(2)   *Fawcus* v. *Sarsfield,* 6 Ell. & Bl. 200.

Where a vessel is sent to sea in a state not fit for a particular voyage, and without encountering any more than ordinary risk, is obliged, owing to the defective state in which she sailed, to put into a port to repair, the shipowner, though the defect were not known to him, and he has acted without fraud, cannot recover against the insurer the expenses of such repairs, though there be no warrant of seaworthiness. *Per curiam*, there is in general no implied warrant of seaworthiness in a *time* policy.

Quebec Marine Insurance Co. v. *Commercial Bank of Canada*,
L.R. 3 P.C. 234.

A policy on a steam-vessel was effected in Lower Canada, at and from Montreal to Halifax, in Nova Scotia. The policy especially excepted the underwriters, *inter alia*, from "rottenness, inherent defects, and other unseaworthiness, bursting or explosion of boilers, collapsing of flues, or breakage of machinery, unless occasioned by unavoidable external cause." At the time of starting there was a defect in the boiler of the vessel, which was not apparent in rivers, but when she got into salt water she became disabled by reason of such defect, and was compelled to put into port to repair, when, after being repaired and detained for some days, she proceeded to sea, but, encountering bad weather, was lost. Held, first, that in a voyage policy there is by implication of law a warranty of seaworthiness, which had not been complied with, as the vessel sailed with a defect of such a nature that, so long as it remained unremedied, it made her unseaworthy for the voyage or stage of the voyage she entered upon, and secondly, that, although the defect was repaired before loss, it avoided the policy.

(3)   *De Hahn* v. *Hartley*, 1 *T.R.* 343.

On the margin of a policy of marine insurance were written the words, "Sailed from Liverpool with fourteen six-pounders, swivels, small arms, and fifty hands, or upwards; copper sheathed." Held, that this amounted to a warranty, and must be literally complied with.

(4)   *Blackhurst* v. *Cockell*, 3 *T.R.* 360.

Goods were insured from the time of lading them on board the ship, "lost or not lost," and warranted well on a particular day. The ship was lost on that day, before the policy was underwritten. Held, that the underwriter was liable, for the warranty was complied with, if the ship were safe at any time of that day.

(5)   *Hore* v. *Whitmore*, 2 *Cowp.* 784.

A ship, warranted to sail on or before a particular day, was prevented from sailing on that day by an embargo. Held, that the warranty was not complied with, and the insurer was exempted from liability upon the loss of the vessel.

(6)   See *Jefferyes* v. *Legendra*, 1 *Show.* 297.

(7)   *Seaman* v. *Fonerau*, 2 *Str.* 1183.

On the 25th of August, 1740, the defendant underwrote a policy on the ship *Davy*, from Carolina to Holland. The agent for the plaintiff had on the 23rd of August received a letter, dated 21st August, wherein it was said, "The 12th of this month I was in company with the ship *Davy*, and at 12 in the night lost sight of her all at once; the captain spoke to me the day before that she was leaky, and the next day we had a hard gale." The ship was not in fact lost, as supposed, but continued her voyage until August 19th, when she was captured by the Spaniards; and there was no pretence of any knowledge on the part of the plaintiff of her actual loss at the time of the insurance. Held, that the defendant was not liable on the policy, as the above letter was not disclosed to him by the plaintiff.

Carter v. Boehm, 3 *Burr.* 1910, *and* 1 *Sm. L.C.*

Insurance on Fort Marlborough, in India, against foreign capture, effected by its governor. The weakness of the fort, and the probability of its being taken by the French, were known to the insured, but not communicated to the insurer. It was also objected that the insurance was against public policy. The plaintiff proved that the office of governor was mercantile, not military ; and that the fort was never calculated to resist European armies. Held, that the jury were justified in finding for the plaintiff. Lord Mansfield : "The special facts, upon which the contingent chance is to be computed, lie most commonly in the knowledge of the insured only ; the underwriter trusts to his representation, and proceeds upon confidence that he does not keep back any circumstance in his knowledge to mislead the underwriter into a belief that the circumstance does not exist, and to induce him to estimate the risk as if it did exist. The keeping back such circumstance is a fraud, and renders a policy void. Although the suppression should happen through mistake, without any fraudulent intention, yet still the underwriter is deceived, and the policy is void. . . . . But the insured need not mention what the underwriter ought to know, what he takes upon himself the knowledge of, or what he waives being informed of. He need not be told general topics of speculation, as, for instance, the underwriter is bound to know every cause which may occasion natural perils, as the *difficulty of the voyage, the kind of seasons, the probability of lightning, hurricanes, earthquakes, &c. He is bound to know every cause which may occasion political perils.*"

(8) *Noble v. Kennoway*, 2 *Doug.* 513.

An underwriter is bound to know the nature and peculiar circumstances of the branch of trade to which the policy relates. To prove the manner of conducting a particular branch of trade at one place, evidence may be given to show the manner in which the same branch is carried on at another place.

(9) *Redman v. Wilson*, 14 *M. & W.* 476.

Where a ship, insured against the perils of the sea, was injured by the negligent loading of her cargo by the natives on the coast of Africa, and in consequence shortly afterwards became leaky, and, being pronounced unseaworthy, was run ashore in order to prevent her from sinking, and to save the cargo—Held, that the insurers were liable for a constructive total loss, the immediate cause of the loss being the perils of the sea, although the cause of the unseaworthiness was the negligence in loading.

Koebel v. Saunders, 17 *C.B., N.S.* 71.

It is not a condition precedent to the attaching of a policy on *goods* against sea-risks that the subject of insurance should, at the commencement of the voyage, be fit to encounter the ordinary vicissitudes of a voyage.

Green v. Brown, 2 *Str.* 1199.

The ship *Charming Peggy* was insured in 1739 from North Carolina to London, with a warranty against captures and seizures. Four years afterwards an action was brought against the insurers, and the loss was laid to be by sinking at sea. All the evidence given was that she sailed out of port on her intended voyage, and had never since been heard of. The underwriter insisted that as captures and seizures were excepted, it lay upon the insured to prove that the loss happened in the particular manner declared on. Lord Chief-Justice Lee said it would be unreasonable to expect certain evidence of such a loss, and that the plaintiff had given the best proof which the nature of the case admitted of. Whereupon, verdict was found for the plaintiff.

(10) *Gordon* v. *Rimmington*, 1 Campb. 123.

The captain of a ship insured burnt her in order to prevent her falling into the hands of a French privateer of superior strength by which she was being pursued. Held, that this was a loss by *fire* within the meaning of the policy.

Busk v. *Royal Exchange Assurance Co.*, 2 B. & Ald. 73.

In an action on a policy on a ship, by which, among other risks, the underwriters insured against fire, it appeared that the vessel having been frozen up for the winter in a Russian port, the captain paid off the crew, and left the vessel in charge of the mate. The mate, one evening, lighted a fire in the ship's cabin, and then, without leaving anyone on board, went away to a Russian vessel lying near at hand; during the night the English vessel was destroyed by fire. Held, that the fact that the burning of the vessel was due to the negligence of the mate did not affect the liability of the insurers upon the policy.

(11) *Butler* v. *Wildman*, 3 B. & Ald. 398.

The captain of a Spanish ship, in order to prevent a quantity of dollars from falling into the hands of an enemy by whom he was about to be attacked, threw the same into the sea, and his vessel was immediately afterwards captured. Held, in an action upon a policy of insurance upon Spanish property subscribed by British underwriters, who, at the time of effecting the policy, knew that the insured were Spaniards, and that Spain was at war with the state to whom the capturing vessel belonged, that this was a loss by jettison—that term in a policy of insurance signifying any throwing overboard of the cargo for a justifiable cause.

(12) *Powell* v. *Hyde*, 5 Ell. & Bl. 611.

By a policy of insurance on goods on board the ship *B.*, a British ship, they were warranted "free from capture and seizure, and the consequences of any attempt thereof." The perils insured against were enumerated as usual, and included "perils of the sea, men-of-war, fire, enemies," &c. The *B.*, in her passage down the Danube, passed within shot of a Russian fort, there being then war between Turkey and Russia, but no war between Great Britain and Russia. The Russian fort fired into her, and sunk her, alleging that the vessel was mistaken for a Turk. Held, that but for the exception introduced by the warranty, the insurers would have been liable. Held, also, that the effect of the warranty was not confined to legal capture or seizure, but that an illegal capture or seizure was within the exception, and in the absence of the exception would have been within the perils enumerated as insured against.

(13) *Nesbit* v. *Lushington*, 4 T.R. 783.

If an armed force board a ship, and take part of the cargo, the underwriters are not liable on a count stating the loss to be by a seizure by *people* to the plaintiffs unknown; for *people* in the policy means "the governing power in the country." Where, after such a seizure, the vessel was stranded, and part of the cargo (consisting of corn) taken by the mob at their own price, the loss could not be recovered as for a general average.

Brandon v. *Curling,* 2 *East* 410.

An insurance on goods from London to Bayonne, shipped on board a neutral vessel, on account and at the risk of Frenchmen, before the declaration of hostilities between Great Britain and France, but exported afterwards, cannot be enforced against the underwriter, even after the restoration of peace, to recover a loss by capture of a co-belligerent during the war. Every assurance on alien property by a British subject must be understood with this implied exception, that it shall not extend to cover any loss happening during the existence of hostilities between the respective countries of the insurer and the insured. And see *Planché* v. *Fletcher,* 1 *Doug.* 251.

(14) *Earle* v. *Rowcroft,* 8 *East* 126.

A shipmaster had general instructions to make the best purchases he could, with despatch. He thereupon went into a settlement belonging to Holland, which country was then at war with Great Britain, to trade, because the purchases could be more speedily and cheaply purchased there than elsewhere. The enemy permitted the transaction, but the vessel was subsequently seized and confiscated by an English frigate for having traded with the enemy. Held, that the conduct of the master was not warranted by his instructions, but was barratrous.

Todd v. *Ritchie,* 1 *Stark.* 240.

Action on a policy of insurance ; the loss was alleged to have arisen from the barratry of the master. After the vessel had started on her homeward voyage, she sprung a leak, and the captain put into port for safety, and before any survey had taken place he broke up her ceiling and end bows with crowbars, in consequence of which the ship was much injured and weakened ; this, it was suggested, was done in order to procure the condemnation of the vessel. Held, this was not necessarily barratry, for it might have been done through error of judgment ; and it was not proved that the captain acted against his better judgment.

(15) *Cullen* v. *Butler,* 5 *M. & S.* 461.

On a policy of insurance on goods in the common form, where the ship and goods were sunk at sea by another ship's firing upon her, mistaking her for the enemy—Held, that this loss was within the general words of the policy, "all other perils and losses." Ellenborough, C.J. : "These general words may have the effect of extending a reasonable indemnity to many cases not distinctly covered by the special words; they are entitled to be considered material and operative words, and to have the due effect assigned to them in the construction of this instrument, which will be done by allowing them to comprehend and cover other cases of marine damage *of the like kind with those that are specially enumerated, and occasioned by similar causes.*"

(16) *Sutherland* v. *Pratt,* 11 *M. & W.* 312.

Three hundred and sixty bales of cotton were insured for £2000, "lost or not lost," at and from Bombay to London. Before the insurance was made, but without the knowledge of the insured, the ship in which the cotton was being carried met with tempestuous weather, whereby the goods were wetted and so damaged as to be rendered useless. Held, that the underwriter was liable on the policy.

Smith v. *Surridge*, 4 *Esp.* 25.

Though unnecessary delay may avoid a policy, that shall not be deemed so which is employed in necessary repairs if the policy is "at and from the place."

(17) *Philpot* v. *Swan*, 5 *L.T.R., N.S.* 183.

A freight was insured for a vessel chartered for a voyage from Hondy Cliff Bay, where there is a roadstead, and then eighty miles up the country for a cargo of copper ore, and then to proceed therewith to Swansea. The vessel proceeded to her destination, and after having taken on board 150 tons, and being ready to complete her loading, a storm arose, which obliged her to put to sea, and in doing so her cable was strained, and her capstan became useless, consequently the remainder of the cargo could not be put on board until the damage was repaired. The vessel did not run for the Cape, where the means of repair could have been obtained, but beat about the coast for some time, when the wind changed, and she then ran to St. Helena, where it was found the damage could not be repaired, and the master, therefore, proceeded to Swansea with the cargo short by 120 tons, which were not shipped. Held, that there was not a total loss of freight by perils of the sea, as the damage was not of an extraordinary character, but such as was capable of repair, and that the means of repair were within a reasonable distance—viz., the Cape—and, consequently, that the loss was occasioned by the master going to St. Helena instead of there. The underwriters were, therefore, held not liable on the policy.

(18) *Mount* v. *Larkins*, 8 *Bing.* 108.

Defendant executed on February 28th, 1824, a policy of insurance on freight from Singapore to Europe, with liberty to sail to, touch, and stay at, any places whatsoever, to load, unload, reload, and for all necessary purposes whatever. The ship sailed from London in September, 1823, and having been detained by the captain, for his own purposes, at Van Diemen's Land, did not arrive at Singapore till March 30th, 1825 ; she sailed thence on the voyage insured on May 3rd, 1825. Held, that by so long a postponement of the risk the defendant was discharged, the jury having found the delay unreasonable.

(19) *Mitchell* v. *Edie*, 1 *T.R.* 613.

When the insured receive intelligence of such a loss as entitles them to abandon, they must make their election in the first instance ; and if they abandon, they must give the underwriters notice in a reasonable time, otherwise they waive their right to abandon, and can only recover as for average loss.

(20) *Livie* v. *Janson*, 12 *East* 648.

An American ship, insured from New York to London, "warranted free from American condemnation," having, for the purpose of eluding her national embargo, slipped away in the night, was by force of wind and tide driven on shore, where she suffered only partial damage ; but the next day she was seized and condemned by the American Government. Held, that the insured could recover, neither for a total loss, because the particular peril by which the vessel was lost was excepted out of the policy ; nor for the previous partial loss, because there had been no actual disbursement to repair it before the total loss occurred.

(21)   *Feise* v. *Parkinson,* 4 *Taunt.* 640.

Where a policy is avoided by fraud on the part of the insured, the insured is not entitled to a return of the premium. But upon a mere misrepresentation without fraud, where the risk never actually attached, there must be a return of the premium.

(22)   *London and N.W. Railway Co.* v. *Glyn,* 28 *Law J.,* Q.B. 188.

The plaintiffs, being common carriers, effected a policy, one of the conditions of which was "that goods held in trust or on commission are to be insured as such, otherwise the policy will not extend to cover such property," and £15,000 was declared to be on "goods their (the plaintiffs') own, and in trust as carriers" in a certain warehouse; by the policy, the funds of the insurers were to be "liable to pay, reinstate, or make good to the insured all damage and loss which they might suffer by fire on the property therein particularized." Held, that the plaintiffs insured the whole value of any goods sent to them to be carried, and not merely their own interest as carriers; and that they could recover from the insurers the value of a packet of silk, destroyed in their warehouse by an accidental fire, although by reason of its not having been declared under the Carriers' Act, they were not liable as carriers for its loss.

(23)   *Sillem* v. *Thornton, Ell. & Bl.* 868.

By a policy executed in London on April 7th, 1851, premises in California were insured against fire for a year from February 1st, 1851. The premises were described in the policy as "a brick building used as a dwelling-house and store, described in the paper attached to this policy." The paper attached gave a minute description of a two-storeyed house, with a certificate that the description was accurate, signed October 30th, 1850. The description was, in fact, accurate up to March, 1851, in which month the insured altered the house by adding a third storey. This was unknown in London when the policy was signed. In May, 1851, the house thus altered was destroyed by fire. In an action on the policy: Held, that the description in the policy amounted to a warranty that the insured would not, during the term insured, voluntarily do anything to make the condition of the premises vary from that description, so as to increase the liability of the insurer; that this warranty was broken; and, consequently, that the plaintiffs could not recover.

(24)   *Busk* v. *Royal Exchange Assurance Co.* See *supra,* p. 312.

(25)   *Worsley* v. *Wood,* 6 *T.R.* 710.

By the proposals of the Phœnix Assurance Co., it was stipulated that "persons insured shall give notice of the loss forthwith, deliver in an account, and produce a certificate of the minister, churchwardens, and some reputable householders of the parish, importing that they know the character of the insured, and believe that he really sustained the loss without fraud." Held, that the procuring of such a certificate was a condition precedent to the right of the insured to recover, and that it was immaterial that the minister, &c., wrongfully refused to sign the certificate.

(26)   See *Godin* v. *London Assurance Co.,* 1 *W. Bl.* 105.

(27)   See *Poole* v. *Adams,* 33 *Law J., Ch.* 639.

(28)   *Halford* v. *Rymer*, 10 B. & C. 724.

A policy effected by a father, in his own name, on the life of his son, he having no pecuniary interest in the life of his son, held void under 14 George III. c. 48, s. 1.

Law v. *London Indisputable Life Policy Company*, 24 Law J., Ch. 196.

A. being entitled to receive a sum of money when B. (in his 29th year) should attain the age of thirty, insured B.'s life for two years. B. attained the age of thirty, and A. received the money. B. then died before the expiration of the two years. Held, that A. was entitled to recover on the policy. And see judgment of Parke, B., in *Dalby* v. *Indian and London Life Assurance Co.*, 15 C.B. 390, overruling *Godsall* v. *Boldero*, 9 East 72.

(29)   *Wheelton* v. *Hardistry*, 8 Ell. & Bl. 232.

Action upon a policy of life insurance. The plaintiffs being interested in the life of J., delivered into the W. Life Insurance Association a proposal for insurance, wherein, *inter alia*, it was declared that J. had not had any fit since childhood. The jury found that the statements made by J., by J.'s usual medical attendant, and his private referee, to the effect that he had not had fits since childhood, were false, and that there was fraud on their parts against the defendants, but no fraud on the part of the plaintiffs. Held, first, that the life insured, the medical referee, and the private referee were not the agents of the plaintiffs so as to make their fraud, misrepresentation or concealment that of the plaintiffs; secondly, that there was no warrantry of the truth of the matters declared in the proposal, and that as there was nothing in the contract to show an intention that the truth of these matters should be the basis of the contract, the plaintiffs were entitled to judgment.

Fowkes v. *Manchester and London Life Assurance Co.*, 3 B & S. 917.

A policy of life insurance was entered into with a company on the life of H. F., which was founded on a written declaration of the insured, agreed to be the basis of the contract between the parties, and contained a proviso that "if any statement in the declaration (which statement should be considered as much a part of the policy as if the same had actually been set forth therein) was untrue, or if the insurance by the policy should have been effected by or through any wilful misrepresentation, concealment or false averment whatever, the policy should be void." The proposal and declaration contained the usual particulars, and proceeded as follows:—"I do hereby declare that the above-written particulars are true and correct throughout, and I do hereby agree that this proposal and declaration shall be the basis of the contract between me and the Manchester and London Life Assurance Association, and if it shall hereafter appear that any fraudulent concealment, or designedly untrue statement, be contained therein, then the policy shall be null and void." Held, that the policy and declaration must be read together, and so reading them the policy was not avoided by an untrue statement in the declaration, unless *designedly* untrue.

(30)   *Horn* v. *Anglo-Australian and Universal Insurance Co.*,
          30 Law J., Ch. 515.

A person, committing suicide while in a state of insanity, commits no legal offence; there is, therefore, no principle of public policy by which, in the absence of an express provision in the contract, a life insurance should be rendered void by such an act.

Clift v. *Schwabe*, 3 *C.B.* 476.

A. effected a policy on his own life, subject, among others, to the following condition: " That every policy effected by a person on his or her own life should be void, if such person should *commit suicide*, or die by duelling, or the hands of justice." A. died in consequence of having voluntarily, and for the purpose of killing himself, taken sulphuric acid, but under circumstances tending to show that he was at the time of unsound mind. Held, that the terms of the condition included all acts of voluntary self destruction, and, therefore, that if A. voluntarily killed himself, it was immaterial whether he was, or was not, at the time a responsible agent.

(31) *Pritchard* v. *Merchants' Life Assurance Co.*, 3 *C.B.*, *N.S.* 642.

A policy was effected in the usual form by B. on the life of A., in consideration of the payment of certain annual premiums on October 13th in each year, with a condition that the policy should be void, amongst other grounds, " if the premiums were not paid within thirty days after they should respectively become due; but that the policy might be revived, within three calendar months, on satisfactory proof of the health of the party on whose life the insurance was made," and payment of a certain fine. An annual premium became due on October 13th, 1855. The thirty days allowed by the condition for payment of the premiums expired on November 12th, on which day A. died. On November 14th, B. sent the company a cheque for the premium, for which they on the following day obtained the cash, giving a receipt as for " the premium for the renewal of the policy to October 13th, 1856, inclusive "—both parties being ignorant that A. was dead. Held, that the payment did not, under the circumstances, revive the policy.

CHAPTER XIV.

NEGOTIABLE INSTRUMENTS.

Assignability. BILLS of exchange and promissory notes were exceptions to the common law rule, now abolished, that choses in action were not assignable.

The usage of merchants requires that they should be in writing; and they differ from ordinary contracts in this particular, that a consideration for a bill or note will be presumed until the contrary appear.

Bill of exchange. (1) A bill of exchange is a written order by one person to another, duly stamped, for the payment of money at a specified time, absolutely, or, at all events, to a third party, or to the order of such third party, and accepted by the drawee.

In order to constitute a bill of exchange there must be a *drawer*, or person making the order; a *drawee*, or person to whom it is addressed; and a *payee*, or person to whom the drawee is requested to pay the amount of the bill. The *payee* may be described in any way. Yet, in order that the bill may be valid, the payee must be a person capable of being ascertained at the time the bill is drawn.

Transfer of bill of exchange. (2) If the written order, duly stamped, is made payable to the payee " or bearer " it is transferable, like a bank note, by mere delivery, so that any *bonâ fide* holder of the instrument may maintain an action upon it in his own name, as soon as it becomes payable.

If the bill is drawn payable to the payee " or order," it can only be assigned by indorsement from the payee.

The indorsement may either be on the face or the back of the bill, and it may either be *special* or *in blank*.

A special indorsement, or an indorsement in full, is where the indorser not only writes his own name on the bill, but also expresses in whose favour the indorsement is made.

An indorsement in blank is where the indorser only writes his own name on the bill, without any mention of the indorsee.

In the first case, the bill can only be transferred by the indorsee by his own indorsement. In the second case, the indorsee may transfer the bill by delivery merely. The difference is the same as that which exists between a bill made payable "to order" and a bill made payable "to bearer."

In order to obtain the security of the drawee, it is necessary to present the bill for his acceptance. No acceptance is binding, unless it be in writing upon the bill, and signed by the acceptor or some person by him duly authorized (19 & 20 Vict. c. 97, s. 6). Acceptance is usually made by the drawee writing the word "accepted" across the bill and signing his name thereto. {Acceptance. (3)}

If the drawee refuse to accept the bill, the drawer and other antecedent parties become liable after due notice to them from the holder.

If the drawee accept the bill *generally*, he undertakes to pay the bill at maturity; and unless the bill be made payable at or after sight, presentment for payment is not necessary in order to charge him. It is his duty to seek out the holder.

If the drawee accept *payable at a banker's* he is held to undertake (1 & 2 Geo. IV. c. 78, s. 1) to pay the bill at maturity when presented for payment *either* to himself or at the bankers.

If he accept *payable at a banker's and not elsewhere*, this is a qualified acceptance; he undertakes to pay the bill at maturity, provided it is presented at the bankers, but not otherwise.

Indorsement. (4)
A bill may be indorsed before the day that it bears date, and before acceptance, and whilst the date and the amount for which it is drawn remain blank. And if the indorsement is made whilst the amount for which it is drawn remains blank, the indorser may become liable to subsequent indorsees or holders, for any amount warranted by the stamp.

Title of holder by indorsement. (5)
The first transfer of a bill of exchange by indorsement is not effected by the mere act of the payee in writing his name on the back of the bill. There must be also an actual delivery of the bill to the transferee or his agent. There is no transfer by indorsement, if the holder merely indorses the bill specially to a third person, and the latter obtains possession of the bill without the holder's consent.

There is no transfer by indorsement, as between the indorser and his immediate indorsee, though the holder gives that person possession of the bill, if the delivery be merely for a collateral purpose, and without the intention of making him the transferee of the property in the bill.

If the party to whose order the bill is payable writes his name on the back of the bill, and hands it over to another, who delivers it over to a third person for value, that is an indorsement from the holder to such third person, and constitutes the latter the absolute owner of the bill.

A *bonâ fide* holder for value is not affected by an intermediate fraud or infirmity of title, of which he had no knowledge at the time he advanced his money on the security of the bill of which he is the holder.

The holder of a bill of exchange indorsed in blank is *primâ facie* the true owner of the bill. But, if it be proved that the bill has been lost by, or improperly obtained from, a former owner, or that the acceptance is a forgery, the onus is thrown upon the holder of proving that he gave value for the bill.

And whenever a bill is proved to have been illegal or fraudulent in its inception, or when the immediate indorser to the holder is proved to have obtained possession of it by fraud, the holder may be called upon for proof that he gave value for the bill, and took it without notice of the illegality or fraud. And if such proof is not forthcoming, he may be prevented from recovering on the instrument.

An innocent indorsee, who has received a bill and given value for it, without notice of the fraud by which it is affected, may, it seems, transfer his right and title to a person who has knowledge of the original fraud, but who was not a party to it. The latter purchases the right and title of the innocent indorsee.

Whenever a bill is due at the time of the indorsement, although the indorsee give full value for it, he takes it on the credit of the indorser, and subject to all the infirmities with which it may be encumbered in his hands, but not subject to claims arising out of collateral matters, such as the right of set off.

One who receives a bill of exchange unindorsed, though for value, acquires no better title under it than that which the person from whom he received it had.

If the payee by special indorsement makes a qualified or conditional transfer of the bill, before acceptance, the drawee who accepts afterwards is bound by the condition. *Restrictive indorsement.* (6)

But when a bill of exchange has been indorsed in blank and rendered generally negotiable, its negotiability cannot afterwards be restrained by subsequent restrictive indorsements.

As between the acceptor and the drawer of a bill, failure of consideration may be a good answer to an action; and the effect of the bill may be restrained by a contemporaneous agreement in writing between the parties. *Liability of acceptor.* (7)

But, as against a *bonâ fide* holder for value, the acceptor is liable at all events, and he cannot escape his

Y

liability by setting up even the forgery of the name of the drawer.

Liability of drawer. (8) The drawer is taken to guarantee that the drawee shall accept the bill, if it is presented to him for acceptance, and that, having accepted it, he shall pay it at maturity.

If the drawee should decline to accept the bill, the holder, upon giving notice to the drawer of the non-acceptance, may immediately sue the latter upon the bill.

If the drawee, after having accepted the bill, should fail to pay it at maturity, the drawer becomes responsible upon it to the holder, provided the latter has made due presentment for payment to the acceptor, and has given the drawer due notice of dishonour.

Liability of indorser. Every indorser of a bill is in the nature of a new drawer, and is liable to every succeeding holder, in default of acceptance or payment by the drawee.

Relative liability of parties to a bill. (9) As between the holder and the acceptor, the acceptor is the principal debtor, and the drawer and the indorsers are his sureties. As between the holder and the drawer, the drawer is the principal debtor, and the indorsers are his sureties. As between the holder and the second indorser, the second indorser is the principal, and the other indorsers are his sureties, and so on.

In accordance, therefore, with the ordinary law of suretyship, a discharge of a former party to a bill who is, *quoad* those subsequent to him, a principal, operates as a discharge of the subsequent parties, who stand towards him in the relation of sureties. So also an agreement to give time to a prior party operates as a discharge of subsequent parties.

Liability of transferror without indorsement. (10) A transfer by mere delivery, without indorsement, does not render the transferror liable to the transferree upon the bill itself, although he may become liable to refund the money he received in exchange for the bill, if the bill is dishonoured at maturity, and turns out to be a forgery.

Presentment for payment. (11) In order that the holder of a bill may charge the drawer and indorsers, in default of the acceptor, it is requisite, as has been pointed out, that he should make due presentment for payment to the latter, and give due notice of dishonour to the parties upon whom he intends to rely.

Presentment for payment should be made to the acceptor, or his clerk, or agent, at his residence, or place of business, or, if so specified, (see p. 319) at his bankers.

If the acceptance is a conditional acceptance, the condition must be strictly accomplished. But the holder is not bound to present the bill on the very day it becomes due, unless there is an express condition to that effect.

If the acceptor absconds, or shuts his house, and cannot be found, presentment is excused, and the bill may be treated at once as a dishonoured bill. Neither the bankruptcy of the drawer or acceptor, nor a declaration by him that he will not pay the bill, is of itself a sufficient excuse for an omission to present for payment. But if a banking firm has notoriously stopped payment, and shut up its ordinary place of business, and immediate notice of the insolvency of the firm is given by the holder to the other parties, he will be entitled to recover on the bill against those parties, although there has been no formal presentment. *Valid excuses for non-presentment. (12)*

Three days of grace are in England allowed to the acceptor, exclusive of the day on which the bill falls due; and presentment for payment, before the last of these three days has expired, is premature, and will not enable the holder to charge the antecedent parties. *Days of grace.*

If the last day of grace should fall on a Sunday, Christmas Day, or Good Friday, the bill becomes payable on the preceding day.

If it should fall on one of the public holidays established by the 34 Vict. c. 17, the bill is payable on the day following.

If the bill, after presentment to the acceptor, remains unpaid, the holder must give immediate notice of dishonour to the drawer and other parties to the bill upon whom he means to rely. The notice should be given by *Notice of dishonour. (13)*

the holder and by each party who means to sue on the bill, generally within twenty-four hours after he has received notice of the dishonour of the bill. But a plaintiff in an action on a bill may avail himself of notice given to the defendant by any other party to the bill.

An action is maintainable immediately after the notice has been received by the party addressed, and it is sufficient to show that the defendant ought to have received it, according to the usual routine of the post-office, prior to the issuing of the writ.

Valid excuses for absence of notice of dishonour. Notice of dishonour may be waived by the conduct or declaration of the person otherwise entitled to it, or where his residence is unascertainable after reasonable inquiry.

(14) Foreign bill. When a foreign bill is refused acceptance or payment, the dishonour must be announced by a protest made by a public notary, and notice of protest should be despatched at the first available opportunity.

Accommodation bill. (15) If the drawer draws on a person who is not his debtor, and who has not received any value for the bill, the bill is called an accommodation bill. In such a case, the drawer is himself the person who ought to provide funds and pay the bill, and he is not consequently entitled to notice of dishonour. This, however, does not do away with the necessity of notice of dishonour to the subsequent indorsers.

Bills taken up supra protest. (16) One who takes up a bill *supra protest*, or for honour, for the benefit of a particular party to the bill, succeeds to the title of the party from whom, not for whom, he receives it, and has all the title of such person to sue upon the bill, except that he discharges all the parties subsequent to the one for whose honour he takes it up, and that he cannot himself indorse it over.

Retiring of bills. (17) Payment by the acceptor, before the bill becomes due, does not extinguish it, any more than if it were merely discounted. If an acceptor retires a bill at maturity, he takes it entirely out of circulation, and the bill is in effect paid. But if an indorser retires it, he merely withdraws it from circulation in so far as he himself is concerned.

Any promise in writing for the payment of a definite sum of money, unconditionally, to a person therein named, or to his order, or to bearer, duly stamped, will constitute a negotiable promissory note (3 & 4 Anne, c. 9, and 7 Anne, c. 25, s. 3). *Promissory notes. (18)*

If the words "or order" or "or bearer" are omitted, the note cannot be treated as a negotiable instrument.

The maker of a promissory note stands in the same position as the acceptor of a bill of exchange. He is primarily liable upon the instrument, and is bound when the note falls due to seek out and pay the holder. He is not entitled to presentment, unless the note is made payable at or after sight, or at some particular place. A promissory note, payable on demand, need not be presented to the maker in order to charge him, the commencement of an action against him being a sufficient demand of the money. But, in order to discharge the indorser, the instrument, whether payable on demand or not, must be duly presented to the maker, and notice of dishonour given. *Liability of maker and indorsers. (19)*

By the 48 Geo. III. c. 88, s. 2, negotiable notes, bills, and drafts for the payment of less than 20s. are made absolutely null and void. But by the 23 & 24 Vict. c. 111, s. 19, it is made lawful for any person to draw upon his banker any draft or order for payment to bearer, or to order, on demand, of any sum of money, though it be less than 20s. *Statutory restrictions.*

A cheque on a banker is a negotiable instrument resembling a bill of exchange. A cheque, however, does not require acceptance to establish its validity. It is not entitled to days of grace. The holder cannot sue the banker upon whom it is drawn, unless the banker has accepted the cheque or promised to pay it to the holder. *Banker's cheques. (20)*

The holder of a cheque does not lose his remedy against the drawer by non-presentment of the cheque within any period short of six years after taking it, unless the banker upon whom it is drawn has become bankrupt in the interval, or unless there is an actual loss to the drawer by the delay. To guard against loss from the insolvency of the drawee, the holder must present the cheque for payment with reasonable promptitude—that is, in the course of the day succeeding that on which he receives the cheque from the drawer.

Forged cheques. (21) A banker who pays a forged cheque, or a cheque which has been fraudulently altered, must sustain the loss, unless the fraud has been facilitated by the carelessness or the negligence of the customer in drawing the cheque.

Crossed cheques. The law relating to crossed cheques is now governed by the 39 & 40 Vict. c. 81. By sec. 4, where a cheque bears across its face an addition of the words "and company," or any abbreviation thereof, between two parallel transverse lines, or of two transverse lines simply, and either with or without the words "not negotiable," that addition shall be deemed a general crossing. Where a cheque bears across its face an addition of the name of a banker, either with or without the words "not negotiable," that addition shall be deemed a special crossing to that banker.

By sec. 7, where a cheque is crossed generally, the banker on whom it is drawn shall not pay it otherwise than to a banker; and where a cheque is crossed specially, the banker on whom it is drawn shall not pay it otherwise than to the banker to whom it is crossed, or to his agent for collection.

By sec. 5, where a cheque is uncrossed, a lawful holder may cross it generally or specially; where a cheque is crossed generally, a lawful holder may cross it specially; and where a cheque is crossed specially, the banker to whom it is crossed may cross it specially to another banker, his agent for collection.

By sec. 12, a person taking a cheque crossed generally or specially, bearing in either case the words "not negotiable," shall not have, and shall not be capable of giving, a better title to the cheque than that which the person from whom he took it had. But a banker, who has in good faith, and without negligence, received payment for a customer of a cheque crossed generally or specially to himself, shall not, in case the title to the cheque proves defective, incur any liability to the true owner of the cheque, by reason only of having received such payment.

A bank note is a promissory note payable to bearer. It is treated as cash, and paid and received as cash. Hence a *bonâ fide* holder of a bank note, who has given value for it, has a valid title to it, although it was stolen by the person from whom he received it. <small>Bank note. (22)</small>

Defences to Actions on Bills and Notes.

Payment made to an intermediate party will not discharge the acceptor, unless the money reaches the holder. Payment to the holder is a good discharge to the acceptor, even though the holder may have stolen the bill, provided the payment be *bonâ fide*, and in the usual course of business. <small>Payment and satisfaction. (23)</small>

Failure of consideration, as it has been seen, is a good answer to an action on a bill, as between the acceptor and the drawer. But if the bill has been indorsed to a *bonâ fide* holder for value, the acceptor cannot set up the failure of consideration between himself and the drawer as an answer to the bill. <small>Want of consideration.</small>

An alteration in a bill or note in a material particular, after it has been negotiated, will avoid the contract. But where the alteration is immaterial, the substance of the contract remaining the same, the contract is not vitiated, although the alteration was made by the holder himself. <small>Alterations in the bill or note. (24)</small>

By the 17 & 18 Vict. c. 125, s. 87, it is enacted that, in actions on a negotiable instrument, the court may order that the loss of the instrument shall not be set up, provided <small>Loss of bills and notes.</small>

an indemnity be given against the claims of any other person upon such instrument. If the instrument was not made payable "to order" or "to bearer," its loss is no defence to an action upon the instrument.

Other Negotiable Instruments.

Bills of lading. (25) Bills of lading made out to the order of the shipper or consignee are negotiable and transferable by indorsement and delivery, so as to vest the right of property comprised therein to a *bonâ fide* holder for value, and to defeat the right of the unpaid vendor to stop them *in transitu*. The contract also is transferred to the indorsee, so as to enable the latter to maintain an action or to be sued upon it.

Dock warrants. (26) Dock warrants have been held negotiable and transferable so as to vest the property deposited in the docks in the holder of the warrant. The contract is not, however, transferred by this means.

Dividend warrants. (27) Dividend warrants issued by the Bank of England for the payment of dividends on stock in the public funds are not negotiable so as to entitle the holder to demand the dividend. But it is the custom of the bank to pay the amount to the holder of the warrant, and these documents are accordingly transferred from hand to hand, and are generally considered negotiable.

ILLUSTRATIVE CASES.

(1) *Yates* v. *Nash*, 29 *Law J.*, *C.P.* 306.

A bill drawn in the following form held to be invalid:—

"Six months after date pay to the order of the *treasurer for the time being* of the Commercial Travellers' Benevolent Institution, the sum of £20 for value received.

"A. B.

"To C. D.

"Accepted, payable at, &c.

"C. D."

Erle, C.J.: "The true construction of the bill is that the defendant undertakes to pay to the order of the person who will, at the maturity of the bill, be the treasurer of the institution. The payee may be described in any way, yet, in order that the bill should be valid, he must be a person capable of being ascertained at the time the bill is drawn."

(2) *Edge* v. *Bumford,* 31 *Beav.* 247.

R., being indebted to the plaintiffs, gave them a bill of exchange, drawn by R. and accepted by the defendant, but made payable to R.'s order. The bill was not indorsed by R., and being sent back for that purpose was destroyed by R. Held, that a suit by the plaintiffs against the defendant to recover the amount of the bill could not be sustained.

Young v. *Glover,* 3 *Jur., N.S.* 637.

The writing of his name by an indorser upon the face of the instrument, Held to be a good indorsement.

Collins v. *Martin,* 1 *B. & P.* 648.

A banker pledged bills, indorsed in blank, that had been deposited with him by a customer. The banker had no authority from the owner to part with these bills; but the court held, that with respect to bills of exchange indorsed in blank, property and possession are inseparable.

(3) *Halstead* v. *Skelton,* 5 *Q.B.* 86.

Since 1 & 2 Geo. IV. c. 78, if the drawee of a bill, drawn without special direction as to place of payment, accepts it, payable at a particular place (without any additional words), he undertakes thereby to pay the bill at maturity, when presented at that place, or to himself; if he accepts payable at such place "and not otherwise or elsewhere," he undertakes to pay it at maturity, if presented at that place, but not otherwise. A declaration against the acceptor of a bill stated that he accepted it "payable at C. & Co., bankers," and that defendant promised to pay it "according to the tenour and effect thereof." Held, that this did not imply that the bill was made payable at the bankers only.

(4) *Passmore* v. *North,* 13 *East* 517.

The defendant, on May 4th, drew a bill of exchange, *which was dated May* 11*th*, and delivered it to T., the payee; T. indorsed it for valuable consideration to the plaintiff on May 5th, and died on the same day. Held, that the indorsee might recover on the bill in an action against the drawer.

Crutchley v. *Mann,* 5 *Taunt.* 529.

A bill made payable to the order of ———— may be filled up by any bearer, who can show that he came regularly to the possession of it, with his own name.

Russel v. *Langstaffe,* 2 *Doug.* 514.

An indorsement written on a blank note, Held to bind the indorser for any sum and time of payment, which the person to whom it was intrusted chose to insert in it.

(5) *Denton* v. *Peters, L.R.* 5 *Q.B.* 475.

A. and B. were partners in a speculation in currants. A. bought the currants, and resold them at a profit to C., who gave A. a bill in payment. The original price of the currants was settled in account between A. and B., and A. held the bill until maturity, when it was presented and dishonoured. Thereupon A., who had, before presentment, indorsed his name on the bill, handed it to B. and requested him to try to obtain payment from C. C. did not pay the bill to B.; and B. then sued A. on the bill. Held, that B. could not recover against A. Mellor J. : " As against the acceptor, this would no doubt have been a valid indorsement. All that is necessary to give a good title against him is the writing of the name of the holder, and a manual delivery of the bill, with intent to transfer the property in it to the indorsee, as between him and the acceptor. But as between indorser and indorsee, there must be the additional element of an intent to stand in the ordinary relation of indorser, that is, to guarantee the payment if the acceptor makes default."

Lloyd v. *Howard*, 15 Q.B. 997.

Action by indorsee against acceptor, averring an indorsement by drawer to M., and by M. to plaintiff. Pleas, traversing the indorsements. The jury found that the drawer wrote his name on the bill and handed it to M., that M. might get it discounted, which was not done; and that plaintiff received it from M., when over due, and without consideration. Held, that there was no indorsement by drawer to M., and that defendant was entitled to have the verdict entered for him on the issue as to that indorsement, plaintiff not being a *bond fide* holder.

Barber v. *Richards*, 6 Exch. 63.

E. drew, and wrote his name on the back of, a bill of exchange, and delivered it to B. to get it discounted. B. deposited it for value with T., upon the terms, that if not redeemed by a certain day it was to be sold. Held, that there was a valid indorsement of the bill from E. to T. [*Lloyd* v. *Howard*, *ubi supra*, distinguished. T., the indorsee, being a *bond fide* holder for value.]

Peacock v. *Rhodes*, 2 Doug. 634.

A bill of exchange with a blank indorsement being stolen and negotiated—Held, that an innocent indorsee might recover upon it against the drawer.

Smith v. *Braine*, 16 Q.B. 244.

A bill of exchange was drawn for the defendant's accommodation; and was by him delivered to M. to get it discounted for defendant. M. gave the bill to C. to get it discounted for defendant, C. took the bill away, promising to get it discounted, and to bring back the money for it in a few hours; instead of doing so, C. indorsed the bill to plaintiff, and did not return. Next day M. saw C., and C. then promised to bring the money for the bill immediately; he then went away, professedly for the purpose of fetching the money, and was not seen afterwards : defendant never received anything on account of the bill. Held, that this amounted to evidence that C., who indorsed to plaintiff, was a *malâ fide* holder, and that the jury might, if they thought right, infer from thence that plaintiff had not given value.

Crossley v. *Ham*, 13 East 498.

The holder in America of two bills of the same tenour, having transmitted them to his agents in England to present them for acceptance, and receive the money when due, and pay over a part of it to the plaintiff, while the bills so remained in his agent's hands, agreed with the defendant, the indorser (who had lent his indorsement to the drawer, from whom the holder received them), that, upon payment of one of the bills, he should be exonerated from both. In the meantime the bills having been presented for acceptance by the agents and dishonoured, *after the dishonour*, the agents, not knowing of such agreement between their principal and the indorser, assigned one of the dishonoured bills to the plaintiff, who was informed of the dishonour, but had no notice of such agreement. Held, that the bill was received by the plaintiff, liable to all its infirmities, and that the plaintiff was bound by the agreement; and that the defendant, having afterwards taken up and discharged the other bill, which had remained in the hands of the same agents, was discharged from both.

Whistler v. *Forster*, 14 *C.B.*, *N.S.* 248.

A. fraudulently obtained a bill from B., and handed it to C. in satisfaction of a *bonâ fide* debt, but *without indorsing it*. Held, that C. obtained no better title under the bill than A. had, and that he could not acquire the right to sue upon the instrument, by obtaining A.'s indorsement after he had received notice of the fraud.

(6) *Robertson* v. *Kensington*, 4 *Taunt.* 30.

The payee of a bill indorsed it, before acceptance, in the following terms:—" Pay the within sum to C., or order, upon my name appearing in the Gazette as ensign in any regiment of the line, between the 1st and 64th, if within two months from this date. R. R." Held, that the drawer who afterwards accepted it was bound by the condition expressed in the indorsement, and that the condition not being performed, the property reverted to the payee, and he might recover upon it against the acceptor.

Walker v. *Macdonald*, 2 *Exch.* 527.

A bill of exchange having been indorsed in blank, was afterwards indorsed by the defendant specially to "B. & W. & Co." The plaintiffs, who carried on business under the respective firms of B. & W. & Co.," and "The E. Company," indorsed the bill by the name of "The E. Company." The bill was duly presented, but payment refused for want of an indorsement by "B. & W. & Co." Held, that the bill having been indorsed in blank, its negotiability could not afterwards be restrained by a special indorsement, and that the presentment was such as to render the defendant liable on his indorsement to the plaintiff.

(7) *Astley* v. *Johnson*, 5 *H. & N.* 141.

Pollock, C. B.: "If a person purchase a bill payable at the end of three months, for goods to be delivered at the end of one month, if the goods are not delivered, and the same party sues on the bill, not having indorsed it to a *bonâ fide* holder, it would be a good answer to say that the consideration for the bill was the delivery of the goods, and that had not taken place."

Mather v. *Maidstone*, 18 *C.B.* 295.

A. accepted a bill for £1000 for the accommodation of B. A bill for that amount, purporting to be drawn by B., and accepted by A., and indorsed by B. to C. and by C. to D. (for value), was afterwards presented to A. for payment. A., having had an opportunity of inspecting the bill, gave D. a cheque for £100, and a renewed bill at three months (similarly drawn and indorsed) for £1000 in exchange for the bill so presented to him. A. afterwards discovered that the acceptance to the bill so delivered up to him was forged. Held, no answer to an action by D. upon the substituted bill.

(8)   *Whitehead* v. *Walker*, 9 M. & W. 516.

Parke, B. : " It is clear that by non-acceptance, followed by protest and notice, the holder acquires an immediate right of action against the drawer —a right of action, not in respect of any special damage from the non-acceptance, but a right of action *on the bill, i.e.,* to recover the full amount of the bill. The effect of the refusal to accept is that the drawee says to the holder, ' I will not pay your bill ; you must go back to the drawer, and he must pay you.' But on failure of acceptance, the holder is bound to give immediate notice to the drawer, and if he omits to do so, he forfeits all rights of action against him, not only in respect of the default of acceptance, but also in respect of the subsequent non-payment."

(9)   *Moss* v. *Hall*, 5 Exch. 46.

Action on a bill of exchange by indorsee against drawer. After the bill had become due it was agreed, for good consideration, between the plaintiff, who was the holder of the bill, and the acceptor, without the authority or consent of the drawer, that the plaintiff should forbear for the period of one month to sue the acceptor. Held, that by this agreement the drawer was discharged from liability on the bill.

(10)   *Gurney* v. *Womersley*, 4 Ell. & Bl. 133.

Defendants took to plaintiffs for discount a bill purporting to be accepted by N. Defendants, however, refused to indorse or guarantee the bill. Plaintiffs agreed to take the bill at the ordinary rate of discount, expressly on the credit of the name of N. The bill turned out to be an entire forgery and worthless. Held, that though there was no indorsement or guarantee, and therefore no warranty of the solvency of the parties to the bill, there was a total failure of consideration, and plaintiffs were entitled to recover back the money which they had paid for the bill.

(11)   *Smith* v. *Vertue*, 30 Law J., C.P. 56.

An acceptance in the following form :—" Accepted, payable, on giving up bill of lading for seventy-six bags of clover-seed, per *Amazon,* at the L. & W. Bank "—Held, to be a conditional acceptance, binding the holder of the bill, upon presenting it for payment, to give up the bill of lading, but not binding him to present on the very day the bill fell due.

(12)   *Bowes* v. *Howe*, 5 Taunt. 30.

Action against makers of certain promissory notes, by which they had promised to pay £5 at Workington Bank. In order to excuse non-presentment, the declaration averred, that after the making of the notes the defendants had become insolvent, and had declared that they "neither could nor would pay any of their notes." Held, that this allegation amounted to no more than a general allegation of insolvency, and, as no request was alleged to which the refusal was to be applied, the necessity for alleging a presentment was not dispensed with. [Here the action was against the makers, who by their contract had made themselves only liable to pay on demand, at a particular place, and the mere fact of their insolvency did not disentitle them from insisting on such demand. As between *third parties,* as will be seen in the next case, the rule is different.]

Turner v. *Stones*, 1 D. & L. 122.

In an action of debt for money had and received, it appeared that on

Saturday evening, January 19th, the plaintiff gave change for a £5 banknote of Messrs. P. & Co.'s bank, to the defendant, at his request; on Monday morning, the banking house of Messrs. P. & Co. was opened for two hours and then closed, and the partners afterwards became bankrupt; no payments were made, and the jury gave an opinion that, if the note had been presented, it would not have been paid; the note was not in fact presented, but on Monday, the plaintiff sent it to defendant, and requested to have his money returned; the defendant at first promised to return it, but afterwards refused. Held, that the obligation on the holder of a note in such a case is to give prompt notice, to the person from whom he received it, of the stoppage of the bank, and to tender the note back to him; and that in the particular case, the plaintiff had done all that he was bound to do, and was entitled to recover, although there had been no presentment of the note.

(13) *Rowe* v. *Tipper*, 13 *C.B.* 256.

A bill indorsed by A. to B. and by B. to C. became due on Saturday, November 15th, and was presented and dishonoured. C. gave notice of dishonour to B. on Monday the 17th, and to A. on the following day, B. having given no notice to A. Held, that the notice by C. to A. was too late. Jervis, C.J.: "If the holder of a bill wishes to avail himself of a notice of dishonour given by him to a remote indorser, he must give it within the time within which he is required by law to give it to his immediate indorser; and he cannot avail himself of *his* laches to gain another day."

(14) *Phipson* v. *Kneller*, 4 *Campb.* 285.

When the drawer stated to the holder of a bill, a few days before the bill became due, that he had no regular residence to which notice could be sent, and that he would himself call upon the acceptor and see if the bill was paid—Held, that the drawer had thereby expressly dispensed with notice of dishonour from the holder.

Bateman v. *Joseph*, 2 *Campb.* 461.

A bill became due on September 27th, and was in the hands of an indorsee in London, who on the 28th sent off a letter by post giving notice of its dishonour to A., his immediate indorser, at Manchester. A. received this on the 30th, and the same day communicated with B., his indorser. B. in turn, desiring to communicate with C., his immediate indorser, and D., another prior indorser, called at the counting house of C. in Manchester, to inquire D.'s address, but could obtain no information on the subject, C. being then from home. Three days later C. returned and informed B. that D. resided at Liverpool. The next day B. wrote to D. giving him notice of the dishonour of the bill. In an action by B. against D. on the bill—Held, that B. had used reasonable diligence to discover D.'s residence, and that notice having been given as soon as this was found, D. had due and sufficient notice of the dishonour of the bill.

(15) *Carter* v. *Flower*, 16 *L.J.*, *Ex.* 199.

In an action on a promissory note by the indorsee against the indorser, to whom it had been indorsed by the payee, the declaration alleged, that neither when the note was made, nor afterwards, and before it became due, nor when it became due, and on presentment for payment, had the maker or the payee any effects of the defendant in his hands, nor was there any consideration or value for the making of the note, for the payment thereof, or its indorsement by the payee to the defendant, and that the defendant had not sustained any damage by reason of his not having had notice of the non-payment of the note. Held, that as against an *indorser* the declaration did not state a sufficient excuse of want of notice of dishonour, as it was consistent with the averments in the declaration that the note might have been indorsed by the defendant for the accommodation of a prior party, in which case the defendant would be entitled to notice of dishonour.

(16)   *See Ex parte Swan, L.R. 6 Eq.* 344.

(17)   *Burbridge* v. *Manners*, 3 *Campb.* 194.

A bill which had been paid and afterwards indorsed, before it became due—Held to be a valid security in the hands of a *bonâ fide* indorsee.

Elsam v. *Denny*, 15 *C.B.* 87.

If an indorser retires a bill of exchange at maturity, he merely withdraws it from circulation, in so far as he himself is concerned, and he may hold it with the same remedies as he would have had if he had been called upon in due course, and had paid the amount to his immediate indorsee. But, if an acceptor retires the bill at maturity, he withdraws it entirely from circulation.

(18)   *Plimley* v. *Westley*, 2 *Bing. N.C.* 251.

A. being indebted to B. for goods sold and delivered, indorsed to him on account of such debt a promissory note made by C. to D. payable two months after date, but without the words "or order," and indorsed by D. to E., from whom A. had received it for valuable consideration. B. kept the note, but did not present it for payment until nine days after it had become due. It was dishonoured and never paid. Held that B. was entitled to recover the price of the goods, notwithstanding he had omitted to give defendant due notice of the dishonour of the promissory note, and therefore could not recover upon it. Tindal, C.J. : "The question is, whether the original claim has been satisfied by the delivery of this note or not : and we must see whether the plaintiff had any means of enforcing payment of the note, or whether it was in his hands merely waste paper. It is clear that unless there be, on the instrument, authority to indorse, the indorsee can enforce payment neither of a promissory note, nor of a bill of exchange. The plaintiff therefore, having no security of which he could avail himself, is remitted to his original right."

(19)   *Mercantile Bank of India* v. *Dickson, L.R.* 3 *P.C.* 574.

The law with regard to time for presentation of a promissory note, payable on demand, requires that the presentation for payment be made within a reasonable time,—that is, a period reasonable with reference to the circumstances connected with each particular case.

Where, therefore, a promissory note dated February 16th, 1864, and indorsed, though made payable on demand, but the payment of which was not contemplated by the makers at any immediate specific date, was not presented to the payee for payment until December 14th of the same year— Held, that since it appeared from the evidence that the note was meant to be, to a greater or less extent, a continuing security, the delay in presentation was, in the circumstances of the case, not unreasonable, and the holders of the note were entitled to recover thereon.

(20) *Robinson* v. *Hawksford*, 9 Q.B. 52.

To an action by holder against drawer of a cheque, it is no answer that the cheque was not presented in reasonable time, unless during the delay the fund has been lost, as by failure of the banker.

Lord Denman, C.J.: "Under ordinary circumstances the only rule is that, if things have continued the same, and no damage has arisen from delay of presentment, the drawer continues liable."

(21) *Hall* v. *Fuller*, 5 B. & C. 750.

Where a cheque, drawn by a customer upon his banker for a sum of money, described in the body of the cheque in words and figures, was afterwards altered by the holder, who substituted a larger sum for that mentioned in the cheque, but in such a manner that no person, in the ordinary course of business, could observe it, and the banker paid to the holder this larger sum—Held, that he could not charge the customer for anything beyond the sum for which the cheque was originally drawn.

Young v. *Grote*, 12 Moore, 499.

A., a tradesman, left with his wife certain blank cheques signed by himself, directing her in his absence to have them filled up for such sums as the purposes of his business might require. The wife requiring £50 2s. 3d., desired one of her husband's clerks to fill up one of the cheques for that sum. The clerk did so, and was sent to get cash for it; but, before he presented the cheque, he altered it by inserting "Three hundred" before the "fifty," having previously left room for the interpolation, and obtained the additional sum, and absconded. Held, that the bankers were not liable to make good the loss, since it was due, not to their negligence, but to that of A. and his wife.

(22) *Miller* v. *Race*, 1 Burr. 452, 1 Sm. L.C.

Action of trover upon a bank note for the payment of £21 10s. to one W. F. or bearer, on demand. It appeared that W. F., being possessed of this bank note on December 11th, 1756, sent it by the general post, under cover, directed to one B. O. at Chipping Norton; that on the same night the mail was robbed, and the bank note in question (amongst other notes) taken and carried away by the robber; and that this bank note on December 12th, came into the possession of the plaintiff, for a full and valuable consideration, and in the usual course and way of his business, and without any knowledge of its having been stolen. W. F. receiving notice of the robbery on December 13th, applied to the Bank of England to stop the payment of the note, which was ordered accordingly, upon W. F. entering into security to indemnify the bank. Subsequently the plaintiff applied to the bank for the payment of the note, and for that purpose delivered it to the defendant, a clerk in the bank; but the defendant refused either to pay the note, or to re-deliver it to the plaintiff. Held, that the plaintiff was entitled to recover; for that property in a bank note passes, like that in cash, by delivery; and a party taking it *bonâ fide*, and for value, is entitled to retain it, even as against a former owner from whom it has been stolen.

(23) *Williams* v. *James*, 15 Q.B. 498.

If the drawer of a bill, payable to his own order, indorses it, and it is accepted and dishonoured, the drawer having received it back, and paid the amount to his indorsee, may return the bill to such indorsee, for the purpose of his suing the acceptor upon it as trustee for the drawer. And the payment is no answer to an action by such indorsee, if there be evidence that when the drawer paid, the bill was left in the hands of the indorsee for the purpose of its being put in suit.

(24) *Master* v. *Miller,* 4 *T.R.* 320, 1 *Sm. L.C.*

An unauthorized alteration having been made in a bill of exchange, after acceptance, whereby the payment would have been accelerated—Held, that the instrument was avoided, and that no action could afterwards be brought upon it, even by an innocent holder for a valuable consideration.

(25)   *See Smurthwaite* v. *Wilkins,* 11 *C.B., N.S.* 842.

(26)   *See Zwinger* v. *Samuda,* 1 *Moore,* 12.

(27)   *See Partridge* v. *Bank of England,* 9 *Q.B.* 424.

CHAPTER XV.

VOID AND VOIDABLE CONTRACTS.

Void Contracts.

A CONTRACT is illegal and therefore void (i.) which has been entered into for the performance of an immoral act, or (ii.) which is contrary to the provisions of statute law, or (iii.) which is contrary to public policy. {Illegal contracts.}

If the illegality of the contract does not appear on the face of it, it may be proved by oral evidence.

(i.) *Contracts Void on the ground of Immorality.*

Contracts founded upon a promise of future illicit cohabitation are void. {Contracts directly promoting immorality. (1)}

Past cohabitation is not an unlawful consideration, but it is an executed consideration, and therefore not sufficient to support a contract. An agreement made in consideration of past cohabitation is, therefore, merely voluntary, and cannot be enforced, unless it is under seal.

Contracts for the future separation of husband and wife are void. But a contract between a husband and a trustee on behalf of the wife, providing the terms of a present separation, will be enforced.

One who makes a contract for sale or hire, knowing that the other party intends to apply the subject-matter to an immoral use, cannot recover upon the contract. {Contracts indirectly promoting immorality. (2)}

Thus, if a landlord knowingly permits a female lodger

to carry on the trade of prostitution under his roof, the courts will give him no assistance for the recovery of his rent. But if a prostitute merely uses the lodging to live in, and plies her trade elsewhere, this is no bar to the landlord's claim for rent.

No contract in relation to the publication of obscene, blasphemous, or immoral writings or prints is enforceable. Neither printer, nor servant, nor workman engaged in publishing such a work can sue on a contract relating thereto, or for works and services connected therewith.

(ii.) *Contracts Void as contrary to the Provisions of Statute Law.*

Construction of prohibitory statutes. (3)

Everything in respect of which a penalty is imposed by statute must be taken to be a thing forbidden; and a contract to do such a thing is absolutely void.

Where a contract is to do a thing which cannot be performed without a violation of law, it is void, whether the parties knew the law or not.

But where the contract is capable of being legally performed, and it is attempted to set it aside on the ground that the intention was to perform it in an illegal manner, this intention must be proved, and to prove it, it is necessary to show that the parties knew what the law was.

Sale of offices. (4)

By 5 & 6 Ed. VI. c. 16, and 49 Geo. III. c. 126, it is enacted that all contracts for money or profit, relating to appointments touching the administration of justice, the collection of the Revenue, or to any office in the gift of the Crown, with the exception of the sale of certain specified offices and commissions, shall be void. Where the business of an office can be transacted by deputy, however, the appointment of a deputy at a fixed salary is legal.

By the 47 Geo. III. c. 25, the assignment by a retired military officer of his pension is void.

By 31 Eliz. c. 6, the sale of ecclesiastical livings and dignities is rendered void. And by 12 Anne, st. 2, c. 12, the purchase of the next presentation to any benefice is rendered void. *Simoniacal contracts. (5)*

These statutes are held not to prohibit the sale of an advowson, or the right of presentation to a living which is filled at the time of the sale.

If an advowson is sold or transferred during a vacancy of the benefice, the presentation upon the vacancy does not pass with the grant.

If an incumbent is sick and dying, and the next presentation is purchased with the intention to present a particular person as soon as the vacancy occurs, the purchase is void.

A bond given by an incumbent for the resignation of his benefice on notice or request generally, or in favour of a particular person named in the bond as soon as the latter should become qualified, is rendered legal by 7 & 8 Geo. IV. c. 25, and 9 Geo. IV. c. 94.

By 8 & 9 Vict. c. 109, s. 18, all contracts or agreements by way of gaming or wagering are rendered void. A colourable contract for the purchase of shares or goods, where neither party intends to deliver or accept the goods, but merely to pay differences according to the rise or fall of the market, are within the statute. *Gaming contracts. (6)*

But an agreement to subscribe towards a prize to be awarded to the winner of any lawful game or sport, is excepted from the statute.

Persons intending to compete in a horse race or other lawful game, may severally deposit money in the hands of a stakeholder, to be awarded to the winner of the race or game; but if the amount of a bet is deposited with a stakeholder, to be awarded to the winner of the bet, the money cannot be recovered by the winner.

By the 16 & 17 Vict. c. 119, betting houses are prohibited, and it is provided that money or valuables received as a deposit on any bet may be recovered back.

Notes, bills, and mortgages, given to secure money won at, or lent for, play are void as between the original parties, but not as against third parties who take them for good consideration and without notice.

Sale by illegal weights and measures. (7)

By the 5 Geo. IV. c. 74, the 5 & 6 Wm. IV. c. 63, and 22 & 23 Vict. c. 56, uniform weights and measures are established, and all contracts made by light or unjust weights and measures, or other weights and measures than those authorized, are declared to be void.

Contracts may, however, be made by any multiple or aliquot part of the pound weight. Thus a contract may be made by "long weight," in which there are 120 lbs. to the hundredweight.

Payment of workmen in coin.

By the 1 & 2 Wm. IV. c. 37 (called the Truck Act), it is enacted that the wages of artificers shall be paid in current coin only, and any contract by which the whole or part of such wages shall be made payable in any other manner shall be void.

Sale of coal.

By the 5 & 6 Wm. IV. c. 63, it is enacted that coal shall be sold by weight and not by measure; and further provisions for the regulation of the sale of coal are made in the 1 & 2 Wm. IV. c. 76, and the 1 & 2 Vict. c. 101.

Sale of spirituous liquors.

The 24 Geo. II. c. 40, takes away the right of action for the price of spirituous liquors, unless the debt shall have been *bonâ fide* contracted for at one time to the amount of 20s. This Act is repealed by the 25 & 26 Vict. c. 38, so far as it relates to spirituous liquors sold, to be consumed elsewhere than on the premises, and delivered at the residence of the purchaser in quantities not less at any one time than a quart.

By the 30 & 31 Vict. c. 142, it is enacted that no action shall be maintainable to recover any sum of money alleged to be due in respect of the sale of any ale, porter, beer, cider, or perry, which was consumed on the premises where sold.

The sale of game, of poisons, of petroleum and other combustible fluids, of chain-cables and anchors, is also regulated by statute (1 & 2 Wm. IV. c. 32; 32 & 33 Vict. c. 117; 32 & 33 Vict. c. 113; 34 & 35 Vict. c. 101, s. 7). *Sale of game, &c.*

By the 29 Car. II., c. 7, tradesmen, artificers, workmen, and labourers are forbidden to exercise their ordinary callings on the Lord's Day, works of necessity and charity excepted. *Sunday trading. (8)*

No action can therefore be brought for the price of goods sold on Sunday, unless the sale is within the exception of the Act, which permits the cooking and sale of food at inns and cookshops, and the sale of milk. The baking of bread on Sunday is permitted by 5 & 6 Wm. IV. c. 37. And if a sale or contract is not made in the exercise of the ordinary trade or calling of the party against whom it is sought to be enforced, it is not invalidated.

If goods are sold abroad, the vendor knowing that they are to be smuggled into this country, this does not make the contract void, so as to preclude the vendor's right of action in this country for the price of the goods, unless he actually assisted the vendee in the act of smuggling, by packing the goods in a particular way, or otherwise. *Goods sold to be smuggled. (9)*

Where a license is required for the sale of goods for mere Revenue purposes, the omission, on the part of a vendor, to take out a license does not render a contract of sale by him unlawful, unless such contract is expressly forbidden. But where such license is required for the protection of the public, a sale without a license is positively illegal. The Excise license of a publican is for Revenue purposes merely; but the magistrate's license, which is also required, is for the protection of the public. A person, therefore, who sells wine, spirits, &c., without the license of the magistrates, cannot recover the price thereof. *Sales without license. (10)*

Unauthorized practitioners, &c.

By the 21 & 22 Vict. c. 90, no person shall be entitled to recover charges for medical or surgical attendance, unless he can prove that he is registered under the Act.

By the 6 & 7 Vict. c. 73, no person shall recover any fee or reward, in respect of business done by him as a solicitor, unless he shall previously have become certificated in due form.

Printers are required (2 & 3 Vict. c. 12 ; 32 & 33 Vict. c. 24) to affix their names and places of abode, or business, to all papers and books printed by them for publication; and if a printer neglects to do this, he cannot maintain an action for his labour or materials supplied.

Contracts in contravention of the policy of statutes. (11)

Contracts in contravention of an Act of Parliament are void. Thus contracts for the evasion of the Registry, Licensing, and Excise Acts, or in fraud of the laws of bankruptcy, are void.

(iii.) *Contracts which are Void as opposed to Public Policy.*

Contracts in restraint of marriage. (12)

Contracts in restraint of marriage generally, are void as opposed to public policy. But a restriction against marriage with one particular person is not void.

Custody of infants. (13)

A covenant by a father that he will abstain from seeing, or exercising any control over, his children is void, unless the father has by gross misconduct shown himself unfit to associate with them.

But by the 36 Vict. c. 12, s. 2, no agreement contained in any separate deed made between the father and mother of an infant or infants shall be held to be invalid by reason only of its providing that the father of such infant or infants shall give up the custody or control thereof to the mother: provided always, that no court shall enforce any such agreement, if the court shall be of opinion that it will not be for the benefit of the infant or infants to give effect thereto.

Agreements to furnish money to be risked on a lawsuit in which the party making the agreement has no interest, are void as amounting to maintenance. And when a party agrees to maintain a suit in consideration of a share in the advantages of it, he is guilty of champerty. *(Maintenance and champerty.) (14)*

All agreements to oust the jurisdiction of the courts of law, to suppress evidence, to compound a felony, to hush up an embezzlement, or to compromise a divorce suit in consideration of a sum of money to be paid by the co-respondent to the petitioner, are void. *(Contracts in obstruction of justice. (15))*

But an agreement to refer future or existing differences to arbitration may be enforced. And an agreement to compound civil rights, or to settle an action which has commenced, is valid.

All contracts tending to induce public officers to violate their duty, or to protect them from the consequences of their misconduct, are void.

All contracts to pay ministers of state for an appointment to a public office of trust, or having for their object the purchase of a dignity or title of honour, or for the purpose of inducing a member of the Legislature to vote in a particular way, or to induce an elector to vote in favour of a particular candidate, are void, as contrary to public policy. *(Contracts interfering with the public administration. (16))*

All contracts to recommend parties for employment in offices of trust, in consideration of the payment of money, entered into without the knowledge of the employer or person who has the office or employment at his disposal, are fraudulent and void. *(Contracts in fraud of employers. (17))*

Contracts in general restraint of trade are void; but contracts restraining the exercise of a particular trade or profession in a particular locality are good, where there is a reasonable ground for the restriction, as in the sale of the goodwill of a business, or of a trade secret, or the taking of an apprentice, or the formation or dissolution of a partnership. *(Contracts in restraint of trade. (18))*

Where such a contract is reasonable the courts will prevent an infringement of it, although a pecuniary penalty may have been stipulated for.

The restraint must be confined within reasonable limits, and the consideration for the restraint must appear upon the face of the contract. It is for the court, and not the jury, to determine whether the restraint is reasonable, and whether the contract is valid. If the restraint is reasonable as to space, the circumstance that it is indefinite in point of time will not affect its validity.

A person who has covenanted not to trade within certain reasonable limits, is bound by his covenant, although the covenantee may have ceased both by himself and by his agents, licensees or assigns, to carry on the trade.

There is no implied covenant, on the part of a vendor or assignor of the goodwill of a business, not to set up the same business in opposition to the purchaser. But the courts will interfere to prevent the vendor from soliciting the customers of the old business to cease dealing with the purchaser, or to deal with himself.

Contracts creating monopolies. (19)

Contracts creating monopolies are void as contrary to public policy.

Contracts with alien enemies. (20)

All contracts for commercial and trading purposes, made between British subjects and subjects of a sovereign who is at war with this country, are null and void, unless such contracts have been made pursuant to a license to trade, granted by the Crown, and such licenses are to be construed liberally.

Judicial Treatment of Unlawful Agreements.

Divisible contracts. (21)

Where there are separate and independent covenants in the same deed, the illegality of one of the covenants does not invalidate the others.

If there are several considerations for separate and distinct contracts contained in the same instrument, and one is good and the other bad, the one may stand and be enforced, although the other fails.

Where there is one entire consideration for two several agreements, and one of these agreements is for the performance of an illegal act, the whole is void. *Indivisible contracts. (22)*

And if an agreement be founded upon a legal and an illegal consideration, and the illegal consideration cannot be separated from the legal consideration and rejected, the illegality of the part vitiates the whole.

So long as an illegal contract remains executory and unperformed, money deposited by one of the parties in pursuance of the contract may be recovered back. *Illegal contract whilst executory. (23)*

Where the unlawful intention has been carried out, and the contract is executed, the courts will not interfere, if the parties are *in pari delicto*. *Illegal contract executed. (24)*

But where the parties are not *in pari delicto*, the more innocent of the two may obtain the assistance of the law to recover money paid by him to another, under the unlawful agreement, although the unlawful act has been accomplished.

Voidable Contracts.

A party is entitled to rescind a contract when he can show that there was a fraudulent representation as to any part of that which induced him to enter into the contract. *False representation. (25)*

Where there has only been an innocent misrepresentation, this is no ground for recession, unless it is such that there is a complete difference in substance between the thing bargained for and the thing obtained.

A contract induced by fraud is not void, but voidable at the option of the party defrauded. He may affirm the contract, and bring an action for its non-performance; or he may disaffirm it, *ab initio*, and bring an action for money which the other party has obtained from him under it. But a party who intends to repudiate a contract on the ground of fraud should do so as soon as he discovers the fraud, otherwise innocent third parties may have acquired rights under the contract, and he will then be left to his action of tort for the deceit.

Duress. (26) A person who has been constrained to enter into an agreement under improper pressure, whether physical or moral, may subsequently disaffirm and avoid it.

Mistake. (27) Where a contract has been entered into upon the faith of a state of things which does not exist, or where one party has made a mistake to which the other party has by his acts contributed, even unintentionally, the contract may be rescinded, provided it is possible to replace the parties in their original condition.

Where in making an agreement between two parties there has been a mutual mistake as to their rights, occasioning injury to one of them, equity will generally grant relief.

A mistake cannot be rescinded which arises from ignorance of a known rule of law, but it may be remedied where it arises in the construction of a document of doubtful meaning.

Failure of consideration. (28) If a thing does not answer the description of that for which it was sold, the buyer is not bound to take it; and if he has paid for it, he may recover back the money, on the ground of failure of consideration. But the purchaser cannot recover back the price, when he has got what he bargained for, although the subject-matter of the sale turn out to be a thing of no value.

ILLUSTRATIVE CASES.

(1) *Robinson* v. *Cox*, 9 *Mod.* 263.

A., for many years a common woman, was kept by B. for some time, and then married C. After her marriage B. continued his visits to her, and gave her a note for £1000 payable on demand. B. died, and upon bill brought by his administratrix, the note was set aside as entered into *ex turpi causa*.

Matthews v. *L—e*, 1 *Mad*. 558.

Bill against an executrix to enforce a parol agreement by her testator to settle an annuity on the plaintiff, a married woman separated from her husband, who had lived with the testator. Held, that the agreement not being founded on any good or valuable consideration was not enforceable.

Merryweather v. *Jones*, 4 *Giff.* 509.

A post-nuptial settlement contained a proviso that, if the husband and wife should live separate, and the wife should require alimony, the wife's interest under the settlement should cease. Held, that the proviso was void.

(2) *Pearce* v. *Brooks*, *L.R.* 1 *Ex.* 213.

The defendant, a prostitute, was sued by the plaintiffs, coach-builders, for the hire of a brougham. There was no evidence that the plaintiffs looked expressly to the proceeds of the defendant's prostitution for payment; but the jury found that they knew her to be a prostitute, and supplied the brougham with a knowledge that it would be, as in fact it was, used by her as part of her display to attract men. Held, that the plaintiffs could not recover.

Lloyd v. *Johnson*, 1 *B. & P.* 340.

Plaintiff was employed to wash clothes for defendant, who was a prostitute, knowing her to be such. Held, that the use to which the clothes might be applied could not bar plaintiff of an action for work and labour.

Poplett v. *Stockdale*, 2 *C. & P.* 200.

A printer cannot recover against a publisher for printing a work which contains the life of a prostitute and the history of her amours, and it is no answer that the parties are *in pari delicto*.

(3) *Waugh* v. *Morris*, *L.R.* 8 *Q.B.* 202.

By a charter-party made by defendant's agent in France, defendant chartered plaintiff's ship, and it was stipulated that the ship should load a cargo of pressed hay in France, and proceed direct to London; and all cargo was to be brought and taken from ship alongside. Defendant's agent verbally told the master that the consignees would require the hay to be delivered at a particular wharf in the port of London, to which the master assented. On arriving in that port the master was unable to land the hay at the wharf, by reason of an Order of Council, forbidding hay from a French port to be landed in the United Kingdom. The order had been made before the charter-party was entered into, but neither party knew of it. After some delay, defendant received the hay from alongside the ship into another vessel, and exported it. There was no legal obstacle to doing this, but eighteen days were allowed by the defendant to elapse beyond the lay days. The plaintiff having brought an action for the detention of his ship, the defendant contended that the contract was for an illegal purpose, and therefore void. Held, that although it was the intention of the parties, when the charter-party was entered into, to land the hay at London, yet as the contract was not made knowingly, with the intention to violate the law, and as it could be carried out, as it ultimately was, without violating the law, it was not void; and defendant was therefore liable for the demurrage.

(4) See *Greville* v. *Atkins*, 9 *B. & C.* 462.

(5) *Sweet* v. *Meredith*, 3 *Giff.* 610.

An agreement was entered into for the sale of an advowson, containing a stipulation that the vendor should pay interest, until the benefice became vacant (the incumbent being a son of the vendor, but not a party to the contract). Held, that the agreement was not simoniacal.

(6) *Coombes* v. *Dibble, L.R.* 1 *Ex.* 248.

The plaintiff and defendant agreed to ride a race, each on his own horse, both the horses ridden to become the property of the winner. Held, that the horses could not be regarded as a contribution towards a prize, within the meaning of 8 & 9 Vict. c. 109, s. 18, and that the contract was therefore void under that section, as being "by way of gaming or wagering."

Bourke v. *Short*, 25 *L.J.*, *Q.B.* 196.

Upon a bargain for the sale of some rags by the plaintiff to the defendant, a difference arose as to the price at which a former sale had been effected, and a written agreement was entered into, that the one who turned out to be wrong should give to the other a gallon of the best brandy, and that the price of the rags then to be sold should be regulated according to what were proved to have been the provisions of the previous sale ; but inversely, *i.e.*, the lower the former price was, the higher was to be the price of the goods sold, and *vice versâ*. Held that, without considering the stipulation with regard to the brandy, the sale was by way of wagering within 8 & 9 Vict. c. 109, s. 89.

(7) *Giles* v. *Jones*, 24 *Law J.*, *Ex.* 259.

A contract for the sale of goods by "the ton long weight"—Held to be legal and valid, as "the ton long weight," though it consists of 240,000 pounds avoirdupois, and is more than twenty hundredweight statutory measure, is yet a multiple of the standard pound.

(8) *Drury* v. *Delafontaine*, 1 *Taunt.* 131.

The plaintiff, who was a horse auctioneer, sold a horse by private contract on a Sunday. Held, that this was not an exercise of his ordinary calling, and that therefore the sale was not void, either at common law, or under 22 Car. II. c. 27.

(9) *Biggs* v. *Lawrence*, 3 *T.R.* 454.

One of several partners resided in Guernsey, and sold a quantity of brandy, which he packed in a particular manner for the purpose of smuggling. Held, that neither he, nor the other partners, who resided in England, and knew nothing of the sale or its purpose, could maintain an action for the price of the goods.

(10) *Johnson* v. *Hudson*, 11 *East* 180.

A factor selling a parcel of prize manufactured tobacco consigned to him from his correspondent at Guernsey, of which a regular entry was made on importation, but without having entered himself with the Excise Office as a tobacco dealer, nor having any license as such, may yet maintain an action against the vendee for the value of the goods sold and delivered, and this though the tobacco were sent to the defendant without a permit, at his desire, there being no fraud upon the Revenue, but at most a breach of Revenue regulations protected by penalties.

Ritchie v. *Smith*, 6 *C.B.* 462.

An agreement entered into for the purpose of *enabling* one of the parties to it to contravene a statute passed for the protection of public morals cannot be enforced in a court of law. An agreement, the object of which is to enable an unlicensed person to sell exciseable liquors contrary to the 9 Geo. IV. c. 61, is, on this ground, illegal.

(11) *Battersby* v. *Smyth*, 3 *Mad.* 110.

A., B. and C. agreed to purchase a ship, and that it should be registered in the name of A. and B. only, but the profits of the ship to be divided amongst the three. C. filed a bill against A. and B. for an account of the profits of the ship. Held, on demurrer, that the agreement was void.

(12) *Topham* v. *Duke of Portland*, 32 *Law J., Ch.* 81.

See judgment of the Master of the Rolls, p. 92 : "The object aimed at by the deeds is not illegal; they are not intended to effectuate any general restraint on marriage, but are for the purpose of preventing the marriage of a daughter of the settlor with one specified person."

(13) *Swift* v. *Swift*, 34 *Law J., Ch.* 209.

A separation deed—Held, not vitiated by an agreement contained therein, on the part of a father, to deprive himself of the control of his children, where the father's conduct was such that his control would be injurious to the children.

(14) *Stanley* v. *Jones*, 5 *M. & P.* 207.

By articles of agreement, T. S. covenanted to communicate to the defendant all such information as he, T. S., possessed or could procure, and to use and exert his utmost influence and means for procuring such evidence as should be requisite to substantiate the defendant's claims against R. M. and W. S. E. ; in consideration of which the defendant covenanted to pay T. S. one-eighth part or share of such sum as should at any time be recovered, or obtained, either by suit in law, or in equity, from R. M. and W. S. E. Held, that the agreement was illegal as amounting to champerty.

(15) *Avery* v. *Scott*, 8 *Exch.* 497.

Any agreement which is to prevent the suffering party from coming into a court of law is illegal, but it is not unlawful for parties to agree to impose a condition precedent, with respect to the mode of settling the amount of damage, or the time of paying it, or other matters which do not go to the root of the action.

Keir v. *Leeman*, 6 *Q.B.* 308.

The law will permit a compromise of any offence, though made the subject of a criminal prosecution, for which offence the injured party might recover damages in an action ; but if the offence is of a public nature, no agreement can be valid which is founded on the consideration of stifling a prosecution for it. Thus, a common assault may be compromised, but not a riot.

Blithman v. *Martin*, 2 *Bulstr.* 213.

The defendant promised the plaintiff, who was a gaoler, a sum of money, if he would release a certain debtor who was in his custody ; the plaintiff did so, and brought his action upon the promise. Held, that he could not recover.

(16) *Egerton* v. *Earl Brownlow*, 4 *H.L.C.* 235.

The Duke of Bridgewater in his will devised large real estates " to Lord Alford for the term of ninety-nine years, if he shall so long live," remainder to the use of the heirs male of his body, with the proviso that, if Lord Alford should die without having acquired the title of Duke or Marquis of Bridgewater to himself and the heirs male of his body, the use and estate directed to be limited to the heirs male of his body should cease, and be absolutely void. Lord Alford entered upon possession of the estates, but died without acquiring either of the titles, and leaving an heir male. Held, that the estate created in favour of Lord Alford's heirs male was not affected by the proviso, which was a condition subsequent, and which was void, as against public policy.

(17) *Waldo* v. *Martin*, 4 *B. & C.* 319.

A., who held the office of bag-man in the Pipe Office of the Court of Exchequer for life, the office being in the gift of B., agreed with C. to resign, and to procure the appointment for C., in consideration of which C. agreed that A. should have half the profits. A. accordingly resigned, and procured the place for C., and a deed was executed for the performance of the agreement. The agreement was not communicated to B. In an action on the covenant, held that the agreement was a fraud on B., and therefore void.

(18) *Mitchell* v. *Reynolds*, 1 *P. Wms.* 181; 1 *Sm. L.C.*

The defendant assigned to the plaintiff the lease of a bakehouse in Liquorpond Street, in the parish of St. Andrew, Holborn, for the term of five years, and entered into a bond in a penalty of £50 not to exercise the trade of baker within that parish during the term mentioned. Held, that the agreement being made on reasonable consideration, and in partial restraint of trade only, was good.

Fox v. *Scard*, 33 *Beav.* 327.

A surgeon at W., upon taking an assistant, required him to give his bond in a penalty not to practice at W. Afterwards he discharged the assistant, who thereupon commenced practice at W. The surgeon then filed a bill to restrain him, to which the defendant demurred. The court overruled the demurrer, holding that, notwithstanding the pecuniary penalty, the plaintiff was entitled to his remedy in equity.

Elves v. *Crofts*, 10 *C.B.* 241.

A butcher on assigning, for the residue of a term, certain premises upon which he had carried on his business, together with the fixtures and the goodwill of the trade, covenanted with the purchaser that he would not *at any time thereafter*, either by himself, or as agent or journeyman for another, set up, exercise, or carry on, or be employed in, the trade or business of a butcher *within five miles* from the premises thereby assigned. Held, not an unreasonable restraint, either in respect of time, or in respect of distance, and that the covenant did not cease to be a binding covenant on the expiration of the term, or on the covenantee's ceasing, by himself or his assigns, to carry on the business assigned.

Labouchere v. *Dawson*, *L.R.* 13 *Eq.* 322.

The vendor of a business and the goodwill thereof may, in the absence of express stipulation to the contrary, set up a business of the same kind either in the same neighbourhood or elsewhere. "He is entitled to publish any advertisement he pleases in the papers stating that he is carrying on such business. He is entitled to publish any circulars to all the world to say that he is carrying on such business; but he is not entitled, either by private letter, or by a visit, or by his traveller or agent, to go to any person who was a customer of the old firm, and solicit him not to continue his business with the old firm, but to transfer it to him, the new firm. Customers, it is true, may be affected by public advertisements and public circulars; but that does not militate against the principle." (Judgment of Lord Romilly, M.R.)

(19)   *See East India Co.* v. *Sandys, Skin.* 169.

(20)   *Flindt* v. *Scott*, 5 *Taunt.* 674.

A license to G. F. and Co., of London, merchants, on behalf of themselves and others, to export on board a ship named, bearing any flag except the French, to a hostile port, and to import from thence specified goods, notwithstanding all the documents may represent the ship to be destined to a neutral or hostile port, and to whomsoever such property may appear to belong, authorizes an enemy, subject of the hostile power, to which the ship is licensed, legally to export from London. Licenses to trade with an enemy are to be construed liberally, and not, like grants of property from the Crown, strictly. And therefore, although the agent, in obtaining the license, did not represent to the Privy Council that he applied on behalf of a hostile trader, the concealment did not vacate the license.

(21)   *Wigg* v. *Shuttleworth*, 13 *East* 87.

The defendant having covenanted in an indenture to pay the plaintiff £300 at the end of a twelvemonth, and in the meantime, and until payment thereof, to pay interest for it at 5 per cent.—Held, no answer to an action of debt for the £300 and the interest accrued thereon to plead that, by the same indenture, it was, amongst other things, covenanted, that the defendant should pay the property tax, payable *for, and in respect of, the said* £300, for the two covenants were independent, and therefore, though the latter was void by the Property Tax Act (46 Geo. III. c. 65, s. 115), yet that did not avoid the other independent covenant in the deed, for the payment of £300 and interest.

Kerrison v. *Cole*, 8 *East* 231.

A bill of sale for transferring the property in a ship, by way of mortgage, may be void as such for want of reciting the certificate of registry therein, as required by 26 Geo. III. c. 60, s. 17. Held, nevertheless, that the mortgagor might be sued upon his personal covenant, contained in the same instrument, for the repayment of the money lent.

(22)   *Hopkins* v. *Prescott*, 16 *L.J., C.P.* 263.

Plaintiff sought to recover £50 on an agreement which was set out in the declaration. It recited that the plaintiff had for a long time carried on business as a law stationer, and also had been a sub-distributor of stamps and collector of assessed taxes, and "that, in consideration of £300, payable by instalments, the plaintiff agreed to sell, and the defendant agreed to purchase, the business of a law stationer, theretofore carried on by the plaintiff; and it was thereby further agreed between them that the plaintiff should not, after the 1st of March then next, carry on the business of a law stationer, or collect any of the assessed taxes, &c., but that the plaintiff would use his utmost endeavours to introduce the defendant to the said business *and offices.*" Held, that the agreement was for the sale of an office within the 5 & 6 Ed. VI. c. 16, and that the declaration was therefore bad. Wilde, C.J.: "The agreement set forth is entire, and the court cannot say that any parcel of the £300 is referable to one part of the agreement, and that the residue of the £300 is referable to the other part."

Featherstone v. *Hutchinson, Cro. Eliz.* 199.

The plaintiff had taken the body of one H. in execution at the suit of J. S., by virtue of a warrant directed to him as special bailiff. The defendant, a third party, in consideration that he would permit H. to go at large, and of two shillings, to the defendant paid, promised to pay the plaintiff all the money in which H. was condemned. After verdict for plaintiff,—Held, in arrest of judgment, that the consideration was not good, being contrary to the 23 Hen. VI. c. 10, and that, though it was joined with another consideration of two shillings, yet, being void and against the statute for part, it was void in all.

(23) *Walker* v. *Chapman, cited* 2 *Doug.* 471a.

The plaintiff paid a sum of money to the defendant to procure him a place in the Customs. The place not having been procured, the plaintiff brought his action to recover back the money. Held, that he was entitled to recover, because the contract remained executory.

(24) *Wilson* v. *Ray,* 10 *Ad. & E.* 82.

Plaintiff being about to compound with his creditors, defendant, a creditor, refused to subscribe the deed, unless he were paid in full. Plaintiff, to obtain his signature, gave a bill, payable to defendant's agent, for the difference between 20*s.* in the pound and 8*s.*, the proportion compounded for. Defendant then signed the deed. Plaintiff did not honour the bill when due; but on subsequent application he paid it to the payee, and defendant received the money. The other creditors were paid according to the deed. Held, that the plaintiff could not recover back the amount paid to defendant above 8*s.* in the pound, for that the transaction had been closed by a voluntary payment, with full knowledge of the facts.

Atkinson v. *Denby,* 30 *L.J., Ex.* 361.

The plaintiff, being indebted to the defendant and others, offered a composition of 5*s.* in the pound, which some of the creditors accepted, but the defendant at first refused. The defendant ultimately accepted this composition, and signed the deed, the plaintiff giving him privately £50 and a bill of exchange for £108, in addition to the 5*s.* in the pound paid to him with the other creditors. Some of the other creditors refused to sign unless the defendant signed, and of this the defendant was aware. Held, in an action by the plaintiff to recover back the £50, as money had and received to the plaintiff's use, that the plaintiff was entitled to recover. Wilde, B.: "Here the parties were not *in pari delicto,* because one was under coercion." [It will be observed that in *Wilson* v. *Ray,* although the bill of exchange was made under coercion, it was paid voluntarily after the coercion had ceased, and although such payment might have been resisted. The parties were therefore simply *in pari delicto.*]

(25) *Kennedy* v. *Panama, &c., Royal Mail Co.,* 36 *L.J.,* Q.B. 260.

A steam-packet company entered into a contract with the Postmaster-General of New Zealand, relating to the mail service of the colony. This contract the government of the colony refused to recognise, on the ground that it was beyond the authority of the Postmaster-General. Meantime the company issued a prospectus, giving notice that they were prepared to receive applications for new shares, "in order to enable the company to perform the contract recently entered into with the general government of New Zealand for a monthly mail service between Sydney, New Zealand, and Panama." The plaintiff, after seeing the prospectus, applied for and obtained an allotment of shares. Held, that he was not entitled, upon finding that the mail service contract was repudiated by the Colonial Government, to recover back the price of his shares; as, although the prospectus contained an implied statement that the contract was binding upon the Colonial Government, yet the misrepresentation was not fraudulent, and was not such as to show that there was a complete difference between the shares which were bargained for, and those which were obtained, so as to constitute a failure of consideration.

Selway v. *Fogg*, 5 *M. & W.* 86.

A. engaged to convey away certain rubbish for B. at a specified sum, under a fraudulent misrepresentation by B. as to the quantity of the rubbish which was to be so conveyed. Held, that in an action for the value of the work actually done, A. could recover only according to the terms of the special contract; although when he discovered the fraud he might have repudiated the contract, and sued B. for deceit. Parke, B. : "If the plaintiff chooses to treat the defendant as a party who has contracted with him, he must be bound by the only contract made between them. Upon discovering the fraud (unless he meant to proceed according to the terms of the contract), the plaintiff should have immediately declared off, and sought compensation for the bygone time in an action for deceit."

(26) *Williams* v. *Bayley*, *L.R.*, 1 *App. Cases*, 200.

A son carried to bankers of whom he, as well as his father, was a customer, certain promissory notes with his father's name upon them as indorser. These indorsements were forgeries. On one occasion the father's attention was called to the fact that a promissory note of his son, with his (the father's) name on it, was lying at the banker's dishonoured. He seems to have communicated the fact to the son, who immediately redeemed it; but there was no direct evidence to show whether the father did, or did not, really understand the nature of the transaction. The fact of the forgery was afterwards discovered; the son did not deny it; the bankers insisted (though without any direct threat of a prosecution) on a settlement, to which the father was to be a party; he consented, and executed an agreement to make an equitable mortgage of his property. The notes with the forged indorsements were then delivered up to him. Held, that the agreement was invalid. A father appealed to, under such circumstances, to take upon himself a civil liability, with the knowledge that, unless he does so, his son will be exposed to a criminal prosecution with a moral certainty of a conviction, even though that is not put forward by any party as the motive for the agreement, is not a free or voluntary agent, and the agreement he makes under such circumstances is not enforceable.

(27) *Emmerson's Ca. L.R.*, 1 *Ch.* 433.

Held, on appeal, reversing the order of the Master of the Rolls, that an agreement for the sale of shares in a company, entered into in ignorance that a petition for winding-up the company had been presented, was not enforceable or valid, so as to make the purchaser a contributory.

Torrance v. *Bolton*, *L.R.*, 14 *Eq.* 124.

Certain property was put up for sale by auction, and in the particulars, which were advertised, was described as being an absolute reversion in a

A A

freehold estate, falling into possession on the death of a lady then in her seventieth year; and by the conditions of sale, which were read for the first time at the auction just previously to the commencement of the biddings, the property was stated to be sold subject to two mortgages. On bill filed by the purchaser at the auction, who stated that he was deaf, and did not understand that by the conditions he was buying only an equity of redemption in the property,—Held, that, although his solicitor paid the deposit on his behalf after having read the conditions, he was entitled to a decree for the recission of the contract, and for a return of the deposit with interest.

Baskcomb v. Beckwith, L.R., 8 Eq. 100.

The owner of an estate put up the whole estate, except a small piece of land, for sale in lots, subject to conditions which provided that no public-house should be built, and no trade carried on upon the property. In the particulars of sale the property was described as the M. estate, and there was nothing to show that any part of the vendor's estate was not included, and in the plan annexed to the particulars the different lots were coloured, and the excepted piece of land was uncoloured, but was not marked with the vendor's name, though the names of the adjoining owners were printed. It was improbable that a public-house would be built on any of the adjoining estates. Held, that a purchaser of one of the lots, consisting of a mansion-house a hundred yards distant from the excepted piece of land, who had purchased in the belief that the whole of the vendor's estate was included in the particulars of sale, and consequently would be subject to the restrictive conditions, could not be compelled to complete his purchase unless the vendor would enter into restrictive covenants as to the excepted piece of land.

Earl Beauchamp v. Winn, L.R., 6 H.L. 223.

Where in the making of an agreement between two parties there has been a mutual mistake as to their rights, occasioning an injury to one of them, the rule of equity is in favour of interposing to grant relief. The court will not, if such a ground for relief is clearly established, decline to grant relief merely because, on account of the circumstances which have intervened since the agreement was made, it may be difficult to restore the parties exactly to their original condition. The rule *ignorantia juris neminem excusat* applies where the alleged ignorance is that of a well-known rule of law, but not where it is that of a matter of law arising upon the doubtful construction of a grant. Lord Chelmsford : "Although when a certain construction has been put by a court of law upon a deed, it must be taken that the legal construction was clear, yet the ignorance, before the decision, of what was the true construction, cannot in my opinion be pressed to the extent of depriving a person of relief on the ground that he was bound himself to have known beforehand how the grant must be construed."

(28)   *Azema* v. *Casella, L.R.,* 2 *C.P.* 678.

The defendants, through brokers, bought of the plaintiff "the following cotton, viz., $\frac{D. C.}{C}$ 128 bales at 25d. per lb., expected to arrive in London per *Cheviot* from Madras. The cotton guaranteed equal to sealed sample in our (the brokers') possession. Should the *quality* prove inferior to the guarantee a fair allowance to be made." The sample was of "Long-staple Salem" cotton. The 128 bales marked $\frac{D. C.}{C}$ which arrived by the *Cheviot* contained "Western Madras" cotton. Upon a special case, in which it was stated that there were, at the time of the contract, different kinds of Madras cotton known in the market, and divided into certain classes and divisions; that the cotton tendered was not "Long-staple Salem," but a particularly good sample of "Western Madras;" that "the cotton was not therefore in accordance with the sample;" and that "'Western Madras cotton' is inferior to 'Long-staple Salem,' and requires machinery for its manufacture different from that which is used for 'Long-staple Salem.'" Held, that the cotton tendered was not that which the defendants bargained for, and that they were not bound to accept it with an allowance; for that the allowance-clause had reference only to an inferiority in quality, and not to a difference of kind.

Lamert v. Heath, 15 M. & W. 488.

The vendor agreed to sell and the purchaser to buy, scrip certificates of shares in the Kentish Coast Railway, and the certificates were delivered by the vendor, and the purchase-money paid, but the Kentish Coast Railway scheme was subsequently abandoned and the company dissolved, and the scrip repudiated on the ground that the secretary had issued it without authority. Held, that the purchaser could not recover from the vendor the money he had paid for it, as he had got what was intended to be bought and sold.

CHAPTER XVI.

TRANSFER OF CONTRACTS.

(i.) *Assignment.*

Judicature Act. By the Judicature Act (36 & 37 Vict. c. 66, s. 24) any debt or other chose in action may now be assigned absolutely by writing under the hand of the assignor; and such assignment, after express notice in writing has been given to the debtor, will be effectual in law (subject to all equities which would have been entitled to priority if the Act had not been passed), to pass and transfer the legal right to such debt or chose in action from the date of such notice, and all legal and other remedies for the same, and the power to give a good discharge for the same without the concurrence of the assignor.

Previously to the passing of the Act, the general rule of the Courts of Equity was that the assignee of a chose in action took it subject to all the equities between the original parties to the contract, and this rule will still prevail; but the parties to the original contract may by express stipulation, or by implication arising from their conduct, agree that the chose in action may be assigned free from such equities.

(ii.) *Covenants running with the Land.*

Real contracts. (1) Covenants running with the land are transferable; they pass from hand to hand with the interest in the realty to which they are annexed, and are called "real contracts."

To enable a covenant to "run with the land," it is not necessary that the covenantor should have any estate in the land. But the covenantor must be clothed with some transferable interest in the land to which the covenant can be attached; for otherwise the covenant is a mere personal covenant.

Although covenants, entered into by the owners of land with covenantees who have not any interest in the land, do not run with the land, yet if a party buys an estate, and accepts a conveyance, with full knowledge of a covenant of this description, he may be compelled to fulfil it. And a purchaser, who does not enquire into his vendor's title, may be affected with notice of such a covenant appearing upon it.

Covenants between landlord and tenant, or reversioner and lessee, affecting the value or enjoyment of the property during the term, are annexed to the estate granted, and run with the land as long as the estate continues. This applies both to covenants made by the lessor and covenants made by the lessee. If the lessee assigns his lease, the assignee may sue or be sued upon any breach which occurs whilst the estate continues in him. The liability of the assignee is extinguished (except as to actually existing breaches) by assigning over his estate to another; and the burden of the covenant will then fall upon the latter. *(Covenants between landlord and tenant. (2))*

Whilst an intermediate assignee may thus extinguish his liability by assigning over, this is not the case with the original lessee; for although by assignment the *privity of estate* between himself and the lessor is extinguished, yet the *privity of contract* remains, and the lessee is liable during the whole of the term, in the nature of a surety for the assignee, for the performance of the covenants.

In order to make an assignee responsible upon the covenants of the lease, he must be clothed with the same estate as that which the lessee had in the land. An under-lessee, therefore, is not liable upon the covenants, inasmuch as he is not possessed of the estate to which they are annexed.

Covenants real run with the estate of the reversioner as well as with that of the lessee. By the 32 Hen. VIII. c. 34, the assignee of the reversion may sue the lessee or his assigns upon the covenants entered into by the lessee with the lessor; and he may himself be sued by the lessee or his assigns upon the covenants entered into by the lessor with the lessee.

Requisites of the covenant. (3) In order to run with the land, the covenant must be inherent in the land; that is to say, the performance or non-performance of it must affect the nature, quality, or value of the thing demised and its mode of enjoyment.

If the covenant relates to things actually in existence, the fact that "assigns" are not expressly mentioned in the covenant is immaterial; but if the covenant relates to things not in existence, it would appear that, in order to bind assignees, they should be expressly mentioned.

Requisites of assignment. (4) Both the lease and the assignment must be under seal, or the benefit and the burden of the covenants will not run with the land. The assignees of the reversion may, however, if there is a lease by simple contract, for a term not exceeding three years in duration, maintain an action against the lessee, or his assignee, for use and occupation.

(iii.) *Transfer by Death.*

Rights of heirs on ancestors' contracts. (5) Real contracts, or covenants running with the land, annexed to an estate of inheritance, descend with the land, in case of death, to the heir-at-law, without his being named in the covenant, and even when the covenant is made with the covenantee and his executors.

The heir-at-law also represents his ancestor upon such personal covenants as relate to the freehold, and affect the value of the inheritance.

When a real contract, or covenant running with the land, has been broken in the lifetime of the ancestor, and the breach remains a continuing breach in the time of the heir-at-law, the latter is the only party entitled to sue upon it, if no actual damage has resulted to the personal estate.

With respect to breaches of real contract not in the nature of continuing breaches, when the covenant, having been broken, is broken once for all, and the entire and ultimate damage has accrued, such damage, if it results in the time of the ancestor, survives to his personal representative. *Rights of personal representatives.* (6)

All real contracts, or covenants running with the land, annexed to reversions for terms of years, leases and chattel interests in land, pass together with the estates to which they are annexed to the personal representatives of the deceased covenantee.

The executor or administrator is alone liable upon, or entitled to sue upon, all bonds and personal covenants and simple contracts entered into with the testator or intestate, and to recover debts of record due to him; and this is the case, even when the bond or other contract is made with a man and his heirs.

The executor or administrator is responsible upon, or entitled to the benefit of, all such of the executory contracts of the deceased as he can fairly and efficiently fulfil.

But when the contract is founded upon the known skill or genius of the deceased (*ex. gr.* as an author, artist, &c.) it is determined by his death.

If there are several executors or administrators, they are jointly liable, in case they have all proved the will, or administered. *Joint liability of executors, &c.*

On the death of one of several executors, either before or after probate, the entire right of representation survives to the others. When the surviving executor, or when a sole *Continuation of representation.* (7)

executor dies after probate his executor, or the executor of such executor, is in law the executor of the first executor.

But on the death of an administrator, or on the death of a sole or surviving executor after probate, no right of representation is transmitted to his administrator; but administration *de bonis non* must be taken out.

(iv.) *Transfer by Bankruptcy.*

Effect of adjudication. Immediately upon the adjudication, the choses in action and obligations of the bankrupt vest in the registrar, and upon the appointment of a trustee they forthwith pass to, and vest in, the trustee (Bankruptcy Act, 32 & 33 Vict. c. 71, s. 17).

Reputed ownership. By the Bankruptcy Act, 1869, s. 15, goods and chattels of which, being a trader, the bankrupt is in possession, at the commencement of the bankruptcy, with the permission of the true owner, of which goods and chattels the bankrupt is the reputed owner, or of which he has taken upon himself the sale or disposition as owner, are property divisible among the creditors. But choses in action, other than debts due to the bankrupt in the course of his trade, are not to be deemed goods and chattels within this section

And by the Bills of Sale Act, 1878 (41 & 42 Vict. c. 31, s. 20) chattels comprised in a bill of sale, which has been, and continues to be, duly registered under the Act, shall not be deemed to be in the possession, order, or disposition, of the grantor of the bill of sale, within the meaning of the Bankruptcy Act.

Property of bankrupt's wife. (8) The bankrupt's disposable interest in his wife's property, not settled on her for her separate use, passes to the trustees under the bankruptcy.

Executory contracts. (9) Executory contracts, in which the bankrupt is interested, and from which benefit may accrue to the estate, and which can be performed on the part of the bankrupt by the trustees, pass to the latter.

Unprofitable contracts may, along with other onerous property acquired by the trustee, be disclaimed in writing by him (s. 23). But after application in writing to ascertain the intention of the trustee, if he does not disclaim within twenty-eight days, he cannot afterwards do so. *Unprofitable contracts.*

By s. 25 of the Act, the trustees are authorized to sell the book debts of the bankrupt and the goodwill of his business; and the purchaser has, by virtue of the assignment, power to sue in his own name for the debts assigned to him. *Book debts and goodwill.*

If one of several partners is adjudged bankrupt, his interest in the partnership contracts and transactions, entered into before the bankruptcy, passes to the trustees. *Interest in partnership.* (10)

The trustees are entitled to sue, if they think fit, upon all contracts entered into with the bankrupt, during the bankruptcy, not being contracts for the personal labour and services of the bankrupt, made for earning his necessary subsistence. *Contracts with bankrupt.* (11)

But if the trustees do not interfere to prevent him, the bankrupt himself may sue upon any contract entered into by him after his bankruptcy.

Whilst the bankrupt remains undischarged, no debt provable under the bankruptcy can be enforced against him, until the expiration of three years from the close of the bankruptcy; and during that time, if he pay to his creditors such additional sum as will, with the dividend paid out of his property during the bankruptcy, make up ten shillings in the pound, he shall be entitled to an order of discharge, in the same manner as if a dividend of ten shillings in the pound had originally been paid out of his property (s. 54). *Liability of undischarged bankrupt.*

At the expiration of a period of three years from the close of the bankruptcy, if the bankrupt has not obtained his discharge, any balance remaining unpaid shall be deemed to be a subsisting debt, in the nature of a judgment debt, and, subject to the rights of any persons who have become creditors of the debtor since the close of the bankruptcy, may be enforced against the debtor, with the sanction of the court which adjudged such debtor bankrupt, or of the court having jurisdiction in bankruptcy in the place where the property is situated.

[With regard to the transfer of a wife's ante-nuptial contracts to her husband, see *supra*, p. 187.]

ILLUSTRATIVE CASES.

(1) *Jay* v. *Richardson*, 30 *Beav.* 563.

The owner in fee of two plots of land demised the first for an hotel, and covenanted that he would not let any house or land, within a certain distance of it, to be used as an hotel. He demised the second plot, which was within the distance, to another person. The defendant purchased the reversion of the second plot, and afterwards bought up the lease of it, but with notice of the restrictive covenants relating to the first lot. Held, that he was in equity bound by the covenant.

(2) *Harley* v. *King*, 2 *C.M. & R.* 18.

The assignee of a lease held liable for the breach of a covenant running with the land, incurred in his own time, though the action was not commenced until after he had assigned the premises.

Barnard v. *Godscall, Cro. Jac.* 309.

An action of covenant will lie against a lessee on an express covenant, notwithstanding he has assigned the term, and the lessor has accepted rent from the assignee. [Parke, B., observes in *Humble* v. *Langston*, 7 *M. & W.* 530, "The assignee of a lease becomes liable to the lessor for the performance of all the covenants which run with the land, and the lessee is also liable in the nature of a surety, as between himself and the assignee, for the performance of the same covenants during the continuance of his interest."]

Halford v. *Hatch*, 1 *Doug.* 186.

Action of covenant brought by a lessor against an under-lessee; the question was whether the action could be maintained against him as *substantially* an assignee, and it was held that it could not.

(3) *Spencer's Ca.* 5 *Co.* 17, *b,* 1 *Sm. L.C.*

In this case it was resolved *inter alia,*—

(i.) Where the covenant extends to a thing *in esse,* parcel of the demise, the thing to be done is *quodam-modo* annexed to the thing demised, and shall go with the land, and shall bind the assignee, although he be not bound by express words.

(ii.) When the covenant extends to a thing, which is not in being at the time of the demise made, the assignee can only be bound by express words.

Thus, if the lessee covenants to repair houses demised to him during the term, the assignee is bound, though not expressly named. But if the covenant be to make a new wall on some part of the demised premises, the assignee is bound, if the lessee covenanted for himself "and his assigns," but not otherwise.

[In *Minshull* v. *Oakes*, 2 H. & N. 793, the court, without overruling Spencer's ca., suggested this qualification of the rules above mentioned, viz., that a covenant to repair a messuage, *and all other erections and buildings which should or might be erected during the term*, runs with the land, and binds an assignee though not named, inasmuch as the covenant is not absolutely to do a new thing, but to do something conditionally, viz., if there be new buildings, to repair them.]

(iii.) It is further laid down in Spencer's ca. that, although the covenant be for a man and his assigns, yet if the thing to be done be *merely collateral to the land*, and do not touch or concern the thing demised in any sort, then the assignee shall not be charged. As if the lessee covenants for himself and his assigns to build a house upon land of the lessor which is no parcel of the demise, or to pay any collateral sum to the lessor, or to a stranger.

(4) *Beely* v. *Parry*, 3 Lev. 15, b.

Tenant for years made a lease for part of the term with covenants, and then granted away his reversion. The assignment of the reversion not having been made by deed,—Held, that the covenants did not pass to the grantee.

Standen v *Christmas*, 10 Q.B. 135.

Where a lease is not under seal, the assignee of the reversion cannot maintain assumpsit against the lessee for breach of his contract with the assignor to repair. Where a lease for a term certain was granted by writing not under seal, and contained an undertaking, on behalf of the lessor and his assigns, for quiet enjoyment,—Held, that his assignee might maintain assumpsit for use and occupation ; for, the lessor having granted for himself and his assigns, the permission of any person who might become assignee of the reversion during the lease was virtually included, so that the occupation became in point of law permissive on the part of the assignee as soon as his interest accrued.

(5) *Lougher* v. *Williams*, 2 Lev. 92.

The plaintiff brought an action of covenant, as heir upon the lease of his ancestor, wherein the lessee covenanted with the lessor, *his executors and administrators*, to repair and to leave the premises in repair at the end of the term. Held, that the heir was entitled to recover on the covenant.

Wotton v. *Cooke*, Dy. 337, b.

Three co-parceners purchased land in fee, paying equal shares of the purchase-money. In a tripartite deed, which recited that the purchase was made with the intent that they and the heirs of each should have and enjoy a just third part of these lands, as well as of the lands in co-parcenary, each covenanted with the others, their heirs and assigns and each of them, to make such conveyance to the heirs of the two who happened to die first. Held, that the heir of a deceased covenantee might maintain an action upon the deed.

Vivian v. *Champion*, 2 Ld. Raym. 1125.

In an action of covenant, by an heir against a tenant, for suffering premises to be out of repair,—Held, that it was immaterial that part of the time during which the defendant suffered the premises to be out of repair was in the lifetime of the plaintiff's ancestor. And in such an action, the plaintiff ought to have such damages as will suffice to put the premises into proper repair.

(6) *Raymond* v. *Fitch*, 2 *C.M. & R.* 588.

Held, that an executor was entitled to sue the lessee of his testator for the breach of a covenant not to fell, stub up, lop, or top, timber trees, excepted out of the demise, such breach having been committed in the lifetime of the testator.

Devon v. *Pawlett*, 11 *Vin. Abr.* 132.

The plaintiff, as administratrix, brought an action against the defendant, upon a promise made by the defendant to the plaintiff to pay to him upon his marriage, or "to his order, his heirs or executors," the sum of fifty guineas. There was no averment that the money was not paid to the intestate's heir. Held, that the declaration was good without such averment, the thing contracted for being a mere personalty; *per curiam*, "if a man enters into an obligation to pay to another or his heirs a sum of money, his executors and administrators, and not his heirs, shall have it."

Marshall v. *Broadhurst*, 1 *Cr. & J.* 40, *b*.

Per curiam, "When the law speaks of executors not carrying on the business of their testator, it means that they are not to buy and sell. We do not say that executors are bound to go on to an indefinite extent, but it is reasonable that they should do so to a certain extent. For instance, if a man make half a wheelbarrow, or half a pair of shoes, and then die, the executors may complete them, and they are not bound to sacrifice the property of their testator by selling articles in an imperfect state. It is otherwise, where the testator enters into a personal engagement to be performed by himself only."

(7) *Elliott* v. *Kemp*, *M. & W.* 306.

L. was possessed of furniture and other property, and on his death, intestate, in 1827, the furniture was removed by his widow to another house, in which she resided until her death in 1832, with her daughter E., and continued during that period to use the furniture. In October, 1820, the widow caused the furniture to be valued, in order to her taking out administration to L., which she afterwards did. In 1838, the furniture was sold by the defendant (who had married another daughter of L.) with E.'s concurrence. In 1840, disputes having arisen about the administration of the proceeds, E. took out administration to her mother. Held, that E. could not maintain trover for the furniture, without having taken out administration *de bonis non* to L.

(8) *Shaw* v. *Steward*, 1 *Ad. & E.* 300.

A testator bequeathed to S. the residue of a term in a house, &c., in case he should so long live, and inhabit the house, and from and after his decease, or giving up possession of the said house, or in case he should mortgage the same, then to M., the wife of S., to hold the premises unto her for the remainder of the term, in case she should so long live therein, and continue the widow of S. and unmarried. S. took possession, but afterwards, being in insolvent circumstances, he went to sea, leaving his wife and family on the premises, where the wife continued to carry on his business. He returned in six months, and resided on the premises as before, till he and his wife were turned out of possession, a commission of bankruptcy having been issued against him, under which the assignees sold the property. S. died, and the widow brought ejectment for the premises. Held, that S.'s going to sea, as above mentioned, was not a "giving up possession" within the meaning of the will; and, *semble*, that his being turned out of the premises, after they were sold by the assignees, had not that effect; but that the interest which the wife took under the will, being contingent upon events, of which some might have happened during the husband's lifetime, was an interest which the husband might assign at law; and that the wife had not an equitable interest sufficiently clear to enable the court to say that the assignees did not become entitled to the premises under the bankruptcy.

(9) *Gibson* v. *Carruthers*, 8 *M. & W.* 321.

Assumpsit by the assignees of T. H., a bankrupt. T. H. before he became bankrupt, at the request of the defendant, bargained for, and agreed to buy from the defendant, 2000 quarters skreened Odessa linseed, at the rate of 30*s*. 10*d*. per quarter. On notice of the bankruptcy of T. H. and of the appointment of the plaintiffs as assignees, the defendant refused, although requested by the plaintiffs, to complete their contract. Held, that the assignees were entitled to recover. Rolfe, B.: "It is clear that assignees of a bankrupt are entitled to the benefit of all contracts entered into by the bankrupt, and which are in *fieri* at the time of the bankruptcy. They may elect to adopt or reject such contracts, according as they are likely to be beneficial or onerous to the estate. In no case can the party, who contracted with the bankrupt, set up the bankruptcy against the assignees as a reason for not doing what he has agreed to do."

(10) *Eckhardt* v. *Wilson*, 8 *T.R.* 142.

To assumpsit by several partners, the defendant pleaded in bar the bankruptcy of one of them. Held, a good plea, because it showed not merely that there were other persons (namely, the assignees of the bankrupt partner), who ought to have sued with the plaintiffs, but that one of the plaintiffs could not sue at all.

(11) *Webb* v. *Fox*, 7 *T.R.* 391.

An uncertificated bankrupt has a right to goods acquired by him since his bankruptcy against all the world but his assignees, and may maintain trover for them against a stranger. Ashurst, J.: "The creditors who have not received twenty shillings in the pound are entitled to receive satisfaction to that amount; but it must be through the medium of his assignees. The creditors who are not assignees have no property in goods acquired by the bankrupt after his bankruptcy; if they take them they are trespassers."

CHAPTER XVII.

DISCHARGE OF CONTRACTS.

(i.) *Performance.*

Demand of performance. (1)
WHERE a penalty or forfeiture attaches for non-payment of money, or for non-performance of a particular act *after demand*, demand of performance is a condition precedent to a right of action for the penalty or the forfeiture, and in these cases a personal demand is generally necessary. When, by the express terms of a contract, the duty to pay money, or to render some particular service, is not to arise until *after demand*, there is no cause of action, until demand has been made.

When, however, there is a debt due, and a covenant or promise by the debtor to pay the debt on request, no request need be made. The law casts upon the debtor the duty of seeking out his creditor, whilst he remains within the realm of England, and paying the money without any request.

When a request, or demand of performance, is by the contract made a condition precedent to any liability for non-performance, if the party who has to do the act has disabled himself from performance, the stipulation as to the request is dispensed with.

Impossibility of performance. (2)
Impossibility of performance is in general no answer to an action for damages for non-performance. If the thing to be done is notoriously physically impossible, and was known to be so by both parties, at the time of making the

contract, the contract is void, unless the promissor has taken it upon himself to warrant that it is possible.

If the thing to be done was possible at the time of making the contract, but has become impossible since, the promissor is liable to an action for damages for non-performance, if he has expressly or impliedly undertaken without any qualification to do it; and whether the impossibility of performance has been occasioned by the act of a stranger, or by the act of the promissor himself, is immaterial.

But where, after the making of the contract, performance has become impossible by the act of God, it would seem that the promissor is excused, unless it clearly appear from the terms of the contract that he was to be liable at all events. And when a man covenants to do a thing which is lawful, and before performance an Act of Parliament renders the thing unlawful, the covenant is repealed.

Every plea of tender, being pleadable only in bar of the costs of an action, must allege the defendant's continued readiness to pay, and must be accompanied by payment into court of the money tendered. *Tender of payment. (3)*

Bank of England notes are a good tender for all sums above £5. But the Bank itself cannot make a legal tender of its own notes to a party requiring gold (3 & 4 Wm. IV. c. 98, s. 6). Gold coin is a good tender for the payment of any amount. Silver coin is a good tender for sums not exceeding 40s., and bronze coin for sums under 6d.

A tender clogged with conditions and reservations is a bad tender, but a tender "under protest" is a good tender.

If a debtor tendering money requires a receipt for the amount, he ought himself to be prepared with the paper and writing materials, and the stamp, when a stamp is necessary, and tender them to the creditor together with the money.

A bill or note usually does no more than suspend the remedy for debt by giving extended credit; it does not deprive the creditor of any lien he may have for the debt; *Payment by bill or note. (4)*

and if it is not paid at maturity, the creditor may sue for his demand as though no bill or note had been given.

But if the creditor has received the bill or note *as cash*, or if, at the time of receiving it, he has agreed to take upon himself the risk of its being paid at maturity; or if the security is marred by the creditor's own laches in omitting to present it, or give notice of its dishonour, the bill or note becomes money in his hands, as between himself and the person from whom he received it.

Payment to agent. (5)
Payment may be made to an agent authorized to receive moneys on account of his principal. And payment to a person found in a merchant's counting-house, in possession of the merchant's account books, and apparently intrusted with the conduct of the business, is a good payment to the merchant himself, although the person receiving the money has in fact no authority from the merchant to do so.

Payment to creditor of the creditor. (6)
If the creditor request his debtor to pay his account to a third party, and the money is paid, this is equivalent to payment to the creditor himself. And payment by a garnishee, on execution levied upon him, in accordance with the Common Law Procedure Act, 1854, is a valid discharge to the garnishee, as against the judgment debtor.

Payment to bankrupt.
By the Bankruptcy Act, 1869, nothing therein contained is to render invalid any payment, made in good faith, and for value received, to any bankrupt, before the date of the order of adjudication, by a person not having at the time of such payment notice of any act of bankruptcy committed by the bankrupt and available for adjudication (32 & 33 Vict. c. 71, s. 94).

Payment by a stranger. (7)
Where one makes a payment in the name and on behalf of another, without authority, it is competent for the debtor to adopt and ratify the payment even after the creditor has commenced an action for the debt.

Payment and acceptance of part. (8)
The payment and acceptance of part of an admitted simple contract debt cannot usually constitute a satisfaction of such debt. But if disputes exist as to the exact amount

due, or the money be paid in advance, or some consideration be given and accepted, then the payment and acceptance of the smaller sum may be a satisfaction and discharge of the claim for the larger amount. And a creditor may agree to take less than the amount of his debt, provided payment is made by a particular day, and, in default, may recover the whole debt. And, in the case of composition deeds, the joint agreement of all, or a certain number, of the creditors to accept the composition, and not to sue the debtor, is a sufficient consideration to each of them for the promise or agreement of each to accept the composition and discharge the debtor.

A receipt is nothing more than a *primâ facie* acknow-ledgment that money has been paid, and may be contradicted or explained. Receipt. (9)

The general rule is that the party who pays money has a right to apply that payment as he thinks fit. If there are several debts due from him, he has a right to say to which of those debts the payment is to be applied. If he does not make a specific application at the time of the payment, then the right of application generally devolves on the party who receives the money. The appropriation by the creditor may be made at any time before the case comes before a jury; and he is not bound at the time he makes the appropriation to give the debtor any notice thereof. If, however, he communicates his election to the debtor, he is bound thereby, and cannot make a different appropriation without the assent of the debtor. Appropriation of payments. (10)

When the creditor has two distinct accounts against the debtor, and the latter makes a general payment on account, the creditor may apply the payment to which account he pleases. But where the account is one entire account, and is so treated by both parties, the payment is deemed in law to be made in discharge of the earlier items of the account.

(ii.) *Discharge by Consent of the Parties.*

Discharge of contracts before breach. (11)   There is no clause in the Statute of Frauds requiring the dissolution of a contract to be in writing; and any contract, whether required by the statute to be in writing or not, may before breach be waived and abandoned by a new agreement not in writing.

Discharge of contracts after breach by release. (12)   After a breach of contract has occurred, the cause of action which thereby arises may be discharged at common law by a *release under seal*.

And in equity an agreement amounting to a release, made upon good consideration, though not under seal, may be enforced. And so may a representation by the creditor of his intention to release the debt, if acted on by the debtor.

Discharge of contracts after breach by accord and satisfaction. (13)   An overdue demand, whether liquidated or unliquidated, may by agreement be discharged by payment of a thing different from that contracted to be paid, though of less pecuniary value, or by a negotiable instrument binding the debtor or a third person to pay a smaller sum (see *supra*, p. 368); and part of a claim may be satisfied by the withdrawal of defence as to the residue.

An accord, to avail, must usually be executed; but the true rule seems to be that, if the new *promise* be received *in satisfaction*, it is a good satisfaction; but if the *performance*, and not the *promise*, is intended to operate in satisfaction, there is no satisfaction without performance.

Discharge of bills and notes. (14)   Bills of exchange and promissory notes have always been an exception to the general rule of law, that a cause of action once accrued could only be discharged by deed of release, or by accord and satisfaction. The liability of an acceptor may be discharged by an express renunciation by the holder of his claim on the bill, although such renunciation be made by word of mouth only.

A covenant by a creditor, not to sue at any time, amounts to a release. *Covenants not to sue. (15)*

A covenant not to sue for a certain time is not a release. It is not pleadable in bar of an action brought contrary to the agreement, but gives rise to a cross claim for the damages resulting from the creditor's suing during the time he had agreed not to sue.

A covenant not to sue for a limited time, with a proviso for forfeiture if an action be brought within the time, operates as a release by force of the condition, if the action be brought within the time.

Generally speaking, the release of one of several joint, or joint and several, contractors, releases all. But the party giving the release may qualify it by a reservation of his right of action against the others, if the original contract reserves to him the power to do so. And the release of one of several joint, or joint and several, contractors, may frequently be construed as a covenant not to sue, not amounting to a release, but giving a claim to damages in case of breach. *Release of one joint contractor. (16)*

(iii.) *Discharge by Operation of Law.*

If a deed, or a simple contract in writing, after it has been finally completed and signed, is altered in any material part, with the privity and assent of the parties to it, a fresh contract is created which puts an end to the first contract. *Material alteration. (17)*

But if the material alteration has been made without the consent of the party against whom the contract is sought to be enforced, either by the party who sues upon the contract, or by some other person, whilst the contract was in the custody of the party who sues, the alteration will discharge the contract, without substituting any fresh contract in its place.

If the material alteration was made by the party against whom the contract is sought to be enforced, or by some third party, without the consent of the party suing upon it, and whilst the contract was out of the custody of the latter, the alteration will have no effect, and the contract will remain as it originally stood, provided the nature and extent of the alteration can be clearly ascertained.

[As to alterations in bills and notes, see p. 327.]

Immaterial alterations. (18) — Whenever the alteration is immaterial, the contract is not vitiated. And when a deed *inter partes* is in progress of execution, and an alteration is made to meet the wishes of the parties who are about to execute it, such alteration, if it does not affect the operation of the deed with respect to the parties who have previously executed it, will not avoid the deed.

Evidence of alteration. — It lies upon the party suing upon an altered contract to account for any material alteration that appears upon the face of it.

Merger of contracts. (19) — If, after a simple contract has been entered into, a contract under seal is executed, for the performance of the same act or duty as that stipulated for by the simple contract, the simple contract becomes merged in the higher security, and can no longer be enforced, provided the contracts are between the same parties, and the remedies upon them are co-extensive.

If a contract has been broken, and judgment has been recovered upon the breach, the judgment is a bar to the original cause of action, which is changed into matter of record, and the inferior remedy is merged in the superior. If judgment is given for the defendant, such judgment operates as an estoppel against the plaintiff, and precludes him from maintaining a second action for the same cause.

Discharge by death. (20) — In contracts for personal services, it is an implied condition that the death of either party shall dissolve the contract.

An order of discharge in bankruptcy discharges the *Discharge by bankruptcy.* bankrupt from all debts and liabilities, present or future, certain or contingent (except demands in the nature of unliquidated damages arising otherwise than by reason of a contract), to which the bankrupt is subject at the date of the order of adjudication, or to which he may become subject during the continuance of the bankruptcy, by reason of any obligation incurred previously to the date of the order of adjudication. A certificate of discharge, under a liquidation by arrangement, has the same effect as an order of discharge in bankruptcy. (Bankruptcy Act, 1869, ss. 31—50, and s. 125).

The provision of a composition under the Bankruptcy *Composition with creditors. (21)* Act, accepted by an extraordinary resolution, will be binding on all the creditors, whose names and addresses, and the amount of the debts due to whom, are shown in the statement of the debtor, produced to the meeting at which the resolution is passed.

If the composition is not paid, the creditors may bring actions for their original debts; and if the composition is payable by instalments, and any instalment is not paid, they may sue for the balance of the original debt remaining unpaid.

By the 3 & 4 Will. IV. c. 27, it is enacted that all actions *The Statutes of Limitation.* brought for the recovery of rent by persons, not being ecclesiastical or eleemosynary corporations, shall be brought within twenty years after the right thereto has accrued to the plaintiff, or to the person through whom he claims. And as regards money secured by mortgage, judgment, or lien, or otherwise charged upon, or payable out of, land, no action shall be brought for the recovery thereof but within twenty years next after a present right to receive such money shall have accrued to some person capable of giving a discharge for the same, unless, in the meanwhile, some part of the principal money or interest thereon shall have been paid, or some acknowledgment of the right thereto shall have been given in writing, signed by the person by whom the same shall be payable, or his agent.

By the Real Property Limitation Act, 1874 (37 & 38 Vict. c. 57), which came into operation on January 1, 1879, the time for the recovery of rent, or money secured by mortgage, judgment, or lien, or otherwise charged upon land, is limited to twelve years instead of twenty years.

By sec. 16 of the 3 & 4 Will. IV. c. 27, persons labouring under the disabilities of infancy, coverture, and lunacy are allowed ten years (reduced by the Real Property Limitation Act, 1874, to six years) from the termination of their disability. But by sec. 17 of the former Act no such action can be brought but within forty years (reduced by the Real Property Limitation Act to thirty years) next after the right of action shall have first accrued.

By the 3 & 4 Will. IV. c. 42, all actions of debt for rent upon an indenture of demise, all actions of covenant or debt upon any bond or other specialty, and all actions of *scire facias* upon any recognisance, shall be commenced within twenty years after the cause of such actions, but not after. Actions for penalties, given by statute to parties aggrieved, within two years of such actions accruing.

And by the 3 & 4 Will. IV. c. 42, just cited, and by the 21 Jac. I. c. 16, and the 19 & 20 Vict. c. 97, six years is fixed as the limit within which must be brought actions of tort or of contract, other than those above referred to, except that in actions of assault, battery, wounding and imprisonment the period is reduced to four years, and in actions for slander to two years.

Under the three last-mentioned statutes, in cases of infancy, coverture and lunacy, the full period of limitation is allowed to run, commencing from the time of the removal of the disability before the right of action is barred. Imprisonment and absence beyond sea no longer have the effect of extending the period of limitation. [19 & 20 Vict. c. 97, s. 10.]

The 3 & 4 Will. IV. c. 27, as we have seen, requires that an acknowledgment, in order to take a case out of the operation of the statute, shall be in writing, and signed by the party making it, or his agent, and the 9 Geo. IV. c. 14, extends this provision to the case of actions upon simple contract debts.

ILLUSTRATIVE CASES.

(1) *Carter v. Ring*, 6 Campb. 459.

To an action of debt on a bond, conditioned for the payment of a sum of money, *on demand*, the defendant pleaded that no demand was made, and upon this issue was joined. Held, that to entitle him to succeed, the plaintiff must prove an express demand, before action brought.

Rumball v. Ball, 10 Mod. 38.

Action of debt upon a note to this effect, "I acknowledge myself indebted to such an one so much, which I promise to pay on demand." It was moved in arrest of judgment, that though upon a note acknowledging a debt it was not necessary to allege a demand; yet where it was part of the agreement, then a demand was necessary. Held, by the court, that no demand was necessary. This is a debt *in præsenti;* and the words, "promise to pay on demand," import no more than that I am ready to pay the money at any time, and do not restrain or qualify the other words, this being no debt arising upon the performance of a certain condition, but a debt plainly precedent to the demand.

Bowdell v. Parsons, 10 East 359.

In consideration of the purchase of hay by the plaintiff of the defendant, the latter promised to deliver to, and suffer the plaintiff to take it away as he wanted it, *when requested*. After suffering the plaintiff to take away a part, the defendant sold and disposed of the residue to other persons. Held, that this superseded the necessity of a request to deliver the residue.

(2) *Wild v. Harris*, 7 C.B. 1005.

A married man entered into mutual promises of marriage with a single woman, who was unaware of his prior marriage. Held, that the woman might recover damages against him for the non-performance of his contract, notwithstanding that its fulfilment would have been illegal.

Clifford v. Watts, L.R. 5 C.P. 585.

Willes, J.: "I am not prepared to say that there may not be cases in which a man may have contracted to do something which in the present state of scientific knowledge may be utterly impossible, and yet he may have so contracted as to warrant the possibility of its performance by means of some new discovery, or be liable in damages for its non-performance, and cannot set up by way of defence that the thing was impossible; but before we arrive at such a conclusion, we must be satisfied, if no other reasonable construction suggests itself, that the party really did intend to warrant that to be possible which was impossible."

Hochster v. *De la Tour*, 2 *El. & Bl.* 678.

Declaration on an agreement to employ plaintiff as courier, from a day subsequent to the date of the writ; averment that plaintiff, from the time of the agreement till the refusal by the defendant, after mentioned, was ready and willing to perform his part of the contract; breach, that before the day for the commencement of the employment, defendant refused to perform the agreement, and discharged plaintiff from performing it, and wrongfully put an end to the agreement. On motion in arrest of judgment—Held, that a party to an executory agreement may, before the time of executing it, break the agreement, either by disabling himself from fulfilling it, or by renouncing the contract; and that an action will lie for such breach before the time for the fulfilment of the agreement. That it sufficiently appeared on the face of the declaration, that there was on the part of the defendant, not merely an intention to break the contract, of which intention he might repent, but a renunciation communicated to plaintiff, on which plaintiff was entitled to act; and consequently that plaintiff was entitled to judgment.

Taylor v. *Caldwell*, 3 *B. & S.* 826.

Where, from the nature of a contract, it appears that the parties must from the beginning have known that it could not be fulfilled, unless when the time for the fulfilment of the contract arrived, some particular specified thing continued to exist, so that, when entering into the contract, they must have contemplated such continuing existence as the foundation of what was to be done; then, in the absence of any express or implied warranty that the thing shall exist, the contract is not to be construed as a positive contract, but as subject to an implied condition that the parties shall be excused, in case, before breach, performance becomes impossible from the perishing of the thing, without default of the contractor.

A. agreed with B. to give him the use of a music-hall on certain specified days, for the purpose of holding concerts. Before the time arrived, the music-hall was, accidentally, and without fault on either side, destroyed by fire. Held, that both parties were excused from performance of the contract.

Baily v. *Crespigny*, *L.R.* 4 *Q.B.* 180.

The defendant covenanted for himself and his assigns not to permit any messuage, &c., to be built on a certain piece of land, which was afterwards taken by a railway company, under their compulsory powers, and built upon. Held, that the defendant was not liable for the act of the railway company.

(3)   *Marquis of Hastings* v. *Thorley*, 8 *C. & P.* 573.

A tender, to be good, must not be made in terms which would cause the other party by taking the money to make an admission. The defendant, in tendering a sum of money, said: "I tender you £21 in payment of the half-year's rent due at Lady-day last." The amount of the half-year's rent amounted, in fact, to £23. Held, that the tender was bad because, by accepting the £21, the plaintiff would have been admitting that that sum was the amount of half a year's rent.

Manning v. *Lunn*, 2 *C. & K.* 13.

A. demanded £20 as rent due from B.; and B. having claimed certain deductions which A. would not allow, B. then put down twenty sovereigns, and said: "I tender you £20 under protest." Held, a good tender, as this was not a conditional tender, the words "under protest" merely importing that B. did not acquiesce in the demand of A., and did not mean to preclude himself from recovering the money back again, if he could.

Laing v. Meader, 1 C. & P. 257.

A plea of tender is not supported by proving that the defendant took a sum of money out of his pocket, and said to the plaintiff: "If you will give me a stamped receipt, I will pay you the money;" as by stat. 43 Geo. III. c. 126, the payer of money may provide the stamp, and charge for it; and a tender must always be unconditional.

(4) *In re London, Birmingham, &c., Banking Co.*, 34 Beav. 332.

A banking company, by its articles, had a first and paramount lien upon the shares of any shareholder "for all moneys due to the company from him." The bank held bills of a shareholder for a debt due to the bank. Held, that the amount of the bills was, before they arrived at maturity, "moneys due to the company," for which it had a lien on the shares, though the remedy for recovering the amount was postponed, and that, therefore, the lien of the bank had priority over a charge created on the shares by the shareholder before the bills arrived at maturity.

Sayer v. Wagstaff, 5 Beav. 415.

Where a debtor delivers to his creditor a promissory note for the amount of the debt, the debt may be considered as actually paid, if the creditor, at the time of receiving the note, has agreed to take it in payment of the debt, and to take upon himself the risk of the note being paid; or if, from the conduct of the creditor, or the special circumstances of the case, such an agreement is legally to be implied. But in the absence of any special circumstances, the transaction does not amount to a discharge of the original debt, but to a mere extended credit.

A solicitor delivered his bill of costs on October 14th, 1842, for which the client, on November 3rd, 1842, gave his promissory note, which was paid on November 17th, 1842. On November 15th, in the following year, the client presented a petition for the taxation of the bill; and upon the question arising, whether this application was made within twelve months, under 6 & 7 Vict. c. 73, s. 41, it became material to consider whether the costs should be treated as having been paid on November 3rd, or November 17th, 1842. Held, that they must be deemed to have been paid at the latter date and not the former.

Peacock v. Pursell, 14 C.B., N.S. 728.

A. received from B., as collateral security for a debt, a bill drawn by C. upon D., and at maturity failed to present it. Held that A.'s laches made the bill equivalent to payment as between A. and B.

(5) *Barrett v. Deere*, M. & M. 201.

To assumpsit for goods sold and delivered, the defendant pleaded payment. There had been disputes between the parties as to certain deductions claimed by the defendant, and the defendant sent W. A. to pay the undisputed amount, and ordered him to deliver, at the same time, a letter stating his objections to the items in dispute. W. A. stated that he went to the plaintiff's counting-house, that the counting-house had a part railed off, and that within this part he found a person sitting, with account books near him, and that he gave him the amount he was directed to pay, and the letter. The person to whom he gave the money and the letter, opened the letter, referred to some of the books, and then said he would say nothing as to the contents of the letter; that that question might remain open, but that he would give a receipt for the sum actually paid. He accordingly gave a receipt in the following form: "Received of J. D., Esq., £6 16s., for B. & Co.   "W. Long."

In fact, the plaintiff had no such person as W. Long in his employment, and the money never came to his hands; it was also proved that no one, except the plaintiff's son, usually sat in the counting-house, and that the money was not paid to him. The money originally in dispute had been paid into court, and the only question now was, whether there had been a good payment of the £6 16s. or not; and on the jury finding the above facts, it was held that the defendant was entitled to the verdict.

(6)   *Roper* v. *Bumford*, 3 *Taunt.* 76.

A landlord directed a tenant, who was overseer of the poor, to pay, on the landlord's account, rates assessed on him, and promised that the levies should eat out the rent. In an action against the tenant for use and occupation,—Held, that the tenant might set-off the levies, or prove them as payment.

(7)   *Simpson* v. *Eggington*, 10 *Exch.* 845.

The treasurer of a corporation paid their clerk (the defendant) the amount of his year's salary, both parties believing, at the time, that he had the authority of the corporation to make such payment; but the treasurer had no such authority, and the corporation afterwards repudiated the payment, and dismissed the defendant from their service. In an action against the defendant for the recovery of certain moneys paid to him on account of the corporation,—Held, that the corporation was entitled, at the trial, to ratify the act of their treasurer; and, consequently, that the defendant could not set-off the amount of his salary as due to him from the corporation.

(8)   *Edwards* v. *Baugh*, 11 *M. & W.* 641.

The declaration stated that disputes were pending between plaintiff and defendant, as to whether defendant was indebted to plaintiff in £173 2s. 6d. for money lent, &c., and that, in consideration that the plaintiff would promise defendant not to sue him for it, and would accept £100 in satisfaction, the defendant promised to pay him £100. Held, a bad declaration, on general demurrer. But, *per curiam*, the declaration would have been sufficient, had it shown some debt due, and a dispute as to the *amount*.

Sibree v. *Tripp*, 15 *M. & W.* 23.

In this case it was held, qualifying the decision in *Cumber* v. *Wane*, 1 *Str.* 426, and 1 *Sm. L.C.*, that a negotiable security may operate, if so given and taken, in satisfaction of a debt to a greater amount, the circumstance of negotiability making it, in fact, a different thing, and more advantageous than the original debt, which was not negotiable.

Thompson v. *Hudson*, *L.R.* 2 *Ch.* 255.

Judgment of Chelmsford, L.C. : " There can be no doubt that a creditor may agree to take less than the amount of his debt, provided payment is made by a particular day, and if the debtor fails of payment on that day, the creditor may recover the whole of his debt. So he may agree to take a mortgage for a less amount than is due to him, payable at a particular day, with a proviso that, if the money is not paid at the day, he shall be remitted to his original demand. But if the agreement is that the debtor shall pay part of the debt, and give a mortgage for the residue, and when the mortgage is prepared [as was the case here], a condition is introduced, forming no part of the original agreement, that if the mortgage money is not paid on the day mentioned in the deed, the creditor shall be entitled to recover the whole of his debt, I apprehend this would be in the nature of a penalty, which could not be enforced in equity."

Pfleger v. *Browne*, 28 Beav. 391.

Judgment of Romilly, M.R. : " It is no consideration for the release of a debt to take a portion of it. But one of the exceptions to this rule is the case of composition with creditors. It is an exception for this reason, that if a person makes a composition with his creditors, it is always assumed that each creditor acts upon the belief and assumption that the others will accept exactly the same amount [in the pound] as he takes, and nothing more."

(9)   *Skaife* v. *Jackson*, 3 B. & C. 421.

In assumpsit by two co-trustees, for money had and received to their use, the defendant produced a receipt for the money given by one of the plaintiffs. Held, that this was not conclusive, and that evidence was properly admitted to show that the giving of the receipt was a fraudulent transaction, and that the money had not been paid.

(10)   *Simson* v. *Ingham*, 2 B. & C. 72.

A bond was given by country bankers to the several persons constituting the firm of a London banking-house, conditioned for remitting money to provide for bills, and for the repayment of such sums, as the London bankers might advance, on account of persons constituting the firm of the country banking-house, or any of them, associated or not with other persons. One of the partners in the country bank died, a considerable balance being then due to the London bankers. It was the course of business between the two houses for the London bankers to send in to the country bankers monthly accounts of receipts and payments. In the month following the death of the deceased partner, the London bankers received sums in payment, more than sufficient to discharge the balance then due ; but during the same time they advanced money on account of the country bankers to an equal amount. In the first instance, the London bankers entered in their books all receipts and payments made after the death of the deceased partner to the account of the old firm, but they did not transmit any account to the country bankers, until two months after the death of the deceased partner, and then they transmitted two distinct accounts : one the account of the old firm, made up to the day of the death of the partner ; and another, a new account, containing all payments and receipts, subsequent to that time. Held, that the entries in the books of the London bankers did not amount to a complete appropriation by them of the several payments to the old account, such appropriation not being complete, until it was communicated to the party to be affected by it ; and, therefore, that the London bankers, notwithstanding those entries, were entitled to apply the payments received subsequently to the death of the deceased partner, to the debt of the new firm. [Compare *Bodenham* v. *Purchas*, 3 B. & Ald. 45.]

Philpott v. *Jones*, 2 Ad. & E. 41.

Plaintiff in an action of debt proceeded for £18, but delivered particulars of his demand, containing items to the amount of £11 for spirits supplied in quantities not amounting to 20s. at a time, and £23 2s. for other articles. It appeared at the trial that defendant had paid plaintiff £17, but there was no proof of any appropriation of the payment by either. The jury found that the plaintiff had appropriated £11 of the £17 already paid, to the demand for spirits, and they gave him a verdict for £17. Held, that such finding was not in contravention of 24 Geo. II. c. 40, s. 12, which prohibits any recovery for spirituous liquors, unless the debt shall have been contracted at one time to the amount of 20*s.* Taunton, J. : "The rule is that if a debtor pays money on account, and does not, at the time, state how it is to be applied, the creditor may make the appropriation. Here the £17 was paid, without any application to particular items of the account. The plaintiff might then apply that payment to the items in question ; and he was not bound to tell the defendant, at the time, that he made such application ; he might make it any time before the case came under the consideration of a jury. There is, therefore, no 'action maintained,' or 'recovery' for the spirits, in this case, according to the terms of the statute. The defendant, if he wished to avail himself of the Act, should have appropriated the payment at the time of making it."

(11) *Goss* v. *Nugent*, 5 *B. & Ad.* 58.

See judgment of Denman, C.J., p. 66, cited *supra*, pp. 181, 182.

(12) *Taylor* v. *Manners*, 35 *L.J., Ch.* 128.

A., being indebted to B., entered into an agreement, not under seal, for the repayment of the money, B. to hold a policy on A.'s life as security. B. died, and her executors reckoned the debt among her assets, and paid probate and legacy duty upon it. Communications took place between the debtor and the executors, on the one hand, and the executors and the residuary legatee, on the other hand, as to not enforcing the debt, upon payment by the debtor of the probate and legacy duty thereon. The debtor did, in fact, pay such duties, and the executors withdrew their claim on the policy, but neither was the agreement surrendered to A., nor cancelled, nor was any release of his debt executed. Held, by Lord Justice Turner, that the communications amounted to an agreement to release the debt. Lord Justice Knight-Bruce, not dissenting, but doubting whether "such a payment, as had been made of the duty, could stand on a better footing than a payment by a debtor to a creditor of a less sum than the whole debt."

Yeomans v. *Williams*, 35 *L.J., Ch.* 283.

Where a father-in-law, to whom his son-in-law owed money upon a mortgage of the house in which the son-in-law lived, wrote to the latter, dissuading him from selling the house to pay off the debt, and saying, " Have you paid me a penny since you had the money ? You can live there just as you do, without paying us any rent ; it is not wished that you should give it up." Held, on bill for redemption, filed by the son-in-law after his father-in-law's death, that he was only liable for the interest which accrued after the father-in-law's death.

(13) *Pinnell's Case*, 5 *Rep.* 117.

Resolved by the whole court, that payment of a lesser sum, on the day, in satisfaction of a greater, cannot be any satisfaction for the whole ; but the gift of a horse, hawk, or robe, &c., in satisfaction is good. For it shall be intended that a horse, hawk, or robe, &c., might be more beneficial to the plaintiff than the money, in respect of some circumstance, or, otherwise, the plaintiff would not have accepted of it in satisfaction.

Cooper v. *Parker*, 15 *C.B.* 822.

Held, that payment of a smaller sum, with an agreement to abandon a defence and pay costs, might be pleaded in satisfaction of a larger demand, whether liquidated or unliquidated.

Evans v. *Powis*, 1 *Exch.* 601.

Two counts by drawer against acceptor of two bills of exchange for £30 and £41 16s. The defendant pleaded as to £13 3s. 2d., parcel of the sum of £30 in the first count, and also as to the second count, that he, the defendant, was in embarrassed circumstances, and indebted to the plaintiff in respect of two causes of action, in the introductory part of the plea mentioned, in the sum of £54 19s. 2d., and to one B. in a certain other sum of money, and was unable to pay the plaintiff and B. their debts in full, and thereupon the defendant agreed with the plaintiff and B. to pay them respectively, and the plaintiff and B. then mutually agreed with each other and the defendant to accept of him 10s. in the pound, as a composition upon, and in full satisfaction and discharge of, their respective debts. The plea then averred readiness and willingness to pay, with a tender of the amount of the composition, and concluded with payment of it into court. The plaintiff replied, traversing the agreement to accept the composition of 10s. in the pound in satisfaction and discharge, upon which issue was joined. At the trial, the agreement proved was to accept a composition of 10s. in the pound, *payable in certain sums, on certain days*. It also appeared that default had been made in payment of the instalments. The learned judge, at the request of the defendant's counsel, amended the plea accordingly. Held, that the plea, as amended, was bad, even after verdict, for not stating that the payments, or at least tenders of payment, were made at the precise times agreed on. *Semble*, that, if the plea had been that a new mutual agreement between plaintiff, defendant, and other creditors, binding on each at the time when it was made, was given as a substitution for, or in satisfaction of, the debt due from the defendant to the plaintiff, such plea would have been good, and in that case it would have been for the jury to decide whether the plaintiff agreed to accept the *agreement* itself, not the performance of it, as a satisfaction for his debt. [See *infra*, (21)].

(14) *Foster* v. *Dawber*, 6 *Exch.* 839.

The defendant, having borrowed of his father-in-law £1000, at 4 per cent. interest, gave his promissory note for the repayment of the amount. The father-in-law subsequently said he would make him a present of the £1000, and got a 10s. receipt stamp, and signed a receipt for the £1000, and interest, and handed it to the defendant; but after that, made a will bequeathing the promissory note to his executors. Held, that although the giving of the receipt did not amount to payment, nevertheless the defendant was discharged from all liability on the note; since, by the law merchant, there may be a release and discharge of a debt due on a bill of exchange, by word of mouth; and promissory notes are by statute put on the same footing as bills.

(15) *Walker* v. *Nevill*, 3 *H. & C.* 403.

A simple covenant, in a composition deed, not to sue for a limited time, is not pleadable in bar of an action, but is itself subject for a cross action, if broken. But a covenant not to sue for a limited time, " and that the deed may be pleaded in bar and discharge of any action brought within that time," may be pleaded in bar of an action, brought either by an assenting or a non-assenting creditor.

Ayloff v. *Scrimpshire*, *Carth.* 64.

" A letter of licence containing the words following—viz., 'that if the creditor sue, &c., within such a time that his debt shall be forfeited,' such licence is pleadable in bar."

(16) *Lacy* v. *Kinaston*, 1 Ld. Raym. 688.

A contract, defeasanced as to one of many joint and several creditors, is defeasanced as to all. An undertaking from a man, with whom many persons have entered into a joint and several contract, to indemnify one of them, is not a defeasance, though an undertaking to indemnify a sole contractor is.

Union Bank of Manchester v. *Beech*, 3 H. & C. 672.

A surety by deed guaranteed the payment of a banking current account, and agreed that no composition with the principal debtor should discharge his liability. The principal debtor entered into a deed of composition with his creditors, which contained an absolute release of his debts. Held, that the surety was not discharged by the release of the principal debtor.

Willis v. *De Castro*, 27 Law J., C.P. 243.

To a declaration for goods bargained and sold, the defendant pleaded that the cause of action accrued to the plaintiff against the defendant and A., B. and C. jointly, and not otherwise, and that the defendant was not separately liable, and that the plaintiff by deed released A., B. and C. from the cause of action. Replication, that the deed was a deed of assignment from A., B. and C. of their estate and effects, for the benefit of their creditors, and contained words purporting, if considered without reference to other parts of the deed, to release, as in the plea pleaded, but that, in another and earlier part of the same deed, it was agreed as follows :—" That it shall be lawful for the creditors to execute these presents, without prejudice to any mortgage, lien, or security which they may have for their respective debts, or any part thereof, or to any claim against any surety or sureties, or any other person or persons who may be liable for the payment thereof." That all the creditors, who executed the deed, executed without prejudice as aforesaid. Held, on demurrer to the replication, that construing the deed as pleaded in the plea, with the qualification introduced by the replication, it amounted only to a covenant not to sue, and not to a release, and that the liability of the defendant was reserved, whether it was originally joint only, or joint and several.

(17) *Henfrey* v. *Bromley*, 6 East 309.

After an award, made under the hand of an umpire, and ready for delivery, pursuant to the terms of reference, of which notice was given to the parties, an alteration by the umpire of the sum awarded, though made on the same day, and before delivery of the award, is void ; but the award is good for the original sum awarded, which was still legible, the same as if such alteration had been made by a mere stranger, without the privity or consent of the party interested. Ellenborough, C.J. : " I consider the alteration of the award by the umpire, after his authority was at an end, the same as if it had been made by a stranger, by a mere spoliator. And I still read it with the eyes of the law, as if it were an award, for the sum at which it originally stood. If the alteration had been made *by a person who was interested in the award*, I should have felt myself pressed by the objection ; but I can no more consider this as avoiding the instrument than if it had been obliterated or cancelled by accident."

(18) *Hutchins* v. *Scott*, 2 M. & W. 816.

By an agreement between the plaintiff and defendant, a house, No. 38, was let to the plaintiff. After the agreement was executed, and delivered to the plaintiff, it was altered (it was not proved by whom) by erasing the figure 8 and substituting 5. The house occupied by the plaintiff was, in fact, No. 35. Held, that the alteration was not material, and that the altered agreement might be given in evidence in an action for an excessive distress.

Lewis v. *Bingham*, 4 B. & Ald. 676.

By deed a mortgagee conveyed to the mortgagor the legal estate, upon being paid the mortgage money, and the latter reconveyed it to trustees, for the purpose of securing an annuity. At the time of the execution by the mortgagee, there were several blanks in the deed, but not in that part which affected him. The blanks left were for the sums to be received by the mortgagor from the grantees of the annuity, and were all filled up, at the time of the execution of the deed by the mortgagor; and several interlineations were made in that part of the deed, after the execution by the mortgagee. Held, that the deed was not therefore void, but operated as a good conveyance of the estate from the mortgagor to the trustees for the payment of the annuity.

(19)   *Ansell* v. *Baker*, 15 Q.B. 20.

One of two makers of a joint and several promissory note gave the holder a deed of mortgage to secure the amount, with a covenant to pay it. Held, that the other maker was not thereby discharged ; for the remedy on the specialty was not co-extensive with the remedy on the note.

King v. *Hoare*, 13 M. & W. 494.

A judgment (without satisfaction) recovered against one of two *joint* debtors, Held a bar to an action against the other: otherwise when the debt is *joint and several.*

Vooght v. *Winch*, 2 B. & Ald. 662.

A verdict obtained by the defendant in a former action is an estoppel, if pleaded in bar, but if it is merely given in evidence under the general issue, it is not conclusive against the plaintiff, but is only evidence to go to the jury.

(20)   See *Farrow* v. *Wilson*, L.R. 4 C.P. 744.

(21)   *In re Hatton*, L.R. 7 Ch. 723.

Where by resolutions under the Bankruptcy Act, 1869, the creditors agreed to accept a composition payable by instalments, and the debtor made default in payment of an instalment to a creditor,—Held, that the creditor could maintain an action against the debtor for the balance of the whole debt remaining unpaid, and would not be restrained by the Court of Bankruptcy. Mellish, L.J. : " At common law, when a body of creditors accept a composition, they may either agree to take the *promise* of the debtor, with or without a surety, in satisfaction of the debts, or they may agree that payment shall be a condition precedent. There is nothing in the Bankruptcy Act to alter this state of things. There may be, as in this case a simple composition, which the creditors agree to accept if paid to the day."

INDEX.

ABANDONMENT,   PAGE
    in cases of marine insurance 305
        notice of . . . . *ib.*

ABATEMENT.
    See NUISANCE.

ABSENCE,
    effect of, under Statute of Limitations . . 11

ACCEPTANCE,
    of offers through post 153
    of part of a debt in satisfaction of the whole . . . 155, 370
    of bills of exchange 319

ACCEPTANCE AND ACTUAL RECEIPT,
    of goods within the Statute of Frauds 166, 261
    articles taken on trial or for inspection 262
    constructive acceptance and receipt . . . . *ib.*
        delivery by vendor to carrier 263
    of delivery orders and dock warrants . . . . *ib.*
    part acceptance and actual receipt . . . . . *ib.*
    effect of acceptance . . . . *ib.*

ACCEPTOR,
    of bill of exchange, liability of . 321
    days of grace 959
    See BILL OF EXCHANGE.

ACCOMMODATION BILLS AND NOTES,
    right of acceptor, maker, or indorser of, to be indemnified . 324
    when holder is bound to prove that he gave value . . . 327

ACCORD AND SATISFACTION,
    discharge by 370
    composition deeds and agreements . . 369, 373

INDEX.

ACKNOWLEDGMENT OF DEBTS,
  contracted during infancy . . .   169
  extending period of limitation . . .   373—375
  authentication of   375

ACT OF GOD,
  loss by . . .   234

ACT OF PARLIAMENT,
  contract in contravention of   338

ADMINISTRATOR,
  rights and liabilities of   359
  promise by, to answer damages out of his own estate . .   163
  de bonis non   360

ADULTERY,
  damages recoverable for   147
  effect of, on contract of married woman   186
  See HUSBAND AND WIFE.

ADVOCATE,
  statements of, in conduct of case, privileged .   119

AGENT,
  contracts with   194
  rights of principals upon   195
    concealment of agency   196
    rights of undisclosed principals . . . .   *ib.*
  rights of principals upon deeds made by agents . .   197
  ratification by principal   194
  revocation of authority . . . . . .   *ib.*
  misrepresentation by agents   195
  warranties by agents . . . .   *ib.*
  purchases by a servant in name of his master . . .   *ib.*
  authority of foremen and managers . . . .   *ib.*
  rights and liabilities of agents on simple contracts . .   196, 197
    notoriety of agency   197
    public officers . . . .   *ib.*
  liabilities of agents on contracts under seal . .   *ib.*
  signature by, under Statute of Frauds   168
  payments through   368
  sales by   198
  indemnification of . . . .   *ib.*

AGENCY,
  contract of   194
    accounting   197
    liabilities of brokers and factors . . .   198
    del credere commissions   197
    payment of commission   198

AGISTER,
  of cattle, liabilities of   233

INDEX.

AGREEMENTS.
    See CONTRACT.

AIR,
	PAGE
grant of right of	45
See LIGHT.	

ALIEN ENEMY,
contracts with	188, 344

ALIMONY.
    See WIFE.

ALTERATION OF CONTRACTS,
release by	371
material and immaterial	ib.
evidence to explain	ib.
of principal obligation discharging surety	292
of bills and notes	327

AMBIGUITY,
latent, or patent	176

AMENDS,
tender of, under statute	96

ANCESTOR,
liability of heir-at-law upon covenants of	358

ANCHORS,
sale of	341

ANIMALS,
injuries from keeping ferocious	30
damages in actions for keeping ferocious	35
right to possession of, *feræ naturæ*	72
trespasser by	18
feræ naturæ not distrainable for rent	64

APPRENTICESHIP,
contracts of	221
liabilities of parties to	ib.
dissolution of	ib.

APPROPRIATION,
of payments	369

ARBITRATION,
agreement to submit disputes to	343

ARBITRATOR,
services of, gratuitous	224

ARREST,

	PAGE
on suspicion of felony	94
for felony, without warrant	ib.
of wrong person	95
for malicious injuries to property	ib.
by servants of railway companies	96
for preservation of peace	93, 94
of soldiers, by superior officer	2
by persons intending to act in pursuance of Act of Parliament	96

ART,

oral evidence to explain terms of	186

ARTIFICERS,

lien of	242
See WORK AND SERVICES.	

ASSAULT,

what constitutes	92
in self-defence, or in obedience to legal warrant	93
in resistance of forcible entry	ib.
by handcuffing unconvicted prisoner	92
distinction between, and battery	ib.
mayhem and wounding	93
on persons wrongfully in possession of land	ib.
by servants of a corporation	96
who to be plaintiffs in action for	ib.
plea of *son assault demesne*	93

ASSENT,

conditional, oral evidence of	177

ASSIGNMENT,

of debts and *choses in action*	356
of policies of life insurance	309
of fire insurance	307
of copyright	169
of securities by creditor to a surety	294

ATTORNEY.

See SOLICITOR.

AUCTION,

sale by	256
puffers	257
without reserve	ib.
conditions and particulars	ib.

AUCTIONEER,

right of, on sales made by him	196
authority of, as agent for both vendor and purchaser	169

AUTHENTICATION,

of contracts under seal, *see* DEED	161
of contracts by joint-stock companies	214

INDEX. 389

AUTHENTICATION—*continued.*   PAGE
    of simple contracts 163
    of executory contracts for the sale of goods . . . 166, 261
        requisites 167
        signature 168
    of promises made by infants 169
    of acknowledgments to bar the Statute of Limitations . . *ib.*
    of leases 165

AUTHORITY,
    false representation of 136
    abuse of, rendering a person a trespasser 21
    acts beyond scope of 104
    of agents to make contracts 194
        revocation of . . . . *ib.*

AVERAGE,
    in cases of insurance 306

AVOIDANCE,
    of contracts, on the ground of fraud 345
        of duress 346
        of mistake . . . . *ib.*

BAILEE,
    conversion of goods by 70
    has no better title than his bailor . . . . . *ib.*
    determination of bailment by . . . . . . *ib.*
    may sue for damage or loss to goods in his possession . . *ib.*
    may compel rival claimants to interplead . . . . *ib.*
    insurance by, against fire 306

BAILIFF,
    responsibility of 108
    See SHERIFF.

BAILMENT,
    gratuitous 231
        liabilities of borrower . . . . . . *ib.*
        deposit or simple bailment . . . . . *ib.*
        mandate or gratuitous commission . . . . *ib.*
    bailment for hire 232
        losses from negligence 233
        losses from robbery . . . . *ib.*
        of materials to workmen 232
    See CARRIERS—WAREHOUSEMEN.

BAILOR,
    when may sue for damage caused to thing bailed . . . 70
    liability of, for not disclosing dangerous nature of goods bailed . 4

BANKER,   PAGE
    refusal by, to cash customer's cheque . . 2
    payment of cheque by 325
    payment by, of forged cheques 326
    crossed cheques 327
    lien of 243

BANK NOTE,
    payment with stolen . 327

BANKRUPT ACTS,
    contracts in contravention of the . 342

BANKRUPTCY,
    malicious proceedings in, when actionable . . . 101
    title to property of bankrupt passes to trustee . . . 73
        onerous property may be disclaimed by trustee . . ib.
    dealings with bankrupt without notice of, valid . . ib.
    execution levied on property when an act of . . 110
    goods in reputed ownership of bankrupt . . . 73
    apparent possession under Bills of Sale Act . . 74
    payment to bankrupt 368
    transfer of executory contracts of . . . 360
    contracts with undischarged bankrupt . . . 361
    release of bankrupt by composition . . . 373
    discharge of bankrupt . . . . . ib.
    liquidation by arrangement . . . . ib.
    effect of an adjudication in 360
        transfer of executory contracts . . . . ib.
        sale of property of which bankrupt was reputed owner . ib.
        sale of bankrupt's book debts, goodwill, &c. . 361
    rights and liabilities of undischarged bankrupts . . ib.
    liability of trustee on executory contracts . . . ib.
        disclaimer by trustee . . . . . ib.
    bills of sale and mortgages constituting an act of . . 282
    bankruptcy of purchaser of chattels before payment . . 266

BARRATRY,
    insurance against . . . 303

BARRISTERS,
    not liable for negligence unless malicious or fraudulent . 82
    honorary character of services of 224
    See ADVOCATE.

BATTERY.
    See ASSAULT.

BEACH.
    See SEA-SHORE.

BENEFICE,
    purchase of . . . 339

INDEX.

BETTING.
    See GAMING.

BILL OF EXCHANGE,
	PAGE
title to	72
given to secure money lost or lent at play	340
recovery of money paid upon forged	226
payment by	367
renunciation of, by parol	370
transfer by indorsement and delivery	318
restrictive indorsement	321
who is *bonâ fide* holder by	320
intermediate infirmities of title	321
when holder must prove he gave value	ib.
accommodation bills	324
acceptance of bills	319
presentment for acceptance	322
liability of acceptor	321
failure of consideration	ib., 327
liability of drawer and indorser	322
giving time for payment	ib.
presentment for payment	ib.
days of grace	323
notice of dishonour	ib.
dispensation of	324
transfer by delivery without indorsement	319
payment and satisfaction of	327
bills taken up *supra protest*	324
retiring of bills	ib.
bills and notes for sums under £1	325
bankers' cheques	ib.
alteration of bills	327
loss of bills and notes	ib.

BILL OF LADING,
acceptance of	263
shipment of goods under	265
countermand of delivery under	266
transfer of	268

BILL OF SALE,
when goods under, are in apparent possession of bankrupt	74, 282, 360
fraudulent	282
of ships	169
of goods and chattels	281
of after-acquired property	282
registration of	281

BOARD AND LODGING.
    See LODGING-HOUSE KEEPER.

BONDS,
transfer of, by death	359
to secure faithful services	292
to secure repayment of advances	291

392 INDEX.

BOUGHT AND SOLD NOTES, PAGE
    signature of, by brokers . . . 169

BOUNDARY WALLS,
    property in 14

BRIDGE,
    obligation of railway company to maintain . 31

BROKERS,
    agency of 169
    rights and liabilities of 198

BYE-LAWS,
    under a statute must strictly follow the statute. . . 7
    imposing penalties . . . . *ib.*
    convictions for breaking 105

BYGONE SERVICES,
    rendered at previous request of promisor . 154

CANAL,
    right to soil of towing paths of 14
    duty of canal company to take reasonable precautions 32
    canal company when bound to fence . . . . *ib.*

CAPTURE,
    loss by 303

CARRIAGE,
    defective construction of . . . 81

CARRIERS,
    delivery of goods to 265
    delivery under bill of lading 267
    carriage of passengers 237
    See COMMON CARRIERS.

CATTLE,
    trespasses by 17, 22
    straying on highway 17, 18
    straying from highways 17, 31
    injuries to, from getting on railway . . . *ib.*
    injuries to, by dogs 30
    trespass by driving or striking 74
    sale of diseased 2
    impounded, must be fed 23
    agistment of 233
    See ANIMALS.

INDEX.

CERTIORARI,
    lies to remove proceedings of justices acting without or in excess of jurisdiction 105

CHAIN CABLES,
    illegal sale of . . 341

CHAMPERTY,
    avoidance of contracts by reason of . . 343

CHANCEL,
    title to, is in rector . . . 15

CHARACTER,
    evidence of, in actions of seduction . 149

CHASTITY,
    reflections on, when actionable 116

CHEQUE,
    payment of, by banker 325
    payment of forged 326
    crossed . . . . *ib.*
    presentment of . . . . *ib.*

CHILDREN,
    father entitled to custody of 146
    subject to controlling power of Court of Chancery and Divorce Court in certain cases . . . . *ib.*
    injuries to, or seduction of . . . . *ib.*
    abduction of, a misdemeanour 149

CHOSES IN ACTION,
    assignment of 356
    husband's right to wife's 185

CHURCH, CHURCHYARD,
    title to, is in rector, but possession in incumbent 15

CLERK OF THE PEACE,
    report by, to Quarter Sessions 118

CLUB COMMITTEES,
    contracts with 215

COACH,
    accidents to, from overturning 81
    injuries from negligent driving of . . . . *ib.*
    hirer of, when liable for negligence in driving . . 84

394 INDEX.

COALS,
  sale of   340

COLLISION,
  liability of ship-owners for damage caused by   86

COMMISSIONERS,
  for enclosing lands   13
  duties of commissioners of wharves and docks . .   32
  cannot create a nuisance   33

COMMODATUM,
  or gratuitous loan .   .   .   231

COMMON,
  rights of 47, 48
  obstructions to 20, 21

COMMON CARRIER,
  who is   233
  nature and extent of duties   234
  public profession by medium of time tables . . .   238
  contracts for carriage of passengers   237
  limitation of liability by notice   235
      Common Carriers Act   234
  limitation of liability by special contract   236
      unjust and unreasonable conditions in special
       contract . . . .   *ib.*
      liability of railway company during sea transit .   237
  losses occasioned by negligence of consignor . . .   *ib.*
  acceptance of goods to be carried beyond the carrier's limit .   238
  carrier's lien   242
  luggage carried by excursion trains   238
  parties to be made plaintiffs in actions against   245

COMPANY.
  See JOINT-STOCK COMPANY.

COMPOSITION DEEDS,
  with creditors   373

COMPOUNDING FELONIES,
  contracts for   343

CONDITIONAL ASSENT,
  admissibility of oral evidence of   .   .   177

CONDITIONAL TENDER   367

CONDITIONS PRECEDENT,
  to payment for work and services   .   .   223

INDEX.   395

CONDITIONS OF SALE,   PAGE
    in auctions. . .   257

CONSENT OF PARTIES,
    discharge by . .   370

CONSIDERATION,
    good and valuable   154
    failure of   156
    moral obligation   155
    forbearance of legal rights. . . . . .   ib.
    unilateral promises   156
    mutual promises . . . .   ib.
    contracts with infants . . . . . .   ib.
    statement of, in guarantees 164, 292
    failure of, in case of bills and notes . . .   321, 327

CONSPIRACY,
    action lies for, if malicious, and damage ensues .   100

CONSTABLE,
    may take person guilty of assault into custody   94
    cannot arrest without warrant, except for felony, or reasonable
      suspicion of felony. . . . .   ib.
    is liable for handcuffing unconvicted prisoners . . .   92
    distinction between arrest by, and by private person for felony . 94
    protection of, where they intended to act in pursuance of an Act
      of Parliament.   96

CONTEMPT OF COURT,
    what is, and committal for   106

CONTINUING BREACHES,
    of real covenants   359

CONTINUING GUARANTEES.
    See GUARANTEE.

CONTRACT,
    definition   153
    unilateral   156
    by matter of record   161
    by deed . . . .   ib.
    parol   163
    consideration for   154
        mutuality of   156
    with married women   185
    by implication of law   154
    with agents   195
    with partners   206
    with corporations   212
    with joint-stock companies   214

CONTRACT—continued.

	PAGE
authentication of, by signed writing	163
sale of growing crops	165
interpretation of	175
illegal	337
performance	366
release	370
accord and satisfaction	ib.
discharge by bankruptcy	373
limitation of suit	ib
assignment of	356
transfer by death	358
by bankruptcy	360
for sale of lands	256
of goods and chattels	259
bailment for hire	232
gratuitous bailment	231
taskwork	222
hiring and service	218
apprenticeship	221
common carriers	233
pledge	283
suretyship	290
marine insurance	299
fire insurance	306
life insurance	307
bills of exchange	318
of partnership	204
torts founded on	3, 4
entered into under false representation	136

CONTRIBUTION,

between shareholders	214
between co-sureties	293

CONTRIBUTORIES,

parties liable to be made	215
limitation of liability of	ib.

CONTRIBUTORY NEGLIGENCE . . 85, 86

CONVERSION,

of chattels	74
refusal to deliver goods	75
sale of goods before a stipulated time	ib.
obtaining goods by abuse of legal process	ib.
when demand and refusal necessary to prove	ib.
by one partner, joint tenant, or tenant in common	73
of trust property	74
of property of bankrupt	73
distinction between, and trespass	74
remedy for, by reception or action	75
damages in actions for	76
effect of judgment for, in altering the property	71

INDEX. 397

CONVICTS,
    contracts with 189

CONVOY,
    stipulation as to sailing with 301

COPYHOLDER,
    cannot prescribe in his own name . . . 47
    waste by, when a forfeiture 59

COPYRIGHT,
    in lectures, or dramatic or musical compositions . 6
    in prints and engravings . . . . . *ib.*
    in useful and ornamental designs . . . 7
    in books 6, 7

CORPORATION,
    liability of, for assault 96
    indictment against 36
    contracts with 212
        with trading corporations . . . 213
    contracts with joint-stock companies . . . 214

CO-SURETIES.
    See CONTRIBUTION, GUARANTEE.

COUNTY COURT JUDGE,
    may commit for contempt 106
    entitled to notice of action . . . . *ib.*

COURT MARTIAL,
    no action lies for malicious proceedings before . 101

COVENANT,
    rights of lien upon 358
        of executors and administrators upon . 359
    running with the land, requisites of . . . 358
        privity of estate and privity of contract . 357
    not to sue 371

COVERTURE,
    liability of women under 185

CREDIT,
    sale of goods on 266

CREDITOR,
    payment according to direction of . . . 369

CROPS AND GROWING PRODUCE,
    sale of 165

CROWD,
    collection of, a nuisance . . 27

CRUELTY.
    See HUSBAND AND WIFE.

CUSTOM,
    conventional servitudes may arise by 44
    must be reasonable and have existed from time immemorial . 46
    right of common claimable by 47
    to search for tin in Cornwall . . . . . . *ib.*
    easements acquired by 47, 48
    and usage, oral evidence of 176
    influence of, upon meaning of words 177
    in the case of policies 302

DAMAGES,
    too remote 2
    in actions for false representation 137
        of libel and slander 122
        of trespass to realty 21
            if wilful and after notice . . . 22
        of trespass and conversion 76
            in actions between bailee and owner . . *ib.*
            if goods have been delivered up . . . *ib.*
        of reduction 149
    when statute imposes a penalty 6, 7
    in actions against sheriff 110
        for malicious prosecution 101
        for unlawful or excessive distress . . . 66
        for negligence 86
        for injuries from ferocious animals . . . 35
        for nuisances . . . . . . *ib.*
    in Divorce Court 147
    appointment between tenant and reversioner . . . 60
    exemplary 22, 86, 110
    for breach of contract for sale of realty 257
    non-performance of contract for sale of goods . . . 268
    wrongful dismissal 220
    actions against apprentices 221
        against carriers 245
    mitigation of, in actions of libel and slander . . . 122
        in actions of seduction 149

DAYS OF GRACE,
    in fire and life insurance 309
    on bills and notes 323

DEATH,
    negligence causing 86
    discharge of contracts by 372
    transfer of contracts by 358
    of master 220
    of partner 207
    of husband 187

INDEX. 399

DECEIT.
    See FRAUD—FALSE REPRESENTATION.

DEDICATION.
    See HIGHWAY.

DEED,
	PAGE
authentication by	161
delivery of, as *escrow*	162
inter partes and deed poll	ib.
made by agents	197
estoppel by	162
when required	ib.

DELAY,
in performance of voyage	305

DELIVERY,
of bill without indorsement	322
of deed	161
as an *escrow*	162
of goods to carriers	265
by carriers	238
actual and constructive	266
non-delivery	268

DELIVERY ORDER,
transfer of possession of goods by	263

DEMAND,
when to be proved in actions of conversion	75
of performance	366

DEPOSIT,
money deposited to abide a wager	339
recovery of, on sale of land	258

DESERTION.
    See HUSBAND AND WIFE.

DESIGN.
    See COPYRIGHT.

DEVIATION,
in a voyage	304

DIRECTORS,
false representation by	133, 215
of projected undertakings	215

DISABILITIES,
of infants	183
married women	185

DISABILITIES—*continued*.   PAGE
 drunkards and lunatics 188
 aliens . . . . *ib.*
 convicts and outlaws 189
 temporary, extending Statute of Limitations . . 374

DISCHARGE,
 of apprentices 221
 of contracts before breach 370
   of bill of exchange . . . . *ib.*
   by accord and satisfaction . . . *ib.*
   by acceptance of securities . . . 367
   by operation of law 371
   by bankruptcy 373
   by death 372

DISCLAIMER,
 by trustee in bankruptcy . . . 361

DISHONOUR,
 notice of 323
  dispensation of . . 324

DISMISSAL,
 of servants for incompetency . . . 219
   for misconduct . . . *ib.*
 wrongful dismissal 220

DISSOLUTION,
 of partnership 207
 notice of 208
 of joint-stock companies 214

DISTRESS,
 at common law a pledge 23
 distrainor must be entitled to immediate reversion . . . 63
 as, power of, against wrong-doer . . . . . *ib.*
 bankrupt tenant . . . . *ib.*
 must not be repeated vexatiously 65
 right of, may be conditional 64
 rent payable in advance . . . . . . *ib.*
 illegal, may be resisted by force 65
 under a licence 64
 what amounts to . . . . *ib.*
 abuse of, renders landlord a trespasser . . . 65
 excessive . . . . *ib.*
 time, mode, and place of . . . . . . *ib.*
 what things are distrainable and what are not . . . 64, 65
 impounding and removal of 66
 unlawful after tender of rent 65
 remedy for wrongful replevin 66
 of goods of lodgers 65
 damage feasant 22, 23

DITCHES,
 boundary, property in 14

DIVIDEND WARRANTS,
 transfer of 328

DIVISIBLE CONTRACTS 223, 344

DIVORCE.
 See HUSBAND AND WIFE.

DOCK,
 negligent management of . . 32

DOCK WARRANT,
 assignment of 263, 328

DOG,
 injuries from attacks of 30
 injury by, to crops 18
 injury to, from traps 27
 when, may be distrained for trespassing 22

DOMESTIC SERVANTS 219

DORMANT PARTNER . . . 205

DRAIN,
 not to be so kept as to constitute a nuisance 27

DRAWER,
 of bill of exchange, liability of . . . 322

DRUNKARD,
 contracts with 188

EARNEST AND PART PAYMENT,
 nature and effect of, in contracts of sale . . . 263

EASEMENT,
 how acquired 44
 when acquired over land let on lease 48
 presumption of lost grant . . . . . *ib.*
 claimed under Prescription Act . . . . . 47—49
 user to be without interruption 51
 of recreation and amusement 49
 of support 45

D D

402 INDEX.

EASEMENT—*continued.* PAGE
    cannot be created by licence 46
    extinguishment of, by unity of possession 50
    reservation of, on sale 46
    of necessity 45

EAVES,
    discharge of water from 45

ECCLESIASTICAL DILAPIDATIONS,
    liability of incumbent to repair 58
    law as to, by statute 59

ENCLOSURE ACT,
    title to highways laid out under 13

ENEMIES,
    contracts with 189

ENTRY,
    peaceable and forcible 19, 93

ESTOPPEL,
    by deed 162, 178
    in pais 178

EVIDENCE,
    of title to realty 11
    of title to goods and chattels 71
    of malice 101
    in mitigation of damages 122, 149
    inadmissibility of oral, to alter written contract . . . 175
    oral, in aid of insufficient written contract . . . 177
    oral, of custom and usage 176
    oral, of conditional assent 177
    discharge of contract before breach by oral agreement . 178, 370
    oral renunciation of claims on bills 370
    oral, to explain alterations 372

EXECUTION.
    See SHERIFF.

EXECUTORS AND ADMINISTRATORS,
    authentication of promises by 164
    rights and liabilities of 359
    continuation of chain of representation . . . *ib.*
    administration *de bonis non* 360

EXECUTORY CONTRACT,
    authentication of 166
    transfer of, by death 359
    of bankrupts 360

FACTOR.
    See AGENT.

FAIR,
    interference with, how far a tort . . . 3

FAILURE OF CONSIDERATION 156

FALSE IMPRISONMENT.
    See ARREST, CONSTABLE.

FALSEHOOD,
    causing damage is actionable 132

FALSE AND FRAUDULENT REPRESENTATION,
    when actionable 2, 132
    by directors of companies 133, 215
    by agents 195
    avoiding contracts 345
    by insurers 301, 309
    in fraud of surety 293
    respecting conduct and credit of third persons . . 132, 134
    fraudulent breach of warranty 133
    respecting matters lying equally within knowledge of both parties 135
    to sheriffs as to ownership of goods . . . 108
    as to title, when one does not sell as owner . . 109
    by manufacturers 135
    by vendors of an article required for a specific purpose . *ib.*
        to absent purchasers . . . . *ib.*
        on sale of goods by sample . . . *ib.*
    of authority by vendors, agents, &c. . . . 136
    when principal liable for 137
    concealment of defects 135
        though goods sold "with all faults" . . 136
    damages for 137
    remedy in equity . . . . . . *ib.*
    indictment for . . . . . . *ib.*

FELONY.
    criminal proceedings for, to be taken before civil . . 5
    conspiracy to charge a person with . . . 100
    arrest for, when justifiable without a warrant . . 94, 95

FEME COVERT.
    See WIFE.

FENCES,
    duty of railway to maintain 31
    trespass by cattle from want of 17, 31
    boundary, property in 14

FERÆ NATURÆ.
    See ANIMALS.

404   INDEX.

FERRY,
    interference with, actionable . . . 3

FIGURES,
    in contracts, controlled by words 175

FIRE,
    injuries by, to house may be waste 58
    liability of householder for safe keeping of . . . 29, 30
    liability of shipowners for loss by 236
    loss by, in maritime insurance 303

FIRE INSURANCE,
    divers insurances on the same property . . . 307
    alteration of premises 306
    fraudulent concealment 309
    risks covered 307
    notice of loss . . . . ib.
    forfeiture of policy 309
    insurances by bailees 306
    assignment of policy 307

FISH,
    right to, when caught . . . 73

FIXTURES,
    right to, as between landlord and tenant . . . 57, 58
    removal of, is waste 57
    are not distrainable 64
    authentication of contracts for sale of . . . 166

FORBEARANCE,
    of legal proceedings, a good consideration . . . 155

FOREMAN,
    authority of . . 195

FORFEITURE,
    of pledges 284
    of policies 309

FORGERY,
    of cheques . 326

FRAUD,
    See FALSE AND FRAUDULENT REPRESENTATION.
    injury caused by, actionable 3
    on creditors, avoiding a bill of sale 282
    by agents on third parties 195
    by directors of companies 215
    determination of power to avoid a contract on ground of . 345
    puffers at auction 257
    on sureties 293

FRAUDS, STATUTE OF,

	PAGE
contracts relating to sale of lands	165
executory contracts for sale of goods and chattels	165
fixtures and shares	ib.
promises by executors and administrators	164
promises to answer for debt, &c., of another	ib.
agreement not to be performed within a year	166

FREIGHT POLICY. 304
See MARINE INSURANCE.

FRUIT,
sale of 165

FURNISHED HOUSES AND APARTMENTS,
letting and hiring of . . . . . . *ib.*

GAME,

right of landowner to preserve	3
right to shoot and carry away	45
waste to destroy	57
sale of	341

GAMING CONTRACTS,

gaming policies of insurance	300
lawful games	339
securities for money won at play	340

GATES,

across public highway	33
at level crossings	31

GOODS AND CHATTELS,

authentication of contracts for sale of	166, 261
mortgage of	280

GOODWILL,
sale of 343

GRANT,

easements acquired by	44
no man to derogate from his own	45
presumption of lost	47

GRASS,

treading down	17
authentication of contracts respecting	165

GRATUITOUS SERVICES 224

INDEX.

GROUSE,   PAGE
- driving away, actionable 3

GUARANTEE,
- nature and effect of 290
- authentication of 163, 290
- bonds to secure faithful services 292
- continuing liabilities 291
- alteration of principal obligation 292
- extension of time of payment . . . . . *ib.*
- release of principal debt 293
- reserve of remedies against surety . . . 292, 293
- release of one of several co-sureties . . . 293
- fraud on sureties . . . . *ib.*
- indemnification of sureties 294
- contribution between co-sureties . . . . *ib.*

GUN,
- injuries from spring-gun 27

HEIRS,
- contracts with expectant 259

HEIR-AT-LAW,
- rights of, upon real and personal covenants of ancestor . . 358
- right of action in respect of continuing breaches of real covenants 359

HEREDITAMENTS,
- sale of corporeal 162
- sale of incorporeal . . . . . . *ib.*

HIGHWAY,
- title to soil of 13, 32
- title to waste land adjoining 13, 14
- of necessity 33
- dedication of 22, 33
- repair of 33
- remedy for non-repair by indictment against parish . 36
- repair of railway bridges over 31
- obstruction to, when actionable at suit of private person . 34
- cattle straying from 17, 31
- fences between, and canal 32
- nuisances adjoining 28

HIRING AND SERVICE,
- yearly hirings 218
- month's warning 219
- service at will . . . . *ib.*
- dismissal . . . . *ib.*
- notice 220
- disability from sickness . . . . . *ib.*
- wrongful dismissal . . . . . . *ib.*
- contracts of apprenticeship 221
  - discharge by award of justices . . . *ib.*

INDEX. 407

	PAGE
HONORARY SERVICES	224

HOUSE,
    injuries from things falling into street from 29
    injuries from fall of . . . . ib.
    alterations in, by tenant 56

HUNDRED,
    liability of, for damage caused by riot 22

HUSBAND,
    right of, to restitution of conjugal rights 143
    right of, to judicial separation 142
    cruelty, what amounts to 144
    desertion, what amounts to 145
    when entitled to a dissolution of marriage 142
    neglect, connivance, and condonation 143, 144
    competency of, to give evidence 146
    may claim damages against co-respondent 147
    right of action upon wife's contracts 185
    remedies of creditors against separate property of wife . 187
    release from liability on wife's contracts after her adultery . 186
    liability for necessaries during separation . . . . ib.
    liability resulting from reputed marriage 187
    right to wife's *choses in action* 185

ILLEGAL CONTRACTS,
    contracts providing for future separation of husband and wife . 337
    contracts in restraint of marriage 342
    maintenance and champerty 343
    contracts obstructing administration of justice . . . ib.
    contracts in contravention of policy of Acts of Parliament . 342
    contracts in fraud of employers 343
    fraud on creditors 282
    sale of offices 338
    simoniacal contracts 339
    contracts in restraint of trade 343
    contracts creating monopolies 344
    contracts with foreign enemies . . . . ib.
    gaming contracts and wagers 339
    notes and bills given to secure money won at play . . 340
    sale by illegal weights and measures . . . . . . ib.
    illegal sale of coals . . . . ib.
    illegal sale of game 341
    illegal sale of spirituous liquors 340
    illegal sale of poison, petroleum, &c. 341
    smuggling . . . . ib.
    illegal sale of exciseable articles . . . . . . ib.
    Sunday sales . . . . ib.
    unauthorized practitioners 342
    the truck system 340
    divisible contracts 344
    indivisible, and void 345
    avoidance on ground of fraud . . . . ib.
    duress 346
    mistake . . . . ib.

INDEX.

IMPLIED CONTRACTS,
    nature of and division of 154

IMPLIED REQUESTS . . . 155

IMPLIED WARRANTY,
    of title by pledgor 284
    in marine insurance 300
    in fire insurance 306

IMPOSSIBILITY,
    of performance of contracts 366

INADEQUACY OF CONSIDERATION 155

INCOMING PARTNERS,
    liabilities of 207

INCORPOREAL HEREDITAMENTS,
    authentication of grants of 162
    growing grass 165
    shares in mining company 166
    transfer of shares . . . . ib.

INCUMBENT,
    is entitled to possession of church and churchyard, though
        freehold in rector 15
    waste by 58

INDEMNIFICATION,
    of agent by his principal 198
    of surety by his principal 294

INDEPENDENT PROMISES 157

INDICTMENT,
    against parish 36
    for public nuisances . . . . . . ib.
    against corporation . . . . . . ib.
    for abduction of unmarried woman . . . 149
    for forcible entry 93
    for fraud 137
    for libel and slander 122, 123
    preferring of unfounded 100

INDIVISIBLE CONTRACTS 345

INDORSEMENT,
    of bills of exchange and promissory notes . . . 320
        transfer by 318

INDEX. 409

INDORSEMENT—*continued.*   PAGE
  of bills of exchange and promissory notes—*continued.*
    restraining negotiability 321
    intermediate infirmities of title . . . . . *ib.*
    liability of indorser 322
    delivery without . . . . *ib.*
  of bill of lading 328
  of dock warrant . . . . *ib.*

INFANT.
  See CHILDREN.
  consideration in contracts with 156
  rights of, *ex contractu* 183
  contracts of, for necessaries . . . . . . *ib.*
  purchase of estates and shares 184
  ratification of contracts of 183
  marriage settlements by 184
  custody of 342

INJUNCTION,
  against commission of trespass 22
  against public nuisances 5, 35
  to prevent waste 60
  to prevent fraud 138
  not granted to stop temporary nuisance 35

INNKEEPER,
  distinction between, and lodging-house keeper . . . 242
  duties and liabilities of innkeepers 240
  statutory limitation of liability of 241

INSURANCE.
  See MARINE INSURANCE, FIRE INSURANCE, LIFE INSURANCE.

INTERPLEADER,
  protection by, to sheriff 109
  protection by, to bailee 245

INTERPRETATION,
  evidence of surrounding circumstances 176
  ambiguity latent and patent . . . . . . *ib.*
  figures and words at length 175
  computation of time . . . . *ib.*

JETTISON,
  insurance against 303

JOINT CONTRACTORS,
  liabilities of executors and administrators 309
  release of 371
  joint and several promissory notes 291

INDEX.

JOINT-STOCK COMPANY,   PAGE
- contracts with 214
- winding up . . . . *ib.*
- parties to be made contributories 215
- fraudulent representations by directors . . . . *ib.*

JOINT TENANTS,
- possession of 12
- of chattel should join in action for negligence . . . 82

JUDGE,
- not responsible for acts done in course of duty 104
-       for slander in reference to suit before him . 118
- disqualification on ground of interest 104
- liable for acts done without jurisdiction 105
- proceedings before inferior, may be removed by *certiorari* . *ib.*

JUDGMENT RECOVERED 372

JUS TERTII,
- between pawnor and pawnee 284

JUSTICE,
- contracts obstructing administration of . . 343

JUSTICES,
- cannot act judicially out of their county, but may ministerially 105
- cannot act if interested 104
- may commit for contempt of court 106
- not liable for erroneous judgment 104
- convictions by, on their own view 105
- must have information to give jurisdiction . . . *ib.*
- must have *some* evidence to justify conviction . . . *ib.*
- convictions by, in excess of jurisdiction 106
- ouster of jurisdiction by claim of title 105
- invalid convictions on bye-laws . . . . . . *ib.*
- actions against 106

LAND,
- title to 11
- authentication of contracts affecting 165

LANDLORD,
- when responsible for nuisance on land demised . . 28
- liability of, for nuisance, though he has parted with the land . 29
- liability of, for non-repair of house . . . . . *ib.*
- acquiescence of, in dedication of a highway when to be inferred 32
- acquiescence of, in user of easements 48
- is entitled to rent in priority to an execution . . . 109

LEAVE AND LICENCE,
- plea of, in actions for trespass to land . . . 21

INDEX. 411

LECTURES,
    copyright in 6

LESSEE,
    liable to lessor for removal of soil . . 18
    right of, to minerals . . . 20

LETTERS,
    property in 72

LETTING AND HIRING.
    See BAILMENT.

LEVEL CROSSINGS,
    gates at 31

LIBEL,
    distinction between, and slander 115
    malice is implied in 116
    privileged communications . . . . . 117—120
    in course of judicial proceedings 118
    by military officer on his subordinate . . . *ib.*
    petitions to the Crown or Parliament . . . *ib.*
    pastoral letters . . . . *ib.*
    communications between friends to prevent an injury . 117
    giving characters of servants . . . . . *ib.*
    reports of trials 119
        of speeches in Parliament 118
        of proceedings at a public meeting . . 119
    by member of House of Commons 118
    newspaper articles 119
    every publisher of, is liable 120
    what is publication 121
    defendants in actions for 120
    plea of apology, &c. 122
    plea of truth of libel 121, 123
    application of libel to plaintiff 121
    defamatory sense of words used 120
    malice 116
    damages recoverable 122
    indictment for 122, 123

LICENCE,
    to commit waste 59
    to go on another's land 21, 46
    to trade with foreign enemies . . . 344

LIEN,
    put an end to, by wrongful sale . . . 71
    conversion of property by person claiming right of . *ib.*
    of bankers 243
    of workmen 242
    of solicitors 243
    general and particular 242
    extinguishment of 244

LIFE INSURANCE,

	PAGE
interest of the assured	307
warranties	308
fraudulent misrepresentations	309
risks covered	308
forfeiture of policy	309
assignment of policy	ib.

LIGHT,

grant of right of	45
right to, under Prescription Act	49
right to, suspended during unity of possession	50
right of obstruction of, where windows are enlarged	51
abandonment of right of	ib.
interruption of enjoyment of	ib.

LIME KILN,

adjoining highway	28

LIMITATION OF ACTIONS,

with regard to recovery of land—

in case of occupation by relations or servants	12
entry or continued claim	11
possession of joint tenants, &c.	12
acknowledgments of title	13
in case of disabilities	11
in case of mortgagees	13
Statutes of Limitation	373
temporary disabilities	374
acknowledgments and promises to pay	169, 373

LIMITATION OF LIABILITY,

of common carriers, by public notice	235
by special contract	236
of carriers by water	ib.
of surety	291
of innkeeper	241
in joint-stock companies	215

LODGING-HOUSE KEEPER,

authentication of contracts with	161
letting lodgings for immoral purposes	337

LONG WEIGHT,

sale by	340

LOSS OR INCONVENIENCE,

a good consideration	154

LOSS OF GOODS

264

LOSS OF BILLS AND NOTES

327

INDEX. 413

LUGGAGE,
    railway passengers' 238

LUNATICS,
    contracts with 188

MAGISTRATES.
    See JUSTICES.

MAINTENANCE 343

MALICE,
    causing damage is actionable 4
    implied in libel and slander 116
    in the assertion of a legal right 101
    in petitioning for an adjudication in bankruptcy . . . *ib.*
    in abuse of legal process . . . . . . *ib.*

MALICIOUS PROSECUTION,
    is a tort, if with malice and want of probable cause . . . 100
    what is evidence of malice and want of probable cause . . 101
    by preferring indictment 100
    before court martial 101
    by proceedings in bankruptcy . . . . . . *ib.*

MANDATE 231

MAN-TRAP 27

MARINE INSURANCE,
    voyage and time policies 299
    valued and open policies . . . . *ib.*
    insurable interest 306
    wagering and gaming policies 300
    express warranties 301
    fraudulent misrepresentation and concealment . . . *ib.*
    risks covered 302
    loss by perils of the sea . . . . *ib.*
    perils of fire and jettison 303
    loss by capture . . . . *ib.*
    restraints and detainments . . . . . . *ib.*
    perils of barratry . . . . *ib.*
    perils, losses, and misfortunes generally 304
    commencement and duration of risk . . . . . *ib.*
    freight policies . . . . *ib.*
    deviation . . . . *ib.*
    total loss and abandonment 305
    partial loss . . . . *ib.*
    general and particular average 306
    return of premium . . . . *ib.*

MARKET,
interference with	3

MARKET OVERT,
definition of	259
sale in	75, 259

MARRIAGE.
See HUSBAND AND WIFE.
loss of, caused by slander	2
authentication of agreements in consideration of	165
contracts in restraint of	342

MARRIAGE SETTLEMENT,
powers of Divorce Court over	145, 146

MASTER AND SERVANT,
liability of master for acts of servant	83
for trespasses to land	17
liability of master for injuries to his servant	84
master bound to comply with statutory regulations for safety of servants	85
master, when liable for injury to servant by negligence of another servant	ib.
master may sue for loss of service of servant through tortious act of another	148
liability of master on contracts made by servant as his agent	195
yearly hirings—domestic servants	218
master's warning or month's wages	219
service at will	ib.
dismissal for want of skill or misconduct	ib.
disability of servant from sickness	220
wrongful dismissal	ib.
death of parties	372
contracts of apprenticeship	221

MEDICAL PRACTITIONERS,
unauthorized	342

MERGER
	372

MILITARY OFFICER,
not liable for injuries caused by inferior officer in carrying out orders	84
cannot be sued for bringing subordinate before court martial	101

MINES,
injuries to, from water from adjoining mines	44
sale of shares in	166
right of lessee in respect of minerals	20

INDEX.   415

MISDEMEANOUR,
    committal of, is actionable . . 5

MISTAKE,
    contracts made under . . . 346

MONOPOLIES,
    illegality of 343

MORAL OBLIGATION,
    when it will support an express promise . . . 155

MORTGAGE,
    of goods and chattels 280
    bills of sale . . . . ib.
    when void as against creditors 282
    possession and apparent ownership . . . ib.

MUNICIPAL CORPORATIONS,
    bye-laws made by 7

MUTUAL PROMISES 156

NECESSARIES,
    for infants 183
    for married woman 186

NEGLIGENCE,
    distinction between, and inevitable accident . . . 2, 81
    of bailor, in not disclosing dangerous nature of goods . . 4
    of coach-proprietors 81
    in driving 82
    of owners and masters of ships 86
    of masters causing injury to servants 84
    of one fellow-servant causing injury to another . . 85
    of contractors and sub-contractors . . . . ib.
    of skilled workmen, &c. 82
    of solicitors . . . . ib.
    of sheriff in execution of writ 106
    of railway companies, in management of stations, &c. . 31
    of canal companies 32
    contributory, by the plaintiff 85
    master responsible for servant's 83
    causing fires 29
    causing destruction of house by fire . . . 58
    when death is caused by 86
    plaintiffs and defendants in actions for . . 82
    damages recoverable for 86
    of hirer of chattels 232
    of borrower 231

INDEX.

NEGLIGENCE—*continued.* PAGE
    of carriers by land 233
    of carriers by water 237
    of common carrier 236
    of consignor 237

NOISE,
    making of, when a nuisance 30

NOMINAL PARTNERS 205

NOTICE,
    of distress 64
    when necessary to abate a nuisance 34
    of dishonour, what amounts to 323
        dispensation of 324
    of assignment 356
    of action, in case of justices, constables, and others intending to
        act under an Act of Parliament 96, 106

NUISANCE,
    what is 27
    carrying on noxious trade 28
    keeping furious animals 30
    non-repair of sewers, &c. 27
    on highways 33
    adjoining highways 27, 28
    necessarily created under Act of Parliament 30
    public, when actionable 35
    when reversioner liable for 28
    tenant always liable for 29
    continuing 35
    abatement of 19, 20, 34
    notice to abate, when necessary 34, 35
    who to be plaintiffs in action for 35
    damages in action for . . . . *ib.*
    indictment for public 36
    injunction against 25

OFFER,
    not binding before acceptance 153

OFFICES,
    sale of 338

ORAL CONTRACTS,
    for sale of land, enforcement of 257

ORAL EVIDENCE,
    inadmissibility of, to vary written contract . 175
    proof of contracts by 177
    of agricultural and mercantile customs . . 176
    of conditional assent 177
    estopples 177, 178
    of renunciations of claims on bills or notes . 370

INDEX.   417

ORDER OF DISCHARGE,
    in bankruptcy 373

OUTLAWS,
    disabilities of 189

PARENT.
    See CHILDREN.
    may sue for injury to child or seduction of daughter, if loss of
        service caused thereby 148
    absence of daughter from parent's house . . . . . *ib.*

PARISH,
    liability of, to repair highway 30

PAROL DISCHARGE,
    of contracts before breach 376

PARTIAL LOSS.
    See MARINE INSURANCE.

PARTNERSHIP,
    participation in profits constituting, or not 204
    joint purchases of goods 205
    tenancy in common of chattels . . . . . *ib.*
    partnerships in profit only 206
    dissolution of partnership 207
    distribution of partnership effects 208
    nominal and dormant partners 205
    liability of partners on simple contracts 206
    transactions out of the ordinary course of business . . *ib.*
    bills, notes, &c., so given in name of firm 207
    representation by partners . . . . . *ib,*
    liability of incoming and retiring partners . . . *ib.*
    notice of retirement or dissolution 208
    specific performance of contract of 206

PART PERFORMANCE,
    of contracts for sale of land 257

PASSENGERS,
    by coach or rail, injuries to 238
    luggage 238

PATENT RIGHT 7

PATENT AMBIGUITY 176

E E

INDEX.

PAWNBROKERS,
    pledges with 285
    warranties on sale of unredeemed pledge 286

PAYMENT,
    and acceptance of part of an admitted debt 386
    to a person found in a merchant's counting house . . . 368
    by bill or note 367
    by a stranger 368
    with a stolen bank-note 327
    receipt 369
    to a bankrupt 368
    appropriation of 369
    tender of 367
    effect of part payment in executory contracts for the sale of goods 263
    of cheques by bankers 326
    into Court, by constables and others 96, 106

PEACE,
    maliciously summoning a person to be bound over to keep the
      peace is actionable 100, 101

PENALTIES,
    given by statute, when a cumulative, exclusive, or alternative
      remedy to that given by common law 6, 7

PERFORMANCE,
    demand of, when necessary 366
    impossibility of . . . . ib.
    of contracts for the sale of land 257

PERILS OF THE SEA 302

PERSONAL CONTRACTS,
    liability of executor upon 359

PERSONAL COVENANTS,
    transfer of, by death 358

PETROLEUM,
    sale of 341

PHYSICIANS,
    qualification of 342
    services by 224

PIGEONS,
    damage feasant, may be shot 18

PILOT,
losses occasioned by incapacity of 237

PLEDGE,
parties entitled to pledge 283
implied warranty of title on part of pledgor 284
right of redemption . . . . *ib.*
forfeiture of pledge . . . . *ib.*
foreclosure 285
custody of pledge . . . . *ib.*
pawnbrokers . . . . *ib.*
warranties on sale of unredeemed pledges 286

POISON,
illegal sale of 341

POLICIES.
See Marine Insurance, Fire Insurance, Life Insurance.

POST,
acceptance of offers made by 153

POUND,
breach of 66

PRESCRIPTION,
title by 47
easements acquired by 49
allowed to supply place of lost grant 48
interruption of enjoyment preventing acquisition by . . . 51
title by, not lost by non-user . . . . *ib.*
periods excluded from computation under Prescription Act . 49

PRESENTATION,
sale of 339

PRESENTMENT,
for payment 319, 323
for acceptance 319

PRINCIPAL AND AGENT.
See Agent.

PRINCIPAL AND SURETY.
See Guarantee.

PRINTS,
copyright in 6

PRIVILEGED COMMUNICATION.
See Libel.

E E 2

PRIVITY OF CONTRACT,
  in covenants running with the land 357

PROFIT A PRENDRE,
  what it is and how claimable 45, 47
  what may be claimed under Prescription Act . . . 49

PROMISE.
  See CONSIDERATION.
  without consideration 155
  unilateral 156
  mutual . . . . ib.
  by an executor to answer damages out of his own estate . . 164
  to answer for debt, &c., of another . . . . . ib.
  in consideration of marriage 165
  without consideration, authentication of 162
  to pay debts barred by Statute of Limitations . . . 169

PROMISSORY NOTE.
  See BILL OF EXCHANGE.

PROSECUTION.
  See MALICIOUS PROSECUTION.

PROSPECT.
  See VIEW.

PROSTITUTION,
  contracts in furtherance of 337
  letting of lodgings for purposes of 338

PROTECTION ORDER.
  See WIFE.

PROTEST,
  of foreign bill 324

PROVISIONAL COMMITTEES,
  liabilities of, to third parties 215

PUBLIC JUSTICE,
  contracts obstructing 343

PUBLIC OFFICES,
  sale of 338

PUBLIC OFFICERS,
  duty of, to perform ministerial functions 4
  not liable for neglect of subordinate officers . . . ib.
  contracts by 197

PUBLIC POLICY,
  contracts in contravention of 342

INDEX. 421

PUFFERS,
 secret employment of, at auctions 257

QUARRY,
 obligation to fence 27

RABBITS,
 remedy for crops injured by 18

RACE STANDS,
 injuries from falling of 81

RAILWAY COMPANY.
 See COMMON CARRIERS.
 not liable for nuisances necessarily created in carrying out their
  powers 30
 duty of, to maintain fences, gates, bridges, &c. . . . 31
 negligent management of stations by. . . . . *ib.*
 arrest or assault by servants of 96

RATIFICATION,
 of the acts of agents . - 194
 of contracts made during infancy 183

RECAPTION.
 See CONVERSION.

RECEIPT,
 effect of 369

RECEIVER,
 when may distrain 63

RECORD,
 contract by 161

RECTOR.
 See INCUMBENT.

REGISTRAR,
 of County Court, to grant replevins 66

REGISTRATION,
 of bills of sale, effect of 281

REGISTRATION ACTS,
 contracts in evasion of 342

INDEX.

RELEASE,   PAGE
- of contracts 370
- of one of several joint-contractors 371
- covenants not to sue . . . . ib.
- merger 372
- judgment recovered . . . . ib.
- of surety 292
- of principal debtor 293
- of one of several co-sureties . . . . . . ib.

RENT,
- receipt of, *primâ facie*, evidence of title 11
- tender of, making distress unlawful 65
- tender of, and expenses, making sale of distress unlawful . . 66
- limitation of suit for 373

REPLEVIN,
- for goods distrained *damage feasant* 23
- writ of 66

REPRESENTATIONS,
- by agents 195
- by partners 207
- *See* FRAUDULENT MISREPRESENTATIONS.

REPUTED MARRIAGE,
- liabilities arising from 187

REPUTED OWNERSHIP.
- *See* BANKRUPT, BILLS OF SALE.

RE-SALE,
- by vendor of realty, in case of non-performance by the purchaser 258
- vendor's power of re-sale of chattels 269

RESERVE OF REMEDIES,
- in release of principal debtor 293

RESTRAINT OF MARRIAGE,
- contracts in 342

RESTRAINT OF TRADE,
- contracts in 343

RESTRICTIVE INDORSEMENT,
- of bills and notes 321

RETIRING PARTNERS,
- liabilities of 208

INDEX.

REVERSIONER,
	PAGE
when, may sue for nuisance	35
right of, to sue for waste	58
right of entry to inspect waste	60
when liable for creation or continuance of nuisance	28, 29

REVOCATION,
of authority of agents 194

RIOT,
liability of hundred for damage caused by . . 22

RIPARIAN PROPRIETOR,
prescriptive right to foul water	27
right of, to use water	43, 44

RIVER,
soil of navigable, title to	14
obstructions in	34

SALE OF GOODS AND CHATTELS,
in market overt, changing the property	71, 259
by sheriff, title under	109
specific performance of contract for	269
out of market overt	260
authentication of	167, 261
signature of memorandum	168
acceptance and receipt	261
receipt for inspection and approval	262
constructive acceptance	ib.
of bills of lading, &c.	263
part acceptance and actual receipt	ib.
earnest and part payment	ib.
transfer of right of property in things sold	264
non-delivery of goods sold	269
non-payment of price	268
lien of vendor for price	265
re-sale by vendor	269
stoppage *in transitu*	266
warranty on. *See* FALSE REPRESENTATION.	
of ships	163
of shares and fixtures	166

SALE OF LANDS,
to infants	184
executory contracts for	165
authentication of	165, 256
sales by auction	256
enforcement of oral bargains for	257
non-performance by the vendor	258
non-performance by the purchaser	257
specific performance of contract for	258

SATISFACTION.
See ACCORD AND SATISFACTION.

SEA-SHORE,
right to soil of 14

SEA WALLS,
erection of, not actionable 28

SEA-WORTHINESS,
in insurance cases 300

SECURITIES,
for money won at play 340

SEDUCTION,
when actionable 148
damages in actions for 149

SELF-DEFENCE,
assaults committed in, not actionable . 93

SERVANT.
See MASTER AND SERVANT.

SERVITUDE.
See EASEMENT.

SHAFT,
obligation to fence 27

SHAREHOLDERS,
in joint stock companies 214
limitation of liability of . . . . *ib.*
liabilities of outgoing and incoming shareholders . . . 215
authentication of contracts for sale of shares 166

SHEEP,
sale of diseased 2
injuries to, from dogs 30

SHERIFF,
duties of, with regard to replevin now transferred to registrar of
    county court 66
sale by, title under 109
must make due inquiry before executing writ *fi. fa.* . . . 108
must execute the first writ delivered to him . . . 107
power to break open a house in execution of process . . . *ib.*
illegality of seizure, if entry illegal 108
remaining in house an unreasonable time . . . . *ib.*
method of levying . . . . *ib.*
seizure of goods and receipt of notice bankruptcy before sale . 110
duty of, to pay rent to landlord 109
sale of goods seized . . . . *ib.*
power of, to protect himself by interpleader . . . *ib.*
damages in actions against 110

INDEX. 425

SHIPOWNERS,
    liability of, for negligence of master 86
    limitation of responsibility of 236

SHIPS,
    sale of 163

SIGNATURE,
    of deed 161
    what is sufficient within Statute of Frauds 168
    of acknowledgments within Statute of Limitations . . . 169

SIMONIACAL CONTRACTS 339

SLANDER,
    distinction between, and libel 115
    repetition of 116
    malice implied in . . . . ib.
    respecting servants 117, 118
    in course of judicial proceedings 119
    interpretation of words used 120
    of title 123
    truth of the charge 121, 123
    damages recoverable in 122
    indictment for . . . . ib.

SMELL,
    when amounting to a nuisance 28

SOLICITOR,
    uncertificated 342
    lien of 243

SPECIFIC PERFORMANCE,
    of sale of lands 258
    of sale of goods 269
    with variation 178
    of contracts of partnership 206

SPIRITUOUS LIQUORS,
    sale of 340

SPORTING,
    right of 45

SPRING GUNS 27

STAKEHOLDERS,
    recovery of money in the hands of . . . 339

STATUTE,
                                            PAGE
  injuries necessarily caused in execution of powers given by . 30
  action for breach of duty created by 6
  duty imposed by, of fencing machinery 28
  protection of persons intending to act in pursuance of . . 96, 106
  contracts made illegal by 338

STEAM ENGINES,
  adjoining highway   28

STOLEN GOODS,
  action to recover 71
  purchase of 259

STOLEN BANK NOTE,
  payment with 327

STOPPAGE *IN TRANSITU,*
  in hands of forwarding agents 266
  goods in hands of purchaser's agents for custody . . . 267
  notice of . . . . *ib.*
  intervention of rights of sub-purchasers 268

STRANGERS,
  to a contract 178
  payment by 368

SUB-AGENTS,
  receipt of money by 198

SUNDAY SALES 341

SUPPORT,
  right of lateral or subjacent 43, 45
  right of, from one house to another 45
  prescriptive right to 49
  where separate stories of house belong to different people . 29

SURETYSHIP.
  See GUARANTEE.

SURGEON,
  unregistered 342

SURVIVORSHIP,
  as between husband and wife 185
  amongst executors and administrators 359

TASK-WORK,
  letting and hiring of 222
  executory contracts for . . . . *ib.*

TASK-WORK—*continued*. PAGE
    honorary services 224
    time of performance 223
    conditions precedent to payment for . . . . . *ib.*
    destruction of materials 224
    prevention of completion, by employer . . . 222
    useless and defective work 223
    safe keeping of materials 232

TENANT,
    for life or years, waste by . . . . . . 56—58
    without impeachment of waste 59
    at will, waste by 58
    liability of, for waste committed by stranger . . . 59
    liability of, for obstruction of entry to inspect waste . . 60
    liability for nuisances . . . . . . 28—30
    cannot dedicate highway 32
    laches of, in permitting easements to be acquired . . 48
    from year to year underletting from year to year may distrain 63
    may resist illegal distress by force 65
    when to be plaintiff in actions for injuries to land . . 35
    may sue for nuisance to lands demised . . . . *ib.*

TENANT IN COMMON,
    when, may maintain trespass against his co-tenant . . 20
    should join in actions for negligence 82
    of chattel not a partner 205

TENDER,
    of amends by constables, &c. 96, 106
    what amounts to a valid tender of money . . . 367

THEFT,
    of things bailed 233
    from carriers by water 237

TIMBER,
    title to, when severed from freehold 72
    cutting and sale of, by tenant for life 57
    right of rector to cut, for repairs 58
    cutting of, by tenant "without impeachment of waste" . 59

TIN,
    right to search for, in Cornwall 47

TITLE,
    to realty from twelve years' possession 11
    by custom 47
    by prescription . . . . *ib.*
    to timber severed from the land 72
    evidence of, from proof of receipt of rents 11
    to personal securities 72
    to goods stolen 71

INDEX.

TITLE—*continued.*   PAGE
    to chattels by finding 71
    to property for the conversion of which damages have been recovered . . . . *ib.*
    by purchase from sheriff, under an execution 109
    by bill of sale 74
    to goods altered by wrongdoer 71
    to birds and animals *feræ naturæ* 72
    to fish 73
    to bills and notes 72
    to letters . . . . *ib.*
    to chattels by purchase in market overt 71, 259
    by delivery order, dock warrant, &c. 72
    to property of bankrupt 73
    warranty of, on sale of chattels 134
    may be tried in an action of trespass 21
    question of, to realty raised before magistrates 105
    slander of 123
    to realty, want of, in the vendor 258
    to chattels 259

TORT,
    what necessary to constitute . . . . 1—5

TOTAL LOSS.
    See MARINE INSURANCE.

TOWING PATH.
    See CANAL.

TRADE,
    interference with, a tort 3
    offensive and noisome 28
    contracts in restraint of 343

TRADE MARKS,
    warranty of 136

TRADING CORPORATIONS 213

TRANSFER,
    of right of property by sale 264
    of right of possession 265
    of contracts by assignment 356
    of covenants . . . . *ib.*
    by death 358
    by marriage 187
    by bankruptcy 360

TREES,
    title to, is in landlord 72
    if standing in a boundary fence 14, 15
    lessee cannot cut, except for repairs 57

TRESPASS,
    to person or personalty :—
        by carrying away goods, or striking cattle 74
        by sheriff 107, 108
        justification of 21
    to realty :—
        what constitutes 17
        after notice 22
        by throwing rubbish, &c. 17
        by cattle, or other domestic animals 17, 18
        by rabbits, pigeons, or dogs 18
        if surface and subsoil belong to separate persons . . 20
        when may be repelled by force 19
        if continuing 22
        by person lawfully entitled, after entry . . . 19
        leave and licence 21
        by tenant in common 20
        by picking up game which has fallen on land of another . 73
        against wrongdoer, mere possession is sufficient . . 70
        title may be tried in action for 21
        damages recoverable in actions of 21, 22
        injunction, against 22

TRESPASSER,
    injuries to, not generally actionable 28, 29

TRUCK SYSTEM,
    illegality of 340

TRUSTEE,
    liabilities of 74
    cutting of timber by 59
    services by 224
        in bankruptcy, property to bankrupt vests in . . 73
        may disclaim onerous property . . . . . ib.

TURF,
    right to cut, a *profit à prendre* 45

UNDER-LEASE,
    under-lessee not liable to lessor on covenants . . . 357

UNDISCLOSED PRINCIPALS.
    See AGENT.

UNILATERAL PROMISE 156

UNITY OF OWNERSHIP,
    extinguishing easements 50

UNREASONABLE CONDITIONS,
    in contracts by railway companies . 236

430　　　　　　　　　INDEX.

USAGE.　　　　　　　　　　　　　　　　　　　　　　　PAGE
　　　See CUSTOM AND USAGE.

VIEW,
　　　interference with, not actionable 2

VOID CONTRACTS.
　　　See ILLEGAL CONTRACTS.

WAGERING POLICIES,
　　　of marine insurance 300

WAGERS,
　　　illegality of 339

WAGES.
　　　See HIRING AND SERVICE.

WAREHOUSEMEN,
　　　goods in the hands of, when *in transitu* 239
　　　safe keeping of goods intrusted to 232

WARNING.
　　　See HIRING AND SERVICE.

WARRANTY.
　　　See FALSE AND FRAUDULENT REPRESENTATION.
　　　by agents 195
　　　in marine insurance 300
　　　in fire insurance 306
　　　in life insurance 308

WASTE,
　　　what it is, different kinds of 56
　　　fire 58
　　　alteration of premises 57
　　　removal of fixtures . . . . *ib.*
　　　in trees and woods . . . . *ib.*
　　　equitable 59
　　　licence to commit . . . . *ib.*
　　　right of entry to inspect 60
　　　by copyholder, when a forfeiture 59
　　　by trustees without impeachment of waste . . . *ib.*
　　　by incumbent 58
　　　action for 60
　　　injunction to prevent . . . . *ib.*

WATER,

	PAGE
natural right to the use of flowing	43
under Prescription Act	49
right to surface	43
right to underground	44
right to discharge of, from eaves	45

WAY,

private, title to soil of	13
right of, under Prescription Act	49
dedication of	32
of necessity	45
repair of, *in alieno solo*	46

WEIGHTS AND MEASURES,

to be used in buying and selling	340

WELL,

abstraction of water from, by an adjoining owner digging a deeper one, not actionable	44
obligation to fence	27

WIFE,

not liable for false representation that she was single	8
persuading, to live apart from her husband	147
right of, to protection order, when deserted by her husband	142
desertion, what amounts to	145
right of, to restitution of conjugal rights	143
when entitled to dissolution of marriage	142
when entitled to judicial separation	ib.
cruelty, what amounts to	144
alimony	145
competency of, to give evidence in cases of adultery	146
settled property of, power of Divorce Court to deal with	145, 146
husband's right on contracts of	185
assent of husband to wife's contracts	186
contract of, how affected by her adultery	ib.
necessaries during separation	187
separate estate of, when liable	ib.
reputed marriages	ib.
liability of wife upon prenuptial contracts	ib.

WINDMILL,

adjoining highway, to be fenced	28

WINDOW,

right to enlarge	51

WITNESS,

not liable for slander in course of judicial proceedings	119
expenses of	224

WORDS,
  control figures 175

WORK AND SERVICES.
  See TASK-WORK.

WRONGFUL DISMISSAL. 220

YEAR,
  authentication of promises not to be performed within . 166
  yearly hirings of domestic servants 218

THE END.

STEVENS AND RICHARDSON, PRINTERS, 5, GREAT QUEEN STREET, W.C.

May, 1880.

A CATALOGUE
OF
LAW WORKS,
PUBLISHED BY
STEVENS AND SONS,
119, CHANCERY LANE, LONDON, W.C.
(*Formerly of Bell Yard, Lincoln's Inn*).

Law Books Purchased or Valued.

Acts of Parliament.—*Public and Local Acts from an early date, may be had of the Publishers of this Catalogue, who have also on sale the largest collection of Private Acts, relating to Estates, Enclosures, Railways, Roads, &c., &c.*

ACTION AT LAW.—Foulkes' Elementary View of the Proceedings in an Action.—Founded on "SMITH'S ACTION AT LAW." By W. D. I. FOULKES, Esq., Barrister-at-Law. Second Edition. 12mo. 1879. 10s. 6d.

"The student will find in 'Smith's Action' a manual, by the study of which he may easily acquire a general knowledge of the mode of procedure in the various stages of an action in the several divisions of the High Court of Justice."—*Law Times.*

Peel.—*Vide* "Chancery."

Prentice's Proceedings in an Action in the Queen's Bench, Common Pleas, and Exchequer Divisions of the High Court of Justice. Second Edition (including the New Rules, April, 1880). By SAMUEL PRENTICE, Esq., one of Her Majesty's Counsel. Royal 12mo. 1880. 12s.

"The book can be safely recommended to students and practitioners"—*Law Times.*

Smith's Action.—*Vide* "Foulkes."

ADMIRALTY.—Boyd.—*Vide* "Shipping."

Lowndes.—Marsden.—*Vide* "Collisions."

Pritchard's Admiralty Digest.—With Notes from Text Writers, and the Scotch, Irish, and American Reports. Second Edition. By ROBERT A. PRITCHARD, D.C.L., Barrister-at-Law, and WILLIAM TARN PRITCHARD. With Notes of Cases from French Maritime Law. By ALGERNON JONES, Avocat à la Cour Impériale de Paris. 2 vols. Royal 8vo. 1865. 3*l*.

Roscoe's Treatise on the Jurisdiction and Practice of the Admiralty Division of the High Court of Justice, and on Appeals therefrom, &c. With an Appendix containing Statutes, Rules as to Fees and Costs, Forms, Precedents of Pleadings and Bills of Costs. By EDWARD STANLEY ROSCOE, Esq., Barrister-at-Law, and Northern Circuit. Demy 8vo. 1878. 1*l*.

"Mr. Roscoe has performed his task well, supplying in the most convenient shape a clear digest of the law and practice of the Admiralty Courts."—*Liverpool Courier.*

*** *All standard Law Works are kept in Stock, in law calf and other bindings.*

[No. 4.] A

AGENCY.—Petgrave's Principal and Agent.—A Manual of the Law of Principal and Agent. By E. C. PETGRAVE, Solicitor. 12mo. 1857. *7s. 6d.*

Petgrave's Code of the Law of Principal and Agent, with a Preface. By E. C. PETGRAVE, Solicitor. Demy 12mo. 1876. *Net, 2s.*

Rogers.—*Vide* "Elections."

Russell's Treatise on Mercantile Agency.—Second Edition. 8vo. 1873. *14s.*

AGRICULTURAL LAW.—Addison's Practical Guide to the Agricultural Holdings (England) Act, 1875 (38 & 39 Vic. c. 92), and Treatise thereon, showing the Alterations in the Law, and containing many useful Hints and Suggestions as to the carrying out of the Provisions of the Act; with Handy Forms and a Carefully Prepared Index. Designed chiefly for the use of Agricultural Landlords and Tenants. By ALBERT ADDISON, Solicitor of the Supreme Court of Judicature. 12mo. 1876. *Net, 2s. 6d.*

Cooke on Agricultural Law.—The Law and Practice of Agricultural Tenancies, with Numerous Precedents of Tenancy Agreements and Farming Leases, &c., &c. By G. WINGROVE COOKE, Esq., Barrister-at-Law. 8vo. 1851. *18s.*

Dixon's Farm.—*Vide* "Farm."

ARBITRATION.—Russell's Treatise on the Duty and Power of an Arbitrator, and the Law of Submissions and Awards; with an Appendix of Forms, and of the Statutes relating to Arbitration. By FRANCIS RUSSELL, Esq., M.A., Barrister-at-Law. Fifth Edition. Royal 8vo. 1878. *1l. 16s.*

ARTICLED CLERKS.—Butlin's New and Complete Examination Guide and Introduction to the Law; for the use of Articled Clerks and those who contemplate entering the legal profession, comprising Courses of Reading for the Preliminary and Intermediate Examinations and for Honours, or a Pass at the Final, with Statute, Case, and Judicature (Time) Tables, Sets of Examination Papers, &c., &c. By JOHN FRANCIS BUTLIN, Solicitor, &c. 8vo. 1877. *18s.*

"A sensible and useful guide for the legal tyro."—*Solicitors' Journal.*

"In supplying law students with materials for preparing themselves for examination, Mr. Butlin, we think, has distanced all competitors. The volume before us contains hints on reading, a very neat summary of law, which the best read practitioner need not despise. There are time tables under the Judicature Act, and an excellent tabular arrangement of leading cases, which will be found of great service . . . . Tuition of this kind will do much to remove obstacles which present themselves to commencing students, and when examinations are over the book is one which may be usefully kept close at hand, and will well repay 'noting up.'"—*Law Times.*

Rubinstein and Ward's Articled Clerks' Handbook.—Being a Concise and Practical Guide to all the Steps Necessary for Entering into Articles of Clerkship, passing the Preliminary, Intermediate and Final Examinations, obtaining Admission and Certificate to Practise, with Notes of Cases affecting Articled Clerks, Suggestions as to Mode of Reading and Books to be read during Articles. Second Edition. By J. S. RUBINSTEIN and S. WARD, Solicitors. 12mo. 1878. *3s.*

"No articled clerk should be without it."—*Law Times.*

"We think it omits nothing which it ought to contain."—*Law Journal.*

Wharton's Articled Clerk's Manual.—A Manual for Articled Clerks: being a comprehensive Guide to their successful Examination, Admission, and Practice as Attorneys and Solicitors of the Superior Courts. Ninth Edition. Greatly enlarged. By C. H. ANDERSON. Royal 12mo. 1864. *18s.*

*** *All standard Law Works are kept in Stock, in law calf and other bindings*

ARTICLES OF ASSOCIATION.—Palmer.—*Vide* "Conveyancing."
ATTORNEYS.—Cordery.—*Vide* "Solicitors."

    Pulling's Law of Attorneys, General and Special, Attorneys-at-Law, Solicitors, Notaries, Proctors, Conveyancers, Scriveners, Land Agents, House Agents, &c., and the Offices and Appointments usually held by them, &c. By ALEXANDER PULLING, Serjeant-at-Law. Third Edition. 8vo. 1862. 18*s.*

"It is a laborious work, a careful work, the work of a lawyer, and, beyond comparison the best that has ever been produced upon this subject."—*Law Times.*

    Smith.—The Lawyer and his Profession.—A Series of Letters to a Solicitor commencing Business. By J. ORTON SMITH. 12mo. 1860. 4*s.*

AVERAGE.—**Hopkins' Hand-Book on Average.**—Third Edition. 8vo. 1868. 18*s.*

    Lowndes' Law of General Average.—English and Foreign. Third Edition. By RICHARD LOWNDES, Author of "The Admiralty Law of Collisions at Sea." Royal 8vo. 1878. 21*s.*

BALLOT.—**FitzGerald's Ballot Act.**—With an INTRODUCTION. Forming a Guide to the Procedure at Parliamentary and Municipal Elections. Second Edition. Enlarged, and containing the Municipal Elections Act, 1875, and the Parliamentary Elections (Returning Officers) Act, 1875. By GERALD A. R. FITZGERALD, M.A., of Lincoln's Inn, Esq., Barrister-at-Law. Fcap. 8vo. 1876. 5*s.* 6*d.*

"A useful guide to all concerned in Parliamentary and Municipal Elections."—*Law Magazine.*
"We should strongly advise any person connected with elections, whether acting as candidate, agent, or in any other capacity, to become possessed of this manual."

BANKING.—**Walker's Treatise on Banking Law.** Including the Crossed Checks Act, 1876, with dissertations thereon, also references to some American Cases, and full Index. By J. DOUGLAS WALKER, Esq., Barrister-at-Law. Demy 8vo. 1877. 14*s.*

"The work has been carefully written, and will supply the want of a compact summary of Banking Law."—*Solicitors' Journal.*
"Persons who are interested in banking law may be guided out of many a difficulty by consulting Mr. Walker's volume."—*Law Times.*

BANKRUPTCY.—**Bedford's Final Examination Guide to Bankruptcy.**—Third Edition. 12mo. 1877. 6*s.*

    Haynes.—*Vide* "Leading Cases."

    Lynch's Tabular Analysis of Proceedings in Bankruptcy, for the use of Students for the Incorporated Law Society's Examinations. Second Edition. 8vo. 1874. *Net*, 1*s.*

    Scott's Costs in Bankruptcy.—*Vide* "Costs."

    Smith's Manual of Bankruptcy.—A Manual relating to Bankruptcy, Insolvency, and Imprisonment for Debt; comprising the New Statute Law verbatim, in a consolidated and readable form. With the Rules, a Copious Index, and a Supplement of Decisions. By JOSIAH W. SMITH, B.C.L., Q.C. 12mo. 1873. 10*s.*

    *** The Supplement may be had separately, *net*, 2*s.* 6*d.*

    Williams' Law and Practice in Bankruptcy: comprising the Bankruptcy Act, the Debtors Act, and the Bankruptcy Repeal and Insolvent Court Act of 1869, and the Rules and Forms made under those Acts. Second Edition. By ROLAND VAUGHAN WILLIAMS, of Lincoln's Inn, Esq., and WALTER VAUGHAN WILLIAMS, of the Inner Temple, Esq., assisted by FRANCIS HALLETT HARDCASTLE, of the Inner Temple, Esq., Barristers-at-Law. 8vo. 1876. 1*l.* 8*s.*

"'Williams on Bankruptcy' is quite satisfactory."—*Law Magazine.*
"It would be difficult to speak in terms of undue praise of the present work."

*** *All standard Law Works are kept in Stock, in law calf and other bindings.*

BAR, GUIDE TO THE.—Shearwood.—*Vide* "Examination Guides."

BILLS OF EXCHANGE.—**Chalmers' Digest of the Law of Bills of Exchange, Promissory Notes, and Cheques.** By M. D. CHALMERS, of the Inner Temple, Esq. Barrister-at-Law. Demy 8vo. 1878. 12s. 6d.

*** This work is n the form of the Indian Codes, besides the English Cases it is noted up with reference to the French Law and the German Code, and on doubtful points to the more recent American Decisions; it also contains a table of overruled or doubted cases.

"Mr. Chalmers has done wisely in casting his book into its present form, and the plan, thus well conceived, has been most effectually carried out. As a handy book of reference on a difficult and important branch of the law, it is most valuable, and it is perfectly plain that no pains have been spared to render it complete in every respect. The index is copious and well arranged."—*Saturday Review*.

"The book is not only well planned, but well executed . . . . . for the rising generations and for men of business this digest will be a gift of no small value."—*Pall Mal Gazette*.

Chitty on Bills of Exchange and Promissory Notes, with references to the law of Scotland, France and America.—Eleventh Edition. By JOHN A. RUSSELL, Esq., LL.B., one of Her Majesty's Counsel, and Judge of County Courts. Demy 8vo. 1878. 1l. 8s.

Eddis' Rule of Ex parte Waring. By A. C. EDDIS, B. A., of Lincoln's Inn, Barrister-at-Law. Post 8vo. 1876. *Net*, 2s. 6d.

BILLS OF SALE.—Cavanagh.—*Vide* "Money Securities."

Millar's Bills of Sale.—A Treatise on Bills of Sale, with an Appendix containing the Acts for the Registration of Bills of Sale Precedents, &c. (being the Fourth Edition of Millar and Collier's Treatise on Bills of Sale). By F. C. J. MILLAR, of the Inner Temple, Esq., Barrister-at-Law. 12mo. 1877. 12s

"The original work is brought down to date, and the latest cases are referred to and considered. The value of the work is enhanced throughout by careful annotation."—*Law Magazine*.

BOOK-KEEPING.—Bedford's Intermediate Examination Guide to Book-keeping.—Second Edition. 12mo. 1875. *Net*, 2s. 6d.

CANAL TRAFFIC ACT.—Lely's Railway and Canal Traffic Act, 1873.—And other Railway and Canal Statutes; with the General Orders, Forms, and Table of Fees. Post 8vo. 1873. 8s.

CARRIERS.—Browne on Carriers.—A Treatise on the Law of Carriers of Goods and Passengers by Land and Water. With References to the most recent American Decisions. By J. H. BALFOUR BROWNE, of the Middle Temple, Esq., Barrister-at-Law, Registrar to the Railway Commission. 8vo. 1873. 18s.

CHANCERY, *and Vide* "**EQUITY.**"

Daniell's Chancery Practice. — Sixth Edition, by LEONARD FIELD and EDWARD CLENNELL DUNN, Barristers-at-Law; assisted by W. H. UPJOHN, Student and Holt Scholar of Gray's Inn, &c., &c., Editor of "Daniell's Forms, Third Edition." 2 vols. 8vo. (*In preparation*.)

Daniell's Forms and Precedents of Proceedings in the Chancery Division of the High Court of Justice and on Appeal therefrom; with Dissertations and Notes, forming a complete guide to the practice of the Chancery Division of the High Court and of the Courts of Appeal. Being the Third Edition of "Daniell's Chancery Forms." By WILLIAM HENRY UPJOHN, Esq., Student and Holt Scholar of Gray's Inn, Exhibitioner in Jurisprudence and Roman

*** *All standard Law Works are kept in Stock, in law calf and other bindings.*

CHANCERY.—*Continued.*

Law in the University of London, Holder of the First Senior Studentship in Jurisprudence, Roman Law and International Law awarded by the Council of Legal Education in Hilary Term, 1879. In one thick vol. Demy 8vo. 1879. 2*l*. 2*s*.

"Mr. Upjohn has restored the volume of Chancery Forms to the place it held before the recent changes, as a trustworthy and complete collection of precedents. It has all the old merits; nothing is omitted as too trivial or commonplace; the solicitor's clerk finds how to indorse a brief, and how, when necessary, to give notice of action; and the index to the forms is full and perspicuous."—*Solicitors' Journal.*

"It will be as useful a work to practitioners at Westminster as it will be to those in Lincoln's Inn."—*Law Times.*

Haynes' Chancery Practice.—The Practice of the Chancery Division of the High Court of Justice and on Appeal therefrom, for the use of Practitioners and Students.—By JOHN F. HAYNES, LL.D. Author of the "Student's Leading Cases," &c. Demy 8vo. 1879. 1*l*. 5*s*.

"Materials for enabling the practitioner himself to obtain the information he may require are placed before him in a convenient and accessible form. The arrangement of the work appears to be good."—*Law Magazine and Review,* February, 1880.

Morgan's Chancery Acts and Orders.—The Statutes, General Orders, and Rules of Court relating to the Practice, Pleading, and Jurisdiction of the Supreme Court of Judicature, particularly with reference to the Chancery Division, and the Actions assigned thereto. With copious Notes. Fifth Edition. Carefully revised and adapted to the new Practice by GEORGE OSBORNE MORGAN, M.P., one of Her Majesty's Counsel, and CHALONER W. CHUTE, of Lincoln's Inn, Barrister-at-Law, and late Fellow of Magdalen College, Oxford. Demy 8vo. 1876. 1*l*. 10*s*.

"This edition of Mr. Morgan's treatise must, we believe, be the most popular with the profession."—*Law Times.*

Morgan and Davey's Chancery Costs.—*Vide* "Costs."

Peel's Chancery Actions.—A Concise Treatise on the Practice and Procedure in Chancery Actions.—By SYDNEY PEEL, of the Middle Temple, Esq., Barrister-at-Law. Demy 8vo. 1878. 7*s*. 6*d*.

"To Chancery practitioners of both branches the volume will doubtless prove very useful."—*Law Times.*

CHANCERY PALATINE OF LANCASTER.—**Snow and Winstanley's Chancery Practice.**—The Statutes, Consolidated and General Orders and Rules of Court relating to the Practice, Pleading and Jurisdiction of the Court of Chancery, of the County Palatine of Lancaster. With Copious Notes of all practice cases to the end of the year 1879, Time Table and Tables of Costs and Forms. By THOMAS SNOW, M.A., and HERBERT WINSTANLEY, Esqrs., Barristers-at-Law. Royal 8vo. 1880. 1*l*. 10*s*.

CIVIL LAW.—**Bowyer's Commentaries on the Modern Civil Law.**—By Sir GEORGE BOWYER, D.C.L., Royal 8vo. 1848. 18*s*.

Bowyer's Introduction to the Study and Use of the Civil Law.—By Sir GEORGE BOWYER, D.C.L. Royal 8vo. 1874. 5*s*.

Cumin's Manual of Civil Law, containing a Translation of, and Commentary on, the Fragments of the XII. Tables, and the Institutes of Justinian; the Text of the Institutes of Gaius and Justinian arranged in parallel columns; and the Text of the Fragments of Ulpian, &c. By P. CUMIN, M.A., Barrister-at-Law Second Edition. Medium 8vo. 1865. 18*s*.

*** *All standard Law Works are kept in Stock, in law calf and other bindings.*

COLLISIONS.—Lowndes' Admiralty Law of Collisions at Sea.—8vo. 1867. *7s. 6d.*

Marsden on Maritime Collision.—A Treatise on the Law of Collisions at Sea. With an Appendix containing Extracts from the Merchant Shipping Acts, the International Regulations (of 1863 and 1880) for preventing Collisions at Sea; and local Rules for the same purpose in force in the Thames, the Mersey, and elsewhere. By REGINALD G. MARSDEN, Esq., Barrister-at-Law. Demy 8vo. 1880. *12s.*

COLONIAL LAW.—Clark's Colonial Law.—A Summary of Colonial Law and Practice of Appeals from the Plantations. 8vo. 1834. *1l. 4s.*

COMMENTARIES ON THE LAWS OF ENGLAND.—Bedford.— *Vide* "Examination Guides."

Broom and Hadley's Commentaries on the Laws of England.—By HERBERT BROOM, LL.D., of the Inner Temple, Barrister-at-Law; and EDWARD A. HADLEY, M.A., of Lincoln's Inn. Barrister-at-Law; late Fellow of Trinity Coll., Cambridge. 4 vols. 8vo. 1869. *3l. 3s.*
"Nothing that could be done to make the work useful and handy has been left undone."—*Law Journal.*

COMMERCIAL LAW.—Goirand's French Code of Commerce and most usual Commercial Laws. With a Theoretical and Practical Commentary, and a Compendium of the judicial organization and of the course of procedure before the Tribunals of Commerce; together with the text of the law; the most recent decisions of the Courts, and a glossary of French judicial terms. By LEOPOLD GOIRAND, Licencié en droit. In 1 vol. (850 pp.). Demy 8vo. 1880. *2l. 2s.*

Levi.—*Vide* "International Law."

COMMON LAW.—Archbold's Practice of the Queen's Bench, Common Pleas and Exchequer Divisions of the High Court of Justice in Actions, etc., in which they have a common jurisdiction.—Thirteenth Edition. By SAMUEL PRENTICE, Esq., one of Her Majesty's Counsel. 2 vols. Demy 8vo. 1879. *3l. 3s.*

Ball's Short Digest of the Common Law; being the Principles of Torts and Contracts. Chiefly founded upon the works of Addison, with Illustrative Cases, for the use of Students. By W. EDMUND BALL, LL.B., late "Holt Scholar" of Gray's Inn, Barrister-at-Law and Midland Circuit. (*Nearly ready.*)

Chitty.—*Vide* "Forms."   Foulkes.—*Vide* "Action."
Fisher.—*Vide* "Digests."   Prentice.—*Vide* "Action."
Shirley.—*Vide* "Leading Cases."

Smith's Manual of Common Law.—For Practitioners and Students. A Manual of Common Law, comprising the fundamental principles and the points most usually occurring in daily life and practice. By JOSIAH W. SMITH, B.C.L., Q.C. Eighth Edition. 12mo. 1878. *14s.*

COMMONS AND INCLOSURES.—Chambers' Digest of the Law relating to Commons and Open Spaces, including Public Parks and Recreation Grounds, with various official documents; precedents of by-laws and regulations. The Statutes in full and brief notes of leading cases. By GEORGE F. CHAMBERS, of the Inner Temple, Esq., Barrister-at-Law. Imperial 8vo. 1877. *6s. 6d.*

Cooke on Inclosures.—With Forms as settled by the Inclosure Commissioners. By G. WINGROVE COOKE, Esq., Barrister-at-Law. Fourth Edition. 12mo. 1864. *16s.*

₊ *All standard Law Works are kept in Stock, in law calf and other bindings.*

COMPANY LAW.—Finlason's Report of the Case of Twycross v. Grant. 8vo. 1877. *Net, 2s. 6d.*

Palmer.—*Vide* "Conveyancing."

Palmer's Shareholders' and Directors' Companion.—A Manual of every-day Law and Practice for Promoters, Shareholders, Directors, Secretaries, Creditors and Solicitors of Companies, under the Companies' Acts, 1862, 1867, and 1877. Second Edition. By FRANCIS B. PALMER, Esq., Barrister-at-Law, Author of "Company Precedents." 12mo. 1880. *Net, 2s. 6d.*

Thring.—*Vide* "Joint Stocks."

CONTINGENT REMAINDERS.—An Epitome of Fearne on Contingent Remainders and Executory Devises. Intended for the Use of Students. By W. M. C. Post 8vo. 1878. *6s. 6d.*

"An acquaintance with Fearne is indispensable to a student who desires to be thoroughly grounded in the common law relating to real property. Such student will find a perusal of this epitome of great value to him."—*Law Journal.*

CONSTITUTIONAL LAW.—Bowyer's Commentaries on the Constitutional Law of England.—By Sir GEO. BOWYER, D.C.L. Second Edition. Royal 8vo. 1846. *1l. 2s.*

Haynes.—*Vide* "Leading Cases."

CONTRACTS.—Addison on Contracts.—Being a Treatise on the Law of Contracts. By C. G. ADDISON, Esq., Author of the "Law of Torts." Seventh Edition. By L. W. CAVE, Esq., one of Her Majesty's Counsel, Recorder of Lincoln. Royal 8vo. 1875. *1l. 18s.*

"At present this is by far the best book upon the Law of Contract possessed by the Profession, and it is a thoroughly practical book."—*Law Times.*

Leake on Contracts.—An Elementary Digest of the Law of Contracts (being a new edition of "The Elements of the Law of Contracts"). By STEPHEN MARTIN LEAKE, Barrister-at-Law. 1 vol. Demy 8vo. 1878. *1l. 18s.*

Pollock's Principles of Contract at Law and in Equity; being a Treatise on the General Principles relating to the Validity of Agreements, with a special view to the comparison of Law and Equity, and with references to the Indian Contract Act, and occasionally to American and Foreign Law. Second Edition. By FREDERICK POLLOCK, of Lincoln's Inn, Esq., Barrister-at-Law. Demy 8vo. 1878. *1l. 6s.*

The Lord Chief Justice in his judgment in *Metropolitan Railway Company* v. *Brogden and others*, said, "The Law is well put by Mr. Frederick Pollock in his very able and learned work on Contracts."—*The Times.*

"For the purposes of the student there is no book equal to Mr. Pollock's."—*The Economist.*

"He has succeeded in writing a book on Contracts which the working lawyer will find as useful for reference as any of its predecessors, and which at the same time will give the student what he will seek for in vain elsewhere, a complete *rationale* of the law.—*Law Magazine and Review.*

"We see nothing to qualify in the praise we bestowed on the first edition. The chapters on unlawful and impossible agreements are models of full and clear treatment."—*Solicitors' Journal.*

Smith's Law of Contracts.—By the late J. W. SMITH, Esq., Author of "Leading Cases," &c. Seventh Edition. By VINCENT T. THOMPSON, Esq., Barrister-at-Law. Demy 8vo. 1878. *1l. 1s.*

"We know of few books equally likely to benefit the student, or marked by such distinguished qualities of lucidity, order, and accuracy as the work before us."—*Solicitors' Journal*, December 28, 1878.

⁎ *All standard Law Works are kept in Stock, in law calf and other bindings.*

CONVICTIONS.—Paley's Law and Practice of Summary Convictions under the Summary Jurisdiction Acts, 1848 and 1879; including Proceedings preliminary and subsequent to Convictions, and the responsibility of convicting Magistrates and their Officers, with Forms. Sixth Edition. By W. H. MACNAMARA, Esq., Barrister-at-Law. Demy 8vo. 1879. 1*l.* 4*s*

Stone.—*Vide* "Petty Sessions."

Templer.—*Vide* "Summary Convictions."

Wigram.—*Vide* "Justice of the Peace."

CONVEYANCING.—Dart.—*Vide* "Vendors and Purchasers."

Greenwood's Manual of Conveyancing.—A Manual of the Practice of Conveyancing, showing the present Practice relating to the daily routine of Conveyancing in Solicitors' Offices To which are added Concise Common Forms and Precedents in Conveyancing; Conditions of Sale, Conveyances, and all other Assurances in constant use. Fifth Edition. By H. N. CAPEL, B.A., LL.B., Solicitor. Demy 8vo. 1877. 15*s.*

"A careful study of these pages would probably arm a diligent clerk with as much useful knowledge as he might otherwise take years of desultory questioning and observing to acquire."—*Solicitors' Journal.*

The young solicitor will find this work almost invaluable, while the members of the higher branch of the profession may refer to it with advantage. We have not met with any book that furnishes so simple a guide to the management of business entrusted to articled clerks."

Haynes.—*Vide* "Leading Cases."

Martin's Student's Conveyancer.—A Manual on the Principles of Modern Conveyancing, illustrated and enforced by a Collection of Precedents, accompanied by detailed Remarks. Part I. Purchase Deeds. By THOMAS FREDERIC MARTIN, Solicitor. Demy 8vo. 1877. 5*s.* 6*d.*

"It should be placed in the hands of every student."

Palmer's Company Precedents.—Conveyancing and other Forms and Precedents relating to Companies' incorporated under the Companies' Acts, 1862 and 1867. Arranged as follows:—Agreements, Memoranda of Association, Articles of Association, Resolutions, Notices, Certificates, Provisional Orders of Board of Trade, Debentures, Reconstruction, Amalgamation, Petitions, Orders. With Copious Notes. By FRANCIS BEAUFORT PALMER, of the Inner Temple, Esq., Barrister-at-Law. Demy 8vo. 1877. 1*l.* 5*s.*

"There had never, to our knowledge, been any attempt to collect and edit a body of Forms and Precedents exclusively relating to the formation, working and winding-up of companies. This task Mr. Palmer has taken in hand, and we are glad to say with much success . . . . The information contained in the 650 pages of the volume is rendered easily accessible by a good and full index. The author has evidently not been sparing of labour, and the fruits of his exertions are now before the legal profession in a work of great practical utility."—*Law Magazine.*

"To those concerned in getting up companies, the assistance given by Mr. Palmer must be very valuable, because he does not confine himself to bare precedents, but by intelligent and learned commentary lights up, as it were, each step that he takes. The volume before us is not, therefore a book of precedents merely, but, in a greater or less degree, a treatise on certain portions of the Companies' Acts of 1862 and 1867. There is an elaborate index, and the work is one which must commend itself to the profession."—*Law Times.*

"The precedents are as a rule exceedingly well drafted, and adapted to companies for almost every conceivable object. So especially are the forms of memoranda and articles of association; and these will be found extremely serviceable to the conveyancer. . . All the notes have been elaborated with a thoroughly scientific knowledge of the principles of company law, as well as with copious references to the cases substantiating the principles. . . . We venture to predict that his notes will be found of great utility in guiding opinions on many complicated questions of law and practice."—*Law Journal.*

⁎⁎* *All standard Law Works are kept in Stock, in law calf and other bindings.*

CONVEYANCING.—*Continued.*

Prideaux's Precedents in Conveyancing.—With Dissertations on its Law and Practice. Ninth Edition. By FREDERICK PRIDEAUX, late Professor of the Law of Real and Personal Property to the Inns of Court, and JOHN WHITCOMBE, Esqrs., Barristers-at-Law. 2 vols. Royal 8vo. 1870. 3*l.* 10*s.*

"We have been always accustomed to view 'Prideaux' as the most useful work out on conveyancing. It combines conciseness and clearness in its precedents with aptness and comprehensiveness in its dissertations and notes, to a degree superior to that of any other work of its kind."—*Law Journal,* February 8, 1879.

"Prideaux has become an indispensable part of the Conveyancer's library. . . . . The new edition has been edited with a care and accuracy of which we can hardly speak too highly. . . . . The care and completeness with which the dissertation has been revised leaves us hardly any room for criticism."—*Solicitors' Journal.*

"The volumes are now something more than a mere collection of precedents; they contain most valuable dissertations on the law and practice with reference to conveyancing. These dissertations are followed by the precedents on each subject dealt with, and are in themselves condensed treatises, embodying all the latest case and statute law . . . Having regard to the wide general knowledge required of all lawyers in the present day, such a work as this must prove highly acceptable to the whole Profession."—*Law Times.*

COPYRIGHT.—**Phillips' Law of Copyright.**—The Law of Copyright in Works of Literature and Art, and in the Application of Designs. With the Statutes relating thereto. By CHARLES PALMER PHILLIPS, of Lincoln's Inn, Esq., Barrister-at-Law. 8vo. 1863. 12*s.*

CORONERS.—**Jervis on the Office and Duties of Coroners.**—With Forms and Precedents. Fourth Edition.
(*In preparation.*)

COSTS.—**Morgan and Davey's Treatise on Costs in Chancery.**—By GEORGE OSBORNE MORGAN, M.P., one of Her Majesty's Counsel, late Stowell Fellow of University College, Oxford, and Eldon Scholar; and HORACE DAVEY, M.A., one of Her Majesty's Counsel, late Fellow of University College, Oxford, and Eldon Scholar. With an Appendix, containing Forms and Precedents of Bills of Costs. 8vo. 1865. 1*l.* 1*s.*

Scott's Costs in the High Court of Justice and other Courts. Fourth Edition. By JOHN SCOTT, of the Inner Temple, Esq., Barrister-at-Law, Reporter of the Common Pleas Division. Demy 8vo. 1880. 1*l.* 6*s.*

"Mr. Scott's introductory notes are very useful, and the work is now a compendium on the law and practice regarding costs, as well as a book of precedents."—*Law Times,* January 3, 1880.

Scott's Costs in Bankruptcy and Liquidation under the Bankruptcy Act, 1869. Royal 12mo. 1873. *net* 3*s.*

Summerhays and Toogood's Precedents of Bills of Costs in the Chancery, Queen's Bench, Common Pleas, Exchequer, Probate and Divorce Divisions of the High Court of Justice, in Conveyancing, Bankruptcy, the Crown Office, Lunacy, Arbitration under the Lands Clauses Consolidation Act, the Mayor's Court, London; the County Courts, the Privy Council, and on Passing Residuary and Succession Accounts; with Scales of Allowances and Court Fees, the Law Society's Scale of Commission in Conveyancing; Forms of Affidavits of Increase, and Objections to Taxation. By WM. FRANK SUMMERHAYS, Solicitor, and THORNTON TOOGOOD. Third Edition, Enlarged. Royal 8vo. 1879. 1*l.* 1*s.*

"In the volume before us we have a very complete manual of taxation. The work is beautifully printed and arranged, and each item catches the eye instantly."—*Law Journal.*

*** *All standard Law Works are kept in Stock, in law calf and other bindings.*

COSTS.—*Continued.*

Webster's Parliamentary Costs.—Private Bills, Election Petitions, Appeals, House of Lords. By EDWARD WEBSTER, Esq., of the Taxing and Examiners' Office. Third Edition. Post 8vo. 1867. 20s.

COUNTY COURTS.—Pitt-Lewis' County Court Practice.—A Complete Practice of the County Courts, including Admiralty and Bankruptcy, embodying the Acts, Rules, Forms and Costs, with Additional Forms and a Full Index. By G. PITT-LEWIS, of the Middle Temple and Western Circuit, Esq., Barrister-at-Law, sometime Holder of the Studentship of the Four Inns of Court, assisted by H. A. DE COLYAR, of the Middle Temple, Esq., Barrister-at-Law, Author of "A Treatise on the Law of Guarantees." In Two parts. 2 vols. (2028 pp.). Demy 8vo. 1880. 2l. 2s.

The parts, each complete in itself, sold separately.

Part I. History, Constitution, and Jurisdiction (including Prohibition and Mandamus), Practice in all ordinary Actions (including Actions under the Bills of Exchange Acts, in Ejectment, in Remitted Actions, and in Replevin), with Appendices, Index, &c. (1184 pp.). 30s.

Part II. Practice in Admiralty, Probate, the Practice under Special Statutes, and in Bankruptcy, with Appendices, Index, &c. (1004 pp.). 25s.

CRIMINAL LAW.—Archbold's Pleading and Evidence in Criminal Cases.—With the Statutes, Precedents of Indictments, &c., and the Evidence necessary to support them. By JOHN JERVIS, Esq. (late Lord Chief Justice of Her Majesty's Court of Common Pleas). Nineteenth Edition, including the Practice in Criminal Proceedings by Indictment. By WILLIAM BRUCE, of the Middle Temple, Esq., Barrister-at-Law, and Stipendiary Magistrate for the Borough of Leeds. Royal 12mo. 1878. 1l. 11s. 6d.

Cole on Criminal Informations and Quo Warranto.—By W. R. COLE, Esq., Barrister-at-Law. 12mo. 1843. 12s.

Greaves' Criminal Law Consolidation and Amendment Acts of the 24 & 25 Vict.—With Notes, Observations, and Forms for Summary Proceedings. By CHARLES SPRENGEL GREAVES, Esq., one of Her Majesty's Counsel. Second Edition. Post 8vo. 1862. 16s.

Haynes.—*Vide* "Leading Cases."

Roscoe's Digest of the Law of Evidence in Criminal Cases.—Ninth Edition. By HORACE SMITH, Esq., Barrister-at-Law. Royal 12mo. 1878. 1l. 11s. 6d.

Russell's Treatise on Crimes and Misdemeanors.—Fifth Edition. By SAMUEL PRENTICE, Esq., one of Her Majesty's Counsel. 3 vols. Royal 8vo. 1877. 5l. 15s. 6d.

This treatise is so much more copious than any other upon all the subjects contained in it, that it affords by far the best means of acquiring a knowledge of the Criminal Law in general, or of any offence in particular; so that it will be found peculiarly useful as well to those who wish to obtain a complete knowledge of that law, as to those who desire to be informed on any portion of it as occasion may require.

"What better Digest of Criminal Law could we possibly hope for than 'Russell on Crimes?'"—*Sir James Fitzjames Stephen's Speech on Codification.*

"No more trustworthy authority, or more exhaustive expositor than 'Russell' can be consulted."—*Law Magazine and Review.*

"Alterations have been made in the arrangement of the work which without interfering with the general plan are sufficient to show that great care and thought have been bestowed. . . . . We are amazed at the patience, industry and skill which are exhibited in the collection and arrangement of all this mass of learning."—*The Times.*

*** *All standard Law Works are kept in Stock, in law calf and other bindings.*

CROSSED CHEQUES ACT.—Cavanagh.—*Vide* "Money Securities."

Walker.—*Vide* "Banking."

DECREES.—Seton.—*Vide* "Equity."

DIARY.—**Lawyer's Companion (The), Diary, and Law Directory for 1880.**—For the use of the Legal Profession, Public Companies, Justices, Merchants, Estate Agents, Auctioneers, &c., &c. Edited by JOHN THOMPSON, of the Inner Temple, Esq., Barrister-at-Law; and contains a Digest of Recent Cases on Costs; Monthly Diary of County, Local Government, and Parish Business; Oaths in Supreme Court; Summary of Legislation of 1878; Alphabetical Index to the Practical Statutes; a Copious Table of Stamp Duties; Legal Time, Interest, Discount, Income, Wages and other Tables; Probate, Legacy and Succession Duties; and a variety of matters of practical utility. PUBLISHED ANNUALLY. Thirty-fourth Issue.

The work also contains the most complete List published of Town and Country Solicitors, with date of admission and appointments, and is issued in the following forms, octavo size, strongly bound in cloth:—

		s.	d.
1.	Two days on a page, plain	5	0
2.	The above, INTERLEAVED for ATTENDANCES	7	0
3.	Two days on a page, ruled, with or without money columns	5	6
4.	The above, INTERLEAVED for ATTENDANCES	8	0
5.	Whole page for each day, plain	7	6
6.	The above, INTERLEAVED for ATTENDANCES	9	6
7.	Whole page for each day, ruled, with or without money columns	3	6
8.	The above, INTERLEAVED for ATTENDANCES	10	6
9.	Three days on a page, ruled blue lines, without money columns	5	0

The Diary contains memoranda of Legal Business throughout the Year.

"An excellent work."—*The Times.*

"A publication which has long ago secured to itself the favour of the profession, and which, as heretofore, justifies by its contents the title assumed by it."—*Law Journal.*

"Contains all the information which could be looked for in such a work, and gives it in a most convenient form and very completely. We may unhesitatingly recommend the work to our readers."—*Solicitors' Journal.*

"The 'Lawyer's Companion and Diary' is a book that ought to be in the possession of every lawyer, and of every man of business."

"The 'Lawyer's Companion' is, indeed, what it is called, for it combines everything required for reference in the lawyer's office."—*Law Times.*

"It is a book without which no lawyer's library or office can be complete."—*Irish Law Times.*

"This work has attained to a completeness which is beyond all praise."—*Morning Post.*

DICTIONARY.—**Wharton's Law Lexicon.**—A Dictionary of Jurisprudence, explaining the Technical Words and Phrases employed in the several Departments of English Law; including the various Legal Terms used in Commercial Transactions. Together with an Explanatory as well as Literal Translation of the Latin Maxims contained in the Writings of the Ancient and Modern Commentators. Sixth Edition. Enlarged and revised in accordance with the Judicature Acts, by J. SHIRESS WILL, of the Middle Temple, Esq., Barrister-at-Law. Super royal 8vo. 1876. 2*l*. 2*s*.

'As a work of reference for the library, the handsome and elaborate edition of Wharton's Law Lexicon' which Mr. Shiress Will has produced, must supersede all former issues of that well-known work."—*Law Magazine and Review.*

"No law library is complete without a law dictionary or law lexicon. To the practitioner it is always useful to have at hand a book where, in a small compass, he can find an explanation of terms of infrequent occurrence, or obtain a reference to statutes on most subjects, or to books wherein particular subjects are treated of at full length. To the student it is almost indispensable."—*Law Times.*

*** *All standard Law Works are kept in Stock, in law calf and other bindings.*

DIGESTS.—Bedford.—*Vide* " Examination Guides."

Chamber's—*Vide* " Public Health."

Chitty's Equity Index.—Chitty's Index to all the Reported Cases, and Statutes, in or relating to the Principles, Pleading, and Practice of Equity and Bankruptcy, in the several Courts of Equity in England and Ireland, the Privy Council, and the House of Lords, from the earliest period. Third Edition. By J. MACAULAY, Esq., Barrister-at-Law. 4 vols. Royal 8vo. 1853. *7l. 7s.*

Fisher's Digest of the Reported Cases determined in the House of Lords and Privy Council, and in the Courts of Common Law, Divorce, Probate, Admiralty and Bankruptcy, from Michaelmas Term, 1756, to Hilary Term, 1870; with References to the Statutes and Rules of Court. Founded on the Analytical Digest by Harrison, and adapted to the present practice of the Law. By R. A. FISHER, Esq., Judge of the County Courts of Bristol and of Wells. Five large volumes, royal 8vo. 1870. *12l. 12s.*

(*Continued Annually.*)

"Mr. Fisher's Digest is a wonderful work. It is a miracle of human industry."—*Mr. Justice Willes.*

"I think it would be very difficult to improve upon Mr. Fisher's 'Common Law Digest.'"—*Sir James Fitzjames Stephen, on Codification.*

Leake.—*Vide* " Real Property " and " Contracts."

Notanda Digest in Law, Equity, Bankruptcy, Admiralty, Divorce, and Probate Cases.—By H. TUDOR BODDAM, of the Inner Temple, and HARRY GREENWOOD, of Lincoln's Inn, Esqrs., Barristers-at-Law. The NOTANDA DIGEST, from the commencement, October, 1862, to December, 1876. In 2 volumes, half-bound. *Net, 3l. 10s.*

Ditto, Third Series, 1873 to 1876 inclusive, half-bound. *Net, 1l. 11s. 6d.*

Ditto, Fourth Series, for the years 1877, 1878, and 1879, with Index.

Each, net, 1l. 1s.

Ditto, ditto, for 1880, Plain Copy and Two Indexes, or Adhesive Copy for insertion in Text-Books (without Index). Annual Subscription, payable in advance. *Net, 21s.*

*** The numbers are issued regularly every alternate month. Each number will contain a concise analysis of every case reported in the *Law Reports, Law Journal, Weekly Reporter, Law Times,* and the *Irish Law Reports,* up to and including the cases contained in the parts for the current month, with references to Text-books, Statutes, and the Law Reports Consolidated Digest. An ALPHABETICAL INDEX of the subjects contained IN EACH NUMBER will form a new feature in this series.

Pollock.—*Vide* " Partnership."

Roscoe's.—*Vide* " Criminal Law " and " Nisi Prius."

DISCOVERY.—Hare's Treatise on the Discovery of Evidence.—Second Edition. Adapted to the Procedure in the High Court of Justice, with Addenda, containing all the Reported Cases to the end of 1876. By SHERLOCK HARE, Barrister-at-Law. Post 8vo. 1877. *12s.*

"The book is a useful contribution to our text-books on practice."—*Solicitors' Journal.*

"We have read his work with considerable attention and interest, and we can speak in terms of cordial praise of the manner in which the new procedure has been worked into the old material. . . . All the sections and orders of the new legislation are referred to in the text, a synopsis of recent cases is given, and a good index completes the volume."—*Law Times.*

Seton.—*Vide* " Equity."

*** *All standard Law Works are kept in Stock, in law calf and other bindings.*

DISTRICT REGISTRIES.—Archibald.—*Vide* "Judges' Chambers Practice."

DIVORCE.—Browne's Treatise on the Principles and Practice of the Court for Divorce and Matrimonial Causes:—With the Statutes, Rules, Fees and Forms relating thereto. Fourth Edition. By GEORGE BROWNE, Esq., B.A., of the Inner Temple, Barrister-at-Law, Recorder of Ludlow. Demy 8vo. 1880. 1*l.* 4*s.*

Haynes.—*Vide* "Leading Cases."

DOMICIL.—Dicey on the Law of Domicil as a branch of the Law of England, stated in the form of Rules.—By A. V. DICEY, B.C.L., Barrister-at-Law. Author of "Rules for the Selection of Parties to an Action." Demy 8vo. 1879. 18*s.*

"The practitioner will find the book a thoroughly exact and trustworthy summary of the present state of the law."—*The Spectator,* August 9th, 1879.

Phillimore's (Sir R.) Law of Domicil.—8vo. 1847. 9*s.*

DUTCH LAW.—Vanderlinden's Institutes of the Laws of Holland.—8vo. 1828. 1*l.* 18*s.*

EASEMENTS.—Goddard's Treatise on the Law of Easements.—By JOHN LEYBOURN GODDARD, of the Middle Temple, Esq., Barrister-at-Law. Second Edition. Demy 8vo. 1877. 16*s.*

"The book is invaluable: where the cases are silent the author has taken pains to ascertain what the law would be if brought into question."—*Law Journal.*

"Nowhere has the subject been treated so exhaustively, and, we may add, so scientifically, as by Mr. Goddard. We recommend it to the most careful study of the law student as well as to the library of the practitioner."—*Law Times.*

ECCLESIASTICAL. — Finlason's Folkestone Ritual Case.—The Judgment of the Judicial Committee in the Folkestone Ritual Case, with an Historical Introduction and brief Notes. By W. F. FINLASON, of the Middle Temple, Esq., Barrister-at-Law. 8vo. 1877. *Net,* 2*s.* 6*d.*

Phillimore's (Sir R.) Ecclesiastical Law.—The Ecclesiastical Law of the Church of England. With Supplement, containing the Statutes and Decisions to end of 1875. By SIR ROBERT PHILLIMORE, D.C.L., Official Principal of the Arches Court of Canterbury; Member of Her Majesty's Most Honourable Privy Council. 2 vols. 8vo. 1873-76. 3*l.* 7*s.* 6*d.*

** The Supplement may be had separately, price 4*s.* 6*d.,* sewed.

ELECTIONS.—Browne (G. Lathom.)—*Vide* "Registration."

FitzGerald.—*Vide* "Ballot."

Rogers on Elections, Registration, and Election Agency.—Thirteenth Edition, including PETITIONS and Municipal Elections and Registration. With an Appendix of Statutes and Forms. By JOHN CORRIE CARTER, of the Inner Temple, Esq., and Midland Circuit, Barrister-at-Law. 12mo. 1880. 1*l.* 12*s.*

"Petition has been added, setting forth the procedure and the decisions on that subject; and the statutes passed since the last edition are explained down to the Parliamentary Elections and Corrupt Practices Act (1880)."—*The Times,* March 27th, 1880.

"We have no hesitation in commending the book to our readers as a useful and adequate treatise upon election law."—*Solicitors' Journal,* April 3rd, 1880.

ENGLAND, LAWS OF.—Bowyer.—*Vide* "Constitutional Law."

Broom and Hadley.—*Vide* "Commentaries."

** *All standard Law Works are kept in Stock, in law calf and other bindings.*

EQUITY, and *Vide* **CHANCERY.**

Seton's Forms of Decrees, Judgments, and Orders in the High Court of Justice and Courts of Appeal, having especial reference to the Chancery Division, with Practical Notes. Fourth Edition. By R. H. LEACH, Esq., Senior Registrar of the Chancery Division; F. G. A. WILLIAMS, of the Inner Temple, Esq.; and the late H. W. MAY, Esq.; succeeded by JAMES EASTWICK, of Lincoln's Inn, Esq., Barristers-at-Law. 2 vols. in 3 parts. Royal 8vo. 1877—79. 4*l*. 10*s*.

⁎⁎* Vol. II., Parts 1 and 2, may be had separately, to complete sets, price each 1*l*. 10*s*.

"Of all the editions of 'Seton' this is the best.—*Solicitors' Journal*.
"We can hardly speak too highly of the industry and intelligence which have been bestowed on the preparation of the notes."—*Solicitors' Journal*.
"Now the book is before us complete; and we advisedly say *complete*, because it has scarcely ever been our fortune to see a more *complete* law book than this. Extensive in sphere, and exhaustive in treatise, comprehensive in matter, yet apposite in details, it presents all the features of an excellent work . . . The index, extending over 278 pages, is a model of comprehensiveness and accuracy."—*Law Journal*

Smith's Manual of Equity Jurisprudence.— A Manual of Equity Jurisprudence for Practitioners and Students, founded on the Works of Story, Spence, and other writers, and on more than a thousand subsequent cases, comprising the Fundamental Principles and the points of Equity usually occurring in General Practice. By JOSIAH W. SMITH, B.C.L., Q.C. Twelfth Edition. 12mo. 1878. 12*s*. 6*d*.

"There is no disguising the truth; the proper mode to use this book is to learn its pages by heart."—*Law Magazine and Review*.
"It will be found as useful to the practitioner as to the student."—*Solicitors' Journal*.

EXAMINATION GUIDES.—Bedford's Guide to the Preliminary Examination for Solicitors.—Fourth Edition. 12mo. 1874. *Net*, 3*s*.

Bedford's Preliminary.—Containing the Questions and Answers of the Preliminary Examinations. Edited by E. H. BEDFORD, Solicitor (No. 15, May, 1871, to No. 48, July, 1879). (*Discontinued*). *Sewed, net*, each, 1*s*.

Bedford's Digest of the Preliminary Examination Questions on English and Latin, Grammar, Geography, History, French Grammar, and Arithmetic, with the Answers. 8vo. 1875. 18*s*.

Bedford's Preliminary Guide to Latin Grammar.—12mo. 1872. *Net*, 3*s*.

Bedford's Intermediate Examination Guide to Bookkeeping.—Second Edition. 12mo. 1875. *Net*, 2*s*. 6*d*.

Bedford's Intermediate.—Containing the Questions and Answers at the Intermediate Examinations. Edited by E. H. BEDFORD. Nos. 1 (Hilary, 1869) to 34 (Hilary, 1877). 6*d*. each. Nos. 35 (Easter, 1877) to 43 (Trinity, 1879). (*Discontinued*). 1*s*. each, *Net*.

Bedford's Student's Guide to Stephen's New Commentaries on the Laws of England. Demy 8vo. 1879. 12*s*.

"Here is a book which will be of the greatest service o students. It reduces the 'Commentaries' to the form of question and answer . . . We must also give the author credit, not only for his selection of questions, but for his answers thereto. These are models of fulness and conciseness, and lucky will be the candidate who can hand in a paper of answers bearing a close resemblance to those in the work before us."—*Law Journal*.

Bedford's Student's Guide to Smith on Contracts. Demy 8vo. 1879. 3*s*. 6*d*.

⁎⁎* *All standard Law Works are kept in Stock, in law calf and other bindings.*

EXAMINATION GUIDES.—*Continued.*

Bedford's Final.—Containing the Questions and Answers at the Final Examinations. Edited by E. H. BEDFORD. Nos. 1 (Easter, 1869) to 33 (Easter, 1877). 6d. each. Nos. 34 (Trinity, 1877) to 42 (Trinity, 1879). 1s. each, *Net.* (*Discontinued.*)

Bedford's Final Examination Digest: containing a Digest of the Final Examination Questions in matters of Law and Procedure determined by the Chancery, Queen's Bench, Common Pleas, and Exchequer Divisions of the High Court of Justice, and on the Law of Real and Personal Property and the Practice of Conveyancing. In 1 vol. 8vo. 1879. 16s.

"Will furnish students with a large armoury of weapons with which to meet the attacks of the examiners of the Incorporated Law Society."—*Law Times*, Nov. 8, 1879.

Bedford's Final Examination Guide to Bankruptcy.—Third Edition. 12mo. 1877. 6s.

Bedford's Outline of an Action in the Chancery Division. 12mo. 1878. *Net*, 2s. 6d.

Butlin.—*Vide* "Articled Clerks."

Dickson's Analysis of Blackstone's Commentaries.—In Charts for the use of Students. By FREDERICK S. DICKSON. 4to. 10s. 6d.

Haynes.—*Vide* "Leading Cases."

Rubinstein and Ward.—*Vide* "Articled Clerks."

Shearwood's Student's Guide to the Bar, the Solicitor's Intermediate and Final and the Universities Law Examinations.—With Suggestions as to the books usually read, and the passages therein to which attention should be paid. By JOSEPH A. SHEARWOOD, B.A., Esq., Barrister-at-law, Author of "A Concise Abridgment of the Law of Real Property," &c. Demy 8vo. 1879. 5s. 6d.

"A work which will be very acceptable to candidates for the various examinations, any student of average intelligence who conscientiously follows the path and obeys the instructions given him by the author, need not fear to present himself as a candidate for any of the examinations to which this book is intended as a guide."—*Law Journal.*

EXECUTORS.—Williams' Law of Executors and Administrators.—By the Rt. Hon. Sir EDWARD VAUGHAN WILLIAMS, late one of the Judges of Her Majesty's Court of Common Pleas. Eighth Edition. By WALTER VAUGHAN WILLIAMS and ROLAND VAUGHAN WILLIAMS, Esqrs., Barristers-at-Law. 2 vols. Royal 8vo. 1879. 3l. 16s.

"A treatise which occupies a unique position and which is recognised by the Bench and the profession as having paramount authority in the domain of law with which it deals."—*Law Journal.*

EXECUTORY DEVISES.—Fearne.—*Vide* "Contingent Remainders."

FACTORY ACTS.—Notcutt's Law relating to Factories and Workshops, with Introduction and Explanatory Notes. Second Edition. Comprising the Factory and Workshop Act, 1878, and the Orders of the Secretary of State made thereunder. By GEO. JARVIS NOTCUTT, Solicitor, formerly of the Middle Temple, Esq., Barrister-at-Law. 12mo. 1879. 9s.

"The task of elucidating the provisions of the statute is done in a manner that leaves nothing to be desired."—*Birmingham Daily Gazette.*

FARM, LAW OF.—Addison ; Cooke.—*Vide* "Agricultural Law." **Dixon's Law of the Farm**—A Digest of Cases connected with the Law of the Farm, and including the Agricultural Customs of England and Wales. Fourth Edition. By HENRY PERKINS, Esq., Barrister-at-Law and Midland Circuit. Demy 8vo. 1879. 1l. 6s.

"It is impossible not to be struck with the extraordinary research that must have been used in the compilation of such a book as this."—*Law Journal.*

*** *All standard Law Works are kept in Stock, in law calf and other bindings.*

FINAL EXAMINATION DIGEST.—Bedford.—*Vide* "Examination Guides."

FIXTURES.—Amos and Ferard on Fixtures.—Second Edition. Royal 8vo. 1847. 16*s.*

FOREIGN JUDGMENTS.—Piggott's Foreign Judgments, their effect in the English Courts, the English Doctrine, Defences, Judgments in Rem, Status.—By F. T. PIGGOTT, M.A., LL.M., of the Middle Royal 8vo. 1879. 15*s.*

"A useful and well-timed volume."—*Law Magazine*, August, 1879.

"Mr. Piggott writes under strong conviction, but he is always careful to rest his arguments on authority, and thereby adds considerably to the value of his handy volume."
Law Magazine and Review, November, 1879.

"M. Piggott donne à l'étude de l'une des questions les plus complexes du droit international privé une forme tout nouvelle : il applique dans toute sa rigueur la méthode des sciences exactes, et ne recule pas devant l'emploi des formules algébriques. C'était là une tentative périlleuse dont le succès pouvait sembler douteux ; mais il suffit d'indiquer la marche suivie et les résultats obtenus par l'auteur pour comprendre l'importance et le mérite de cette publication."—*Journal du Droit International Privé*, 1879.

FORMS.—Archibald.—*Vide* "Judges' Chambers Practice."

Chitty's Forms of Practical Proceedings in the Queen's Bench, Common Pleas and Exchequer Divisions of the High Court of Justice: with Notes containing the Statutes, Rules and Practice relating thereto. Eleventh Edition. By THOS. WILLES CHITTY, Esqr. Demy 8vo. 1879. 1*l.* 18*s.*

Daniell's Forms and Precedents of Proceedings in the Chancery Division of the High Court of Justice and on Appeal therefrom; with Dissertations and Notes, forming a complete guide to the Practice of the Chancery Division of the High Court and of the Courts of Appeal. Being the Third Edition of "Daniell's Chancery Forms." By WILLIAM HENRY UPJOHN, Esq., Student and Holt Scholar of Gray's Inn, Exhibitioner in Jurisprudence and Roman Law in the University of London, Holder of the First Senior Studentship in Jurisprudence, Roman Law and International Law, awarded by the Council of Legal Education in Hilary Term 1879. In one thick vol. Demy 8vo. 1879. 2*l.* 2*s.*

"Mr. Upjohn has restored the volume of Chancery Forms to the place it held before the recent changes, as a trustworthy and complete collection of precedents."—*Solicitors' Journal.*

"We have had this work in practical use for some weeks, and so careful is the noting up of the authorities, so clearly and concisely are the notes expressed, that we have found it of as much value as the ordinary text books on the Judicature Acts. It will be as useful a work to practitioners at Westminster as it will be to those in Lincoln's Inn."—*Law Times.*

FRENCH COMMERCIAL LAW.—Goirand.—*Vide* "Commercial Law."

HIGHWAYS.—Baker's Law of Highways. By THOMAS BAKER, of the Inner Temple, Esq., Barrister-at-Law. (*In the press.*)

Chambers' Law relating to Highways and Bridges, being the Statutes in full and brief Notes of 700 Leading Cases; to which is added the Law relating to the Lighting of Rural Parishes under the Lighting Act, 1833. By GEO. F. CHAMBERS, Esq., Barrister-at-Law. Imperial 8vo. 1878. 18*s.*

Shelford's Law of Highways.—The Law of Highways; including the General Highway Acts for England and Wales, and other Statutes, with copious Notes of the Decisions thereon; with Forms. Third Edition. With Supplement by C. MANLEY SMITH, Esq., one of the Masters of the Queen's Bench. 12mo. 1865. 15*s.*

*** *All standard Law Works are kept in Stock, in law calf and other bindings.*

INCLOSURES.—*Vide* "Commons."

INDIAN LAW.—Norton's Leading Cases on the Hindu Law of Inheritance.—2 vols. Royal 8vo. 1870-71.
Net, 2*l.* 10*s.*

INJUNCTIONS.—Seton.—*Vide* "Equity."

INSURANCE.—Arnould on the Law of Marine Insurance.—Fifth Edition. By DAVID MACLACHLAN, Esq., Barrister-at-Law. 2 vols. Royal 8vo. 1877. 3*l.*

"As a text book, 'Arnould' is now all the practitioner can want, and we congratulate the editor upon the skill with which he has incorporated the new decisions."—*Law Times.*

Hopkins' Manual of Marine Insurance.—8vo. 1867. 18*s.*

INTERNATIONAL LAW.—Amos' Lectures on International Law.—Delivered in the Middle Temple Hall to the Students of the Inns of Court, by SHELDON AMOS, M.A., Professor of Jurisprudence (including International Law) to the Inns of Court, &c. Royal 8vo. 1874. 10*s.* 6*d.*

Dicey.—*Vide* "Domicil."

Kent's International Law.—Kent's Commentary on International Law. Edited by J. T. ABDY, LL.D., Judge of County Courts. Second Edition. Revised and brought down to the present time. Crown 8vo. 1878. 10*s.* 6*d.*

"Altogether Dr. Abdy has performed his task in a manner worthy of his reputation. His book will be useful not only to Lawyers and Law Students, for whom it was primarily intended, but also for laymen. It is well worth the study of every member of an enlightened and civilized community."—*Solicitors' Journal.*

Levi's International Commercial Law.—Being the Principles of Mercantile Law of the following and other Countries —viz. : England, Ireland, Scotland, British India, British Colonies, Austria, Belgium, Brazil, Buenos Ayres, Denmark, France, Germany, Greece, Hans Towns, Italy, Netherlands, Norway, Portugal, Prussia, Russia, Spain, Sweden, Switzerland, United States, and Würtemberg. By LEONE LEVI, Esq., F.S.A., F.S.S., Barrister-at-Law, &c. Second Edition. 2 vols. Royal 8vo. 1863. 1*l.* 15*s.*

Vattel's Law of Nations.—By JOSEPH CHITTY, Esq. Royal 8vo. 1834. 1*l.* 1*s.*

Wheaton's Elements of International Law; Second English Edition. Edited with Notes and Appendix of Statutes and Treaties, bringing the work down to the present time. By A. C. BOYD, Esq., LL.B., J.P., Barrister-at-Law. Author of "The Merchant Shipping Laws." Demy 8vo. 1880. 1*l.* 10*s.*

"Mr. Boyd, the latest editor, has added many useful notes; he has inserted in the Appendix public documents of permanent value, and there is the prospect that, as edited by Mr. Boyd, Mr Wheaton's volume will enter on a new lease of life. . . . . It is all the more important that their works (*Kent and Wheaton*) should be edited by intelligent and impartial Englishmen, such as Dr. Abdy, the editor of *Kent*, and Mr. Boyd."—*The Times.*

"Both the plan and execution of the work before us deserves commendation. Mr. Boyd gives prominence to the labours of others. The text of Wheaton is presented without alteration, and Mr. Dana's numbering of the sections is preserved. Mr. Boyd's notes, which are numerous, original, and copious, are conveniently interspersed throughout the text; but they are in a distinct type, and therefore the reader always knows whether he is reading Wheaton or Boyd. The Index, which could not have been compiled without much thought and labour makes the book handy for reference, and, consequently, valuable to public writers, who in these days have frequently to refer to International Law."—*Law Journal.*

"Students who require a knowledge of Wheaton's text will find Mr. Boyd's volume very convenient."—*Law Magazine.*

Wildman's International Law.—Institutes of International Law, in Time of Peace and Time of War. By RICHARD WILDMAN, Barrister-at-Law. 2 vols. 8vo. 1849-50. 1*l.* 2*s.* 6*d.*

JOINT OWNERSHIP.—Foster.—*Vide* "Real Estate."

_{*} *All standard Law Works are kept in Stock, in law calf and other bindings.*

JOINT STOCKS.—Palmer.—*Vide* "Conveyancing" and "Company Law."

Thring's (Sir H.) Joint Stock Companies' Law.—The Law and Practice of Joint Stock and other Public Companies, including the Statutes, with Notes. a Collection of Precedents of Memoranda and Articles of Association, and all the other Forms required in Making, Administering, and Winding-up a Company. By SIR HENRY THRING, K.C.B., The Parliamentary Counsel. Third Edition. By G. A. R. FITZGERALD, Esq., Barrister-at-Law, and Fellow of St. John's College, Oxford. 12mo. 1875. 1*l*.

"This, as the work of the original draughtsman of the Companies' Act of 1862, and well-known Parliamentary counsel, Sir Henry Thring is naturally the highest authority on the subject."—*The Times.*

Jordan's Joint Stock Companies.—A Handy Book of Practical Instructions for the Formation and Management of Joint Stock Companies. Sixth Edition. 12mo. 1878. *Net*, 2*s.* 6*d.*

JUDGES' CHAMBERS PRACTICE.—**Archibald's Forms of Summonses and Orders**, with Notes for use at Judges' Chambers and in the District Registries. By W. F. A. ARCHIBALD, M.A., of the Inner Temple, Barrister-at-Law. Royal 12mo. 1879. 12*s.* 6*d.*

"The work is done most thoroughly and yet concisely. The practitioner will find plain directions how to proceed in all the matters connected with a common law action, interpleader, attachment of debts, *mandamus*, injunction—indeed, the whole jurisdiction of the common law divisions, in the district registries, and at Judges' chambers."—*Law Times,* July 26, 1879.

"A clear and well-digested *vade mecum*, which will no doubt be widely used by the profession."—*Law Magazine,* November, 1879.

JUDGMENTS.—Piggott.—*Vide* "Foreign Judgments."

Walker's Practice on Signing Judgment in the High Court of Justice. With Forms. By H. H. WALKER, Esq., of the Judgment Department, Exchequer Division. Crown 8vo. 1879. 4*s.* 6*d.*

"The book undoubtedly meets a want, and furnishes information available for almost every branch of practice."

"We think that solicitors and their clerks will find it extremely useful."—*Law Journal.*

JUDICATURE ACTS.—**Ilbert's Supreme Court of Judicature (Officers) Act, 1879;** with the Rules of Court and Forms, December, 1879, and April, 1880. With Notes. By COURTENAY P. ILBERT, Esq., Barrister-at-Law. Royal 12mo. 1880. 6*s.*

(*In limp leather,* 9*s.* 6*d.*)

*** A LARGE PAPER EDITION (for marginal notes). Royal 8vo. 8*s.*

(*In limp leather,* 12*s.*)

Forming a Supplement to "Wilson's Judicature Acts."

Leys' Complete Time-Table to the Rules under the Supreme Court of Judicature Act, 1875. Showing all the periods fixed by the Rules within or after which any proceedings may be taken. By JOHN KIRKWOOD LEYS, M.A., of the Middle Temple, Esq., Barrister-at-Law. Royal 8vo. 1875.
Net, 1*s.* 6*d.*

Lynch's Epitome of Practice in the Supreme Court of Judicature in England. With References to Acts, Rules, and Orders. For the Use of Students. Fourth Edition. Royal 8vo. 1878. *Net*, 1*s.*

Morgan.—*Vide* "Chancery."

Stephen's Judicature Acts 1873, 1874, and 1875, consolidated. With Notes and an Index. By Sir JAMES FITZJAMES STEPHEN, one of Her Majesty's Judges. 12mo. 1875. 4*s.* 6*d.*

*** *All standard Law Works are kept in Stock, in law calf and other bindings.*

JUDICATURE ACTS.—*Continued.*

Swain's Complete Index to the Rules of the Supreme Court, April, 1880, and to the Forms (uniform with the Official Rules and Forms). By EDWARD SWAIN. Imperial 8vo. 1880. *Net.* 1s.

Wilson's Supreme Court of Judicature Acts, Appellate Jurisdiction Act, 1876, Rules of Court and Forms. With other Acts, Orders, Rules and Regulations relating to the Supreme Court of Justice. With Practical Notes and a Copious Index, forming a COMPLETE GUIDE TO THE NEW PRACTICE. Second Edition. By ARTHUR WILSON, of the Inner Temple, Barrister-at-Law. (Assisted by HARRY GREENWOOD, of Lincoln's Inn, Barrister-at-Law, and JOHN BIDDLE, of the Master of the Rolls Chambers.) Royal 12mo. 1878. (pp. 726.) 18s.
(In limp leather for the pocket, 22s. 6d.)

*** A LARGE PAPER EDITION OF THE ABOVE (for marginal notes). Royal 8vo. 1878. *(In limp leather or calf, 30s.)* 1l. 5s.

"As regards Mr. Wilson's notes, we can only say that they are indispensable to the proper understanding of the new system of procedure. They treat the principles upon which the alterations are based with a clearness and breadth of view which have never been equalled or even approached by any other commentator."—*Solicitors' Journal.*

"Mr. Wilson has bestowed upon this edition an amount of industry and care which the Bench and the Profession will, we are sure, gratefully acknowledge. . . . . . A conspicuous and important feature in this second edition is a table of cases prepared by Mr. Biddle, in which not only are cases given with references to two or three reports, but every place in which the cases are reported. . . . . . Wilson's 'Judicature Acts,' is now the latest, and we think it is the most convenient of the works of the same class. . . . . . The practitioner will find that it supplies all his wants."—*Law Times.*

JURISPRUDENCE.—Amos, Law as a Science and as an Art.—An Introductory Lecture delivered at University College at the commencement of the session 1874-5. By SHELDON AMOS, Esq., M.A., Barrister-at-Law. 8vo. 1874. *Net,* 1s. 6d.

Phillimore's (J. G.) Jurisprudence.—An Inaugural Lecture on Jurisprudence, and a Lecture on Canon Law, delivered at the Hall of the Inner Temple, Hilary Term, 1851. By J. G. PHILLIMORE, Esq., Q.C. 8vo. 1851. Sewed. 3s. 6d.

Piggott.—*Vide* "Foreign Judgments."

JUSTINIAN, INSTITUTES OF.—Cumin.—*Vide* "Civil Law."

Greene.—*Vide* "Roman Law."

Mears.—*Vide* "Roman Law."

Ruegg's Student's "Auxilium" to the Institutes of Justinian.—Being a complete synopsis thereof in the form of Question and Answer. By ALFRED HENRY RUEGG, of the Middle Temple, Barrister-at-Law. Post 8vo. 1879. 5s.

"The student will be greatly assisted in clearing and arranging his knowledge by a work of this kind."—*Law Journal.*

JUSTICE OF THE PEACE.—Burn's Justice of the Peace and Parish Officer.—Edited by the following Barristers, under the General Superintendence of JOHN BLOSSETT MAULE, Esq., Q.C. The Thirtieth Edition. Vol. I. containing titles "Abatement" to "Dwellings for Artisans;" by THOS. S. PRITCHARD, Esq., Recorder of Wenlock. Vol. II. containing titles "Easter Offering" to "Hundred;" by SAML. B. BRISTOWE, Esq., Q.C., M.P. Vol. III. containing titles "Indictment" to "Promissory Notes;" by L. W. CAVE, Esq., Q.C., Recorder of Lincoln. Vol. IV. containing the whole title "Poor;" by J. E. DAVIS, Esq., Stipendiary Magistrate for Stoke-upon-Trent. Vol. V. containing titles "Quo Warranto" to "Wreck;" by J. B. MAULE, Esq., Q.C., Recorder of Leeds. Five vols. 8vo. 1869. 7l. 7s.

*** *All standard Law Works are kept in Stock, in law calf and other bindings.*

20   STEVENS AND SONS' LAW PUBLICATIONS.

JUSTICE OF THE PEACE.—*Continued.*
Paley.—*Vide* "Convictions."
Stone's Practice for Justices of the Peace, Justices' Clerks and Solicitors at Petty and Special Sessions, in Summary Matters and Indictable Offences, with a List of Summary Convictions and of Matters not Criminal. With Forms. Eighth Edition. By THOMAS SIRRELL PRITCHARD, Esq., Barrister-at-Law, Recorder of Wenlock. Demy 8vo. 1877.   1*l.* 10*s.*
Wigram's The Justices' Note Book. By W. KNOX WIGRAM, Esq., Barrister-at-Law, J.P. Middlesex. Royal 12mo., 1880.   10*s.* 6*d.*

In the first portion, or 'Preliminary Notes,' the constitution of courts of Summary Jurisdiction, together with the whole course of ordinary procedure, as modified by the recent Act, are explained in a series of short chapters, under the following heads:—
I. Justices—Jurisdiction—Divisions—Petty and Special Sessions. II. Summary Jurisdiction upon Information—Preliminary Proceedings. III. Summary Jurisdiction upon Information—the Hearing and Punishment. IV. Indictable Offences—Committal for Trial. V. Summary Jurisdiction as regards Indictable Offences; (children—young persons—and adults). VI. Summary Jurisdiction upon Complaint. VII. Quarter Sessions and Appeal. VIII. Note on the Summary Jurisdiction Act, 1879.

In the second part, entitled 'Notes of Matters and Offences alphabetically arranged,' will be found an account of most subjects which from time to time occupy the attention of Justices, either in Petty or Special Sessions.

"We have nothing but praise for the book, which is a justices' royal road to knowledge, and ought to lead them to a more accurate acquaintance with their duties than many of them have hitherto possessed."—*Solicitors' Journal.*

"This is altogether a capital book. Mr. Wigram is a good lawyer and a good justices' lawyer."—*Law Journal.*

"We can thoroughly recommend the volume to magistrates."—*Law Times.*

LAND TAX.—**Bourdin's Land Tax.**—An Exposition of the Land Tax; its Assessment and Collection, with a statement of the rights conferred by the Redemption Acts. By MARK A. BOURDIN, of the Inland Revenue Office, Somerset House (late Registrar of Land Tax). Second Edition. Crown 8vo. 1870.   4*s.*

LANDLORD AND TENANT.—**Woodfall's Law of Landlord and Tenant.**—A Practical Treatise on the Law of Landlord and Tenant, with a full Collection of Precedents and Forms of Procedure. Eleventh Edition. Containing an Abstract of Leading Propositions, and Tables of certain Customs of the Country. By J. M. LELY, of the Inner Temple, Esq., Barrister-at-Law. Royal 8vo. 1877.   1*l.* 16*s.*

"The editor has expended elaborate industry and systematic ability in making the work as perfect as possible; and we doubt not that this eleventh edition will be a greater success than any of its predecessors."—*Solicitors' Journal.*

LAW LIST.—**Law List (The).**—Comprising the Judges and Officers of the different Courts of Justice, Counsel, Special Pleaders, Draftsmen, Conveyancers, Solicitors, Notaries, &c., in England and Wales; the Circuits, Judges, Treasurers, Registrars, and High Bailiffs of the County Courts, District Registries and Registrars under the Probate Act, Lords Lieutenant of Counties, Recorders, Clerks of the Peace, Town Clerks, Coroners, Colonial Judges, and Colonial Lawyers having English Agents, Metropolitan and Stipendiary Magistrates, Law Agents, Law and Public Officers, Circuits of the Judges and Counsel attending Circuit and Sessions, List of Sheriffs and Agents, London Commissioners to Administer Oaths in the Supreme Court of Judicature in England, Conveyancers Practising in England under Certificates obtained in Scotland, &c., &c., and a variety of other useful matters so far as relates to Special Pleaders, Draftsmen, Conveyancers, Solicitors, Proctors and Notaries. Compiled by WILLIAM HENRY COUSINS, of the Inland Revenue Office, Somerset House, Registrar of Stamped Certificates, and of Joint Stock Companies. Published annually. By Authority. 1880.   (*Net cash* 9*s.*)   10*s.* 6*d.*

*** *All standard Law Works are kept in Stock, in law calf and other bindings.*

LAW REPORTS.—A large Stock of second-hand Reports. Estimates on application.

LAWYER'S COMPANION.—*Vide* "Diary."

LEADING CASES.—Haynes' Student's Leading Cases. Being some of the Principal Decisions of the Courts in Constitutional Law, Common Law, Conveyancing and Equity, Probate, Divorce, Bankruptcy, and Criminal Law. With Notes for the use of Students. By JOHN F. HAYNES, LL.D., Author of "The Practice of the Chancery Division of the High Court of Justice," "The Student's Statutes," &c. Demy 8vo. 1878. 16s.

"We consider Mr. Haynes' book to be one of a very praiseworthy class; and we may say also that its editor appears to be a competent man. He can express himself with clearness, precision, and terseness."—*Solicitors' Journal.*

"Will prove of great utility, not only to Students, but Practitioners. The Notes are clear, pointed and concise."—*Law Times.*

"We think that this book will supply a want . . . . the book is singularly well arranged for reference."—*Law Journal.*

Shirley's Leading Cases made Easy. A Selection of Leading Cases in the Common Law. By W. SHIRLEY SHIRLEY, M.A., Esq., Barrister-at-Law, North-Eastern Circuit. Demy 8vo. 1880. 14s.

"Mr. Shirley writes well and clearly, and evidently understands what he is writing about."—*Law Times,* April 10, 1880.

LEXICON.—*Vide* "Dictionary."

LIBRARIES AND MUSEUMS.—Chambers' Public Libraries and Museums and Literary and Scientific Institutions generally, a Digest of the Law relating to. Second Edition. By G. F. CHAMBERS, of the Inner Temple, Barrister-at-Law. Imperial 8vo. 1879. 8s. 6d.

LICENSING.—Lely and Foulkes' Licensing Acts, 1828, 1869, 1872, and 1874; Containing the Law of the Sale of Liquors by Retail and the Management of Licensed Houses; with Notes to the Acts, a Summary of the Law, and an Appendix of Forms. Second Edition. By J. M. LELY and W. D. I. FOULKES, Esqrs., Barristers-at-Law. Royal 12mo. 1874. 8s.

"The notes are sensible and to the point, and give evidence both of care and knowledge of the subject."—*Solicitors' Journal.*

LIENS.—Cavanagh.—*Vide* "Money Securities."

LIFE ASSURANCE.—Scratchley's Decisions in Life Assurance Law, collated alphabetically according to the point involved; with the Statutes. Revised Edition. By ARTHUR SCRATCHLEY, M.A., Barrister-at-Law. Demy 8vo. 1878. 5s.

LIGHTS.—Woolrych's Practical Treatise on the Law of Window Lights.—Second Edition. 12mo. 1864. 6s.

LOCKE KING'S ACTS.—Cavanagh.—*Vide* "Money Securities."

LORD MAYOR'S COURT PRACTICE.—Candy.—*Vide* "Mayor's Court Practice."

LUNACY.—Elmer's Practice in Lunacy.—The Practice in Lunacy under Commissions and Inquisitions, with Notes of Cases and Recent Decisions, the Statutes and General Orders, Forms and Costs of Proceedings in Lunacy, an Index and Schedule of Cases. Sixth Edition. By JOSEPH ELMER, of the Office of the Masters in Lunacy. 8vo. 1877. 21s.

MAGISTERIAL LAW.—Burn.—*Vide* "Justice of the Peace."
Leeming and Cross.—*Vide* "Quarter Sessions."
Pritchard.—*Vide* "Quarter Sessions."
Stone.—*Vide* "Petty Sessions."
Wigram.—*Vide* "Justice of the Peace."

*** *All standard Law Works are kept in Stock, in law calf and other bindings.*

MANDAMUS.—Tapping on Mandamus.—The Law and Practice of the High Prerogative Writ of Mandamus as it obtains both in England and Ireland. Royal 8vo. 1848. *Net*, 1*l*. 1*s*.

MARITIME COLLISION.—Lowndes.—Marsden.—*Vide* "Collision."

MAYOR'S COURT PRACTICE.—Candy's Mayor's Court Practice.—The Jurisdiction, Process, Practice, and Mode of Pleading in Ordinary Actions in the Mayor's Court, London (commonly called the "Lord Mayor's Court"). Founded on Brandon. By GEORGE CANDY, Esq., Barrister-at-Law. Demy 8vo. 1879. 14*s*.

"The 'ordinary' practice of the Court is dealt with in its natural order, and is simply and clearly stated."—*Law Journal*.

MERCANTILE LAW.—Boyd.—*Vide* "Shipping."

Russell.—*Vide* "Agency."

Smith's Compendium of Mercantile Law.—Ninth Edition. By G. M. DOWDESWELL, of the Inner Temple, Esq., one of Her Majesty's Counsel. Royal 8vo. 1877. 1*l*. 18*s*.

"We can safely say that, to the practising Solicitor, few books will be found more useful than the ninth edition of 'Smith's Mercantile Law.'"—*Law Magazine*.

Tudor's Selection of Leading Cases on Mercantile and Maritime Law.—With Notes. By O. D. TUDOR, Esq., Barrister-at-Law. Second Edition. Royal 8vo. 1868. 1*l*. 18*s*.

METROPOLIS BUILDING ACTS.—Woolrych's Metropolis Building Acts, with Notes, Explanatory of the Sections and of the Architectural Terms contained therein. Second Edition. By NOEL H. PATERSON, M.A., Esq., Barrister-at-Law. 12mo. 1877. 8*s*. 6*d*.

MINES.—Rogers' Law relating to Mines, Minerals, and Quarries in Great Britain and Ireland; with a Summary of the Laws of Foreign States and Practical Directions for obtaining Government Grants to work Foreign Mines. Second Edition Enlarged. By ARUNDEL ROGERS, Esq., Judge of County Courts. 8vo. 1876. 1*l*. 11*s*. 6*d*.

"The volume will prove invaluable as a work of legal reference."—*The Mining Journal*.

MONEY SECURITIES.—Cavanagh's Law of Money Securities.—In Three Books. I. Personal Securities. II. Securities on Property. III. Miscellaneous; with an Appendix containing the Crossed Cheques Act, 1876, The Factors Acts, 1823 to 1877. Locke King's, and its Amending Acts, and the Bills of Sale Act, 1878. By CHRISTOPHER CAVANAGH, B.A., LL.B. (Lond.), of the Middle Temple, Esq., Barrister-at-Law. In 1 vol. Demy 8vo. 1879. 21*s*.

"We know of no work which embraces so much that is of every-day importance, nor do we know of any author who shows more familiarity with his subject. The book is one which we shall certainly keep near at hand, and we believe that it will prove a decided acquisition to the practitioner."—*Law Times*.

"The author has the gift of a pleasant style; there are abundant and correct references to decisions of a recent date; and, in the matter of newly-enacted statutes; attempts are made, and, as we think, not without success, to grapple with points of practice and interpretation which as yet remain judicially unsolved. An appendix, in which is embodied the full text of several important statutes, adds to the utility of the work as a book of reference; and there is a good index."—*Solicitors' Journal*.

"In the second book bills of sale extend over some sixty-three pages; and the treatise on them seems on the whole well written, especially with reference to the alterations made by 41 & 42 Vict. c. 31."—*Law Journal*.

"May be the means of saving enormous labour to thousands of readers."—*Bullionist*.

MORTGAGE.—Coote's Treatise on the Law of Mortgage.—Third Edition. Royal 8vo. 1850. *Net*, 1*l*.

MORTMAIN.—Rawlinson's Notes on the Mortmain Acts; shewing their operation on Gifts, Devises and Bequests for Charitable Uses. By JAMES RAWLINSON, Solicitor. Demy 8vo. 1877. Interleaved. *Net*, 2*s*. 6*d*.

⁂ All standard Law Works are kept in Stock, in law calf and other bindings.

NAVY.—**Thring's Criminal Law of the Navy**, with an Introductory Chapter on the Early State and Discipline of the Navy, the Rules of Evidence, and an Appendix comprising the Naval Discipline Act and Practical Forms. Second Edition. By THEODORE THRING, of the Middle Temple, Barrister-at-Law, late Commissioner of Bankruptcy at Liverpool, and C. E. GIFFORD, Assistant-Paymaster, Royal Navy. 12mo. 1877. 12s. 6d.

"A full series of forms of warrants, minutes, charges, &c., and a good Index, complete the utility of a work which should be in the hands of all who have to deal with the regulating and governing of the Fleet."—*Law Magazine.*

"In the new edition, the procedure, naval regulations, forms, and all matters connected with the practical administration of the law have been classified and arranged by Mr. Gifford, so that the work is in every way useful, complete, and up to date."—*Naval and Military Gazette.*

NISI PRIUS.—**Roscoe's Digest of the Law of Evidence on the Trial of Actions at Nisi Prius.**—Fourteenth Edition. By JOHN DAY, one of Her Majesty's Counsel, and MAURICE POWELL, Barrister-at-Law. Royal 12mo. 1879. 2l. (*Bound in one thick volume calf or circuit, 5s., or in two convenient vols. calf or circuit, 9s. net, extra.*)

"The task of adapting the old text to the new procedure was one requiring much patient labour, careful accuracy, and conciseness, as well as discretion in the omission of matter obsolete or unnecessary. An examination of the bulky volume before us affords good evidence of the possession of these qualities by the present editors, and we feel sure that the popularity of the work will continue unabated under their conscientious care."—*Law Magazine.*

Selwyn's Abridgment of the Law of Nisi Prius.—Thirteenth Edition. By DAVID KEANE, Q.C., Recorder of Bedford, and CHARLES T. SMITH, M.A., one of the Judges of the Supreme Court of the Cape of Good Hope. 2 vols. Royal 8vo. 1869. (*Published at 2l. 16s.*) *Net*, 1l.

NOTANDA.—*Vide* "Digests."

NOTARY.—**Brooke's Treatise on the Office and Practice of a Notary of England.**—With a full collection of Precedents. Fourth Edition. By LEONE LEVI, Esq., F.S.A., of Lincoln's Inn, Barrister-at-Law. 8vo. 1876. 1l. 4s.

NUISANCES.—FitzGerald.—*Vide* "Public Health."

OATHS.—**Braithwaite's Oaths in the Supreme Court of Judicature.**—A Manual for the use of Commissioners to Administer Oaths in the Supreme Court of Judicature in England. Part I. containing practical information respecting their Appointment, Designation, Jurisdiction, and Powers; Part II. comprising a collection of officially recognised Forms of Jurats and Oaths, with Explanatory Observations. By T. W. BRAITHWAITE, of the Record and Writ Clerks' Office. Fcap. 8vo. 1876. 4s. 6d.

"Specially useful to Commissioners."—*Law Magazine.*

"The work will, we doubt not, become the recognised guide of commissioners to administer oaths."—*Solicitors' Journal.*

PARTITION.—Foster.—*Vide* "Real Estate."

PARTNERSHIP.—**Pollock's Digest of the Law of Partnership.** By FREDERICK POLLOCK, of Lincoln's Inn, Esq., Barrister-at-Law. Author of "Principles of Contract at Law and in Equity." Demy 8vo. 1877. 8s. 6d.

*** The object of this work is to give the substance of the Law of Partnership (excluding Companies) in a concise and definite form,

"Of the execution of the work, we can speak in terms of the highest praise. The language is simple, concise, and clear; and the general propositions may bear comparison with those of Sir James Stephen."—*Law Magazine.*

"Mr. Pollock's work appears eminently satisfactory . . . the book is praiseworthy in design, scholarly and complete in execution."—*Saturday Review.*

"A few more books written as carefully as the 'Digest of the Law of Partnership,' will, perhaps, remove some drawbacks, and render English law a pleasanter and easier subject to study than it is at present."—*The Examiner.*

*** *All standard Law Works are kept in Stock, in law calf and other bindings.*

24   STEVENS AND SONS' LAW PUBLICATIONS.

PATENTS.—**Hindmarch's Treatise on the Law relating to Patents.**—8vo. 1846. 1*l*. 1*s*.

Johnson's Patentees' Manual; being a Treatise on the Law and Practice of Letters Patent, especially intended for the use of Patentees and Inventors.—By JAMES JOHNSON, Barrister-at-Law. and J. H. JOHNSON, Solicitor and Patent Agent. Fourth Edition. Thoroughly revised and much enlarged. Demy 8vo. 1879. 10*s*. 6*d*.

"A very excellent manual."—*Law Times*, February 8, 1879.

"The authors have not only a knowledge of the law, but of the working of the law. Besides the table of cases there is a copious index to subjects."—*Law Journal*, March 1, 1879.

Thompson's Handbook of Patent Law of all Countries.—Third Edition, revised. By WM. P. THOMPSON, C.E., Head of the International Patent Office, Liverpool. 12mo. 1878. *Net* 2*s*. 6*d*.

PERSONAL PROPERTY.—Smith.—*Vide* "Real Property."

PETITIONS.—Palmer.—*Vide* "Conveyancing."

Rogers.—*Vide* "Elections."

PETTY SESSIONS.—**Stone's Practice for Justices of the Peace,** Justices' Clerks and Solicitors at Petty and Special Sessions, in Summary Matters and Indictable Offences, with a List of Summary Convictions and of Matters not Criminal. With Forms. Eighth Edition. By THOMAS SIRRELL PRITCHARD, of the Inner Temple, Esq., Barrister-at-Law, Recorder of Wenlock. In 1 vol. Demy 8vo. 1877. 1*l*. 10*s*.

"The book, as a whole, is thoroughly satisfactory, and, having gone carefully through it, we can recommend it with confidence to the numerous body of our readers who are daily interested in the subjects to which it relates."—*Solicitors' Journal*.

POOR LAW.—**Davis' Treatise on the Poor Laws.**—Being Vol. IV. of Burns' Justice of the Peace. 8vo. 1869. 1*l*. 11*s*. 6*d*.

POWERS.—**Farwell on Powers.**—A Concise Treatise on Powers. By GEORGE FARWELL, B.A., of Lincoln's Inn, Esq., Barrister-at-Law. 8vo. 1874. 1*l*. 1*s*.

"We recommend Mr. Farwell's book as containing within a small compass what would otherwise have to be sought out in the pages of hundreds of confusing reports."—*The Law*.

PRECEDENTS.—*Vide* "Conveyancing."

PRINCIPAL AND AGENT.—**Petgrave's Principal and Agent.**—A Manual of the Law of Principal and Agent. By E. C. PETGRAVE, Solicitor. 12mo. 1857. 7*s*. 6*d*.

Petgrave's Code of the Law of Principal and Agent, with a Preface. By E. C. PETGRAVE, Solicitor. Demy 12mo. 1876. *Net, sewed*, 2*s*.

PRIVY COUNCIL.—**Finlason's History, Constitution, and Character of the Judicial Committee of the Privy Council,** considered as a Judicial Tribunal, especially in Ecclesiastical Cases, with special reference to the right and duty of its members to declare their opinions. By W. F. FINLASON, Barrister-at-Law. Demy 8vo. 1878. 4*s*. 6*d*.

Lattey's Handy Book on the Practice and Procedure before the Privy Council.—By ROBERT THOMAS LATTEY, Attorney of the Court of Queen's Bench, and of the High Court of Bengal. 12mo. 1869. 6*s*.

PROBATE.—**Browne's Probate Practice:** a Treatise on the Principles and Practice of the Court of Probate, in Contentious and Non-Contentious Business, with the Statutes, Rules, Fees, and Forms relating thereto. By GEORGE BROWNE, Esq., Barrister-at-Law, Recorder of Ludlow. 8vo. 1873. 1*l*. 1*s*.

"A cursory glance through Mr. Browne's work shows that it has been compiled with more than ordinary care and intelligence. We should consult it with every confidence." —*Law Times*.

Haynes.—*Vide* "Leading Cases."

⁎⁎* *All standard Law Works are kept in Stock, in law calf and other bindings.*

PUBLIC HEALTH.—Chambers' Digest of the Law relating to Public Health and Local Government.—With Notes of 1073 leading Cases. Various official documents; precedents of By-laws and Regulations. The Statutes in full. A Table of Offences and Punishments, and a Copious Index. Seventh Edition, enlarged and revised, with SUPPLEMENT containing new Local Government Board By-Laws in full. Imperial 8vo. 1875-7. 1*l.* 8*s.*

⁎⁎ The SUPPLEMENT may be had separately, price 9*s.*

FitzGerald's Public Health and Rivers Pollution Prevention Acts.—The Law relating to Public Health and Local Government, as contained in the Public Health Act, 1875, with Introduction and Notes, showing all the alterations in the Existing Law, with reference to the Cases, &c.; together with a Supplement containing "The Rivers Pollution Prevention Act, 1876." With Explanatory Introduction, Notes, Cases, and Index. By G. A. R. FITZGERALD, Esq., Barrister-at-Law. Royal 8vo. 1876. 1*l.* 1*s.*

" A copious and well-executed analytical index completes the work which we can confidently recommend to the officers and members of sanitary authorities, and all interested in the subject matter of the new Act."—*Law Magazine and Review.*

" Mr. FitzGerald comes forward with a special qualification for the task, for he was employed by the Government in the preparation of the Act of 1875; and, as he himself says, has necessarily, for some time past, devoted attention to the law relating to public health and local government."—*Law Journal.*

PUBLIC MEETINGS.—Chambers' Handbook for Public Meetings, including Hints as to the Summoning and Management of them; and as to the Duties of Chairmen, Clerks, Secretaries, and other Officials; Rules of Debate, &c., to which is added a Digest of Reported Cases. By GEORGE F. CHAMBERS, Esq., Barrister-at-Law. 12mo. 1878. *Net,* 2*s.* 6*d.*

QUARTER SESSIONS.—Leeming & Cross's General and Quarter Sessions of the Peace.—Their Jurisdiction and Practice in other than Criminal matters. Second Edition. By HORATIO LLOYD, Esq., Recorder of Chester, Judge of County Courts, and Deputy-Chairman of Quarter Sessions, and H. F. THURLOW, of the Inner Temple, Esq., Barrister-at-Law. 8vo. 1876. 1*l.* 1*s.*

" The present editors appear to have taken the utmost pains to make the volume complete, and, from our examination of it, we can thoroughly recommend it to all interested in the practice of quarter sessions."—*Law Times*

Pritchard's Quarter Sessions.—The Jurisdiction, Practice and Procedure of the Quarter Sessions in Criminal, Civil, and Appellate Matters. By THOS. SIRRELL PRITCHARD, of the Inner Temple, Esq., Barrister-at-Law, Recorder of Wenlock. 8vo. 1875. 2*l.* 2*s.*

" We can confidently say that it is written throughout with clearness and intelligence, and that both in legislation and in case law it is carefully brought down to the most recent date."—*Solicitors' Journal.*

RAILWAYS.—Browne and Theobald's Law of Railways. By J. H. BALFOUR BROWNE, of the Middle Temple, Registrar of the Railway Commissioners, and H. S. THEOBALD, of the Inner Temple, Esqrs., Barristers-at-Law. (*In preparation.*)

Lely's Railway and Canal Traffic Act, 1873.—And other Railway and Canal Statutes; with the General Orders, Forms, and Table of Fees. By J. M. LELY, Esq. Post 8vo. 1873. 8*s.*

⁎⁎ *All standard Law Works are kept in Stock, in law calf and other bindings.*

RATES AND RATING.—Castle's Practical Treatise on the Law of Rating. By EDWARD JAMES CASTLE, of the Inner Temple, Barrister-at-Law. Demy 8vo. 1879. 1l. 1s.

"Mr. Castle's book is a correct, exhaustive, clear and concise view of the law."—*Law Times.*

"The book is a useful assistant in a perplexed branch of Law."—*Law Journal.*

Chamber's Law relating to Rates and Rating; with especial reference to the Powers and Duties of Rate-levying Local Authorities, and their Officers. Being the Statutes in full and brief Notes of 550 Cases. By G. F. CHAMBERS, Esq., Barrister-at-Law. Imp. 8vo. 1878. 12s.

REAL ESTATE.—Foster's Law of Joint Ownership and Partition of Real Estate. By EDWARD JOHN FOSTER, M.A., late of Lincoln's Inn, Barrister-at-Law. 8vo. 1878. 10s. 6d.

"Mr. Foster may be congratulated on having produced a very satisfactory *vade mecum* on the Law of Joint Ownership and Partition. He has taken considerable pains to make his treatise practically useful, and has combined within the fifteen chapters into which the book is divided, brevity of statement with completeness of treatment."—*Law Magazine.*

REAL PROPERTY.—Greenwood's Recent Real Property Statutes. Comprising those passed during the years 1874-1877 inclusive. Consolidated with the Earlier Statutes thereby Amended. With Copious Notes, and a Supplement containing the Orders under the Settled Estates Act, 1878. By HARRY GREENWOOD, M.A., Esq., Barrister-at-Law. 8vo. 1878. 10s.

"To students particularly this collection, with the careful notes and references to previous legislation, will be of considerable value."—*Law Times.*

"The author has added notes which, especially on the Vendor and Purchaser Act, and the Settled Estates Act, are likely to be useful to the practitioner . . . so far as we have tested them, the statements appear to be generally accurate and careful, and the work will be found exceedingly handy for reference."—*Solicitors' Journal.*

"Mr. Greenwood's book gives such of the provisions of the amended statutes as are still in force, as well as the provisions of the new statutes, in order to show more clearly the effect of the recent legislation."—*Law Journal.*

Leake's Elementary Digest of the Law of Property in Land.—Containing: Introduction. Part I. The Sources of the Law.—Part II. Estates in Land. By STEPHEN MARTIN LEAKE, Barrister-at-Law. 8vo. 1874. 1l. 2s.

*** The above forms a complete Introduction to the Study of the Law of Real Property.

Shearwood's Real Property.—A Concise Abridgment of the Law of Real Property and an Introduction to Conveyancing. Designed to facilitate the subject for Students preparing for Examination. By JOSEPH A. SHEARWOOD, of Lincoln's Inn, Esq., Barrister-at-Law. Demy 8vo. 1878. 6s. 6d.

"The present law is expounded paragraphically, so that it could be actually *learned* without understanding the origin from which it has sprung, or the principles on which it is based."—*Law Journal.*

Shelford's Real Property Statutes.—Eighth Edition. By T. H. CARSON, Esq., Barrister-at-Law. 8vo. 1874. 1l. 10s.

Smith's Real and Personal Property.—A Compendium of the Law of Real and Personal Property, primarily connected with Conveyancing. Designed as a second book for Students, and as a digest of the most useful learning for Practitioners. By JOSIAH W. SMITH, B.C.L., Q.C. Fifth Edition. 2 vols. Demy 8vo. 1877. 2l. 2s.

"He has given to the student a book which he may read over and over again with profit and pleasure."—*Law Times.*

"The work before us will, we think, be found of very great service to the practitioner."—*Solicitors' Journal.*

*** *All standard Law Works are kept in Stock, in law calf and other bindings.*

REGISTRATION.—Browne's(G.Lathom)Parliamentary and Municipal Registration Act, 1878 (41 & 42 Vict. cap. 26); with an Introduction, Notes, and Additional Forms. By G. LATHOM BROWNE, of the Middle Temple, Esq., Barrister-at-Law. 12mo. 1878. 5s. 6d.

Rogers.—*Vide* "Elections."

REGISTRATION CASES.—Hopwood and Coltman's Registration Cases.—Vol. I. (1868-1872). *Net*, 2l.18s. Calf. Vol. II. (1873-1878). *Net*, 2l. 10s. Calf.

RIVERS POLLUTION PREVENTION.—FitzGerald's Rivers Pollution Prevention Act, 1875.—With Explanatory Introduction, Notes, Cases, and Index. Royal 8vo. 1876. 3s. 6d.

ROMAN LAW.—Cumin.—*Vide* "Civil."

Greene's Outlines of Roman Law.—Consisting chiefly of an Analysis and Summary of the Institutes. For the use of Students. By T. WHITCOMBE GREENE, B.C.L., of Lincoln's Inn, Barrister-at-Law. Third Edition. Foolscap 8vo. 1875. 7s. 6d.

Mears' Student's Ortolan.—An Analysis of M. Ortolan's Institutes of Justinian, including the History and Generalization of ROMAN LAW. By T. LAMBERT MEARS, M.A., LL.D. Lond., of the Inner Temple, Barrister-at-Law. *Published by permission of the late M. Ortolan.* Post 8vo. 1876. 12s. 6d.

Ruegg.—*Vide* "Justinian."

SAUNDERS' REPORTS.—Williams' (Sir E. V.) Notes to Saunders' Reports.—By the late Serjeant WILLIAMS. Continued to the present time by the Right Hon. Sir EDWARD VAUGHAN WILLIAMS. 2 vols. Royal 8vo. 1871. 2l. 10s.

SETTLED ESTATES.—Middleton's Settled Estates Act, 1877, and the Settled Estates Act Orders, 1878, with Introduction, Notes and Forms, and Summary of Practice. Second Edition. By JAMES W. MIDDLETON, B.A., of Lincoln's Inn, Barrister-at-Law. 12mo. 1879. 4s. 6d.

"A complete work as a practical edition of the Settled Estates Act, 1877, and will be found exceedingly useful to legal practitioners."—*Law Journal.*

"The book is a well-timed and useful manual of the Act."—*Solicitors' Journal.*

"The book is excellently arranged, particularly in the summary of practice."—*Saturday Review.*

SHERIFF LAW.—Churchill's Law of the Office and Duties of the Sheriff, with the Writs and Forms relating to the Office. By CAMERON CHURCHILL, B.A., of the Inner Temple, Barrister-at-Law, assisted by A. CARMICHAEL BRUCE, B.A., of Lincoln's Inn, Barrister-at-Law. Demy 8vo. 1879. 18s.

"This is a work upon a subject of large practical importance, and seems to have been compiled with exceptional care. . . . . There is an appendix of forms which will be found useful."—*Law Times.*

"Under-Sheriffs, and lawyers generally, will find this a useful book to have by them, both for perusal and reference."—*Law Magazine.*

SHIPPING, and *vide* "Admiralty."

Boyd's Merchant Shipping Laws; being a Consolidation of all the Merchant Shipping and Passenger Acts from 1854 to 1876, inclusive; with Notes of all the leading English and American Cases on the subjects affected by Legislation, and an Appendix containing the New Rules issued in October, 1876; forming a complete Treatise on Maritime Law. By A. C. BOYD, LLB., of the Inner Temple, Esq., Barrister-at-Law, and Midland Circuit. 8vo. 1876. 1l. 5s.

"We can recommend the work as a very useful compendium of shipping law."—*Law Times.*

SIGNING JUDGMENTS.—Walker.—*Vide* "Judgments."

⁎ *All standard Law Works are kept in Stock, in law calf and other bindings.*

SOLICITORS.—Cordery's Law relating to Solicitors of the Supreme Court of Judicature.—With an Appendix of Statutes and Rules. By A. CORDERY, of the Inner Temple, Esq., Barrister-at-Law. Demy 8vo. 1878. 14s.

"Mr. Cordery writes tersely and clearly, and displays in general great industry and care in the collection of cases."—*Solicitors' Journal.*

"The chapters on liability of solicitors and on lien may be selected as two of the best in the book."—*Law Journal.*

SOLICITORS' GUIDES.—*Vide* "Examination Guides."

STAMP LAWS.—Tilsley's Treatise on the Stamp Laws.—Being an Analytical Digest of all the Statutes and Cases relating to Stamp Duties, with practical remarks thereon. Third Edition. With Tables of all the Stamp Duties payable in the United Kingdom after the 1st January, 1871, and of Former Duties, &c., &c. By E. H. TILSLEY, of the Inland Revenue Office. 8vo. 1871. 18s.

STATUTES, and *vide* "Acts of Parliament."

Biddle's Table of Statutes.—A Table of References to unrepealed Public General Acts, arranged in the Alphabetical Order of their Short or Popular Titles. Second Edition, including References to all the Acts in Chitty's Collection of Statutes. Royal 8vo. 1870. (*Published at 9s. 6d.*) *Net,* 2s. 6d.

Chitty's Collection of Statutes.—A Collection of Statutes of Practical Utility; with Notes thereon. The Third Edition, containing all the Statutes of Practical Utility in the Civil and Criminal Administration of Justice to the Present Time. By W. N. WELSBY and EDWARD BEAVAN, Esqrs., Barristers-at-Law. In 4 very thick vols. Royal 8vo. 1865. (*Published at 12l. 12s.*)

Reduced to, net, 6l. 6s.

Supplements to the above. By HORATIO LLOYD, Esq., Judge of County Courts, and Deputy-Chairman of Quarter Sessions for Cheshire. Royal 8vo. Part I., comprising the Statutes for 1873, 7s. 6d. Part II., 1874, 6s. Part III., 1875, 16s. Part IV., 1876, 6s. 6d. Part V., 1877, 4s. 6d. Part VI., 1878, 10s. Part VII., 1879, 7s. 6d., sewed.

*** Continued Annually.

"When he (Lord Campbell) was upon the Bench he always had this work by him, and no statutes were ever referred to by the Bar which he could not find in it."

*The Revised Edition of the Statutes, A.D. 1235–1868, prepared under the direction of the Statute Law Committee, published by the authority of Her Majesty's Government. In 15 vols. Imperial 8vo. 1870–1878. 19l. 9s.

Vol. 1.—Henry III. to James II.,	1235–1685	1l. 1s. 0d.
„ 2.—Will. & Mary to 10 Geo. III.,	1688–1770	1 0 0
„ 3.—11 Geo. III. to 41 Geo. III.,	1770–1800	0 17 0
„ 4.—41 Geo. III. to 51 Geo. III.,	1801–1811	0 18 0
„ 5.—52 Geo. III. to 4 Geo. IV.,	1812–1823	1 5 0
„ 6.—5 Geo. IV. to 1 & 2 Will. IV.,	1824–1831	1 6 0
„ 7.—2 & 3 Will. IV. to 6 & 7 Will. IV.,	1831–1836	1 10 0
„ 8.—7 Will. IV. & 1 Vict. to 5 & 6 Vict.,	1837–1842	1 12 6
„ 9.—6 & 7 Vict. to 9 & 10 Vict.,	1843–1846	1 11 6
„ 10.—10 & 11 Vict. to 13 & 14 Vict.,	1847–1850	1 7 6
„ 11.—14 & 15 Vict. to 16 & 17 Vict.,	1851–1853	1 4 0
„ 12.—17 & 18 Vict. to 19 & 20 Vict.,	1854–1856	1 6 0
„ 13.—20 Vict. to 24 & 25 Vict.,	1857–1861	1 10 0
„ 14.—25 & 26 Vict. to 28 & 29 Vict.,	1862–1865	1 10 0
„ 15.—29 & 30 Vict. to 31 & 32 Vict., and Supplement,	1866–1867–8	1 10 6

*** The above Work is now completed.

*** *All standard Law Works are kept in Stock in law calf and other bindings.*

STATUTES.—*Continued.*
   *Chronological Table of and Index to the Statutes
   to the end of the Session of 1878. Fifth Edition, imperial 8vo.
   1879. 14s.
   *Public General Statutes, royal 8vo, issued in parts and in
   complete volumes, and supplied immediately on publication.
   * Printed by Her Majesty's Printers, and Sold by STEVENS & SONS.
   Head's Statutes by Heart; being a System of Memoria
   Technica, applied to Statutes, and embracing Common Law, Chancery, Bankruptcy, Criminal Law, Probate and Divorce, and Conveyancing. By FREDERICK WILLIAM HEAD, of the Inner
   Temple, Student-at-Law. Demy 8vo. 1877. *Net*, 1s. 6d.
SUMMARY CONVICTIONS.—**Paley's Law and Practice of Summary Convictions under the Summary Jurisdiction Acts, 1848 and 1879**; including
   Proceedings preliminary and subsequent to Convictions, and the
   responsibility of convicting Magistrates and their Officers, with
   Forms. Sixth Edition. By W. H. MACNAMARA, Esq., Barrister-at-Law. Demy 8vo. 1879. 1l. 4s.
   "We gladly welcome this good edition of a good book."—*Solicitors' Journal.*
   Templer's Summary Jurisdiction Act, 1879.—
   Rules and Schedules of Forms. With Notes. By FREDERIC
   GORDON TEMPLER, of the Inner Templer, Esq., Barrister-at-Law. Demy 8vo. 1880. 5s.
   "We think this edition everything that could be desired."—*Sheffield Post*, Feb. 7, 1880.
   Wigram.—*Vide* "Justice of the Peace."
SUMMONSES AND ORDERS.—**Archibald.**—*Vide* "Judges' Chambers Practice."
TORTS.—**Addison on Wrongs and their Remedies.**—
   Being a Treatise on the Law of Torts. By C. G. ADDISON, Esq.,
   Author of "The Law of Contracts." Fifth Edition. Re-written.
   By L. W. CAVE, Esq., M.A., one of Her Majesty's Counsel,
   Recorder of Lincoln. Royal 8vo. 1879. 1l. 18s.
   "Since the last edition of this work was published, by the operation of the Judicature Acts, great changes have been effected in practice and pleading. . . . In
   the present edition the nature of the right infringed has been taken as the basis of
   the arrangement throughout. . . . Every effort has been made, while assimilating
   this edition in form to the companion treatise *On Contracts*, to maintain the reputation which the work has already acquired."—*Extract from Preface.*
   "As now presented, this va'uable treatise must prove highly acceptable to judges and
   the profession."—*Law Times*, February 7th, 1880.
   "Cave's 'Addison on Torts' will be recognized as an indispensable addition to every
   lawyer's library."—*Law Magazine and Review*, February, 1880.
TRADE MARKS—**Rules under the Trade Marks' Registration Act, 1875 (by Authority).** Sewed. *Net*, 1s.
   Sebastian on the Law of Trade Marks.—The Law
   of Trade Marks and their Registration, and matters connected therewith, including a chapter on Goodwill. Together with Appendices
   containing Precedents of Injunctions, &c.; The Trade Marks Registration Acts, 1875—7, the Rules and Instructions thereunder;
   The Merchandise Marks Act, 1862, and other Statutory enactments; and The United States Statute, 1870 and 1875, and the
   Treaty with the United States, 1877; and the New Rules and
   Instructions issued in February, 1878. With a copious Index.
   By LEWIS BOYD SEBASTIAN, B.C.L., M.A., of Lincoln's
   Inn, Esq., Barrister-at-Law. 8vo. 1878. 14s.
   "The book cannot fail to be of service to a large class of lawyers."—*Solicitors' Journal.*
   "Mr. Sebastian has written the fullest and most methodical book on trade marks
   which has appeared in England since the passing of the Trade Marks Registration
   Acts."—*Trade Marks.*
   "Viewed as a compilation, the book leaves little to be desired. Viewed as a treatise on
   a subject of growing importance, it also strikes us as being well, and at any rate carefully
   executed."—*Law Journal.*
   "Mr. Sebastian's book is a careful statement of the law,"—*Law Times.*

*** *All Standard Law Works are kept in Stock, in law calf and other bindings.*

TRADE MARKS.—*Continued.*

Sebastian's Digest of Cases of Trade Mark, Trade Name, Trade Secret, Goodwill, &c., decided in the Courts of the United Kingdom, India, the Colonies, and the United States of America. By LEWIS BOYD SEBASTIAN, B.C.L., M.A., of Lincoln's Inn, Esq., Barrister-at-Law, Author of "The Law of Trade Marks." Demy 8vo. 1879. 1*l.* 1*s.*

"A digest which will be of very great value to all practitioners who have to advise on matters connected with trade marks."—*Solicitors' Journal*, July 26, 1879.

Trade Marks' Journal.—4to. Sewed. (*Issued fortnightly.*)
Nos. 1 to 192 are now ready. *Net,* each 1*s.*
Index to Vol. I. (Nos. 1—47.) *Net,* 3*s.*
Ditto, „ Vol. II. (Nos. 48—97.) *Net,* 3*s.*
Ditto, „ Vol. III. (Nos. 98—123.) *Net,* 3*s.*
Ditto, „ Vol. IV. (Nos. 124—156.) *Net,* 3*s.*
Ditto, „ Vol. V. (Nos. 157—183.) *Net,* 3*s.*

Wood's Law of Trade Marks.—Containing the Merchandise Marks' Act, 1862, and the Trade Marks' Registration Act, 1875; with the Rules thereunder, and Practical Directions for obtaining Registration; with Notes, full Table of Cases and Index. By J. BIGLAND WOOD, Esq., Barrister-at-Law. 12mo. 1876. 5*s.*

TRAMWAYS.—Palmer.—*Vide* "Conveyancing."

Sutton's Tramway Acts.—The Tramway Acts of the United Kingdom, with Notes on the Law and Practice, and an Appendix containing the Standing Orders of Parliament, Rules of the Board of Trade relating to Tramways, and Decisions of the Referees with respect to Locus Standi. By HENRY SUTTON, B.A., of Lincoln's Inn, Barrister-at-Law. Post 8vo. 1874. 12*s.*

TRUSTS AND TRUSTEES.—**Godefroi's Digest of the Principles of the Law of Trusts and Trustees.**—By HENRY GODEFROI, of Lincoln's Inn, Esq., Barrister-at-Law. Joint Author of "Godefroi and Shortt's Law of Railway Companies." Demy 8vo. 1879. 1*l.* 1*s.*

"No one who refers to this book for information on a question within its range is, we think, likely to go away unsatisfied."—*Saturday Review,* September 6, 1879.
"Is a work of great utility to the practitioner."—*Law Magazine.*
"As a digest of the law, Mr. Godefroi's work merits commendation, for the author's statements are brief and clear, and for his statements he refers to a goodly array of authorities. In the table of cases the references to the several contemporaneous reports are given, and there is a very copious index to subjects."—*Law Journal.*

USES.—**Jones (W. Hanbury) on Uses.**—8vo. 1862. 7*s.*

VENDORS AND PURCHASERS.—**Dart's Vendors and Purchasers.**—A Treatise on the Law and Practice relating to Vendors and Purchasers of Real Estate. By J. HENRY DART, of Lincoln's Inn, Esq., one of the Six Conveyancing Counsel of the High Court of Justice, Chancery Division. Fifth Edition. By the AUTHOR and WILLIAM BARBER, of Lincoln's Inn, Esq., Barrister-at-Law. 2 vols. Royal 8vo. 1876. 3*l.* 13*s.* 6*d.*

"A standard work like Mr. Dart's is beyond all praise."—*The Law Journal.*

WATERS.—**Woolrych on the Law of Waters.**—Including Rights in the Sea, Rivers, Canals, &c. Second Edition. 8vo. 1851.
Goddard.—*Vide* "Easements." *Net,* 10*s.*

WATERWORKS—Palmer.—*Vide* "Conveyancing."

WILLS.—**Rawlinson's Guide to Solicitors on taking Instructions for Wills.**—8vo. 1874. 4*s.*

WILLS.—*Continued.*

Theobald's Concise Treatise on the Construction of Wills.—With Table of Cases and Full Index. By H. S. THEOBALD, of the Inner Temple, Esq., Barrister-at-Law, and Fellow of Wadham College, Oxford. 8vo. 1876. 1*l*.

"Mr. Theobald has certainly given evidence of extensive investigation, conscientious labour, and clear exposition."—*Law Magazine.*

"We desire to record our decided impression, after a somewhat careful examination, that this is a book of great ability and value. It bears on every page traces of care and sound judgment. It is certain to prove of great practical usefulness, for it supplies a want which was beginning to be distinctly felt."—*Solicitors' Journal.*

"His arrangement being good, and his statement of the effect of the decisions being clear, his work cannot fail to be of practical utility, and as such we can commend it to the attention of the profession."—*Law Times.*

"It is remarkably well arranged, and its contents embrace all the principal heads on the subject."—*Law Journal.*

WRONGS.—*Vide* "Torts."

REPORTS.—*A large stock new and second-hand. Estimates on application.*

BINDING.—*Executed in the best manner at moderate prices and with dispatch.*

The Law Reports, Law Journal, and all other Reports, bound to Office Patterns, at Office Prices.

PRIVATE ACTS.—*The Publishers of this Catalogue possess the largest known collection of Private Acts of Parliament (including Public and Local), and can supply single copies commencing from a very early period.*

VALUATIONS.—*For Probate, Partnership, or other purposes.*

STEVENS AND SONS,

𝕷𝖆𝖜 𝖕𝖚𝖇𝖑𝖎𝖘𝖍𝖊𝖗𝖘, 𝕭𝖔𝖔𝖐𝖘𝖊𝖑𝖑𝖊𝖗𝖘, 𝕰𝖝𝖕𝖔𝖗𝖙𝖊𝖗𝖘 𝖆𝖓𝖉 𝕷𝖎𝖈𝖊𝖓𝖘𝖊𝖉 𝖁𝖆𝖑𝖚𝖊𝖗𝖘,

119, CHANCERY LANE, LONDON, W.C.

NEW WORKS AND NEW EDITIONS.

IN PREPARATION.

Archibald's Handbook of the Practice in the Common Law Divisions of the High Court of Justice; with Forms for the use of Country Solicitors. By *W. F. A. Archibald*, Esq., Barrister-at-Law, Author of "Forms of Summonses and Orders, with Notes for use at Judges' Chambers, &c. (*In the press*).

Baker's Law of Highways in England and Wales, including Bridges and Locomotives. Comprising a succinct code of the several provisions under each head, the statutes at length in an Appendix; with Notes, Forms, and complete Index. By *Thomas Baker*, of the Inner Temple, Esq., Barrister-at-Law. (*Nearly ready*.)

Ball's Short Digest of the Common Law; being the Principles of Torts and Contracts, chiefly founded upon the works of Addison, with Illustrative Cases, for the use of Students. By *W. Edmund Ball*, LL.B., late "Holt Scholar" of Gray's Inn, Barrister-at-Law and Midland Circuit. (*Nearly ready*.)

Browne and Theobald's Law of Railways. By *J. H. Balfour Browne*, of the Middle Temple, Esq., Barrister-at-Law, Registrar to the Railway Commissioners, and *H. S. Theobald*, of the Inner Temple, Esq., Barrister-at-Law.

Bullen and Leake's Precedents of Pleading. Fourth Edition. By *T. J. Bullen*, Esq., Special Pleader, and *Cyril Dodd*, of the Inner Temple, Esq., Barrister-at-Law. (*In the press.*)

Coote's Treatise on the Law of Mortgage. Fourth Edition, thoroughly revised. By *William Wyllys Mackeson*, Esq., one of Her Majesty's Counsel. (*In the press.*)

Daniell's Chancery Practice.—Sixth Edition.—By *L. Field* and *E. C. Dunn*, Esqrs., Barristers-at-Law. Assisted by *W. H. Upjohn*, Esq., Student and Holt Scholar of Gray's Inn, &c., Editor of the Third Edition of "Daniell's Forms."

Jepson's Lands Clauses Consolidation Acts; with Decisions, Forms, and Table of Costs. By *Arthur Jepson*, of Lincoln's Inn, Esq., Barrister-at-Law. (*In the press.*)

Jervis on the Office and Duties of Coroners; with Forms and Precedents. Fourth Edition. By *R. E. Melsheimer*, of the Inner Temple, Esq., Barrister-at-Law. (*In the press.*)

Morgan and Davey's Treatise on Costs in Chancery. Second Edition. By *George Osborne Morgan*, of Lincoln's Inn, Esq., one of Her Majesty's Counsel; assisted by *E. A. Wurtzburg*, of Lincoln's Inn, Esq., Barrister-at-Law. With an Appendix, containing Forms and Precedents of Bills of Costs.

Smith's Treatise on the Law of Negligence. By *Horace Smith*, B.A., of the Inner Temple, Esq., Barrister-at-Law, Author of "The Law of Landlord and Tenant," Editor of "Roscoe's Criminal Evidence." (*Nearly ready*.)

Stone's Practice for Justices of the Peace, Justices' Clerks, and Solicitors at Petty and Special Sessions, &c. Ninth Edition. By *F. G. Templer*, of the Inner Temple, Esq., Barrister-at-Law, Editor of "The Summary Jurisdiction Act, 1879."

STEVENS AND SONS, 119, CHANCERY LANE, LONDON, W.C.

*** *See also Catalogue at end of this Volume.*

STEVENS AND SONS, 119, CHANCERY LANE, W.C.

Bedford's Guide to Stephen's New Commentaries on the Laws of England. *Seventh Edition.* By QUESTION AND ANSWER. 8vo. 1879. *Price* 12s. *cloth.*

"Here is a book which will be of the greatest service to students."—*Law Journal.*

Bedford's Final Examination Digest.—Containing a Digest of the Final Examination Questions in matters of Law and Procedure determined by the Chancery, Queen's Bench, Common Pleas, and Exchequer Divisions of the High Court of Justice; and on the Law of Real and Personal Property; and the Practice of Conveyancing. By EDWARD HENSLOWE BEDFORD, Solicitor. Author of "The Guide to Stephen's Commentaries," &c. 8vo. 1879. *Price* 16s. *cloth.*

Haynes' Student's Leading Cases.—Being some of the Principal Decisions of the Courts in Constitutional Law, Common Law, Conveyancing and Equity, Probate and Divorce, Bankruptcy, and Criminal Law. With Notes for the use of Students. By JOHN F. HAYNES, LL.D. *Demy* 8vo. 1878. *Price* 16s. *cloth.*

"Will prove of great utility, not only to Students, but Practitioners. The Notes are clear, pointed and concise."—*Law Times.*

Greenwood's Manual of Conveyancing.—A Manual of the Practice of Conveyancing, showing the present Practice relating to the daily routine of Conveyancing in Solicitors' Offices. To which are added Concise Common Forms and Precedents in Conveyancing, Conditions of Sale, Conveyances, and all other Assurances in constant use. *Fifth Edition.* By H. N. CAPEL, B.A., LL.B., Solicitor. *Demy* 8vo. 1877. *Price* 15s. *cloth.*

"The information under these heads is just of that ordinary practical kind which is learned from experience, and is not to be gathered from treatises. A careful study of these pages would probably arm a diligent clerk with as much useful knowledge as he might otherwise take years of desultory questioning and observing to acquire."—*Solicitors' Journal.*

Smith's Real and Personal Property.—A Compendium of the Law of Real and Personal Property, primarily connected with Conveyancing. Designed as a second book for Students, and as a digest of the most useful learning for Practitioners. By JOSIAH W. SMITH, B.C.L., Q.C. *Fifth Edition.* 2 vols. *Demy* 8vo. 1877. *Price* 2l. 2s. *cloth.*

"He has given to the student a book which he may read over and over again with profit and pleasure."—*Law Times.*

Pollock's Principles of Contract at Law and in Equity.—Being a Treatise on the General Principles concerning the Validity of Agreements, with a special view to the comparison of Law and Equity; and with references to the Indian Contract Act, and occasionally to Roman, American, and Continental Law. *Second Edition.* By FREDERICK POLLOCK, of Lincoln's Inn, Esq., Barrister-at-Law. *Demy* 8vo. 1878. *Price* 1l. 6s. *cloth.*

"He has succeeded in writing a book on Contracts which the working lawyer will find as useful for reference as any of its predecessors, and which at the same time will give the student what he will seek for in vain elsewhere, a complete *rationale* of the law."—*Law Magazine.*

Wharton's Law Lexicon, or Dictionary of Jurisprudence, Explaining the Technical Words and Phrases employed in the several Departments of English Law; including the various Legal Terms used in Commercial Business; with an Explanatory as well as Literal translation of the Latin Maxims contained in the Writings of the Ancient and Modern Commentators. *Sixth Edition.* Revised in accordance with the Judicature Acts, by J. SHIRESS WILL, of the Middle Temple, Esq., Barrister-at-Law. *Super-royal* 8vo. 1876. *Price* 2l. 2s. *cloth.*

"As a work of reference for the library, the handsome and elaborate edition of 'Wharton's Law Lexicon' which Mr. Shiress Will has produced, must supersede all former issues of that well-known work."—*Law Magazine and Review.*

Wheaton's Elements of International Law.— Second English Edition. Edited with Notes and Appendix of Statutes and Treaties, bringing the work down to the present time. By A. C. BOYD, Esq., LL.B., J.P., Barrister-at-Law. Author of "The Merchant Shipping Laws." *Demy* 8vo. 1880. *Price* 1l. 10s. *cloth.*

"Both the plan and execution of the work before us deserves commendation. The text of Wheaton is presented without alteration."—*Law Journal.*

Wilson's Supreme Court of Judicature Acts, Appellate Jurisdiction Act, 1876, Rules of Court and Forms, with other Acts, Orders, Rules, and Regulations relating to the Supreme Court of Justice, with Practical Notes. *Second Edition.* By ARTHUR WILSON, of the Inner Temple, Barrister-at-Law. Assisted by HARRY GREENWOOD, of Lincoln's Inn, Barrister-at-Law, and JOHN BIDDLE, of the Master of the Rolls Chambers. *Royal* 12mo. 1878. *Price* 18s. *cloth (or limp leather for the pocket. Price* 22s. 6d.*)*

*** A Large Paper Edition of the above (for Marginal Notes), *Royal* 8vo. *Price* 1l. 5s. *cloth (or limp leather, price* 30s.*).*

"The practitioner will find that it supplies all his wants."—*Law Times.*

www.ingramcontent.com/pod-product-compliance
Lightning Source LLC
Chambersburg PA
CBHW051235300426
44114CB00011B/746